DATE DUE

A HISTORY OF NAMIBIA

MARION WALLACE
with JOHN KINAHAN

A History of Namibia

From the Beginning to 1990

Columbia University Press
New York

Columbia University Press
Publishers Since 1893
New York   Chichester, West Sussex
© Marion Wallace and John Kinahan, 2011
All rights reserved.

Library of Congress Cataloging-in-Publication Data

Wallace, Marion.
A history of Namibia : from the beginning to 1990 / Marion Wallace
with John Kinahan.
   p. cm.
Includes bibliographical references and index.
ISBN 978-0-231-70194-5 (cloth: alk. paper)
ISBN 978-0-231-80061-7 (ebook)
1. Namibia—History. I. Kinahan, John. II. Title.

DT1575.W35 2010
968.8—dc22

2010042796

∞

Columbia University Press books are printed on permanent and durable acid-free paper. This book is printed on paper with recycled content.
Printed in India

c 10 9 8 7 6 5 4 3 2 1

CONTENTS

LIST OF ILLUSTRATIONS

ABBREVIATIONS

AACRLS	Archives of Anti-Colonial Resistance and the Liberation Struggle
AG	Administrator-General
AMEC	African Methodist Episcopal Church
BAB	Basler Afrika Bibliographien (Basel Africa Library)
CANU	Caprivi African National Union
CDM	Consolidated Diamond Mining
DEK	Deutsche Evangelische Kirchengemeinde (German Lutheran Church)
DKG	Deutsche Kolonialgesellschaft (German Colonial Society)
DKGSWA	Deutsche Kolonialgesellschaft für Südwestafrika (German South West Africa Company)
DTA	Democratic Turnhalle Alliance
ELK	Evangelical Lutheran Church
ELOK	Evangelical Lutheran Ovambo–Kavango church
FMS	Finnish Mission Society
FNLA	National Front for the Liberation of Angola
ICJ	International Court of Justice
ICRC	International Committee of the Red Cross
JAH	*Journal of African History*
JNS	*Journal of Namibian Studies*
JNSS	*Journal of the Namibia Scientific Society*
JSAS	*Journal of Southern African Studies*
JSWASS	*Journal of the South West Africa Scientific Society*
LMS	London Missionary Society
MHAG	Missions-Handels-Aktien-Gesellschaft (mission trading company of the RMS)

MPLA	Popular Front for the Liberation of Angola
NAD	(South African) Native Affairs Department
NAN	National Archives of Namibia
NANSO	Namibian National Students' Organisation
NASA	National Archives of South Africa
NGK	Dutch Reformed Church
NLO	Northern Labour Organisation
NMC	Native Military Corps
NNF	Namibia National Front
NP	National Party
NNC	Namibia National Convention
NPCC04	National Preparatory Committee for the Commemoration of 2004
NUDO	National Unity Democratic Organisation
NWV	Namibia Women's Voice
OAU	Organisation of African Unity
OMEG	Otavi Minen und Eisenbahngesellschaft (Otavi Mines and Railway Company)
OPC	Ovamboland People's Congress
OPO	Ovamboland People's Organisation
PHFHC	Conference on 'Public History, Forgotten History', University of Namibia, Aug. 2000
PLAN	People's Liberation Army of Namibia
RMS	Rhenish Mission Society (Rheinische Missionsgesellschaft)
SADF	South African Defence Force
SAHJ	*South African Historical Journal*
SLO	Southern Labour Organisation
SWA	South West Africa
SWACO	South West Africa Company
SWANLA	South West African Native Labour Association
SWANLIF	South West Africa National Liberation Front
SWANU	South West African National Union
SWAP	South West Africa Police
SWAPA	South West Africa Progressive Association
SWAPO	South West Africa People's Organisation
SWASB	South West Africa Student Body
SWATF	South West Africa Territorial Force
SWC	SWAPO Women's Council

ABBREVIATIONS

SYL	SWAPO Youth League
TGNU	Transitional Government of National Unity
UN	United Nations
UNIA	Universal Negro Improvement Association
UNITA	National Union for the Total Independence of Angola
UNSWP	United National South West Party
UNTAG	United Nations Transition Assistance Group
WBMC	Walfish Bay Mining Company
WNLA	Witwatersrand Native Labour Association
UNIN	United Nations Institute for Namibia
UNSCR	UN Security Council Resolution
UNSWP	United National South West Party

GLOSSARY

Angra Pequena	Former name for Lüderitz(bucht)
Baaiweg (Afrikaans)	Jonker Afrikaner's road between Windhoek and Walvis Bay
Bambuse, pl. Bambusen (German)	African boy in employment of German troops
Baster, Bastaard	Person of mixed race
(Berg/Hill) Damara/Dama/ Daman	Historical and variant terms usually equated with modern Damara people
Bezirk (German)	(Administrative) region
(Cattle) Damara	Historical term usually equated with modern Herero people
Deutschtum (German)	Approximately, 'Germanness', German identity
Distrikt (German)	(Administrative) district
Eanda (Otjiherero)	Female line in the Herero double descent system
Efundula (Oshikwanyama)	Female initiation ceremony
Ehi rOvaherero (Otjiherero)	Land of the Herero
Eingeborene (f.)/Eingeborener (m.) (German)	Native
Frauenbund (German)	Women's League/Association
Gariep	Orange (River)
Great Namaqua	Historical term denoting ancestors of modern Nama people

Kaptein (Afrikaans)	Captain, chief, leader
Landesrat (German)	Territorial Council
Mwanamwalie (Silozi)	Lozi representative in the Caprivi
Ohamakari (Otjiherero)	Site of battle at the Waterberg
Ohango (Oshindonga)	Female initiation ceremony
Ohorongo (Otjiherero)	Name of Maharero's clan
Omaheke (Otjiherero)	Desert/very arid area in eastern Namibia
Omalenga, sing. elenga (Oshiwambo languages)	Senior headman/woman
Ombuke (Otjiherero)	Prophet
Omutandu, pl. omitandu (Otjiherero)	Praise song
Omuhona, pl. ovahona (Otjiherero)	'Big man', leader
Oorlam (Afrikaans)	Person usually of Khoekhoe origin, but adopting Dutch cultural traits
Oruuano (Otjiherero)	Herero church with strong emphasis on tradition, lit. 'communion'; Protestant Unity Church
Oruzo (Ojtiherero)	Male line in the Herero double descent system
Otjiserandu (Otjiherero)	Maharero branch of the *oturupa*
Oturupa (Otjiherero)	Herero troop movement(s); also known as *Truppenspieler*
Ovaherero, sing. Omuherero (Otjiherero)	Herero people/person
Police Zone	The settler-occupied areas of southern and central Namibia
Red Line	Term denoting the boundary between the Police Zone and the areas to the north
Reichskanzler (German)	Imperial chancellor
Reichstag (German)	German Parliament
Schutztruppe (German)	(Lit.) protection troops; German colonial military forces
Veld (Afrikaans)	field, plain, pasture, hunting ground
Vernichten (German)	Destroy, annihilate

ACKNOWLEDGMENTS

This book has been a long time in the making, and its completion is as much a surprise to me as it must be to my long-suffering publisher. It would not have been finished without the help, advice, encouragement and commitment of numerous friends and colleagues. Special thanks are due in this regard to Dag Henrichsen, who read and commented on virtually the entire manuscript, plied me with books and articles, references, source material and chocolate and, most importantly, encouraged me to keep going throughout the project. I am grateful, too, to Patricia Hayes for her incisive comments on my text and her long-term support and friendship, and to Tilman Dedering, John Kinahan, Henning Melber, Giorgio Miescher and Jeremy Silvester, who also read and commented on draft chapters. I am also thankful to John Kinahan for his willingness to provide an expert archaeological view and thus greatly enhance the book's coverage of Namibia's precolonial past.

Many others also provided generous help and support. Helle Jensen sent me books and articles from Namibia. Martha Akawa, Lawrence Flint, Werner Hillebrecht, Anette Hoffman, Justine Hunter, Jill Kinahan, Premesh Lalu, Karl-Johann Lindholm, Ellen Namhila, Ciraj Rassool, Lorena Rizzo, Felix Schürmann, Vilho Shigwedha, Napandulwe Shiweda, Piers Vigne and Günther Volker variously supplied references, sources, expertise, unpublished theses and papers, stimulating conversation and general support. I would also like to thank my employer, the British Library (and in particular Stephen Bury), which granted me a short sabbatical in 2008 to work on this book.

For the images published in the book I am very grateful for the help of the staff of the National Archives of Namibia, in particular to

Werner Hillebrecht. Many others also assisted with the images: Martha Akawa; Dag Henrichsen, Regula Iselin and Giorgio Miescher at the Basler Afrika Bibliographien; Malcolm Harman at the Powell-Cotton Museum, Kent; Rainer-Maria Kiel at Bayreuth University Library; Conny Berry at the Sam Cohen Library, Swakopmund; Boris Löffler at the Staatsarchiv Bremen; Susannah Rayner at the School of Oriental and African Studies Library, London; Silke Seybold at the Überseemuseum, Bremen; Martha Smalley at Yale University Library; John Liebenberg; Patricia Hayes; and Mrs Jess Hahn. I am also very much indebted to Sebastian Ballard for producing the maps on the following pages.

Last but certainly not least, I am more grateful than I can say to Andrew Pearson, who has given me a fabulous amount of practical and moral support throughout this project; and to our daughters, Ruth and Bea, for being there.

MAPS

Note: With the exception of Map 5, these maps do not relate to a particular period in Namibia's history.

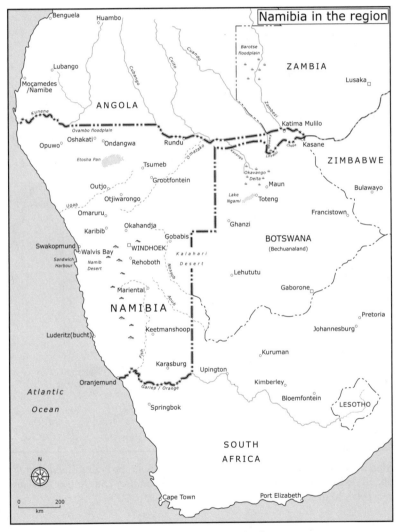

Map 1: Namibia in the region (© Sebastian Ballard).

Map 2: Southern Namibia (© Sebastian Ballard). Sources: Nuhn, *Feind überall*, pp. 60–1; Kinahan, *Cattle for Beads*, p. 31; *Kriegskarte*; Lau, *Jonker Afrikaner's Time*, Map 1; Mendelsohn, *Atlas of Namibia*, p. 30

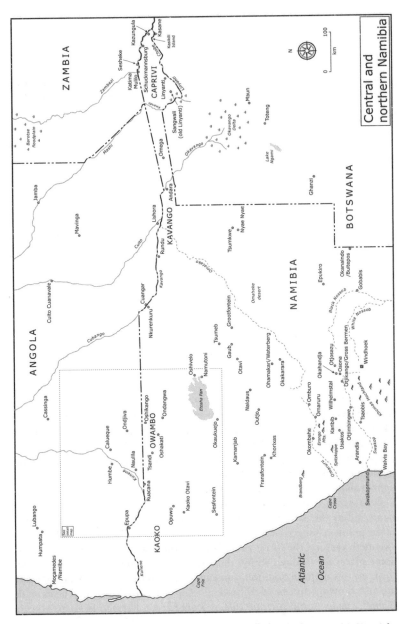

Map 3: Central and northern Namibia (© Sebastian Ballard). Sources: McKittrick, *To Dwell Secure*, Map 2.1; Hayes *et al.*, *Namibia under South African Rule*, p. xviii; Fisch, 'Tawana's Military Campaign', p. 118; Gibson *et al.*, *Kavango Peoples*; *Kriegskarte*; Mendelsohn, *Atlas of Namibia*, pp. 20–7

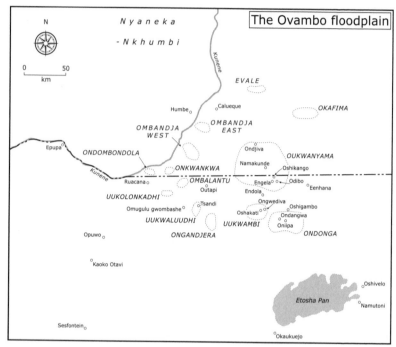

Map 4: Inset of Map 3 (overleaf), the Ovambo floodplain (© Sebastian Ballard). This map shows places mentioned in the text, rather than the Ovambo floodplain at any particular period. The international border shown here is the modern one; before 1928 the Neutral Zone lay to its south. The map shows, *approximately*, the location of the Ovambo polities in the nineteenth century; Oukwanyama is also shown extending some distance into Namibia, as it certainly did by the early twentieth century. It should be noted that the borders of the polities changed over time, in some cases markedly, and that, during the twentieth century, the forest zones between them were needed for settlement. Some places now falling within these states may therefore be shown outside them on this map. In addition, some modern foundations, such as Oshakati, are also shown. Sources: McKittrick, *To Dwell Secure*, Map 2.1; Hayes *et al.*, *Namibia under South African Rule*, p. xviii; Kreike, *Recreating Eden*, Map 4.

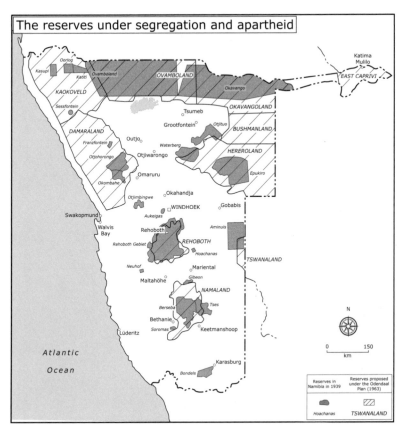

The reserves under segregation and apartheid

Map 5: The reserves under segregation and apartheid (© Sebastian Ballard). This map shows the reserves as they stood, firstly, in 1939, before the introduction of apartheid, and, secondly, in 1963, when the Odendaal Report set out new reserve boundaries (not all of which were implemented). Sources: Hayes *et al.*, *Namibia under South African Rule*, p. xv; Katjavivi, *History of Resistance*, Map 8.

INTRODUCTION

On 21 March 1990, Namibia gained its independence after a bitter, decades-long struggle against South African rule. The transition took place a quarter-century after decolonisation swept most of the continent, but four years before South Africa itself achieved majority rule. Namibia's colonial history was, thus, a long one: originally occupied by Germany in 1884, it was conquered by South Africa in 1915, ruled by the latter from 1921 as a Mandated Territory of the League of Nations and, after the Second World War, effectively as part of South Africa itself.

Although this colonial past is recent, and memories of it remain very intense, it was, nevertheless, a relatively short interlude in the long span of human activity in what is now Namibia. For thousands of years, humans have migrated into and across the region, building power, creating art, music and literature, exercising religious beliefs, producing food and goods, trading across wide distances and introducing new solutions to old problems. Over the last few centuries, semi-nomadic societies have kept cattle, sheep and goats, or foraged and hunted for food, or both, across much of the very dry and marginal central and southern parts of Namibia; in most of the more fertile north, small polities, usually ruled by kings or queens, established themselves on the basis of farming, cattle-rearing, fishing, foraging and hunting. From the late eighteenth century, and especially from the middle of the nineteenth, all areas of Namibia began to see significant political, economic and cultural change, as its residents were affected by, and indeed grasped and shaped, the new forces of merchant capitalism and Christianity. By the time Namibia became a colony in formal terms, it had already been considerably transformed.

1

Today, more than twenty years after independence, Namibia is inhabited by over two million people. Its land area is 832,690 square kilometres—more than double the size of Germany and nearly 70 per cent that of South Africa.[1] It shares borders with South Africa, Botswana and Angola, and, in the north-east (where a finger of land called the Caprivi Strip was added to the territory in 1890) with Zambia.[2] To the west, Namibia abuts the Atlantic Ocean; most shipping goes through Walvis Bay, its only deep-water port, which was annexed by the British in 1878, and only returned to Namibia from South African rule in 1994.

In the west and south of the country, the land rises from the coastal plain to form a steep ridge or escarpment; beyond, much of the land mass of the country consists of a generally flat plateau, lying between 900 and 1,300m above sea level. Namibia's very sparse population density is explained by its harsh climate and above all by its extreme dryness. The country has two deserts—the Namib in the west and the Kalahari in the east—and median annual rainfall in the extreme south and west is below 50mm. Precipitation rates rise towards the north and east, reaching a maximum of 550–600mm in the wettest areas, although most of the country receives much less. In addition, the unreliable rains fall only between October and March. Namibian history has thus been characterised by cycles of drought, and agriculture has only been possible in the more fertile northern areas. These climatic conditions have also had a decisive effect on current settlement patterns: the most densely populated areas are in the north, which has long been home to relatively large communities, and the towns, to which people migrated both after independence and during the colonial period.[3]

This book is an attempt to bring together what has been written on Namibia's past, covering the period to independence in 1990. It opens with a chapter, by John Kinahan, based largely on archaeological research and dealing with the period from the first recognisable evidence of human activity to the mid-nineteenth century. For the period from (roughly) the mid-eighteenth century, I have then tried to pull together the existing published historiography of Namibia and to weave it into something approaching a coherent whole. Such an attempt to construct a single narrative out of complicated and multi-layered histories is, of course, necessarily problematic. It carries the danger not only of doing violence to history by attempting to summarise very complex events in a line or two, but also of reflecting, at least to some extent, the limitations and emphases of the existing literature, and thus of eclipsing alternative narratives.

Yet there are also enormous advantages to writing a general history. One of these is that the gaps in what has already been written resolve into sharp perspective. There can, of course, be no question of a neutral process of 'filling the gaps': the definition of such lacunae is never stable because they are always constructed by historians. Nevertheless, some things do stand out. Conversely, the most popular research choices among historians and anthropologists also become evident, and in some cases throw other areas into the shade. I discuss examples in both these categories below.

Looking at the *longue durée* of Namibian history also brings home the fact that the period for which written historical sources exist is only a fraction of the duration of human settlement in Namibia. John Kinahan's chapter is crucial to the book in that it makes possible coverage of the period before the mid-eighteenth century, and brings the conclusions of the most recent archaeological investigations to a general audience. He also shows how material and archival sources can be used to critique each other, in the period for which historical archaeology is possible.

Kinahan deals separately with the history and current state of archaeological research and writing. Here, it is necessary briefly to discuss the historiography of Namibia, before moving on to raise some of the general issues important for this book. The need for a new synthesis is clear: the last general history based on academic research, Peter Katjavivi's *A History of Resistance in Namibia*, was published in 1988, while Klaus Dierks's *Chronology of Namibian History*, although both extensive and useful as a reference source, is, as its title suggests, a list of dates and events rather than a narrative history.[4]

Most of the societies of precolonial Namibia developed their own historical practices, creating, maintaining and adding to coherent (if often partisan) narratives. Such expertise was preserved orally, from generation to generation, by specialist historians. Other practices and literatures, for example the genre of praise songs, also allowed Africans—frequently women—to perform and memorialise historical knowledge and historically-based claims to resources. Arguably the first major written historical work on Namibia, however, was Heinrich Vedder's *Das alte Südwestafrika* (1934).[5] This text is deeply flawed:

not only does it present precolonial Namibia as incessantly riven by wars among savages, for whom the coming of German colonialism was a blessed relief, but it is very inadequately referenced and full of errors, as a detailed analysis of Vedder's treatment of the exploration of the Namibian coast has shown.[6] For these reasons, I have not used *Das alte Südwestafrika* as a source for the present book.[7]

After the Second World War, the historiography of Namibia expanded considerably. In 1962, the courageous South African journalist Ruth First visited Namibia and conducted both interviews and archival research, which resulted in a radical history of the territory: ground-breaking at the time, it remains worth reading for its insights and vivid descriptions.[8] First's work was followed in 1971 by another general history by Israel Goldblatt which, although less analytical, is interesting for its attention to precolonial sources.[9]

It was primarily the long-drawn out struggle over the fate of Namibia that was to generate an astonishing amount of debate and research at this period. Volumes were filled with arguments for and against South African rule over Namibia. These debates produced, among other works, John Wellington's *South West Africa and its Human Issues*, for which he researched and analysed the Odendaal Plan (under which apartheid was implemented in Namibia).[10] Helmut Bley and Horst Drechsler researched government records in East Germany to construct conceptually new and radical histories of German rule in Namibia, including of the genocide perpetrated by the German colonial government against the people of central and southern Namibia between 1904 and 1908.[11] Somewhat later, from inside the South West Africa People's Organisation (SWAPO), the major national liberation movement, came work including the 'official history', *To Be Born a Nation*,[12] and Katjavivi's *History of Resistance*; academic work from members of the South West Africa National Union (SWANU), the minority nationalist organisation, included Zedekia Ngavirue's research on the inter-war years.[13] Analysis of the capitalist exploitation of Namibia through the migrant labour system was carried out in particular by Richard Moorsom,[14] and social history began to develop through the work of Brigitte Lau and others.[15] A literature of short publications in support of the liberation struggle, based on research into conditions in Namibia, also flourished during the 1970s and 1980s. Important historical conferences on Namibia also produced significant collections of papers.[16]

4

The broader context for these writings was the emergence of nation-alist history in Africa in the period of decolonisation and, even more importantly, of the rise in the 1950s and 1960s of the resistance para-digm in African studies.[17] As SWAPO had it in *To Be Born a Nation*, a long history of 'popular resistance to foreign intrusion'[18] began long before the formal colonisation of Namibia, culminating in the struggle for national independence. Such studies played a tremendously impor-tant role in showing the extent to which Africans had resisted colonisa-tion and oppression. Nevertheless, the assumptions behind these accounts—essentially, of a bipolar conflict between coloniser and colo-nised and of continuous resistance to colonial rule—have increasingly been questioned. As James Scott argued, Africans employed the 'weap-ons of the weak'[19]—avoidance and subversion of colonial control—far more frequently than overt opposition. More fundamentally, historians have come to a better understanding of conflict generated by stratifica-tion within African societies, the intersections of power and gender and generation, and continuities before, during and after colonialism. As Van Walraven and Abbink have written about the nature of libera-tion wars, for example, 'recent scholarship has produced more anthro-pologically oriented studies that tend to view wars as very complex social phenomena, rather than as struggles in straightforward support of modern political ideologies'.[20]

Such considerations are apposite in the Namibian context. There is, for example, very little social and economic history for the period fol-lowing the Second World War, and particularly from the 1960s:[21] no comprehensive analysis, for instance, of how and when apartheid leg-islation was extended to Namibia. Much remains to be done to situate the struggles of the period, including the war of independence, in social and economic, as well as political, terrain, and to move beyond the narrowly political emphasis of the existing (plentiful) literature. On the other hand, historians have already moved beyond the resistance/col-laboration dichotomy to construct more complex analyses of subjects including the nineteenth-century protection treaties with Britain and Germany, and the role of figures such as Samuel Maharero.[22]

By the same token, state and settler power has come to be under-stood as frequently fractured, partial, and limited by circumstances and resources, rather than an all-powerful machinery that was able to enforce, in Drechsler's words, 'the peace of the graveyard'[23] after the genocide. This is not to deny that there were moments when European powers mobilised huge resources to inflict crushing defeats on African opponents, or that military technology played a critical role in the establishment and maintenance of colonial rule. But it is important to understand the conflicts and reluctances in German and South African political formations, the divergence of settler and state interests, the huge difficulties in administering a territory the size of Namibia efficiently, and the importance of the cooperation of African elites for the maintenance of colonial power.

With independence, historical writing in and about Namibia flowered. The National Archives were now open to those previously unable to consult them, and extensive oral research also became possible. Academic history based in Namibia grew in strength. The History Department at the University of Namibia has, at certain periods, been a crucible of change, hosting three major international history conferences,[24] publishing working papers, and encouraging its students to carry out and disseminate original research. As a result (and with the support of a few key external institutions), at the time of writing a number of Namibians have history PhD theses at or near completion.[25] Historical research within a more or less nationalist paradigm, as well as the acquisition of relevant archives, has also been actively promoted by the Archives of Anti-Colonial Resistance and the Liberation Struggle (AACRLS), a project set up in 2001 within the National Archives and funded by the German government.[26] Indeed, history frequently appears in the public domain, through the memorialisation of sites, events and people; the continuing practice of oral historians; and the debate and contestation about, in particular, national reconciliation after independence, the genocide of 1904–8 and the role of the nationalist struggle in the symbolic life of the new nation.

Work published during the post-independence period is referenced extensively throughout this book. Among the strengths of this scholarship are a focus on social, economic and cultural as well as political history; detailed research on many previously neglected or under-researched areas, such as the north of Namibia; and the insistence of many authors—although not all[27]—on adopting African-centred perspectives and on trying to understand historical processes as both dynamic and complex. These works, like their predecessors, draw on a substantial range of sources. Written records on Namibia date from the first European interest in the area, in the second half of the eighteenth century; they include the archives not only of European travellers and other individuals, Christian missions and colonial governments, but also of a number of African leaders, for whom correspondence had become an essential tool of power well before the end of the nineteenth century. By the early twentieth century, too, literacy had spread and letter-writing had become a means of communication among the African population.[28] In addition, the new scholarship has been quick to explore and analyse other categories of source material, particularly oral history and tradition, and diverse forms of text and image.[29]

For all the strengths of this historiography, academic historical writing on Namibia remains a minority interest—a fact that partly (although not fully) explains why there are so many lacunae in the historiography. There are relatively few Namibia specialists internationally; such scholarship has developed most strongly in countries with a historic link to Namibia through colonialism and/or the independence struggle. In the country itself, the growth in academic history since independence has been rather fragile overall, the archive and academic sectors are small, and it remains difficult to make a living as a historian. The majority of historical texts on Namibia have thus been produced by academics based in Europe and America (the present book, apart from Chapter 1, not excepted). This situation is not, of course, peculiar to Namibia, and in one sense reflects existing power relations;[30] on the other hand, the field is so far-flung both because of the internationalism of SWAPO's work before independence, and because history is in general an international discipline, a fact which encourages rigour, challenge and the cross-fertilisation of ideas.

Nevertheless, the imbalance remains an issue. As Jeremy Silvester writes, work by Lovisa Nampala and Vilho Shigwedha 'provides an important window on to the "collective memory" of the meaning of tradition in northern Namibia'.[31] Namibian historians have the ability to unpack the linguistic and cultural riches and complexities of Namibian communities more subtly than their Western counterparts, and to combine perspectives thus gleaned with insights from the archives in new and fruitful ways. If there are also dangers in being close to the communities being researched, which may generate the writing of ethnically exclusive histories, then it should be remembered that Western historians too have fallen into this trap. Work by emerging African historians also forcefully reminds us how deeply the past—with its pain—is still inscribed in the present. Nampala and Shigwedha's work is shot through with debate and argument about issues—such as polygyny and compulsion used by the missionaries—that still matter today in the context of societies whose cultural worlds changed irrevocably through colonial and Christian intervention.[32] History cannot be other than public property, and it is the work of Namibian historians in particular that has the potential to bring the public and academic sides of the debate together in a spirit of critical enquiry.

Throughout this book, I have tried to construct an Africa-centred narrative of Namibia's history, and to be mindful of Nancy Rose Hunt's insistence that 'the politics of representation cannot be confined to European geographies and imaginaries, but must extend to African ways of conceptualising time, space, and social relations'.[33] This has implications for the structuring of both space and time. Historians, writes Norman Etherington, 'need to be able to position themselves imaginatively in a landscape where the agents of colonialism appear first as specks on a distant horizon':[34] if, he argues, we see South African history spatially from the viewpoint of the Cape Colony, we place ourselves, perhaps unconsciously, with the colonisers. Exactly the same can be argued for Namibia, and it is with this perspective that John Kinahan's chapter opens the book. Furthermore, an Africa-centred approach also calls into question the idea of a bounded space called 'Namibia' or 'South West Africa', since many pre-existing political units extended far across the borders that were imposed during the colonial period. Although this book constructs a single narrative about widely differing regions and people, whose only common ground is that they are now part of the nation-state Namibia, I have tried as far as possible to look at the larger context and to understand national borders for what they were—sometimes fictional, almost always permeable, and with meanings that changed over time. It is with these caveats that I have used 'Namibia' to describe the area of the modern nation-state, even before that name came into general use. In this, I have followed a common practice among historians of describing ex-colonies by their modern names. (I have also used the abbreviation 'SWA' to describe the colony of South West Africa during both the German and South African colonial periods.)

Similarly, internal boundaries must be understood as much less rigid, and more complex, than has been assumed in much of the literature. In particular, the division of Namibia into the northern areas and the 'Police Zone'—the settler-occupied areas of the south and centre—had become a standard spatial conceptualisation by the apartheid period (after the Second World War). This separation, because it has also affected the way in which history has been written, has also influenced the construction of this book: in Chapters 2 to 6, the north is discussed separately from the south and centre. Nevertheless, this division must be understood as partial, permeable (especially in the early period) and constructed in stages.

The northern boundary was first erected, running from east to west (roughly between Grootfontein and Fransfontein), by the Germans in 1896–97; it delimited the extent of effective German control in an attempt to protect settlers (living to the south) from an epidemic of cattle disease. The Police Zone was first defined by the government in Berlin in 1907, in a move to confine German responsibility for protecting settlers to an area that excluded the north and some of the western and eastern parts of Namibia. In 1925 the first map showing a red line (a term that became shorthand for the boundary) was published. The line passed roughly along the original German boundary, but now extended to the eastern and western borders of the territory, and was put in place in order to prevent cattle from the northern areas being exported to South Africa. The Police Zone and the Red Line were legally defined by the Prohibited Areas Proclamation of 1928. Even thereafter, the boundary continued to shift.[35]

Like space, periods of time cannot be limited absolutely: many of the dates that have been conventionally understood as markers of change in Namibia have been called into question, and at the very least must be understood as indicating messy and gradual transition rather than rigid historical cut-off points. In this case, too, an Africa-centred—and indeed Namibia-centred—perspective has the potential to disrupt existing chronologies. Some historians now argue that, viewed from half a century after decolonisation, the impact of colonialism has been less profound than previously thought.[36] In Namibia, colonialism and apartheid clearly did have very deep effects, not least because of the genocide of 1904–8, and more generally through the fairly consistent, and largely successful, efforts of state and settlers to exploit the colony's black population within a capitalist framework. Nevertheless, the way in which these arguments can decentre the colonial period is important: as already noted, Namibia was under European rule for a relatively short period of its past, and there were significant limitations to German and South African power. In addition, if the dates of the advent (and change) of formal colonial rule are not always those of

9

greatest significance for Namibia's history, neither should the territory automatically be assumed to have followed the same chronological trajectory as South Africa. Although South African 'native policies' were usually (although not always) applied in SWA, the latter had its own critical moments of change—for example the 'referendum' of 1946, which was crucial for raising consciousness and sparking political opposition to the South African administration.

If a book such as this one must therefore problematise time and space, it must also be concerned with the reclaiming of submerged histories, those that differ from dominant, primarily political narratives. Of course, it is impossible to do this comprehensively: as Verne Harris has written, 'the marginalised are...legion. Naming them all is an impossible task'.[37] In addition, the limitations of both sources and historiography make it difficult to disentangle and conceptualise histories of—for example—women, or the poor, or the young. Nevertheless, throughout this book I have tried in particular to think about gender and power, to consider the effects of historical change on women as well as men, to try to uncover women's agency, and to keep in view the extent to which political power was actively created through the deployment of constructions of masculinity.[38] For any success I have had in doing this, I am indebted to those historians who have written about women and gender; it remains a depressing constant, however, that gender is frequently not incorporated into the paradigm in which many new works are written. For example, the Native Ordinances of 1907 were imposed on all Africans over the age of seven.[39] Yet the authors who examine these measures do not pause to discuss the social, cultural and economic implications of the fact that this extreme level of regulation applied to women as well as men. In this, as in so many other areas, as Lita Webley argues, 'a feminist approach advocates not necessarily a different or even a more subjective view of the past but in fact a *better* understanding of past societies and events'.[40] Women's part in the independence struggle, too, although widely and somewhat formulaically praised in the literature, is hardly as yet understood in a nuanced and analytical way.[41]

Another aspect of Namibian historiography that needs thorough and urgent review is the way in which ethnicity and ethnic groups have habitually been conceptualised. It is now a commonplace in African historiography that ethnic groupings and affiliations do not necessarily have a deep past, and that many are recent constructs. As Etherington writes for South Africa, 'In 1800 there were no Ndebele, no Swazi, no "Bhaca" or "Shangaan" (though of course there were people living who were the ancestors of those who later came to think of themselves as belonging to such groups)'.[42]

In precolonial Namibia, people spoke the languages, or forerunners or variants of the languages, that are still spoken there today, including Otjiherero, Oshiwambo, Khoekhoegowab (Nama-Damara), Afrikaans, San languages, Rukwangali and Silozi; people also shared some of the cultural traits that have now come to be linked to the definitions of modern ethnic groups. Yet, as Kinahan argues in Chapter 1, reading the 'ethnographic present' back into the past can be dangerous—and the archaeological record can reveal complexities not apparent from written records. For the nineteenth century, even talking about groups such as 'the Herero' or 'the Ovambo' is highly misleading. At this period, most polities encompassed far fewer people than later ethnic groups such as 'the Ovambo', whose forbears lived in several (mainly) monarchical states, or 'the Nama', who were melded from a number of southern polities, themselves formed through highly complex processes involving a merging of incomers from the Cape ('Oorlams') with the original inhabitants. The designation of people of mixed racial heritage as 'Coloured' occurred in Namibia largely after the Second World War; before this date, their identity formation and its labelling were varied and flexible.[43] There is debate about how old 'Damara' identity or identification is. Certainly, ancestors of the present-day 'Damara' lived scattered over much of the country, without political unity; they may originally have been Bantu-speakers, but adopted Khoekhoegowab at a very early date.[44] Conversely, the Lozi Empire, which included part of the Caprivi Strip in its far southern reaches, ruled groups speaking many different languages.

The worlds in which people lived were, essentially, constituted not by ethnicity in the modern sense, but by their immediate networks of kin, which framed the structure of their day-to-day lives, and at the same time by the political dispensations under and in which they lived. Again, the South African example is instructive: in the nineteenth century and before, African societies were essentially constituted around powerful leaders who could offer military protection, access to stock, land, grazing and water and, increasingly, opportunities to acquire trade goods; the strongest of such 'chiefly families and followers' attracted many outsiders into their ranks.[45] This interpretation is, I would argue, also an accurate way of describing the situation in Namibia, where leaders such as Hendrik Witbooi were able to attract large followings. In this book, I have used Namibian words for leader—in Otjiherero, *omuhona* ('big man'); in Afrikaans, which was widely spoken by Nama-Oorlam in the nineteenth century, *kaptein* ('captain')—in preference to 'chief', which carries negative connotations and does not distinguish between different forms of leadership. I have, however, used 'king' or 'queen' for the rulers of the north, since the concept of royalty is appropriate there.

An explicit, self-ascribed identification as 'Herero' *did* emerge before colonial rule, but most other modern ethnic identities in Namibia were created, if not exclusively by European travellers and colonial governments, then with a great deal of help from them. They were inscribed into the territory's political framework throughout the course of its colonial history, but in a particularly dogmatic way during the apartheid period. Such distinctions went deep—although in some cases the categories constructed under apartheid have not worn well. 'White', for example, did not become a unifying construct that overrode perceived differences between Afrikaner, German and British, nor did 'Kavango' replace Kwangali, Gciriku, Mbunza, Shambyu and Mbukushu. Nevertheless, ethnic origin and belonging is a reality negotiated by all Namibians today. Ethnic identities are, however, realities that have been constructed through historical processes, not uncontested, primordial and unchanging sets of cultural and linguistic attributes.

Perhaps inevitably, the strength of the ethnic paradigm in Namibia today has been influential in shaping the way that history has been written, and there has been a marked tendency to read modern ethnic categories back into the past and to construct histories of individual ethnic groups. The imagining of communities as mono-ethnic is, however, called into question by settlements like that at Otjeru, south of the Police Zone boundary, which was of mixed ethnic composition.[46] In addition, this type of historiography tends to obscure the ways in which ethnic divisions have been constructed and reinforced, or alternatively softened, as well as the mutual relations, for example, of 'Herero', 'San' and 'Damara'. The researching of regional rather than ethnic studies, as I and others have argued elsewhere, is surely the way to move beyond these limitations. In addition, there has been a fascination, on the part of both historians and anthropologists, with particular narratives. One of these is that of the Herero, stereotyped variously as 'proud' and sometimes as 'tragic', but also attractive to researchers for other reasons including the 'exotic', 'Victorian' dresses worn by Herero women. While the suffering of Otjiherero-speakers during the genocide should in no way be minimised, one result of this historiographical treatment has arguably been to overshadow the genocidal war in the south; the social and political history of this region, particularly in the later nineteenth and early twentieth centuries, has also been very much neglected.[47] Another popular topic of research has been the San ('Bushmen') peoples of Namibia and Botswana, about whom more than six hundred books and articles have appeared.[48] This interest has much to do with the idea of San as 'original' and 'primitive' people; the story of the transformation of the majority of San in Namibia into a rural, and extremely poor, proletariat received little attention before the publication of the work of Robert Gordon and James Suzman. The latter has reflected that 'in a strange way' he had written 'about a "lost" race'—'marked out not by their geographic isolation from others, but rather their conceptual marginalisation by others'.[49]

A further word on the subject of orthography is necessary. I have tried to use the most up-to-date spellings possible, but the orthography of Namibian languages is not consistent, and I have not always succeeded. I have also followed conventional rather than logical practice in some cases: thus, for example, I have applied prefixes to the names of Bantu languages spoken in Namibia ('Otjiherero' rather than 'Herero'), but chosen the more usual form 'Herero' rather than 'Ovaherero' to describe people of that group. For the 'Ovambo' people, however, I followed conventional practice in using the prefix; 'Owambo' is used to designate the area they inhabited. In Khoekhoegowab/Nama-Damara, the four clicks are written | ‖ ! and ǂ (the first three correspond to the Isizulu clicks c, x and q).

This book attempts, however inadequately, to address the questions raised in this introduction, to provide a new synthesis of the history of Namibia, and to suggest fresh insights into many aspects of that history. Like all historical texts, it is a work in progress. It is to be hoped that it will not simply act as a reference book, but also generate new debate and research on the history of one of Africa's least understood and studied countries.

1

FROM THE BEGINNING

THE ARCHAEOLOGICAL EVIDENCE

John Kinahan

The history of south-western Africa, now Namibia, extends deep into the past, well beyond reach of memory and the written record. Traces of modern humans and their ancestors, including graves, dwelling places, stone tools and an unparalleled wealth of rock art, provide the only secure evidence of what happened here over the last one million years. This archaeological record, while continuous with the documentary sources and oral traditions of recent time, presents as many problems as it does insights into the Namibian past. Archaeological evidence is abundant, but it is also patchy, and often ambiguous; it is won by hard and slow manual labour under difficult conditions, and requires specialised methods of analysis.

This summary of Namibian archaeology aims to provide the general reader with an overview of the evidence, as well as current interpretations and likely prospects for future research. It is important, especially for the historian, to appreciate that archaeological investigation of the precolonial African past is rarely structured by calendar events, and almost never relates to known individuals. Lacking the element of personal or even ethnic identity, archaeological reconstructions have often appeared to be too generalised and therefore unsatisfactory. However,

15

this is a deceptive impression, for modern archaeological approaches attend more than previously to the fine detail of evidence in which human individuality is sometimes discernible.[1]

Ultimately, all archaeological investigation is limited by the vagaries of natural preservation. In Namibia, the archaeologist is faced with something of a paradox: preservation is generally good in the most arid parts of the country where conditions were hostile to human settlement, except during brief periods when there was sufficient water to be found, but the moister parts of the country, which are most suitable for cultivation and sedentary life, are characterised by rather poor archaeological preservation. This means that archaeological knowledge of settled farming communities in northern Namibia is quite scant, in comparison to that of small nomadic communities who lived in the Namib Desert. Future research may help to alleviate this geographical and thematic imbalance.

Archaeological evidence not only extends the Namibian documentary record into the past, it also brings to the reconstruction of history issues of human ecology, such as methods of hunting, the processing of plant foods and techniques of animal husbandry. Added to this is evidence of local trade networks, metallurgy, ritual practices and burial traditions, most of which escaped the notice of even the most astute among early colonial visitors, whose accounts form the basis of early documentary history in Namibia. Indeed, the great historical value of the archaeological record is that it demonstrates the dynamic and adaptable nature of precolonial society. The account of indigenous Namibian communities given by early ethnographers is in comparison but a snapshot of an ever-changing cultural landscape.

An overview of the history of archaeological research in Namibia will help to explain the emphasis of work in some areas and periods, and the apparent neglect of others. The archaeological research agenda is set by general questions of human development, the possibilities of investigation that arise in any particular region, and the interests of individual archaeologists or research programmes. Archaeological research is not therefore directed towards a broad-based investigation of the Namibian past. Nonetheless, archaeology in Africa has always reflected the social and political climate of the time, and in Namibia it is possible to identify some of the major influences of colonial rule in the practice of the discipline.[2]

A Brief History of Archaeology in Namibia

Late nineteenth century travellers such as W.C. Palgrave[3] noted the presence of rock paintings, and others including colonial officials and military officers noticed artefacts on the ground surface in several places. Significant discoveries of rock art were made after the turn of the century, the most notable being the so-called White Lady of the Brandberg. Reinhard Maack, who brought the painting to public notice, was himself an artist of note, and deeply concerned at the plight of the Bushmen, or San.[4] The settler community in Namibia was reluctant to believe that these fine works were executed by the very people whom the colonial authorities treated as mere vermin. Their prejudices were confirmed—at least temporarily—by the eminent French prehistorian Henri Breuil, who declared that the paintings were not African at all, but the work of more advanced Mediterranean people, precursors of the European settler community.[5]

Breuil's views were dismissed by archaeologists as nonsense,[6] although the controversy over the authorship of the rock art provided a stimulus for legitimate research. This set in train a series of surveys, excavations and large scale rock art documentation projects that still continue more than half a century later.[7] However, one of the immediate consequences of colonial rule was the disruption of San society, and the loss of both economic independence and cultural affinity to the rock art traditions by these and other communities such as the Damara.[8] The separation of the rock art from the social history of its creators was compounded in Namibia by a strong empiricist tradition, mainly among German archaeologists, who tended to study the rock art in isolation from the ethnographic and historical record.[9] This approach has been challenged in the last two decades, and supplanted by an anthropologically based understanding of hunter-gatherer art and ritual practice.[10]

Such changes in the study of rock art illustrate a general tendency in Namibian archaeology: most investigations are carried out in response to earlier work, often in the same area or in comparable circumstances. As a result, Namibia has seen an overwhelming concentration of effort in the Namib Desert and along its inland margin.[11] Most research since the 1950s has focused on the last 5,000 years, and the archaeology of hunter-gatherer communities associated with the rock art.[12] There has been some diversity of approach, with attempts to reconstruct the cultural ecology of the desert,[13] and most particularly the role of plant foods in subsistence.[14] During the South African era, some archaeologists adopted the ethnological framework of colonial rule as a template of research.[15] This highly simplified view of the Namibian past was also common among ethnologists and otherwise critical historians.[16]

Archaeologists, being much concerned with the technology and economy of past societies, have played a peripheral role in the development of critical history in Namibia.[17] In some ways this was the inevitable result of restricted research opportunities prior to independence in 1990. Thus, no archaeological investigations have ever been carried out in the central northern regions, the heartland of settled agriculture and of modern anti-colonial resistance. Very limited work was carried out in the northern parts of the country as a whole, and little is known

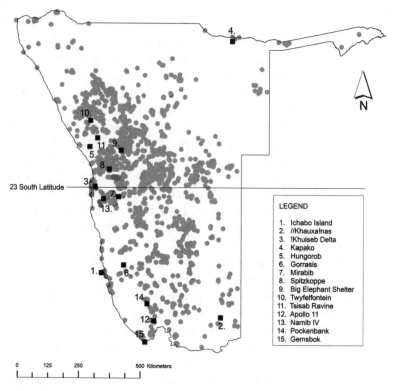

23 South Latitude

LEGEND

1. Ichabo Island
2. //Khauxa!nas
3. !Khuiseb Delta
4. Kapako
5. Hungorob
6. Gorrasis
7. Mirabib
8. Spitzkoppe
9. Big Elephant Shelter
10. Twyfelfontein
11. Tsisab Ravine
12. Apollo 11
13. Namib IV
14. Pockenbank
15. Gemsbok

0   125   250   500 Kilometers

Map 6: Distribution of archaeological sites in Namibia. Source: John Kinahan

of the earliest arrival of farming communities in Namibia.[18] More detailed research in neighbouring countries has had to suffice as a basis for understanding the most important recent precolonial developments in Namibia,[19] including the rise of powerful centralised kingdoms, such as did not exist in the more arid central and southern parts of the country.[20]

During and after the 1980s, a new generation of researchers began to question the most basic premises of conventional history, including the historical reality of ethnic identities,[21] the link between indigenous social formations and the early colonial economy,[22] and the treatment of ethno-historical sources by colonial apologists.[23] This general shift in intellectual climate also brought changes in archaeological thinking. For the first time, archaeological evidence was used to counter the prevailing belief that indigenous economies were static and incapable of innovation. New research showed that nomadic pastoralism arose in Namibia as a local response to the spread of farming throughout southern Africa.[24] Archaeological evidence was also used for the first time in southern Africa to investigate indigenous responses to early European contact, a period hitherto represented only by the voice of colonial documentary accounts.[25]

These broad trends primarily reflect shifts in theoretical orientation. Archaeological methods and techniques also changed, and during the last fifty years the quality of field research has greatly improved.[26] The advent of radiocarbon dating brought greater chronological control, and with it a correlation of the Namibian and southern African sequence. Despite differences of interpretation, archaeological research is based on common standards of survey, excavation, description and analysis. Most of the research that is cited here as forming the basis of present archaeological knowledge in Namibia has been published in peer-reviewed journals. Furthermore, the archaeological finds referred to in these publications are in most cases housed in museum collections where they may be consulted for further research. In most cases, the archaeological sites themselves may be visited, some having been proclaimed as national monuments.

The Emergence of Modern Humanity in the Late Pleistocene

The archaeological sequence as it is presently known in Namibia starts with the late Pleistocene evidence of the Early and Middle Stone Age, with Later Stone Age evidence first appearing before the Last Glacial Maximum[27] and the commencement of the Holocene about 10,000 years ago, when the classic hunter-gatherer cultures of the recent pre-colonial period developed. Possibly much older are informal pebble tools which might even date to the Plio-Pleistocene boundary at about two million years. The Holocene period, mainly characterised by the Later Stone Age record, also includes the first appearance of ceramics, metallurgy and farming within the last 2,000 years. In general, research covering the early part of the archaeological sequence refers to questions of human evolution, while the middle part of the sequence provides evidence of cognitive and technological advances as well as the rise of regional diversity. The final and most recent part of the sequence includes the richest evidence of human adaptation to the Namibian environment, and of development towards complex social traditions. In Namibia there is particularly well preserved evidence of early trading contact with the outside world, the moment when documentary history commences.

Evidence of evolutionary continuity in southern Africa currently favours the hypothesis that Pleistocene human ancestors spread from Africa throughout the Old World.[28] Dated hominid remains are scarce, however, and none have been found so far in Namibia. This may be due, in part, to the fact that much of the country remains archaeologically unexplored, but stone artefacts from this period are common, so it appears that conditions were not suitable for the preservation of early human skeletal remains. Elsewhere in southern Africa, Pleistocene human remains have been found in deep cave deposits, preserved in long sequences of occupation debris.[29] Such deposits are uncommon in Namibia and the extreme aridity prevailing here over long periods of human prehistory was not conducive to sustained occupation.[30] Pleistocene stone artefact finds are particularly common below the Namibian escarpment, where natural deflation of the surface has preserved artefact quarry and workshop sites in relatively pristine condition. Sheet erosion in the highlands has removed almost all trace of such sites, and over large areas of the Namib and Kalahari Deserts, archaeological sites lie deeply buried beneath the surface sands.

Late Pleistocene dates are available from several sites in the Namib Desert. At the site Namib IV, immediately south of the lower !Khuiseb River, bones of the extinct elephant *Elephas recki* indicate an age of

Fig. 1. Typical Pleistocene Early Stone Age hand-axe from Namibia (© John Kinahan.)

between 400,000 and 700,000 years,[31] and one site at Gemsbok, imme-diately north of the Orange River, has been dated to 800,000 years.[32] Firmly dated finds increase with time, as a consequence of differential preservation, and from about 50,000 years reliable dates are more eas-ily obtained within the limits of the radiocarbon method.[33] From 10,000 years until the recent past, there is a very steep increase in the number of dated sites and in the quality of organic preservation.[34] Unfortunately, the precision of radiocarbon dating decreased markedly in the last two centuries, owing to the effect of increased atmospheric carbon emissions during the Industrial Revolution.[35] For this reason, archaeological dating of early contact sites relies almost entirely on the comparative study of glassware and ceramics introduced to Namibia by passing European traders.[36]

The poorly resolved chronology of the Early Stone Age in southern Africa poses acute problems for the comparison of stone artefact assemblages in different parts of the region. In southern Africa generally, artefact typology provides a basis of comparison for the more recent Middle Stone Age assemblages, because these are more diverse in terms of tool design and often occur in sufficient volume to allow quantitative description. Thus, broad developmental stages based on technological similarity provide a quasi-chronology for the region as a whole.[37] Very few Middle Stone Age dates are available for Namibia, and recent advances in dating[38] tend to confirm that the Namibian evidence does not differ greatly from the regional pattern as far as it is known. The available evidence from Namibia is of human settlement in the escarpment zone, near to the few water sources that existed, and hunting of species such as mountain zebra, which still occur in the area today.[39] Population density appears to have been very low, and Middle Stone Age communities in Namibia probably represented the outer limits of human adaptation to desert conditions in southern Africa.[40]

Middle Stone Age artefact assemblages from Namibia include large numbers of blades and points, some with bifacial working that exemplifies the mastery of technique and raw material characteristic of this period. Secondary working, or retouch, is relatively uncommon among the Namibian assemblages, and examples of stone components for composite hafted tools are also rare. The use of raw materials shows a preference for fine grained quartzite and crypto-crystalline materials such as silcrete and chert, and some of these were carried over considerable distances.[41]

Evidence hinting at population movement and social organisation is scarce, and it is highly significant that the earliest rock art in Namibia is associated with one of the late Pleistocene escarpment sites, Apollo 11.[42] The dating of the rock art between 19,000 and 25,000 years suggests that the cognitive system evident in much more recent southern African rock art has been continuous over an extraordinarily long period of time. Even earlier evidence from South Africa, in the form of etched red ochre and dating to approximately 70,000 years, has added support to the view that modern humanity largely evolved in Africa.[43]

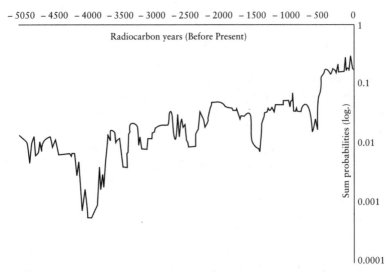

Fig. 2. Radiocarbon dates from Namibia showing peaks in human occupation over the last 5,000 years. The data, approximately 400 radiocarbon measurements, are mainly from the drier northwestern parts of the country, and reflect the human responses to climatic variation (© John Kinahan.)

Human settlement in southern Africa has always been decisively influenced by climate, and in the more arid parts of the region rainfall is the main environmental limiting factor.[44] Earlier palaeo-environmental models linked apparent changes in the archaeological sequence with a series of African pluvial (high rainfall) episodes, but the study of deep-sea cores has shown that global temperature changes provide a more robust framework which also accommodates changes in atmospheric circulation and rainfall.[45] Precise correlation of warming and cooling events with archaeological evidence remains difficult, although the Last Glacial Maximum, peaking at 18,000 years, corresponds with significant gaps in the sequence, suggesting local depopulation, and apparent extensions of human settlement related to shifts in rainfall distribution.[46] The lowering of the sea-level by approximately 100m exposed a littoral margin which might have drawn human settlement as the resource-rich coastline extended, in some places by more than 100km.[47] When sea-level was restored by global warming at the start of the Holocene approximately 10,000 years ago, human settlement

23

contracted to the present shoreline, and archaeological evidence of its larger distribution was inundated.

Interestingly, the advent of the Holocene did not bring an immediate reoccupation of Namibia west of the escarpment. The available evidence is that the region remained deserted for several thousand years, or so thinly populated that little trace of occupation has been found. More detailed field investigations may close this gap in the sequence of occupation, but it is significant that human settlement in southern Namibia is again evident about 6,500 years ago, coinciding with a subsequent global climatic event associated with a brief rise in sea-level and, very likely, rainfall.[48] The influence of climatic conditions is further underlined by the fact that the central and north-western[49] parts of Namibia, below the escarpment, were occupied more or less continuously through the late Holocene, following this improvement in the climate.[50] In contrast, the dated archaeological record for the southern part of Namibia is generally sporadic, with some significant gaps in occupation.[51] This latitudinal difference is best explained by the fact that while the north of Namibia is directly exposed to episodic high rainfall from seasonal atmospheric circulation anomalies,[52] the influence of these events is weaker in the south of the country.[53] The overall density of Holocene sites decreases southward, and the gaps in the sequence become larger with distance from the heartland of the Later Stone Age in Namibia, the desert and mountain zone between the escarpment and the Atlantic coast, and north of the !Khuiseb River. There is as yet little knowledge of human responses to climatic shifts in other, less arid parts of the country, such as the more tropical north-eastern regions. However, conditions in the Namib are clearly so marginal that evidence of sustained occupation can be taken as proxy evidence for climatic amelioration.

Human Adaptation During the Holocene

Summer rainfall over much of Namibia is brought by isolated convective storms that move over the landscape in an almost random fashion.[54] However, mountainous terrain in the desert and along the escarpment is associated with localised rainfall, which sustains reliable springs and seepages through groundwater recharge as a result of the very high runoff of water from the exposed rocks. These scattered water sources were most important in the driest parts of the country,

Fig. 3. Remains of an encampment site, dating to the most recent reoccupation of the Namib Desert, approximately 4,000 years before present (© John Kinahan.)

and the archaeological evidence shows that in the last 5,000 years, the movement of people was essentially tethered to such places during the long dry season.[55] It seems that the seasonal replenishing of these water sources was predictable enough, over the long term, to support a regular pattern of hunter-gatherer aggregation during the dry season, and dispersal during and immediately after the summer rains, before ephemeral pools in the desert dried up.[56]

There are well preserved food remains from this period, with abundant evidence of hunting and gathering equipment, so that it is possible to reconstruct the subsistence economy in some detail.[57] Most of the evidence is from the dry season sites because these tend to be large rock shelters that were repeatedly used, as opposed to temporary bivouacs used during hunting expeditions after the summer rains. In the dry season, people depended on a wide range of smaller species, such as hyrax, tortoises, various lizards and the occasional rare antelope. The archaeological evidence shows that some animals were probably roasted whole in shallow pits, while others were skinned and dismembered according to remarkably consistent preferences. Animal foods were supplemented with wild melons in the early months of the dry

25

season, as well as various corms. A range of fruits is evident from seed remains, and although some tubers would also have been exploited, these have left no identifiable remains except perhaps in the form of the pointed sticks used to dig them out of the ground.[58]

Stone artefact assemblages from these sites are characterised by a high diversity of items, including an array of small components for composite tools. Crescents and segments, sometimes less than 10 mm in length, were prepared as barbs to be hafted with vegetable mastic into the points of projectiles, such as arrows and light spears. All the component parts of these tools are found, either partly made, complete, or broken, so it is possible to reconstruct their manufacture and use with some certainty. The crescents and segments were struck as flakes from small cores of crystalline quartz or chert, and then modified further.[59] Wooden components such as arrow shafts were made with stone blades and scrapers, both abundantly represented in the evidence. Larger stone artefacts, including informal butchery tools, grooved stones, slate pendants, grindstones and even a single example of a stone palette for the preparation of pigments, occur in the archaeological deposits from this period. Finished items account for a very small proportion of stone fragments recovered from the excavations, usually less than 1 per cent by volume.

The variety of stone artefact raw material recovered from Holocene hunter-gatherer sites in Namibia provides a tantalising indication of human mobility, and of the extent of regional connections through networks of exchange, possibly based on kinship.[60] Materials such as crystalline quartz and chert of the highest quality are scarce and localised in their occurrence, yet they are found at virtually every major dry season site, sometimes in minute quantities.[61] The generalised distribution of these materials is the result of movement patterns that would have covered every possible source of water in the desert, as random rainfall events could be followed after the dry season over great distances.[62] Other materials recovered from the excavation of these sites illuminate different facets of hunter-gatherer life, such as the working of wood and leather, both being occasionally preserved. Suspected ritual objects have also been recovered, as well as a variety of bone artefacts, including awls, points, possible divining bones and large quantities of ostrich eggshell beads.[63]

Holocene hunter-gatherer sites in the Brandberg and other mountainous parts of Namibia west of the escarpment contain some of the largest concentrations of rock art in the whole of Africa.[64] This art, as discussed earlier, has been the focus of study, and of controversial interpretation, for almost a century.[65] Detailed archaeological investigation showed that the occupants of the rock shelters were not foreign visitors, but African hunter-gatherers with a material culture much the same as is found in similar sites throughout the region.[66] Having proved the indigenous affinity of the art, archaeologists had for more than fifty years nothing further to add to its interpretation. Indeed the study of rock art became largely the preserve of the amateur, early archaeologists having noted too many unrealistic depictions to treat the paintings and engravings as a useful source of information on hunter-gatherer life. Besides, the rock art on the walls and surrounding rock surfaces seemed impossible to date, and without dating the subject matter could not be assigned to any place in the sequence.

Rock art research in southern Africa changed decisively in the early 1980s with the comparative study of rock art, historical ethnography of the southern San peoples, and the anthropology of hunter-gatherer ritual practice.[67] The field moved rapidly once it became possible to recognise in the art evidence of the most central of southern San religious rituals: the trance dance. Evidence of trance experience and the work of specialised ritual practitioners, or shamans, occurs abundantly throughout the distribution of southern African rock art, thus demonstrating that the whole genre belongs to a common regional cognitive system.[68] The fact that the art referred largely to supernatural concerns meant that it could no longer be taken as a literal depiction of hunter-gatherer life, nor could its meaning be taken as self-evident. Moreover, the highly specific links between the rock art and the ethnographic record showed that interpretation should henceforth proceed on this basis. Much debate ensued, principally around regional differences in subject matter and details of depiction, and general objections to this new interpretative framework diminished.

Some limitations of the shamanistic approach to rock art interpretation emerged, one of these being its somewhat a historical view of hunter-gatherer society.[69] While the archaeological evidence did not point to any important changes during the Holocene, it seemed unlikely that something subject to as much social negotiation as ritual practice would remain unchanged for millennia.[70] In Namibia, the rock art is overwhelmingly associated with dry season aggregation sites in the arid parts of the country lying below the escarpment. Recent ethnographic studies of San communities in the Kalahari suggest that prolonged dry season aggregation was a major source of social tension, exacerbated by food shortage at this time of the year. The same studies indicate a marked increase in ritual activity during times of social tension, the trance dance being the most efficacious method of healing social discord. Another important ritual task during the dry season, at least in the past, was rain-making, a particular speciality of some Kalahari shamans.[71]

Human figures predominate in the Namibian rock paintings, where they account for more than 80 per cent of all images. The rest is made up of a range of animals, varying in importance from site to site. Giraffes are consistently prominent among the animals, as are springbuck and the larger antelope, including eland, kudu and oryx. Significantly, these animals hardly feature among the remains of hunted game found at the sites, and their occurrence in the rock art does not correspond with their natural abundance: the animal motifs clearly represent a culturally mediated selection. Close examination of the animal paintings reveals many clues to their probable importance in ritual; some antelope are shown with human feet, while others are shown with their natural markings altered to emphasise those parts of the human body that are identified in the ethnographic record as sites of ritual potency.[72]

The ethnographic record shows that the animals chosen as religious symbols possessed certain qualities that exemplified social values important to the southern San, and that the animals in the rock art are in many instances ritual healers who have temporarily assumed the form and supernatural power of that animal.[73] This reasoning, by which all animate subjects are actually people, might explain why human figures are largely absent from the rock engravings in the same area. A subtle clue linking the two genres is found in the depiction of birds, quite rare in the paintings but common in the engravings,[74] as at the site of Twyfelfontein. Whether painted or engraved, however, the birds are all non-passerine, or striding, species, such as ostrich and bustard. They are often shown proceeding in a line, like people, and occasionally with body decorations like those of trance dance participants.[75]

Rock art interpretation, and the archaeology of Holocene hunter-gatherers in southern Africa, rest on a general model that accommodates regional variation within the framework of the archaeological, ethno-historical, physical anthropological and linguistic evidence. This framework provides for comparison of hunter-gatherer adaptations across the great range of southern African environmental diversity, as well as providing a context for local specialisation, whether in the form of subsistence practices or ritual emphasis in the selection of animal metaphors in rock art. The explanatory robustness of this model came under attack in the 1980s, with the celebrated 'Kalahari Debate', launched with Edwin Wilmsen's critique of positivist anthropology.[76] Archaeologists, more than other scholars, had relied upon the ethnography of the most intensively studied Kalahari group, the Jul'hoansi,[77] as representing Holocene life,[78] while paying less attention to evidence of regular contact between such hunter-gatherer groups and farming peoples as had moved into the region over the preceding 2,000 years. The revisionist analysis went further, to argue that not only was the cultural landscape of the Kalahari far more diverse and complex than most archaeologists believed, but that communities such as the Jul'hoansi might be best understood as a marginalised underclass of dominant agro-pastoral society.[79]

Although the conventional model of Holocene hunter-gatherer society is not so flawed as to be unusable, the critique of its application to archaeology has revealed its particular weakness as a conceptual framework for understanding historical processes such as innovation, contact and economic decline. Archaeologists in southern Africa have used as units of description, analysis and comparison an array of constructions which are labelled as cultures, industries and traditions, and these have been treated as equivalent to the ethnographic record, which has led almost inevitably to a somewhat static view of precolonial society. This approach usually treats evidence of economic and cultural change as indicating outside influence, with innovation generally attributable to the arrival of immigrant peoples. Without doubt, some *a priori* changes in the archaeological sequence are best explained as the result of migration, and the spread of iron-using agro-pastoral communities is a prime example. But there is also regional variation in the evidence, which archaeologists have generally explained as due to sampling differences, local adaptation and other causes, rather than pointing to more subtle cultural evolutionary trends. In Namibia, as elsewhere, it is important to consider such evidence of more complex changes in the form of adaptation and response to innovation if we are to achieve a nuanced understanding of the processes that shaped the indigenous society encountered by the first European visitors.

Fig. 4. An example of the elaborate shamanistic rock art that developed in Namibia during the last 2,000 years (© John Kinahan.)

Complex Economies of Precolonial Namibia

The earliest archaeological site showing evidence of farming settlement in Namibia is Kapako, near Rundu, where pottery—an archaeological signature of food production—as well as bone and iron slag were dated to approximately 850 AD.[80] The pottery from Kapako belongs to the so-called Kalundu Tradition, or the western stream of the movement into this region by Bantu-speaking farming peoples.[81] Then, as today, settled farming in Namibia was limited to the far north, where rainfall conditions were suitable for the staple cereals of millet, sorghum and, recently, maize.[82]

This area was already inhabited by hunter-gatherer communities who acquired pottery from farming settlements,[83] and soon learned to make pottery themselves.[84] From the early first millennium AD, pottery had been in circulation in the wider region, occurring in archaeological sites thousands of kilometres beyond the limits of farming settlement. Little of the pottery is attributable to specific farming traditions as recognised on the Kavango River, but this might only reflect the small extent of archaeological survey in northern Namibia and the adjacent parts of Angola.[85] The important observation is that, before the establishment of farming settlements, hunter-gatherer peoples adopted and spread pottery (in this instance) rapidly, and over a very wide area. Other innovations arrived in this part of southern Africa with the spread of food-producing economies, principally domestic sheep, goats, cattle and dogs, and their distribution is attributed to the southward migration of Khoe-speaking peoples, ancestors of Namibia's Nama pastoralists.

Nomadic pastoralism in southern Africa is historically associated with the Khoekhoen peoples, of whom the precolonial Nama are the best known from early historical accounts of Namibia. On linguistic grounds, the Khoekhoen clearly originate within southern Africa; this is generally agreed on the basis of genetic studies, as well as evidence of common systems of kinship and religious practices.[86] They apparently diverged from the broader Tshu-Kwe group in northern Botswana, about 2,000 years ago,[87] having acquired livestock and pottery from the Bantu-speaking peoples who had begun to settle in that region as farmers. The Khoekhoen are thought to have advanced rapidly southward via a number of hypothetical routes suggested by historical and other evidence,[88] to occupy the more arid western parts of the subcontinent. This model is satisfactory as a general explanation for the evident fact that while the pastoral Khoekhoen encountered by the first European settlers were clearly related to their hunter-gatherer neighbours, their livestock must have come from elsewhere. Archaeological evidence, mainly in the form of pottery and domestic animal bone dated to about 2,000 years ago, at first suggested just such a rapid migration.[89] But, as more evidence accumulated, it appeared that pottery arrived in some cases up to a thousand years before livestock,[90] indicating first, that pottery was not a reliable indicator of pastoralism,

31

and second, that the rapid dispersal of pottery might simply reflect the extensive and interconnected nature of hunter-gatherer exchange networks. Thus, while Khoekhoen pastoralists surely spread as some of the evidence indicates, the movement was perhaps slower, and the process of interaction with other peoples more complex, than at first supposed.[91]

In archaeological models of hunter-gatherer and pastoral interaction in precolonial southern Africa, the historical ethnography of the western Cape has long exercised a certain hegemony. Records of early European settlement at the Cape contain highly detailed accounts of indigenous peoples and these have provided literal flesh to the bones of archaeological reconstruction. Conventionally, archaeologists have treated the historical sources as the 'ethnographic present' of the archaeological record, portraying Khoekhoen and hunter-gatherer society as essentially static until their catastrophic encounter with Europe in the seventeenth century.[92] This model has been widely applied by historians and archaeologists, but its validity is questionable, especially considering the revisionist critique outlined above. In Namibia, the archaeological evidence points to a series of local developments involving an increasingly complex cultural landscape, where the adoption of pastoralism was but one of several specialised economic adaptations. The fact that some of these complex forms of behaviour disappeared before the advent of written ethnography further underlines the importance of the archaeological record as a historical source.

The reoccupation of the Namib Desert during the mid-Holocene climatic amelioration about 5,000 years ago led to the establishment of increasingly specialised hunter-gatherer subsistence patterns. Intensive exploitation of marine resources, mainly mussels, is evident from about 2,000 years ago.[93] There are also clear indications of hunting forays deep into the Namib where few traces of earlier human occupation are found. Some of these groups gathered large quantities of land snails, and other resources such as melons.[94] Specialised techniques were developed to extract and process large quantities of wild grass seed from the underground caches of harvester ants.[95] In a number of places, hunting parties erected extensive systems of low rock barriers to drive migrating antelope into carefully prepared ambushes.[96] These innovations and adaptations improved the efficiency of hunting and gathering and, in the case of food that could be stored, reduced fluctuations in food supply. The available evidence thus points to a process in which specialised techniques provided a measure of food security in an uncertain environment. Greater food security conceivably led to an increase in population, in turn requiring further intensification of hunting and gathering. Whatever the explanation, the degree of control over food supply that developed in the Namib implies a complex form of hunting and gathering, which approached a form of husbandry. The difference between this and pastoralism was not as great as archaeologists sometimes suppose.[97]

Ownership of domestic stock was widespread in the Namib Desert and the interior 1,000 years ago. Although there is suggestive—but insecure—evidence of an earlier arrival as much as 2,000 years ago,[98] it seems that in both Namibia and South Africa the majority of reliable radiocarbon dates are from the second millennium AD.[99] In Namibia, there is compelling evidence that pastoralists used pottery in the intensive exploitation of wild plant foods such as melons and grass seed, rather than in tasks related to animal husbandry, where indeed it has no obvious function.[100] Interestingly, there is similar evidence from South Africa, where pottery was used by pastoralists to render fur seal blubber.[101] The Namibian evidence suggests that at least in a technological sense, the acquisition of pottery and the adoption of domestic animals might be best understood as an elaboration of the evolving complexity of the hunter-gatherer economy. There are indications that involvement in pastoralism varied, with specialist rainmakers and metal-smiths, for example, who were paid in livestock but remained on the periphery of the pastoral economy.[102]

Evidence of social transformations associated with pastoralism is uncertain, mainly because it is for the moment confined to the rock art and is, therefore, undated. The rock art of the Brandberg, primarily the Hungorob Ravine, shows what appears to be a clear shift from monochrome depictions of men and women participating in communal trance rites to polychrome men, painted as individuals with richly elaborate symbolic elements such as body markings, dance rattles and ritual fly whisks.[103] There are similar indications of a shift towards specialisation in the rock art of the Drakensberg in South Africa.[104] The change from egalitarian ritual activity to highly individual and seemingly powerful shamans has some parallels in recent Kalahari ethnography where successful healers were able to establish themselves as wealthy livestock owners.[105] In the Namib Desert and elsewhere in southern Africa, this development may have been a direct response to interaction with immigrant agro-pastoralist communities. Whether this was the mechanism that transformed some hunter-gatherer groups into pastoralists is a matter for continuing debate.[106] It is, however, noteworthy that early in the second millennium AD the rock art sites of the Hungorob Ravine were abandoned in favour of the open air homesteads characteristic of pastoralist settlement.

Notwithstanding the geographical bias towards archaeological investigation in the north-western parts of Namibia, there is a clear concentration of evidence in this area relating to the early arrival of pottery, an overwhelming concentration of rock art[107]—including images of domestic livestock—and an abundance of nomadic pastoralist sites dating to the second millennium AD. One of the pastoral migration routes favoured by the conventional model has it that pastoralists moved into Namibia from the northeast, crossed to the Namib Desert and then moved southward into South Africa.[108] The evidence that has accrued in the last twenty years does not support this hypothesis. Not only is there the strong concentration of archaeological sites in the northwest, but the evidence is that the southern part of the country was more sporadically occupied during the first millennium AD. On balance, therefore, the Namibian evidence is of a core or nucleus of response to the innovation of pastoralism, restricted to the northwest, where highly specialised adaptations to the desert environment had developed since the mid-Holocene climatic amelioration. Long gaps in the occupation of the southern part of the country appear to be borne out by a very low abundance of rock art and an absence of early pastoral evidence. This evidence suggests that the spread of pastoralism involved a process of localised acquisition of livestock by hunter-gatherer communities in optimal environments, the northwestern parts of Namibia being one example. While this model does not exclude the introduction and spread of livestock through the movement of farming peoples into the region, the Namibian archaeological evidence does not favour the immigration of Khoekhoe people as a general explanation for the spread of pastoralism in southern Africa, the view favoured by many scholars.[109]

The pattern of pastoral settlement and land use that developed in the Namib Desert is a very close adaptation to the prevailing environmental conditions.[110] Small, isolated homestead sites, comprising a few huts and some stock enclosures, were occupied during the long dry season. These sites were situated within a few kilometres of reliable water supply, usually hand-dug wells in dry river courses. Dry season pastures included perennial grasslands in the mountains and scrub browse along the river courses. Summer rain in the desert produces a flush of grass cover that is highly nutritious but short-lived. Pastoral homesteads aggregated in large encampments on the annual pastures and the remains of the stone-built hut foundations show that within the encampment, household units remained distinct and separate, each centred about a complex hut with storage cells and other indications of status. The pastoral household layout appears to have been structured according to both status, presumably patriarchal, and gender, cooking shelters being associated with pottery and stone pestles used in the grinding of wild grass seed. Recent ethnographic studies confirm that seed gathering and processing was the concern of women, to the extent that harvester ant nests were recognised as the property of individual women.[111] There is also archaeological evidence to suggest that women congregated at seed processing sites up to several kilometres away from the main encampment. Very rarely do these seed processing sites have evidence of hunting activities such as stone artefact production or animal butchery.

A direct counterpart to the exploitation of grass seed is found elsewhere in the Namib, in the !Khuiseb Delta. Nomadic pastoralist communities in the !Khuiseb adapted the use of pottery to process the flesh of !nara melons, a major component of the diet which could be stored for use over several months. As with the harvester ant nests, !nara bushes were recognised as the property of the families who used them, to the extent that these rights could be inherited, via the female line.[112] Pastoral communities in the !Khuiseb Delta established regular trading contacts with European vessels calling at Walvis Bay from the mid-eighteenth century. A unique eye-witness account of pastoral life in the !Khuiseb Delta, including the first portraits of Namibian people as seen by outsiders, is the 1786 description by Thomas Bolden Thompson of HMS *Nautilus*.[113]

Beef was in considerable demand by visiting ships, and this was obtained in exchange for glass trade beads, porcelain and a variety of other goods including, eventually, liquor and firearms. Relatively permanent pastoral encampments were maintained in the dune-fields immediately inland of Walvis Bay, the focus of pastoral settlement having shifted northwards and nearer to the anchorage, to maintain control over trading contact. This move made it necessary to keep cattle and other stock further inland at the nearest pasture and water, and traders' accounts mention having to wait several days for the animals to be brought down to the Bay. Archaeological evidence of this trade includes one site with perfectly preserved hoof impressions of the cattle and small stock, together with the tracks of the people, including adults, children, as well as dogs, that herded the animals over the tidal mudflats of the lagoon.[114]

WOMAN IN WALWICH BAY. CAFFRARIA.

Fig. 5. One of the illustrations from the 1786 journal of Captain T.B. Thompson, R.N., probably the earliest portrait of a Namibian as seen by an outsider. The subject is shown wearing a sealskin cloak over her shoulders; hanging about her neck are a bodkin and bone !nara knife with punctuate decorations identical to those found on archaeological examples. The earring ornament appears to be a Royal Navy button, bearing the fouled anchor insignia first adopted in 1774. (Reproduced courtesy of Quentin Keynes.)

The archaeological evidence suggests that wealth in trade goods was unevenly distributed, and that dependence on marine foods as well as !nara melons might indicate the growth of a marginalised class of people who no longer possessed livestock and could not benefit directly from trade with visiting ships. Later, towards the end of the nineteenth century, poverty was a noticeable feature of the Walvis Bay area and many people lived from hand-outs and missionary charity.[115] The phenomenon of marginalisation among pastoral communities was noticed in the Cape, where people who had lost their animals and lived as outlaws and stock raiders were known by specific ethnic names.[116] Sharp economic divisions, combined with the practice of ethnic labelling, could explain historical references to the existence of two separate sections of the ‡Aonin at Walvis Bay: the !Khuisenin, who kept livestock, and the Hurínin, who subsisted on fish, mussels and whatever they could find on the coast.[117] The potential for economic marginalisation was apparently intensified during this period.

Relative dating of pastoral encampments, using trade items of known age, shows that contact with Europeans greatly intensified local economic activity, with glass beads and other items achieving a wide inland distribution. Hostile exchanges sometimes occurred at Walvis Bay, and it appears from the documentary record that the ‡Aonin, ancestors of today's Topnaar people, did not encourage visitors from ships to go further inland than the first line of dunes, where lookouts were placed to warn of approaching ships.[118] The items recovered from the archaeological sites at Walvis Bay show that the ‡Aonin were highly selective in their acceptance of trade goods. The range of glass beads found at Walvis Bay is far smaller than was available at the time and it seems that the ‡Aonin were primarily interested in beads that could be absorbed into the pre-existing indigenous exchange of livestock and copper and iron beads. Thus glass beads for the ‡Aonin were not mere truck, as the Europeans may have thought. In fact, the European visitors were being drawn deliberately into the indigenous economy.[119] European porcelain, or earthenware, reveals a similar selectivity on the part of the ‡Aonin, who particularly favoured annular ware bowls, a distinctive and useful type of vessel, eschewing flat plates and fancy items that had no equivalent in the indigenous assemblage.

However, the ‡Aonin and the masters of passing ships were not trading as equals; the trade goods acquired by the ‡Aonin did not have the same value in labour and livestock production in the merchant economy, and as the volume of trade goods increased, their value would have begun to decline. It is likely that the root of this inflationary tendency lay partly in the pastoral economy itself, where livestock could be transformed into commodities such as copper if the number of animals exceeded the herding labour capacity of the household. Livestock exchanges and loans were also employed, as a risk management strategy, but as long as copper remained relatively scarce it could serve as a temporary repository for wealth in livestock. The ǂAonin faced all the usual risks of pastoralism, including drought, disease and raiding, and so their position was highly vulnerable even before the advent of trade with Europeans. As it happened, the trade at Walvis Bay began in earnest early in the nineteenth century, at the same time as the Oorlam Nama moved into southern Namibia and engaged in large-scale raiding to feed the overland livestock trade to the Cape Colony. Within decades, the Oorlam depredations were felt even in northern Namibia. The most strategic site for the Oorlam was in the centre of the country, where the capital, Windhoek, stands today. Jonker Afrikaner, the visionary leader of the Oorlam, established a trading route to Walvis Bay and in that way eclipsed the influence of all other indigenous traders.[120]

Conventional accounts of the Oorlam expansion into Namibia rely on documentary sources which generally imply that the Oorlam—a term that in fact means 'experienced' in the vernacular Dutch of the Cape[121]—were acculturated to the extent that they were no longer Nama pastoralists in the traditional sense.[122] They possessed guns and ox wagons, dressed in European clothes, and had apparently lost the Nama kinship-based social structures. In this sense, the Oorlam might be considered to represent the vanguard of European expansion into Namibia, although some writers dispute the degree to which the Oorlam had been 'Europeanised'.[123] Part of this uncertainty rests on the fact that there are few documentary sources containing direct observations of the Oorlam in the 1790s,[124] when they moved across the Orange River to avoid attack by colonists who held the Oorlam under Klaas Afrikaner responsible for the murder of one of their compatriots, Pieter Pienaar.[125]

Fortunately, the ruins of the encampment established by the Oorlam on a remote bend in the Bak River in south-eastern Namibia still exist. The site, known as ǁKhauxaǃnas, occupies a low hill, overlooking a waterhole that is reputed never to fail. A perimeter wall almost 700 m in length encloses an area of approximately 35,000 square metres, containing the ruins of up to thirty dwellings. The method of dry-stone construction, using throughband stones at key points and rubble filling, is typical of colonial stock enclosures dating to the nineteenth century. So, too, are drainage holes and the use of rectangular layout in some of the buildings.[126] Although these features provide material confirmation of the documentary record and the general consensus of historians, the site contains other evidence that casts light on the detailed links between colonial and indigenous societies, and this helps to define the subtle transitionary status of the Oorlam.

The southern part of the ‖Khauxa!nas boundary wall faces the approach that would have been used by visitors from Cape Colony. Here the walling is well finished and the slope below provides a natural *glacis* that would slow any attackers on foot. A rectangular building on the outside of the wall probably served as a reception point, and once through the entrance alongside it, the visitor would next encounter the large and elaborate main household, with perimeter walls of well-laid stone. The boundary wall of the encampment has a total of twenty-two gateways, but none is wide enough to have admitted an ox-wagon. If at the time of their residence at ‖Khauxa!nas the Oorlam had possessed wagons, they are unlikely to have left them outside the protective screen of the boundary wall. This alone suggests that the documentary record only reflects the circumstances of the Oorlam at a later stage, when wagons had been added to their equipment. A similar contradiction lies in the question of firearms. Historians state that the Oorlam had rifles, but the gunflints found on the site suggest the use of smoothbore guns such as were more commonly in use at that time.[127] The southern defences of the site are appropriate for such inaccurate weapons, but quite unnecessary for rifles with a longer effective range.

There is crucial evidence in the internal layout of the site to show that the Oorlam had not abandoned the indigenous kinship system, as has been claimed.[128] Indeed, the evidence of the site itself provides valuable insights that augment the documentary sources. Nearly all of the gateways on the northern perimeter of ‖Khauxa!nas lead directly into discrete groups of huts and cooking shelters, and a number of the gateways have screening walls that would have enhanced the privacy of these household groups. The northern perimeter wall seems to have been a continuous rear side of a string of households, many having a small ash midden against the outside of the perimeter. The grouping of the huts, their individual and separate access points, and the lack of communal facilities directly parallel the structure of earlier nomadic pastoral aggregation camps in Namibia. The layout of the traditional encampments expressed the relative autonomy of family groups within the aggregation and was therefore structured on kinship lines. ‖Khauxa!nas is known to have been the camp of Klaas Afrikaner and his two sons, Jager and Titus. It is therefore no surprise to find that there are two particularly elaborate household clusters at the northern end of the site; these were probably occupied by the two sons, while the largest household cluster, just inside the southern boundary, was probably occupied by Klaas himself.

From the mid-nineteenth century, documentary sources are relatively plentiful and the archaeological record is of supplementary rather than prime importance. This is especially so when alternative and perhaps conflicting documentary evidence lessens the historian's dependence on single authoritative sources. However, large parts of Namibia remained out of reach and relatively unknown to European colonists until the early twentieth century. In such circumstances recent archaeological evidence can add much detail to the historical record. One example is the guano rush of 1844 when thousands of foreign ships congregated around Namibia's offshore islands, notably Ichabo. There is little documentary record of the intense interaction between the ships and indigenous people living on the coast, but recent archaeological research has located several sites with evidence of this contact.[129] A second illustrative example is provided by the catastrophic rinderpest epidemic which reached Namibia in 1897, leading to very high mortality of cattle and the effective collapse of pastoralism.[130] There are no documentary records of the impoverished people who moved out into the Namib Desert to live on wild grass seed, but numerous archaeological sites attest to this tragic event.[131]

The Fragile Heritage of the Archaeological Record

Our current understanding of the Namibian archaeological sequence is based on a very small sample of sites where systematic investigations have been carried out. The normal practice in Namibian archaeology is to limit excavation to a representative fraction of the site, the remainder being left undisturbed to allow for future investigation.

Furthermore, field surveys often involve documentation of rock art and other features that cannot be moved. This means that most of the archaeological material representing the great span of Namibian pre-colonial history lies not in the controlled storage of a museum or archive, but on the open landscape, exposed to both natural decay and damage from modern human activities. It is not physically possible to excavate, collect and house every item of the Namibian archaeological record. Nor is it desirable to do so, for context—the original physical setting of archaeological remains—is as informative as the find itself.

In keeping with international practice, the legal protection of archaeological sites in Namibia makes provision for archaeological impact assessment of large projects such as mines and infrastructure development. Development projects can have major impacts on vulnerable archaeological sites, and several large-scale archaeological investigations have taken place as a result. Mineral exploration is mainly carried out by foreign-based mining houses which are frequently subject to domestic legislation concerning archaeological impact mitigation in overseas projects. This greatly strengthens the Namibian measures, as does the imposition of international standards by major lending institutions that provide funding for Namibian utility expansion projects.[132]

Archaeological remains in Namibia are protected under the National Heritage Act (27 of 2004),[133] which makes provision for the proclamation of archaeological and other heritage sites as national monuments. There are about ninety national monuments in Namibia: only twelve are archaeological sites, the remainder being colonial buildings, memorials and other sites of interest. The limited attention to precolonial history is thus mirrored in the selection of sites as national monuments. This could be partly explained by the divergence of archaeology and history that was pointed out at the beginning of this chapter. Such divergence is exacerbated by the lack of narrative continuity between the archaeological past and the modern history of anti-colonial struggle in Namibia.

The Namibian school curriculum addresses the teaching of history based on evidence other than the documentary record, by emphasising the value and specific nature of sources including oral tradition and archaeological evidence. The school curriculum links the precolonial and colonial history of Namibia, and uses the archaeological evidence to frame a wider African context for precolonial Namibia. The curriculum also stresses the unique nature of archaeological evidence and its vulnerability to damage through modern developments, in this way carrying a strong conservation message.

Namibia became a signatory to the World Heritage Convention within a few years of independence, and in 2007 gained World Heritage listing of Twyfelfontein, an outstanding example of a late Holocene hunter-gatherer rock art site. The site contains over 2,000 engravings, and with 150,000 visitors per year, is the most heavily visited rock art site in Africa. Very few Namibians visit the site, however, in marked contrast to neighbouring Botswana, Zimbabwe and South Africa, where site visits by school pupils account for a significant proportion of visitor numbers. The Namibian situation may illustrate the fragility of traditional practices and the relative ease with which their historical continuity can be broken. In Zimbabwe, by contrast, some continuity in the ritual importance of rock art sites is evident.[134]

Foreign institutions and research programmes have always played an important—even dominant—role in Namibian archaeology. The early link with France did not continue after the work of Henri Breuil in the 1950s, although post-independence Namibia has seen a renewal of interest through co-operative programmes involving the National Museum. Sporadic British, North American and Swedish based research initiatives were launched after independence, replacing the strong links that previously existed with various South African museums and universities. However, the strongest and most consistent foreign research effort is based in Germany, with almost fifty years of continuous fieldwork and research publication. None of the foreign research initiatives has led to the establishment of permanent facilities, institutional support or significant training programmes which arose elsewhere in Africa where former colonial powers remained active in archaeological research.

In conclusion, it is worthwhile to sketch out a number of likely directions for future research, and to identify some critical questions that archaeologists could attend to in Namibia. Moving backwards in time, one of the most necessary areas for research is the archaeology of agricultural settlement in northern Namibia—its time span, its ecological setting, its links with the powerful kingdoms of southern Angola[135] before and during the slave trade, and its impact on small-scale hunter-gatherer communities to the south, within Namibia. The evolution of traditional settlement layout in north-central Namibia might be pursued archaeologically, to investigate the development of complex settlement design possibly as a response to the threat of attack, and as a metaphorical expression of social hierarchy. The influence of mixed agriculture on hunter-gatherer society may be less easily ascertained, but frontiers or zones of contact can provide critical insights into the history of precolonial Namibia.[136]

Archaeological research can contribute to an understanding of the environmental effects of agriculture and animal husbandry over the last two millennia, providing time-series data that reveal such longer-term consequences as arise from disturbance of tree savannah and arid scrub vegetation systems. This would require both conventional archaeological investigation, in the form of settlement mapping and dating, and specialised reconstruction of vegetation systems. Equally important as ecological responses would be the economic risk-management strategies of precolonial society, including livestock loans and marriage practices.[137] While archaeological investigation might not provide comprehensive insights into issues such as these, its unique temporal perspective will always provide a necessary complement to African history.

Material evidence from archaeological investigation is always a useful complement to the documentary record, and the early history of settler communities in Namibia provides many instances of idealised description which make illuminating comparison with evidence found at farms, mission stations and other places. Ancestral land claims may in some cases find support from the archaeological record, while in others the evidence may be less accommodating of political ambition.[138]

2

POLITICS, TRADE AND TRANSFORMATION

SOUTHERN AND CENTRAL NAMIBIA, 1730–1870

The period between 1730 and 1870 was a time of rapid transformation. At its beginning, much of what was to become central and southern Namibia was inhabited by foragers, hunters and herders, and was traversed by extensive precolonial trade networks. By its end, the region's political, social and economic dynamics had been radically reshaped, not least by the rise and fall of a form of centralised control over the entire region, as Jonker Afrikaner won and then lost effective dominance. In the same period, economic relations were fundamentally reoriented as central and southern Namibia became incorporated into the Cape economic nexus, and indigenous societies seized the opportunities offered by the advent of merchant capital. By 1870, too, Christian missions had put down firm roots, white traders had begun to play important economic and political roles, and the question of formal colonisation loomed on the horizon. The fact that Namibia, sandwiched between the much older colonies of Portuguese Angola and the Dutch/British Cape, had hitherto been spared European occupation had much to do with its marginal environment and inaccessible coast.

This chapter begins, somewhat arbitrarily, in 1730, because at about that point it begins to be possible to trace some of these histories through historical, as well as archaeological and linguistic, sources. As discussed in the Introduction, the written records we have are far from perfect; for the eighteenth century in particular they are extremely patchy, shedding no light on huge expanses of space and time and casting their beam disproportionately on areas and events witnessed by Europeans. Oral traditions, now published for Herero and Mbanderu, provide an invaluable source, but tend to concentrate on military and political events, and to construct particular narratives of the rise and fall of the power of Otjiherero-speakers.

The chapter's end point, 1870, is more closely bound up with the course of Namibia's history, since this was the year of the signing of the Okahandja peace accords, which marked the end of Oorlam Afrikaner dominance and the rise to power of the Herero paramount, Maharero. Spatially, the chapter deals with the centre and south of the country, defined by nineteenth-century European observers as 'Damaraland' and 'Great Namaqualand' respectively.[1] The former was understood as the land of the 'Cattle Damara'—a term later equated with 'Herero', although things were not as simple as that, as we shall see below. Great Namaqualand was defined as the region between Damaraland and the Orange (Gariep) River, and understood to 'belong' to Nama Oorlam groups. In fact, these neat definitions of territory and ethnicity would have been contested from many different angles by the region's contemporary African inhabitants. Central and southern Namibia was a complex political environment, in which groups of people speaking Otjiherero, Khoekhoegowab, Cape Dutch and San languages maintained varied and intertwined relationships, and where claims to rights to land, water and grazing sometimes flared into conflict.

One reason for considering Great Namaqualand and Damaraland together in this chapter is that they began to develop a certain geographical coherence during this period, becoming deeply enmeshed in the Cape trade and, later, subject to the full force of German colonialism. By contrast, most of the people of the north lived in relatively settled communities, unlike the originally semi-nomadic peoples to the south, and were governed through centralised kingdoms that did not begin to come under direct colonial rule until 1909. For this reason Chapter 3 deals with the history of Owambo, Kaoko, Kavango and Caprivi in the precolonial period. The spatial (and temporal) divisions used in this work should, however, be understood as an organising device, not a physical barrier. There was much contact between Ovambo societies and their southern neighbours at this period, particularly through trade, and there were also close connections—and migration—between Otjiherero-speakers in the Kaoko and those living to the south.

Land, People and Power

As we saw in the previous chapter, by the end of the eighteenth century the southern and central part of Namibia was inhabited by small and highly mobile groups of people who lived from herding cattle, sheep and goats, foraging for a wide range of food from the bush (*veldkos*), hunting and trapping game, and possibly some small-scale agriculture;[2] they also ran both short- and long-distance trade networks. Although historians and archaeologists still debate fiercely whether people could and did move between different 'lifeways' as economic circumstances changed—for example, whether hunter-gatherers always remained so, or could become pastoralists when conditions were right—there was undoubtedly some fluidity. Both flexibility and mobility were vital to survival in this fragile ecology, where water was usually short, drought frequent, and pasture and other resources could quickly become exhausted. The difficulties of obtaining sufficient food, especially in lean years, compromised the health of the population, particularly those without cattle; however, the disease environment was not as harsh as the more fertile and well-watered areas to the north, where malaria and in some places sleeping sickness were endemic.[3]

Control of productive resources centred, not on the ownership of specific portions of land, but on rights to wells, pasture and other resources such as ants' nests and beehives. As the anthropologist Winifred Hoernlé, writing in the early twentieth century, put it:

Before the coming of the missionaries these people [the Nama] wandered about from fountain to fountain, seeking pasture for their stock. Large permanent fountains, or pools in river beds were claimed as their property by the different groups, rather than areas enclosed by definite territorial boundaries.[4]

Water and grazing, people and herds, were thus 'bound…into a network of political interests and equally into a structure of political control'[5] which was not static and could become the subject of contestation and conflict. Claims to resources might be asserted or reasserted at particular historical moments, as land was abandoned or (re)occupied.

At the beginning of the nineteenth century, the broader political framework seems to have been largely characterised by decentralised power and authority. For example, although the leader of the Kai ‖Khaun or Red Nation had theoretical superiority (based on a hereditary claim) over other Nama groups, in practice his power was heavily circumscribed. According to Hoernlé, a Nama chief '…was acknowledged to be the head of the senior sib [clan] and, if a person of fine character, was accorded a great deal of respect, but the heads of the other sibs acted as his council and he could not do much without their cooperation'.[6] The ancestors of the present-day Damara, too, generally seem to have placed authority in each individual (male) family head.[7]

The nineteenth century saw the rise of leaders—'big men' in anthropological terminology—who acquired power on a new scale (even though their authority was still fairly circumscribed in comparison, for example, with that of the Ovambo kings to the north). These men were drawn mainly from within Oorlam groups (newcomers from the Cape province to the south) and, from the 1860s, from among Otjiherero-speakers. Their ability to acquire and maintain a leadership position depended little, if at all, on hereditary claims, but rather on attracting followers (since labour was a critical resource) and building up herds (the key to wealth). The acquisition of guns, ammunition and horses—usually through trade with the Cape—was also critical. The development of broader forms of authority was not, however, exclusive to pastoralist groups: by the late nineteenth century forms of chieftainship also seem to have emerged among the Hai‖Om in north-central Namibia, perhaps as a result of the (so far successful) struggle to preserve their autonomy from both the Herero groups to the south and the Ovambo polities to the north. In the long term, however, the rise of the 'big men' and the trading, raiding and warfare that developed during the nineteenth century put the Damara and San groups scattered across the country under great pressure.[8]

Control of the bodies and productive capacities of women was a particularly important source of power for aspiring leaders, who were almost always men. Women were bound into complex networks of exchange and alliance, principally through marriage. They (as well as children) were also taken as booty in cattle raids, and they were also disadvantaged in particular ways, for example through the legal system. Lita Webley has argued that the situation of Khoekhoe women probably worsened during the nineteenth century. In 1800, Nama women could own property and livestock, and control most of their own production; in the early nineteenth century a female chief named Games even appears to have ruled the Red Nation until the heir, her brother, came of age. The arrival of groups using guns and practising aggressive raiding (of which more below) probably undermined the position of women significantly.

Relative wealth, seniority and kinship ties also played a part in determining the limits to women's autonomy and mobility. For example, among Herero and Damara, older, high-status women played an important role at the holy fire (an important focal point for both groups). The sources also record differentiation among women: a woman of the powerful Oorlam society ruled by Amraal had a number of female servants, some of them Damara.[9]

Although nineteenth-century networks of power were loosely based on the support (or submission) of those sharing affinities of kinship and language, they were by no means ethnically exclusive. Indeed, the cohesive ethnic groups of modern Namibia—'the Herero', 'the Damara', 'the Nama' and so on—were largely a development of the late nineteenth and twentieth centuries. It is true that certain common cultural and linguistic threads were present at an earlier period, for example among Otjiherero-speakers, who by the 1870s had developed both a strong emphasis on cattle for ceremonial purposes and as a store of wealth, which may well have drawn on older roots, and a quite unusual 'double descent' system (in which goods were inherited through both the male and female lines) that was not shared by either the patrilineal peoples around them or the matrilineal societies to the north. Early European observers, however, as Dag Henrichsen has argued, attested to a much more fluid situation earlier in the century, often describing people in central Namibia as 'Cattle Damara' or 'Hill Damara' (*Vieh-* or *Bergdamara or dama*). Although these terms have frequently been understood as 'Herero' and 'Damara' respectively, they were in fact used as economic, as much as ethnic or linguistic, markers: they indicate not which language people spoke, but whether they owned cattle. The term 'Herero' did not emerge as an important label until the second half of the century, and at that date it was still necessary to have cattle in order to 'be Herero'; impoverished Otjiherero-speakers were called 'Ovatjimba', not 'Ovaherero'. Only in the 1870s did 'Omuherero' truly come to signify ethnicity, as the process of defining Herero identity took shape.[10]

The reality of nineteenth-century Namibia, was, then, one in which kin relations helped to construct, but did not dictate, political units: 'Descent ideology is not identical with political authority. It is the language of political authority'.[11] People of varied origins and language groups might join together to obtain the protection of a strong leader; political and social identity was frequently remoulded through the dispersal and making (or remaking) of small polities around individual leaders; individuals and groups might be captured or conquered in raids, and incorporated into militarily stronger societies by marriage, as bonded labourers, or as tribute-payers; disparate groups might assemble temporarily to take advantage of the opportunities offered by trade or European explorers.[12] The nineteenth century therefore saw the creation, and in some cases the dissolution, of diverse and stratified polities.

The Expansion of the Frontier

Even from the early eighteenth century, the area north of the Gariep (which today forms the southern boundary of Namibia) was beginning to be affected by the expansion of Cape Colony from the south. Founded by the Dutch in 1652, the Colony grew as settler numbers, and thus the demand for farmland, increased. This expansion took place mainly through a series of bitter and protracted wars with the pre-existing inhabitants—San, Khoekhoe and Xhosa—a process that involved 'the conquest of indigenous lands, the depletion of Khoikhoi herds, the invasion of the traditional hunting-grounds of hunter-gatherer communities, and the ultimate loss of independence by indigenous peoples'.[13] By 1809, the conquest of the Khoekhoe and San communities south of the Gariep was effectively complete: proclamations of 1809 and 1812 formally incorporated them into the economy of what was now a British colony.[14]

As early as 1738, a trading expedition of Boers and their Khoekhoe and San servants from the Cape Colony crossed the Gariep into Great Namaqualand. This journey culminated in a surprise attack on the homestead of a chief or *kaptein* called Gal, killing seven people and stealing more than a thousand cattle. The chief's son, Captain Gaaren, travelled to Cape Town to complain; the episode fuelled more general unrest, which erupted into open warfare south of the Gariep in 1739 and ended in crushing defeat for Khoekhoe and San.[15]

In the 1730s, southern Namibia was still far beyond the bounds of the Cape Colony, but by the 1780s the population of the northern frontier areas was coming under intense pressure from settler expansion. Some colonists seem to have been settling, or at least grazing their animals, north of the Gariep, as shown by complaints made by representatives of the Great Namaqua at the time of another uprising in Little Namaqualand, in 1798–99.[16] In addition to the better-known journeys of whites to the river and beyond—particularly those of Jako-bus Coetzé (1760), Hendrik Hop (1761–62), Hendrik Wikar (1778–79), and Robert Gordon (1779)—there was obviously much unrecorded contact. In the early 1790s, it was also claimed that gold deposits existed several days' journey north of the Gariep. If this had proved true, much of present-day Namibia would probably have been annexed immediately by the Cape; however, the supposed gold ore turned out to contain only copper.[17]

Despite the interest of the colonists, it was in fact fugitive and Oor-lam groups that exerted the most significant outside influence on Namibia at this period, creating the first substantial and long-term links between the Cape and Great Namaqualand.[18] It is probable that refugees from the violence of the 1730s fled northwards into southern Namibia, arriving in significant numbers by the end of the century. These might be individuals—fleeing slaves and servants, escaped crim-inals—or groups migrating with their stock. In many cases these new-comers were the cultural products of the frontier,[19] which was not only violent—although it was certainly that—but also a place where incor-poration, cultural shifts and interracial sexual relationships occurred, enabling some individuals of relatively low status in the colonial dis-pensation to acquire new skills and often identities. These were often people of Khoekhoe, mixed race or slave origin, who usually worked for the settlers, perhaps growing up in their houses and on their farms; others were the children of white colonists and African women. In time, groups with a new 'Oorlam' identity emerged—that is, 'people living outside the [Cape] colony but possessing attributes acquired within the colony'.[20] These qualities included the ability to speak Cape Dutch, the possession of firearms, wagons and horses, and frequently the adoption of Christianity. The term 'Oorlam' essentially indicated an economic and cultural identity, and also a deeply gendered one: Oorlam groups depended heavily on cattle-raiding, which they carried out by means of the commando, a mounted group of men armed with guns. They had adopted this institution from the colonists, who used it to form mounted citizen militias in order to launch raids on neigh-bouring societies. Groups of 'Basters' ('Bastaards'), people of mixed white and African ancestry, also emerged on the frontier.

The 'Great Namaqua' whom the Oorlam encountered on entering Namibia consisted of a number of different Nama-speaking pastoralist groups. The Kaiǁkhaun, or Red Nation, were generally recognised as senior and are known to have lived in the Karas Mountains in the early nineteenth century; they probably granted the Oorlam incomers settlement rights. The other Nama-speaking groups of whom there is evidence are the !Kami‡nûn (Bondelswarts), who probably lived in south-eastern Namibia from the late sixteenth century; the ǁKhaulgôan (Swartboois), who perhaps separated from the Red Nation around 1800 and at this time lived at the Fish River, around Keetmanshoop; the !Kharakhoen (Fransman people), also living near the Karas Mountains at this time; the ǁHaboben (Veldschoendragers); the !Gomen or ǁO-gain (Groot Doode); and the ‡Aonin (Topnaar) at Walvis Bay.[21]

Among the incoming Oorlam groups, the Afrikaners were to have the most significant impact on Namibia. First recorded in the sources in 1761, by the early 1790s the Afrikaner family, under Klaas Afrikaner, were working for Petrus Pienaar, a successful white farmer based in the Orange River District. Pienaar employed the male members of the group as a commando, and they acquired a fearsome reputation for aggressive (and profitable) raiding. In 1796, however, they rebelled and killed Pienaar and most of his family and fled to the Orange River area, where they engaged in banditry, killing and trade in ivory and arms, attracting a group of Khoekhoe and San followers, and using southern Namibia as a refuge.[22] Despite their (well-deserved) violent reputation, however, they eventually made peace with the Cape government in 1819, when Jager Afrikaner (who had been baptised four years earlier) and his son Jonker travelled to Cape Town under the aegis of the missionary Robert Moffat.

Some of the Oorlam groups, like the Afrikaners, emerged as coherent units before they crossed the Orange, while others did so thereafter. The Bethany people probably crystallised as a group from the related Boois and Frederiks families, who settled at Klipfontein (later Bethany); they seem to have left the Cape around the beginning of the nineteenth century, both because of the possibility of conscription during the brief Dutch reoccupation of the Cape in 1803–6 and because their leader, Jacobus Boois, was illegally trading in guns on Jager Afrikaner's behalf.[23] The Khauas people, by contrast, were formed under missionary influence. Piet Vlermuis, leader of one Oorlam group, settled with his people at the mission stations at Heirachabis and, from 1813, at Bethany; in the 1830s he placed his people under the leadership of Amraal Lambert, who had arrived at Bethany in 1814, and later moved with his followers to Naosonabis and then

THE NAMAQUA KRAAL.

Vol. I., p. 428.

Fig. 6. This illustration of a Nama/Oorlam village, captioned 'the Namaqua kraal', appeared in James Chapman's account of travelling through South Africa, Namibia and Botswana in the 1850s. Although the location of the picture is not discussed, it appears in the book alongside text describing encounters with Amraal's people in the east. Note the circular houses, which were constructed from mats laid over a framework of reeds and could be taken apart in order to move to a new settlement. The men on the right are riding oxen, a common practice in Namibia at this date. (From James Chapman, *Travels in the Interior of South Africa* [London: Bell and Daldy, 1868], facing p. 426. SOAS Library. Photographer: Glenn Ratcliffe.)

Gobabis. The combined group came to be called the Khauas people or Kailkhaun.

As these histories imply, the people of Great Namaqualan were influenced in a variety of ways by Namibia's first missionaries, who arrived under the aegis of the London Missionary Society (LMS)[24] and established their first station at Warmbad in 1806. Both Nama and Oorlam, probably especially the poor, gathered at mission stations, which offered access to resources, and developed an atmosphere of religious enthusiasm. Even though Oorlam leaders also demanded missionaries because of their potential for opening up trade routes, these early missions were precarious. Warmbad had to be abandoned in 1811 because of Jager's attacks, and again in 1818. Heirachabis had a much shorter life, closing as early as 1808, while Bethany (Klipfontein), the third and final station to be founded at this time, opened in 1814 but closed in 1822 (Warmbad was reopened in 1834 by the Wesleyan Methodist Mission Society, and Bethany in 1842 by the Rhenish Mission Society).

These first tentative Christian ventures, unlike later missions, did not attempt to remould indigenous societies. Although the mobility of pastoralists was later to be condemned by both missionaries and colonial authorities as a signifier of 'savagery', at this date some missionaries found that the only way to maintain contact with their followers in times of drought was to pursue the same semi-nomadic lifestyle; they lived, like everyone else, in reed huts. They were also heavily dependent on the work of African converts, as preachers and catechists—a role frequently taken on by elite families—and linguists. In fact Johann Schmelen, the LMS missionary at Bethany, married a Nama-speaking woman named Zara, who was the main author of a number of Nama translations of religious works begun by her husband. The Schmelens became the founders of a mixed-race missionary dynasty; their marriage, despite being the target of some disapproval by the mission authorities, was praised by a number of nineteenth-century commentators as a practical means of mission and a way of creating a Christian elite.[25]

Despite the limitations of early mission work, it is clear that the missionaries were significantly tied in to temporal power relations. Jonker Afrikaner's destruction of Warmbad in 1811 was part of a pattern of attacks on Nama groups in the area, but it may have been triggered by the fact that the missionary, Johann Albrecht, had appealed to the Cape for a commando to be raised against the Afrikaners. The dissolution of Bethany in 1822 was a result both of the drought gripping the area and of violent conflict between Johann Schmelen, Piet Vlermuis and Jantje Kagab (the latter was probably chief of the !Kharakhoen). The dispute may have originated in the loss of missionary control over arms and ammunition, after the route to the sea at Angra Pequena (now Lüderitz(bucht)) had been successfully opened up by Piet Vlermuis and his followers in 1815, giving them the opportunity to trade directly for weaponry. The events at Bethany gave rise to further hostility towards the mission and a general increase in conflict during the 1820s, which in turn created the conditions in which the missionary William Threlfall and his African companions Jacob Links and Johann Jager, attempting to found a new mission station, were killed near Warmbad in 1825.[26]

Brigitte Lau argued that this rise in tension resulted from an increasingly violent 'Oorlam invasion', which followed an initial period of cooperation between Oorlam and Nama and lasted through the 1820s, destroying the herds, political autonomy and traditional social structures of the latter. The institution of the commando was particularly important in this process. However, as we saw in the previous chapter, subsequent research by both Tilman Dedering and John Kinahan has revealed complexities beyond the Nama-Oorlam polarisation posited by Lau. Specific, local circumstances, and competition over economic resources and political influence, had greater significance than a more generalised hostility between Nama and Oorlam. Indeed, we know that Nama and Oorlam sometimes fought together, that Oorlam groups were sometimes in conflict with each other, and that both Nama and Oorlam settled on mission stations.

In addition, in the early nineteenth century Nama and Oorlam modes of production were not as much at variance as has been supposed. Dedering argues that, given the marginality of the environment in southern Namibia, the Nama were never 'a cattle-rich, self-sufficient African society that perpetuated itself in ecological balance'.[27] Although they had cattle, they relied mainly on sheep and goats and other strategies such as foraging; raiding was also a widely used accumulation strategy even before the arrival of the Oorlams. Conversely, the latter were not always dominant. Only the Afrikaners had significant firepower, and even though they represented a major political and to some extent military force in southern Namibia and the northern Cape from the early years of the century, they did not attain a commanding position until the 1830s. Nor, although they were eventually to have (like the missionaries) enormous cultural and economic influence on the societies of southern Namibia, did they enter the country carrying 'the "merchant capital factor" on their backs across the Orange as they carried their guns'.[28] Although there was early trade at the coast and into the interior (as we shall see below), and some new southbound trade in the early decades of the nineteenth century, Nama-Oorlam communities in the south only began to engage seriously in long-distance commerce from the 1830s, and a significant volume of trade or engagement with merchant capital did not develop until the 1840s. Before this, Oorlam groups remained dependent on pastoralism.[29]

The conflicts of the 1820s, and in particular the murder of Threlfall in 1825, encouraged the Cape government to take a greater interest in the area north of the Gariep. In 1830, it concluded its first alliance with a local *kaptein*—Abraham Christian, leader of the Bondelswarts, who had requested help against the Oorlam Afrikaners—with the idea of developing a 'buffer zone' on the northern frontier through cooperation with African leaders. This was in part an attempt by the Cape government to counter a new (perceived) threat from the increased mobility of Khoekhoe and San, who had, in theory, been freed from forced labour by Ordinance 50 of 1828. In 1834 the mission at Warmbad was reopened and its new leader, Edward Cook, began to liaise between the Cape government and Abraham Christian—the first time a missionary had taken on such a role in Namibia. In 1837 the first public visit of an emissary of the Cape government was made by James Alexander (an earlier secret mission had been carried out by Andrew Smith in 1828). Alexander recommended increasing the level of cattle imports from Namibia, particularly because of fears about the food supply in the Cape following the exodus of Boer farmers from the Colony in 1837 (the so-called 'Great Trek').

This cattle trade existed already because Africans in Namibia's coastal settlements had, besides connecting with a network of precolonial trade routes, been engaging in commerce with European shipping for some considerable time.[30] In 1786 the captain of the British ship HMS *Nautilus* encountered a 'village' of people speaking a click language and possessing cattle and dogs, as well as eating 'the fruit of a small thorny plant which the [ship's] Botanist found to be a kind of Cucumber' (the !nara melon, a staple food at the coast).[31] Although these coastal peoples—discussed in the previous chapter—had probably been trading with Europeans since the mid-eighteenth century, it was only in the 1770s that the advent of whaling off the Namibian coast led to a significant increase in the volume of trade. By this date whale products had become essential commodities in Europe and the American colonies. Whalebone was used to make umbrellas and corsets, while the oil was used for street lighting and to make paints and lubricants and tan hides. With the exhaustion of the whaling grounds off New England in the 1760s, the resources of the Namibian coast became increasingly important to American, French and particularly British whalers. Whaling here peaked between 1790 and 1810, although it continued until stocks became depleted in the 1840s. Shore stations were founded from 1810, and seal hunting also became important.[32]

Walvis Bay was at the centre of this trade, although other coastal settlements including Sandwich Harbour and Angra Pequena were also involved. There is some evidence that the new commerce was incorporated into pre-existing networks. The people at ‡Khisa-ǁgubus (near to Walvis Bay) dealt in, among other things, copper beads from the mountains of the interior, cowrie shells from the Indian Ocean, European glass beads from the ships, and cattle. The latter trade, probably supplied from as far away as modern Botswana, was already sizeable by the 1830s: one individual captain is recorded to have expected to buy between two and three hundred head of cattle. It has been argued that Otjiherero-speakers, Tswana, and San-speaking cattle-owners supplied cattle for this trade.[33] There was also some trade in arms and ammunition, although this does not seem to have reached significant proportions until the nineteenth century.

It was not only the offshore trade that attracted ships to Namibia. One of the aims of the 1786 mission of HMS *Nautilus* had been to discover whether Namibia would be a suitable place for a penal colony, to which convicts from Britain could be transported. The ship's captain found emphatically that it would not do: 'So inhospitable and so barren a Country is not to be equalled except in the Desarts [*sic*] of Arabia, at least from the appearance of the Shore...'[34] Indeed, the proverbial bleakness of the coastline had largely deterred Europeans from attempting to settle or trade until the second half of the eighteenth century, although the coast had been known to them since the early 1480s (when Diogo Cão landed at Cape Cross, north of Swakopmund, followed by Bartholomeu Dias at Angra Pequena, which he named). The political context changed, however, with the Dutch occupation of the Cape in 1652, and this, together with the increasing value of the offshore trade, was eventually to encourage attempts to establish political control of the waters to the north. In 1793 the captain of the *Meermin* annexed Walvis Bay for the Dutch. Two years later the British took possession of the Cape Colony, and in 1796, in an attempt to undermine American commercial competition, Captain Alexander of the *Star* claimed Walvis Bay (and Angra Pequena) for the British. However, these claims were not enforced, and Walvis Bay was not to be formally annexed by Britain until 1878.[35]

While we know something of both the far south of Namibia and the coastal areas in the eighteenth and early nineteenth centuries, there is much less evidence on the regions to the north and east.[36]

There are, however, oral histories of Otjiherero-speakers describing their migration into what is now central Namibia and Botswana. Oral histories of Mbanderu—a section or phratry of the broader group of Otjiherero-speakers—give a detailed, although undated, narrative of the migration of several clans from Kaoko via Tsumeb to the Waterberg area, including a journey by one leader, Kaimu, and his people to the sea and back again to the centre of the country. At this point— some time before 1800—all the Mbanderu clans are said to have migrated eastwards as far as Ghanzi in modern Botswana: 'in that time Okanaindo (today Buitepos [the settlement at the border post]) did not exist for them'.[37] Herero traditions also speak of the migration of various clans southwards from Kaoko, and record expansion as far east as Maun (also in Botswana) by about 1820. Although it is impossible to verify the detail of the traditions of migration—which may themselves have been influenced by Vedder's writings—there is nevertheless good evidence of Otjiherero-speaking settlements in Botswana around this date.[38]

Mbanderu traditions also refer to war between Tswana-speaking people and Mbanderu, apparently some time before 1800 and probably over access to grazing land and water. The 1820s was a period of violence over much of modern South Africa, and it seems that Otjiherero-speakers found themselves on the western fringes of these confrontations.[39] A Sotho-speaking group (later to become known as the Kololo) was defeated at the Battle of Dithejwane in 1823 and moved northwards, successfully attacking the Tawana at Toteng on Lake Ngami, only to be defeated by Mbanderu to the west of the lake. In about 1826 Mbanderu were also fighting Ngwaketse near modern Lehututu, and around 1832 there was fighting between Rolong and Mbanderu (possibly with Herero) to the east of the Nossob River. In 1834 the Ngwaketse leader Sebego was able to extract tribute from Herero near Ghanzi. These events gave rise, according to oral traditions, to the 'War of the Shields', so named because Herero were unsuccessful in battle until, copying their enemies, they learned to make shields from cattle hides.[40] The rise of the *ohorongo* (Maharero) clan can also probably be dated from around this period. Tjirue, the grandfather of Maharero, who was to become the predominant Herero leader of the second half of the nineteenth century, had lost his cattle during conflict with Tswana in the late eighteenth century. Tjamuaha, Tjirue's son, was able to rescue his family from poverty and to begin building up his following and herds when he was sent cattle by the wealthy Tjipangandjara.[41]

Afrikaner Hegemony[42]

The oral traditions of Otjiherero-speakers also allude to their first engagement with the Oorlam Afrikaners, as they moved southwards on the western side of Namibia in the early nineteenth century in the quest for access to land and water. In the late 1820s, it seems likely that ‖Oaseb, the leader of the Red Nation, called on Jonker Afrikaner for protection; Jonker and his commandos successfully countered this migration, pushing many Otjiherero-speakers back to the north of the Swakop River, although some were also absorbed by the conquerors.

These struggles were the first success in the rise to power of Jonker Afrikaner, the third son of Jager Afrikaner and grandson of Klaas, who had led the Afrikaners north across the Orange. For three decades, until Jonker's death in 1861, the state he created was to dominate the trade and resources of southern and central Namibia, conquering the inhabitants of the region or bringing them into alliances, many of an unequal, patron-client character. Some observers stressed his leadership qualities: according to the missionary Henry Tindall, he was 'an eloquent speaker, an able politician, a skilled commander and undaunted warrior, a deadly marksman and a generous friend'.[43] Many of those who came under his sway will have had a less positive view. Under Jonker, a new trade relationship with the Cape flourished and a Christian community was established among the Afrikaners; his people and other Oorlam groups founded some of the first permanent settlements in south and central Namibia. Yet his edifice was fragile, and after his death the patron-client relations he had established were soon destroyed.[44]

The origins of Jonker's polity apparently lie in the years after 1823, when the Afrikaners defeated the Bondelswarts in battle. At this point Jonker moved northwards with a minority of the group. This had the effect of segmenting the main Afrikaner lineage and allowing a new power base to be created by a younger son without sparking a succession struggle.

Jonker's power, then, was initially grounded in his control of a section of the Afrikaners' herds and people; it was vastly increased by his ability to mobilise men, ride-animals[45] and guns in what could be a fearsome display of military force. By 1858, according to the calculations of the trader Charles John Andersson, he had 2,000 armed men at his disposal. His commandos raided both cattle, many of which were sent to the Cape as trade goods, and people (male and female, including children), who were used as labourers, in particular to tend the cattle. His military expeditions covered a wide area of north-central Namibia, extending on occasion as far as the Ovambo kingdoms.[46] Arms, ammunition, horses, wagons and other trade goods came in large quantities from the Cape, and Jonker kept very firm control of this trade, which had reached significant proportions by the 1840s. He restricted the activities of the white traders who began to arrive in the early 1840s (of which more below), and in 1844 led an expedition to Walvis Bay that ended the independence of the ǂAonin, who had been important coastal traders. This put Jonker in control of the trade route between Walvis Bay and Lake Ngami, on which Nama-Oorlam groups were to levy tolls for the next thirty years.[47]

Jonker did not rely only on direct violence, however: his hegemony over central and southern Namibia was consolidated through incorporative processes. Jonker made cattle loans to Tjimba (people without cattle) on mission stations and formed alliances—on a patron-client basis—with a number of Otjiherero-speaking leaders in the early 1840s, including Tjamuaha, the father of Maharero, and Kahitjene. Other Oorlam leaders forged what appear to have been similar relationships, Amraal Lambert at Gobabis, for example, recognising Kandjake Uahandura as leader of the local Mbanderu.[48] These arrangements allowed the *ovahona* to begin to build power and wealth through attracting followers and acquiring cattle.

Nevertheless, Jonker's military campaigns precipitated the impoverishment of many of the existing inhabitants of the central part of the country. In the 1840s it was exceptional for Otjiherero-speaking leaders to be well-off, and at the turn of the decade more were impoverished by cattle raids; at this time Kahitjene's people became Tjimba after a conflict with Jonker. Many also fled to Kaoko. Jonker's patronage and demands for payments were also liable to create internal tensions and increase inequalities within client groups: there is evidence that Otjiherero-speaking groups raided cattle from each other at this period, and of frequent disputes over inheritance. Damara and San groups were equally if not more affected by this immiseration, and by the 1850s observers were describing a foraging (rather than a pastoralist) economy in much of central Namibia; hunting for subsistence was also compromised by the rapid increase in commercial hunting, which depleted game stocks. Damara in particular turned to waged labour, working for example on road-building, guano extraction and seal-hunting, from the 1840s.[49]

Jonker appears to have established alliances, rather than relationships of domination and subordination, with the other Nama-Oorlam *kapteins* who set up new polities in the south-central area of the country from the 1840s; some of them had moved northwards to be closer to him. At this period the term 'Oorlam' was coming to denote difference within rather than between polities, as Nama and Oorlam completed the process of merging; the Oorlams now formed the (Christian) elite strata of these groups. Below these there was usually a mixed population (Damara and Herero as well as Nama and Oorlam) in varying degrees of dependence and subordination.[50] Relations of the other polities with Jonker were in practice unequal: in particular, ‖Oaseb competed with the Afrikaners for control over Otjiherero-speaking groups, and the pattern was one of shifting alliances and periodic conflict. ‖Oaseb could usually rely on some support from Willem Swartbooi, while Jonker's firmest ally was Amraal Lambert. The years 1854–57 saw heightened conflict between ‖Oaseb and Jonker and their allies, perhaps intensified by increasing competition for resources with the arrival of copper prospectors in the region, but the outcome was the confirmation of Jonker's superiority and a new accommodation with ‖Oaseb.

The largest of the new Nama-Oorlam polities was Jonker's. This was based at Tsebris in 1840 and Windhoek by 1842, when the population consisted of some 2,000 people (half of whom were identified by the missionaries as 'dependents'), and where Jonker erected a stone chapel and held services, though he had not been granted a missionary. The Dutch name 'Windhoek', meaning 'windy corner', comes from Jonker's time rather than the colonial period.[51] ‖Oaseb and the Kai‖khaun (Red Nation) established a headquarters at !Hoaxa!nas in 1853, but in the 1840s and 1850s many of them lived near to Jonker along the Kubakop River, and later at Rehoboth. The Khauas people under Amraal Lambert established a polity at Naosanabis (Leonardville) in the early 1840s; the Goliath and Isaak families formed the Berseba settlement in 1850; the Swartboois (led by Willem Swartbooi) moved to Rehoboth in 1845 (abandoning it in 1864); and the Veldschoendragers formed a polity at Schans Vlakte in the 1840s. Tseib's people, an offshoot of the Red Nation that emerged as a group around 1850, set up an independent settlement, apparently against ‖Oaseb's wishes, at |Nu|goaes, also known as Zwartmodder (renamed Keetmanshoop in 1866).[52] Of greatest long-term significance, the Witboois, an Oorlam group previously living at Pella in the northern Cape, entered southern Namibia in the 1850s, although it was not until 1863 that they established a permanent settlement—a 'rather close-knit, politically active community'[53]—at Gibeon.

It was thus in this period that the first settled Nama-Oorlam polities were established. This policy was encouraged both by *kapteins*, because it facilitated trade, and by missionaries, who were in almost all cases associated with the new settlements and who saw the abandonment of a semi-nomadic lifestyle as a critical marker on the road to 'civilisation'. For their part, African leaders largely welcomed missionaries as intermediaries in the Cape trade (missionaries engaged in commerce themselves, buying goods to sell on to Africans, as well as encouraging secular traders) as well as for the diplomatic advantages they offered; some leaders also had varying degrees of religious motivation. Once established, missionary stations constituted alternative nodes of power and an implicit threat to the authority of the *kapteins*, although the missionaries' influence throughout this period remained limited by the continued independence of African leaders and their own vulnerability to raiding and war.[54]

After its early setbacks, missionary work in Namibia greatly expanded, with the arrival of missionaries Carl Hugo Hahn and Franz Heinrich Kleinschmidt of the Rhenish Mission Society (RMS) in Namibia in 1842. The RMS, which had been founded in Germany in 1828, was to become the dominant mission society in central and southern Namibia. In the early 1850s it agreed with its potential competitors (that is, other missions) a near-exclusive right to operate in this 'mission field' and organised itself administratively into the 'Namaland' and 'Hereroland' conferences.

In the south the RMS provided missionaries to the Nama-Oorlam polities, achieving early success with the baptism of Willem Swartbooi at Rehoboth (which took its name from a well dug by Isaac in Genesis 26:22) in 1845. The society established a presence at the headquarters of ‖Oaseb and Amraal Lambert, as well as among some groups based further south, at Schans Vlakte, Bethany and Berseba; in the 1860s it also sent missionaries to Gibeon and Hoachanas. (The Bondelswarts, however, remained linked to the mission station at Warmbad, which stayed in Wesleyan hands until 1867.) In central Namibia, however, where the mission set its sights on evangelising the Otjiherero-speaking population, it encountered much greater difficulties. Initial cooperation with Jonker foundered on the latter's unwillingness to allow access to Otjiherero-speaking groups, resulting in long-term hostility between the mission and the Afrikaner *kaptein*.

After the breakdown of relations with Jonker, the RMS established a station at Otjikango (Neubarmen, now Gross Barmen). For the next thirty years, Hahn was the driving force in the mission in central Namibia. His mission work would not, however, have been possible without Johanna Uerita Gertze, the earliest convert, who played a significant role from about 1848/49 and, in particular, supported (or perhaps authored) Hahn's linguistic work. The mission work of other Africans, and of Hahn's wife Emma, was also crucial; indeed, in 1842, the missionary Kleinschmidt had married Johanna Schmelen, who, like her Nama-speaking mother Zara Schmelen, became a lifelong active missionary.

By the end of the 1840s the RMS had two further stations in central Namibia, at Otjimbingwe and Scheppmansdorf (near Walvis Bay). Its work in the area, however, suffered both from continued conflict with Jonker Afrikaner, whose men razed the mission at Otjimbingwe to the ground in 1853, and from the extreme unwillingness of Africans to convert to Christianity. Although many of the *ovahona* cultivated good relations with the missionaries, they did not at this date accept Christianity, and many of the people gathering on mission stations were marginalised, impoverished Damara and Tjimba attracted by the prospect of food and work. By 1871, there were only three Otjiherero-speaking converts, although there may have been more Damara Christians, since there is evidence of their receptiveness to the new religion from as early as 1840.[55]

Notwithstanding these difficulties, and in contrast to the early missions in the south, the new RMS and Wesleyan stations made active attempts to reshape the societies in which they lived 'on the terrain of everyday practice', according to a specific Christian and European model of godliness. In southern Africa in the nineteenth century (as has been shown in particular for the Tswana), missionaries promoted a salvation that lay not only in faith, a rigid sexual morality and the abandonment of what they saw as 'heathen' practices, but also in the adoption of the features of an idealised, orderly, European peasant society: Western clothes, literacy, square houses, a Christian education, a rigid assignment of male and female roles confining women to the domestic space, and the use of the plough.[56] In Nama-Oorlam societies, many of these cultural practices had already been developing for decades, and by the 1840s the wearing of Western clothes was widespread and mission education popular among the elite—although the transition was not always smooth, as witnessed by the refusal of women to abandon traditional hut-making techniques at Rehoboth in 1843. Many of these polities also adopted written constitutions, such as the Ryksboek of 1847 at Bethany, which owed something to missionary influence.[57]

Cultural transformation was much harder to achieve in central Namibia than in the south, given the slow rate of conversion, although Hahn made strenuous attempts, introducing the plough in 1848, for example. Attempts to set up European-style agriculture generally proved an expensive failure, given the climatic conditions; the policy of creating static mission stations in itself placed new demands on the already fragile ecology, and environmental degradation was commonly reported by missionaries. Certain selected aspects of European culture were however adopted, and adapted to, more quickly than Christianity itself. The origins of Herero women's 'long dress', the Victorian-style dresses widely worn today, appear to lie in the sewing classes established by Emma Hahn and (probably) Johanna Uerita Gertze in 1846, which were enthusiastically attended by Otjiherero-speaking women; the adoption of Western-style clothing by both women and men probably signalled a willingness to engage with certain symbols of modernity rather than openness to the new religion.[58]

As the Nama-Oorlam polities increasingly brought the southern and central parts of Namibia within the ambit of the Cape trade network, the influence of (mainly) white traders, both missionary and secular, grew. Traders unconnected with the missions began to arrive overland from the Cape from 1843/44, when James Morris and Sidney Dixon became the first to make the trek successfully. The 1840s saw a rapid expansion of trade with the Cape, centred on the Afrikaners' capital at Windhoek, where 'a crowded, bustling market the whole year round'[59] attracted people from central, southern and probably northern Namibia. The trade also helped to stimulate road-building, so that ox-

Figs. 7. and 8. These photographs of Otjiherero-speaking women, taken in 1885, vividly show the contrast between traditional, predominantly leather, clothes and styles inspired by Western fashions and made from fabric. In central Namibia, although the missions brought cloth garments, the adoption and adaptation of Victorian-style clothes progressed much faster than conversion to Christianity. These are the forerunners of the more elaborate dresses worn by Herero women today. (Reproduced courtesy of the National Archives of Namibia [Figure 7: no. 11455, Figure 8: no. 11456] and Staatsarchiv Bremen [Figure 7: StaB 7.15—Luederitz, Adolf—21 No. 44; Figure 8: StaB 7.15—Luederitz, Adolf—21 No. 46]).

wagons, which were essential for transporting large volumes of goods, could be used. Jonker's roads from Windhoek, across the Auas mountains towards the Cape and to Walvis Bay (the 'Baaiweg'), are well known, but other *kapteins* also commissioned the paving of routes between Bethany and Berseba, and to Warmbad and Rehoboth. In 1844 Hahn commented that the high quality of the work on the Baaiweg was unmatched by anything he had seen in the Cape Colony.[60]

The early activities of European traders were encouraged by a guano boom in 1844. Guano (sea-bird excrement) was first promoted in Britain as a miracle fertiliser in the early 1840s, and was discovered on Ichabo Island, off the Namibian coast, in 1843. This resulted in a rush on the island by (mainly) British ships. By October 1844 there were 350 vessels and 6,000 seamen on the outcrop, resulting in such anarchic conditions that a British naval ship was sent to impose order.[61] Although the Ichabo guano deposits were temporarily exhausted early in the following year, the demand generated boosted the activities of the Cape traders, and commerce burgeoned. No systematic figures exist for the value of the import-export trade of southern and central Namibia at this period, but it was clearly large-scale. In 1851/52 the trader and adventurer Andersson estimated that 8–10,000 head of cattle, and many more small stock, were sent overland annually to the Cape.[62] Another extremely important field of trade and production at this period was hunting. As in many parts of Africa, commercial exploitation led to the rapid depletion of stocks of game, as elephants were hunted for ivory and ostriches for their feathers. The trader Frederick Green alone is estimated to have shot more than seven hundred and fifty elephants between 1854 and 1876; contemporaries reported that game had been exhausted in Ngamiland by 1860, after only a decade of commercial hunting, and in central Namibia by 1880. This intense exploitation led to mixed consequences for Africans: on the one hand, hunting and foraging groups found it more difficult to meet their own subsistence needs, while on the other, some Africans became involved in, and profited from, commercial hunting.[63]

At this period, too, the first concessions—rights to prospect, mine and exploit resources within a defined area—were granted by African leaders to Europeans; copper was of especial interest. The de Pass family, who arrived in the territory in the 1840s, obtained a monopoly over the guano trade and were granted fishing and mining rights of great long-term profitability by David Christian at Bethany. Mining concessions were also granted by the Afrikaners, the Bondelswarts, and the Swartboois at Rehoboth.[64] The trader Robert Lewis, later granted huge concessions by Maharero, arrived in 1858.

The missionaries continued to play a pivotal role in this commerce into the 1850s, particularly after the founding of the mission at Otjimbingwe in 1849. This station became a particularly important trading centre, attracting European artisans as well as Tjimba and other settlers. In 1856 the Walfish Bay Mining Company (WBMC) established a copper mine there—tapping the resources formerly used by indigenous metalworkers[65]—and operating on the basis of a concession granted by the Afrikaners in 1854. This (secular) enterprise also had interests in guano, trading and fishing. It has been described as 'the decisive catalyst for the first systematic integration of southern Hereroland into the trade and capital network of the Cape Colony',[66] and was employing many of the smaller European traders by 1856. The mine proved unprofitable, however, and closed in 1860.

The pattern and development of this trade and industry was complex. Although, from the 1830s, direct trade with the Cape came to predominate, there were still some links with other seaborne traders and networks connecting to an extensive hinterland, particularly to modern Botswana and northern Namibia. The consequences of these trading relationships, too, were varied. Missionaries and secular traders did not foist arms and ammunition onto unwilling African leaders. On the contrary, these and other commodities were very much in demand, and a missionary's credibility might depend on his ability to supply them. Nor, particularly in the early days, were the traders always necessarily in an advantageous position: on the ground they were often dependent on local leaders for labour and other necessary resources. In addition, their enterprises were usually undercapitalised and their number remained small: there were only perhaps a dozen in the 1840s, and most had become impoverished by the end of the decade.[67]

Nevertheless, these agents often held the advantage. They were frequently able to command a quick profit and to charge high prices. The engagement with merchant capital increasingly began to destabilise even the Nama-Oorlam groups that had so far profited from it, as, by the 1840s, their leaders found themselves increasingly indebted, and less able to control the terms of trade. This sparked an increase in raiding; in the 1850s, attacks in the area bounded by Gobabis, Windhoek, Walvis Bay and Okahandja included in their targets some Herero leaders allied to Jonker, and thus led to a breakdown in his system of allegiances. Mbapupua, for example, fled to Nangolo, King of Ondonga, at this period; some Otjiherero-speakers seeking refuge in Owambo worked as herders, and some may even have been sold into slavery.

Paradoxically, however, it was partly engagement with capitalism that led to the tentative beginnings of a process of (re)pastoralisation among Otjiherero-speakers. In the 1850s many Tjimba managed to acquire cattle through cultivation and waged labour. To do this they often drew on the resources of mission stations, while the people of the *omuhona* Zeraua, who had been deprived of most of their stock through raiding in 1851/52, were able to regenerate their herds through supervising cattle-posts for the WBMC and working in its mine. At this period, too, Herero began to use the trade networks to acquire arms and ammunition, successfully beginning to subvert Jonker Afrikaner's control of this trade—which meant that, when they moved to overthrow Afrikaner hegemony in the early 1860s, they had the means to do so.[68]

Ovita Vyongombongange [69]

The 1860s were to witness a radical shift in power relations in Namibia. As the decade opened, trade with the Cape had reached new levels of importance in the economy of the southern and central part of the country. In 1860 Andersson, fast becoming the most successful European trader in the region, signalled his own intention to undermine Jonker's control of this commerce by establishing a centre at Otjimbingwe. Yet, at the same time, long-distance trade was proving extremely vulnerable to epidemics of lungsickness, a cattle disease that now hit many of the herds. In order to protect their own stock, Nama-Oorlam leaders tried, with some success, to prevent traders exporting cattle through the areas under their control: although Andersson got through to the Cape in 1860, he was forced to turn back in 1861. Tension was further increased by a severe smallpox epidemic that peaked around 1860–61.

The deaths of both Jonker Afrikaner and Tjamuaha in 1861 thus came at a critical time. Jonker was replaced by his son Christian Afrikaner, who died two years later, to be succeeded by Jan Jonker Afrikaner. If the accidents of history thus weakened the Afrikaner dynasty, the opposite is true for the *ohorongo* clan. Tjamuaha was succeeded by his son Maharero, a man of great ability who had also been close to Jonker Afrikaner, and had learned military skills on commando with him.[70] Under his leadership, Herero groups established dominance over central Namibia within a decade, successfully acquiring much of the Nama-Oorlam cattle wealth.

Maharero acted to resist Afrikaner control soon after he took his father's place. In 1863 he began with a symbolic theft, sending his nephew, Hirarapi, to take a sheep from Christian Afrikaner. Maharero thus indicated his desire to break his allegiance to the Afrikaners and initiated the *ovita vyongombongange*, the raid of the grey, white and brownish-spotted cow (an animal said to give bravery and strength).[71] Meanwhile Andersson, increasingly determined to resist the Afrikaners, had been arming and training mercenaries from the Cape (the 'Otjimbingwe Volunteers') and Tjimba living on the mission station at Otjimbingwe. In 1861/62 he even imported two cannons into the country. His actions were supported by the white population of Otjimbingwe and, on his return to the 'mission field' in early 1864, by Hahn, who was also frequently in conflict with the Afrikaners.

Hirarapi's raid provoked what was probably the largest-scale fighting in Namibia to that date. The numbers of people involved—and killed—in this war were far higher than in ordinary cattle-raiding excursions. In response to the raid, Christian Afrikaner, leading a commando of 4–500 men, attacked the forces gathered at Otjimbingwe— that is, the Otjiherero-speaking leaders and their people who had gathered to Zeraua and Maharero, and Andersson's men. The attack failed, and in the subsequent battle (on 15 June 1863) about 200 Nama-Oorlam and 60 Herero died, including Christian, his ally Piet Koper and Hirarapi.[72]

In the months that followed, Maharero's forces, together with those of Andersson and his lieutenant Green, attempted to consolidate this success. In March 1864 they attacked Windhoek. In June a force of about 2,500 marched towards Rehoboth, to support the Swartbois, who had recently joined with Maharero, against an alliance of Nama-Oorlam leaders. The result was an inconclusive pitched battle from which the Afrikaners retreated. In the aftermath the Swartbooi people were attacked and defeated by an Afrikaner commando. Towards the end of the year the *kaptein*s at Berseba, Bethany and Gibeon managed to prevent the Afrikaners attacking Otjimbingwe by cutting off their supplies of ammunition. However, although the balance of power had begun to tip away from the Afrikaners, neither side had achieved a clear military victory. As a result Maharero once more moved northwards from Otjimbingwe, apparently deserting his brief alliance with Andersson (who was to die in 1867) and these more formal methods of warfare. Open conflict continued nevertheless.

The events of 1863–64 have proved a fertile debating ground. For Heinrich Vedder, following the RMS view, they were a 'Herero war of freedom' in which Maharero led a fight for liberation from the Oorlam Afrikaner overlords, supported and even inspired by the Rhenish missionaries. Oral tradition, as related by Alex Kaputu, records Tjamuaha on his deathbed declaring that '...the time had come to lift the Nama yoke from the Hereros'. Heinrich Loth was the first to oppose this interpretation of the war, arguing that the missionaries were to a large extent responsible for the conflicts; Lau later emphasised the role of the traders, particularly Andersson, who had strong economic reasons for wanting to break Afrikaner political dominance.[73]

Lau and Loth, however, exaggerate the importance of Europeans in Namibia at this period. Henrichsen's subsequent research has revealed the role of Herero leaders in these conflicts, particularly that of Maharero, who rose to a position of leadership among Herero groups largely because of his prowess in these wars—he became known as 'Muniovita', 'owner of the raid'—and went on to consolidate his strength through the skilful creation of marriage and other alliances.[74] Maharero's active leadership can be seen, for example, in the symbolism used in the 1864 campaign. In the expedition to Rehoboth not only was a new 'national flag', invented by Thomas Baines (the artist, trader and traveller) and Andersson, borne aloft, but Herero fighters were also smeared with ash from the holy fire. In a letter to Andersson before the march to Rehoboth, the trader Frederick Green relayed Maharero's words: 'It was to be his [Maharero's] war'.[75] Nor is it likely, as averred by earlier writers, that Andersson was recognised as 'regent and military commander' by Maharero and other leaders. A document making this claim does exist, but it is not signed, and there is no proof that the ovahona ever agreed to it.[76]

If this revision successfully restores African agency to a more central and credible place in the events of the early 1860s, it does not resurrect unproblematically the idea of a 'Herero war of liberation'. There is some truth in this formulation: many Otjiherero-speaking leaders took the opportunity to emerge from subordinate relationships with the Afrikaners, and the origins of the Herero paramountcy lie in this period. Yet, on the one hand, a wider 'Herero' identity would only begin to develop in earnest in the following decade; on the other, many alliances and enmities did not follow a simple Nama/Herero division, as evidenced for example by the dynamics of the intense period of conflict that followed the battles of 1863–64, which would eventually destroy Afrikaner hegemony. Up to about 1868 there was a great deal of fighting between the Afrikaners (usually supported by ‖Oaseb and !Nanib Hendrik Zes) and other Nama-Oorlam groups. The Afrikaners staged assaults on several of the Nama-Oorlam polities, including those of the Witboois at Gibeon and the Lamberts at Gobabis. Over the period, the Afrikaner alliance was defeated several times, particularly in November 1865 by a Rehoboth commando and in 1867, when ‖Oaseb was overwhelmed by a commando from Gibeon and Berseba. As late as May 1868 the Cape authorities warned the southern *kapteins* against taking up arms, because of fears that they might assist the Koranna in the northern Cape, who had risen against the British. In response, the *kapteins* of Bethany and Berseba requested a formal alliance with the Cape. This was refused, but in January 1870 the Cape government did conclude an agreement with Willem Christian of the Bondelswarts, with whom an alliance had first been made forty years earlier.[77]

The aim of much of the fighting in the south was economic as well as political: to raid cattle as much as to achieve military superiority. Herero leaders, too, pursued cattle raids intensively between 1863 and 1866—Maharero, Kambazembi and Kapekaha were particularly active in this regard—with the result that many Herero became cattle-rich and many Nama-Oorlam were reduced to poverty, while the Herero 'big men' were successfully able to assert their independence from Afrikaner dominance. The fighting of these years encompassed a wide area, reaching as far as Ondonga and the Kaoko north of Otjitambi, and was fuelled by large quantities of weaponry obtained both from Andersson and from previous raids; it was also in part a result of indebtedness to traders. The violence of the 1860s also impoverished the Damara and (probably) the San groups scattered around the country. For example, during the two-week march to Rehoboth in 1864, Maharero's and Andersson's forces robbed Damara settlements of sheep and goats to provision the troops.[78]

The violence of the 1860s, coupled with Andersson's death in 1867, meant that many white traders withdrew from central and southern

Namibia at this period. Trading was carried on, however, by the 'mission colony' founded by Hahn at Otjimbingwe in 1864. This consisted not only of missionaries and converts, but also of a group of European artisans and traders and their families. The colony was based on the theological idea of *Volksbekehrung*, the conversion to Christianity of whole communities rather than individuals, and was intended by Hahn to encourage cultural and religious change among Africans.[79] Conversion of Herero continued at a very slow pace: only sixty-nine had been baptised by 1870. The founding in 1866 of the Augustineum, the RMS teacher training college in Otjimbingwe, however, opened the way for longer-term cultural transformation. On the trading front, the mission colony was heavily involved in hunting for ivory and feathers, and equipped a network of hunters, many of whom were stationed in Ondonga. It also imported arms and ammunition, despite a prohibition from RMS headquarters.

By 1868, conflict in southern and central Namibia had more or less come to an end, and the Afrikaner Oorlam hegemony had been destroyed. About this time, around 20,000 Otjiherero-speakers under Maharero, Kandjii, Kavingava and Kambazembi, as well as the largest group of Mbanderu, moved southward to the area between Windhoek and Okahandja, thus consolidating their gains by occupying land formerly under the Afrikaners' control. In 1870, Jan Jonker arrived at Windhoek and made a formal peace treaty with Maharero, assisted by the missionaries Brincker, Diehl and Irle. Hahn, arriving a little later in the same year, managed to get this treaty replaced with one that gave greater rights to traders and missionaries and further reduced the power of the Afrikaners. Windhoek was now deemed to be legally Maharero's. The second treaty also gave permission to a group of Cape Basters (people of mixed race), who had entered the south of the country in the 1860s, to settle at Rehoboth; this was the origin of the modern settlement there. The treaty also makes clear that Maharero was recognised as paramount by the south-eastern Herero and the Mbanderu, although not by Kambazembi and Kamureti.[80]

The treaties of Okahandja formally recognised the *de facto* end of Afrikaner hegemony, and marked the rise of a new elite of cattle-rich, well-armed Otjiherero-speakers in central Namibia. The period since 1730 had seen the rapid and fundamental transformation of the region, as it became firmly locked into the merchant capital network extending from the Cape, and, as we shall see in the next chapter, northwards as far as the Ovambo kingdoms and beyond from the mid-1860s. This engagement had complex effects. Although Jonker Afrikaner's polity benefited hugely, in the short term, from his control of the Cape trade, the destabilising effects of this commerce became increasingly felt in indebtedness and higher levels of raiding. In the end, the downfall of the Afrikaners owed much to the fact that the Herero *ovahona* were able to seize the opportunities for accumulation offered by the new economic conditions, using them successfully to arm themselves and build up their herds. The fact that the Afrikaners fell so quickly points also to the fragile conditions imposed by Namibia's environment, which (in the centre and south) necessitated production through pastoralism rather than agriculture. Wealth stored in cattle was mobile and readily transferable: it is easier to carry off a herd of cattle than to deprive people of their land. Thus dominance could be achieved relatively simply, with an effective commando, but it could also be quite easily undermined. This, the newly wealthy were to find out to their cost over the next three decades, as we shall see in Chapters 4 and 5.

3

MONARCHY, POWER AND CHANGE

THE NORTH, 1750–1907

This chapter deals with the northern regions of present-day Namibia, those that were defined later as Kaoko, Owambo, Kavango and Caprivi.[1] By the nineteenth century, the majority of the people of these areas lived in centralised states, ruled by kings or queens. These polities were mainly matrilineal (that is, inheritance and the royal line was traced through the mother's lineage), and most were small. Owambo was by far the most populous area in precolonial Namibia: late nineteenth-century estimates vary between about 80,000 and 143,000 for the whole floodplain. The earliest estimates for Kavango, Caprivi and Kaoko give totals of about 7–8,000, 11,000 and 5,000 respectively.[2] The main means of production in these societies were agriculture and herding and, along the rivers, fishing. To the west, Kaoko had a much more marginal economy and was inhabited by pastoralists, with rather weaker forms of authority than the kingdoms. Hunting and foraging also remained important everywhere.

For most of the northern areas, rich and multi-layered oral histories (some of which have been published) make it possible to trace the probable lineaments of some past events—although they are imbued with symbol and metaphor as much as literal 'fact'. These narratives give expression to African understandings of time and space, landscape and environment, and history and politics; arising out of complex struggles for power and resources, and influenced by the political moment of retelling or recording as a historical text, they also sometimes contradict each other, and many function as justifications of the claims of royal lineages.[3]

Written sources, by contrast, date only from the mid-nineteenth century, when the region began to engage with merchant capital. It was still to be more than fifty years until any part of the north experienced direct colonial presence, with the occupation of the Caprivi Strip in 1909, but the second half of the nineteenth century was to be, nonetheless, a period of profound and in many respects devastating change. During that time the effects of long-distance commerce (including the slave trade), the rising influence of Christian missionaries and the incursions of colonising powers caused far-reaching changes in the social fabric of the north.

The areas discussed in the chapter were all to fall outside the Police Zone (that part of the colony designated for white settlement by the Germans in 1907), giving their colonial history a very different character from that of the rest of German South West Africa. At an earlier period, however, there was significant contact with regions to the south, through trade and also through the many kin-based and political ties that connected Otjiherero-speakers in Kaoko with those living in central Namibia; the later isolation of the north from the Police Zone—never absolute—was largely brought about by deliberate colonial policy. Generally speaking, nevertheless, the peoples of the north had as close, or closer, links with regions outside the boundaries of modern Namibia. The Ovambo floodplain now falls into both Namibia and Angola. The precolonial borders of the different polities of the Kavango area cut across the river at right angles,[4] so that people moved frequently from one bank to the other; when the colonial boundary between Namibia and Angola was charted in this area, it followed the river's course instead. In the far north-east, the Caprivi Strip was an integral part of the Lozi state, whose heartland in the Barotse floodplain is now in Zambia.

Migration Histories

From a very early date, groups of foragers and hunters, the majority of whom probably spoke Khoe and San languages, were scattered across north and north-eastern Namibia. In the nineteenth century, Khoe-speaking Hai‖Om lived in Owambo; San-speaking Ju|'hoansi and Khoe-speakers, including the ‖Ani-Khoe ('river-bank dwellers', who fished and engaged in metal-working), inhabited many parts of the north-east. Bantu-speaking Yeyi, also dependent on foraging and fishing, had lived at the Linyanti River (which now forms the southern boundary of the Caprivi Strip) until most of them migrated southwards under pressure from the expanding Lozi kingdom in about 1750.[5]

The origins of the Bantu-speaking states that had emerged in the region by about the seventeenth century are very obscure. On the basis of linguistic and environmental evidence, Jan Vansina argues that the Bantu languages spoken in Namibia today originated in what is now the south-western part of the Democratic Republic of Congo between 300 BCE and 400 CE, and were brought southwards both by language transfer (the adoption of a new language) and the migration of people, particularly after about the year 900. Agropastoralists, he suggests, had moved into the Owambo region by the thirteenth century, and when the climate became drier in (approximately) the next century, they stayed and learned to manage within the new environmental constraints.[6] The oral histories, however, emphasise migration, which they date back about ten generations, thus either 'flattening' time, or concentrating only on relatively recent population movements.[7]

The migrations described by the oral narratives were probably responses to political and economic pressures on land and resources, as well as periodic drought, in central Africa, and perhaps in some cases to the slave trade. The traditions emphasise the search for good land and game: an early place of settlement of the Ovambo peoples '... was deep in the bush where wild animals could be found in their thousands and where grazing areas for cattle, sheep and goats could be found'.[8] These narratives are often explicit in claiming immediate places of origin. Kaokolanders locate their point of departure as Okarundu Kambeti, a hill north of Ruacana (the latter is now on the Namibia–Angola border).[9] Many of the clans that were to form the Ovambo kingdoms have roots in the Nyaneka-Nkhumbi polities of southern Angola. Their migration histories record the importance of Oshimholo (north-east of Evale in modern Angola) as a stopping place, before they moved on to Oshamba, the origin of the Ondonga kingdom. It was from here that the clans are said to have separated to establish, initially, Oukwanyama, Uukwambi and Ongandjera.[10]

There are also traditions that ascribe joint origins to the Herero and Ovambo, and to the Ovambo and Kwangali—the latter being the people who settled at the westernmost point within Namibia of the Kavango River. Indeed, the Kwangali, together with other peoples now living along the Kavango—the Mbunza, Shambyu and Gciriku—all possess close linguistic links to Umbundu, spoken to the north-west, in present-day Angola, but also have oral histories that site their origins to the east, referring to migrations, starting allegedly in about the mid-eighteenth century, from the floodplains between the Kwando and Zambezi Rivers (often called the Mashi area) under pressure from the Lozi kingdom. Such apparent contradictions are perhaps a result of multi-layered migrations into the Kavango polities. Remarkably, a migration history has also been preserved for the Tjaube, a group which was probably Khoesan-speaking and also entered the Kavango area perhaps in the eighteenth century, but was later effectively wiped out by conquest.[11]

There are different versions of the history of the fifth group later classified as 'Kavango', the Mbukushu. They seem to have been conquered by Mwanambinje, a brother of Mboo, the first Lozi king, perhaps in the early seventeenth century. This may have resulted in a division into three groups, one of which emerged as the separate Subiya people, who migrated to the Chobe River, thus establishing themselves in and around present-day Caprivi. A large group of Mbukushu migrated eventually to their current home at Andara (named after one of their kings). Other accounts, however, also claim a common migration with the Shambyu.[12]

Oral traditions, although they say little about how far violence was a cause of the migrations, tell us much else about their dynamics. As well as the fission of larger groups into smaller, they record the fusion of people from different clans or polities into one state. For example, Uukwaluudhi is said to have been formed from people originating from both Owambo and Kaoko. Many of the new kingdoms were created by people who had lived mainly by hunting and foraging, and the traditions also record the adoption of new modes of production—and with them new claims to the land. The acquisition of knowledge about cattle is explained in the chronicle of the Kwangali and Mbunza:

People began to eat milk. When they saw something white coming out of the udder, they pointed at it, saying: 'Look at that! What is this white thing?' They tried to milk it into wooden pitchers, they ate it. They observed whether perhaps someone would die. They did not die, and then they went on eating it. They did like that, milking and eating it; and they called it *masini* (milk).[13]

In Ongandjera, an Nkhumbi princess is said to have introduced the pastoral people to agriculture, and thus married their leader and became their first queen. Shambyu traditions record the adoption of iron-working to make elephant traps, with the admonition that, 'If you want to survive you must be clever. Cleverness is wealth'.[14] Production also depended on adaptation to new environments: in Kaoko, for instance, palm trees were an important source of sustenance.[15]

The New Polities

Oral traditions also provide some insights into the establishment of the new monarchies and the construction of authority in the northern regions. In the long run, agropastoralists generally established dominance over the existing population. This sometimes came about through conquest, but incorporative strategies were also used: some Khoesan intermarried with Bantu-speakers, or took leading roles in ritual events. The case of Uukwambi is particularly interesting in this respect. Oral tradition records that, at an early date, Kwambi people established a kingdom under the authority of the 'Bushmen'. This state of affairs lasted for four reigns, during which time the Kwambi kings married Khoesan women; after this Neyema became king and fought and defeated the Khoesan, apparently reducing those who remained in the kingdom to slavery. Not all the earlier societies were obliterated, however, and in the late nineteenth and early twentieth centuries there was still a degree of interdependence between the two groups. There also seem to have been early conflicts with other groups of Bantu-speakers. Ondonga, for instance, is said to have been invaded by people from Ombwenge, perhaps in the late seventeenth century; the invaders were defeated a few years later.[16]

This process of migration, settlement, conquest and absorption resulted in the establishment of the polities of the north that, despite some changes of ruling dynasty and location, are still recognisable today. In the Ovambo floodplain, the southernmost kingdom was Ondonga, with Uukwambi to its north. Westwards lay the kingdoms of Ongandjera and Uukwaluudhi, and a number of decentralised communities including Uukolonkadhi, Ondombondola and the largest, Ombalantu.[17] To the north, in modern Angola, were the two Ombandja kingdoms and Evale. Oukwanyama also lay mainly in Angola in the nineteenth century. West of Owambo, Kaoko was inhabited by pastoralists without centralised authority. To the east, along the Kavango River, monarchies (often ruled by queens rather than kings) were established from west to east by the Kwangali, Mbunza, Shambyu, Gciriku and Mbukushu. Most of the Ovambo states called the monarch 'omukwaniilwa', while Oukwanyama used 'ohambo';[18] most of the Kavango polities used 'hompa', while the Mbukushu used 'fumu'. Further east, in what is now Caprivi, some form of kingship or paramount leadership was established by the Subiya, most likely under the overrule of the Lozi kingdom, of which more below; other groups, including the ancestors of the modern Fwe group, seem to have lived under more decentralised rule.

The majority of the people of the north thus came under royal authority at some point before the beginning of the nineteenth century. It has been conjectured that the rise of the monarchies occurred in part because they could offer security, defence and access to the means of production in situations of conflict.[19] In the long term—and particularly in Owambo, where the monarchs were stronger than in Kavango—royal rule also appeared to offer a means of ensuring fertility, production and security in fragile natural environments. Indeed, the association of the fertility of the land with hierarchical order and royal power is very much a feature of the oral narratives, which are themselves essentially royal sources.[20] Kings and queens owned, or held rights to, all the land in their polities and were thus able to control its distribution. Monarchs decreed when harvesting should start, exercised authority over a proportion of the fruit-tree production, held grain in store for emergencies and directed the timing of expeditions to hunt, trade and extract resources such as salt and iron. They also exercised significant control over the Ovambo female initiation ceremony (efundula in Oukwanyama, ohango in Ondonga), and thus symbolically over fertility in the kingdoms. This coming-of-age ceremony was central to the Oshiwambo-speaking societies (unlike male circumcision, which began to die out, except in Ombalantu, in the second half of the nineteenth century).[21]

Monarchs also claimed for themselves a proportion of the produce of commoners, and (in the case of kings) direct control of the fertility of individual women through marriage and other sexual rights. The rulers thus ensured their own material wealth, as well as the resources with which to govern and to perpetuate the royal line. Over time, they also reinforced their authority through the development and control of judicial systems, making or expressing laws and establishing wards administered by headmen. In Owambo, much of the work was done by a group of senior headmen and women called *omalenga* (sing.: *elenga*), who also formed the king's council. The *omalenga*, the royal clan and other wealthy people formed the elite of these societies, which had developed hierarchies before they were affected by contact with Europeans in the mid-nineteenth century. Such divisions were reflected, for example, in the very different clothes worn from an early date by the rich, who used the skin of leopards and giraffes, and the poor, who often wore goat-skins.[22]

These rather practical foundations of monarchical power do not entirely explain its rise to predominance. Ideas and symbolic practices were also crucial. The 'adoption of titles as symbols of authority'[23] was an important ideological innovation, probably introduced in northern Namibia as a result of the new arrivals' previous experience in neighbouring kingdoms. Just as important, the kings and queens claimed a form of sacred authority through explicit association with Kalunga (the supreme God) and the ancestors, and through the exercise of ritual powers. For example, monarchs of the hyena clan, which came to rule Ondonga, Ukwangali and Umbunza, claimed the ability to make rain, while Mbukushu royalty had a strong reputation—recognised by the Lozi kings—for similar powers.[24]

The kings and queens did not, however, hold uncontested or exclusive rights over the collective rituals and observances that ensured peace with the spiritual world, bound societies together, promoted fertility and controlled production. Female initiation was not entirely controlled by the monarchs: Ombalantu, which was a republic, became 'the centre of Owambo culture',[25] and princesses of the other Ovambo communities went there for initiation. Kings created sacred spaces both by conferring refuge on fugitives, and by creating symbols of power (often stones), but others, to a lesser extent, did the same. As this might suggest, royal power in northern Namibia was deeply ambiguous. On the one hand, kings and queens were revered as sacred and had wide powers on which the checks provided by the state were often weak, even though decision-making was theoretically a consensual process. On the other, in practice their authority was insecure, and frequently challenged and undermined by important councillors and members of the royal family. The system under which a council of advisers chose the monarch's successor from a number of matrilineal relatives also created systemic instability.

Such circumstances led to repeated episodes in which members of the royal family were killed by a newly installed monarch or else fled into exile. They also created the conditions for some of the monarchs to oppress their people and to undermine production and fertility, with the result that they are remembered in the traditions as 'cruel'.[26] Kwanyama histories refer, in what is probably a series of dramatic metaphors, to the reign of King Haita, when agricultural production was allowed to decrease and the king 'made people cultivate their lands with their fingers; and ordered his counsellors [sic] to cut a baobab tree with knives, and women to spread flour on top of water'.[27] In extreme cases, monarchs were killed by their subjects. Such was the fate of King Mpepo of Ukwangali, who is portrayed as hiding in deep water in order to kill little children with a knife—perhaps an image of his destruction of the nation. Most decisively, the killing of the tyrannical King Kampaku of Ombalantu in the early nineteenth century brought the Ombalantu monarchy to an end; authority within the polity was dispersed among lineage heads and a spiritual leader. Conversely, the traditions also feature monarchs demonstrating positive royal characteristics: care for their subjects, the ability to ensure fertility, reverence for ancestors, bravery in battle and energy in promulgating laws to establish order in the realm. Queen Mushinga, who ruled the Shambyu in the first half of the nineteenth century, 'is described as very kind...she taught the people how to work [properly] with hoes in the fields'.[28]

While not all queens are remembered so positively, it has been argued that, in the Kavango, they were usually less interested than their male counterparts in amassing riches, assassinating rivals or acquiring spouses already attached to others.[29] Such attitudes to female rulers also reflect the relatively high status of women in the matrilineal societies of northern Namibia. Although overall these polities were patriarchal, and male dominance was established and reinforced through a range of social and legal practices, nevertheless the fact that inheritance and rights passed from mother to daughter meant advantages for both royal and commoner women. Matriliny, generally speaking, gave women 'greater degrees of independence, autonomy, formal authority in local politics and ritual, control of income, decisions concerning child-bearing, [and] family relations' than patriliny. Gender largely dictated women's and men's roles in production—as in other Bantu-speaking societies, the growing of crops was mainly women's responsibility[30]—but in both Owambo and Kavango, women had some land ownership rights. They were also protected in significant ways by their matrilineal kin; divorce was relatively easy; and elite women could claim both formal and informal power. Under colonial rule, women were to lose many of these rights.[31]

The experience of a number of elite women is recorded in the traditions. Women occasionally came to the throne in polities dominated by kings, for example in Ongandjera. More significantly for Owambo, the mothers of kings could gain significant power, and elite women could become *omalenga*.[32] It is in the Kavango River area, however, and particularly in the Kwangali and Shambyu polities, that the genealogies record large numbers of female rulers: in Ukwangali, there were some seven queens and ten kings up to the mid-twentieth century.[33] The traditions contain a most interesting debate on the right of women to rule. Two male matrilineal relatives of the Kwangali queen who had been brought up in Oukwanyama attempted to take the Kwangali throne by a combination of force and trickery, proclaiming, 'Let us go and take over, we are men, how can a woman rule? Instead we are men!' Having killed the queen and her family, however, they were killed in their turn by her subjects.[34] This narrative seems to act both to affirm the right of women to rule in Ukwangali, and to assert independence from Oukwanyama.

As this tradition also suggests, there is a great deal of evidence for conflict among the polities of the north before the 1840s, caused among other things by succession disputes and conflicts over resources. The *ekumbu*, a raiding party organised by a king, was a long-standing institution which aimed to capture both cattle and people from neighbouring polities—although not to take territory, nor, usually, to kill. In the hands of ambitious and able kings, such expeditions could be an important means of building centralised power. For example, Haimbili, King of Oukwanyama in the first half of the nineteenth century, is said to have strengthened his position by raiding the neighbouring polities. Raids also resulted in a form of slavery when the prisoners taken, instead of being ransomed, were enslaved. At this period slaves were often incorporated (ceremonially and practically) into kin groups; while this granted them a place in their new society, it also defined them in significant ways as inferior.[35]

It is not easy to trace specific historical developments beyond these rather general conclusions on the dynamics of the north up to the 1840s. Nevertheless, some tentative observations can be made. At an early point, Ongandjera rose to a position of military dominance in the Ovambo floodplain through access to superior technology, having obtained poisoned arrows through an alliance with Khoesan (who formed an important element within the Ngandjera polity). The larger eastern kingdoms also gained in strength during the first half of the nineteenth century. In Ondonga, the reign of King Nangolo, beginning in about 1820, is said to have brought unification, military strength and prosperity to the kingdom. By about 1850, Oukwanyama, too, had freed itself from Nkhumbi rule; the refusal of Mweshipandeka to undergo circumcision before becoming king (in the 1850s) may have been connected with this.[36]

To the east, the people of present-day Caprivi were directly affected by events that shook the Lozi state. This kingdom (sometimes called an empire), which was much larger than the polities of northern Namibia, had developed sophisticated methods of government and administration and, at its height, brought people of between twenty-five and thirty-five different ethnic affiliations into an overarching Lozi identity. According to Lozi and Fwe traditions, in a second period of conquest King Ngombala (c. 1725–75)[37] once again brought the Subiya and other groups in the south under his control. The Subiya chief had earlier been appointed *mwanamwalie*, that is, Lozi representative in the Caprivi; now, Ngombala placed his own officials, *lindumeleti*, in the area. This version of events is, however, contested by the Subiya historian D.M. Shamukuni, who argues that the Subiya had their own independent kingdom ('Itenge') from the time of their arrival in the Chobe area. While this argument cannot be accepted in its entirety—the evidence for Lozi overrule is good, and the waters are further clouded by contemporary disputes between Subiya and Fwe—Lozi traditions may overemphasise the mildness of Lozi authority and the extent to which it was exercised through a rather indirect form of rule. The fact that the Subiya rose in rebellion against the ruling powers in the Caprivi a number of times also suggests, perhaps, a desire to achieve some form of autonomy.[38]

One of these interventions seems to have occurred in the 1830s, when Liswani I of the Subiya probably assisted the forces of the Kololo, a large Sotho-speaking group led by the 'charismatic and astute Sibituane',[39] to cross the Zambezi. Over the next decade the Kololo went on to conquer the Lozi kingdom. That the Kololo kings expected support from the people of the south is attested by the fact that by 1851 Sebitwane had based himself at Linyanti (now Sangwali, in modern Caprivi),[40] situated between the Linyanti and Kwando Rivers. Here, the swamps offered some security, although they also caused many deaths from disease among the incomers.[41]

Trade and Government in the Era of Merchant Capital

It is unlikely that the inhabitants of northern Namibia made direct contact with the agents of capitalism from north or south before the 1840s. Prior to this date there was, nevertheless, vigorous short-distance and regional trade in commodities including food, pottery and other specialised products. Long-distance commerce linked the Ovambo kingdoms with Kaoko, Kavango, southern Angola and central Namibia. Iron was extracted and processed in southern Angola by

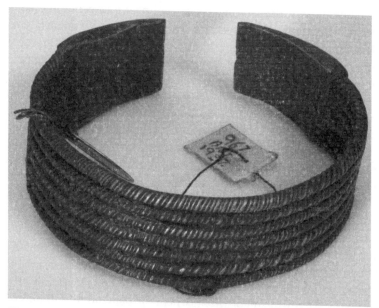

Fig. 9. Iron was smelted by Kwanyama smiths in southern Angola and used to make a variety of products. This fine Kwanyama iron anklet was collected in 1937 by the Powell-Cotton sisters. The iron-working industry, and the trade routes through which its products were distributed, are much older. (Photographers: Arne Sjogren and Gerrit Swanepoel. Item A 37/179 from the collections of the Powell-Cotton Museum, Kent, UK. Collected by Miss A. Powell-Cotton and Miss D. Powell-Cotton.)

Kwanyama smiths; copper ore was bought by Ndonga from Hai‖Om traders, who controlled the deposits to the south of Owambo; and salt was gathered from the Etosha Pan by expeditions from Ondonga. Other trade goods included ostrich eggshells, sold by San and by Kaoko pastoralists.[42]

In the second half of the nineteenth century, northern Namibia was to feel the full force of engagement with merchant capital and to suffer from many of its more destructive effects. The region entered into long-distance trade rather later than many other parts of Africa, in part because of its geographical remoteness. The Cape frontier was expanding fairly slowly from the south: although the traders and explorers Francis Galton and Charles John Andersson visited Ondonga in 1851, King Nangolo did not allow them to travel further into Owambo and showed little interest in trading with them. To the north, a Portuguese-led trade in slaves for export to the Americas had been developing, with devastating social, political and economic conse-quences, for about three centuries. The area south of Benguela, how-ever, did not become a target until the late eighteenth century at the earliest—partly because of its low population density and strong politi-cal formations—and the Ovambo monarchs refused to sell people until the mid-nineteenth century. To the east, the Lozi kings also came into contact with the wider slave-trading network through Ovimbundu traders from Angola, but at least until the end of King Mulambwa's reign in 1835, they also refused to export people, one reason being that their agricultural heartland in the Barotse floodplain relied on large supplies of labour.[43]

With the establishment of the southern Angolan port of Moçamedes in 1840, Portugal began to take a greater interest in the southern part of its Angolan colony. In 1834, the Portuguese government had moder-ated its tightly protectionist policies, thus facilitating rapid growth in the ivory trade. The slave trade also continued unabated despite the official ban on exports in 1836. Many enslaved people were absorbed within the colony of Angola itself, where the demand for labour grew as the plantation sector in the south prospered in the second half of the nineteenth century; the number of slaves in the Moçamedes area grew from 400 in 1840 to 7,000 in 1877. It is likely that male captives, who had been most in demand for export, now became less attractive to traders than women, whose labour and reproductive capacity were more valued by African societies. Children were also enslaved. Even after slavery was formally abolished in 1879, it was replaced by a form of contract labour that was the same in all but name, and the practice was not finally ended until 1911–13.[44]

By 1851—if not before—developments in Angola were starting to influence trade in the Ovambo kingdoms, where African entrepreneurs imported glass beads and alcohol in exchange for ivory. White, mainly Portuguese, traders also began to make their way to the northern Ovambo kingdoms at about this time.[45] A stronger reason for these communities to engage in long-distance trade, however, appeared when, in the 1850s, Jonker Afrikaner's forces began to launch devastating raids on Ovambo territory. Over the period 1858–62, Nama-Oorlam commandos engaged intensively in the north, helping Shikongo, a claimant to the throne of Ondonga, to unseat his rival, assisting Ndonga forces to destroy and burn the kingdom of Ongandjera—thus ending its military dominance of the region—and capturing some 20,000 cattle from a number of Ovambo kingdoms. Soon Jonker Afrikaner's forces also turned their attention to the north-west, where they began raiding the people of Kaoko. Although the Afrikaners had lost their military and political supremacy by 1870, Swartbooi and Topnaar commandos, based in southern Kaoko, carried out raids—whose devastating effects are still remembered—until the 1890s.[46]

Confronted with attackers equipped with horses and firearms, the targeted populations varied in their response. In Kaoko, although heroic resistance by figures such as Mureti is remembered, the pastoralist communities were largely forced into flight. Some went to the mountains of northern Kaoko to live mainly from foraging (eventually assuming a 'Tjimba' identity), while the majority crossed the Kunene into Angola and remained pastoralists, although with diminished herds. Many of this group were able to increase their income by working for settlers, hunting, and trading ivory, feathers and cattle for blankets, alcohol and guns. A third path was taken by the leader Kakurukouje (also known as Kasupi), who co-operated with the Swartboois.[47] In Owambo, however, the Nama-Oorlam raids persuaded the kings that they needed urgently to acquire firearms, which were hardly known before the late 1850s.[48] What guns could do had also been demonstrated by another early European visit. In 1857, the missionaries Hahn and Rath (along with several other non-clerical white men) arrived in Ondonga to explore the prospects for mission in the north, but managed to offend King Nangolo. On their departure violence flared, and the Europeans shot and killed three Ndonga, including the king's son. The king himself died the following day, probably of a stroke.[49]

The only way to acquire guns was through trade with Europeans, and items of value were needed in exchange. The Portuguese, by and large, demanded slaves in payment for arms and ammunition. The sale of people, usually those accused of crimes or captured in raiding, thus began on a noticeable scale during the 1860s in Ondonga, Oukwanyama and Uukwambi, and a decade or so later the traveller Gerald McKiernan visited a Portuguese trader's camp near the Kwanyama palace and discovered female slaves in chains, wearing iron collars. Portuguese traders also imported cheap jewellery, glass beads, tobacco and alcohol—the latter, known locally as *aguardente*, was a product of the sugar plantations of southern Angola—and exchanged them for people, cattle and ivory. European traders from the south, who used the Walvis Bay export route, began to appear in southern Owambo by the mid-1860s, importing beads, clothes and ammunition in return for ivory and ostrich feathers. The Cape authorities' ban on slavery, however, prevented them from buying and selling people.

Both groups of Europeans stimulated an intensive period of hunting that was quickly to result in the rapid depletion of game in and around the Ovambo kingdoms. In both cases, too, trading was a high-risk but often extremely profitable venture, normally carried out by undercapitalised individuals, although larger-scale investment was also provided by more prosperous figures such as Charles John Andersson and Axel Eriksson. By the end of the 1870s the Walvis Bay traders had obtained the upper hand in the firearms market, since they, unlike the Portuguese, were able to provide modern weapons. Trade in ivory became large-scale in the 1860s, but with the continual depletion of game, the cattle trade rose to prominence in the 1880s and 1890s. At the same time, the plantation sector in southern Angola became increasingly important, and trade was further stimulated by the establishment of a colony of Boers, who provided transport for trade goods, at Humpata in southern Angola in 1881. Despite stiff competition between the Portuguese and Walvis Bay traders, many of the latter moved northwards across the Kunene in the 1880s when war broke out in central Namibia.[50]

To the east, the Kololo state also began to participate in long-distance trade at about mid-century. Engagement with the slave trade probably began at some time between 1835 and 1850: as in Owambo, slaves were necessary as payment for firearms, in this case for defence against the Ndebele. The Caprivi had become 'the pivot of decision making for the Makololo polity',[51] and it was here that a long-distance trading hub developed. There is some evidence that King Sebitwane had already been trying to open up a new trade route to the west when, in 1851, the British missionary David Livingstone and his party arrived at Linyanti. As well as spreading the Christian gospel, Livingstone was passionately committed to fighting the slave trade, and aimed to replace it with what he called 'legitimate commerce'.

The Kololo kings welcomed Livingstone, partly because they saw his arrival as an opportunity for increased access to long-distance trade networks. Sebitwane died in 1851 and was succeeded briefly by his preferred candidate, his daughter Mamochisane, who soon, however, gave way to his son Sekeletu—a king who was to prove much less popular and successful than his father. Sekeletu and his advisers commissioned and equipped an expedition under the joint leadership of Livingstone and a senior Kololo, Pitsane, which after a very arduous journey managed to open up a new route to the coast in Angola, arriving at Luanda in 1854; en route, as Sekeletu's representative, and under his authority, Livingstone was able to mediate between the king and some of the groups who had been alienated by the Kololo conquest of the Lozi state. In subsequent years, Kololo parties seem to have continued to trade westwards, and thus the expedition probably had longer-term effects. Having returned to Linyanti in 1855, Livingstone and another Kololo elder, Sekwebu, led a successful journey to the east coast.[52]

On the Kavango River, the Mbukushu made contact with long-distance trade networks about mid-century. Griqua traders arrived at their capital at Andara in 1852 (thus connecting it with Toteng and, via this route, Walvis Bay); they were shortly followed by white traders, and at some point by Mambari (African agents in the slave trade network). In the Kavango, enslaved people were a very important item of exchange, but by the 1880s, cattle, which stimulated Mbukushu pastoralism, were also being traded. Further west, Andersson visited Ukwangali in 1859, and a number of white hunters and traders arrived there in the ensuing years. In the 1890s, however, commentators noted a rather limited amount of commerce in the Kavango area, with very few modern guns in evidence—although the area was certainly subject to slave raiding.[53]

The effects of long-distance trade on northern Namibia in the second half of the nineteenth century have been most fully explored in relation to the Ovambo kingdoms. Most historians concur that the terms of trade were generally favourable to Europeans, on occasion extortionately so; nevertheless, kings possessed some bargaining power and purchased with discrimination, in particular opting for modern weapons, whatever the cost. The polities of the northern floodplain thus became very well armed, and it was essentially this military strength that kept the colonial powers at bay until the early twentieth century. The monarchs also retained a tight hold over long-distance trade, which tended to strengthen their power, allowing them to accumulate wealth rapidly and to create networks of patronage.

In many ways, however, the trade introduced new weaknesses and intensified existing rivalries and internal divisions. From the 1870s, a new era of raiding began under the pressures of increasing demand for slaves and other exigencies such as drought. These conditions were exacerbated in the following decade by the decline of hunting. At the same time, society was becoming more militarised, firearms were more often used for raiding, and a version of the commando institution had emerged. Up to a point, this intensification of trade and raiding reinforced the stronger eastern kingdoms, Oukwanyama, Uukwambi and Ondonga. Mweshipandeka was famous because 'he liked war very much', launching a large number of raids and capturing both people and cattle. His rule 'was accepted among his people. He urged them to cultivate their crops...People had enough food to eat'.[54] The dominance of the eastern kingdoms was, in a sense, formalised when, probably at a date between the late 1880s and late 1890s,[55] peace agreements were concluded among them. They now increasingly directed their raiding against the decentralised and less powerful communities. Republican Ombalantu (which had not engaged in trade to the same extent as its neighbours) had some capacity to resist, and Uukolonkadhi obtained limited protection from Uukwaluudhi, but the smaller societies of Onkankwa, Ehinga and Okafima were effectively dissolved as a consequence. Ongandjera, which had not recovered from conquest in 1862, was effectively excluded by its more powerful neighbours from contact with the traders.[56]

Even the eastern kingdoms, however, began to suffer from the destabilising effects of rapid accumulation, which provided the *omalenga* and members of the royal family with opportunities to enrich themselves and to challenge the kings. In the late nineteenth century the Kwanyama king was virtually powerless to control the *omalenga*, while in 1884 the Ondonga kingdom was split between King Kambonde and his brother Nehale. In addition, all three of the powerful kingdoms had at least one monarch who became alcoholic—a direct result of the long-distance trade. The new enrichment of the elite also led to the imposition of heavier burdens on the poor. Although guns could be a productive resource, very little of the profits of trade went otherwise into boosting production on the floodplain, and few commoners had access to the new sources of income. The institution of *okashava*, an irregular form of taxation, was now increasingly used to take the possessions of the poor in order to pay for the purchases of royalty and *omalenga*. Those on the receiving end did not accept this 'taxation': '*Okashava* is the name given to the people who robbed others…They came from the king…They took many things including cattle'.[57]

Witchcraft accusations also became more common, and individuals thus marginalised were increasingly sold into slavery: in 1887, for example, ten or more citizens of Ondonga were sold each month in order that the king could buy alcohol. In response to such exactions, people fled to neighbouring kingdoms, sometimes in large numbers. By 1896, about two thousand Kwanyama had moved to Humbe in southern Angola.[58]

Some of the kings tried to resist the entanglement in trade and the growing rapaciousness of the times. Both Negumbo of Uukwambi and Weyulu of Oukwanyama succeeded more despotic kings (in 1875 and 1885 respectively) and moderated their predecessors' policies. Nevertheless, as the 1890s dawned, the outlook for the African communities of northern Namibia was becoming increasingly bleak. Over the next two decades tensions and inequality grew more and more pronounced, and violence and raiding intensified. Conflict was exacerbated by increasing indebtedness to traders,[59] by growing alcohol imports and, critically, by a succession of natural disasters. Droughts, famines and, most damagingly, the cattle disease rinderpest put further strain on productive resources. Rinderpest swept the north in 1897, killing between 80 and 95 per cent of cattle and, together with drought, led to great hardship. Although cattle herds had recovered significantly by 1910, the epizootic spurred increased raiding, violence and impoverishment.[60]

To the west, rinderpest also destroyed most of the herds of those Himba who had previously migrated from Kaoko into Angola. They now increasingly turned to waged labour in order to replace their livestock. Many became mercenaries for the Portuguese under leaders such as Vita Tom (also known as 'Oorlog' or 'war') and Muhona Katiti, and in the period 1895–1906 they participated almost every year in expeditions against the Nkhumbi, Ngambwe or Ovambo peoples. When a change in Portuguese government policy meant that their services were no longer required, they turned to banditry and then, in the case of Vita Tom, to policing bandits on behalf of the Portuguese. At some time in the late nineteenth and early twentieth centuries, too, the Kwangali king, Himarwa, fought for the Portuguese.[61]

The influx of European goods into the northern communities not only had long-lasting political and economic consequences, but was also a catalyst for cultural change, especially in Owambo. Western clothes were initially very expensive: in 1866 Mweshipandeka bought a European suit priced at a hundred head of cattle. Like traditional clothing, Western garments were used to express status, and at first served mainly to reinforce the power of the monarchs. Guns and

Fig. 10. Leaders from the Kaoko, taken in 1918. Vita Tom (Oorlog) is second from the right. The second figure from the left is probably Muhona Katiti; although he is usually identified as the man on Tom's right, this person is wearing Western clothes, which were never adopted by Katiti.[62] (Reproduced courtesy of the National Archives of Namibia [No. 9391, Dickman collection, South African Museum, Cape Town]).

horses, too, both became symbols of royal power, and also signalled the creation of new, male hierarchies based on military prowess.[63] It was, however, the Christian missions that were the most significant nineteenth-century agent of cultural change in Owambo.

Hahn, frustrated by his inability to achieve more than a handful of converts in central Namibia, viewed the Ovambo kingdoms as a potentially more fruitful mission field, and in 1866 made a second, more successful visit to the region. The Rhenish Mission Society did not have the resources to send its own missionaries to Owambo, but instead encouraged the Finnish Mission Society (FMS), which was also Lutheran, to do so. A group of seven Finnish missionaries thus arrived in the north in 1871, and quickly established stations in Ondonga, Oukwanyama, Uukwambi and Ongandjera. In the following year, however, the kings evicted them from everywhere except Ondonga, which for the next thirty years was to remain the only Ovambo kingdom open to the FMS. The expulsions seem to have been partly caused by the failure of the missionaries to deliver trading and even supernatural advantages, and their propensity to preach against slavery, thus disappointing the kings' expectations and threatening to undermine their authority. As elsewhere in Africa, monarchs trod a knife-edge, aiming to use the missionaries' diplomatic and commercial influence, but threatened by their creation of alternative power bases and their often close relationship to colonial powers. In Ondonga, the mission was led by the influential Martti Rautanen. He cultivated good relations with the Ndonga kings partly by offering them medical treatment: 'Trusted by the king [Kambonde KaNankwaya], Rautanen would visit the royal court every day to treat the king'.[64]

Elsewhere in Owambo, the Roman Catholic missionary Father Duparquet negotiated the entry of the Holy Ghost Fathers to Oukwanyama in 1884. However, when King Namhadi died in the following year, tensions in the kingdom exploded, the missionaries were accused of his death, and two of them were killed. The Catholics thus withdrew from Oukwanyama; mission work was resumed there by the RMS itself in 1891. Ongandjera, Uukwambi and Uukwaluudhi allowed FMS stations to be established in their territories in 1903, 1908 and 1909 respectively.[65]

The rest of northern Namibia received far less attention from missionary societies in the nineteenth century. It was the Holy Ghost Fathers who first attempted the Kavango, braving the difficulties of even reaching the area (the first three missions failed to arrive) and its adverse disease environment to establish a short-lived station in Ukwangali in 1903. It was not until 1910 that a mission was success-fully founded among the Gciruku, and three years later another was established at Andara, the Mbukushu capital (after a failed attempt in 1909). The complex politics of the founding of these missions can be traced to the intricacies of the external relations of Kavango monarchs, without whose backing the missionaries could not succeed. There was no mission in the eastern Caprivi until about 1924, when the Seventh Day Adventists arrived (although the Paris Evangelical Missionary Society set up bases on the borders of modern Caprivi, at Sesheke and Kazungula, in 1885 and 1889 respectively). Missionaries were not allowed to enter Kaoko until the 1950s.[66]

In Ondonga, the FMS was slow to prosper, and by 1890 still only had a hundred converts.[67] Missionary progress was restrained by the unifying potential of Ovambo cultural institutions and the strength of a world-view that wove religious beliefs into everyday life and ritual. Conversion to Christianity meant thoroughgoing cultural change, including the abandonment of polygyny, non-participation in rituals such as female initiation, and rejection of traditional hairstyles and clothing in favour of European-style clothes made at the missions (although in the early days, given the weakness of the missionaries, these rules could not be rigorously enforced).[68] Partly because of these prohibitions, the elite in particular were reluctant to convert, and it was mainly the young who were initially attracted to Christianity. The majority of the first converts were children brought up at, and edu-cated by, mission stations. By the 1890s, many young people had been exposed to violence, and were thus attracted to the mission stations by the language of security used in explaining the new religion. They were also influenced by the material benefits the missions offered, as well as by peer pressure. Compulsion on the part of the missionaries was also probably a factor.[69]

In the last years of the century, the influence of Christianity in the north increased considerably in the context of the rinderpest epidemic and other crises, and by 1900 there were just over eight hundred Christians in Ondonga (although they still only constituted about 2.5–5 per cent of the kingdom's population). In the following decades, the missionaries consolidated their position by expanding their schools, focusing on education as a crucial tool in the shaping of a new generation of Christians. By 1910 there were about 2,000 pupils in elementary schools, and in 1913 a teacher-training college was founded. Formal medical missionary work began in 1911, with the arrival of Dr Selma Rainio.[70]

A shift in the culture of Owambo was also heralded by the small-scale beginnings of labour migration to the settler colonies of German South West Africa and Angola in the 1880s. Although the number of these contract workers gradually increased, it was never very large until diamonds were discovered in southern Namibia in 1908. At this period African rulers were able keep some control over the migrants, sending them out in organised parties and reaping a share of their earnings. Contracts generally lasted only six months; workers were expected to return in time to help with the harvest, and the majority did so, although Ovambo settlements also emerged in some of the southern towns.

Just as much of the early interest in Christianity came from young people, so it was young men and boys who were the first migrant workers. Going on contract involved a perilous journey to south or north and the likelihood on arrival of poor working and health conditions and harsh treatment. Nevertheless, migrant labour offered an escape from increasing poverty in Owambo. Workers used their earnings to acquire goods, including cattle, which in turn gave them the means to marry and gain land rights; guns, often for self-defence; and high-status items such as clothing. Contract work thus gave these young men not only access to economic resources, but also the ability to define new meanings of modernity in their behaviour, dress and language. Young women, however, were excluded from this new rise in status: only a few left Owambo, both because only men were formally recruited in German South West Africa, and because their year-round labour was essential for agricultural productivity.[71]

In the east, political and cultural change took a rather different course, characterised on the one hand by developments in Kololo and Lozi dynastic politics, and on the other by engagement with long-distance trade, although not initially the slave trade, which Sekeletu had banned, under Livingstone's influence. By the 1870s, however, Mambari slave-traders were active in the Caprivi. The intrusion of merchant capitalism into the area was also signalled by the extensive influence gained by the British trader, adventurer and philanderer George Westbeech, who became a member of the Barotse Council of State in the 1870s.[72]

As in Owambo, commerce in ivory tended to concentrate power in the hands of the kings, some of whom became very unpopular. Although Kololo rule under Sebitwane had gained acceptance partly through his use of incorporative practices, his successor Sekeletu—also based in the Caprivi—became much more dictatorial. He died in 1863 and in the following year an uprising, in which the Totela, Subiya and Fwe apparently took part, put the Lozi prince Sipopa on the throne. In 1865 the new king brought the Fwe leader, Simaata Kabende, into his administration, giving him the title of *mamili* and appointing him to guard the Lozi kingdom in the south. This appointment essentially marked the origin of the modern Fwe ethnic group, bringing together Fwe, Yeyi, Totela, Mbukushu, Lozi and Kwengo people, with different remembered places of origin, under one leader.

Other groups in the south refused to accept Sipopa, however, and in 1865–66 the king put down a rebellion by Subiya and others with much violence. The king's rule became increasingly tyrannical and in 1876 he, like the Kololo monarchs before him, moved his capital from the Barotse floodplain to the south, this time to Sesheke in modern Zambia. This probably caused some of the residents of the Caprivi to flee southwards, and it seems to have been at this time that the main body of Subiya under Nkonkwena sought the protection of the Mangwato people under Khama in modern Botswana; according to Shamukuni, the Subiya remaining in the Caprivi now came under the rule of the king's sister, Ntolwa. Some Subiya may have subsequently migrated back to Caprivi from Botswana.[73]

Further conflict resulted in the killing of Sipopa in 1878. He was eventually succeeded by the Lozi king Lubosi, who was deposed in his turn in 1884. Lubosi took refuge in the Kavango with the Shambyu people, and successfully fought his way back to power the following year, assisted by the Mbukushu and Simaata Kabende Mamili, among others. After this he took the title of Lewanika, the 'unifier'. Lewanika was a skilled and versatile politician, and his long reign until his death in 1916 heralded a new period of stability. For the inhabitants of the Caprivi, the consequences of his restoration were immediate and long-lasting. Violent retribution was taken on the Subiya and Toka living around Sesheke, who had taken part in the king's deposition. Thereafter, Lewanika reformed the administrative structures in the Caprivi area, which had previously been ruled by members of Lozi royalty from Nalolo to the north. Mamili and his people now came directly under Lewanika's authority; most other Caprivians were governed from the newly created province of Sesheke, under Lewanika's niece Akanangisa Mukwai, who soon gained a reputation for cruelty and self-aggrandisement. From 1892, her control of the Caprivi was undercut by the stationing of Lewanika's son Letia at Kazungula. A second new province, Mashi, based at Kaunga (on the Kwando River, on the present Angola–Zambia border), had responsibility for the less densely populated western Caprivi. Lozi rule over the Caprivi remained nevertheless rather indirect, although tribute was levied in the late nineteenth century, and occasional slave raids against Subiya, Yeyi and Mbukushu people are recorded.[74]

Conquest and Entrapment

In the 1880s, colonial expansion began to affect those parts of Africa that had hitherto escaped direct European rule. As a result of the Berlin Conference that formalised the 'scramble for Africa' in 1884–85, most of what is now Namibia became, on paper at least, a German colony. In 1886 a treaty between Germany and Portugal fixed the boundary between Namibia and Angola at the 'cataracts on the Kunene River'. Since it was later discovered that *two* sets of cataracts in fact existed, a border dispute resulted: a strip of Ovambo land running east-west along the colonial border was claimed by both countries and eventually became known as the Neutral Zone. In the Kavango, Portugal and Germany agreed in 1886 to divide their territory along a line down the middle of the Kavango River. Further east, in 1889–90 Lewanika had been induced, with missionary encouragement, to agree to British 'protection' for the Lozi kingdom. Although this strategy had the limited success of ensuring the integrity of the Barotse heartland, he had not suspected that the British—who had occupied Northern Rhodesia (now Zambia) and Bechuanaland (now Botswana)—would immediately alienate the area that became known as the Caprivi Strip, exchanging it for German territory elsewhere. Germany hoped eventually to use the Caprivi to open up access to the east African coast.[75]

These new borders cut across numerous existing boundaries, bisecting the polities of the Kavango, detaching part of the Lozi kingdom and slicing through the Ovambo floodplain. In practice, however, it took time for direct colonialism to have any deep impact—a result partly of the strength of the African states, even though they had been considerably weakened by the crises of the late nineteenth century. European governments, too, acted under significant constraints, and were reluctant to devote resources to their colonial projects. In addition, relations among the three major colonial powers in southern Africa (Germany, Portugal and Britain) were frequently characterised by suspicion, double-dealing and conflict over boundary claims. The pursuit of these rivalries was at least as important a concern to the European countries as the exercise of direct or indirect power over Africans.

Although the Portuguese began to take a serious interest in conquering southern Angola in the late 1860s, the military strength of the African states made the process slow and difficult. In 1896 King Weyulu refused to allow a Portuguese fort on Kwanyama territory. It was not until the early twentieth century that the Portuguese invaded the Ovambo floodplain, and in 1904 they were roundly defeated by Ombandja West and East, aided by forces from Oukwanyama; three years later, however, they returned and secured the conquest and dissolution of the Ombandjas. Among the many consequences of the Portuguese advance southwards was the relocation of the Kwanyama polity. In the early 1890s this had been situated mainly north of the modern border between Namibia and Angola, but by 1904 a significant number of Kwanyama villages had been founded inside Namibia.[76]

It was only in 1908, when an administrator was sent to the Caprivi Strip, that any of the northern parts of the new colony of German South West Africa came under direct colonial rule. Caprivi continued to be administered by the Lozi authorities until 1904, when Letia began, under pressure, to withdraw his officials. The Caprivi Strip, which had been the royal hunting grounds and thus remained well-stocked with game, became a haven for unregulated hunting and trading by European adventurers and criminals.[77] In other regions of the north, monarchs continued to rule much as before.

The German strategy towards the north—if such it can be called—developed gradually. In the 1890s and early 1900s, a succession of governmental and non-governmental visitors entered Owambo, Kavango, Caprivi and Kaoko to explore these regions, assess whether their natural resources—minerals, and land for settlement or railway-building—were such as to justify occupation, and establish relations with local leaders. Indeed, in a dubious transaction, the southern half of Kaoko had been sold by the Swartbooi and Topnaar to concession companies in the 1880s. Overall, the colonisers were unimpressed with the north's natural resources except for its people, who could supply labour for the nascent industry in German South West Africa; this was particularly true of Owambo, the most populous area. These conclusions were an important factor behind the German policy of encouraging African settlement in the northern parts of South West Africa, allowing Kavango residents to move into the colony in order to flee the Portuguese, for example, and sending Kakurukouye to persuade Himba in southern Angola to return to Kaoko. In the latter case, Muhona Katiti's group came back in 1910, and Vita Tom's in 1917.[78]

The north's remoteness was a further brake on direct colonisation. Most important, the Germans were cautious in the face of African military power, and unwilling to provoke what could be a costly war by too rash an intervention. German colonial strength developed slowly in the south, against determined resistance; the colony did not have the resources to conquer the strong northern kingdoms. On several occasions, however, the government in Berlin had to restrain officials on the ground from taking military action. African states were most endangered when whites were killed or robbed in their territories. The colonial press reported these incidents as insults to German authority (which, of course, the kings did not recognise) and they were often exaggerated by the settler community to the status of a *casus belli*. In 1903, in revenge for the expulsion of Catholic missionaries from Ukwangali, Volkmann, the administrator of the Grootfontein District,[79] launched an unauthorised punitive expedition against the polity, attacking King Himarwa's palace and killing six people. Volkmann went on to meet some of the other Kavango monarchs and learned of the killing of the Paasch family by the Gciriku and Shambyu. The infamous 'Paasch incident', as it came to be called, aroused further anger among whites in SWA; plans for a punitive military campaign resulted, but were cut short by the Bondelswarts uprising in the south in 1903 (see Chapter 6).[80]

The most immediate threat to the eastern Kavango polities, however, came from the Tawana, a people based at Toteng in Botswana. In 1893 or 1894, the Gciriku king Nyangana found himself embroiled in struggles with the neighbouring kingdoms and successfully called on the Tawana to attack the Shambyu polity. After defeating the latter, however, the Tawana-led army turned on their Gciriku allies, apparently tricking the men into believing that they could offer supernatural protection in battle, and then massacring almost all of them at a place that came to be called Lishora, the 'place of destruction'. Nyangana:

> was seduced with the following words: 'You King Nyangana, we want to make you bullet-proof lest you do not die even if you are shot with a gun. Well, take off all your weapons and pile them on one heap'....Only a little later, the war started already. The Rwa [Tawana] massacred the Gciriku.[81]

The Tawana took large amounts of booty in the form of both goods and people, and also killed the ‖Ani-khoe leader Mukekerume, ostensibly for his past rudeness to the Tawana king.

Nyangana himself, with some close relatives, was held prisoner for three years until, under British pressure, he was released and allowed to return home, where he began to rebuild his kingdom. The Shambyu and especially the Gciriku polities had by now been impoverished by Tawana exactions. The Mbukushu also suffered: nominally under Lewanika's less harsh jurisdiction, between 1895/96 and 1910 they nonetheless had to pay annual tributes to the Tawana. This contestation of Lewanika's authority points to the regional dimension of these events. Colonial influence was also exerted by the British, who gave some backing to the Tawana; the Portuguese and Germans, by contrast, were largely absent.

By the end of the nineteenth century the Kavango had become extremely vulnerable, and the sale of citizens to slave traders by their own kings or relatives, or through raids on neighbouring polities, seems to have become endemic.[82] Oral traditions from Ukwangali recall that:

> The yimbali [slave traders] brought goods; blankets and things from the Portuguese and also gunpowder...If the child of one's sister is stubborn, then [he/she is disciplined by saying:] 'your uncle will sell you'. And also the chiefs acted in the same manner...He who sells people [must be aware that] also he himself could be sold.[83]

In Owambo, by contrast, there was early tension with the Germans when, in 1886, the trader William Jordan was killed in the territory of Nehale (the Ndonga king Kambonde's brother). Jordan was the founder of the Boer colony of Upingtonia, a source of considerable conflict among Namibian leaders.[84] Although the Germans were too weak to mount a punitive expedition against Nehale at this date, by 1894 a line of forts in north-central Namibia at Gobabis, Okahandja, Okombahe and Omaruru marked the consolidation of colonial power in the south and offered a base from which to extend northwards;

soon thereafter, Leutwein toured the areas immediately south of Owambo and, in 1896, established an extensive *Nordbezirk* (northern district) centred on Outjo. By the following year there were about a hundred and fifty German troops in the district, attempting unsuccessfully to quarantine the areas of white settlement from rinderpest.[85]

As the number of German victories in the north of the Police Zone increased, the Ovambo kings became increasingly aware of the threat posed by the new colonial government. Differing circumstances—the extent of missionary influence, the relative proximity of the Germans and Portuguese, and the effect of power struggles among the kingdoms and their royalty—led to differing policy responses. In 1899 Lieutenant Viktor Franke, the new district chief of the *Nordbezirk*, visited the north and met with Kambonde and Weyulu, who hoped that a non-provocative stance would avert the German threat. Kambonde, in particular, had adopted a neutral policy by about 1897, and was courted by the Germans with both arms and alcohol, although he and Weyulu had no illusions about their intentions—four years earlier he had expressed to Rautanen 'his great amazement that strange people should come to his country and try to possess it and place it under their rule'.[86] Nehale and King Negumbo of Uukwambi, however, began to plan an attack on the German party. Although this was not put into action, Franke left quickly, having also been dissuaded by the missionary Rautanen from trying to obtain treaties of friendship or to implement plans for a military post in Uukwambi. In this and other situations, Rautanen and the other missionaries acted as interpreters and mediators between the Ovambo kings and the German government, sometimes mitigating the potential effects of German intervention but, particularly after Leutwein agreed a monopoly for the Lutherans in Uukwambi and Ongandjera in 1900, increasingly taking a pro-colonial position.[87]

Tensions were heightened in 1900 by an attack on German traders in Uukwambi. This time, a large military response was authorised by Leutwein and was only prevented by an edict from Berlin of February 1901 forbidding the conquest of the north, largely on economic grounds. Although a punitive expedition of twenty-five men was authorised, it had to make a hasty retreat from Uukwambi when confronted with an army of about seven hundred men (from Uukwambi, Oukwanyama and that part of Ondonga under Nehale's authority).

The Germans thus failed to make much headway in the north itself. At the same time, however, they pursued a strategy of encircling Kaoko and Owambo from the south, gradually isolating them from the rest of the colony. This was partly for military purposes. Between 1900 and 1903 the defensible boundary of the colony was shifted northwards by the erection of forts at Okaukuejo, Namutoni and Sesfontein: the first two of these directly impinged on lands to which Ovambo kings laid claim. With the outbreak of the Namibian War in 1904 (see Chapter 6), the fort at Namutoni was razed to the ground by Nehale's forces, and that at Okaukuejo was raided repeatedly by Ngandjera troops after being attacked by Herero. Although the Germans made plans for an invasion to punish Nehale for the attack on Namutoni, the vast resources needed to prosecute the war in the south made this an impossibility.

After the colonial government began to get the upper hand in the south, the policy of encirclement and containment was applied with new force. By a decree of 25 January 1906, Ovamboland was declared a reserve. Partly intended as a defensive measure, the edict also had very significant long-term economic and social implications. Government permission was now needed for trade with the Ovambo communities, labour recruitment from the area, and indeed any entry into Owambo by whites. The sale to Owambo of arms, ammunition, alcohol and horses was also banned. These new controls were an attempt to cut off long-distance trade, which had made something of a recovery since the rinderpest epidemic; the arms trade prohibition also reflected the fact that, despite German bans in the late 1880s and early 1890s, there was still a vibrant illegal trade from Angola through Owambo into central Namibia. By 1910 there were estimated to be about 15,000 guns, half of them of a modern type, in Oukwanyama alone. Kaoko was also forced into isolation by its exclusion from the Police Zone in 1907: this was to put severe restraint on its pastoral economy during the colonial period.[88]

By the end of the period covered in this chapter, the economic viability of the north had been seriously undermined. A flourishing centre of trade throughout the second half of the nineteenth century, by 1906 Owambo had been deliberately cut off from international trade routes and its future as an underdeveloped reserve set in motion. Across the north, older social formations had been undermined, and new forms of modernity were emerging, most strongly in Owambo. Nevertheless, a combination of African military strength (especially in Owambo), German weakness and the effects of resistance in the south meant that the polities still retained their political independence. This was to change within little more than a decade, as we shall see in Chapter 7.

4

THE SHADOW OF PROTECTION, 1870–93

In 1870, as we saw in Chapter 2, the warring parties in central Namibia came to an agreement in Okahandja. The resulting peace lasted a decade. From Windhoek northwards, Otjiherero-speaking groups consolidated and expanded their prosperity, engaging increasingly in merchant capital networks; at the same time, they developed an identification as 'Ovaherero'—people with cattle, guns and horses. Less powerful groups in the same area, however, were increasingly deprived of access to land and water, and began to be compelled to work as migrant labourers. The Nama-Oorlam polities had also undoubtedly lost some of their wealth in the wars of the 1860s. The absence of a social and political historiography focusing on the south at this period, however, means that our understanding of their histories remains very limited.

If the 1870s were largely peaceful, this was nevertheless the time when the first serious moves were made to bring Namibia within a colonial sphere of influence—at this period unsuccessfully (with the exception of Walvis Bay, annexed by the (British) Cape Colony), but with successful moves following in the next decade by Germany. Although this path was slow and difficult—and the historiography remains patchy, particularly for the south—it was thus at this period that these two powers began to cast what I have termed a 'shadow of protection' over SWA. 'Protection' was the term used by British, German and African leaders to describe initial arrangements made between colonial powers and African polities, the latter hoping to use European arms and influence to bolster their own authority. In the earliest phases, however, protection agreements usually meant little; later on, they provided the ground on which the German colonial government could begin to build its domination of the new colony.

In 1880, economic tensions, combined with old and new rivalries, led to renewed outbreaks of fighting. The same period also witnessed the meteoric rise to power of Hendrik Witbooi, who had gained ascendancy over all the Nama-Oorlam groups in Namibia by about 1890, and until 1894 successfully resisted capitulation to German colonial rule. By this point, the balance of power was firmly shifting against the *ovahona* and *kapteins*. In 1870, the critical dynamics of power were still those within and among African leaders and societies. The formal colonisation of Namibia by Germany in 1884 made little appreciable difference, since the German administration was remarkably weak for the following decade. Nevertheless, African leaders were gradually being undermined, and when this chapter ends, in 1893, the German colonial administration was about to acquire meaningful power for the first time.

The Politics of Protection

As we have seen, the peace accord of 1870 sealed the transformation of central Namibian politics begun in 1861. It recognised the ground gained by Otjiherero-speaking groups, and the fact that the influence of Nama-Oorlam communities no longer extended as far north as Windhoek. From this period, Herero identity went through a substantial process of redefinition, so that 'from the 1880s Herero were regarded as wealthy cattle-owners *par excellence*, despite the fact that they were frequently not cattle-owners in the first half of the nineteenth century';[1] in the 1870s the term 'Herero' first gained general currency. Otjiherero-speakers were also the largest group in central and southern Namibia: in 1876 the missionary Irle estimated their numbers at between 64,000 and 96,000.[2] Population figures given by Cape Commissioner Palgrave at about the same time (using the conventional ethnic categories that in some respects belied a more disparate reality) gave estimates of 85,000 Herero, 30,000 (Berg) Damara, 3,000 San, 16,850 Nama-Oorlam, 1,500 Basters and 150 whites, excluding Boers.[3]

The military success of a number of Otjiherero-speaking leaders in the wars of the 1860s allowed them to develop substantial power bases. The most influential *omuhona* (or 'big man') in the 1870s was Maharero. His people numbered some 23,000 and his cattle herds perhaps as much as 40,000 (although his wealth diminished in the cattle raiding of the following decade). Kambazembi, who was based at the Omuramba Omatako, having entered central Namibia from Kaoko in 1863, had about 12,000 people and (by the 1890s) 70,000 cattle. Kamureti, who had pursued a similar migration, had about 6,000 people living north-west of Omaruru around the Omatako River. Zeraua, at Omaruru, was one of the most politically influential of the *ovahona* and controlled over 4,000 people. In the east, the Mbanderu *omuhona* Kahimemua ruled approximately 13,000 people at the Nossob River.[4]

The Oorlam Afrikaners, and probably other Nama-Oorlam groups, had been impoverished by their defeats in the 1860s and consequent losses of stock, grazing and goods. It was in this context that the political configuration of the south shifted substantially so that, in the 1880s, the Witboois at Gibeon were to emerge as one of the most powerful Nama-speaking groups. By 1871 they were already estimated to number 3,000. Like the other Nama-Oorlam communities, they were organised according to the commando system, controlled by a small, male elite that was both military in character and mission-educated.[5] In 1870, a new group of incomers also settled at Rehoboth, and became known as the Rehoboth Bastaards or Basters. Of mixed race, Dutch-speaking and Christian, and with a constitution first adopted in 1868, they were one among a number of Baster groups arriving about this time. The crucial geographical position of their headquarters, which straddled the main north-south route between southern and central Namibia and acted as a gateway to Windhoek and Okahandja, created the conditions under which their *kaptein* would later have to negotiate a difficult political path between the competing interests of Herero, Nama-Oorlam and Germans.[6]

In the 1870s, political power rested largely with the more influential *ovahona* and *kaptein*s. Maharero, in particular, exerted some control over most of the Herero leaders in central and eastern Namibia, and intervened particularly in matters of inheritance; Zeraua and his successors at Omaruru, and Kambazembi at the Waterberg, tried to restrict this influence, the former certainly with some success.[7] Nevertheless, the international political climate was changing, and little more than a decade later the major European powers would claim possession of almost all of Africa, with most of South West Africa falling to Germany. In the 1870s, however, it seemed more than possible that central and southern Namibia would become a British protectorate.

In 1874, Zeraua, Maharero and Kambazembi wrote jointly to the Cape government, requesting British protection against an impending incursion by Boers from the South African Republic, to whom the *ovahona* feared losing land.[8] This catalysed intervention on the part of the Cape government. In 1875, the Cape Legislative Assembly voted for the annexation of Walvis Bay and of an unspecified amount of territory inland from the port, and in the following year William Coates Palgrave, an official with previous experience as a trader in the region, was sent from the Colony to Namibia. Between 1876 and 1885 Palgrave was to head five separate missions to the territory.[9] Broadly, his intentions were to create a British sphere of influence there, to aid the flow of trade with the Cape and to initiate labour recruitment. There was, however, a gulf between the additional aims of the Cape authorities, which wanted to protect their strategic interests by a policy of direct annexation, and those of the British government, which was far more cautious about taking on new imperial commitments. Because of this, and because the initial success of Palgrave's diplomatic overtures could not be sustained in view of the very different expectations of Namibia's rulers, the only land his mission annexed for Britain was Walvis Bay and the surrounding territory (in 1878). He did, however, achieve the recruitment of hundreds of labourers for the Cape Colony (as we shall see below).

It is clear that the leaders of many communities in central and southern Namibia perceived Palgrave's mission as a means of pursuing their own political and economic aims. This was particularly true of Maharero, who took up this 'politics of protection' with energy, hoping not only to safeguard his and his people's interests against the Boers, but also to promote his own overlordship of central Namibia. He and other Herero leaders used the negotiations with Palgrave—a series of large meetings of senior men—to assert their claims to power and status, displaying their wealth by arriving with large numbers of wagons and horses; Palgrave, on the other hand, brandished his counter-claims to authority and modernity through the use of the camera (there was an official photographer in his party) as well as the written word. Interestingly, one of the principles shaping this photography was the classification of subjects into preconceived ethnic groups ('Damara', i.e. Herero, 'Berg Damara', i.e. Damara, and 'Namaqua', i.e. Nama), showing how Palgrave's mission both drew on, and helped to consolidate, existing stereotypes.

In 1876, Maharero's negotiations with Palgrave appeared to reach a successful conclusion. *Ehi rOvaherero* (the land of the Herero) was, for the first time, formally defined—as covering an area between Rehoboth, Waterberg and Omaruru—in a letter signed by the *ova-hona*. This attempt to define control over land through the definition of rigid borders contrasted sharply with older methods of legitimating territorial claims, which specified rights to waterholes and grazing. The same letter granted some land for use by Boer settlers and agreed to a 'protection' arrangement in which Herero would be defended against attack by the installation of a British resident in Namibia. As Henrichsen points out, in pursuing this course Maharero was following a policy that both ignored the claims of Damara and Nama-Oorlam, and offered the chance for Herero groups to consolidate their hold on land and cattle (a function also fulfilled by Herero praise songs for places (*omitandu*), which bound people, cattle and land together as well as acting as claims to rights for water and grazing).[10] Maharero's policy was, thus, very far from being a capitulation to the British. His approach was supported by Riarua, Wilhelm Maharero and the Mbanderu leader Japona, although others, including Kamureti, Kambazembi and Tjaherani, took a more cautious position, opposing protection arrangements. Maharero himself also soon began to have doubts, and the agreement with the British was effectively undermined when Palgrave failed to keep him informed about the annexation of Walvis Bay (although hopes remained on both sides for a successful resumption of the negotiations).

Palgrave also met almost all the Nama-Oorlam *kaptein*s in central and southern Namibia. Both Andries Lambert at Gobabis and the Basters at Rehoboth requested British protection. Jan Jonker Afrikaner, however, hoping to bring some of the areas of southern Hereroland back under Afrikaner control, used the negotiations to argue for changes to the peace agreements of 1870; Palgrave did not give him a sympathetic hearing. Jacobus Isaak of Berseba also had reservations about protection arrangements, saying that he would agree to an 'English Resident' as long as he 'does not deprive us of our land, or of our capacity as Captains...But if I was to be subservient to the Resident I see no existence for us...'.[11] However, David Christian at Berseba accepted protection, in view (he said) of the threat posed by Boer incursions, and Palgrave also claimed the support of Moses Witbooi. No written agreement with the southern *kaptein*s was reached, how-

Fig. 11. This image of Maharero appears in an album of photographs produced by Palgrave's trip to Namibia in 1876. Maharero sits on the left, with
Riarua, his military commander (also known as Amadamap), to his left; behind them stands Maharero's eldest son, Wilhelm. (Reproduced courtesy of
the National Archives of Namibia [no. 2770]).

ever, with the exception of Willem Christian and the Bondelswarts,
who already had a longstanding alliance with the Cape. The Bondelswarts also requested a magistrate to deal with their external affairs
and to 'be the guardian of our land, and manage it for the benefit of
our people'[12] without, however, having the right to alienate territory
without their consent.

When Palgrave's missions began, central and southern Namibia had
been at peace since 1870. The following decade saw the expansion of
both missionary enterprise and the Cape trade, as well as the deep
incorporation of Herero as well as Nama-Oorlam groups into capitalist
and mission networks. Herero *ovahona*, like their counterparts in the
south, were now frequently requesting missionaries to settle with them,
in an attempt to gain access to political influence and long-distance
trade. The operations of the Rhenish Mission Society expanded at this
period, as it opened or reoccupied stations in the centre of the country,
at the coast and in the south. Thus, 'a vulnerable, locally orientated

RMS [was turned] into a functioning social network on a small, but steadily growing scale, running educational institutions, the first hospitals for Africans, farming businesses and mission stations'.[13]

The Nama missions, dealing with communities long acquainted with Christianity, were much more successful in encouraging conversion and church-going than their counterparts among Otjiherero-speakers. Nevertheless, Christianity did begin to make significant inroads among the latter: in 1869 the Herero mission of the RMS had only 150 members, but by 1876 this total had grown to 983 and by 1883 to 1,448. At this period the Herero elite began to take a serious interest in the new religion: many of the *ovahona*, including Maharero, Zeraua, Kandjii and Riarua, although unwilling themselves to convert, sent their children to church and in some cases to be educated at the Augustineum, the RMS's educational institution at Otjimbingwe, founded in 1866. While the RMS divided its work by ethnic group, there is evidence that the reality was somewhat more complex: for example, some Damara and Nama-Oorlam assembled on the stations of the Herero mission. Mission stations also continued to be a refuge for the poor of central Namibia, for example in the work begun in the late 1860s at Omaruru by Daniel Cloete among impoverished Damara and Swartboois. The Damara mission station, at Okombahe, was a slightly different case, in that it was founded in 1870 among a community that dated from the mid-nineteenth century, and had quite probably been successful before the mission came. The people there produced crops of mealies, pumpkins and tobacco as well as keeping goats and cattle.[14]

In addition to its spiritual and political work, the mission (which had persistent financial problems of its own) continued to engage actively in long-distance trade, which in the 1870s reached a different order of magnitude from the undercapitalised ventures of the 1860s. The peak probably came in 1877/78 when, according to Palgrave, there were ten stores in central Namibia, and up to a hundred and twenty wagons trading there. In 1869, the pro-imperial head of the RMS, Friedrich Fabri, set up a mission trading company, the Missions-Handels-Aktien-Gesellschaft (MHAG). The MHAG, like its competitors, imported arms (despite prohibitions from mission headquarters) and alcohol, and exported the products of hunting, as well as cattle. It was surpassed in scale—although there were now other large business concerns in central Namibia—only by the associates Axel Wilhelm

Eriksson and Anders Ohlsson (the latter based in Cape Town), who in the mid-1870s possessed capital to the approximate value of £200,000. At the same period, Otjimbingwe lost its position as the most important trading station in central Namibia, with the rise of Omaruru, Zeraua's base, on which Eriksson and Ohlsson also centred their operations, and Okahandja, Maharero's settlement.[15]

These traders' main exports were ivory and ostrich feathers, which were sent to the Cape and thence to Europe. As in many parts of Africa, this was a time when game was aggressively hunted and animal populations depleted for the sake of vast profits from these luxury goods. Ivory was used for piano keys as well as jewellery and other high-value items: elephants' tusks had thus replaced whaling products as the prime export commodity. To obtain these items the large companies, as well as a number of smaller businesses and individuals, used a system of commercial hunting in which traders (white, Baster, Griqua and sometimes black), working on credit, controlled a network of Nama-Oorlam and San hunters; an active trade to and from the Ngami area also continued at this period. Otjiherero-speakers also participated in these activities, but were frequently able to remain outside this system and to operate on their own behalf.

The Herero groups—unlike the Nama-Oorlam—were relative newcomers to the Cape trade: it was in the 1870s that they engaged deeply for the first time with these networks, using the proceeds of hunting to import modern weapons and horses. In the short term, at least, this entry to the markets allowed them to build their military strength (and to develop commando groups) and thus to increase their control over trade, herds, people and access to water and grazing. This process of (re)-pastoralisation among Otjiherero-speakers was paralleled by an increasing self-identification as 'Herero'—defined not only as people who spoke Otjiherero, but also as people with cattle, guns and horses.[16]

One consequence of this rise in prosperity was an increase in tension, both among those dispossessed in the process of the construction of *ehi rOvaherero*, as the growth of the herds created pressure on water and grazing, and among Herero, as the new trade brought increasing indebtedness. These tensions were to explode after the crash at the end of the decade, when the plentiful rains of the 1870s came to an end with the drought of 1879–81. By this time, too, supplies of game were almost exhausted, and the world recession of the early 1880s led to the collapse of the market for the products of hunting.

Armed conflict, particularly in the form of cattle raids, was the result, as drought forced Herero herders to move their stock southwards into the area around Windhoek. This sparked fighting between (in broad terms) Jan Jonker Afrikaner and the Rehoboth Basters on the one hand, and Maharero on the other, although it was, as Lau reminds us, 'a very complex pattern of shifting, cross-ethnic alliances'.[17] In 1880, apparently provoked by an incident at a cattle post, Maharero ordered the killing of all Nama-Oorlam in and around the Okahandja region.[18] After several months of heavy fighting, the pattern of violence shifted to a more decentralised but nevertheless fairly intense succession of cattle-raids. In western and north-western Namibia, too, Nama, Damara and San fought Herero over cattle.

These years were also a turning point for the small Damara groups dotted around central Namibia. Already impoverished by the expansion of the Herero herds and increasingly used by them as labourers, they experienced severe suffering in the drought of 1880—exacerbated by the depletion of game, usually a resource in hard times, by commercial hunting. Damara who had lived at Okombahe, paying tribute to the local *ovahona*, were forced by poverty to move to the neighbouring mountains, and an Otjiherero-speaking group under Daniel Kariko (who in turn was subject to the Omaruru polity) subsequently settled there and claimed ownership. At the same time, Damara were increasingly recruited as migrant labourers, at first (1879–82) by the Cape authorities, who recruited at least 200 men, 50 women and perhaps 100 children (but probably many more) for domestic and farm work and other occupations in the Cape. Manasse Tjiseseta at Omaruru (who succeeded Tjaherani, Zeraua's successor, in 1884) subsequently made agreements allowing South African labour agents to recruit Damara, especially for work on the mines; such recruitment was, in some cases, carried out forcibly. Some Damara managed to resist these pressures by fleeing to the Swartboois; together, in 1887, they successfully defended Otjitambi against Herero attacks.[19]

The new conflicts of the 1880s were fuelled by the indebtedness of both sides, and their dependence on finding grazing for, and raiding, cattle. The violence undid much of the progress made by the RMS since 1870, as well as undermining large- and small-scale trading operations. The MHAG went bankrupt in 1881; Eriksson & Co., which had already been trading to Lake Ngami and Owambo, now moved northward, centring its operations on Moçamedes in southern Angola, and trading mainly in cattle—now in heavy demand for the mines of South Africa. With the Cape government attempting (from 1880) to ban arms exports to Namibia, the *ovahona* and *kapteins* became increasingly dependent on the few remaining traders, especially those who could find a way to circumvent the new regulations and import weaponry. In many cases cattle, mining and trading concessions, and even land, were sold to the traders or used to repay debts. The best known of these men was Robert Lewis, with whom Maharero had a long association, and to whom he granted far-reaching concessions in 1877, 1883 and 1885, including trading rights over a large part of central Namibia.[20]

The Rise of Hendrik Witbooi

In 1883, despite the conflict besetting southern and central Namibia, a German merchant named Adolf Lüderitz arrived in the territory and laid the foundation for its colonial occupation (and, indeed, for the definition of 'South West Africa' as an entity). Lüderitz's arrival, however, and the protection treaties he was to conclude over the following two years, must have appeared inconsequential in the eyes of Namibian leaders in comparison with the rise of Hendrik Witbooi, which began about the same time.

Of the three best-known nineteenth-century leaders in central and southern Namibia—Jonker Afrikaner, Maharero and Hendrik Witbooi—it is Witbooi who is most often commemorated today as a hero of the struggle against colonialism. He held out against German rule, refusing agree to a protection treaty until his defeat by the German administrator, Leutwein, in 1894; ten years later, at a great age, he led another uprising in which he was killed. Between 1894 and 1904, however, he remained faithful to the peace agreement he had made with the Germans, on a number of occasions sending his own troops to fight alongside the *Schutztruppe* (the German military) against those who were resisting colonial rule. Witbooi is indeed a contradictory figure: educated and an able carpenter, he became a religious visionary after a narrow escape from the killing of Nama in Herero territories in 1880, and developed into a charismatic leader who was able to attract followers through the force of his personality. He was also a gifted politician and military leader, blending sincere religious conviction with a strategy to establish Witbooi dominance based on the armed raiding of other groups in the centre and south.

Fig. 12. Hendrik Witbooi, the predominant leader in the south for the two decades until his death in 1905, photographed c. 1898. (Photographer: probably August Wulff. Reproduced courtesy of the National Archives of Namibia [no. 056] and Übersee-Museum Bremen no. P00056]).

Hendrik Witbooi was a keen correspondent and many of his letters, exchanged with African and German leaders and others including his community of followers, have survived. It is, therefore, possible to hear his voice with remarkable immediacy and to an extent not paralleled by any other Namibian leader at this date (although others also kept their own archives). This makes it doubly disappointing that there is as yet no substantial study of the social and political history of Witbooi and his people, nor indeed of the south of Namibia after 1870.[21] Nevertheless, the outlines of the story are clear. Hendrik Witbooi was born in about 1830 at Pella, in the northern Cape, the son of Moses and !Nanses (Lena) Witbooi. Moses became *kaptein* of the Witboois in 1875, on the death of his father Kido. From the 1820s the Witboois had begun a series of migrations in search of a place to settle, and in 1863 they established a base, together with a missionary, at Gibeon (formerly Kachatsus). As far as we know, they built up and maintained their power through seizing or requiring cattle from other population groups. They, like the other groups of southern Namibia, were also closely tied into the Cape-based exchange networks, importing large quantities of goods—clothes, food, alcohol, arms and horses.[22]

From the age of about thirty-eight, Witbooi became a committed member and then an elder of the mission church in Gibeon, developing a close friendship with the RMS's first representative in there, Johannes Olpp. In this he may have been encouraged by his wife, Katharina, who joined missionary Olpp's classes shortly before her husband. By 1884, however, Hendrik Witbooi had decided to lead his people away from Gibeon and thus to separate from his father, whose attempts to resist Herero attacks since 1880 had been largely unsuccessful. With a band of about 300 (probably all male) followers, Hendrik Witbooi travelled northwards; near Windhoek, after some initial fighting, he negotiated with Maharero and obtained safe-conduct through his lands. The following year he again travelled northwards from Gibeon, this time with a group consisting of between five and six hundred men, women and children, including a number from other Nama-Oorlam groups; only around 40–50 people were left behind.[23] The journey ended in disaster. Although Maharero seems to have made promises of safe-conduct, his troops attacked the incomers at Osona, south of Okahandja, forcing the Witboois to flee in disarray.

That Maharero should have taken this action is perhaps not surprising, in view of the conflicts of recent years[24] and the increased competition for water and grazing that the arrival of the Witboois would have brought. Witbooi, on his side, believed that migration northwards was a task laid on him by God. His letters are vague as to the exact nature of this mission, which seems to have involved continuing his grandfather Kido Witbooi's journey northward; the missionaries also thought that he aimed to bring a general peace to the land.[25] At the same time, he was aiming to establish a power base independent of his father, and to gain access to better grazing lands than the area around Gibeon. His initial use of essentially peaceful methods—even returning stolen stock to the Basters, who were allied with Maharero—epitomises these complexities. On the one hand, he seems to have believed at this stage that such actions were God's will, and he was also probably influenced by the church's prohibition on stealing; on the other, this was part of a clever political strategy to reach a non-violent accommodation with the much stronger Maharero.

Hendrik Witbooi's actions cost him the approval of the missionaries, who saw his claim to direct knowledge of the will of God as an implicit challenge to the basis of their own authority, and were concerned about the spiritual movement he inspired; Witbooi's intended migration also contravened their policy of encouraging settled communities. In 1884 Witbooi was relieved of the office of church elder. He continued, however, to act as pastor and preacher for that part of the Witbooi community (the majority) remaining under his control, among whom Christianity flourished independently of a missionary. This community settled at Garumanas, north of Rehoboth, after the defeat of 1885.

Early in 1886, Hendrik Witbooi (commanding forces from both Witbooi and other Nama-speaking groups) made a third unsuccessful attempt to establish a base further north, launching a surprise attack on Okahandja, which was driven back with some difficulty. Witbooi's forces were then engaged in battle near Rehoboth, and defeated, by a Herero force.[26] Further south, however, he had more success. When, in 1887, Paul Visser overthrew Moses Witbooi as head of the Gibeon people, Hendrik struck back, defeating Visser and his allies in July 1888, and taking up the captaincy of Gibeon (Moses Witbooi and Visser were both killed in this conflict). He was now poised, as we shall see below, to move into a position of ascendancy in the south comparable with Jonker Afrikaner's; although he did not attain a similar dominance over Otjiherero-speakers, he posed a constant military challenge to them.

The Coming of the Germans

The expansion of formal colonial power into Namibia coincided with this rapidly changing period in the territory's history. In 1883, the German trader Adolf Lüderitz kick-started the process that was to lead to the German occupation of SWA by beginning a series of land purchases. Although, in the 1870s, it had not been a foregone conclusion that Germany would establish an empire, in the 1880s other major European powers moved to annex large areas of African (and other) territory; in the event Germany, which had not hitherto held overseas possessions, opted decisively to play a similar role. Its occupation of

SWA was facilitated by the fact that Britain, which might have laid claim to what the Cape government saw as its own hinterland, did not put up substantial opposition. Nevertheless, in the early years Germany's commitment to colonise the territory wavered frequently, and even as late as 1892, it seriously considered pulling out.

Although a growing enthusiasm for empire, and its attendant profits, emerged in Germany after its unification in 1871, Otto von Bismarck, the Imperial Chancellor (*Reichskanzler*), urged caution. Arguing that Germany's true interests lay in Europe, he warned that acquiring colonies would be costly both financially and in diplomatic terms. As the decade progressed, however, his position changed, as economic nationalism grew and the scramble for Africa of the European powers accelerated. The delicate politics of a Germany divided by the consequences of recent rapid industrialisation and its attendant rise in unemployment may also have encouraged him to seize on colonisation as a project likely to unify and distract all but the left. By 1884 Bismarck was prepared to support colonisation, although his position (in the long run untenable) was that colonies should be administered by private German companies. At the same time, the European powers agreed on the legal basis of their occupation and partition of Africa at the (in)famous Berlin Conference (1884–85). By the end of the decade, Germany had established the beginnings of colonies in the Cameroons, Togoland, East Africa and the Pacific islands as well as in South West Africa.[27]

It was in this context that Lüderitz acquired vast tracts of land in what is now Namibia. He was not the only trader seeking to make a profit from Namibian resources:[28] in the early 1880s a number of others also obtained new concessions in the territory, despite the continued intermittent violence. Nevertheless, his special significance lay in the sheer size of the deals he was able to strike, in his grandiose political ambitions—he hoped to found a German sphere of influence stretching into central and east Africa—and in the fact that his acquisitions came at the right historical moment to trigger political intervention.

Lüderitz began by sending his agent Heinrich Vogelsang, assisted by the Rhenish missionary Johannes Bam, to negotiate with Joseph Fredericks of the Bethany people for the land around Angra Pequena (soon to be rechristened 'Lüderitzbucht', 'Lüderitz Bay'). Lüderitz bought this land by an agreement of 1 May 1883. On 25 August, Fredericks and the Bethany people agreed to a second sale, this time of the territory stretching from the Gariep (Orange) River, which formed the northern border of the Cape Colony, to the 26th parallel, north of Angra Pequena. By these two transactions, the trader acquired the coastal strip stretching inland for twenty *geographical* miles; it was not explained to the Bethany people that a geographical mile is 7.4 km, in contrast to an English mile, which is 1.6 km. They were therefore duped into selling off far more land than they had realised. The price was £600 (apparently paid in goods) and 260 rifles.[29]

Bam's role in these negotiations illustrate the importance of individual RMS missionaries (or former missionaries), with their language skills and contact with Africans, in negotiating 'protection' and purchase. In Germany the head of the mission, Friedrich Fabri, had been an active supporter of the German annexation of South West Africa since 1880. Yet the RMS' support for German rule was not as unequivocal as historians like Drechsler have implied. It was not until 1884 that the Society gave public backing to annexation, and as late as 1878, when Walvis Bay was annexed by the British, Fabri requested *British* protection for RMS missionaries in SWA. Although there was much German patriotism among missionaries on the ground, there was also a pragmatic desire for security from the violence of the times; in addition, missionaries like Bam, who favoured German intervention, differed from those, like Gottlieb Viehe, who identified themselves more closely with the interests of Africans and attempted to remain neutral. As Oermann writes, the RMS:

… had immense problems in defining what level of political involvement by the missionaries was still acceptable. The primary focus for the headquarters was on the expansion of mission activities, but the fact that RMS missionaries at home and abroad were German citizens always had an underlying influence.[30]

The land purchases in the south gave Bismarck a basis on which to begin the process of installing German authority in Namibia. By a telegram of 24 April 1884 he effectively created the colony by placing Angra Pequena under German 'protection'; he also sent gunboats to gain effective possession of the coast. Lüderitz was then invited by the German government to acquire the coastal strip from the 26th parallel to the Angolan border. This he did through dubious means, concluding purchase agreements with leaders who had little or no control over the land they claimed to sell, while those with *de facto* control of most of the area steadfastly refused to alienate it. In August 1884, the section from 26 to 22 degrees south (that is, from north of Angra Pequena to north of Walvis Bay) and stretching inland for 20 geographical miles was bought from Piet Haibib of the Topnaars (who were based at Rooibank, near Walvis Bay). Lastly, in 1885 he was sold land stretching from 22 degrees south, northwards to Cape Fria and the Cunene River, as well as more territory in the Kaoko region, by the Swartboois at Fransfontein and those Topnaars settled at Sesfontein under Jan Uichamab. He also acquired prospecting rights and some land in central Namibia, including Windhoek, from Jan Jonker Afrikaner.

With these purchases, the incipient German colony acquired—in name at least—almost the entire coast of Namibia and land stretching eastward for, roughly speaking, 150 km.[31] The fact that Joseph Fredericks, Piet Haibib, Cornelius Swartbooi, Jan Uichamab, Jan Jonker Afrikaner and their *raad*s agreed to sell this land—which left them with very little—requires some explanation. Money was one obvious motivation: all these groups were small, relatively powerless and largely impoverished—Jan Jonker, for example, now had only fourteen men capable of fighting—and their economic situation was also worsened by the arms embargo. Lüderitz paid for land, and usually guaranteed the *kaptein* an annual income in addition. Also, at least in the case of Fredericks, deception was practised and alcohol was supplied in some quantity.

The *kaptein*s, however, were also clearly trying to use German influence in existing power struggles. Jan Jonker Afrikaner's attempt to sell Windhoek to Lüderitz was consistently contested by Maharero, who argued his own claim to the place (in accordance with the second 1870 Treaty of Okahandja). The Swartboois' struggle was with Manasse Tjiseseta of Omaruru, one of the most powerful Herero leaders. In 1867 the Swartboois had established a base at the strategically important Ameib, south-west of Omaruru, which was also claimed by Manasse. Tensions were not relieved by their subsequent move to the Kaoko, where their settlement at Fransfontein was seen by Manasse Tjiseseta as a threat to trade routes between Omaruru and the north. Cornelius Swartbooi used the opportunity of the land sale to Lüderitz to issue a proclamation defining his land as stretching from Karibib and Okombahe northwards to Cape Fria and the Cunene River; much of this area was actually ruled by Manasse. In return, the Germans made a promise—never fulfilled—to obtain Okombahe and Waterberg (both places under Herero authority) for the Swartboois. The latter thus used their agreement with the Germans as a vehicle for sweeping land claims. This considerably heightened conflict with the Herero at Omaruru, although in the late 1880s the Swartboois established peace and some sort of alliance with Manasse. A further example of a minor *kaptein*'s use of land sales in local power struggles occurred in 1890, when the Veldschoendragers in the south made a deal with the German trader Theophilus Hahn; Hendrik Witbooi contested this sale, arguing that he had conquered the land in question, which was therefore legitimately his.[32]

At the same period, agents of the German government also negotiated protection treaties with the peoples of central and southern Namibia in order to establish a political foothold for the German occupation of SWA. Generally speaking, these agreements guaranteed the security of German nationals and their right to trade freely, and prevented African leaders from entering into relations with other European powers. In return, the Germans were to protect the *kaptein*s and *ovahona*, and to respect their jurisdiction over their own people. Between them, the imperial Consul General Gustav Nachtigal, his agent Dr Hoepfner and the former Rhenish missionary Carl Büttner concluded protection treaties with the Bethany people, the Topnaars and the Rehoboth Basters in 1884, and with Jan Jonker Afrikaner, the Berseba people and the Red Nation in 1885; the (unfulfilled) hope of protection against Hendrik Witbooi was a factor in some of these decisions. Other Nama-Oorlam groups, however, most notably the Witboois but also the Khauas and the Bondelswarts, refused to sign protection treaties at this date. The latter held out against severe pressure, including threats of war, from Büttner, their *kaptein* (Willem Christian) infuriating him by his brief and categorical replies: 'In response to my question as to what I [Büttner] should tell His Majesty, the Kaiser, about the negotiations, he said that this was my business and that his answer remained "No"'.[33] The Bondelswarts' resistance was conditioned by their longstanding alliance with the Cape, and they did not enter into an agreement with the Germans until 1890.[34]

Maharero was initially very reluctant to sign a treaty with the Germans. He continued to pursue a policy of consolidating his own influence, and that of the *ohorongo* clan, over much of northern and central Namibia, and on 19 September 1884 had promulgated a document defining the boundaries of Hereroland as extending from Kaoko to the mouths of the Swakop and Omaruru Rivers, and south to the

Rehoboth Gebiet; concessions or purchases within this area were only to be valid with his consent. He also still considered British protection to be an option, writing in October 1884 to the Cape for advice. The British were not, however, prepared to act, having decided in June 1884 not to oppose German expansion into South West Africa. In addition, Hendrik Witbooi had erupted onto the scene, and it was in October 1885, in the aftermath of the fighting at Osona, that Maharero signed a protection treaty with Heinrich Göring, the newly arrived Imperial Commissioner for SWA (and the father of the future Nazi leader Hermann Göring). Besides apparently offering German military support against Witbooi, the 1885 treaty also allowed Maharero to enhance his own position symbolically through the European symbols of sovereignty—a uniform and a 'throne' decorated with an inlaid, gilded crown—presented to him by the Germans. The following month, in November 1885, Manasse Tjiseseta also agreed a protection treaty with the colonisers.

Thus, with a few important exceptions, most of the people of central and southern Namibia had been drawn into formal relations with the Germans in the brief period 1884–85. It is perhaps true, as Schürmann argues, that the engagement of African leaders with the Germans was partly conditioned by the expectation that, as had been the case with white traders and politicians in the past, the new arrivals from Europe offered little threat and would soon be gone. Indeed, for some years to come Maharero remained the most effective political force in central Namibia. The German official presence remained tiny: until the arrival of German troops in 1888, Göring was supported only by a secretary and a police superintendent.[35] The continued power of Maharero and other local rulers was illustrated by the Upingtonia incident of 1885, when a group of migrating Boers founded a settlement of this name at what is now Grootfontein. The fear of incursion by Boer pastoralists, which had caused Maharero and his colleagues to appeal to the Cape for assistance eleven years earlier, had finally been realised. Maharero, aided by the Ndonga king Kambonde and Robert Lewis, successfully exerted his influence to force the settlers out. The land in question was, however, also claimed, and actually occupied, by San groups, who launched attacks on Upingtonia and were thus also instrumental in achieving the Boers' eviction.[36]

Internationally, however, the colonial powers were increasingly agreeing the boundaries marking the territory to which they laid claim.

Considerable tension between Britain and Germany led the British to annex Bechuanaland in January 1885 (thus dashing Lüderitz's hopes of extending German influence from SWA to the east coast, with the cooperation of the Boer republics); later in the year, however, the British acknowledged Germany's interest in Great Namaqualand and Hereroland.[37] In 1886, Germany also agreed to British ownership of the guano islands off the coast of Namibia, and in the same year Portugal accepted German demands that the northern boundary of SWA should be fixed at the Cunene (although the northern border of Owambo remained in contention until it was finally agreed in 1926). The north-eastern boundary was demarcated in 1890 through an agreement with Britain, under which Germany acquired the Caprivi Strip; at the same time, the other boundaries between Britain and Germany (with the exception of the southern border of the Walvis Bay enclave) were confirmed. This agreement also allowed British companies to operate in the territory.[38]

Uncertain Occupation

In 1885 Lüderitz, as yet unable to make a profit, was forced to sell his land holdings, which constituted about a quarter of the total area of Namibia. The buyer was the Deutsche Kolonialgesellschaft für Südwestafrika (German South West Africa Company, DKGSWA),[39] founded on 30 April of that year with the support of leading German businessmen. It was given very generous concessions, including all prospecting and mining rights for the whole territory (not just for the land it owned), and exclusive rights to build railways, roads, harbours and canals and to control trade in its areas. The German government's hope in pursuing this course was that the DKGSWA would at some point accept a charter committing it to administering SWA. Had this strategy succeeded, it would have meant that Bismarck could have avoided asking the *Reichstag* (Parliament) for funds for the colony and thus encountering the resistance of its anti-imperialist members.

If, however, this model had been found to work, up to a point, in the British empire, in the Namibian case it was a failure from the beginning. The DKGSWA, undercapitalised at its inception, could not immediately make a profit and was thus ill-fitted to play the role of colonial administrator that Bismarck had envisaged for it. Only after the apparent discovery of gold in 1887 did it begin to move in this direction, but these developments—along with a minor gold rush—halted abruptly in the following year, when the 'discovery' was exposed as a hoax. In the meantime the *Reichstag* had been persuaded to agree funding for the new colony: in 1886 the grant was 22,000 Marks, and it rose continually thereafter, reaching 166,000 Marks as early as 1888. Finally, the demise of any realistic hope of chartered company government was signalled when Maharero pulled out of the protection treaty with the Germans in 1888.[40]

In the intervening years, Herero in central Namibia had become increasingly disillusioned with German 'protection'. If they had hoped to mobilise German firepower against Witbooi, they were disappointed, since the failure of the German government to send any troops to SWA made this impossible. One Herero summed up this frustration: 'Where is your protectorate? We thought you would come to our aid in the event of an attack on us. What kind of protectorate is yours? What we want is protection'.[41] In addition, the influx of (male) German settlers caused by the gold rush had created discontent, particularly because the settlers had sexual relations with Otjiherero-speaking women. With the treaty in tatters, Göring was forced to retreat to Walvis Bay. As Oermann suggests, German power at this time was largely illusory: 'the events of 1888...can be treated as an illustration not of the formal, but of the real balance of power before 1890'.[42] The work of the Rhenish missionaries, now seen by Maharero as allies of the German authorities, also suffered a severe setback.

While these events were taking place, Hendrik Witbooi and his people were gaining increasing dominance, winning 'uncontested dominion over enormous territories'[43] in southern and, to some extent, central Namibia. After defeating Paul Visser in 1888, Witbooi found himself in opposition to Visser's former allies, Manasse !Noroseb of the Red Nation, Jan Jonker Afrikaner, Kol of the Grootedoden, ‡Arisemab and many of the Veldschoendragers, and Frib of the Khaiǁkhaun—that is, the effective powers in central Namaland. By about 1890, through a series of brilliant military campaigns, Witbooi had established his authority over all these groups, defeating some including the Afrikaners (Jan Jonker was killed in battle in August 1889) and gaining the allegiance of others, such as Frib; he also extended his authority to the far south by obtaining the cooperation of Willem Christian of the Bondelswarts against the Veldschoendragers.[44] In addition, he periodically engaged Herero, particularly Maharero's people, in battle. The details of the establishment and consolidation of Hendrik Witbooi's military gains have not been fully analysed, although it is clear that he was able to amass wealth through successful cattle-raiding or the demanding of tribute, and that he was involved in the Cape trade, which he used to procure supplies.

Witbooi's personal charisma, and his ability to convince people that he knew the will of God, also meant that he could attract and retain followers by peaceful rather than coercive means. In 1889 he established a base at Hoornkrans, west of Rehoboth, where the Witbooi group settled together with 'a great many leaderless people'[45] including most of the followers of Jan Jonker, Visser and ‡Arisemab. Here he built a tightly disciplined, Christian community. Economically, the settlement was based on stock raiding (the products of which were distributed among all households) and, to some extent, husbandry; the creation of effective military force; and trade for horses, arms and a range of other commodities, including such luxury items as musical instruments. The role of its leader was critical. As one visitor recorded (with perhaps some hyperbole), the people 'believe in [Witbooi's] mission and his visions and follow him, urged on in particular by his own indeed extraordinary courage, even to death and ruin'.[46]

The continued violence between Otjiherero-speaking groups and Hendrik Witbooi at this period illustrates the ambiguities embodied in Witbooi's personality and actions, as well, perhaps, as the correspondence of his territorial ambitions with his religious beliefs. His biographer Günter Reeh argues that he saw himself, in Old Testament terms, as an instrument of God's punishment, and that he considered Maharero worthy of such punishment, since he had obstructed Witbooi's divinely inspired northwards migration. As he wrote in 1889 to Hermanus van Wyk, *kaptein* of Rehoboth, 'there are times when [God] shall rule among men through peace, and…at another time He shall rule through war. And God pursues certain purposes through war. So do not always speak to me of peace only. For I myself beseech God for true peace…'[47]

The violence contributed to a sense of mounting crisis, as many groups lost much of their cattle and became vulnerable to disease, particularly smallpox. This situation was fuelled by (and in turn helped to intensify) conflict within Otjiherero-speaking societies, as Christianity gained in popularity and as the younger generation (particularly, it seems, young men) increasingly ignored the authority of their elders and formed themselves into armed troops.[48]

Into this unstable situation the German government sent Captain Curt von François, together with twenty soldiers, in 1889, in an effort to restore its authority. Von François' diplomatic and military gifts, however, left much to be desired. He soon exceeded his orders, which were to evict Robert Lewis from South West Africa but not to come into conflict with Herero or other Africans. The Germans were against Lewis because they blamed him for Maharero's rejection of the protection treaty (overestimating his influence in these events), and because he held probably the most valuable economic interests in the country, based on concessions from Maharero. Von François, however, pursued his own strategic objectives from the outset. He began by antagonising the Herero at Otjimbingwe by establishing without their permission a base at nearby Tsaobis, from which he attempted to control the trade route between Otjimbingwe and Walvis Bay and to cut off supplies of arms and ammunition. Although the *ovahona* of Okahandja, Omaruru and Otjimbingwe combined to challenge von François, the increasing military conflict with Hendrik Witbooi forced them to back down.[49]

Despite unhappiness with von François' course of action, the German government increased the armed force for SWA, the *Schutztruppe* (protectorate troops), to fifty men in January 1890. Maharero accepted German protection for the second time shortly thereafter—and perhaps as a consequence, although he was also motivated by the ongoing conflict with the Witboois. The Germans now allowed Maharero to buy arms, while trying to impose a complete embargo on Witbooi. Otherwise, however, 'protection' remained a cipher, and indeed intensified the conflict by giving rise to tension while failing to supply any actual protection from attack. Von François wrote letters to Witbooi demanding peace, but could do little more. The latter's military superiority at this juncture was demonstrated when, in September 1890, returning from an expedition to collect tribute (and, when resisted, raid cattle) from Herero and Damara settlements, he demanded permission to water his cattle at von François' headquarters at Tsaobis. The German commander did not have the troops to resist Witbooi, and was only saved from the embarrassment of acceding to his request by the fact that Witbooi eventually left of his own accord. Von François then hastily retreated to Windhoek, where he immediately had built the fort now known as the Alte Feste, strategically placed on a central ridge.[50]

It was in response to the second 'protection' agreement between Maharero and the Germans that Witbooi wrote a prophetic and deservedly famous letter, accusing Maharero of failing to understand the hidden dangers of his alliance with the Germans. The sovereignty of the Herero and the 'Red nations' (that is, the Nama-speaking people) was, he argued, equivalent to that claimed by European countries over their own territories. The letter is worth quoting at length:

> Hereroland belongs to the Herero nation, and is an autonomous realm. And Namaland belongs to all the Red nations, and these too are autonomous realms—just as it is said of the White man's countries...But you, dear Captain, you have now accepted another rule, and have handed yourself over to a human supremacy for protection against all dangers—primarily, and most immediately against me...But, my dear Captain! Do you realise what you have done?...surrendering yourself over to government by another, by White people, thinking it wisely planned: that will be to you like the sun which the jackal carried on his back (and which burned him nearly to death)...For I tell you you will not understand Göring's dispensations, you will not be satisfied for he will not act according to your will, or traditional law, or customs...Then it will be too late for you have already given him every right, and he will no longer bend to your ways.[51]

This letter, although it perhaps underestimates the sophistication of Maharero's tactics, is astounding for its accuracy, political acumen and urgency (it is also interesting for its use of essentially European concepts of territoriality in the Namibian context). It amply demonstrates the political grounds on which Hendrik Witbooi based his resistance to the German incursion, resistance that was to be the greatest obstacle to the early establishment of colonial power.

At the same time—although Namibian leaders could not have known this—Germany was, for the last time, seriously considering abandoning Namibia. The expulsion of 1888 panicked the Deutsche Kolonialgesellschaft's investors and weakened the pro-imperialists in Germany. By 1890, with the company's capital almost gone and in the absence of mineral discoveries, Bismarck toyed with the idea of giving the territory to the British in exchange for Heligoland (an island in the North Sea), or selling it to British-based capitalists. Crises in a number of German possessions had caused a wider disillusionment with colonial policy, and in 1890 Bismarck declared himself 'weary of colonies'.[52]

After Bismarck's resignation in the same year, his successor, Count Leo von Caprivi, was initially even less sympathetic to the South West African project and to the pleas of von François and Göring for a military campaign against its inhabitants. In 1891 he noted that 'The Emperor is prepared to give up South West Africa if necessary so that all energies may be focused on East Africa'.[53] In these years, too, politicians at the Cape did everything they could to encourage Britain to wrest South West Africa from Germany; the government in London, however, aware of the risks of such action, held back. The colonial lobby in Germany (including the Colonial Department of the Foreign Office) responded by pushing harder for the colonisation of Namibia, and by mid-1892 had gained the upper hand.

One of the factors behind this shift in policy was the acceptance of a new version of the policy of 'empire on the cheap' in South West Africa. By 1892, given the failure of company administration in SWA, the authorities were willing to accept a compromise in which the German state paid for the running of the territory and its army, while a number of large companies were given very generous concessions: freehold land and exclusive rights to mining and construction work, and the right to distribute land to settlers. Little was required of the companies in return except that they should facilitate the economic exploitation of SWA. The implementation of this policy was made possible both by the 1890 treaty with Maharero and by a new willingness to allow British capitalists to invest in Namibia (in the absence of German funds, since the DKGSWA's investors were unwilling to invest further, and Cecil Rhodes acted to prevent the success of another German concern, the Groll Syndicate).

Between 1892 and 1901 the German government granted or confirmed concessions to eight companies to operate in Namibia. These concessions were partly, but by no means wholly, based on land sales and the granting of mining and other rights by Namibian *kapteins* and *ovahona*. Large commercial syndicates began to snap up concessions to land and other resources, drawn by the prospect of sizeable (if not short-term) profits. Their activities were also to have profound political as well as economic consequences, as we shall see in the next chapter.

The largest of the companies, and politically the most significant, was the South West Africa Company (SWACO), which was led by an investor named Joseph Scharlach and an Anglo-German board of directors, but drew the majority of its capital in the first years of its existence from British investors. In 1892 SWACO acquired the 'Damaraland concession', 13,000 km^2 of land (in northern Hereroland, lying outside the holdings of the DKGSWA) and 72,000 km^2 of mining and railway-building rights. In the same year the Kharaskhoma Syndicate, which was also largely British-held, bought much of the holdings of the DKGSWA in the south. The syndicate was already involved in the politics of this area, negotiating with (and intervening in the affairs of) the Bondelswarts, the Veldschoendragers and the Keetmanshoop people; in 1890 it had succeeded, apparently through prolonged bribery, in persuading the Bondelswarts to accept German protection, five years after their stiff resistance to German officials. A third company to obtain concessions in this early phase was the Hanseatische Land- und Minengesellschaft, which was given large amounts of land as well as mining concessions in the Rehoboth and Gobabis areas.[54]

Although these developments presaged a radical shift in the control of land and mineral rights, they were not yet matched by practical consequences, since the companies did not yet have the ability to exercise the rights granted by the German government. Exploitation of SWA's resources was impeded by the actual balance of power in the territory—a fact underlined by Hendrik Witbooi's attack on the DKGSWA's station at Kubub in the south, which had been established without his permission. Ownership of much of the land granted to the companies was contested, and a large part of it was occupied by Africans, while further tracts came into use for grazing in time of drought. European mining and farming operations thus remained small-scale, and there were still few white settlers. Their numbers began to grow, however, after the Siedlungssyndikat für Südwestafrika (Settlement Syndicate for SWA) was founded in Germany in 1891, with the specific aim of encouraging Germans to emigrate to the territory. The first notable—although still small—influx occurred after the government granted the use of Klein Windhoek for settlement. Samuel Maharero and Zacharias Zeraua also sold off portions of their land (in order to buy goods) at about this time. The new settlers were mainly traders and small-scale farmers, Boers from South Africa as well as Germans, and it was at this period that the Voigts brothers and Fritz Wecke settled in Namibia and set up their trading company, Wecke und Voigts (which still exists). Nevertheless, in practice Namibians remained in control of most of their land and retained effective political independence until after Leutwein arrived to head the administration in 1894.[55]

Realignment

Maharero died on 27 October 1890. He had been the most powerful leader of Otjiherero-speakers in Namibia since forging his reputation in the battles of the 1860s. He had presided over a population whose herds had expanded vastly and whose territory had also grown, and who had forged a new 'Herero' identity. By the time he died, however, the power of the *ohorongo* clan was on the wane, and old rivals—the Afrikaners—had given way to new ones, the Witboois and the Germans.

Maharero's death gave rise to a fierce succession struggle. The Herero 'double descent' system of inheritance resulted in a complex (although flexible) set of rules governing the transmission of property and position through the female and male lines (*eanda* and *oruzo* respectively). Maharero's cattle and other possessions were divided among a number of claimants, mostly relatives from his *eanda*. Little apart from a brick house came to his son, Samuel Maharero (one of the poorer Herero leaders). Samuel Maharero did, however, eventually succeed to his father's position as leader of the *ohorongo* clan and the people at Okahandja, and by implication the wider Otjiherero-speaking community. His claim to this inheritance was weak. Although the succession went through the patrilineal line (the *oruzo*), there were two men with a stronger claim, Nicodemus Kavikunua (the son of Maharero's brother, also known as Kambahatuza or Kambahiza) and Riarua (Maharero's military commander and half-brother). The fact that Samuel Maharero was a Christian, and therefore perceived as occupying an ambiguous position—perhaps not fully 'Herero'—further disadvantaged him. As conflict developed over the inheritance, Samuel Maharero persuaded the German authorities in SWA to recognise him as Herero paramount, and in August 1891 Hugo von François (Curt's brother) went to Okahandja to do so.[56]

At the same time, Hendrik Witbooi's attacks were causing crisis among Otjiherero-speaking groups. His cattle raids were on a considerable scale: according to one estimate, he netted 7,000 cattle, as many as 1,700 sheep and 20 horses in 1890 alone. The *ovahona* also raided Witbooi's people, attacking Hoornkrans with a large force in April 1892, when they were driven back after fierce fighting.[57] Although, in these circumstances, many of the *ovahona* withdrew northwards with their people, Samuel Maharero remained at Okahandja, and made peace with Witbooi (Hermanus van Wyk acting as intermediary) in November 1892. Although this agreement has been described as a peace settlement between 'the Herero' and 'the Nama', Samuel Maharero's very circumscribed authority meant that it was in fact no such thing. He may, indeed, have hoped that the new alliance would aid him in his struggles against the other *ovahona*; it was probably also a response to increasing anti-German feeling among Herero at Okahandja.[58]

Despite its limitations, the peace agreement alarmed the German authorities. The fact that the Witboois were the most prominent group in central Namibia not to have accepted German 'protection' had long caused von François to demand permission to conquer them militarily. On 17 March 1893 a further 215 German soldiers arrived at Walvis Bay, and he quickly seized the chance to launch a surprise attack on Witbooi's headquarters. On the night of 12 April German forces fell on Hoornkrans, killing 80, including 30 women, and wounding 100 (according to official figures). The press reported that some women and children who remained in the settlement after the battle were shot by German troops; about 70 were taken prisoner, and transported to Windhoek (where they became prey to sexual violence from settlers). A few days later Witbooi described how:

Captain [von François] attacked us early in the morning while we were unsuspectingly asleep, and although I took my men out, we were unable to beat them back...and the Captain entered the camp and sacked it in so brutal a manner as I would never have thought a member of a White civilised nation capable of...But this man robbed me, and killed little children at their mother's breast, and older children, and women, and men. Corpses of people who had been shot he burned inside our grass huts, burning their bodies to ash.[59]

Among the prisoners were Hendrik Witbooi's wife and one of his daughters. The latter declared, according to a German source, that the colonial victory was only temporary: 'her father would one day fall upon us [the German forces] like a lion and take his revenge'.[60] Witbooi himself escaped and, with 200 fighters, mounted a successful campaign against von François, who had very little idea of how to counter guerrilla tactics. As his successor was to write later, of a different context, 'In Africa, the hardest aspect of fighting a war is locating the enemy in this vast expanse of land...'[61] The Witboois launched attacks on the German forces from their base in the Naukluft Mountains, on one occasion appearing suddenly just outside Windhoek; they also managed to disrupt German supplies significantly, and to attract others to join them.[62]

The Germans in SWA thus now found themselves facing sustained armed resistance. At the end of a decade of German 'rule', the colony of SWA had barely begun to take shape on the ground. Although formal agreements had been reached with a number of African leaders, these had, as yet, little meaning in practice. Nevertheless, the period since 1870 had been crucial for laying the foundations of colonial rule. Beginning in 1894, Africans now began to be confronted with a very different experience of German domination.

5

UNDER GERMAN RULE, 1894–1903

On 1 January 1894, Theodor Leutwein arrived in SWA to replace von François as the head[1] of the colonial administration (rudimentary as it was). The balance of power was now to swing decisively in favour of the colonisers for the first time. By the end of 1896 Leutwein had quelled immediate opposition to German occupation, concluded agreements with those groups that had previously held aloof from Göring and von François, and begun to set up the structures of colonial rule. In the following year, African pastoralists were devastated by the epidemic of rinderpest. Thus the conditions for colonial development were created: for the first time, German settlers arrived in South West Africa in some numbers, and an infrastructure of roads, railways and harbours began to be created. The costs of this enterprise were devastating, however, to Africans in the Police Zone (as central and southern Namibia was now redefined by the Germans). They lost much of their political power and autonomy, and suffered losses of land, water and grazing rights. A decade after Leutwein's arrival, most of the African groups in the Police Zone took up arms in the Namibian War, and were answered with genocide.

The first Defeats

Although Leutwein's most important goal after his arrival in SWA was to defeat the Witboois in battle, he aimed first at an easier target. A German had recently been killed in the territory of the Khauas people at Gobabis. When Leutwein demanded the handing over of those

131

Fig. 13. Theodor Leutwein, the first effective architect of German power in Namibia, was in charge of the colony between 1894 and 1904. This undated photograph was probably taken in the garden of Leutwein's residence in Windhoek. (Reproduced courtesy of the National Archives of Namibia [no. 053]).

responsible for the killing, the *kaptein* of the Khauas, Andries Lambert, refused. Leutwein took this, along with other 'offences' and a general reputation among the Khauas for lawlessness, as grounds for armed intervention and, with a hundred troops at his back, arrested Lambert. In March 1894 he negotiated a settlement under which the Khauas recognised German sovereignty, Lambert remained *kaptein* and the polity was left more or less intact. However, this was soon to change: Lambert and most of his people were caught trying to escape from the Germans, and this time the *kaptein* was court-martialled and executed, the people disarmed and much of their land and cattle confiscated. These events also persuaded Simon Kopper, leader of the Fransmann people at Gochas (south-east of Mariental), to sign a protection treaty with the Germans—something he had hitherto strenuously resisted.

Leutwein's success in bringing the Khauas and Fransmanns under control not only provided an immediate demonstration of German power, but also helped to provide security for the German forces in their planned campaign against Hendrik Witbooi; at this time the Germans also established a chain of small and isolated garrisons in the south. This accomplished, Leutwein delayed further in taking on Witbooi's well-armed and experienced commandos and agreed to a two-month truce, lasting until August 1894. Both he and Hendrik Witbooi saw this as a chance to strengthen their forces. During this time there was a surprising degree of contact between the opposing sides, with Witbooi women washing German soldiers' clothes in return for tobacco and coffee.[2] At the same time, Witbooi and Leutwein were arguing over the question of sovereignty through an extensive correspondence. '...[T]he rulers of different countries and kingdoms make treaties as brothers', wrote Witbooi on 21 May, 'to live in peace, and to confer on great and weighty matters affecting their nations and peoples. Yet each ruler stays on his land and among his people as their autonomous chief'. To which Leutwein succinctly replied: 'The real issue is that there is a captain in Namaqualand who believes he can do as he will, when Namaqualand is a protectorate under His Majesty the German Kaiser'.[3]

Hendrik Witbooi's hopes of remaining independent were destroyed by a short military campaign between 27 August and 5 September. Although the results of the fighting were inconclusive, Witbooi offered a conditional peace, which Leutwein accepted. Witbooi's willingness to settle seems to have reflected the difficulty of survival in the mountains and of resisting the stronger fire-power of the Germans, who possessed heavier guns and—probably—a larger number of troops (Leutwein estimated the Witboois' strength at about 250 fighters, compared with around 350 on the German side).[4] Despite fears about the long-term intentions of the Germans, Witbooi probably also saw this compromise as a means of retaining as much of his former independence and authority as possible. On his side, Leutwein agreed to the settlement because the complete military defeat of the Witboois—if achievable at all—could only have come at high cost.

Under the peace settlement, Witbooi agreed to accept German authority. In return, he retained his position and his people kept their stock and land (returning now to Gibeon), and even their arms. Because they had been impoverished by their campaign in the mountains, Leutwein was now able to encourage their long-term economic dependence by making them a loan of a hundred and fifty cattle.[5] A year later Witbooi agreed to provide troops for the Germans and, despite some tensions, did so on many occasions. African soldiers were to form a very significant element of the early German military campaigns in Namibia, supplying both vital local knowledge and the skills to survive in the arid bush, and Leutwein, being familiar with British methods of conquest, was well aware of their potential. These arrangements also brought benefits to the African troops, for example the possibility of acquiring cattle from defeated enemies;[6] there were thus, perhaps, some continuities between these early colonial wars and a longer history of cattle-raiding. Witbooi himself remained loyal to the German authorities until he and his people rose against them in October 1904. Writing to Leutwein shortly thereafter, he reflected on his ambiguous feelings about the previous decade:

I have for ten years stood in your law, under your law, and behind your law... For this reason I fear God the Father. All the souls which have for the last ten years perished from all the nations of Africa...without guilt or cause, without the justification of warfare in times of peace, and under treaties of peace, accuse me.[7]

In addition to direct military intervention, Leutwein also engaged in the succession politics of Otjiherero-speaking groups during the first months of his command. The struggle for the Herero paramountcy (discussed in the previous chapter) was still unresolved, and in June 1894 Samuel Maharero (whose claim was recognised by the Germans) had been forced to leave Okahandja by his half-brother Riarua (probably the legitimate claimant). Samuel Maharero appealed to Leutwein for assistance, successfully emphasising his support for German authority, and induced the German commander to intervene directly—thus making German 'protection' a reality for the first time. Leutwein set out for Samuel's camp, on a hilltop at Osona near Okahandja—where the German flag was flying—with forty-one troops and a field-gun. This threat of force, combined with the knowledge of what had happened to Andreas Lambert, proved enough for both Riarua and Nicodemus Kavikunua to recognise the authority of Samuel Maharero and the German government. Riarua also had to surrender much of his authority and cattle-wealth to Samuel Maharero. The latter now embarked on a period of close and mutually advantageous cooperation with the German authorities, who installed a garrison at Okahandja.[8]

By September, Leutwein and his deputy von Lindequist, who had arrived in the territory in 1894 (and was later to become Governor himself), felt able to turn their attention to the polity at Omaruru, whose *omuhona* Manasse Tjiseseta was now among the strongest of the Herero leaders. His authority was built on solid foundations: the ability to control and export the labour of Damara-speakers; agricultural self-sufficiency (partly provided by tribute-paying Damara farmers at Okombahe); the development of well-armed commandos; fiscal and judicial control, including the taxation of traders passing through Omaruru; and a firm grip over land, water and mining rights. This economic and political strength enabled Manasse to maintain a high degree of *de facto* independence from the Herero paramountcy. It also presented—despite his previous acceptance of a protection treaty—a potential challenge to German authority, which Leutwein would not ignore.

The latter had already been given an opening for intervention in July 1894, when Cornelius Goroseb, *kaptein* of those Damara living at Okombahe, travelled to Windhoek to request freedom for his people from Manasse's control. Then, in December, Leutwein, who was fresh from his victory over Hendrik Witbooi, was able to take advantage of a dispute relating to Manasse's judicial authority. In September 1894, a British settler in Manasse's territory named Christie had killed a Baster named Buijs. Christie had fled beyond Manasse's area of control; the latter sent men to arrest him, who killed him instead (possibly in self-defence). Leutwein took the view that, since Christie was a settler, his killers should be handed over to the German authorities for trial, rather than falling under Manasse's jurisdiction. He enforced this decision by marching on Omaruru with a hundred men and a cannon, accompanied by Samuel Maharero, Zacharias Zeraua of Otjimbingwe (a former ally of Manasse), some of Zeraua's men and Cornelius Goroseb. With the example of the Khauas presumably in mind, and hoping to retain at least part of his wealth and authority, Manasse did not deploy his own armed forces, but delivered the men in question to the Germans. In the negotiations that followed, Leutwein recognised that Manasse should be autonomous of Samuel Maharero at Okahandja, but forced him to accept a garrison and deprived him of control of the Damara community at Okombahe, thus seriously weakening his polity at Omaruru. At about the same time, colonial authority over this north-western part of central Namibia was also further cemented by German intervention in a succession struggle among Manasse's rivals, the Swartboois. Their *kaptein*, Cornelius Swartbooi, had died in January 1894 and his nephew, David Swartbooi, was installed as his successor with German help.[9]

With the loss of Okombahe, Manasse's authority over its Damara-speaking population was transferred to Cornelius Goroseb, whom the colonial authorities now created paramount chief of 'the Damara'. This was a reward not only for his role in undermining Manasse, but also for the commitment he now made to provide unspecified amounts of labour to the Germans. In reality, he could hope to exercise little power beyond Okombahe, since his new 'subjects' consisted of scattered groups of Damara-speaking people who, although they may have identified themselves as sharing (aspects of) a common Bergdamara culture (the point is debated), certainly had no political unity.

In the following year Leutwein engaged further with small, relatively powerless groups of Damara and San, apparently attempting to obtain some control over these very diverse and decentralised communities. He recognised Johannes (Jaq) Kruger, a Baster who also played a leadership role at the Waterberg, as captain of the San and Damara living at Gaub (near Grootfontein); in return Kruger was to be accountable to the local representative of SWACO, as well as supplying labour for local farmers. Leutwein also signed an agreement with a San 'captain', Aribib, at Naidaus.[10]

Land, Cattle and Resistance

1894 was thus, for Leutwein and von Lindequist, a year of intense diplomatic and military activity, and by its end a rough '*pax Germanica*' had been established throughout south and central Namibia. German domination of the three most powerful political units—that of the Witboois, and the Okahandja and Omaruru polities—had been implemented in such a way as to allow their rulers some continued autonomy, and numerous other agreements had been completed. Although the threat of colonial violence was never far below the surface, only in the case of Andreas Lambert and the Khauas people had a polity been destroyed by force—so far. Leutwein had thus deployed a very effective combination of tactics, refraining from the use of direct violence where possible and choosing instead to exploit political divisions and conflicts and to implement versions of indirect rule, which were always given legal justification (in colonial terms) through the signing of formal agreements. This policy may have involved the flaunting of colonial strength, but it also stemmed from underlying weakness. The number of German troops in the country remained very small—a fact that made it impossible as yet to mount a challenge to the strong Ovambo kingdoms to the north. In the east, however, tension was about to increase rapidly as the German administration now attempted to make colonial power a reality on the ground.

Leutwein's new policy was, in essence, to try to push Namibian pastoralists back within 'agreed' boundaries, thus freeing land for German occupation and exploitation. His focus was on 'Hereroland', which had greater potential for cattle-ranching than the more barren south, and where he hoped further to undermine (some of) the still relatively strong Herero polities by capitalising on his alliance with Samuel Maharero. In December 1894, the two men signed a treaty moving the southern boundary of Hereroland northwards from its former (effective) position; in the south and east, it now ran along the White Nossob River. Otjiherero-speakers were banned from living, or grazing their stock, in the area beyond the new border. The boundary changes put the important grazing areas at Seeis and Gobabis under German control. Their effects were felt most heavily by Otjiherero-speakers living in the east, particularly Kahimemua, the Mbanderu *omuhona*, and Nicodemus Kavikunua, one of the defeated claimants to the Okahandja paramountcy, and their people, who were living together at Otjihaenena on the White Nossob.

Unlike many of the protection agreements, this treaty was worth more than the paper it was written on: intense and immediate efforts were made to enforce it, as Leutwein used the power of (part of) the Herero elite to implement effective land dispossession. A frontier commission, in which Assa Riarua (Riarua's son) as well as Samuel Maharero's son and nephew were involved, was sent out to negotiate the precise borders, enforce grazing restrictions and remove Otjihererospeakers to the northern side of the boundary. The following year, in August 1895, Samuel Maharero agreed to further loss of territory by signing treaties redefining the northern border of Hereroland. He and Leutwein toured the new boundary, obtaining the cooperation of the very wealthy *omuhona* Kambazembi at the Waterberg (who accepted Samuel Maharero's authority). Agreements were also signed with the Topnaar and Swartbooi at Fransfontein (as well as with the San and Damara groups mentioned above).[11]

Leutwein, aware of the dangers of colonial warfare, might have refrained from acting so quickly had he not been subject to strong political pressure. This came both from the small but vocal German settler community (particularly the newer arrivals) and from the concession companies. Both groups demanded the removal of all land and cattle from Herero; this, they argued, would provide the Germans at a stroke with access to land, stock and labour. The South West Africa Company wanted military action against the eastern Herero and dispossession in the north; the DKGSWA called for a campaign to protect its interests in the Spitzkoppe area (territory claimed by Manasse Tjiseseta); and the Kaoko Land- und Minengesellschaft (formed in 1894, taking over the rights of the DKGSWA in the Kaoko)[12] wanted the Swartboois driven from their land. These demands were partly fulfilled through the new treaties. The northern agreements, among other provisions, gave new land and mining rights to SWACO, and aimed to expel Africans from the land assigned to the company.

As for Samuel Maharero, his cooperation in the enforcement of the new boundaries brought frequent opportunities to establish his authority over rival *ovahona*—which he exploited with considerable political acumen—as well as for personal economic gain, including a salary from the administration. His actions facilitated colonial encroachment on African authority and territory and, as Helmut Bley has observed, he 'seemed far less aware of the long-term consequences of his dependence on the German Government than Hendrik Witbooi or Manasse [Tjiseseta] of Omaruru'.[13]

On the ground, the enforcement of the boundaries aroused strong opposition in both east and north. In some cases removals took place in the shadow of a cannon, and the shifting of the northern frontier was accomplished with the help of a force of eighty German cavalrymen. In addition, violations of the treaty—that is, allowing cattle to graze beyond the boundaries set out—led to the confiscation (from November 1895) of 5 per cent of the stock found on the wrong side of the line, an act the herders saw—with justification—as robbery. Although rich pastoralists were the main target, it is likely that members of smaller, isolated Damara and San groups also suffered, although we know little of their (probably varied) experiences of the new policy.

Nevertheless, Leutwein and Samuel Maharero did not have it all their own way. In early 1895, Nicodemus Kavikunua and a force of armed Herero were able to wring concessions from von Lindequist and his colleagues. In May Leutwein, von Lindequist, Samuel Maharero and Assa Riarua went to Otjihaenena for renewed talks with the well-armed Nicodemus Kavikunua, Kahimemua and other Otjiherero-speaking leaders, at which Samuel Maharero's claims to authority were as much at issue as the new boundary. The outcome of the negotiations was to establish Nicodemus Kavikunua in a chieftaincy independent of the paramount (but heavily reliant on the German authorities) in the east, in return for some territorial concessions. The agreement meant a partial defeat for Leutwein, who softened some of his demands in order to avoid armed conflict. It also, however, gave him the opportunity to extend his divide and rule policy, since the very senior leader Kahimemua, who (oral tradition states) saw himself as Maharero's counterpart in the east—and independent of the Okahandja paramountcy—was now subordinated to Nicodemus Kavikunua.[14]

The latter—despite his efforts to remove his subjects north of the boundary agreed in May—still represented a substantial potential threat to the Germans and the accommodation between the two did not last long. Leutwein prevented him from establishing a permanent headquarters at Gobabis (a place that Kahimemua also claimed, and where the Germans established a garrison in June 1895).[15] The people of the east were seeing their means of production comprehensively undermined: the German authorities continued to expropriate cattle; the threatened loss of control of Gobabis would put Nicodemus Kavikunua's arms supplies from Botswana in jeopardy; Kahimemua wrote to Leutwein asking 'why you refuse to grant me part of the land';[16] and the Khauas people had been politically and economically devastated by Leutwein's actions in 1894. With drought exacerbating these already tense conditions, the situation exploded into war in March 1896. Although the African resistance to colonial encroachment was fractured by pre-existing divisions and conflicts over questions of seniority and power, the uprising nevertheless presented the colonisers with their most sustained challenge since the arrival of Leutwein.

The war began when a group of Khauas launched a surprise assault on a German patrol. The attack threw the colony into a ferment, provoking a frenzy of rumours, for example that the Witboois would turn against the Germans. The following month, the Khauas, probably Nicodemus Kavikunua[17] and perhaps Kahimemua[18] made an attack on the German garrison at Gobabis. This was heavily, but not easily, defeated, with perhaps a hundred losses on the African side, and six on the German.[19] At this stage, Nicodemus withdrew from the fighting: he appears to have gone, with very few followers, to seek refuge with Tjetjo Kandjii (Maharero's sister's son, who had challenged Samuel Maharero's authority but had eventually submitted to his leadership without bloodshed). At the same time, Kahimemua and the main body of Otjiherero-speakers, together with the Khauas, moved into the *veld*, successfully evading their pursuers until the latter found them at Otjunda (which they named Sturmfeld), near Epukiro, and after a hard-fought battle defeated them. The victorious force included Germans, Basters, the followers of Witbooi and Samuel Maharero, and two disaffected Mbanderu *ovahona*.

After the defeat at Otjunda, Kahimemua gave himself up. His forces had experienced heavy losses (including his brother and two of his sons), and supplies of food and ammunition seem to have been exhausted. Oral tradition also links his surrender to the fact that he was believed to be an *ombuke* (prophet); such people were rare, and it was even more unusual for a political leader to assume this identity. Kahimemua, then, spoke with his ancestors and, with a sense of imminent doom, effectively laid a curse on the new dispensation, declaring 'I have utterly destroyed the whole country!' before sending messengers to Samuel Maharero with the words 'I am here. Come and fetch me'.[20] These words fit with the general tendency of the oral traditions relating to Kahimemua to construct a narrative of his prophetic and uncompromising life and death: at the talks in May 1895, for example, he had declared that 'As long as I live, I shall have no land to give to strangers'.[21] If some of his sayings are perhaps later constructions rather than contemporary utterances, they nevertheless eloquently suggest the imprint that Kahimemua's character and politics have made on Mbanderu historical memory, as well as the significance of the defeat of 1896. Carow's version of Kahimemua's message to Leutwein after Otjunda also has a prophetic ring: '"I want to give myself up, and then die, for I have lived long enough [*ich bin alt genug*]"'.[22] Nicodemus Kavikunua, meanwhile, went from Tjetjo to Assa Riarua, and thence into German custody. Both he and Kahimemua were imprisoned in

Okahandja, where they were tried, condemned to death and executed by firing squad on 12 June 1896. Other participants in the fighting were also shot.[23]

If this spelled the end of one of the most determined, and tragic, episodes of armed resistance against the German occupation of SWA, the focus of the sources on the two contrasting leaders—Kahimemua dying with dignity and courage, Nicodemus Kavikunua in fear—should not be allowed to obscure what kind of war this was. It involved not only male fighters, but whole groups of Khauas, Mbanderu and Herero as they fled together after the defeat at Goba-bis. Carow records the arrival of starving Khauas women and children at the German camp as they came to surrender; Khauas women are even said to have intervened in the April battle by attempting to shield the men from gunfire.[24] In the aftermath of the uprising the Germans removed the Khauas (or all those defined as such) from the east. Some were placed under Witbooi's authority; many were imprisoned and taken to Windhoek, were they were interned in prison camps and used as labourers by the Germans; others were also probably taken on as servants by German troops.[25] At the same time, the economic basis of the eastern Otjiherero-speakers was further undermined. The latter had lost some of their herds in the fighting and, in addition, according to Leutwein, the German authorities seized 12,000 head of their cattle in 1896–97. After the fighting, many were brought under the authority of Samuel Maharero and his followers, while others fled across the border to the British territory of the Bechuanaland Protectorate. Sam-uel Maharero also stepped up his raiding in the east, targeting among others his erstwhile opponent Tjetjo Kandjii, and extending his sphere of influence eastward. The colonial military presence was further strengthened as Leutwein took the opportunity to establish a perma-nent garrison of seven hundred troops, spread through the south and centre as well as the east.[26]

That the war in the east did not become a wider conflict was partly due to Leutwein's successful use of divide and rule tactics. By the end of 1895, the situation within other Otjiherero-speaking polities had become explosive. Even the Okahandja people had been affected by the new boundary treaties, which forced them to withdraw their stock from grazing land. Leutwein did not hesitate to confiscate cattle from Samuel Maharero's people; the paramount received a half-share of the proceeds. The Okahandja polity was thus becoming increasingly

Fig. 14. This photograph is almost certainly of the Khauas people,[27] captured after their defeat by Leutwein in 1896 and subsequently imprisoned in Windhoek. The image is a powerful visual reminder that women and children as well as men experienced the privations of war, captivity and forced labour under German rule. (Reproduced courtesy of the National Archives of Namibia [no. 01880]).

divided, and Samuel Maharero's popularity was dwindling. His wider standing—and the economic well-being of Otjiherero-speakers—were further compromised by his practice of selling land (much of it in areas that he did not traditionally control), particularly in order to settle his debts to traders.

In contrast to his approach in the east, Leutwein eased some of these tensions by allowing the Okahandja Herero temporary use of grazing land south of the new boundary, as far as Seeis. However, he and Samuel Maharero could not prevent other moves to evade the grip of the Windhoek-Okahandja power nexus, as dispossessed pastoralists began to turn beyond the boundaries of Hereroland for support. Thus, subjects of Samuel Maharero complained of the situation to the Ndonga king Kambonde late in 1895. The German authorities subsequently accused the Herero *omuhona* Katarre, a subject of Manasse Tjiseseta, of theft, and disarmed him. In doing so, they probably intended to pre-empt cooperation between Kambonde and Katarre, whose headquarters were situated on the trade route between Omaruru and the Ovambo kingdoms—an important source of arms for the people of central Namibia, and one that the Germans took action to control by also placing a garrison at Outjo.

Another conflict blew up between the German authorities and Daniel Kariko, based at Okombahe and under Manasse Tjiseseta's authority. After the German settlement with Manasse deprived him of his control over the Damara at Okombahe, Kariko increasingly felt his position to be under threat. At the end of 1895 he successfully approached Kambonde for permission to settle in Ondonga. The move enabled Kariko to establish better access to arms through the northern traders, and to send captured Damara labourers to South African enterprises such as the Damaraland Guano Company based at Cape Cross. In an apparent attempt to withdraw from the German-controlled state, he also began claiming to be a British subject. The subversive implications of this stance were not, however, something the Germans were prepared to countenance. In June 1896 Kariko was summoned to Omaruru by Manasse Tjiseseta and arrested. He was found guilty of treason and banished, but later escaped to Walvis Bay. A cattle fine was also imposed, so that his people were probably impoverished.[28]

If, by the end of 1896, all the Namibian societies lying to the south of the Ovambo kingdoms had been severely affected by the German occupation, it was in the following year, with the arrival of rinderpest, that a time of peril became one of disaster. Rinderpest is a virulent and contagious cattle disease, leading to high mortality if not treated. It affected much of southern Africa, and had reached Namibia by April 1897. The territory presented ideal conditions for its spread: large herds pushed into crowded grazing lands, following the forced removals of previous years; a very limited number of passable routes along which the virus was quickly communicated; and a state lacking the resources to enforce quarantine procedures or vaccination rigorously. The Germans had, indeed, attempted to defend the colony by erecting a line of forts between Gobabis in the east and Tswawisis near Fransfontein in the west in late 1896 and early 1897; although this boundary, which delineated the limits of effective German control of SWA, was of great long-term significance in that it was the origin of the later division of SWA into the 'Police Zone' and the territories to the north, it was of no use in containing the epidemic.

The rinderpest epizootic thus had a catastrophic effect on African pastoralists. The mortality figures are disputed but, among Herero, at least two-thirds of cattle died.[29] Settlers' losses were lower. Even in the worst-hit districts, between 75 and 95 per cent of their cattle survived,[30] largely because of the authorities' vaccination programme; this had been made possible by the work of the great German bacteriologist Robert Koch[31] and his assistant Kohlstock who, invited to South Africa by the British South Africa Company, quickly produced a vaccine that Kohlstock then brought to Namibia in June 1897. Settlers' herds were given priority, leaving inadequate supplies for Africans' cattle. In addition, many Namibian pastoralists, already highly suspicious of the colonial state and its intentions, were distrustful of a vaccine that was not always reliable: in Otjosazu, for example, 2,000 out of 3,000 inoculated cattle died. The manufacture of the vaccine also required gall from healthy cows, which were requisitioned from Africans. Resistance to the vaccination programme thus flared periodically.

The epidemic had all the hallmarks of a major colonial public health crisis. It was caused by the rapid spread of disease, but met with coercive control measures—resisted by those on the receiving end—and with resources distributed unequally along racial lines. In its aftermath, the people of central Namibia experienced widespread malnourishment because of the loss of a major food source. When infectious diseases, including malaria and typhoid, broke out in 1897–98, they caused high mortality: the missionary Irle estimated that 10,000 people died in the severe epidemic (possibly typhoid) that occurred at the beginning of 1898.[32] Those who escaped embarked on a number of strategies aimed firstly at survival, but also at managing the economic consequences of the disaster.

Impoverished former cattle-owners and their families converged on mission stations, such as those at Omaruru and Otjimbingwe, in search of agricultural land, or migrated within and beyond the protectorate in search of work. Some went to Windhoek or the new urban centres of Karibib and Tsumeb, while others sought refuge in Botswana (following an earlier agreement with the king of the Batawana, Sekgoma Letsholathebe) or in Kaoko or Owambo; some ended up as labourers on Boer farms in Botswana; some went to the South African mines. At the same time, some of the *ovahona*, principally Samuel Maharero, increasingly sold off large areas of land in order to settle debts and increase their own patronage networks. While the epidemic effectively undermined the power and autonomy of the Omaruru polity, of Kambazembi at Waterberg and of Tjetjo Kandjii at Gobabis, in the short term it increased the influence of Samuel Maharero, who used it to reinforce his power in the east.[33]

It can be assumed that the tragic consequences of rinderpest were shared by the population of the south and by smaller groups in central Namibia, although very little has been written on this subject. The effects of the epidemic were no doubt complex. Poorer groups, which owned few or no cattle, may not have been as devastated as richer pastoralists; on the other hand, some groups were certainly further marginalised by the general crisis. Gewald notes, for example, that after the epidemic Damara herders of Herero cattle were being replaced by impoverished Otjiherero-speakers. San 'were rapidly forced into the colonial economy'[34] and it is likely that many Damara, too, continued to be coerced into migrant labour of various kinds. In the far south, attempts to contain the epidemic led to armed resistance and further tragedy when the Germans established a twenty-kilometre-wide quarantine belt on the border with South Africa, which encompassed land on which the (Oorlam) Afrikaners were settled. Military conflict was triggered when the authorities found and killed cattle belonging to the Afrikaners inside this zone. It took the Germans almost a month to win this war, but on 2 August 1897 they defeated the Afrikaners, killing thirty-seven (including some women), in a battle during which British troops prevented any possible escape southwards across the Gariep. The Afrikaner *kaptein*, his sons and other leaders were court-martialled and shot; what happened to the survivors is unclear. In any event, the Afrikaners had been broken as a cohesive political force.[35]

The tensions arising from the rinderpest crisis were also partly responsible for provoking a rising among the Swartboois at Fransfontein and other groups in the north-west. Other causes of this conflict included German intervention in the succession to Cornelius Swartbooi, who had died in 1894. Resistance to German control ebbed and flowed throughout 1897, and at the end of that year a large group led by David Swartbooi left for the *veld* where, together with disaffected Topnaar under Jan Uichamab and a small group of western Herero under the *omuhona* Kambatta, they carried out raids on settlers' cattle. The German authorities viewed the new situation as an opportunity to gain *de facto* possession of the Swartboois' land for one of the major concession companies, the Kaoko Land- und Eisenbahn Gesellschaft. They launched a military campaign (to which Samuel Maharero and Hendrik Witbooi each contributed 100 men) and by March 1898 had defeated the Swartboois, whom they then took to Windhoek; they imprisoned approximately 150 men and 400 women and children, and forced them to remain in the capital even after their release. The Topnaar escaped with a fine of 1,000 small stock, while twenty-five of Kambatta's men, including his son, were convicted of high treason and turned over to the railways as forced labour.[36]

In 1897, the government in Windhoek considered itself strong enough to pass an ordinance for the stamping of weapons, with the aim of gradually disarming Africans without appearing to do so. As well as registering guns, the authorities tried to exchange South African for German rifles in order to try to undermine weapons smuggling from British territory. The registration policy has found a place in the Herero oral record, where it is remembered as the 'vaccination' of weapons—perhaps a comparison with vaccination of cattle during the rinderpest epidemic. In the years that followed, the implementation of this policy triggered conflict with a number of smaller groups. In 1899, Samuel Maharero sent an armed force to compel Tjetjo Kandjii to accept the stamping of his fighters' weapons; when this demand was met with resistance, the old *omuhona* was treated leniently, but his son was disarmed and removed to Okahandja with his people. In 1900, the Germans fought a three-week military campaign against a group of Basters living at Grootfontein who had been trying to resist the registration of their horses. Their *kaptein*, Klaus Swart, was killed, and the people were deprived of their land and cattle and forced to labour for the colonisers. In 1898, Willem Christian, the *kaptein* of the Bondelswarts at Warmbad, and Paul Fredericks, at Bethany, also unsuccessfully opposed the registration of their weapons. In response, Leutwein marched south with a hundred men and four cannon, joined by fifty of Witbooi's fighters. After their defeat Christian and Fredericks were found liable for the costs of this expedition and, since they could not pay, had much of their land confiscated as a result.[37]

Small-scale armed resistance thus continued to flare periodically, and Namibia was never fully pacified before the eruption of war in 1904. Nevertheless, a rudimentary form of German rule over south and central Namibia became effective in the period 1894–97. It was then that, for the first time, the German colonial state became something more than an idea in the minds of administrators and politicians in Berlin and Windhoek, and that independent political power in Namibia was quickly and effectively destroyed. Those leaders who did retain a measure of autonomy—the most powerful being Samuel Maharero and Hendrik Witbooi—did so only through reaching an accommodation with the German authorities. How did it come about that the power of African rulers was so quickly broken?

The first and most obvious answer is the military might of Germany. The question is complex, however. While colonial firepower was an essential precondition of conquest, it was by no means always the deciding factor. The German garrison in Namibia was weak in numbers, and Leutwein relied heavily on the local knowledge and military skills of his African allies. As this suggests, Leutwein used his undoubted political, diplomatic and military abilities to great effect in exploiting and deepening the pre-existing divisions among polities whose struggles for land, water and power had been defined by the conflicts and alliances of previous decades, and to many of whom the Germans initially seemed no more dangerous than older enemies. In many cases, too, African leaders accepted compromise settlements for fear of losing everything through armed resistance. If Hendrik Witbooi perceived the threat more clearly than most, even he could not, or would not, act consistently on that understanding, and his ten years' alliance with the Germans helped to ensure the colonisers' domination of the other polities—as did the active collaboration of Samuel Maharero. Conversely, those who resisted the Germans did not always do so from an explicit desire to throw off their control; such conflicts were sometimes generated by the desire for immediate political gains, a desperate struggle for survival, or internal political dynamics. Resistance, therefore, like collaboration, occurred within the constraints of the broader situation and the compass of what was politically possible.

Despite these complexities, Leutwein employed direct force (relying on the skills and knowledge of local troops) on numerous occasions; when he exercised restraint, it was nevertheless the threat of violence that usually encouraged African compliance with his demands. Even had armed resistance to the Germans been far more unified and determined, it is doubtful whether it would have been successful against the underlying power of a German state that—by and large—was determined to hold on to its colonial territories. When major armed conflict

147

broke out, in 1904, Germany proved willing to pour large numbers of troops into SWA.

A further factor in the conquest was the level of the penetration of merchant capital into SWA. It is true that involvement in trade did not automatically draw people into underdevelopment: in central Namibia Otjiherero-speakers had been able to use commerce to arm themselves and to attain increasing autonomy and power (although, at the same time, this led to the impoverishment of others, helping to spark raiding and war).[38] By the 1890s, however, the disadvantages of capital penetration were becoming increasingly clear, as Samuel Maharero and other *ovahona* sold land to pay their debts, thus exacerbating crises of land hunger and widening divisions within the Otjiherero-speaking polities.

The Construction of the State

The conquest of Namibia in the period 1894–97 enabled, and was aided by, the construction of a fledgling German state in Namibia. German domination was now to be exercised through the creation of bureaucratic boundaries, regulations and offices, the establishment of judicial institutions, and the parcelling out of land to white settlers. In Germany, meanwhile, the growing importance of empire was signalled by that country's first colonial exhibition in 1896. Over a hundred people from German colonies, including one of Samuel Maharero's sons, were sent to this event to embody the nascent German empire for European eyes.[39] German foreign policy had become more resolutely pro-imperial after the resignation of Chancellor von Caprivi in 1894, and during the next few years Germany pursued an expansionist policy in southern Africa, which led to diplomatic clashes with Britain; in 1898, however, Germany (with Bernhard von Bülow now foreign secretary)[40] and Britain signed an accord, and relations improved.[41]

The establishment of German rule in Namibia was tempered by the fact that the new regime remained markedly fragile. Its ability to enforce its authority on a day-to-day basis was restricted by the very slight resources of men and equipment available to it, and the practical difficulties of policing such a huge, dry and hot territory. Nevertheless, the scale and depth of the transformation in the decade before the war of 1904 were unprecedented. As we have seen, African polities were put under ever-increasing pressure by the rapid expansion of both the settler population and the operations of the concession companies, as well as by the rinderpest epidemic. In 1896, the white population of Namibia (including the armed forces) was only 2,000; by 1903, it had more than doubled, to reach 4,700, and settlers received some financial support from the state.[42]

The dispossession that accompanied this increase is starkly represented in the statistics. By 1902 the number of Otjiherero-speakers' cattle had fallen to 46,000, from about 100,000 in the early 1890s; by the same year, cattle owned by Germans numbered roughly 44,500. By 1902, 29.2 million hectares of land was held by the concession companies, 10.2 million by the state and 3.7 million by white settlers, out of a total of 83.5 million.[43] Large numbers of Africans were turning to waged work for the first time. There were, nevertheless, still significant brakes on colonial expansion. One was that the concession companies did not yet have effective control over much of the land they had been granted, another that they were very slow in distributing land for settlement, preferring to hold onto their assets in the expectation that prices would rise.[44] This situation pertained until 1907, when the government reached a deal with the companies.[45]

Leutwein sought to root the expanding German presence firmly in Namibian soil through the construction of 'modern' and bureaucratic—if initially rudimentary—state mechanisms. These were to provide for the government of the settlers and to give a legal framework to the appropriation, definition and control of land and other concessions—just as the protection and purchase agreements provided a legal cover for the assumption of power over African leaders. As early as 1894, Leutwein attempted to inscribe German authority onto the landscape by dividing the colony into three administrative districts (*Bezirke*), excluding the northern areas of Owambo, Kaoko and the northern parts of Hereroland. The *Bezirke* were subdivided as the white population grew, and in 1896 a new *Nordbezirk* (northern district), based on Outjo, was also established. As we have seen, the northern boundary was formalised and fortified in the face of the rinderpest epidemic; at this period, however, control of the border could not be fully enforced.[46]

Although before 1904 the German administration was in practice staffed mainly by army officers, in principle Leutwein (himself both governor and chief military commander) aimed to signal the modernity of the nascent state in SWA by differentiating between military and civilian authority.[47] This aim was somewhat undermined by the fact that policing was carried out by the *Schutztruppe* until 1905. On the other hand, the administration in Windhoek was given a rudimentary departmental structure, which included sections for finance, customs, health and mining, and procedures to regulate the registration of land and other concessions were set up. These not only had the broad effect of facilitating the transfer of African land and rights into European hands, but on occasion were used to exert pressure on the course of African politics. After Manasse Tjiseseta's death in 1898, the German authorities were able to exert influence over the choice of his successor through their control of land registration procedures: many of the Omaruru councillors needed to sell land to recoup their losses from the rinderpest epidemic, and could only do so with German permission.[48]

Despite these attempts to establish structures of government, Leutwein's power was significantly limited in a number of ways. The governor's room for manoeuvre was restricted by the demands of his African allies and opponents, and the difficulties of imposing foreign rule with limited resources. Nor did the new regime in Namibia represent a homogeneous German interest. Ultimately constrained by policy decisions taken in Berlin, Leutwein's administration was frequently under pressure for more aggressive action against African societies, both from the settlers—themselves not a unified group, since many of the newer arrivals were more belligerent than those of longer standing—and the concession companies, whose activities, Leutwein warned, were likely to cause unrest among Africans.

These companies—whose numbers now increased with the addition of the Otavi Minen und Eisenbahngesellschaft (OMEG) in 1899 and the Gibeon Schiff- und Handelsgesellschaft in 1903—were exciting opposition in Germany, as well as in some quarters in South West Africa. SWACO, which had a controlling interest in many of the other companies, was particularly unpopular in Germany, where it was seen as politically dangerous (because its capital was predominantly British) and as unwilling to contribute to the development of the colony. The first of these objections was exaggerated, since the company's ownership was in fact increasingly falling into German hands.[49] Nevertheless, it was becoming clear that the policy of 'empire on the cheap' was leaving the territory prey to large companies that—partly because their operations were not yet very profitable—could not be compelled to support the cash-strapped German administration by carrying out major infrastructural work. After the rinderpest disaster, the collapse of ox-wagon transport made the building of a railway between the coast at Swakopmund and Windhoek imperative for the colonial economy. SWACO, which held the monopoly on this work, refused to carry it out, and the problem was only resolved when the company relinquished these rights in return for a large concession in the north. This allowed the government to employ the Railway Regiment of the German army and African labourers to carry out the work; it was completed in 1902.[50]

The Swakopmund–Windhoek railway was the largest infrastructural work to be completed under German rule before 1904, but not the only one. Roads and dams were built, and water-boring carried out; many of these activities directly benefited settler farms. The Woermann Line began regular steamship sailings between Germany and Swakopmund in 1896, and three years later the construction of an artificial harbour basin at the port town began. In 1903, OMEG started work on a new railway-building project, this time to replace the existing line between Swakopmund and Windhoek and to continue it north to Tsumeb, in order to facilitate the transport of copper from the Tsumeb mine and of labour recruits. The new line and the land dispossession it heralded caused tension, as we shall see in the next chapter, and its construction was interrupted by the outbreak of war in 1904. It was eventually completed in 1905.[51] During Leutwein's term of office, the colonisers thus began to put in place the infrastructure—both physical and administrative—to enable them to exploit the economic potential of SWA. Many aspects of this process were not new: Africans had built roads, constructed wells and dams and, indeed, given concessions for many years before the advent of direct colonialism. Nor did the developments of the period before 1904 match the rapid economic expansion in the era of copper and diamonds thereafter. Nevertheless, developments in this decade presaged the construction of a new form of capitalist economy, with much greater industrialisation and increased access to technological resources.

It was the work of Africans, who built the infrastructure and laboured on farms and in the towns for both large and small employers, that made this 'development' possible. This period is key for the history of labour in Namibia. It was in the 1890s that migrant workers from the north, mainly from Owambo, began to be employed in the German colony, at first on a small scale, but in their hundreds when the big infrastructural works began. Although before 1907 the number of such workers remained comparatively small, in some years there may have been as many as 1,700 in the Police Zone at any one time.[52] During the same period, Africans in the south and centre of the country (both male and female) turned to waged labour on an unprecedented scale, particularly, as we have seen, after the devastation of the rinderpest epidemic. By the early 1900s, they were working on the railways and in the SWACO mines, for missionaries and German troops, and on settler farms. Nevertheless, the colonial government experienced persistent labour shortages, and in 1901 attempted to restrict the export of labourers from the colony; a brief exception was made in 1903, when the Witwatersrand Native Labour Association (WNLA) was allowed to recruit for the South African mines.[53]

The underlying economic principle of these developments was to channel the benefits of Namibia's resources in the direction of German nationals, other settlers and European business interests. In the 1890s, however, the capitalist exploitation of a *black* workforce by a white minority government was still subject to many constraints. Although race signified one boundary between exploiter and exploited, this division was not yet as clear-cut as it was later to become. The alliance of some African leaders with the colonial government meant that their economic and political interests were tied to those of the German authorities, and that wide divisions opened up between part, at least, of the elite and their peoples. On the other hand, the relative autonomy of African polities at this stage—which their alliances with the German authorities, paradoxically, helped temporarily to preserve—meant that local leaders managed to retain some control over the employment of their people by Europeans, gaining financial benefits and providing them with some protection against ill-treatment. In many cases, they continued to be able to do this even after the rinderpest epidemic.

In the rural areas of the Police Zone, too, conflict was not always the keynote, as the isolated situation of individual settlers meant that they needed to maintain good relations with local *ovahona* and *kapteins* in order to obtain the workers on whom their farms depended (although they often resented having to do so). In the early 1890s, working for Europeans was in some cases a high-status activity, and Herero, for example, would send young girls to be educated in European households. Older-established settlers in particular, like Gustav Voigts, maintained good relationships with Africans. In many cases

German settlers—who were predominantly male[54]—entered into sexual relationships with African women, from which children were often born. Although some of these were characterised by rape and violence, others were more consensual or even long-term. Senior African men were, probably, using women's productive capacity to create and maintain strategic alliances with the settler population, although the extent of women's agency in these arrangements is less clear, and their position was certainly quite tenuous. The wide prevalence of these relationships also worried some settler and government circles, as we shall see in Chapter 7.[55]

When such strategies failed, conflict resulted. Young women living in German households as servants might be mistreated, and settlers, ignorant of African social relations, mocked these girls for behaving like princesses; as Gesine Krüger comments, they 'overlooked the fact...that they were actually dealing with princesses'.[56] Sexual violation also became a common part of early colonial relations. Cases of rape are recorded, for example, in Windhoek, where a number of women had been brought as prisoners after the conquest of the polities to which they belonged.[57]

Despite the flexibilities that remained in African–European relations in the 1890s, German administrators and settlers were already attempting to construct a coercive system of labour relations and to extend colonial order more generally. To this end, they used administrative decree, the power of the courts and direct violence. As early as 1892, officials began to introduce controls over African workers' movements and behaviour when they made provision for written employment contracts in urban areas. In 1894 and 1896, regulations controlling workers were introduced in the Otjimbingwe and Gibeon districts respectively. In some areas, particularly the south, passes were also being issued to Africans giving them permission to travel. Territory-wide measures to control African labour and impose passes were under discussion by officials before 1904, but were not imposed until after the Namibian War began.[58]

Although, in theory, African leaders retained jurisdiction over their people, the protection treaties allowed for any cases involving whites to be taken to colonial courts. Africans were thus prosecuted for offences including allowing stock to stray and minor theft. In the year 1902/3, 473 Africans received sentences of corporal punishment, and 326 were sent to prison. In more serious cases, too, whites patently received more lenient sentences than Africans. Between 1894 and 1900, the murders of four African men and one African woman by whites were punished with sentences ranging from three months to three years, while in the same period fifteen Africans were executed for killing six Europeans. In addition, many offences did not come before the courts, partly because the territory was impossible to police comprehensively, but also because employers often did not want to lose their workers' time by having them taken into custody. Farmers were allowed to administer a punishment of up to twenty-five lashes themselves, without recourse to the courts.[59]

Tensions also emerged in the towns, points of intense contact between settlers and Africans. Many of these urban centres had been founded before 1884, often as mission stations and/or the headquarters of semi-nomadic groups, but the first two decades of German rule saw rapid growth. By 1903 Windhoek—then, as for the rest of the century, the predominant urban settlement in Namibia—had a white civilian population of around 500, and 2,000 African residents,[60] many of whom, as we have seen, had arrived in the capital under coercion. Karibib, too, grew rapidly from 1901 as a result of the building of the railway. In some towns, racially based spatial segregation was beginning to emerge, based on the ad hoc construction of separate areas for Africans, including detention camps, accommodation for those serving the army, and in some cases an older and often complex form of segregation that had grown up around the mission stations. All these developments would intensify in the last decade of German rule.[61]

By 1903, there were thus many sources of tension between Africans and Europeans in the Police Zone. Some African leaders benefited from their alliance (however uneasily this was adhered to) with Leutwein, while others felt the brunt of this power politics. Poorer members of some of the Otjiherero-speaking polities, in particular, became increasingly alienated from, and impoverished by, the leaders' more self-serving actions. On the other side, settlers (with some important exceptions) and concession companies were now broadly in favour of a war of dispossession, in the belief that the way to the untrammelled exploitation of Namibian resources would not be clear unless the power of African leaders were completely broken.

6

THE NAMIBIAN WAR, 1904–8

In 1904, the conflict and tension that now prevailed in southern and central Namibia exploded into wars of resistance against the colonising power. By the time of the last major military engagement, in 1908, Germany had committed genocide against the peoples of south and central Namibia. Most of those who survived battle and flight were imprisoned in concentration camps, where many of them died,[1] and the survivors were deprived of almost all their land and cattle. The events of 1904–8 were thus crucial in creating the structure of unequal, and racially determined, land ownership that Namibia obtained until independence (and has proved remarkably robust thereafter).

These events are of great historical significance, and their repercussions are still powerful. Debates around the Namibian War[2] emerged with new vigour at the time of its centenary in 2004, when arguments over compensation and memorialisation reflected the pain, anger and sense of injustice felt by the descendants of those affected, and at the same time revealed fault-lines in contemporary Namibian politics as well as the still-controversial nature of many aspects of this history. The implications for German history and politics, too, are substantial. It has been vigorously argued—and equally vigorously denied—that the Namibian genocide, the first of the twentieth century, planted the seeds of the genocide later committed by the Third Reich.

The Wars of Resistance and the Genocide

In October 1903 a dispute over a stolen sheep at Warmbad, in the far south of Namibia, triggered an uprising on the part of the Bondelswarts living there; deeper grievances included new white settlement on land that had previously been theirs.[3] In December, Leutwein rode south to quell the unrest, which had spread to other places including Maltahöhe, although it remained localised and mainly spontaneous. On 12 January, however, fighting of a completely different order broke out between Herero and German troops in Okahandja. Over the next ten days, Herero fighters attacked settlements across central Namibia, wrecking most of the existing 267 white farms in the area. They launched assaults on towns, villages, telegraph lines and the Windhoek–Swakopmund railway, besieged the German fortifications at Windhoek and Okahandja as well as Omaruru, Otjimbingwe, Gobabis and Outjo, and killed between 123 and 150 settlers.

These events took the authorities in Windhoek completely by surprise. With armed Herero in effective possession of the entire central region, and the governor and much of the armed forces twenty days' march away, the settler population was thrown into a state of panic. Lieutenant Franke and his company, however, returned quickly from their march southward, and Herero forces pulled back from Windhoek, Okahandja and Omaruru—although not without a pitched battle near Omaruru which left six or seven Germans, and perhaps a hundred Herero, dead. In this very early stage of the war, Nehale, the ruler of the southern part of Ondonga, responded to Herero overtures by sending troops to attack the five Germans holed up in the fort at Namutoni; the latter were forced to vacate the fort, but Ndonga losses were very heavy.[4] Nehale's aims were apparently to assert rights to the copper workings at Tsumeb, and to do away with the German post at Namutoni, which he feared might act as a bridgehead to the north. The Ndonga king, Kambonde, had taken a more cautious line, however, and after Namutoni the Ovambo polities largely withdrew from active conflict; nevertheless, they acted as a conduit for the supply of arms and ammunition to the forces opposing the Germans, and received Herero refugees after the defeat at Ohamakari (Waterberg). Support was not forthcoming from the south, however: in January 1904[5] Samuel Maherero had written to both Hermanus van Wyk, the leader of the Rehoboth Basters, and Hendrik Witbooi, but van Wyk, who remained loyal to the Germans throughout, turned over the letters to the German authorities. Hendrik Witbooi's troops initially fought on the German side.

Leutwein, meanwhile, was forced to conclude a compromise peace settlement with the Bondelswarts, under which they were disarmed.

They were also supposed to cede land, and the leaders of the uprising were to be extradited; these conditions could not be enforced because of the war situation, however, and about six hundred Bondelswarts crossed the border into South Africa to avoid capture. Arriving back in central Namibia in mid-February, Leutwein found that the towns were now relatively safe for the Germans, but that, as Jon Bridgman puts it, 'the Hereros in a month had destroyed the whole structure of German order so painfully built up in the preceding decade'.[6]

Why, and how, had almost all the Herero polities gone to war? The uprising was led by Samuel Maharero, and it is likely that it had been planned, or at least that military action had been discussed, at gatherings of Otjiherero-speakers during the previous year. It is possible, however, that it was triggered by events in Okahandja in January 1904, where the aggressive actions of the district administrator (*Distriktschef*) Zürn led to considerable tension, and that it spread rapidly to other parts of central Namibia rather than being fully co-ordinated in advance. Indeed, some Herero leaders, particularly those at Omaruru and Otjimbingwe, were initially reluctant to join the uprising (although they were committed by the end of the month).[7] Whatever the case, Herero forces under Samuel Maharero's command behaved with considerable discipline and co-ordination, achieving rapid military success and, in almost all cases, following his direction that Africans of other ethnic groups and white women and children, missionaries and non-German men were to be spared.

War was joined as the Herero communities reached breaking point under the increasing demands of the German regime and the settlers, and the steadily (if unevenly) declining authority of the Herero polities, within which tensions had been emerging for some decades. Indeed, oral sources cite the migration of young men to an uncertain future on the South African mines, and the loss of 'traditional' culture through the influence of church and school, as causes of the war.[8] In the earliest years of the twentieth century land loss continued, with sales of rich grazing grounds to settlers in the Okahandja district and to the east. In 1901, for example, headmen representing the people living at the Wit Nossob River (east of Windhoek) petitioned Leutwein to ban future land sales, listing properties that were being taken from them, and blaming Samuel Maharero. *Ehi rOvaherero*, the land of the Herero defined in Maharero's day, was under serious and immediate threat, together with the pastoral economy it supported.[9]

Many of these land sales were made in order to pay the debts of Samuel Maharero and the other *ovahona*, for indebtedness had now also reached a critical stage. Under German rule, the number of traders operating in Namibia had rapidly increased, and additional markets for consumer goods such as clothing, alcohol, coffee and sugar had developed. The traders, often operating on small margins but seeking large profits, generally gave out goods on credit, later demanding payment in cattle. In July 1903, the German authorities, fearing instability because of the high level of African indebtedness, decreed that all such debts would lapse if not repaid within a year. As a result traders set about immediately collecting what they claimed was owed to them, sometimes by violence. This, together with the unequal operation of the judicial system, caused deep resentment. In the early years of the century, there were several high-profile cases in which German settlers received light penalties for the murder or other mistreatment of Africans; in other instances, whites who had committed rape were not brought to court at all. Even Assa Riarua was severely flogged by a baker called Schäfer, who merely received a fine of 20 Marks. The authority of the *ovahona* and their ability both to control and to protect their subjects—particularly women—was thus increasingly weakened.[10]

In addition, in 1903 SWACO began to implement plans to build a railway line between Otavi and the coast at Swakopmund. In July, under pressure from Leutwein, Samuel Maharero agreed to cede the land required for the track (although he did not concede a 20 km-wide strip on either side that the Germans also hoped to obtain). Partly in response to these developments, both the missions and the Governor now proposed the creation of reserves. The missionaries hoped to protect their congregations (in both the south and centre of Namibia) from land loss, at the same time as consolidating their own interests and influence among these communities. Leutwein, on the other hand, while appreciating the benefits of providing indigenous pastoralists with sufficient means of production to defuse political tensions, also hoped to free further land for German exploitation. In central Namibia these proposals were generally unpopular: not only did they offer insufficient and poorly watered land, but they also meant the loss of Okahandja, Omaruru, the Waterberg and Omburu—some of the Herero polities' richest grazing grounds. In the event, the work of the Land Commission, set up to create reserves, was interrupted by the outbreak of the Namibian War (by which time very few reserves had come into existence).[11]

It was, thus, the expansion of colonial domination—enacted through land loss, disarmament, profit-taking and physical assault—that was at the root of the Namibian War.[12] To these causes should be added the fact that the Herero polities still possessed the organisation, skills and weaponry to make war. Indeed, oral testimony cites a new threat of disarmament, or the 'vaccination' (registration) of weapons, as one of the main reasons for taking up arms.[13]

This broad-brush picture obscures some of the complexity and heterogeneity of central Namibia at this period, whose shifting fractures, divisions and alliances helped to shape the outbreak and course of the war. Within the Herero polities, there was a good deal of popular support for the uprising. It is likely that younger men were particularly

Fig. 15. Surveying for the Otavi–Swakopmund railway line. Work on the line began in 1903 and proved a major cause of the tension that led to the Namibian War. This photograph is also a reminder of the importance of the work of Africans, in both skilled and unskilled roles, in the construction of the colony's infrastructure. (Reproduced courtesy of the National Archives of Namibia [no. 5345] and the Scientific Society Swakopmund [no. 2890, album S, p. 27]).

enthusiastic: they had little to gain from land sales, and were the most likely to be in waged labour and therefore at greatest risk of being mistreated by their employers. There is also some evidence of support from Herero women. They were certainly with the men in the *veld*, and are recorded to have encouraged the fighters from behind the lines with chants proclaiming 'Hereroland belongs to us'. Communities directly affected by land sales were, we know, extremely discontented, and among the older men Assa Riarua led opposition to these changes, calling for the proposed reserve to be extended, in opposition to Samuel Maharero, who had argued for it to be reduced in order to have more land to sell. On the other hand, the missionary Kuhlmann's view, after visiting the Herero encampment in February, was that some of the poorer people feared that the *ovahona* might take their cattle if the Herero won the war. However, those with the least to gain from taking up arms were undoubtedly Samuel Maharero and others of the elite who had begun to participate in land sales and who were most deeply enmeshed in the German colonial project. The decision of the Herero paramount to lead the resistance can, therefore, best be explained as the result of strong pressure from his own people, as he found himself caught up in 'a maelstrom from which he could not escape'.[14] Nevertheless, he was certainly aware of the negative effects of encroaching German domination, and in his letters about the war he spoke of German injustices and atrocities towards Herero.[15]

There were also differences among the Otjiherero-speaking leaders, not all of whom were initially eager to take up arms. As we have seen, some joined Samuel Maharero after an initial period of vacillation. Most important, there was considerable tension between the Okahandja leaders and the eastern Otjiherero-speakers, whose leaders, Kahimemua and Nikodemus Kavikunua, had been executed with Samuel Maharero's connivance only eight years previously, and who had suffered considerable losses of cattle and land in the intervening period. Mbanderu of Kahimemua's clan migrated to Botswana rather than participating in the war, arriving there well before the defeat at Ohamakari.[16] There were also some Otjiherero-speakers who found themselves outside the main political formations. Some fought with or worked for the German forces, particularly boys whom the Germans called *Bambusen*,[17] and some (especially women) had family networks extending into both the German and Herero communities and may therefore have found themselves in an ambiguous position.

The diversity of the settlement patterns in central Namibia also meant that, even here, the war was never a purely Herero–German affair. For one thing, some Damara had been absorbed into the social structures of the Herero polities. More important, the non-Otjiherero-speaking communities scattered around central Namibia could not escape the effects of the war. In particular, Damara groups at the Waterberg, Gobabis, the Omaruru valley, Okahandja, Windhoek and the Khomas Hochland were literally in the firing line. The authority of the Damara leader Cornelius Goroseb ran no further than Okombahe, and it was 'the local complexities of [Damaras'] relationship with both the Germans and the Herero' that dictated their attitude to the war. For example, in Gobabis Damara fought on the Herero side; a man known as Gariseb is remembered to have led resistance in the mountains; and in other places Damara fought or worked for the Germans, remained neutral or fled before advancing troops. Although the effects of the Namibian War on San communities are harder to trace, partly because the violence they faced after the war was more severe, they are likely to have had similarly varied encounters, and there is some oral evidence that they faced a 'second wave' of violence from Herero and Nama in flight from the Germans.[18]

The Course of the War

By 22 February the main body of Herero, under Samuel Maharero, Tjetjo and other commanders, was based at Otjosasu, about thirty miles east of Okahandja; within a few weeks they moved east and south to the Onjati hills.[19] During March and April 1904 the Herero forces pursued a largely successful military campaign, making skilful use of their mobility and knowledge of the ground by repeatedly ambushing the Germans and drawing them into fighting in areas of dense bush, where heavy guns were of the least use.

Leutwein, for his part, was handicapped by poor communications, a lack of experienced troops and the difficulties of fighting in arid and hot conditions. His troops, divided into three sections, had some success in the west, but in the east, under the impatient Major Glasenapp, they sustained heavy losses when Tjetjo's forces twice caught them in major ambushes.[20] Meanwhile, the forces under Leutwein's direct control, based in Okahandja, attempted to take on Samuel Maharero. The Governor at first concentrated on holding the garrisons of central

Namibia, and protecting the railway, but as reinforcements arrived from Germany, and under pressure from Berlin to achieve a victory in open battle, he marched out of Okahandja on 7 April. Samuel Maharero attacked the German forces near Mount Ongandjira, to the northeast of Okahandja, but was eventually driven back—despite the courage of the Herero troops who charged twice onto the German guns—with, according to German sources, over a hundred losses; fourteen Germans were killed. Two days later, however, Leutwein's men were ambushed by the Herero troops at a waterhole at Oviumbo, and, after several hours of fighting, forced to retreat to Okahandja, with twenty-five dead.[21]

By early May, the German forces were in a very demoralised condition, exacerbated in the east by a typhoid outbreak. The Herero forces had destroyed almost all the settler farms in central Namibia and gained possession of their occupants' herds; they effectively controlled the entire area apart from the garrisons and towns. At this point Samuel Maharero moved his base northwards, to the plateau at Ohamakari, where there was better grazing: perhaps 6,000 fighters and 40,000 women and children as well as numerous cattle, wagons and horses gathered there.[22]

In the wake of Leutwein's failure to deliver a crushing blow against the Herero forces, he was replaced in June as military commander by General Lothar von Trotha, an experienced soldier who had led German campaigns in East Africa and China, and whose understanding of the proper relations between coloniser and subject was considerably more brutal than Leutwein's. The latter remained Governor, albeit with effectively circumscribed powers, until he left the colony in November 1904. The German government also poured men and supplies rapidly into South West Africa, and it was these resources—even though the soldiers suffered from disease, exhaustion and failures of supply—that were ultimately to prove decisive. Almost 5,000 German troops had arrived by 17 June, and the total eventually rose to almost 20,000.[23]

Von Trotha spent the months before August building up supply lines and encircling the Waterberg. As the German troops gradually moved into position, Samuel Maharero failed to take the chance to withdraw, despite shortages of food and water in the Herero camp. It is probable that he stayed where he was in expectation of a peace offer—which knowledge of Leutwein's normal *modus operandi* would have led him to expect. Indeed, one oral record retained in the Maharero family holds that Samuel Maharero thought the war was over at this point.[24] The restraint of the Herero forces during the war strongly suggests that their aim was not so much to put an end to German rule (as assumed by an earlier generations of historians)[25] as to combat 'the settlers, the practices of the traders and...the way in which the chiefs were being increasingly despised and their authority undermined'.[26] Possibly, too—although this remains speculation—there was disagreement over strategy among the Herero leaders.

Von Trotha's aim, by contrast, seems to have been—at the very least—to achieve complete military victory as expounded in contemporary German theories of total warfare. The German objective at Ohamakari was thus, in the general's words, 'to attack the enemy simultaneously with all forces in order to annihilate [*vernichten*] him'.[27] On 11 August 1904 the Germans attacked the Herero positions at the Waterberg, with six sections consisting of some 4,000 men, 36 artillery pieces and 14 machine guns.[28] The Battle of Ohamakari was over in a day. Colonel von Deimling, advancing from the west, took the Waterberg plateau, while the forces approaching from the north and east met little opposition. In the south and south-east, however, the Herero troops put up stiff resistance and towards the end of the day almost overwhelmed the Germans under Lieutenant Colonel von Mueller. By nightfall, however, it was clear that the battle was lost to the Herero, particularly because the women, men and children at the rear were unprotected from German fire. Those who were able fled to the south-east, where General von der Heyde's incompetence had created a weak point in the German defences.[29]

Thus began the desperate flight of the Herero peoples, pursued by German troops, into the *omaheke*, the desert area to the east of the Waterberg that stretched into the British territory of Bechuanaland. They took a route fully navigable to them under normal circumstances; there had been traffic and migration between eastern Namibia and western Botswana for many years.[30] But under conditions of defeat and mass migration, the route across the *omaheke* became a death-trap. As a German officer described the scene, 'The Hereros' cattle... lay in the bush with the mass of their people, dead of thirst, strewn along the path of their death march...When we unsaddled in the bush, our feet bumped up against corpses'.[31]

This trauma is vividly recalled in Herero oral traditions. According to its *omutandu* (praise song), Ohamakari 'is the site where people died at the place of war/The land where the people split'.[32] A mourning song for Omaruru runs:

I am a young woman, belonging to those of Tjiyaku,
(the one) with the necklace that fell off from his Adam's apple, without some-one who will gather (the beads)

In these typically metaphorical lines, the necklace symbolises the scattering of the community in 1904.[33] Today, real rather than symbolic jewellery can still be found where fleeing women abandoned it because its weight slowed them down.[34] During Samuel Maharero's flight to Botswana:

> He had horses of hunger
> He was riding with horses of hunger
> He was riding, he was riding
> And still he had horses of hunger
> He went to foreign homes
> TRULY!

'Horses of hunger' are normally those that are ridden out early in the day without having been fed; here, the term encapsulates the desperation of the refugees.[35]

Memories within the Herero communities do, however, encompass resistance as well as defeat. In the late 1940s it was recalled that 'the troops protected their Chief [Samuel Maharero] armed only with knob-kerries until they brought him into a land where he could be sheltered', because 'as long as their Chief had not been captured or killed, it could not be said that the land had been captured'.[36] There is also remembrance of military engagements and some Herero victories after Oham-akari. The German official record, however, notes only one further battle in which Herero attacked the Germans, at Omatupa on 15 August; thereafter, a further twenty-five engagements up to 22 December essentially consisted of German attacks on fleeing Herero.[37] It soon became clear to the Germans, however, that the pursuit of a final, decisive victory—their military objective—would mean chasing the Herero across the *omaheke*. This was impractical for their soldiers, themselves weakened by the desert conditions. Instead, von Trotha adopted the simple but brutal strategy of occupying the waterholes at the edge of the desert, thus sentencing a people in flight to death from dehydration and starvation. Although some prisoners were taken, many Herero men, women and children were simply shot dead or subjected to worse atrocities by German soldiers.[38] Von Trotha refused peace terms—the obvious next step under 'normal' conditions of colonial warfare. Nearly two months after the battle, on 2 October, he issued a proclamation:

I, the Great General of the German soldiers, address this letter to the Herero people...The Herero people will have to leave the country. Otherwise I shall force them to do so by means of guns. Within the German boundaries, every Herero, whether found armed or unarmed, with or without cattle, will be shot. I shall not accept any more women and children. I shall drive them back to their people—otherwise I shall order shots to be fired at them.[39]

There followed a proviso that soldiers should shoot warning shots at women and children, thus driving them away rather than killing them. In the conditions of the *omaheke*, however, this was tantamount to a death sentence.[40]

Not all the fugitives died during these terrible events: some reached Botswana, some survived in the *veld*, and some escaped to other parts of Namibia or British territory in Walvis Bay. But, ultimately, the majority of the Herero perished, in the *omaheke* or in the concentration camps in which they were later imprisoned, as Germany committed the first genocide of the twentieth century.

The War in the South[41]

As 1904 wore on, the slaughter in central Namibia combined with other circumstances to make war in the south inevitable. The German-language press—which many Nama-speakers were able to read—was full of threats that the Nama would suffer a similar fate to that of the Herero. The German authorities, with Leutwein's eventual agreement, were moving in a similar direction, turning their attention to the 'settlement of the native question' and disarmament in the south. Tension was heightened in September when a group of Witbooi fighters brought shocking eye-witness reports of the new German methods of conquest.

New fears were thus heaped on to the accumulated grievances—the land loss and defeat—of the last two decades.[42] Two further events also combined to precipitate the southern polities into a state of war. First, Jakob Morenga, who had been a leader of the Bondelswarts uprising of the previous year, returned in August to the Karas Mountains, attracting followers and beginning a campaign of guerrilla attacks on German forces and farms. Of both Herero and Nama parentage, he was well educated and a talented military strategist (which helps to explain his position of leadership among the Bondelswarts despite the fact that he did not come from the small elites governing the polities of southern Namibia). His allies Abraham and Edward Morris were sons of the British trader James Morris and a daughter of one of the leading Bondelswarts families.

At the same time, the Witboois were being increasingly radicalised by the arrival of Shepherd Stuurman, a self-styled prophet from South Africa. Also known as Hendrik Bekeer, this maverick individual claimed to have received a call from God to lead a movement to drive the whites out of Africa. Stuurman became influential with Hendrik Witbooi and many of his followers. Nevertheless, the profoundly religious *kaptein*, despite his great age, remained in control of his people, and it seems certain that the decision to break with the Germans was ultimately his. Prophecy may have given the Witboois the immediate impetus to act, but underlying this was a deep reservoir of despair created over the previous ten years. Their alliance with the Germans had left them significantly impoverished. With cattle raiding, formerly an important means of production, now prevented, Hendrik Witbooi[43] and the elite of his polity had turned increasingly to land sales for the payment of their debts (which in turn were partly caused by unequal trading relations). According to one estimate, by 1899 most Witbooi families owned no more stock than one goat, and in Gibeon signs of social breakdown were in evidence. As Hendrik Witbooi wrote in response to German peace proposals in July 1905, '...I was right there with you many times during your peace, and have come to see in it nothing but the destruction of all our people'.[44]

The trigger for war came when, at the beginning of October 1904, the local district administrator was shot by a Witbooi (probably not on Hendrik's orders); a missionary was also killed. The Witboois now rose against the Germans, and were soon joined by the Fransmann people under Simon Kopper, the Red Nation under Manasse Noroseb and the Veldschoendragers under Hans Hendrik. The Bondelswarts, like the Witboois a sizeable population, were divided: about a third were interned with their leader Johannes Christian at Warmbad; a third were absent from the territory, working in the South African mines; and the remainder joined the war to fight under Morenga.

Other Nama-speaking groups—Tseib's people at Keetmanshoop and the Topnaars and Swartboois in the north-west (who were disarmed and interned)—took little part in the war. In Bethany, Paul Fredericks was interned (with a minority of his people) under appalling conditions; his rival for the *kaptein*ship, Cornelius Fredericks, joined Hendrik Witbooi early in 1905. Johann Christian Goliath at Berseba, however, remained allied with the colonial regime, his men providing labour to the German forces. The Basters at Rehoboth, under Hermanus van Wyk, fought with the Germans, although not without some doubts.

At the beginning of this new period of warfare, perhaps 2,350 Nama fighters faced a German force in the south of only about 1,000.[45] For the colonial government, the new rising was both a shock and a disaster, as well as a clear indication that von Trotha's attempts to pacify the territory were not meeting with universal success. In Germany, too, it provoked political conflict, strengthening the voices of those (particularly on the left) disturbed by events in SWA. Tension escalated in December 1906, as the *Reichstag* (Parliament) voted against increasing funds for the rapidly expanding military operations in SWA. The *Reichstag* was dissolved as a result, and the election that followed was won by the pro-imperialists, thus cementing Germany's will to end the resistance in South West Africa.[46]

The initial period of fighting saw both failures and successes for the Nama forces. The Witboois and the Veldschoendragers suffered heavy defeats in December 1904, at Naris and Koes respectively. Hendrik Witbooi (together with Simon Kopper) was able to regroup in the Auob Valley and to offer stiff resistance, despite being eventually forced to flee, at the Battle of Gross-Nabas in January 1905. After a further series of engagements, the Witboois retreated to the relative safety of the Kalahari, and the German commander decided—against his more cautious orders—to launch an attack on Morenga in the Karas Mountains. Morenga's men met and defeated one of the German divisions at the Aob waterhole (with the loss of Edward Morris among others); the Germans eventually forced them into flight at Narudas in March.

By this point, with the Witboois and Morenga pushed back, the German position looked relatively hopeful. In fact, however, this was only the beginning of a protracted armed conflict in which Nama fighters used the tactics of guerrilla warfare and the harshness of the country to great effect. Time and again, gains won by the Germans in hard-fought battles—at Gross-Nabas, for instance, extreme thirst caused insanity among the troops and twenty-two Germans died[47]—were negated by the ability of the African forces to escape, the German troops being too exhausted to pursue them over long distances. The Europeans also frequently found it difficult to obtain supplies, especially water. As was usual for military campaigns at this date, disease was also rife: by November 1905, the hospital in Keetmanshoop was overflowing with troops suffering from scurvy, dysentery, typhoid, heart conditions, rheumatism and battle wounds.

The Nama groups ranged against the German forces, although far more able to make the local conditions work to their advantage, also experienced intense suffering. They had problems with supplies, which they patched together from captured enemy property, weaponry smuggled from the Cape and Bechuanaland, holdings of stock and the foodstuffs available in marginal areas. African military success was predicated on mobility: on the ability of guerrilla fighters to elude the German forces by fleeing to desert and mountainous areas and by crossing and re-crossing international borders (which they, implicitly and explicitly, refused to recognise). This placed great demands not only on the fighting men but also on the women, children and other non-combatants who set out together to escape and resist the Germans. In some instances the fighters left non-combatants behind within SWA; some groups also crossed the border in late 1905 and early 1906 into the Cape, where many of the women and children were placed in refugee camps by the British, while the men escaped to continue fighting in Namibia.[48] On many occasions, however, women and children remained with the men: German records of surrender list the presence of women and children as well as men on almost every occasion.[49] In these circumstances non-combatants shared the general privations, hardship and danger. An informant from Gibeon, speaking in 2007, recalled that his grandfather '...grew up during the war and was always on the run with his parents. He also told me how the people were wiped out by the German soldiers...Some babies were shot dead whilst they were on the backs of their mothers. Many soldiers were also shot dead'.[50]

Women and children were present on long forced marches undertaken by Cornelius Fredericks and his followers to escape the German troops. They were also among the Witbooi group journeying across southern Namibia in 1905. In October, forced out of the Kalahari by conditions of intense drought, they were confronted with German occupation of the wells stretching along the eastern side of Namaland from Gochas via Koes to Hasuur; women were denied water, and the people were reduced to drinking their animals' blood. According to one German officer:

...the Hottentots, who already seemed to be extremely shattered and exhausted...wandered about...aimlessly between Koes, Geibis and Geiachab. They suffered severely from lack of water...Here the fate of the Witbooi people was to be fulfilled. The first sign of the incipient *Auflösung*[51] was the crowds of women and children, half dead through hunger and thirst, who arrived at the German garrisons and pleaded for water.[52]

Towards the end of April 1905, von Trotha assumed personal command of the German forces in the south, and on 28 April he issued a proclamation that shared many of the features of the earlier decree against the Herero, without going quite as far. The general offered food and work (that is, presumably, forced labour with subsistence rations) to those who gave themselves up, but also threatened the Nama with the fate of the Herero, and stated: 'He who believes that mercy will not be extended to him[53] should leave the land for as long as he lives on German soil he will be shot—this policy will go on until all such Hottentots have been destroyed [*vernichtet*]'.[54] This proclamation did nothing to end the war.[55] From June 1905, von Trotha faced not only Hans Hendrik and Simon Kopper in the east and Cornelius Fredericks in the south, but also the Witboois, who had slipped undetected through the German lines, together with a Herero leader known as Andreas, in the west. Von Trotha now directed his forces against the Witboois, whose 750 fighters, armed with a mixture of old and modern rifles, faced about double that number of German troops with twenty artillery pieces and two machine guns.

The Witboois managed to thwart von Trotha's first attempt to surround and defeat them by escaping from the Gibeon area. After periodic heavy fighting, however, Hendrik Witbooi was fatally wounded on 29 October at the battle of Vaalgras, and died soon afterwards. His death, together with the physical hardships of the war, undermined the Witbooi resistance. In November, Samuel Isaak, Hans Hendrik and their followers were the first of the Witboois and their allies to surrender; Isaak Witbooi, who had opposed this move, eventually sued for peace in February 1906. In all, 278 men and 306 women and children surrendered.[56] The peace terms were relatively lenient, but were later rescinded by the next governor, Friedrich von Lindequist. As for Stuurman, he had slipped away from SWA in mid-1905, after conflict with the Witboois as his poor leadership and military ineptitude became evident.[57]

Despite the fate of the Witboois, the other southern leaders, including Morenga and Cornelius Fredericks (the core of whose followers consisted of the Bondelswarts and Fransmann people),[58] fought on, with considerable military success. On 24 October 1905, the Germans suffered one of their worst defeats of the war. Trapped and exposed to Morenga's guns at Hartebeestmund on the Orange River, they were unable to escape until nightfall, when 17 lay dead; Morenga probably had no losses. Meanwhile, Cornelius Fredericks planned and executed a number of successful attacks; he was later described in the German official history of the war as a leader of 'virtually unparalleled celerity and skill'.[59] Nevertheless, the forced marches that he and his people endured to escape German pursuit took a heavy toll, and they were able to resist no longer after their defeat at Gochas in January 1906. By early March, Cornelius Fredericks, 235 men and 176 women and children had surrendered and been imprisoned; others fled to the northern Cape, where they stayed until after the South African conquest of Namibia. The Fransmanns and the Red Nation, meanwhile, had gathered together in the area between the Middle Nossob and the Bechuanaland border, where they seem to have focused more on surviving in these marginal, semi-desert conditions than on further fighting. War-weariness was clearly a feature of this long and harsh conflict, as has been noted in oral records (in this case for the Witbooi): 'If the war stopped for some time, they tried to live a normal life by making fires and celebrating weddings and other traditional events as if there was no war'.[60] However, German harassment, coupled with the death of Manasse Noroseb in battle in December 1905, led to the surrender of 250 of the Red Nation, mainly women and children, while the rest fled across the border.

The Germans' other opponents split into small groups, the better to use the tactics of guerrilla warfare, and, as Bridgman puts it, for 'months the bands of Morenga, Johannes Christian and Morris...quite literally [ran] circles around the whole German army'.[61] In May 1906, however, the Germans followed Morenga's forces south across the border and defeated them in British territory. Morenga gave himself up to the Cape police, who refused to hand him over to the German authorities. This failure to co-operate reflected a situation in which

German–British relations blew hot and cold. The British, for example, often cut off German supplies from South Africa by closing border posts. British hostility to the German authorities was exacerbated by the fact that, in November 1906, a group of disaffected Boers who had migrated to Namibia launched a short-lived and disorganised insurgent raid into South Africa. On other occasions, however, the British authorities, who also had to consider the possibility that unrest might spread to South Africa, actively supported the Germans, sometimes even in military action.[62]

In June 1906 Colonel von Deimling replaced Dame as military commander in the south, and set up a new system under which German patrols shared the responsibility for pursuing the African bands so that the troops no longer had to give up the chase through exhaustion. He also moved as many cattle as possible northwards, thus depriving his opponents of one of their main sources of supply. Towards the end of the year, these measures helped to bring the Bondelswarts into peace negotiations. On the German side, pressure for peace came especially from the military, who had failed to defeat Johannes Christian's fighters despite engaging them in numerous battles—twenty-seven between 26 July and 1 November 1906. So great was von Deimling's anxiety to end the conflict that he actually defied the orders of the Colonial Department and Governor von Lindequist in order to settle for more lenient terms than they would have allowed.

The Peace of Ukamas/Heirachabis was thus agreed in December, in the face of considerable mutual distrust but with the authority of Johannes Christian and, eventually, of Abraham Morris. The treaty was a sign of the effectiveness of the Bondelswarts' guerrilla campaign and their success, if not in achieving outright victory, at least in establishing a military stalemate. This fact is an important counterpoint to the overall narrative of African defeat in the Namibian War. Under the treaty, the Bondelswarts were resettled on part of their old lands, with the use of three waterholes; they were loaned goats and cattle; and the *kaptein* received 300 sheep and a team of oxen. By April 1907, 769 of the group had arrived back from the Cape. They were, however, disarmed, forced to enter waged labour, and barred from leaving the newly defined location without passes.

With the Treaty of Heirachabis signed, the German authorities declared peace on 31 March 1907. One result of this was, however, that Morenga was released by the British authorities, and returned to

SWA with 400 followers to continue the fight. In September, he was finally killed in battle on the British side of the border. Even the death of this most resourceful, courageous and persistent leader did not quite bring the war to an end. In Bechuanaland, survivors of Simon Kopper's and Manasse Noroseb's forces had formed two settlements. The inhabitants of one, in Lehututu, eventually became British subjects. The other group, under Simon Kopper, acted as a magnet for members of the scattered and disaffected peoples of southern Namibia, growing from about seventy combatants in April 1906 to between 400 and 500 (together with 2,000 non-combatants) by September 1907. A German force, armed with machine guns, attacked the settlement in March 1908. Despite heavy losses on both sides, however, the action was inconclusive and Simon Kopper remained undefeated. Under British pressure to resolve the situation, the Germans finally agreed in 1909 to make him regular payments in return for keeping the peace—which he did until his death in 1913.

There were still isolated bands under arms—generally more interested in survival outside the confines of the state than in directly challenging the Germans. The year 1909 saw the execution of the leaders of a group under Abraham Rolf, who had been carrying out raids in southern Namibia. Nevertheless, it was the settlement with Simon Kopper that effectively brought the Namibian War to an end. As Drechsler summed it up, 'a major European power, with about 15,000 soldiers in the field, was locked for years in a struggle with what were initially only 1,000 to 2,000 and later no more than some hundred Nama whose methods proved unanswerable'.[63] The costs of both war and defeat were, however, extremely high.

The Concentration Camps

If the period of open conflict was one of great suffering, its immediate aftermath was a time of desperate tragedy. The German authorities set up concentration camps in which the defeated African groups—men, women and children—were imprisoned. Terrible conditions in the camps and forced labour for their inmates led to extreme misery and very high mortality.[64]

On 12 December 1904, at Berlin's command, von Trotha rescinded his order for the extermination of the Herero. German policy now shifted to the imprisonment of the defeated population—although there were still, in central Namibia and in the south, arbitrary shootings and numerous public hangings of those accused of fighting the Germans. Military patrols had little success in bringing the survivors from the *veld*, and when von Lindequist became Governor in November 1905, he allowed the Rhenish missionaries to establish collection camps.[65] For the Herero survivors, leaving the harsh conditions of the bush was a difficult choice: 'Some people were collected in the camps and others were living on the open *veldt*, afraid of being killed by the Germans. In those days, people were killed, [as for example] if you were found in the bush or at the poisoned water holes. Many people were afraid of going to the camps of the colonisers'.[66]

photo: Weyrauther

Hereros stellen sich in Omaruru zur Gefangenschaft (Februar 1905)

Fig. 16. This photograph shows Herero prisoners presenting themselves for detention in Omaruru in 1905. After the defeat and slaughter of 1904, missionaries set up collection camps where the survivors, often destitute, could hand themselves in. This image comes from the little-known collection of Georg Weyrauther, a marine transferred to South West Africa soon after the beginning of the Namibian War.[67] (Photographer: Georg Weyrauther. Reproduced courtesy of Historischer Verein für Oberfranken [Historical Association of Upper Franconia] and Bayreuth University Library.)

Although many stayed in the *veld*, and a minority continued to fight, 11,000 people eventually arrived at the missionary camps. The missionary Diehl recorded the despair with which many came in, expecting to be killed, but 'ready to die, if only to finally have peace'.[68] From the missionary camps, the prisoners were transported to centres where labour was needed, principally Windhoek, Okahandja, Karibib, Swakopmund and Luderitz. A number of camps were established around these centres, some run by the government, some by private employers or other bodies such as the police. The largest camps were in Windhoek, where there was an average of 5,000 prisoners (about double the town's civilian population).

The defeated Nama, with the exception of the Bondelswarts, were also imprisoned in the camps. In contravention of the agreements made with the Germans, the groups surrendering under Samuel Isaak and Hans Hendrik were sent to the Windhoek camp in February 1906, and then to Shark Island, off Luderitz. The Bethany people, under Cornelius Fredericks, were sent to Karibib to labour on the Tsumeb railway, and then to Shark Island. By the end of 1906, there were over 2,000 Nama-speaking prisoners on the island. Isaak Witbooi and his people were eventually imprisoned at Okandjande, near Otavi. Meanwhile, 119 Witboois who had been serving with the German forces in October 1904 were deported to Togo and then Cameroon; almost two-thirds had died by June 1906.[69]

Conditions in the camps were desperate. The nutrition, housing, clothing and sanitation provided were woefully inadequate and, on the coast in particular, the prisoners experienced the further torment of cold and windy weather, against which they had virtually no protection. In these circumstances many fell ill from tuberculosis, dysentery, scurvy, typhoid and typhus. In addition, the level of sexual violence was high, as white settlers and soldiers habitually took advantage of female prisoners.[70] The missionaries reported on the camps in unsparing terms: 'Like cattle, hundreds were driven to their death, and like cattle they were buried', wrote Heinrich Vedder of the situation in Swakopmund.[71] In some cases, missionaries and sometimes local officials managed to have conditions slightly improved through protest to the authorities and through private charity, but death rates in the camps remained extremely high throughout the period of detention.[72]

The camps were not intended merely for the detention of defeated enemies: they were also a means of extracting labour, in the harshest manner possible. The prisoners, half-starved and in poor health, were violently forced to carry out the heaviest kinds of manual labour. They worked, in large numbers and without pay, on building the railways between Luderitz and Keetmanshoop, and between Windhoek and Otavi, and they carried out harbour works at Luderitz and Swakopmund—infrastructure that was to underpin the economy of South West Africa in future years. In April 1906, for example, the prisoners working on the Otavi line numbered 900 men, 700 women and 620 children. The detainees also worked as domestics, as servants of the troops, and on farms. They worked both directly for the regime and for private employers, who, in 'a human trade tantamount to slavery',[73] paid the authorities 10 Marks per month for each man or woman; these employers included private companies such as OMEG, Arthur Koppel and Lenz, which were contracted for big projects such as the railways.[74]

Conditions for the labourers were terrible. Migrant workers from the Cape were shocked by the treatment they saw meted out to the prisoners in Swakopmund:

These unfortunate women are daily compelled to carry heavy iron for construction work, also big stacks of compressed fodder. I have often noticed cases

Fig. 17. Herero women unloading a crate, Swakopmund, 1905. Forced labour was the fate of most prisoners held in the camps after the defeats of the Namibian War. (Reproduced courtesy of the National Archives of Namibia [no. 5041].)

where women have fallen under the load and have been made to go on by being thrashed and kicked by soldiers and conductors.[75]

There were some attempts to resist these harsh conditions, for example by escape and even suicide. Flight from the Swakopmund camp to Walvis Bay (where the men enrolled for work in South Africa) was quite common, on one occasion involving a group of 120 prisoners aided by Michael Tjiseseta of Omaruru.[76] The detainees also made pleas to sympathetic listeners, particularly missionaries, and struggled to find family members.[77] Kaera (Ida Leinhos), a woman of mixed descent and some social standing, managed to shield members of her own family from imprisonment.[78] Ngatitwe (Rupertine), the mother of Zacharias Zeraua, is remembered as having intervened successfully to prevent hangings at the concentration camp in Omaruru:

At one point she challenged the Germans who were hanging people, saying 'these people were only following the orders of my son... If you want to kill them you should kill me instead'...After Rupertine's intervention, we never heard of people being hanged again.[79]

Nevertheless, for the vast majority this was an experience of unparalleled degradation and suffering, and very many died.

The mortality figures are contradictory and difficult to assess, but even the official statistics, which do not account for all the prisoners, show that nearly half died: that is, between October 1904 and March 1907, there were 7,682 deaths out of approximately 15,000 Herero and 2,000 Nama.[80] Things were particularly bad in the Luderitz district, where the notorious Shark Island was situated, and where the most extreme effects of the concentration camp policy were felt. Herero prisoners began to arrive at the beginning of 1905. Eyewitness reports published in the *Cape Argus* on 25 September 1905 testified to the conditions they faced: 'The women who are captured and not executed are set to work for the military as prisoners...saw [*sic*] numbers of them at Angra Pequena [Luderitz] put to the hardest work, and so starved that they were nothing but skin and bones..'.[81]

Nama prisoners, who were sent to the island from September 1906, were to have built a deep-sea harbour, but by January only twenty of them were thought to be capable of work, and the project had to be abandoned. Photographs taken on Shark Island by a German officer, Lieutenant von Düring, in 1905, both illustrate the desperate conditions endured by the prisoners and construct a visual choreography of domination by the military, of which the sexual degradation of female prisoners was an integral part.[82]

The death rates in the Luderitz district starkly illustrate the results of this treatment. Between 1905 and 1908, between 3,000 and 4,000 prisoners-of-war probably died; mortality on Shark Island itself was in the region of 70 per cent.[83] Cornelius Fredericks was among those who met his end here. On the railway, on which many of the Herero prisoners worked, 1,359—67.48 per cent—of the labourers were estimated to have died between January 1906 and June 1907.[84]

Shark Island was closed in April 1907, after Major von Estorff, who had negotiated the original peace agreement with the Witboois, became head of the German army in Namibia. The Nama survivors were, however, held in captivity until the end of German rule in 1915; Samuel Isaak died shortly before the German surrender. According to the Luderitz District Commissioner's official figures, when the camp on Shark Island was closed there were about 450 survivors of the original total of over 2,000 Nama prisoners: at least 1,550 had thus died. Estorff, however, put the mortality figure at 1,900.[85] The rest of the concentration camps were closed in January 1908,[86] and their inmates released—albeit to a new and highly regulated colonial dispensation.

Genocide and the Historiography of the Namibian War

Genocide, as defined by the United Nations Genocide Convention of 1948, consists of acts 'committed with intent to destroy, in whole or in part, a national, ethnical, racial or religious group'. Such acts include 'killing members of the group' and 'deliberately inflicting on the group conditions of life calculated to bring about its physical destruction in whole or in part'.[87] It is, in the view of this author and of most historians currently working on the subject, beyond reasonable doubt that genocide, thus defined, was committed in Namibia in the early twentieth century.

Firstly, the mortality statistics. Despite some uncertainty (and much argument) about the precise figures, it is clear that very large numbers died as a result of the German campaign against the Herero. Most contemporary sources put the number of Otjiherero-speakers before the Namibian War at somewhere between sixty and a hundred thousand. By the beginning of 1908 their numbers were estimated to be 16,363; the census of 1911 recorded a total of 19,423.[88] Perhaps between 3,000 and 10,000[89] also survived in Botswana, South Africa,

Owambo, Kaoko and Angola. Thus, using even the most conservative of these figures, more than half the population classified as Herero was wiped out. The true proportion of deaths is almost certainly higher, and probably very much so.

There is much less clarity as to the number of deaths of Nama-speakers, because the size of the total population before the war is unclear. An estimate of 1892 put their numbers at 15–20,000.[90] Some natural increase could normally be expected, meaning that, even if the lower end of the 1892 estimate is correct, a guess of 20,000 for the Nama population in 1904 would not be wildly inaccurate and could well be a conservative estimate. On this basis, the Nama-speaking population may have declined by about a third: in 1908 their numbers were estimated at 13,114, and the 1911 census gave a figure of 14,236.[91] We do know for certain that specific groups of Nama-speakers—the Veldschoendragers, Witboois and Bethany people, all of whom were sent to Shark Island—were almost wiped out in the concentration camps. 517 Witboois had died in detention in 1906 even before arriving on the island; there is likely to have been a similar death rate at this period among the other two groups; at least 1,550 Nama died on the island (out of a total of over 2,000), and perhaps as many as 1,900; and there were further deaths after April 1907. The result was that, by 1909, only 248 Nama prisoners survived.[92] Well over 2,000 Witboois, Bethany people and Veldschoendragers thus died in the camps. Among those deported, there were also very high mortality rates. The overall decline in the Nama population can also be explained by the deaths due to the privations endured during the war, including the German policy of sealing off waterholes—deaths that are impossible to quantify but, given the nature of the military campaign, are likely to have been numerous—and by the flight into British territory of many Nama-speakers.

It is likely that there was also considerable mortality among San and Damara-speakers caught up in the cataclysm that hit Namibia at this time: for example, there is a good deal of evidence that Germans indiscriminately attacked Damara in central Namibia. However, the difficulties of untangling these histories, and the effects of the ethnic prism through which the Namibian War is—albeit for good reasons—viewed, means that no statistical analysis of these deaths exist.

The genocidal acts of the Namibian War did not occur accidentally—they were, to quote from the United Nations definition of genocide, 'committed with intent'. As early as June 1904, von Trotha issued orders for the shooting of all those fighting the Germans, thus already indicating the brutal and aggressive nature of the campaign that he intended to pursue. This created an atmosphere in which many German soldiers (although there were exceptions) perpetrated massacres of civilians and other atrocities, both before and after Ohamakari.[93] Some recent—and contested—work suggests that von Trotha's strategy at the Battle of Ohamakari (11 August) was not yet to destroy (*vernichten*) the Herero as a people, but rather to achieve a complete military victory of the kind demanded in contemporary German strategic thinking. Even at this stage, however, the difference between these two objectives was blurred in practice, given the presence of far more Herero non-combatants than fighters on the battlefield. As the events of the next few weeks took shape, it is clear that von Trotha quickly now, if not earlier, adopted a strategy aimed explicitly at destroying the Herero.[94] Some time after a massacre of seventy captured Herero in the first week of September, he told subordinates that 'The entire Herero people must be exterminated',[95] and when von Estorff protested about the policy of pushing the Africans into the *omaheke* (which he was ordered to lead), he was told that von Trotha 'wanted their entire destruction [*gänzliche Vernichtung*]'.[96] The Extermination Order of 4 October not only formalised a policy that was already in place, but also ruled out peace negotiations, thus setting the seal on the genocide.[97]

In contrast to von Trotha's aggressive project to 'destroy the rebellious tribes by shedding rivers of blood and money',[98] Leutwein's more moderate (although still self-serving) position was that the destruction of the Herero would be 'a grave mistake from an economic point of view' because of the long-term need for labour.[99] The conflict between the two is mirrored in the broader struggle between the military and civilian authorities in Germany. Under von Trotha, SWA essentially became a military dictatorship, and his genocidal policies received active support from the head of the General Staff, von Schlieffen, and implicitly from Kaiser Wilhelm II. The Colonial Department and Chancellor von Bülow attempted a negotiated solution to the Herero war but could make no headway until von Schlieffen reluctantly agreed to rescind the Extermination Order in December. Even now, although surrenders were to be accepted, von Schlieffen would not agree to peace talks.[100]

After von Trotha's departure from Namibia, genocidal policies continued, in the concentration camps, under Governor von Lindequist and Acting Governor Tecklenburg. The authorities in SWA were informed of the colossal death rates from an early point in the camps' history by both local officials and missionaries, and politicians in Berlin also knew what was happening. Yet not only was very little done to stop the deaths, but in February 1907 Tecklenburg actively prevented Nama women and children from being taken off Shark Island.[101] The genocide therefore not only continued against the Herero, but was also deliberately implemented against the Witboois, Bethany people and Veldschoendragers. This is particularly significant because the case for arguing that genocide was carried out in the south is otherwise not quite as clear-cut as for central Namibia, although there are nevertheless strong arguments in its favour.[102] As we have seen, wells were sealed off on the edge of the Kalahari, and after the Witboois escaped to the desert regions in the east the Germans planned to oblige them to stay there.[103] Although von Trotha's order of April 1905, unlike the Extermination Order, offered the possibility of surrender to some, it also threatened the Nama with a similar fate to that of the Herero, and essentially prepared the ground for a period of lawlessness in which German soldiers and settlers were able to kill with impunity.[104]

The genocide in Namibia cannot simply be explained by Germany's (eventual) greater military strength—nor, indeed, as an expedient adopted as a response to military failure, although this also played a part. The war in Namibia went much further in slaughter and atrocity than any conflict in the Europe of the time. This can be attributed partly to the ideology of racial superiority current in European discourse. In politics and popular culture in both Germany and Namibia, Africans were systematically dehumanised. Herero were seen as 'wild beasts', 'savages' and 'insolent barbarians' who, according to widely circulating rumours, had raped, killed and dismembered white women;[105] Nama were called 'predators' by German politicians. Such ideas had a long history, and many soldiers subscribed to them, as is evident from their diaries. Thus, Africans were imagined by Germans as the epitome of savagery and the antithesis of civilisation. This dehumanisation fostered an atmosphere in which Africans could be killed with impunity, in which the status of non-combatant was not recognised, and in which military aggression could easily slide into mass murder.[106] The nadir of this process was perhaps reached when, from the concentration camps, the skulls of prisoners—including that of Cornelius Fredericks—were sent to Germany for research into the nature of racial hierarchy.[107]

Genocide was, thus, committed in Namibia between 1904 and 1908. Germany was not alone among the European powers in its imposition of force in order to impose its authority and, eventually, to extract the maximum economic value from its colonies. The atrocities in Namibia can be understood as standing at the extreme end of a continuum of violence and repression in which all the colonial powers participated. Nevertheless, it is important to name what happened in 1904–8 as genocide, not least because those who deny this continue to foster a debate that is really 'a constant exercise in denial of historical evidence'.[108] Because of the tenacity with which they make their arguments, it needs to be restated that the way in which they minimise African suffering is contrary to the weight of historical evidence and the conclusions of most recent research.[109]

The question of genocide is also politically explosive because of the complex politics of the history and remembrance of the Namibian War among those taking a generally anti-colonial position in Namibia itself. In 2004, the centenary of the genocide was commemorated by two different organisations—the National Preparatory Committee for the Commemoration of 2004 (NPCC04), which had the support of government, the churches and representatives of the Nama-speaking groups in the south, and the Genocide Commemoration Committee, which was politically close to Kuaima Riruako, the Herero paramount and opposition leader.[110] The latter body demanded reparations to Otjiherero-speakers from the German government. Although the NPCC04 did not support this strategy, in August 2004 the two organisations came together for a commemoration ceremony at the Waterberg attended by the German Minister of Economic Co-operation and Development, Heidemarie Wieczorek-Zeul, who asked for forgiveness for 'the guilt incurred by Germans at that time'.[111]

The political importance, and sensitivity, of defining what happened in Namibia as genocide has, however, perhaps had a detrimental effect on the spirit of historical inquiry and on the ways in which historical narratives have been framed. Large amounts of energy have been expended in justifying positions on both sides, to the point that evidence begins to be treated in a rather instrumental way. Certainly there have been some very good recent analyses, which have helped to develop our understanding of the events of 1904–8 as a process of historical development.[112] But the genocide debate can also be a hindrance to inquiry, and, above all, to situating the Namibian War as an event in *Namibian*, rather than German, history.[113]

Because the question of intent is central to proving genocide, much consideration has been given to the policies of the perpetrators. Yet the war cannot be properly understood without more analysis of the internal dynamics of the African polities, their motivations in going to war and seeking peace, and the relations of the different polities and leaders to each other. The historiography on these points remains thin, particularly for the south.[114] More research—including oral history—would tell us much, about the war not simply as heroic resistance to colonialism but as a harsh and difficult lived experience that affected whole African populations, often forced into migration and flight. Such a recasting might add much to what we already suspect: that at many points during the war the struggle for survival could be as crucial as engaging the enemy; that reasons for fighting or for making peace, springing both from earlier social processes and the circumstances of the moment, could be less than clear-cut; and that women and other non-combatants were as heavily involved as the fighters in the circumstances of war and peace. Indeed, although the war was broadly 'African' against 'German', resulting in a crushing defeat for the Africans, it might also reveal more of the counter-narratives of individuals: those Africans, for example, who fought with rather than against the Germans, and those whose military success forced their opponents to a negotiated settlement. And it would surely also tell us that, whatever the label given to the events of 1904–8, the atrocious experiences endured by almost all Africans in central and southern Namibia deserve to be remembered and understood, and had a profound effect on shaping the twentieth-century history of Namibia.

7

BUILDING A GERMAN COLONY, 1908–15

By 1908, a significant proportion of the African population in the Police Zone had been slaughtered in the Namibian War. Thousands had been driven from the territory, the social and political structures of the Herero had been destroyed and some Nama groups had almost been exterminated. Of the pre-war Herero leaders, only Zacharias Zeraua of Omaruru remained in the Police Zone. Of the southern leaders, Hendrik Witbooi, Jacob Morenga, Cornelius Fredericks and Paul Fredericks were dead, Samuel Isaak and Edward Fredericks (brother to Paul Fredericks and his successor as leader of the Bethany people) remained prisoners-of-war, and Simon Kopper, Manasse Noroseb and Jacobus Christian (son of the Bondelswarts leader Willem Christian) were in exile.[1] In the years that followed, the German colonial authorities imposed punitive control measures to try to create a disciplined proletariat out of the defeated African population. Colonial domination was, however, always contested by African subjects, and never completely imposed. Indeed, the nature of that domination—what exactly it meant to construct a German colony on African soil—was also fiercely contested among German settlers and officials. In the event, the Germans were to have less than a decade in which to try to resolve these questions: in 1915, shortly after the outbreak of the First World War, they lost SWA to South Africa.

The Survivors and the Labour Laws

In the aftermath of the war, the survivors had clear priorities: survival, and reconnection with kin and social networks. The level of African mobility was high. In one year alone, official figures showed that 11 per cent of workers had moved between districts.[2] Correspondence seized by the German authorities shows that Herero were using the written word to locate and communicate news of family and friends, and that they were constructing far-flung support networks in very difficult circumstances. A flavour of the correspondence is given by a letter from one Matthias Karl, dated 25 December 1908:

The world here is full of tribulations and difficulties, everywhere. Levi is in Okanona, Traugott has disappeared, I hear nothing from him and where he may be. Kamapuenisa is in Karibib...A person who has been in Swakopmund must weep...[3]

In the years after 1907, Africans were also taking whatever opportunity they could find to regenerate the herds they had lost. By 1913, they owned more than 25 per cent of the small stock in the colony, as well as more than twenty thousand head of large stock.[4] These efforts at reconstruction took place in spite of new legislation which, the colonial government hoped, would establish a 'seamless...system of control' over the Police Zone. With the Native Ordinances (*Eingeborenenverordnungen*) of 1907, the authorities aimed to transform the Africans into a landless proletariat, destroy their political organisation and culture, and force them to work in a disciplined and orderly manner for white employers. The three ordinances dealt with control measures, passes and work contracts, and together they set out a system in which all Africans—both female and male—over the age of six had to be registered with the local authorities and carry pass tokens (metal discs) allowing them to be identified by officials. The breaking of employment contracts was also punishable by law. Travel between districts was only allowed to those in possession of a travel pass signed by a white person, and vagrancy—essentially, travel without a pass—was an offence. On the farms, African settlements (*Werften*) were restricted to ten families, in an attempt to ensure that labour was distributed widely. There were, however, some limits to the reach of the Native Ordinances, which did not actually ban Africans from moving to other districts between contracts and thus aimed in theory to create, in Juergen Zimmerer's view, a 'half-free labour market' (although in practice these limited freedoms were often undermined, for example by the distribution of 'vagrants' to farmers needing labour). Some protections for the workers were also built into the legislation, but these generally proved weak and ineffective. In addition to the Native Ordinances, taxation was imposed on Africans (usually exempting women) by most local authorities from about 1910; a proposal for a colony-wide tax was, however, vetoed by the Colonial Office in 1911.[5]

The state's ability to extract labour from the Africans of the Police Zone rested on the expropriation of the latter from all their land and livestock, with the intention of making it impossible for Africans to earn an independent living. This had been accomplished, under separate legislation, by September 1907. Africans could not now own cattle or horses without special permission, and they lost all their land, except in a few cases, including those of the Bondelswarts, who had negotiated peace at Heirachabis, the Berseba people, who had remained neutral, and the Rehobothers, who had fought with the Germans.[6] Relations with the latter were generally fairly harmonious (although issues such as taxation caused conflict), because both sides appreciated the advantages of cooperation: the Germans valued Rehoboth as a political buffer and ally, and the Basters achieved a relatively favoured status under German rule, based partly on their mixed-race status. The colonial government was, however, much less happy with the arrangements regarding the Bondels and Berseba people, from whom both government and settlers were constantly expecting rebellion. Unwilling to take them on directly because of their potential military strength, the authorities deported three very small Nama groups, largely as a warning of the consequences of 'disobedience'. The Stuurmann people, a group under 'Klein Hendrik Witbooi' (Hendrik Witbooi's son), and the Veldschoendragers were first imprisoned in Grootfontein, and subsequently ninety-three of them, including forty women and twenty-seven children, were deported to Cameroon in 1910; nearly two-thirds of them died before the remainder were allowed to return to Namibia in 1912.[7]

Such harsh measures were necessary, in the view of the authorities, in order to extract as much labour as possible from the African population of the territory. The late German period saw a particularly acute shortage of workers, both because of the genocide and because the mining industry now flowered rapidly. Industrial copper working began at the Tsumeb mine in 1906, and, most important, diamonds were discovered by Zacharias Lewala, an employee of August Stauch, near to Lüderitzbucht in 1908. The mines, and the infrastructure of the colony that the Germans were now rapidly putting in place, all demanded large supplies of labour, as did the white farms, whose numbers quickly expanded with the settlement policy of Governor von Lindequist.[8] This encouraged the rapid acquisition by settlers, particularly members of the *Schutztruppe*, of mainly small-scale farms, aided by state funding (500,000 Marks in 1906 alone). In the Governor's view, the physical occupation of large tracts of land was necessary in order to make good the German conquest; ex-soldiers would also be easily able to form a citizens' militia in the case of further unrest. Although the new policy quickly increased the number of white settlers—to nearly 15,000 by 1914—in practice, many farms, under-capitalised and in debt, were soon in a parlous economic state. This, coupled with the fact that many of these farmers probably carried the enmities of the Namibian War into the post-war period, and that they, like most of the whites in the colony, subscribed to an aggressive ideology of white racial supremacy, led to a situation in which African workers were routinely exploited and abused. On the isolated farms, where the owners frequently suspected their servants of poisoning them, and where rumours of new uprisings often circulated, a culture of violence, fear and the denigration of Africans for their supposed 'cheekiness' and 'laziness' prevailed.[9]

The labour laws were enforced through a judicial system that imposed punitive measures, particularly corporal punishment (which usually meant flogging), on Africans found to be breaking the rules. The number of sentences to physical punishment applied by the courts rose from 534 in 1907/8 to 1,713 in 1912/13.[10] There was also considerable unrecorded violence directed at Africans by their employers, who were permitted by law to exercise a 'right of paternal correction' (*väterliches Züchtigungsrecht*) over their workers—that is, to apply extra-judicial corporal punishment. The worst abuses—heavily criticised by the centre and left in Germany—came to light in a much-publicised series of trials in 1911–13 of farmers who had shot at African servants and farmworkers, beaten them, caused them to miscarry and in some cases killed them. Although some commentators argued that these were isolated events, there was vehement support for the accused in the local press, indicating a widespread opinion among settlers that they should be able to discipline workers by whatever means they deemed necessary; this included the 'right' to beat black women, which had been outlawed in 1896.[11]

The state also energetically deployed violence against San groups, who were seen by most settlers and officials as both an armed threat and a people impossible to induce to labour (although, in fact, by 1912 997 out of a population of 2,829 were in employment, mainly on settler farms).[12] In 1911 San bands, increasingly squeezed by white settlement on their land and by drought, launched a series of stock thefts and armed attacks on farms and parties of Ovambo migrants in the Grootfontein district. Governor Seitz responded by authorising police patrols to shoot any San trying to run away, and in 1911–12 alone four hundred such patrols were sent out. Captured San were punished, subjected to forced labour and in some cases deported to other parts of the colony.[13] Patrols also sought out Africans attempting to make a living from *veldkos*, hunting and sometimes stock theft beyond the reach of the white authorities: Herero settled near to waterholes in the arid regions to the east, or Damara living in the mountains. A community of two hundred under the Herero leaders Kandiapu and Kanjemi, based to the east of the Omuramba Omatako, which sent out raiding parties to farms, was eventually tracked down in 1911 and its leaders killed. Some groups living in the *veld* were, however, brought in by negotiation rather than violence.[14]

Nevertheless, the authorities found that pass and vagrancy laws could not solve the labour shortage—partly because of determined and widespread African resistance, and partly because the population of the Police Zone was so sparse (standing at around 69,000, including migrant workers, in 1913). By 1911, there were estimated to be 15,000 more jobs than workers within the colony.[15] Migrant workers were thus brought in both from the north (of which more below) and from South Africa, and violence was also deployed against both categories. African and Coloured workers from the Cape had first been employed in SWA during the Namibian War, and this trend continued in the post-war period. In 1910, at a place called Wilhemsthal, at least fourteen South African railway workers were massacred by soldiers during a labour dispute.[16]

The very severity with which white power was enforced indicates that the Germans' attempt to establish total control was proving to be little more than a colonial fantasy. On the farms and in the homes of whites in urban areas, African workers gained a reputation among settlers for 'insolence'—better understood as a refusal to recognise white authority, whether generally or as represented by individual employers. When the settler Carl Schlettwein asked one of his workers 'who was master and who servant', he received the reply, 'Are all the whites masters, or are you just trying to be one?'[17] Throughout the Police Zone, Africans repeatedly left their jobs and threw away their pass discs in order to change their identity and escape punishment for 'desertion': in some cases they left the farms for other employment, in others, particularly after good rains, for the bush. Their resistance was aided by a number of factors hampering efficient German administration of the Native Ordinances, including lack of administrative manpower and the fact that the small, under-strength police force was unable to patrol Namibia's vast area comprehensively. Settlers—who, as a body, had an antagonistic relationship with the more upper-class civil authorities in the colony—also undermined the provisions of the legislation, for example by allowing more than ten families to live on their farms, and in some cases engaging in more traditional African patron-client relations by paying Africans with stock in lieu of cash wages. Such measures tended to make for better labour relations, and one farm in the Grootfontein area even used a system of labour tenancy that allowed African farmers use of land on which to grow crops and keep livestock. (On the other hand, many employers' actions, for example the refusal to grant Africans travel passes, also undermined the minimal protection written into the legislation.)[18]

Whether Africans' resistance went as far as attempting to revitalise pre-war forms of authority is doubtful. According to rumours that frequently circulated among settlers, Africans were rejoining their old 'tribes' and planning further rebellion. In reality, however, there was no serious attempted uprising through the remainder of the German period. Given that the most important of the old leaders were largely dead or absent and that, among Herero, the basis of authority—cattle—had been wiped out, it seems unlikely that political reconstitution seemed a serious possibility until after the German defeat.[19]

The reality on the farms was that the workforce—to whom the settlers attributed almost supernatural malevolent powers—were having the greatest difficulty in simply surviving. In 1907 the population of the Police Zone had been defeated, demoralised and deeply traumatised. Their health was already undermined by malnutrition, disease and forced labour, in the post-war period many farm-workers were often quite literally starving: a 1912 study of farms in 'central Hereroland' found that, in 75 per cent of cases, African workers were receiving too little food to satisfy their minimum nutritional requirements.[20] The mental trauma of the survivors is illustrated in songs about the war composed by Otjiherero-speakers in Botswana, which speak, with rich and vivid imagery, of flight, sacrifice, and a world turned upside down: 'People are distraught; the child has lost its mother; the mother has lost her husband; the lambs have gone to suckle the goats'.[21]

On the part of the German authorities, conditions in the Police Zone led to some rather weak moves toward liberalisation—for example, there were discussions about whether to end the ban on cattle owner-ship or to create reserves for Africans—which ultimately, however, came to little beyond the appointment of Native Commissioners, part of whose function was to try to safeguard African interests, from 1912, and new legislation against the worst abuses of workers. In this, the colonial government was influenced both by the threat of political scandal in Germany over abuses in the colony and by the fear that the harsh labour laws might drive Africans once more to rebel. In Germany itself, the elections early in 1907—although won on a right-wing, imperialist programme—paradoxically brought in a mildly reforming agenda under Bernhard Dernburg, the new head of the Colonial Office. Both Dernburg and his successor Wilhelm Solf visited Namibia, in 1908 and 1912 respectively, but did little to improve conditions for Africans in the face of determined local white resistance.[22]

New Forms of Consciousness and Social Change

Africans in the Police Zone dealt with the new situation not only by trying to rebuild more traditional social forms, but also by engaging with, and shaping, new identities. These processes arose partly out of the massive social breakdown experienced in the post-war years, with its accompanying generational and gender tensions. At this period, many Africans not only adopted but also transformed and subverted European symbols and practices, deploying them in some cases to cri-tique white rule as well as forms of authority wielded by Africans.

The most important cultural development in the immediate post-war period was the mass conversion of Otjiherero-speakers to Christianity, so that by 1914 the RMS had 25,000 members in the Police Zone. The Catholic Church, which had been given the right to operate in SWA on an equal basis with the Protestants in 1905, had 2,672 African mem-bers by 1919.[23] Many of the conversions took place in the concentra-tion camps—certainly, at least in part, through genuine religious belief on the part of the prisoners. The social and cultural consequences of this shift were profound, particularly among Otjiherero-speakers, only a minority of whom had accepted Christianity before 1904. Africans were now able to use—and reshape—the structures of leadership and community offered by the churches to fill the void left by the collapse of their old social and political arrangements.

To some extent, it was (male) members of the former elite who assumed authority in the mission churches. In the immediate aftermath of the genocide, missionaries had called on Christian, mission-educated survivors, often the relatives of the *ovahona*, to encourage those remaining in the *veld* to come to the collection camps. These men included Gustav Kamototo, formerly a teacher at Otjihaenena; Erastus, a relative of the previous *omuhona* there; and Friedrich, himself the previous *omuhona* of Omburo. Samuel Kariko showed great bravery in going, under RMS auspices, to minister to the prisoners on Shark Island. After the concentration camps were dissolved, the number of African evangelists, teachers and elders expanded, and in 1911 the RMS opened a seminary at Gaub. Together with stints in the mines and other new forms of employment, the missions now offered career paths for young African men that had hardly existed before. Their numbers included Andreas Kukuri, the grandson of the senior man at Otjosazu, a life-long teacher who trained at Gaub; Hosea Kutako, later to become Herero paramount, who taught at the RMS mission in Omaruru; and Frans ‖Hoesemab, an important leader in the location in Windhoek as well as a mission teacher (of whom more below). On the farms, missionaries and mobile evangelists—including Kido at Sesfontein, Daniel at Okombahe and Philippus at Keetmanshoop—now offered one of the most important means of communication between people living in otherwise very isolated conditions. At this period, too, church publications in Namibian languages first began to appear.[24]

Despite the significance of these changes, the missionaries who ran the RMS were not, as yet, prepared to cede any meaningful degree of authority to African leaders. Politically, the stance of white missionaries at this period was rather complex. Most supported German authority, and even corporal punishment, overall, but there were also many occasions on which they criticised the treatment of Africans by settlers and the state.[25]

A second strong new source of identity for Africans was the *Bambuse* institution. During the Namibian War, hundreds of boys—some

Fig. 18. This image is described as showing 'Catechist Johannes' holding a lesson in Grootfontein, almost certainly some time during the German period. It shows the importance of African leaders within the churches. After the concentration camps were closed, church elders played a key role in reconstituting social networks. (Reproduced courtesy of Special Collections, Yale Divinity School Library.)

orphaned—had been absorbed into the *Schutztruppe* as servants or *Bambusen*. Andreas Kukuri, for example, became a *Bambuse* after his group was captured. Girls, too, were present in some numbers in military camps as domestics and sometimes prostitutes; many would have continued in similar roles after the end of the war. The *Bambusen*, who were often given uniforms by their masters, emerged as discrete groups with their own hierarchies and identities. In many ways, these groups formed an alternative, and more youthful, approach to modernity from that presented by the Christian hierarchies, at times resorting to forms of social banditry.[26]

The post-war period also saw rapid growth in the black and white population of Namibia's towns. In Windhoek, for example, the black population doubled, to around 4,000, between 1903 and 1912, and the settled white population grew from 457 in 1903 to about 1,700 in 1915. This increase in the number of urban residents resulted from a rapid influx of German officials and other settlers, the dissolution of the concentration camps—many of whose inmates remained in urban areas—and the arrival of Africans attempting to escape difficult rural conditions. In the authorities' view, these new urban black populations posed the danger of 'indiscipline' and potential unrest; legislation was enacted to compel Africans to live in locations separate from areas of white settlement, and to impose a night-time curfew. Like the Native Ordinances, however, these harsh racial measures had limits. The Germans do not seem to have placed explicit limits on the numbers who could migrate into urban areas—although in 1911 travel passes became subject to a fee of two shillings in order to make such migration more difficult—or to have designated them as temporary rather than permanent dwelling places for Africans; indeed, in the absence of a system of rural reserves it would have been difficult to do so. Nor, it seems, was thoroughgoing social segregation imposed.[27]

In this context, new forms of authority began to develop among urban Africans, especially when the state began to appoint black headmen in the towns. The best known of these was the Frans ‖Hoesemab, the leader of the Damara section of the Windhoek location and an important figure in the RMS in Windhoek. The conflicts that dogged his career pivot around the question of authority, in the church and in the location. ‖Hoesemab quarrelled with the missionary Becker after the latter failed, in his view, to consult him sufficiently on mission business; Becker was also scandalised by ‖Hoesemab's refusal to conform to the church's rules on sexual morality. When Damara members of the RMS congregation began to assert identity and confidence by wearing top hats, Becker saw this as open mockery of whites (although it may have had much more to do with generational conflicts within the black community). In 1913, the government exiled ‖Hoesemab to Lüderitzbucht, at the RMS's request.[28]

Authority—of the state, but also of senior African men—was at issue, too, in the question of the behaviour and control of African women. Although black women were clearly absorbed into the workforce as agricultural labourers as well as domestics,[29] they were also able to subvert both German and African patriarchal controls in significant ways. For one thing, married women, and those with children, often successfully resisted being forced into paid work, and in most cases were exempt from taxation. For another, as officials in the rural districts complained, some left their families on the farms for the towns; others migrated with their families to the towns. These dynamics are reflected in the figures: the black female population of Windhoek, for example, was higher than that of black men from at least 1903 until at least 1915.[30] Once in the urban areas, although some women engaged in prostitution (and many will have been coerced into sexual relationships with white men), many others worked as domestics and in other roles; the fact that labour was short offered the leverage to demand higher wages or to change jobs relatively easily.[31] Some African women had, thus, succeeded in wresting a relatively high degree of autonomy for themselves, despite the very difficult conditions they faced.

The Construction of 'Germanness'

Clearly, then, there was much anxiety among settlers in the towns, as well as on the farms and mines, about the construction of white domination and what Bley has called the employers' 'everyday struggle for "distance"'.[32] In these circumstances, African women in both rural and urban areas became a strong focus for the fears of (particularly) male settlers. In other southern African colonies at this period, social tensions exploded around incidents in which African men were accused of raping white women; in Namibia, by contrast, African *women* were the focus for moral panics onto which broader conflicts were projected. In newspapers and in novels they were constructed as strong, malevolent and dangerous, sexually alluring to German men but ultimately destructive.[33] The Germans' failure to differentiate between combatants and non-combatants during the Namibian War arguably was produced by, and also helped to mould, a settler discourse in which African women and children hardly figured as categories deserving of protection.

These settler imaginings resulted directly in aggression towards black women, as illustrated for example by the Cramer case. African women also became subject to general, regular, brutal and degrading compulsory examinations for venereal disease. Although VD scares were a staple of settler panics about supposed African threats, there is little doubt that sexually transmitted infections had been brought to Namibia by white men, and that they had been widely spread by the pervasive sexual violence that pertained during and after the Namibian War.[34] The examinations for VD began in the concentration camps and continued after the prisoners were released, although some reforms were made following protests by the German Women's Association for Nursing in the Colonies and the RMS in 1910.[35]

Indeed, both gender and race were set at the heart of the colonial project in the late German period. In Germany itself, the colonial movement had long been associated with the ideas of radical nationalists who saw imperial expansion as essential to the maintenance of Germany's honour and its hopes of becoming a world power. In this thinking, the colonies were spaces in which Germany could be reinvented in its supposed essentials: a rural idyll, free from industrialisation and urban 'moral degeneration'. The empire would thus serve as a bulwark against both communism and capitalism, and resolve, in a profoundly conservative direction, conflicts that were threatening to break Germany itself apart. The colonies were projected as ideal spaces in which to construct 'Deutschtum'—very roughly, 'Germanness'—and to which emigration from Germany could be rerouted from its most popular destination, the United States. German South West Africa took pride of place in this thinking. Of Germany's large colonies, it was the one that could provide the healthiest conditions to settlers; it had also, in imperial thinking, been bought with the blood of German soldiers. The victory of the pro-empire lobby in the elections of 1907 only strengthened the power of these ideas.

The idea of Deutschtum rested on a concept of the purity and superiority of the white, and specifically the German, race. In this it was informed by the rigid racial hierarchy of Social Darwinism as well as the proto-National Socialist ideas of writers such as Frieda von Bülow and Carl Peters; more liberal thinkers such as Paul Rohrbach, settlement commissioner for SWA from 1903, also acted as advocates for the settlers and for German expansionism.[36] The actual situation in German South West Africa, however, militated against the establishment of white 'racial purity'. Sexual relations between white men and African women (many born in violence or in the commoditisation of sex, but a minority consensual) were extremely common—a situation that had its roots both in an older multicultural elite and in the massive influx of settlers and soldiers since 1890. In a very few instances, African women had married white men (not all of them German) in accordance with colonial law: there were thought to be forty-two such civil marriages by the beginning of 1903.[37] Most of the wives of Germans seem to have been Rehoboth women who, because of their mixed ancestry, were seen by their husbands as 'half-white'.[38]

194

Inter-racial sex and marriage threatened the whole idea of settler colonialism in the eyes, not only of colonial ideologues, but also of successive governors and many settlers. Because marriage to German men conferred German citizenship on African women and their children,[39] it became a particular target, and in 1905 Tecklenburg, the deputy governor, put a stop to 'mixed marriages'—that is, those between 'natives' and 'non-natives'. In addition, in 1907 such marriages contracted before 1905 were declared invalid, and a 'native' (*Eingeborene/Eingeborener*) was defined as anyone with any non-white ancestry—a move that rejected any idea of assimilation of dual-descent individuals into the white population. African women married to white men, and their children, now stood to lose land, rights and education, as for example was the fate of Ida Leinhos (Kaera) and her family—although 'mixed' marriages made in the Cape Colony were supposed to be (and usually were) legally recognised by the German authorities.

The colonial government also took measures to try to reduce the number of births of children of African–European liaisons, which, according to official statistics, reached about four hundred in 1909 alone.[40] Under the constitution of the Landesrat (Territorial Council), white men in relationships with black women were now barred from voting; they were also denied certain forms of financial help and the right to buy land from the government—a policy largely enforced, although a few individual exceptions were later made for those married before 1905. Compulsory registration of the births of 'mixed race' children was introduced in 1912, and at the same time their fathers were forced to make a compensation payment to the mother of the child.[41] Nevertheless, continued growth in the 'mixed' percentage of the population showed that these measures had little effect.

If black women were seen by colonial ideologues, and many settlers, as the ultimate disruptive force, there was no shortage of propaganda promoting female German settlers as the opposite: the panacea that would bring order and the values of *Deutschtum* to the colonial domestic sphere. By May 1910, the Frauenbund[42] (Women's League), founded in Germany in 1907, had sent 158 women to the colony; by 1913, the ratio of male to female whites stood at three to one.[43] There were, however, significant tensions between the upper- and middle-class leadership of the Frauenbund and the mainly working-class emigrants. White women were, according to the former, not only to be the bearers of German culture to the colonies, but also to embody a whole range of practical domestic and agricultural skills. Ideal male settlers, too, were supposed to be rugged individualists, able to cope with the 'freedom' offered by the colonial space, but also gifted with all the attributes necessary to become successful farmers. Most of the young working-class people emigrating, however, did so for mainly economic reasons, and became considerably disillusioned by the harshness of life and tense social relations in the colony; the 'freedom' of the colony became, for many settlers, the freedom to shoot and beat Africans.[44] Nor was SWA quite the rural colony so desired by the radical nationalists: by 1914, 30 per cent of the male European population was employed in the civil service and the military,[45] and more were working in small-scale manufacture and commerce rather than on farms.

In fact, the efforts made by the colonial government to control the behaviour of the white settler population illustrate both the difficulties of creating and sustaining whiteness and 'Germanness' as dominant racial categories, and the extent of class tensions within the colony. Successive governors endeavoured to create a state free of the spectre of white poverty—and in the process to rid SWA of lower-class individuals. The discovery of diamonds in particular encouraged the immigration into the territory of adventurers considered 'undesirable' by the authorities, and settlers were deported to Germany for alcoholism, poverty and homosexual activities among other reasons. Particularly before and during the South African War (1899–1902), considerable numbers of Boers from South Africa had arrived in SWA, among whom the poorer groups of migrant Trekboers were particularly unwelcome to the authorities.[46]

Creating *Deutschtum* was carried out not only through the exclusion of 'undesirables', but also through the active promotion of cultural institutions, and the memorialisation and marking of the land. In the towns, the German communities formed a plethora of sporting, musical, charitable and religious clubs and associations, and the Deutsche Evangelische Kirchengemeinde (DEK; German Lutheran Church) established a number of branches for the German population. The central districts and white settlement areas of towns like Windhoek, Swakopmund and Lüderitzbucht came to be dominated by buildings in the contemporary German style, and memorials to German sacrifice and victory were also erected. In Windhoek, the names of Germans killed in the Namibian War were inscribed in the Christuskirche (1910), a DEK church that still dominates the centre of the city, and in

Fig. 19. This photograph, dating from 1904, shows Afrikaner women and children in Gibeon and hints at the conditions faced by poor white settlers in Namibia. Boer incomers, who arrived in relatively large numbers before 1915, were a source of anxiety to German policy-makers and commentators seeking to establish a white-ruled, German colony. (Reproduced courtesy of the National Archives of Namibia [no. 4996].)

1912 an equestrian statue (the Reiterdenkmal) that has since become iconic was erected outside the old fort (the Alte Feste.)[47]

Administering the Colony

Such development was made possible partly by the introduction of municipal self-government for the settlers in 1909, followed in 1910 by elections to the Landesrat. This body had limited powers over policy areas including roads, water, hunting and farming, but other matters, including defence, finance and most of the basic business of government, were reserved to the governor, who continued to rule by decree, subject to the authority of the Colonial Office in Berlin. Because the right to vote was restricted to propertied, white German men, the Landesrat largely represented the male settler elite, especially

197

the farmers, who thus achieved a political power disproportionate to their economic importance within the territory. This section of the settler population had in fact already become a strong political force, gaining from the German government the large sum of ten million Marks in compensation for losses during the Namibian War. In 1911 the Landesrat voted to increase the supply of labour to the farms by preventing residents of the Police Zone from working on the mines; in 1913, with the founding of the Land Bank, the state began to provide more generous financial help to white farms.[48]

At the same time, civil government was both expanding and being placed on a more organised footing. The number of administrative districts (*Bezirke*) rose to eleven by the end of the German period. The central administration was divided into four departments in 1908 (for internal administration, transport, legal matters and military security), and two more (native affairs and public works) were added in 1910/11. The police became a civilian body in 1907, and the *Schutztruppe* was reduced to a permanent strength of 1,967 Germans plus 600 African auxiliaries. The German government improved and standardised conditions for civil servants in the colonies, and funded research into exploration, agriculture and health. These developments were echoed in Namibia, where mapping was undertaken and research into water provision and agriculture carried out. Production increased, and in 1907 the governor helped to make commercial farming in the arid south viable in the long-term by importing, from Uzbekistan, the first karakul sheep, whose valuable pelts could be sold at high prices on international markets.

It was, however, the boom in mining, particularly diamonds, that was the most striking economic development of the late German period. Diamond revenues formed two-thirds of the state's income between 1909 and 1913, and put GSWA well on the way to becoming financially self-sufficient (except for the cost of the *Schutztruppe*, which was met by the German imperial government); between them, diamonds and copper accounted for 66,830,000 Marks' worth of exports in 1913, out of a total of 70,302,830 Marks. Soon after the discovery of diamonds, Dernburg excluded small operators from the diamond fields, thus creating a monopolistic situation and making it possible for the DKGSWA and its subsidiary the Deutsche Diamanten Gesellschaft (founded in 1909) to make a profit for the first time. A consortium of German banks also benefited substantially from the diamond industry. OMEG, meanwhile, also profited heavily from the copper boom.

The authorities also put significant resources into the infrastructure of the colony. The railways were of particular significance, because of their practical role in facilitating capitalist development and their symbolic significance as markers of civilisation and modernity. By 1913, a rail network of 2,104 km had been built. Education and health services for the white population were also put in place across SWA. For Africans, such services, where they existed, were mainly provided by the missions (which placed a much greater emphasis on education than on health care), with minimal state subsidies, although towards the end of the German period the government showed interest in increasing this funding in order to create a more educated (and German-speaking) workforce.[49]

The North: Direct and Indirect Rule

Nothing could be mined without a sufficient supply of cheap labour, and it was primarily to Namibia's northern regions that the Germans turned in their search for workers. This requirement for labour, and the continued military strength of the Ovambo kingdoms, were both strong factors in Germany's eventual decision not to occupy Owambo directly. This was not, however, a foregone conclusion. In 1908 Franke toured the area and for the first time obtained declarations of obedience from the kings of Ondonga, Oukwanyama, Uukwambi, Uukwaluudhi and Ongandjera. The monarchs were persuaded to cooperate both by the hope of obtaining some protection from the Portuguese threat, which was particularly obvious to the Kwanyama, and by fears aroused by the outcome of the Namibian War. In June 1909, the Colonial Office in Berlin agreed to the establishment of a Resident Commissioner for Ovamboland, but this move towards occupation came to nothing when the *Reichstag* refused funds. A few months later Görgens, the colony's chief land surveyor, finally extracted permission from the new Ndonga king, Kambonde kAngula,[50] to station a German post on his territory, but the Colonial Office vetoed this arrangement.[51]

Thereafter, the colonial administration confined its direct involvement in Owambo to annual official visits, which were concerned above all with the recruitment of migrant labour. The colonial government was also able to use the mission stations for intelligence on and communication with the region. In addition, the authorities cultivated 'soft power' by sending substantial amounts of famine relief to be distributed by the missions. In the years after 1907, the people of the north experienced widespread deaths from hunger and disease, as they were hit by famine and drought in 1907–8 and again in 1910–12. At the same time, young, reforming kings came to power in the two most powerful Ovambo kingdoms. Mandume ya Ndemufayo became king of Oukwanyama in 1911. He quickly brought in measures to centralise power, curbing the activities of the *omalenga*, to reduce the levels of violence within the kingdom, and to promote, in the tradition of 'good' Ovambo kings, the cultivation of the land. He is remembered as defending the poor against the depredations of the rich: although he himself perpetrated some violence, 'King Mandume had laws that protected his country and his people'.[52] In Ondonga, which had once again been unified after the death of Nehale in 1908, Nambala Kadhikwa took the throne in 1912. Like Mandume, he also was concerned to centralise power and to undercut the *omalenga* and their violence against commoners. Politically, however, the two kings diverged radically. Nambala espoused Christianity, drawing on it as a source of political power, and was baptised Martin soon after his accession; until his death in 1942 he remained the colonial authorities' closest ally in the region. Mandume, however, opposed the new religion, and came into conflict with the missionaries over the question of female initiation; his reign ended with a direct military challenge to the government of SWA, as we shall see below.[53]

Across Owambo, kings encouraged their subjects to respond to the Germans' demand for labour as a means of warding off more direct intervention by the colonial power. The monarchs were also motivated to co-operate by the benefits, including 'gifts' from returning migrants, that they received. For commoners, too, it made sense in famine conditions to look for the means of survival elsewhere. In most years between 1910 and 1914, the annual number of Ovambo migrants to the Police Zone stood at over 9,000, although it fell to just over 6,000 in 1912 after good rains. The length of most contracts at this period, eight to nine months, was still advantageous to Owambo, allowing workers to come home for the harvest. As the numbers going south increased, however, it seems unlikely that kings managed to maintain their previous tight control of migrant groups.

The contract workers went principally to the mines at Tsumeb and Luderitz, although some were also sent to settler farms. They were paid more than Police Zone workers, but were treated as more expendable and subjected to harsh conditions: twelve-hour days, usually without a day off, poor food, inadequate clothing and corporal punishment. In 1911, 181 of the 2,300 migrant workers on the diamond mines died of ill-health (mainly scurvy and lung infections). In the same year the colonial government brought in new legal regulation of workers' conditions, but the efforts of the Native Commissioner at Luderitz, Hermann Tönjes (formerly an RMS missionary), to make improvements were met with determined resistance by the mines.[54]

Despite the hopes of the colonial administration, the more sparsely populated and remoter regions of Kaoko, Kavango and Caprivi never provided much migrant labour for the Germans. Kaoko was cut off from trade and largely ignored, beyond some attempts to encourage migration from Angola. In both Caprivi and Kavango, however, the Germans established a direct occupation of sorts. In Caprivi, the German colonial government instituted direct rule early in 1909, in the person of Captain Streitwolf who, with a force of twenty-three men, established a mission at a place he called Schuckmannsburg, opposite Mwandi in modern Zambia. This apparently bizarre decision to situate an outpost in the part of GSWA furthest from Windhoek was explained at the time as a measure taken to control the unregulated activities of settlers in eastern Caprivi, particularly Germans who were using the area as a conduit for arms and cattle (possibly diseased) to the Police Zone. The strategic importance of the Caprivi, abutting as it did three British colonies, and hopes of finding minerals there, also played a role.

On Streitwolf's arrival, many of the local population left with their cattle for Lozi territory in modern Zambia, partly on the orders of Letia (King Lewanika's son), but also through fear of the Germans. Streitwolf encouraged their return, with some eventual success. He also began to create a separate Caprivi identity, mainly through the recognition of two chiefs—Simaata Kabende Mamili for the Fwe, and Chikamatondo for the Subiya. The former had previously been under Lewanika's authority, a link now broken, while the latter replaced Mwanamwalie, who retained his authority on the British side of the river. Streitwolf also separated the eastern Caprivi further from the rest of the Lozi kingdom, causing considerable hardship, by restricting the rights of Lozi subjects living in Zambia to harvest reeds and fish on the South West African side of the river. He expelled most of the whites in the Caprivi, and explored and mapped the area. After his departure in 1910, his successors continued these policies and were under orders to intervene in African politics as little as possible, although Viktor von Frankenburg, who arrived in 1911, had a reputation for strict punishments of African 'offenders'.[55]

In Kavango, direct occupation by the Portuguese of the Angolan side of the Kavango River was to have far more significance for the local population than the stationing of Germans in the region. In mid-1909, Portuguese forces arrived at the northern bank of the Kavango River (where, at the time, most of the Kavango peoples lived), and threw up a series of five forts, some with a substantial garrison. The consequences of this sudden occupation for local residents were severe. The Shambyu fruitlessly attempted armed resistance, and seem to have fled to Shikambakamba in southern Angola for some years before returning in about 1915. The Mbukushu had just been visited by Streitwolf and appealed, in vain, for his help. All the polities suffered depredations of their crops and livestock by Portuguese soldiers, and the rape of women seems to have been rife. In consequence, the majority of the Kwangali, Mbunza, Gciriku and Mbukushu escaped across the river to German territory, where control was much lighter, although in 1909 the Germans had induced the Kwangali king, Kandjimi, to sign a 'protection' treaty. The following year a German police post was erected at Nkurenkuru, opposite the Portuguese fort at Cuangar. Although the post exercised some supervision over the Kavango area, particularly Ukwangali, its primary purpose was to observe Portuguese activity. Its functions were restricted both by lack of resources and by the Germans' hope of keeping the population on their side of the river: to do this, they had to present themselves as more liberal masters than the Portuguese. This strategy delivered very few migrant workers for the Police Zone, however—the highest total, in 1913, was 122.[56] Although there was some appetite for consumer goods in the Kavango, migrants were deterred by the harsh conditions on the mines at Tsumeb and the difficulties of the journey, as well as by the fact that there was still plentiful farmland in the Kavango. European influence in the area nevertheless also increased at this period through the establishment of Catholic missions in Gciriku territory (1910) and at Andara (1913), where the Mbukushu king Diyeve II hoped that the missionaries and German authorities would protect him against Tawana domination.[57]

German rule over the north, then, when it was not absent, was indirect and rather liberal—if by force of circumstance rather than design. In the case of Owambo, the position was to be quickly reversed with the coming of South African rule.

8

SOUTH AFRICAN RULE, 1915–46

With the outbreak of the First World War in 1914, the colonies of southern Africa were abruptly plunged into hostilities. These events were to have traumatic consequences for the Germans in South West Africa, whose attempts to defend the territory from invading South African forces were quickly defeated. The effects of the war on the African population were mixed. Some suffered during the campaign, while others benefited. During the first few years of South African rule (when martial law was imposed), government policy towards Africans was characterised by a mild liberalism in the Police Zone, but by an unprecedented level of intervention in the north, where the Kwanyama king Mandume was overthrown. In 1921, South Africa (representing Britain) began to govern Namibia on the new legal basis of a League of Nations mandate, and there followed two decades in which the South African administration systematically applied its policies of racial segregation to Namibia, seeking, as the German government before it had done, to extract as much wealth from the colony as possible.

The new colonial government was not, however, particularly effective or efficient in the early years of the mandate. The 1920s was a time of fierce struggle against an administration that was still chronically short of resources. These events played a part in shaping colonial policy, and it was not until the 1930s, in the context of drought and depression, that the state was able significantly to increase its control over African mobility and labour—although this domination still remained partial. Resistance and conflicts—as in the past—were generated by the internal dynamics of African societies and the immediate pressures facing them, as well as by explicit opposition to colonial policies. Nevertheless, from the repression of the inter-war period a sustained nationalist movement was later to emerge.

The most decisive early action of the First World War on Namibian soil occurred on 21 September 1914, when the German post in the Caprivi at Schuckmannsburg, now isolated in hostile territory, surrendered to the British without a fight. The Caprivi was administered by the Bechuanaland Protectorate Police for the rest of the martial law period. Further west, hostilities erupted between the Germans and Portuguese when the latter killed the administrator of Outjo and several of his party at Naulila, near the Kunene River on the Angolan side of the border, in October 1914. Shortly thereafter, a small German force overwhelmed the fort at Cuangar, and went on to destroy the remaining four Portuguese forts along the Kavango. In December, German troops routed the Portuguese garrison at Naulila. The defeated Portuguese and victorious Germans both then withdrew from Owambo and Kavango, leaving southern Angola in a state of revolt and Mandume in a strong position to extend his power in the area. In the Kavango, according to the oral historian Nakare, the Kwangali assisted the Germans in the attack on Cuangar. 'Afterwards they went back and Kandjimi stayed behind': in other words, the Kwangali king was the true victor of the attack, which left him in full possession of his lands once the Germans had departed.[1]

From the point of view of the colonial powers, however, these engagements were little more than skirmishes. South Africa, like the other British dominions (Australia, New Zealand and Canada), actively participated in the First World War on the Allied side, and between September and December 1914 its forces invaded Namibia, attacking both overland and from the sea.[2] With a much larger force than the Germans,[3] composed partly of experienced Boer commandos, as well as better transport and equipment, South African troops overwhelmed their opponents in a matter of months, taking Windhoek in May. The Germans surrendered at Khorab, near Tsumeb, on 9 July 1915. Namibia now effectively passed into South African hands, and was at first ruled by the military under martial law. During this period the South Africans maintained a substantial presence: in 1917 the Administrator estimated that there were some 6,000 troops and civilian officials in the territory.[4] The martial law period ended formally on 1 January 1921 when South Africa became the mandatory power for Namibia.

The 'Famine That Swept' and Colonial Rule in the North[5]

The martial law period was a time of trauma for the population of Owambo. By the time of the South African invasion, the region was being ravaged by one of the most destructive famines of the twentieth century—remembered as *ondjala yawekomba*, the 'famine that swept'—which peaked after the failure of the rains in 1914 and 1915, forming a terrible climax to the series of droughts and famines that had plagued the region throughout the late German period. People had little resistance or resources with which to combat the famine, and the result was mass starvation, the breakdown of normal social relations, the denial of hospitality to refugees—normally a strong tradition—and huge population movements both within Owambo and to the south. Although the famine's effects were uneven—southern Angola, for example, was particularly hard-hit, while a successful melon harvest in 1915 slightly eased the situation in Ondonga—all the Ovambo communities experienced intense suffering. Mortality during the famine was high, although South African estimates that 25,000 died out of a population of 156,000 are probably exaggerated; in southern Angola, missionaries put the number of deaths at 50,000.[6] The highest death rates were probably among the most vulnerable—children, old people and women. In these desperate circumstances, many turned to the missions, which began to grow rapidly for the first time in the years following the famine: the number of converts rose from 1,418 in 1904 to 3,205 in 1914.[7]

Of those people—mainly, but not exclusively, men—who made for the Police Zone in the hope of finding work, many died on the way, but thousands of weak and starving would-be labourers reached their destination.[8] In the railway town of Karibib (where there were 5,000 'excess' workers during the famine) mortality was very high, despite the rudimentary medical care provided by the territory's new South African medical officer and his staff.[9] Some of the famine migrants also managed to establish small, permanent settlements in the south, particularly at Luderitz. In the Kavango, too, the rains failed in the same period, and 1915 is remembered as a year of extreme hardship, generating recourse to migrant labour in some numbers for the first time: in 1917/8 about 250 Kwangali and Mbunza men are recorded to have gone on contract.[10]

After the famine, Owambo gradually began to recover and migration dropped to well below the level of the late German period:

between October 1916 and November 1917 only 3,168 labourers went south, and in 1921 the total was only 4,000.[11] Establishing the labour supply had, however, been one of the first objectives of the new regime. In August 1915 Stanley Pritchard, who had been director of the Native Labour Bureau in the Transvaal, was sent to the north by the new military government in Windhoek. Here, he negotiated permission from King Martin for a South African base in Ondonga; in return, the king, whose authority with his subjects had been weakened during the famine, accepted aid (which, however, never amounted to much in practice) from the South Africans. The latter were now able to set up the first colonial administrative framework in Owambo, at a time when, in Pritchard's view, it was 'difficult to imagine so unique an opportunity of establishing a political administration in a country in which, in other circumstances, resistance to authority might...have been anticipated'. A Resident Commissioner (Major Charles Manning, seconded from the South African Native Affairs Department) was installed at Ondangwa, and there was also a Resident at Namakunde, just south of the Angolan border.[12]

If, in the end, the South Africans had achieved the occupation of Ondonga without bloodshed, the opposite was to be true of Oukwanyama. There, King Mandume was initially well disposed to the new administration, partly because of his need for allies after a disastrous encounter with the Portuguese. In April 1915, a large military force from Portugal arrived at Moçamedes and subdued a number of areas in southern Angola, including Ombandja. The main fighting, however, was against Mandume, who, despite fielding up to 30,000 troops,[13] was defeated in four days of heavy fighting in August. A few days later, in the face of the Portuguese advance, Mandume ordered his palace at Ondjiva to be burnt and retreated behind the South West African border.

Mandume now found his authority constantly challenged, in an atmosphere of tension caused by famine, war and increasing lawlessness as the Kwanyama *omalenga* reasserted themselves and began to carry out raids without Mandume's permission. Relations with the South Africans gradually broke down as Mandume was accused of causing trouble in the border region, of crossing unauthorised into Portuguese territory and the Neutral Zone, and finally of refusing to go to Windhoek to meet South African officials (his headmen prevented this on the grounds that a king was not allowed to leave his kingdom). As

Fig. 20. King Mandume and his troops, 1916, probably at Oihole. Pictures of Mandume famously do not capture his face, shaded as it is by his broad-brimmed hat.[14] This image suggests the impressive forces at his command, which allowed the Kwanyama kingdom to resist European rule for so long. It was taken by C.H.L. Hahn, the Native Commissioner in the north. (Photographer: C.H.L. Hahn. Reproduced courtesy of the National Archives of Namibia [no. 11920] and Mrs Jess Hahn.)

tension grew, Mandume routed a small Portuguese force that entered the Neutral Zone on 30 October 1916, killing nineteen. Manning warned that his success was likely 'to unite his people on both sides of the border and create a dangerous position',[15] and the South Africans responded with a military expedition. A large force, equipped with Maxim guns, attacked and defeated Mandume's army in half an hour on 5 February 1917. Mandume lost his life in the battle, and with him went the last hopes of the independence of Oukwanyama.

Although official accounts state that Mandume was shot dead, a very strong and unanimous Kwanyama oral tradition holds that the king committed suicide (as he had previously threatened to do). Photographs of the king's body taken after the battle—which inscribed the South African triumph in the photographic record—suggest that this is indeed a possibility. A monument erected to the memory of the South African soldiers who died in this campaign, in front of the railway station in Windhoek, is also reappropriated as a memorial to Mandume by the Kwanyama belief that the king's head is buried underneath it.[16] Whatever their literal truth, such traditions concerning the dismemberment of the king's body symbolised the dismemberment of Oukwanyama and the final loss of its independence. At the same time, however, through the assertion that Mandume took control of his own death, they held the seeds of an alternative to colonial visions of dominance and held out the possibility of a different process of remembering—of the past, and of the Kwanyama polity and the north in general. As Hayes argues, the idea of the king's suicide corresponded with long-standing royal claims of the monarchy's ability to safeguard the land: 'In a time of disorder and fragmentation, the threat of royal suicide was in a sense a response to the trauma of famines, violence and the dissection of Oukwanyama. It was a means of keeping the world intact'.[17]

After the defeat of Mandume, the Kwanyama kingship was abolished and eventually replaced by a compliant council of headmen. In Ondonga, the South Africans strengthened their alliance with Martin, and they also intervened occasionally in the affairs of the other polities. The new government, for example, brought significant change to Ombalantu, where, in March 1917, it appointed a man called Aipanda, chosen by a meeting of the people as 'spokesman', to rule most of the territory; Aipanda and his successors seem to have had little popular support, probably because of Ombalantu's previous decentralised form of government. In Ongandjera, King Shaanika periodically attempted to involve an unwilling colonial administration in the affairs of government, in order to deflect the blame for unpopular decisions on to the authorities, and thus to strengthen his own position against the *omalenga*.

On the whole, and with the exception of Oukwanyama, South African policy in Owambo at this period was cautious, usually non-interventionist and even tinged with a certain amount of paternalism.[18] With less than ten officials responsible for the area, resources for the administration of this troubled border region were very thinly stretched, and the extraction of labour continued to be the authorities' main concern. The latter was facilitated by the continuation of key German policies by the South Africans, so that Owambo remained formally cut off from wider trading networks, both to the south and to Kaoko. South African policy was also to attempt to please the League of Nations—which would decide ownership of SWA after the war—by trying to ban both slave and arms trading, and to deal with lawlessness and raiding in the region. The effectiveness of the new measures was patchy, given the colonial government's weakness in the north—the arms trade, for example, certainly continued in some form[19]—and, except in Oukwanyama, the famine was certainly a far more important event than the establishment of the new administration. Yet the coming of direct South African rule to the north was significant because it heralded much tighter control in the years to come.

Officials also made expeditions to Kaoko in 1917 and 1919; during the first of these, Manning appointed Vita Tom, whom he perceived as 'civilised', in contrast to the more traditionally oriented Muhona Katiti, as chief of northern Kaokoland. In the Kavango, Kandjimi established good relations with the South Africans partly in order to gain protection from the Portuguese, who began to rebuild their forts in 1916 and were again acting repressively towards the local population, even attempting to prevent them using the river for transport. Besides (unsuccessfully) demanding the arrest of Kandjimi, the Portuguese appointed rivals of the Gciriku and Mbukushu monarchs as chiefs of their respective peoples on the Angolan side of the river. The South Africans, however, like the Germans, preferred indirect rule in the region, apart from a short-lived reoccupation of the fort at Nkurenkuru in 1917; they also exercised some control over Kandjimi through the payment to him of an annual salary.[20]

The Invasion and After: Reconstruction and Repression in the Police Zone

In the Police Zone, the South African invasion of Namibia had an immediate impact on some African groups, particularly the Bondelswarts, whom the German administration had long hoped to remove from their existing lands. In August 1914 they were herded onto trains and taken to the north to work on the planned railway to Owambo. The Rehobothers, for their part, now broke with a thirty-year tradition of loyalty to the Germans, refusing to fight against the South Africans because they feared losing their land should the latter be victorious; they were rescued from defeat at Tsamkhubis by the timely arrival of a South African force. The campaign also resulted in stock losses as large herds (belonging to both black and white farmers) were requisitioned to supply the forces on both sides. Again, both Bondelswarts and Rehobothers were particularly hard-hit: the former were reckoned to have lost 15,227 small and 123 large stock, leaving just 600 and 30 respectively. Overall, however, few of Namibia's black population actually participated in the fighting. General Botha (who together with Smuts led the South African forces) declared the conflict to be 'a white man's war' and restricted the role of Africans largely to that of auxiliaries and labourers.[21]

Overall, in the short term the arrival of the South Africans greatly facilitated African access to land and stock, and the tentative repastoralisation that had begun in the latter years of German rule was tremendously hastened and reinforced. These processes were assisted by the fact that, across the Police Zone, there were still large tracts of land not yet settled by whites: in 1916 farmland surveyed, but not yet occupied by white farmers, covered just over 33.6 million hectares. In addition, the settlers' grip on their land had to be relaxed during the campaign as many German farmers joined the armed forces, later (except for the officers) to be detained at a camp at Aus in southern Namibia; others fled to the towns. Up to 1919, too, the agricultural sector struggled economically, and this meant that many farmers were more or less forced to accept a form of labour tenancy, allowing workers to graze their own stock on their employers' land.[22] The settlers' control over their workers was also weakened by the incoming government's abolition of some forms of punishment, as we shall see below.

The South African invasion thus intensified the movements of people and stock and the rebuilding of herds that had already been evident in the later German period. In the Windhoek area, Africans established new pastoral settlements at Orumbo-Okatana, Aukeigas and Fürstenwalde; in the Karibib district, black pastoralists settled at the government farm of Neubrunn; in the Keetmanshoop district, 139 black stock-owners with stock on 17 farms had acquired grazing licences by March 1918; Hoachanas, near Rehoboth, was occupied by African pastoralists during the invasion; and Africans occupied crown lands and established new communities around water-holes in the Gobabis, Okahandja, Omaruru and Windhoek districts.[23]

On the political level, this movement meant the (re)constitution of leadership that had been broken or banished by the defeat of 1904. In the south, Edward Fredericks returned to lead the Bethany people, while Hendrik Witbooi's sons Isaak and Hendrik arrived back in

Gibeon in 1915, having survived imprisonment and deportation. Further north, Herero chiefs were re-establishing their authority: Traugott Maharero, a brother of Samuel Maharero, gathered his people at Okahandja; Kambazembi's family returned from southern Angola to the Waterberg area; and Daniel Kariko, or Kavezemba, moved back to the Otjohorongo area from Owambo. In 1920 Frederick Maharero proclaimed Hosea Kutako (who had become headman of Herero in Windhoek in 1917) his father Samuel's representative in Namibia. The Damara leader Frans ‖Hoesemab returned to Windhoek and became location foreman in August 1915.

But if the descendants of the old power-bearing lineages were returning, it was within the new constraints of South African authority. In 1918 Isaak Witbooi and some of his councillors were arrested and imprisoned after Witbooi, attempting to reassert his father's judicial authority, appointed his own officials on white farms. Their task was to refer people accused of crimes, mainly adultery, to his court at Gibeon. Witbooi men expressed their support for Isaak by reviving Hendrik Witbooi's practice of wearing white cloths on their hats.[24]

State and settlers were also unnerved by the quasi-military activities of the (mainly) Herero troop movement (*oturupa*), which became newly active in the martial law period. The *oturupa* had probably developed out of Herero involvement in the *Schutztruppe*; its members, divided into districts, wore German military uniform, held German military ranks and engaged in drilling exercises. The *oturupa* organisations also provided mutual support to their members, collecting money and disbursing it to those in need. They posed no immediate military threat to the colonisers, however, but rather operated (despite some social tensions) as a unifying force among Herero in this period of reconstitution, 'a symbolic resurrection of the Herero army in the eclectic style which it had adopted before the risings of 1904 and 1907'.[25]

The years of martial law were thus, in many ways, a time of hope for the African population of the Police Zone, many of whom seem to have genuinely expected that the new colonial masters would return land confiscated by the Germans. As Wolfgang Werner has put it, 'Since the 1860s Herero mythology had invested Britain with the ability to come and liberate them'.[26] The new regime had, however, no intention of returning well-watered land to the Africans of the Police Zone. During the martial law period, while Namibia's status remained uncertain, it turned a blind eye to the takeover of crown and unoccupied lands and allowed the short-term occupation of a number of farms; after 1920, this *de facto* permission to settle was in most cases quickly rescinded.

In the meantime, the new South African regime also introduced a number of reforms.[27] Although these helped to create spaces in which Africans could manoeuvre for land and freedom, they were not motivated by any deep-seated commitment to humanitarianism or Cape liberalism on the part of the South African authorities. Rather, they arose from South Africa's desire to present itself as the liberator of Africans in the territory, in order to be permitted to retain SWA after the war ended; they also reflected a distancing of the state from the ('enemy') settler community. While intending to curb the worst excesses in the existing labour system, the new regime, like the old, nevertheless continued to depend on this system. The South Africans thus abolished flogging as a punishment for workers, and the settlers' 'right of paternal correction', as well as raising the age at which Africans were compelled to carry passes from seven to fourteen, and rescinding the ban on African ownership of livestock (although not land). On the other hand, Masters and Servants legislation was tightened up twice during the martial law period, and there were also new regulations for the control of vagrants and of African labourers on mines and works. The propaganda campaign was brought to a climax with the publication in 1918 of the so-called 'Blue Book', which detailed the excesses of German rule.[28]

Other factors were also responsible for the weakening of colonial control—however limited—in 1915. The conquerors, wary of a potential military threat from the hostile German population, found it prudent not to antagonise the African residents of the territory. Moreover, the resources necessary for efficient repression were not available to the new regime. This was partly because of the territory's economic weakness: between August 1915 and March 1920 the total state revenue of Namibia was £1,236,957, considerably less than the £2,071,157 the German colonial regime collected in the last single year of its operation, 1914–15.[29] Administrative weakness was to be a feature of government in Namibia until the early 1930s and beyond.[30]

If 1915 brought some amelioration in the living conditions of many Africans, the opposite was the case for the German population. It is true that the conquest and occupation of German South West Africa was one of the least traumatic episodes of the First World War. Mortality among the combatants was 266 on the South African side, with 263 wounded, while 34 Germans were killed and 65 wounded.[31] After the conquest, officers and reservists were allowed to remain at home, while regular soldiers were, as we have seen, interned. Nevertheless, many settlers suffered in the ensuing difficult economic conditions, particularly the crisis in the white farming sector. In addition, German civil servants could not be paid because funds from Germany were cut off, assets in local banks were frozen and the value of the Mark dropped. The German settlers also found their civil rights heavily restricted under martial law. Permits were necessary for travel out of the country and between major towns, letters were censored and the spreading of 'false reports' banned. After the war, about half the territory's German population—1,619 military personnel, 1,226 officials, 873 police, 1,223 'undesirables' and their families, and 1,433 volunteers—were deported to Germany.[32]

Such hardships were, however, dwarfed by the worldwide influenza pandemic of 1918, which hit Namibia very hard and quickly caused large numbers of deaths among both the white and black populations. The form of influenza that had arrived in many parts of the Police Zone in October 1918 was highly infectious, and was communicated (from South Africa) at great speed via passengers travelling on the territory's rail system. It was also extremely virulent, quickly causing fatal complications in many cases. Worldwide, the pandemic caused some twenty million deaths, up to a tenth of them in sub-Saharan Africa. In Windhoek, where mortality was highest in Namibia, the disease probably killed about 10 per cent of the population of the location, and the same proportion of the South African garrison; mortality among the German population was between 3 and 4 per cent. Workers on the diamond fields were also particularly hard-hit. The epidemic led to a severe crisis, and the military authorities were hard-pressed to deliver even the most basic medical care. By the end of the year, however, it was over, although it recurred in less severe form in 1919, this time affecting Owambo.[33]

South Africa's New Colony

The South African takeover conditioned the history of SWA for the rest of the twentieth century. South Africa's motives for both capturing and possessing Namibia thus invite further examination. The conquest itself was triggered when Britain, on the first day of the war, requested South Africa to invade Namibia; the willingness of the South African government to comply was partly a result of existing tensions with the German administration in SWA. South Africa, however, was not united in its attitudes to Germany and Britain, and the invasion of Namibia was opposed by Afrikaners sympathetic to the Germans, who rose in rebellion in 1914. This was forcibly suppressed, and the subsequent campaign in Namibia not only served to cut off further German support for disaffected Boers, but was also led by the Boer generals Botha and Smuts and largely carried out by Boer commandos—thus, perhaps, seeking to construct a new unity within the South African state.[34]

There were also longer-term advantages to be gained from the takeover of SWA. The occupation of Namibia had been an objective the Cape Parliament in the 1870s; now, its conquest formed part of a broader and largely unsuccessful expansionist strategy aimed at Portuguese East Africa and ultimately at the British territories of Bechuanaland, Basutoland, Swaziland and the Rhodesias as well as SWA. This policy seems all the more ambitious when it is remembered that at this date South Africa remained 'weak, divided [and] poor'.[35] The Union of South Africa had been created as recently as 1910 through the political unification of two former British colonies, Cape Colony and Natal, and two former Boer republics, the Transvaal (formerly the South African Republic) and the Orange River Colony (formerly the Orange Free State). At the same time South Africa had become a self-governing British dominion. For its government, therefore, the conquest of Namibia meant 'enter[ing] the prestigious adult world of colonial power'.[36] Nevertheless, although South Africa was thus beginning to establish its new status as a nation, the symbols of conquest deployed in Namibia—the Union Jack and a banner proclaiming 'Britannia Still Rules the Waves'—remained those of the British empire.[37] In the long term, too, the territory did not play a major role in public consciousness or imagination in South Africa where, except at times of conflict or moments of political decision, it was to remain a forgotten, marginal and neglected hinterland. Nevertheless, its possession carried some very significant advantages for the South African government, and in the martial law period, the Administrator described it with disarming frankness as 'a very valuable asset for the Union'.[38]

For one thing, SWA opened up the prospect of jobs and land for the growing numbers of impoverished whites in South Africa itself, where landlessness, disaffection and the threat of social unrest were rising, and were to culminate in the white miners' strike ('Rand revolution') of 1922. The authorities in SWA responded with a mass land settlement programme for poor whites, as we shall see below. For another, the territory's mineral resources, particularly diamonds, were an extremely attractive asset; indeed, South African investors, not least Cecil Rhodes, had long had financial interests in the territory. Crown land passed from the German to the South African authorities at the time of the conquest. The diamond mines were taken over by the Custodian of Enemy Property during the occupation, and after the war were bought by Anglo-American (which effectively became a South African company ten years later when it bought up the de Beers diamond empire).[39]

South Africa's authority over Namibia was formally established through the mandate system set up at the end of the First World War by the Allied powers (in which Smuts, a member of the (British) Imperial War Cabinet from 1917, participated). The colonial powers carved up Germany's former territories among themselves according to a tiered system of mandates, designated 'A', 'B' and 'C'. A new Permanent Mandates Commission of the League of Nations was responsible for overall supervision of these arrangements. South West Africa was put under a 'C' mandate—the category assigned to those colonies thought least able to govern themselves—that was granted formally to Britain, to be administered by South Africa. Under Mandate Article (22) of the Covenant of the League of Nations, South West Africa was to be administered as an integral part of South Africa (which might reasonably expect the territory's eventual formal incorporation). The mandatory power was, however, to govern Namibia as a 'sacred trust of civilisation' and to 'promote to the utmost the material and moral well-being and social progress of the inhabitants'.

The mandate, once agreed, took two-and-a-half years to come into force (a fact that explains some inconsistencies in the history books about the date of the end of the period of martial law). Hostilities ended with the armistice of 11 November 1918. South Africa was agreed as the mandatory power for Namibia under the Treaty of Versailles on 7 May 1919; the Treaty itself was not signed until 28 June. In September, South Africa passed the Treaty of Peace and South West Africa Mandate Act (no. 49, 1919), under which the South African Parliament delegated authority over SWA to the Governor-General of South Africa (at that time, Lord Buxton), who in turn delegated these powers to the Administrator of SWA (appointed by the South African government). At the end of 1919 South African law, as applied in the Cape, replaced German law in Namibia, and during 1920 a civil administration was set up. It was not until 17 December 1920, however, that the Council of the League of Nations formally confirmed the mandate and defined its terms. On 1 January 1921, military rule was withdrawn from South West Africa and a new, civilian government instituted.[40] A swift and bitter disillusionment accompanied this transition.

Segregation

The South African administration now moved swiftly to quash the limited control over land and mobility seized by Africans during the period of martial law. The government's objective was to establish a new colonial order, including a smooth-running economy of direct benefit to South Africa. Governance of the Africans in the territory was intimately linked to this aim, as the Administrator's dictum—'the Native question is synonymous with the labour question'[41]—neatly sums up. Among Africans in the Police Zone, however, there were rather different hopes and expectations: land, 'a desire for more liberty' and better conditions for workers, as petitioners told the Governor-General on his visit to Namibia in 1922.[42] Such aspirations meant that the repressive policies implemented from the beginning of the mandate period inevitably set the administration on a collision course with African societies.

If the 'native question' was the 'labour question' it was also, in the Administrator's eyes, 'the land question',[43] and the new regime immediately gave its attention to both issues. For Africans, the land policy implemented in the Police Zone meant the establishment of reserves; since they had lost so much territory during the German period, these measures actually led to a net gain in the extent of the land on which they were officially permitted to settle. The reserves thus created, however, were in general situated on the most marginal land, without adequate water, and became places of extreme poverty.

The new administration's policies in the Police Zone were hammered out by the Native Labour Commission, set up in 1920 to investigate the state of the labour market (including black women's labour and mobility, perceived as hardest to control) and to report on the reserves and (urban) locations. Its remit was soon extended to include the question of reserves (it is thus also known as the Native Reserves Commission) and to 'secure contentment and welfare of the Natives as far as possible, to establish certainty to the whites as to the permanent places of abode of the Natives, and...to tighten up Native Affairs and to prevent vagrancy and idleness'. The Commission's recommendations called for racial segregation as a general principle, and the establishment of (better-controlled) reserves. 'Black islands', that is, small African settlements near to land occupied by whites, were to be avoided.[44]

In Namibia, the creation of reserves was explicitly intended to engineer thoroughgoing racial segregation; these measures stemmed directly from the segregationist policies being energetically implemented in South Africa itself at this time.[45] Yet the administration, like the previous German regime, also aimed to prevent the re-establishment of 'tribal organisation'. Thus, although most reserves had a majority ethnic group and leadership, they were not intended to be ethnically exclusive, and in fact the state prevented Frederick Maharero, still in exile in Botswana, from becoming Herero paramount, in order to try to prevent the emergence across the reserves of a greater degree of pan-Herero identity and organisation.[46] The reserves were also intended to act as pools of labour, to assist with the costs of reproducing that labour (for example, by providing some support for older people) and, together with sweeping legislation introduced at the same time, to control African mobility. In addition, they were to be a means of 'containing, counting and controlling the black pastoral economy'[47]—whose resilience led the authorities and settlers to fear competition with white farming enterprises—particularly through the imposition of grazing fees on owners of livestock in the reserves.

At the same time as the reserves policy was being put together, the administration was hammering out plans for the settlement of 'poor whites' from South Africa. A Land Board was set up; by the end of 1925, 880 farms had been allotted to new settlers (a substantial increase in the number of white-owned farms, which had stood at 1,138 in 1915); and by 1926 the white population had almost doubled from its 1914 level. These farms, like those already in existence, were utterly dependent on black labour, and by 1928, about 60 per cent of Africans in the Police Zone were resident on them.[48]

New settlers were required to show that they possessed only the relatively small sum of £500 (later reduced to £250), which could be made up of livestock and other items such as furniture. This meant that many of the incomers were stock farmers from the Cape who possessed little except their animals, and were often as poor as black stockowners, or poorer. They also engaged in similar farming practices, particularly periodic migration with their herds to better pastures in response to the aridity and unpredictability of Namibia's climate, especially in the south. The Drought Commission of 1924 reported that a 5,000 ha. white-owned farm might, in practice, have access to 15,000 ha.;[49] similarly, black pastoralists were often able to range their stock widely because many farms and reserves—and indeed the borders of the territory itself—were not fenced in the 1920s.[50] To the authorities and other commentators, however, this kind of mobility was a marker of race and difference: both white and black pastoralists were encouraged to abandon their nomadic habits, while at the same time the 'fact' that the black stockowner, 'even when he lives under civilised conditions...from time to time...insists on making a change for no apparent reason' was seen as an indication of the difficulty of 'civilising' Africans.[51] African mobility was, in reality, motivated by many factors including the struggle to survive, the demands of kinship, the search for grazing and (particularly in the case of migration to the urban areas) the desire to escape patriarchal authority, and it remained common for people to move frequently around the country, despite the state's attempts to control movement and to prevent black people from settling in the towns (which were now designated white areas).

Indeed, the significance of the towns as spaces where Africans tried to evade and resist colonial control should not be underestimated. It is true that the urban population remained small—Windhoek was by far the largest town, with a population of 7,859 in 1921, rising to 14,929 in 1946—but so did the population at large: about one-seventh was living in urban areas by 1946. In Namibia, there was a high proportion of African women in the towns by comparison, for example, with many cities in South Africa—because of the events of the German period and, perhaps, also because migration was easier for women in pastoral societies than for those who were tied to the fields. The urban areas remained closely linked to the countryside through economic, kinship, leadership and cultural ties, and many urban residents (particularly Otjiherero-speakers) still considered their real homes to be on the land. Movement out of the towns during this period was both voluntary, as Africans rebuilt their herds (acquiring stock both on the reserves and on white farms), and forced, as the reserves policy was implemented. Although proletarianisation was, thus, one factor in the increase of the urban population, it was, for some, at least partially reversed by what has been called the repastoralisation of the 1910s and 1920s. Nor was urban growth particularly marked around the two largest centres of industry, Luderitz and Tsumeb, where the work-force consisted of male migrant labourers who continued to return to the north at the end of their contracts. There were, thus, complex processes of both urbanisation and ruralisation in Namibia that differed significantly from trajectories in South Africa, where the largest conurbations grew up in the mining areas of the Rand.[52]

The Means of Control?

To implement its segregatory policies, the administration introduced a body of new law mostly derived directly from legislation passed in South Africa at the same period or slightly earlier. Proclamation 3 of 1917 dealt with labour on the mines, and the Masters and Servants Proclamation (34/1920) with the negotiation of contracts for Police Zone workers, who could be punished for 'desertion'—that is, leaving their jobs. The Vagrancy Proclamation (25/1920) allowed the arrest and distribution to employers of those found 'wandering' outside the reserves 'without visible means of support'; there was also legislation forcing African men in the Police Zone to take up employment[53] unless they owned ten cattle or fifty small stock. It has been argued that the vagrancy laws were specifically targeted at San communities, who continued through the 1920s and 1930s to be hunted down, and in many cases shot, by police patrols; those caught were imprisoned and forced to labour.[54] 1922 saw the introduction of the Native Administration Proclamation, which established the reserves and made provision for passes for African men—women were not required to carry passes, although many believed that they were, a fact of which the state took full advantage.[55] The legal basis for the adminis-tration of the reserves rested on the Native Reserves Regulations of 1924 and the Native Administration Proclamation of 1928, which also made the Administrator 'supreme chief', with the power to appoint chiefs and headmen. Control of Africans in urban areas was imposed through the Natives (Urban Areas) Proclamation of 1924 and the introduction of a night-time curfew for Africans in white areas of the towns (Proclamation 33/1922). Various forms of taxation were introduced in both the urban and rural areas of the Police Zone (while the white population of the territory paid no personal tax at this period). In the reserves, grazing fees were paid into reserve trust funds, in theory to pay for improvements to infrastructure and agriculture; in practice, however, the administration often blocked such expenditure, with the result that large credit balances built up, totalling about £80,000 by the late 1940s.[56]

The fact that the territory was a League of Nations mandate seems to have had little substantial impact on policy. There was a *de facto* ban on explicit racial discrimination in individual laws, but this did little to restrain the imposition of segregation in practice. For example, although Africans were not explicitly prevented from owning land, residential segregation was effectively established through the urban areas and reserves legislation. Similarly, a report by Lord Hailey found in 1946 that a system of informal racial discrimination in employment pertained, despite the lack of a legal colour bar.[57] Moreover, legislation applying to 'natives' as a class, for instance the Natives Administration Proclamation, was permitted.

If the legal framework of state control was put firmly in place during the 1920, the practical means of enforcing it were not. Policing of the vast land area was minimal: in 1923 the police numbered only 503 (278 whites and 225 Africans), and even by 1939 this total had only reached 520 (359 whites and 161 Africans). Unlike in South Africa, 'native administration' was not, except in the north, a recognised career. The Secretary for South West Africa (the second in command below the Administrator) doubled up as Chief Native Commissioner, and across the Police Zone district magistrates, on tours of duty from South Africa, also functioned as local native commissioners. The Native Affairs Department operated with very few staff, and expenditure in this area was also minimal.

In these circumstances, Africans were frequently able to circumvent or ignore the plethora of regulations purporting to dominate their lives. Indeed, it has been argued that the intent of some of the new legislation was more to reassure white settlers of their own dominance than to control labourers in significant numbers. The government's weakness was exacerbated when SWA was hit by drought and recession in the early 1920s; mining and agricultural exports, the state's main source of revenue, were particularly hard-hit. The decision to continue with the land settlement programme despite these conditions was, as the SWA Commission of 1935 later admitted, economically disastrous. The state subsidised the new white farmers heavily by raising loans from South Africa, so that by 1928/9 public debt stood at £406,800. To compound matters, the administration also realigned Namibia's economy to the benefit of South Africa. The territory's railway had been linked with that of its southern neighbour via a new line through Upington early in the martial law period, and SWA officially became part of the South African Customs Union in 1921. Both customs dues and the management of railway tariffs tended to favour South African economic interests over those of SWA.[58]

The Struggles of the Early 1920s

In 1921 the Native Reserves Commission recommended that the existing German reserves should be confirmed. Otjohorongo and Aukeigas, in the east and the Windhoek district respectively, had been founded in the martial law period, while in 1923 reserves were established at Neuhof and Tses in the south (the latter was, in fact, land bought from the Berseba community), Otjimbingwe in the centre, and Waterberg East, Otjituo, Aminuis and Epukiro in the north-eastern part of the Police Zone. Others were later added, including Gibeon and Warmbad in the south, Eastern (between Otjituo and Epukiro) and Ovitoto.

The implementation of the reserves policy generated a degree of overt resistance that would not recur until the late 1950s, and the state's response was frequently violent. It is true that the creation of the reserves was partly a response to African leaders' expectations of the return of land, and that in some cases Africans were not, initially at least, put at a disadvantage. For example, in 1925 black stockowners were removed from a government-owned farm at Neubrunn to Otjimbingwe, 'an alternative that was acceptable to them' because the land there was known to be fertile.[59] Overall, however, the reserves were created on tracts of poorly watered land that were too small to support their populations, and although not all their occupants were thrown into immediate crisis, the long-term consequences of this policy were severe, as 'the inhabitants were ground into poverty'.[60]

The earliest to be severely affected were the Bondelswarts, who had lost large numbers of stock in 1915, at the time of the invasion, and were also being pressurised by an influx of settlers into the Warmbad district. In 1921 they were faced with new regulations forcing younger men into exploitative labour contracts, and the imposition of a heavy tax on the ownership of dogs, which they used for hunting; these measures, as well as the effects of drought and recession, reduced them to desperate poverty. They were radicalised by the fact that the South Africans had not allowed their leader, Jacobus Christian, to resume formal authority after returning from exile in 1919, and by the arrival of Abraham Morris, Jakob Morenga's lieutenant, in May 1922. Within the reserve, Adam Pienaar and other leaders also vocalised the general discontent. The result was that, in 1922, the Bondelswarts rose in arms against the South African administration.

Fearing a more general uprising, the government panicked, and the Administrator, Gysbert Hofmeyr, personally led a military force against the rebels. On 29 May two aeroplanes from Pretoria bombed Guru-chas, where the Bondelswarts had taken refuge. By 7 June, the rebel-lion had been crushed. The dead—men, women and children—totalled about 100 out of a population of 1,000 (of whom about 200 were armed). Abraham Morris and Adam Pienaar were killed and Jacobus Christian taken prisoner (to be released and recognised as headman in 1924), and once again the Bondelswarts' livestock was confiscated. Not only the Permanent Mandates Commission of the League of Nations, but even the settler press in Namibia, were shocked by the brutality of the state's response.[61]

The defeat of the Bondelswarts set the pattern for the first half of the 1920s, as the South African regime proceeded to ride roughshod over African resistance to removal. It is true that there were still instances in which the state could be forced into concessions, as when the Wit-boois managed to resist being removed to the Tses reserve in 1923.[62] But these occasions were few. In the east, the Herero and Mbanderu leaders Hosea Kutako and Nikanor Hoveka had initially been pre-pared to support a move to new reserves at Aminuis and Epukiro from better-watered but less secure land in central Namibia. Yet their hopes were disappointed as the harsh economic realities of these eastern, semi-desert areas became clear: in 1924, they discovered that the area offered by the government was not at Epukiro, but thirty miles *beyond* it, on land described by Kutako as 'a desert where no human being ever lived before'.[63] Kutako now opposed the removal, but bombing in 1925 in the hills around Orumbo in the Windhoek district, where Otjiherero-speakers were living, effectively forced the move.[64]

Namibia's towns were also a significant arena of unrest in this period. In Windhoek, resistance to the collection of taxes from loca-

Fig. 21. Hosea Kutako, long-lived Herero leader and one of the founders of the post-war nationalist movement in Namibia. This portrait was taken by Anneliese Scherz in 1956 in Windhoek, when Kutako was aged about eighty-six.[65] (Photographer: Anneliese Scherz. Reproduced courtesy of Basler Afrika Bibliographien.)

tion residents peaked in 1924 with a widespread tax boycott. There was also an attempt to impose passes on black adults (excluding married women) in the locations. The protests were eventually gradually quelled through the application of the Natives (Urban Areas) Proclamation to the town in 1925. In the rural areas, too, there was much low-level resistance both to the state and to white settlers, for example through acts of evasion or non-compliance by farmworkers, or attacks carried out by persecuted San communities.[66]

Direct resistance to the state peaked with the Rehoboth rebellion of 1923–25. Initially, the Baster community of the Rehoboth Gebiet had been given the impression by the South African authorities that the rather privileged position they had held under the Germans would be maintained. In the early years of South African rule, the Gebiet became home to large numbers of black pastoralists, who rented land from Basters: by 1925 the population consisted of 3,500 Basters, 2,500 black people (many, but not all, Herero) and about thirty whites. Such 'squatting' was made illegal by Proclamation 11 of 1922, but this legislation could not be implemented in Rehoboth until after the suppression of the rebellion.

In 1923, the state tried to impose a new 'Baster Agreement' on the Rehoboth Gebiet. This was rejected by a majority of the Rehoboth burghers, who now set up their own institutions of government. Although this 'rebel' faction drew many of its members from the reserve's elite, it also elicited widespread support among 'squatters', whose interests were threatened by the state's intention to remove them to other reserves. The administration eventually forced a showdown by demanding compliance with new cattle branding regulations by 1 March 1925. Unrest resulted, and on 5 April Rehoboth was surrounded by South African forces and overflown by three South African Air Force planes. The armed forces then moved in, arresting 632 people (recorded as 289 Basters, 218 Herero, 75 Nama and 50 Damara).[67]

The suppression of Rehoboth effectively signalled the end of the intense rural and urban protest of the first half of the 1920s. This unrest had been partly sustained, not by an explicitly nationalist agenda—that was to come later—but by a variety of ideologies and new organisations, some of which flared brightly and briefly, while others, with deeper roots, attained much wider influence. The South African Industrial and Commercial Workers' Union (ICU)—mainly representing workers from South and West Africa and the Caribbean—established a branch at Luderitz in 1920; the South West African National Congress was founded by S.M. Bennett Ncwana in Luderitz in 1922; and the African People's Organisation and African National Bond, both representing Cape Coloureds, were established in Windhoek in 1923 and 1925 respectively. The influence of all these organisations was limited by the fact that they represented a narrow range of interests and were subjected to 'divide and rule' policies by the administration. The Universal Negro Improvement Association (UNIA), by contrast, was much more effective: its first branch was founded in Luderitz in 1921, but by January 1922 it had a base in Windhoek and its executive included Hosea Kutako, Aaron Mungunda (his brother) and other Herero leaders, as well as the two most prominent Damara leaders in the capital, Frans ‖Hoesemab and Alpheus Harasemab.

The UNIA had been founded by Marcus Garvey in Jamaica in 1914, and, with its demands for African rights and its anti-colonial and pan-Africanist ideology, gained a mass following in the US from 1916. In Namibia, the organisation's call that '…black men [should] pull together and …unite as one and then they will get their liberty as this is their land'[68] spread quickly in the towns and countryside, and indeed as far north as the kingdom of Uukwambi. Many (to the frustration of the movement's leaders) interpreted its message as a kind of millenarian promise that the Americans would come to liberate them. The movement had significant support among all ethnic groups in central Namibia. It helped to contribute to a climate of tension and fear among settlers and the authorities, and this formed the backdrop for the two major uprisings of the period and many smaller incidents of unrest. When, however, the Americans failed to arrive, support for the UNIA quickly dissipated from its peak in 1923.[69]

In the ferment of ideas and action in Namibia in the early 1920s, new ideologies meshed with older institutions and practices. The prominence of Otjiherero-speakers in the UNIA suggests that the new Herero traditionalist movement and the *oturupa* (the Herero troop movements) may have been influenced by Garveyist ideas. From about 1920 Otjiherero-speakers began to reject the mission churches for subverting their older social structures and cultural norms, and to revive practices such as the lighting of the holy fire (*okuruuo*), the centre of Herero ritual life, and polygyny and teeth filing.[70] This movement was greatly accelerated by the ceremonial burial of Samuel Maharero at Okahandja in 1923 (after his death earlier that year in Botswana), which helped to create a new sense of Herero identity. At the same time, the *oturupa* movement was becoming increasingly active. Until the late 1930s it acted partly as a voice for younger, disaffected and poorer men (and probably also some women), and was frequently the target of Kutako's criticism. Troop organisations also existed among Damara and Ovambo. Given the level of repression during this period, however, these movements perhaps inevitably retreated from direct protest, cultivating instead an 'alternative vision' of a space beyond colonial authority in which (a version of) traditional cultural practices could be pursued, even if political power was no longer a reality.[71]

The popular protests of the early 1920s arose directly from the government's failure to fulfil the expectations aroused—often deliberately—during the period of martial law. It was above all the state's military superiority that allowed it to crush this resistance, thus pre-serving the huge racial inequalities in land, wealth and rights that had been established during the German period. In particular, the use of the aeroplane both to destroy and to threaten destruction 'changed the whole complexion of guerrilla warfare in the territory and provided a powerful symbol of colonial supremacy with which to intimidate the colonised'.[72] Paradoxically, however, the state's reach on a day-to-day level was far more circumscribed than at times of crisis. It was only with the coming of depression and drought at the end of the 1920s that this began to change.

The Depression and the Famine of the Dams

The year 1928/9 heralded the beginning of the driest period of the inter-war years: in the next five years rainfall over the whole territory was 60 per cent below average. At about the same time, the mines first cut production, and then closed down, as the effects of the worldwide depression hit Namibia. Diamond sales dropped from over £2 million per annum before the slump to just £91,000 by 1933. The administration's annual revenue fell disastrously, resulting in a large deficit and heavy cuts in expenditure.[73]

The human cost of drought and depression was high. In the Police Zone, black stockowners were forced off white farms into reserves, and large numbers of the newly destitute, both white and black, made for Windhoek and other urban centres. White farmers and workers received state help, and in the capital, the Avis Dam was built by white workers as a relief project. Assistance for black stockowners was on a much smaller scale, and there was little in the way of relief works for the numerous African unemployed, although in Windhoek about a hundred labourers were employed to reorganise the layout of the location in 1932–33.[74]

In Owambo, however, the state responded much more actively to the famine and economic recession, seizing the chance for decisive intervention.[75] Despite the defeat of Mandume in 1917, the power of the administration in the north remained very limited—although it was already undermining the area's independence through its isolationist policies, which resulted in the gradual closing of the border with Angola, the policing of internal boundaries, and exclusion from SWA's markets. In addition, although the people of the north retained most of their land (at least on the South West African side of the border), in 1926 the South Africans ceded the disputed 'Neutral Zone' along the Angola–Namibia border to Portugal. The resulting new boundary became known as *onhaululi*, 'the dividing road', and in the 1990s, according to the historian Petrus Ndongo, was still 'hated by many'.[76] Large numbers of Kwanyama residents of the Neutral Zone, many of whom had already fled from the harsher tax and labour regime in Angola, now moved southwards; in the 1930s many of them went on to create settlements on previously uncultivated 'wilderness' land in eastern Oukwanyama.[77]

Nevertheless, in the 1920s, the experience of colonialism remained shallow in Owambo. Until the late 1920s no attempt was made to disarm its population, and no taxation was imposed; the western areas especially had little direct contact with Europeans. The machinery of government also remained minimal. C.H.L. ('Cocky') Hahn, Native Commissioner between 1920 and 1947, laid the foundations of a system of indirect rule by governing through nominally compliant councillors, headmen or kings in each of the Ovambo polities.[78] Ovambo societies also retained some control over their engagement with the migrant labour system, as the continued labour shortages in the mines of SWA indicate. The number of workers migrating from the north into the Police Zone—on average, about 6,000 per year between 1926 and 1930[79]—remained consistently below the levels of the late German period. The fact that most—though not all—returned to the north at the end of their contracts was a product of social cohesion in the north as well as colonial regulations. In the 1920s, migrant labour was still largely confined to young men, who did not expect to go on contract after getting married. Recruits sought choice in their place of employment and contested poor working conditions, for example by boycotting the diamond mines in the early 1920s because of high death rates among workers.

In response to their difficulties in securing labour, employers and the state sought to provide incentives to encourage migration—a store was set up in Ondangwa in 1925 in order to foster the growth of a cash economy—and to regulate and discipline contract workers, for example subjecting them to degrading physical examinations and categorising them according to their apparent health status, and forcing them to carry passes. In 1924, the northern boundary of the Police Zone was formally brought into operation as a veterinary border, and the following year was mapped, for the first time, as a red line. This meant that the administration now took steps to staff the border posts, so that the movement of workers between Owambo and the Police Zone became subject to much greater surveillance and control. The recruitment process was also reorganised in 1925, when the Southern Labour Organisation (SLO) and the Northern Labour Organisation (NLO) were formed. The South African-owned diamond mines, recruiting through the SLO, had the first choice of labourers from Owambo, while the NLO obtained workers for the German-owned copper mine at Tsumeb and white farms, operating at first mainly in the sparsely populated Kavango, and from 1929 in Caprivi.[80]

Nevertheless, in the 1920s the colonial government was far less interested in the other northern regions than in Owambo, although it did intervene directly on a number of occasions. In 1923 the northern part of Kaoko was divided into three reserves for (the actually fluid categories of) Herero, Tjimba and Himba; in southern Kaoko there were also Herero, Nama and Damara communities. The state was not seriously interested in the area as a source of migrant labour, because of its very sparse population (some recruitment took place there between 1950 and 1954, but was not considered a success). The administration's main aim was rather to isolate Kaoko, partly to protect white settlers in the Police Zone from competition with skilled black pastoralists. This policy could not be enforced very effectively in the 1920s—Africans were able to evade border controls, and Garveyite ideology also penetrated the region at this time—but its introduction nevertheless indicated the government's intentions for these pastoral societies, whose economy and ultimately survival depended on their mobility. In Kavango, the administration vetoed the Shambyu council of elders' choice of a new king in 1924, and installed its own candidate. Overall, relations between the Kavango rulers and the South African authorities seem to have been characterised by cooperation; even though this alliance was forced on the monarchs, it nevertheless helped to strengthen their influence in their own domains. By contrast, in the 1920s the SWA administration showed no interest in Caprivi, which was governed from the Bechuanaland Protectorate between 1922 and 1929; it was split into eastern and western regions and administered by the district commissioners of Kasane and Maun respectively. Eastern Caprivi especially was not as isolated as Namibia's other northern regions at this date, and trade in particular flourished.[81]

Hence it was the large potential workforce in Owambo that formed the focus of the government's interest in the north, and when the rains failed in eastern Owambo in 1928, the administration perceived an opportunity to shift the balance of power further to its own advantage. As the mines laid workers off, road-building and other projects for male Ovambo labourers were set up in the Police Zone. In Owambo itself, as the population exhausted its usual strategies for coping with famine, the administration established food-for-work projects on which mainly women and children laboured, building dams first in Ondonga (beginning in August 1929) and, as the famine progressed, in other areas (although little was done in the west, where hunger came later but ultimately with even more suffering). Notably, King Martin of Ondonga also took effective action to feed his people, buying grain at his own expense.

These policies thus forced large numbers of able-bodied men into contract work in the Police Zone—partly through preventing wives from working on the dams if their husbands remained in the north. In the late 1920s, too, health provision for migrant workers was improved, as was transport to and from Owambo. Through such measures, the administration clearly hoped to increase the labour supply from the north for such time as it would be needed again. Meanwhile, for most of the women, this was the first direct contact with the colonial state, which was now attempting to position them as 'a contained, agriculturally self-supporting rural populace, dominated by traditional leaders and male lineage elders'.[82] Such a conservative view of Ovambo society and 'traditions' acted directly to disempower women and to limit their room for manoeuvre, as we shall see below. Although few people died in this famine, memories of it remained bitter: "'People were told they would be provided with food, but in fact they were made to work'".[83] At this period 'Ovamboland' was also officially declared a reserve, and the state formally introduced a head tax on Ovambo men (suspended until after the depression). Since it could be paid in grain as well as cash, this measure also affected women directly, since it was they who cultivated and owned the crops.[84]

Although the historiography of the north-eastern areas is very thin for this period, the famine was probably general there too: hunger is certainly recorded among the Gciriku in the Kavango.[85] In Kaoko, famine struck in 1928 and became known as *katurambanda*, the pounding (for eating) of leather clothes. Conditions were particularly desperate there both because the administration made very little relief provision and because the isolation of Kaoko imposed by the colonial authorities, if not yet fully effective, nevertheless made trading for food very difficult and increased pressure on grazing and water. In 1929–31, the situation was compounded when about 1,200 people were removed from the south to the centre of Kaoko, 'one of the major forced removals in Namibia's colonial history'.[86]

Tightening Controls: The 1930s

The state's intention to impose its authority more effectively on Owambo became clear in stark terms as the depression came to an end. Iipumbu, king of Uukwambi, had defied Hahn with impunity in the early 1920s, refusing to pay a large fine. He was also coming into conflict with local missionaries, as they made increasing numbers of converts in his kingdom, and early in 1932 he conducted an armed, although bloodless, siege of the Finnish mission station in order to retrieve one of his subjects, Nekulu ya Shivute, who had fled there, probably in order to escape Iipumbu's sexual advances. The administration, although often at odds with the missionaries, took this opportunity to impose a fine on Iipumbu. When the king refused to pay, the South Africans sent a small armed force against him, and completely destroyed his palace by aerial bombing. Although bloodshed had been avoided, this intimidation was enough to force the king to flee to the Kavango; the administration proclaimed that 'no trouble with the natives [in Ovamboland] need be anticipated for very many years to come, if ever'—a statement that must rank as one of the least accurate political prophecies in the history of Africa. Despite the strong element of anti-colonial resistance in Iipumbu's actions, however, he was a complex figure who responded to the increasing tensions of the colonial era by imposing his authority violently on certain of his subjects, including a number of women whom he is said to have raped, and men accused of homosexual relations, whom he had shot; discontented Kwambi had fled the kingdom before his deposition. Divisions within Uukwambi itself were thus important in generating the crisis that gave the colonial authorities the opportunity to intervene.[87]

After the defeat of Iipumbu, the administration tightened its hold over the Ovambo kingdoms. Councils of headmen—Hahn's preferred choice—had now been imposed on Uukwambi as well as Oukwanyama. In Ondonga, Uukwaluudhi and Ongandjera, where the rulers who had derived their legitimacy from the time before colonialism were ageing, Hahn was increasingly able to exert his authority by promoting the influence and ensuring the succession of younger men deemed more 'progressive'. He was also able to divest the Ovambo polities of most of their weapons, so that disarmament was more or less general by 1937. The newer monarchs, like Sheya and Uushona in Ongandjera, are remembered in terms very similar to the narratives of 'bad kings' of precolonial times: Sheya, for example, is said to have allowed his horses to feed in poor people's fields. After the Second World War, the unpopularity of this new generation of rulers and their cooperation with the administration would lead to a crisis of legitimacy for traditional authority, as their subjects turned instead to the churches and to the new nationalist movements.[88] By contrast, King Mwaala of Uukwaluudhi, who reigned between 1909 and 1959, is essentially remembered as an independent king who corrected the abuses of the past, and at the end of his life came into conflict with the administration; he is seen, according to Shigwedha, as 'the model of a good Omukwaniilwa'.[89]

In Kaoko, too, this period saw a greater level of colonial intervention. In 1935, after a court case concerning murder and elephant-killing, the administration imprisoned Vita Tom, the Himba leader, and his ally Thomas Mutate. The authorities thus ended their decade-long alliance with these men, which had allowed the latter to impose their often violent rule on the region. Hahn replaced Tom with a 'tribal council' of seven Herero members, which later expanded into the Kaokoland Tribal Council. The isolation of the region was also further enforced when, in 1939–40, six police posts were established on the Kunene to prevent trade into Angola.[90]

In the Kavango, a direct colonial presence was instituted in 1936 with the founding of Rundu as the Native Commissioner's residence. The Caprivi was transferred to the control of Windhoek, apparently at the behest of the Permanent Mandates Commission, in 1929. Police were stationed in the eastern and western sides, and there was some intervention, including the construction of a road from the Kwando River to Katima Mulilo and Schuckmannsburg in 1930; Chikamatondo and Lefani Mamili (Simaata Mamili's successor) also received allowances from the state. In 1930 the administration introduced the taxation of adult men, and the following year registration of firearms was carried out. Nevertheless, the Caprivi remained 'an appendix of or footnote to South West Africa' during this period. In 1939 the Caprivi Strip was placed under the direct control of South Africa, ostensibly because of the difficulties of administering it from Windhoek but possibly, as Kangumu argues, because the South Africans already realised its potential strategic importance.[91]

These changes were accompanied by major social transformations, caused in large part by the experiences of migrant labourers and, crucially, the spread of Christianity. In Owambo, from about 1920, several hundred people (and sometimes more) were becoming Lutherans every year; it has been calculated that, by 1951, there were 71,000 Christians (Lutheran, Catholic and Anglican) out of a total population of 198,000. The majority of converts were to be found among the poorer commoners, to whom in many cases Christianity gave new freedoms or protection. Members of the elite were also gradually beginning to turn to the new religion in some of the polities, although not in all: Uukwaluudhi, for example, did not have a Christian king until 1961.[92]

The missionaries opposed many aspects of Ovambo culture—including dress, ritual and bridewealth—on ideological grounds. In the 1930s female initiation, and bridewealth in particular, became arenas of fierce struggle, as the heads of the matriclans and the Ovambo kings saw the missions increasingly undermine their power. However, Hahn and the administration in general gave little support to the missions in these conflicts. The state's policy was to prevent 'detribalisation' and to ensure that Owambo continued to operate as a base for the reproduction of migrant labour. In order to achieve this, they aimed for a socially stable population, anchored in particular by the productive and reproductive roles of women—who had been banned from migrating out of Owambo as early as 1918.[93] In the 1930s, officials also sought these goals through recording and promoting traditions that they saw as fixed and timeless. Hahn was particularly active in this respect, for example attending and photographing female initiation ceremonies—a sharp contrast to the approach of the missionaries. In truth, the state's understanding of 'tradition' was a newly rigidified version of what had in the past been a set of rather flexible governmental and cultural rules and precepts, and this served in practical ways to objectify and disempower women. The administration's very conservative view of their position in Ovambo society seems, for example, to have led directly to a loss of land rights for women; the mission campaigns against polygyny also led to the marginalisation of divorced wives.[94]

The changes in the north occurred in the context of general economic recovery. In November 1933 the drought broke, with widespread flooding, and eleven years of reasonable rainfall followed (broken only in 1940–41). By 1936 the land settlement programme had been restarted, the *veld* had been regenerated, and both the farming and mining sectors had recovered. Although there was once again a shortage of labour in the Police Zone, the number of contract workers recruited from the northern areas grew to significantly higher levels than before the depression, so that totals ranged from 8,458 to 9,705 in each of the years from 1937 to 1940. In 1935, Proclamation 29 raised the minimum length of contracts to eighteen months. Although workers were now losing much of the leverage they had previously had over the system, they were still able successfully to contest it on occasion: in 1938 Consolidated Diamond Mining (CDM) had to stop recruiting in Owambo because of protests about new X-ray machines at Oranjemund.[95]

The most important economic shift was the increasing success of white-owned agriculture. Mining was *not* the mainstay of the economy at this period: although it formed 58 per cent of GDP in 1921, it failed to reach this level again until after the Second World War. The rise of the farming sector was largely due to the growth in karakul farming at this period. Farmers were able to sell the highly prized pelts of day-old lambs for cash, and were thus able to overcome liquidity crises and to compete with heavy industry for labour (although they only paid about a third of the amount of mine wages): from 1935, more migrant workers went to farms than to mines. The farming sector's leverage was to increase still further in the Second World War, when the mines closed while farming boomed because of demand for food in South Africa and overseas. This led in 1943 to the merging of the NLO and the SLO into one organisation, the South West Africa Native Labour Association (SWANLA), which would now control all contract workers employed in the Police Zone.[96]

In the 1930s, white farming was also aided by new state support, partly in the form of new marketing boards for agricultural products, as well as increased controls on the reserves in order to prevent competition from black farmers. The latter found their access to markets within the Police Zone heavily restricted, so that traders buying stock from Africans were generally able to fix prices at well below the market rate. This, together with increasing pressure on a fragile ecology, led in general to greater impoverishment in the reserves, although in some places black pastoralists still had room for manoeuvre—for example in the Otjimbingwe reserve, where the fertility of the river-bed resulted in reasonable food security. Even here, however, cash was needed to pay government taxes and fees, which made migrant labour a necessity and increasingly undermined the local economy.[97]

At a political level, there were varied responses to these pressures. In the eastern reserves, Herero leaders including Hosea Kutako were to some extent prepared to compromise with the administration, as well as promoting the interests of the elite, for example by calling for a poll tax to replace grazing fees. Dissension within the reserves was directed at wealthier stockowners as well as the government, and was expressed partly through the *otjiserandu*. Yet Kutako also continued to mount verbal challenges to the administration, for example making an 'articulate and searing condemnation of South African rule in Namibia' to the South West Africa Commission of 1935, in which he compared the government to the German regime and Africans to 'prisoners'. By contrast, headmen were deposed by the administration in 1938 in both Soromas (Joseph Frederick) and Berseba (Diedrich Goliath); the latter event is particularly revealing of how complex the interplay of local politics with the state could become. Goliath, who became *kaptein* in 1933, gained considerable popular support by opposing grazing fees, administering justice and issuing passes himself, and refusing to call the location superintendent 'Sir'. Yet he was embroiled in struggles not only against the state, but also against the rival Izaaks family, and his deportation to Hoachanas in 1938 was hastened by loss of support on the reserve board.[98]

The authorities also tightened their control of the towns in the 1930s, extending the 1924 Natives (Urban Areas) Proclamation and, in 1932, imposing further controls on the entry of black women into urban areas. In Windhoek, the municipality now began (although still on a fairly small scale) to remove 'undesirables' to the reserves, and there were also probably forced removals of locations within a number of towns.[99] African women were a particular focus of urban policies. They were, for example, the target of periodic crackdowns on illegal beer-brewing, as well as of the state's attempt in 1939 to carry out compulsory examinations for venereal disease; these measures were fiercely resisted, with some, limited, success. The authorities' focus on black women is partly explained by the fact that, as in the north—and as, indeed, in South Africa, where much more rapid urbanisation meant that these debates carried greater intensity—settlers and officials attributed to them the potential to disrupt the social order and to intensify 'detribalisation' and 'moral degeneration'.[100]

The resulting attempts to fix women in 'traditional' roles drew on official and settler understandings of 'the native'. In other ways, too, 'knowledge' of Africans was elaborated at this period and also became an important element in defining and constructing colonial policy. Ethnographic stereotyping already had a long history in Namibia. In the nineteenth century, commentators had begun to assign Africans to primordial and unchanging 'tribes'—which were far more the product of European imagination than an accurate reflection of a fluid and changing history—and missionaries had divided their congregations on ethnic lines. As we saw in Chapter 6, such racial stereotyping had been influential in creating the conditions for genocide.[101] The inter-war period saw the continued development of such ideas through a number of new studies (with varying degrees of academic respectability). Two of these were particularly important in influencing popular white (and to some extent black) consciousness: *The Native Tribes of South West Africa* (1928), by the missionary, ethnographer and historian Heinrich Vedder,[102] the Medical Officer to the administration, Louis Fourie and the Native Commissioner of Ovamboland, Hahn;[103] and *Das Alte Südwestafrika* (1934), also by Vedder. The former consisted of discrete ethnographies of Namibia's 'tribes'—defined as the Ovambo, Herero, Nama, Damara and Bushmen—while the latter described the precolonial history of Namibia as a long series of conflicts, from which only German rule could provide liberation.[104]

The creation of this ethnographic knowledge helped to sustain white rule by reinforcing, in the context of contemporary Social Darwinist thought, the idea of Africans' (supposed) innate inferiority to whites. Damara and San came off particularly badly in this regard. Vedder declared that the former belonged on the lowest rung of the evolutionary ladder, while the latter were usually constructed as 'vermin' or dangerous savages, who would somehow 'disappear'; at the same time a more positive but very romanticised narrative of the San was beginning to emerge, for example through filming carried out by the 1925 Denver expedition to the Kalahari. Both versions ignored the fact that San were, at this time, being actively hunted down by police and settlers.[105]

On the ground, however, there was still much flexibility in ethnic identification. It is true that the ethnic identities that developed in Namibia were not purely colonial constructions: they generally developed out of older political configurations, and in some cases there was a significant degree of self-ascription to ethnic categories, as seen, for example, in the emergence of Herero identity from the 1870s. Nevertheless, in many places ethnic boundaries remained both blurred and porous in the inter-war period, and in some cases changed considerably; Garveyite ideology crossed ethnic lines; and there was also considerable willingness to co-operate across perceived ethnic lines in the different reserves. Towards the end of the 1930s, however, the state began, as we shall see in the next chapter, to (re)turn to the policy of governing Africans on the basis of 'tribe', as a way of countering perceived social disintegration (which seemed a relatively safe option now that the old African political units had been undermined). These policies would lead both to the increased fixing of ethnic categories and to greater conflict between different groups.[106]

White Politics, Nazism and the Second World War

While the state spent a good deal of energy on promoting African quiescence in the period to 1948, it could not take the consent of whites to its policies for granted. For one thing, preserving the white community *as white* still required state action. Farms awarded under the land settlement programme could be confiscated if the occupant cohabited with an African, and in 1934 the Immorality Proclamation made 'illicit carnal intercourse' between black and white illegal. While the definition of whiteness may have blurred at the edges, the many people of mixed heritage were uniformly excluded from white social, political and economic arenas.[107]

The deep ethnic divisions among the settler population also strongly conditioned government policies. Relations between Germans and the incoming South Africans after the First World War were characterised by bitter disputes, focusing particularly on the question of whether German-speakers should be entitled to government-funded education in German. The London Agreement of 1923, however, led to an accommodation between the two communities. Copies of the 'Blue

Book' (the anti-German report published during the martial law period)[108] were shredded, and automatic naturalisation was offered to German citizens.[109] The South West Africa Constitution Act of 1925 set up a limited form of representative government, consisting of an eighteen-member Legislative Assembly, two-thirds of whose members were elected by white men (until 1939, when white women also got the vote), and the remainder appointed by the Administrator. This system allowed the latter to maintain an equal balance between the South African and German 'sections', regardless of the outcome of the elections. The Legislative Assembly was excluded from a number of major policy areas, however, and its ordinances were subject to the Administrator's consent. The latter, who governed through two influential smaller bodies, the Executive Committee and the Advisory Council, remained the effective power in the territory (subject to the authority of the Governor-General in Cape Town).[110]

Although General Smuts (Prime Minister of South Africa 1919–24) set in train the negotiations leading to the constitutional settlement in SWA, it was actually implemented by the National Party, which came to power in South Africa in 1924. Anxious to establish independence[111] from Britain—both practically and symbolically—the new government moved toward the *de facto* annexation of South West Africa. As we have seen, in 1926 the South African government ceded the Neutral Zone on the Angola–Namibia border to Portugal: in doing so, it effectively made its first claim to formal sovereignty over South West Africa. Two years later, when a new South African flag was inaugurated to fly alongside the Union Jack within South Africa, Pretoria decreed that the South African flag alone would be flown in SWA.[112]

Although the London Agreement had dealt with the immediate crisis in relations between the German and South African populations, white national politics nevertheless remained divided mainly on ethnic lines for the entire inter-war period.[113] The Deutscher Bund (German party) was founded in 1924 and won the first elections to the Legislative Assembly in 1926, mainly because the South Africans were divided between the National Party, which promoted the policies of Hertzog's Nationalists in South Africa, and the Union Party, which aligned itself with Smuts. The following year, however, these two merged to form the United National South West Party (UNSWP), which went on to win the 1929 elections to the Legislative Assembly. The UNSWP campaigned on a platform of incorporating SWA into South Africa, while the Deutscher Bund hoped to maintain the mandate, as well as promoting German cultural and educational rights. In 1932 the two parties tried and failed to reach a compromise that would have allowed a greater degree of self-government.[114]

The two main white ethnic groups also maintained a high degree of social and political segregation. To some extent, class divisions followed this divide. German farmers formed a wealthy elite in relation to the incoming Afrikaner pastoralists, and (despite declining economic influence in many areas) Germans continued to dominate the retail trade. In 1928, a further layer of complexity was added when 301 extremely poor 'Angola Boer' families—Afrikaner settlers from Angola—were resettled in SWA by the state. This was part of the administration's project to ensure South African numerical superiority, and the new arrivals were heralded by the press as symbolising 'the spirit of the Voortrekkers'; generous state funding for the new arrivals managed, however, to excite hostility among both 'sections' of existing settlers and to deepen German hostility to the administration.[115]

Overall, until about 1933, the administration seems to have more or less successfully incorporated the white settler population in its project of establishing white domination while using black labour to extract the territory's resources. By this time, however, the rise of Hitler in Germany was having profound effects on Namibia. The Nazis' stated objective of regaining the former German colonies offered hope to German settlers that they might once again take control of SWA, while at the same time making them a more serious potential threat to the administration. In addition, Nazi influence inside Namibia became insidious and widespread: Nazi officials arrived from Germany to promote the message and 'nazify' existing institutions, and branches of the Hitler Youth and the National Socialist (Nazi) party were set up. Although there was some opposition to the new ideology among Germans, one estimate puts their support for Nazism after the annexation of Austria at between 80 and 95 per cent.[116] The Legislative Assembly responded with the Criminal Law Amendment Ordinance of 1933, which banned Nazi propaganda, and the following year both the Hitler Youth and the Nazi party were outlawed. In 1937 the Deutscher Bund was also banned (to be replaced by the Deutscher Südwest Bund) because of its support for Nazism. In 1936, SWA was also nudged further down the path to integration with South Africa when the report of the South West Africa Commission, set up to advise on forms of government for the territory, argued for incorporation (although this was not yet accepted by the South African government).[117]

By 1939, according to the traveller Negley Farson, being '"Heil Hitlered!" and given the Nazi salute in the African bush'[118] was a common experience. In April, the South West African police force was strengthened by the arrival of 350 armed police from South Africa, and in September, after the outbreak of war and amid rumours of a possible *coup d'état*, German men and other suspected rebels (numbering 1,220 by the end of 1940) were rounded up and interned in South Africa (German women were allowed to remain at liberty).

There was some vocal support for Hitler in the *otjiserandu* and among Ovambo contract workers, although this undoubtedly stemmed from a desire to subvert the British imperial narrative of freedom rather than a belief in 'the Nazi version that Hitler was trying to free the world from Jews who were exploiting Africa'.[119] The war's more lasting impact on the black population of Namibia was large-scale recruiting to the (South African) Native Military Corps (NMC), which took place between 1941 and 1943 (despite the fact that the League of Nations prohibited recruitment of indigenes from the mandated territories). About 5,000 African men were recruited in all, the majority from Owambo. Famine conditions in the north in 1941 encouraged enlistment, and in eastern Owambo this seems to have been a mainly voluntary process; in the western areas, however, news of the harsh treatment of recruits deterred men from joining up, and officials apparently then coerced thousands into the NMC.[120]

In the eastern Caprivi, a Special Company of Native Soldiers was formed in August 1940 to protect the bridge at Victoria Falls, but disbanded in 1943 when there seemed little likelihood of action.[121] The Namibian members of the NMC, meanwhile, were stationed in South Africa and did not see active service. In 1943 recruiting was stopped, and by January 1945 all black Namibian soldiers had been discharged. This was at least partly due to fears of the uncontrollability of black troops. There were other signs, too, that the war had the effect of 'heighten[ing] the "conscientisation of oppression"', even if 'this did not automatically translate into a rise in "national consciousness"'.[122] Ovambo workers went on strike several times in 1941, and African servicemen protested that their gratuities after discharge—a few pounds or nothing—were in stark contrast to the farms granted to Afrikaner soldiers.

Nevertheless, the Second World War was not as important for Namibia's later history as the referendum (of sorts) of 1946, which triggered the incorporation of SWA into South Africa, and the rejection by the latter of the United Nations Trusteeship. These events led to new direct resistance to South African rule in Namibia, and eventually to the birth of the nationalist movements. This, then, was a decisive moment in Namibia's history, and it is to these events that we now turn.

9

NATIONALISM AND APARTHEID, 1946–70

The period 1946–70 was characterised by two main developments. First, South Africa repudiated its 'sacred trust' to govern SWA as a mandate, and began to incorporate the territory ever more closely into its own structures of government. The apartheid system that was being worked out in South Africa during these years was also applied to Namibia, a process that culminated in the report of the Odendaal Commission, published in 1964. At the same time, the more aggressive manifestations of the early implementation of apartheid fostered the growth of protest, as did the increasing reach of the migrant labour system as well as the growing ability of Namibians to make contact with broader international developments. Resistance to South African rule led to the foundation of explicitly nationalist organisations from the late 1950s.

Writing the history of the period between the Second World War and independence in 1990 is facilitated by the fact that African-authored sources are much more plentiful than for earlier periods: the views and experiences of black people in Namibia are evidenced at this period through autobiography, scholarship, letters, oral history, works of devotion and political statements. Yet, in other ways, historical narratives are more difficult to construct. This is a period still very much in flux, as new facts and arguments are put forward and debated, and which—perhaps even more than the Namibian War—holds continued political significance and resonance. Indeed, the process of historicising the years 1946–90, which are still well within living memory, has hardly begun.[1]

Protest and Nationalist Organisations[2]

The period immediately following the Second World War saw major international change with the rise of nationalism and the retreat of colonialism. In 1947, Britain withdrew from its largest and most important territory, India; Britain and France had granted most of their colonies independence by the end of 1960s. Against this background, however, South Africa pursued a different course, aiming for regional expansion.[3] Namibia played a central role in these plans.

The United Nations replaced the League of Nations in 1945, and responsibility for the Mandated Territories was handed to a new Trusteeship Council. The South African Prime Minister, Jan Smuts, resisted the new arrangements and tried to persuade the UN to accept the incorporation of Namibia into South Africa as a fifth province. To support his argument he had a 'referendum' carried out among Africans in Namibia, between December 1945 and April 1946, which resulted in a 'vote' of 208,850 for incorporation and 33,250 against.[4] However, there had been no individual voting: at a series of meetings called by chiefs and headmen, and held only in the reserves, Africans had been asked not whether they backed incorporation, but rather, whether they wanted 'any other nation to rule them',[5] suggesting that they had a choice between South Africa and Germany.

The 'referendum' and its apparent conclusion were strenuously opposed by a number of African leaders, the most important of whom was the Herero paramount Hosea Kutako. Although he had been prepared to makes some compromises with the authorities during the inter-war period, Kutako and the Herero Chief's Council had been increasingly disillusioned by growing land loss and impoverishment. In the south, the Berseba, Tses and Soromas reserves had also rejected incorporation. Kutako had the support of Frederick Maharero, and was also backed by Tshekedi Khama and other chiefs in Botswana, by Dr A.B. Xuma, leader of the African National Congress in South Africa and, as decolonisation became a reality, by India and other newly independent countries. For the first time, the opposition forces in Namibia were gaining an effective international presence—one they would retain and develop until independence in 1990.

In the south, 1946 also saw an African breakaway from the Rhenish Mission, when the black leaders Zachäus Thomas, Petrus Jod and Markus Witbooi headed a secession to the African Methodist Episcopal Church (AMEC). This was partly because they discovered, through a South African newspaper, that Vedder, now head of the RMS in Namibia, was considering handing over the mission churches to the South African Dutch Reformed Church (NGK)—a proposal, they felt, to sell them 'like live slaughter stock'.[6] The split was also inspired by their increasing frustration with the conservative and gradualist policies of the RMS leadership in Namibia.[7]

The United Nations refused South Africa's request for the incorporation of SWA in December 1946. South Africa did not accept this decision, although Smuts did advocate limited reform in SWA, and in 1947 marked out substantial new amounts of land for reserves (although much of it was arid).[8] In 1948, however, the National Party (NP) won the elections in South Africa and began to implement apartheid. The new government, prepared to defy international opinion and eager to foster a closer relationship with Afrikaans-speaking whites in Namibia, formally stated in the following year that it would no longer submit annual reports on Namibia to the UN.[9] There was little the Trusteeship Council could do as SWA effectively, if not legally, moved towards becoming South Africa's fifth province.

These events signalled the beginning of a new phase of resistance to South African policy in Namibia, and soon indeed to South African rule of Namibia itself. This grew in four separate, but intermittently connecting, strands. In addition to the activities of the traditional leaders and mounting discontent in the churches, migrant workers from the north became increasingly politicised, as did the tiny Namibian intelligentsia. The latter two groups were to form the backbone of the organized nationalist movement that emerged at the end of the 1950s.

The most important and vigorous opposition in the immediate post-referendum period was led by the (small and embattled) existing African elites, particularly Kutako and the Herero Chief's Council. Kutako moved quickly to invite the radical Anglican priest Michael Scott to take the Namibian case to the United Nations (Kutako himself not being permitted to travel). This Scott did in late 1947, after visiting Namibia, where he listened to the arguments of Kutako and his people, David Witbooi, and representatives of the Damara and Windhoek Ovambo communities. Once at the UN, he worked through the 1950s to keep Namibia on the international agenda.[10]

The radical turn taken by the churches was an important factor in expressing and disseminating discontent and protest. A prayer used by Kutako in the late 1940s suggests an early reaching for a new theology

245

grounded in experience: 'Help us who have been placed in Africa and have no dwelling place of our own. Give us back a dwelling place…'[11] In 1955, many Otjiherero-speakers left the RMS to form the *Oruuano* church (known in English as the Protestant Unity Church; literally, 'communion'), which soon gained Kutako's support. In part a cultural movement, the *Oruuano* accepted some forms of Herero traditional practice, including the holy fire and ancestor-worship; it was also a reaction to the conservatism of the RMS and particularly to the stance of Vedder, who in 1949 had become a member of the South African Parliament as the representative of the Africans of SWA, and in this capacity declared his support for apartheid.[12] Partly in response to the challenges posed by the two major schisms, the Rhenish Mission in Namibia became the autonomous Evangelical Lutheran Church (ELK) in 1957.

The RMS had been preceded in this move by the Finnish mission in the north, which had first ordained Africans in 1925, handed its parishes over to African pastors in the late 1930s and 1940s, and became an independent body, the Evangelical Lutheran Ovambo–Kavango Church (ELOK), in 1956 under its first African supervisor, Leonard Auala. By the 1950s missionaries were claiming, perhaps with some exaggeration, that half the population of Owambo had become Christian, and in the early part of that decade an intense revivalist movement, *Epaphuduko* (the 'great awakening' or 'enlightenment'), led to new waves of conversion. By the 1980s, the vast majority in the region had become church members.[13]

The most important factor, however, in the creation of the formal nationalist movements was the success of contract workers from the north in organising themselves and converting deep-seated discontent with the status quo into a sustained mass movement. Beginning in 1939, hundreds of workers from across the north of Namibia had been recruited to work in South Africa, entering via Botswana, by the Witwatersrand Native Labour Association. They thus entered what had previously been 'a sealed door to the outside world',[14] allowing them access to South African protest politics and, in a few cases, to formal education. In 1949 the authorities attempted to bar Namibians from migrating to South Africa, although this had little effect on the flow of labour.[15]

In 1957 a group of mainly Oshiwambo-speaking contract workers living in Cape Town formed the Ovamboland People's Congress

(OPC); their best-known member was Andimba Toivo Ya Toivo, who had been in the South African army during the Second World War and, after experience as a teacher and on the mines, now worked on the railways at Cape Town. This group was influenced by the politics of resistance in South Africa, where the 1950s saw mass mobilisation; their contacts included the African National Congress, members of the South African Liberal Party (including Randolph Vigne and Patrick Duncan), and a number of Communist Party activists including Ray Alexander, who had already, in 1952, tried to start organising a trade union branch in Luderitz. In April 1959, nationalist activity gained a base in Namibia itself with the founding of the Ovamboland People's Organisation (OPO) in Windhoek by Sam Nujoma—who had been organising workers there for some time—and Jacob Kuhangua, with Nujoma as its first president. The OPO took on the mantle of the OPC and, according to Ya Toivo, also incorporated an underground resistance organisation formed in the north in the early 1950s called 'Nghuwoyepongo' or 'the call of an orphan who is rescued by God'.[16]

The OPO organised inside Namibia as well as campaigning for national independence at the United Nations. Because of Namibia's history as a League of Nations mandate, the UN remained a very important focus of the campaign for self-determination until independence in 1990. In 1957 Michael Scott was joined there by Mburumba Kerina, an important figure in the early history of SWAPO, and the following year by Jariretundu Fanuel Kozonguizi, delegated by the Herero Chief's Council.

Besides contract workers, the Namibian activists in Cape Town in the 1950s included members of the first generation of Namibian students to pursue higher education in South Africa. By this date a tiny incipient Namibian intelligentsia was emerging, as a few individuals managed to progress beyond the teaching offered by the mission schools. The latter remained the main provider of education to African children (only 30 per cent of whom were in school by 1958); most only offered a basic education,[17] and provision was particularly poor in the north, although there were some exceptions including the Anglican and Lutheran secondary schools at Odibo and Oshigambo respectively. By the mid-1940s, however, some state schools were being opened for black pupils, mainly in the (largely) Otjiherero-speaking reserves, as a result of campaigns led by Hosea Kutako.[18] In the same decade night classes, attended by the young Sam Nujoma among

Fig. 22. Sam Nujoma was the leader of the South West Africa People's Organisation from its inception, and became the first President of independent Namibia in 1990. This poster is one among very many images created by both SWAPO and the international solidarity movement to assist in making SWAPO's case both at home and abroad. Words from this text recur in the title of Nujoma's autobiography, *Where Others Wavered*. (SWAPO poster [Luanda, 1980?] Published in Giorgio Miescher and Dag Henrichsen, *African Posters* [Basel, 2004], p. 21, no. X 1460. Reproduced courtesy of Basler Afrika Bibliographien.)

others, were held in Windhoek under the auspices of a self-help group, the African Improvement Society. Nevertheless, by the late 1950s the tertiary sector in the territory consisted solely of four teacher training colleges. For the white population, schooling had been compulsory since 1921 and there was considerable state provision.[19]

Like the nucleus of the OPO, with which they had contact, the Namibian students and intellectuals in Cape Town were influenced by the new radical movements in South Africa and beyond. Their ranks included Ottilie Schimming Abrahams, Kenneth Abrahams, Fanuel

Kozonguizi, Emil Appolus, Mburumba Kerina and Zedekia Ngavirue. It was members of this group who were responsible for creating Namibia's early political *cum* educational organisations. The SWA Student Body (SWASB) was founded in 1952, and was superseded later in the decade by the South West Africa Progressive Association (SWAPA), which 'captured the imagination of the youth and incipient intelligentsia, particularly in Windhoek'.[20] SWAPA provided scholarships to South Africa and in 1960 briefly published *South West News*, the first black-authored newspaper in Namibia, thus attempting to seize the terms of the debate and make political information available to Africans—if only, in practice, to a small urban minority.[21]

The creation of a formal, broad-based nationalist organisation had been under discussion since about 1955, and in August 1959 the Herero Chief's Council and SWAPA together established the South West Africa National Union (SWANU), bringing in leading members of other organisations, including Sam Nujoma. However, as early as April 1960 this first attempt to create an umbrella nationalist movement was fatally ruptured when the HCC withdrew its backing for SWANU.[22]

This conflict arose partly from the differing outlooks of the HCC and Kutako on the one hand, and the intelligentsia grouped in SWAPA on the other. The radical nationalism of the latter was strongly entwined with an appeal to modernity and education—their own source of legitimacy—which was at odds with an idea of indigenous authority based on older structures of power. Although the conflict was largely fought out within the Otjiherero-speaking community, rather than between ethnic groups, ideas about ethnicity nevertheless played a role. The Herero Chief's Council made efforts to be inclusive, bringing in Damara and Ovambo members, but essentially its power base was ethnically defined; Herero processes of self-identification had also recently been assisted by government policy, through 'tribal meetings' held in the reserves which encouraged the emergence of a firmer pan-Herero identity.[23] The policies of Kutako and his successor Clemens Kapuuo[24] tended to reflect these dynamics, particularly in a willingness to espouse federalist constitutional options based on ethnically defined power blocs. By contrast, both SWANU and the OPO stood for an explicit form of nationalism in which the struggle for national independence was the unifying force, and ethnic differences were downplayed.

After the April split, the OPO took the decision to reconstitute itself as a national movement, offering an alternative to the weakened SWANU. Thus was born the South West Africa People's Organisation (SWAPO), which was to become the dominant liberation movement of the next thirty years, and the party of government after independence in 1990.[25] Sam Nujoma, already in exile, became president; Nathaniel Maxuilili (in Namibia) became acting president, and Mburumba Kerina (in New York) party chairman. The parting of the ways between SWAPO and SWANU could perhaps have been avoided had the two most experienced nationalist activists, Ya Toivo and Kozonguizi—under house arrest in the north and away at the UN respectively—been present at the crucial time. The creation of two separate nationalist organisations thus, perhaps, reflected accidents of history as much as political or doctrinal differences.

State, Economy and Migrancy in the 1950s

The growth of protest in the decades following the Second World War resulted as much from the social and economic effects of South African policy within the territory as from the political debate over incorporation. Constitutional changes were bringing Namibia into closer alignment with South Africa. In 1949, under the South West Africa Affairs Amendment Act, the Advisory Council was abolished and SWA's white population given the right to elect representatives directly to the South African Parliament—where they assisted the NP in pushing through apartheid policies.[26] The National Party of SWA won a large majority in these (whites-only) elections, and subsequently became a branch of the National Party in South Africa. In Namibia, it advocated apartheid and opposed the UN mandate; its main opponent, the United National South West Party, took a more moderate stance and argued against incorporation. At the same time, the number of white-owned farms in Namibia was again expanding, following the report of the Social Security Commission (Lardner-Burke Commission) of 1945–47 (which dealt with whites only). In response to its findings, the government shifted the Red Line in the north-west and north-east to bring more land into the Police Zone, some for reserves, but most for white settlement. The latter increased exponentially in the next decade and a half, assisted by the fact that the Police Zone boundary was moved ten more times during the same period. By 1963/4, the number of white-occupied farms increased to some 7,000, a rise of over 80 per cent; the number of settlers grew from 37,858 in 1946 to 66,000 in 1958.[27]

If South African policy favoured the white, and particularly the Afrikaner, community, SWA as a whole, and particularly the African population, were brought under much tighter direct control during the 1950s. In 1955, the South African Minister of Native Affairs, H.F. Verwoerd, took over direct responsibility for policy concerning Namibia's African population following the passing of the 1954 South West Africa Native Affairs Administration Act.[28] SWA thus came strongly under the influence of the increasingly authoritarian and ideologically driven South African Native Affairs Department (NAD).[29] Within South Africa itself, in the early 1950s, the Nationalist government extended and deepened the previous segregationist approach to 'native policy' to create the more thoroughgoing apartheid system, under which racial discrimination, spatial separation and the control of black labour in white interests were all secured by heavy repression. Apartheid was implemented through a number of key pieces of legislation including the Mixed Marriages Act (1949), the Group Areas Act (1950), which created more extreme residential segregation and led to a large number of forced removals, the Population Registration Act (1951), the Reservation of Separate Amenities Act (1953), which kept the better public facilities for use by whites only, thus creating 'petty apartheid', and the Bantu Education Act (1953).[30]

This legislation did not automatically apply to Namibia, where the trajectory of apartheid was 'slower and less elaborate...than in South Africa'.[31] The 1950s and 1960s saw the introduction of three main categories of legislation: new constitutional laws, a plethora of security legislation, and measures imposing further racial discrimination. The segregationist laws promulgated in the inter-war years nevertheless continued to play an important role in the apartheid era, and not all apartheid legislation was applied to Namibia. One reason for this was that the challenges to the state were not as great there as in South Africa, where apartheid emerged partly as a response to growing economic and social crisis, as increasing numbers left the land for the cities. Urbanisation did not occur on this scale in Namibia, although there does seem to have been an increase in migration to the towns, as agricultural land became less productive: the number of black residents of urban areas grew from 30,000 in 1946 to 49,000 in 1955.[32] Nor did significant organised protest emerge until the end of the first decade of apartheid. On the other hand, the fact that a good deal of *de facto* control was already applied through informal discrimination also restrained the government from introducing new laws. For example, although the sections of the Population Registration Act assigning individuals to racial categories were not extended to Namibia, in practice such racial classification was informally in place already.[33]

The most important new law passed during the 1950s was the Natives (Urban Areas) Proclamation of 1951,[34] which (together with the somewhat later Aliens Control Act (1963)) imposed comprehensive new controls on African mobility. Essentially, the new legislation sought to create a very small African urban elite with rights to remain in the towns, while the majority of the black population were conceived as a transient proletariat. It also reinforced the pass system, providing for African men aged eighteen and over to carry passes; women were not required to do so,[35] although those from the north could not enter the Police Zone without a permit, which was seldom granted. The urban areas legislation and subsequent town planning ordinances also set up new means of enforcing spatial apartheid in the towns, using the title deeds of individual properties to prevent land in 'white' and 'Coloured' areas being sold to Africans. The success of these measures meant that the Group Areas Act was not extended to Namibia.

Further apartheid legislation imposed in Namibia included the Industrial Conciliation Ordinance of 1952, which barred Africans from joining trade unions, and the Prohibition of Mixed Marriages Ordinance (1953). The Education Ordinance (1962), introduced on the recommendation of the van Zyl Commission of 1958, initiated Bantu education—in effect, a very basic, functional education for the black majority—in Namibia, bringing changes in the syllabus, the state takeover of many mission schools, and an official policy of restricting the education of most Africans to a period of four years.[36]

This legislation, despite its limitations, provided the basis for an aggressive and fairly well-defined 'native policy' in Namibia in the 1950s, which attempted to implement a new level of control over the African population. In the rural areas, the authorities began to reconstitute the reserves as ethnic units—a new development, since, as we saw in the previous chapter, ethnically mixed reserves had previously been created in order to limit their potential as power bases for the leaders of the old African polities. Once the older political formations had been comprehensively undermined, however, the state developed a new strategy of resurrecting and sponsoring 'tribal' groups, with the objective of ensuring order and quiescence. After the Second World War (on the basis of the Natives Trust Funds Proclamation of 1939), a number of tribal trust funds and councils were set up; the latter were established for the Damara in 1947, the Herero in 1950 and the Nama in 1953. The takeover of South West African 'native affairs' by the Native Affairs Department in 1955 brought the reserves strategy under its direction and was eventually to hasten the progress of the reserves to 'homeland' status.

The new emphasis on ethnic segregation and cohesiveness was supported intellectually by a new series of ethnologies, encompassing urban as well as rural areas, produced by the NAD. These laid down key ideas on the nature of the supposed tribal groupings in Namibia. Kaoko, for example, which was proclaimed as a reserve in 1947, was designated home to three main 'tribes', the Himba, Tjimba and Herero. This new arrangement contrasted with the existing long-established divisions based on the lineages of three 'big men'—Kakurukouye, Vita Tom and Muhona Katiti. These ideologies of tribe began to permeate African groups and their self-understandings, but the extent to which the people came to identify with, and shape, the broad categories 'Nama', 'Ovambo' and so on varied with time and place, depending among other things on previous ideologies of ethnicity, the dynamics of local politics and the increasing economic pressures on the reserves.[37]

In pursuit of increased control and ethnic segregation, the South African administration in Namibia implemented a limited number of forced removals in the 1950s. The Aukeigas reserve near Windhoek was closed in 1958, despite opposition from a Damara organisation called 'Fakkel' (torch). The last inhabitants were sent to the barren territory of Sorris-Sorris in the west, and Aukeigas became the Daan Viljoen game reserve. Attempted removals from the Hoachanas reserve in the south were met with stiff resistance and, although a small group of residents were taken to new land at Itsawisis, their leader, Rev. Markus Kooper, managed to travel to New York in order to protest at the United Nations. In 1954, around two hundred Hai‖Om were evicted from the Etosha game reserve; most, like the majority of the Hai‖Om population outside the reserve, became farm labourers.[38]

There were also forced removals in the towns, where contradictions between the government's drive to restrain African urbanisation and employers' labour needs were becoming plainly apparent. The authorities applied the pass laws vigorously in an attempt to control Africans' freedom of movement and choice of employment, and to prevent unrest. In Windhoek, the tensions caused by these policies were soon to explode, with far-reaching political repercussions.

As early as 1954, the municipality began planning to remove the location—the home of most black people in the capital, now known as the Old Location—to a new site north of the town. This measure was intended not only to increase residential segregation, but also to seal off the white population from any possibility of infection from the location—a spurious argument commonly used in South Africa to justify spatial separation—as well as to free land for white housing. A separate township was to be built for the Coloured population, which had grown significantly through immigration from South Africa since the Second World War.[39] Most of the population of the location opposed the move and, by extension, the apartheid policies behind it: when asked to provide a name for the new township, the Location Advisory Board[40] dubbed it 'Katutura', 'we have no dwelling place'. The promised conditions might be better in the new township, but rents would be higher, the distance to central Windhoek further, and an existing community ripped apart.[41]

In late 1959, protests erupted in the form of two women's marches from the location to central Windhoek. The demonstrators objected not only to the planned removal, but also to increasing attempts to control the illicit beer trade on which many of them depended for their livelihood. Boycotts of the buses and the location beer hall, apparently organised by the OPO and SWANU, and in which women played a prominent role, had been agreed by 8 December; Fakkel was also involved in the resistance. Two days later, unrest outside the beer hall exploded into violence and the police shot and killed at least eleven[42] people.[43]

The shock caused by the Old Location shootings was palpable: 'We never thought the South Africans would shoot...this was a mandated territory...We also thought the UN would do something'.[44] This pivotal historical moment thus served further to radicalise the population and to unite opposition to South African rule, as well as causing Nujoma and other OPO leaders to take the decision to go into exile. It also intimidated some of the Old Location's population into moving to Katutura, although it was not until 1968 that the last residents were forced to do so.[45]

Fig. 23. Residents of the Old Location in Windhoek preparing to move. Despite fierce resistance, which led to the infamous shootings of 1959, the black location was eventually demolished and most of its residents were removed to the new township of Katutura. (Reproduced courtesy of the National Archives of Namibia [no. 4370].)

Another major object of state policy during the 1950s was the control of migrant labourers.[46] At the same time, the contract labour system was now affecting life in the north to an unprecedented extent. The numbers recruited from the northern regions overall (including Angola) grew from 17,494 in 1948 to 30,129 in 1960.[47] This rise was largely the result of growing poverty in Owambo, as pressure on land heightened because of population growth[48] and decreased access to grazing and other resources when the boundaries to north and south (the Namibia–Angola border and, especially, the Red Line) were fenced, following a devastating epizootic of foot-and-mouth disease in the Police Zone in 1961–62. The population was also hard-hit by a major drought in the late 1950s and early 1960s. Continued commercial isolation and the virtual absence of formal employment meant that the contract labour system offered one of the few opportunities to supplement the products of subsistence farming. It is true that there were some new agricultural developments—the increasing use of ploughs in the north from the late 1940s, and the construction of canals and dams for a major water system (complete by the late 1960s)—and it is also true that migrancy had its own momentum, allowing young men access to status and cash for bridewealth and land occupancy fees, and for commodities including sewing machines and bicycles. But, overall, it was the increasingly difficult circumstances that were driving people—often now married as well as unmarried men—to turn to contract labour. In Kavango, by contrast, the continued availability of new agricultural land meant that the numbers recruited as migrants were very much lower than in the Oshiwambo-speaking areas.[49]

As far was Owambo was concerned, then, the balance of power within the migrant labour system had now shifted decisively in favour of the colonial authorities. In 1941, contracts were lengthened to two years (although in 1950 protests succeeded in reducing this to eighteen months, except for farm workers), and in 1948 the Native Labourers Commission ruled that all first-time Ovambo migrants must work on (the less popular and less well-paid) farms.[50] Overall, contract labour was increasingly experienced as oppressive in all its aspects. The grievances of the workers are documented in many accounts. These included the demeaning ways in which they were treated; the hardships of travel to and from their places of employment; the tough and brutal conditions—extending in some cases to murder by employers—encountered once there; and the low level of wages, which were not always paid.

The enforced separation of wives, husbands and family members was also keenly felt on both sides. A husband might leave a pregnant wife to go on contract: 'When he returned, the child was already walking'.[51] The workload of women and children in the north increased substantially with periods of male absence and it is likely that their nutritional levels fell, as food production became harder. Although in some cases there were probably temporary shifts in gender roles as, for example, some women took responsibility for cattle, both the power to make decisions and access to the (increasingly important) cash economy remained in the hands of men, undermining women's economic independence. The men's work of reproducing the settler economy was thus built on the further exploitation of women's and children's labour. In general, too, the increasing power of mission churches to restrict divorce, prevent polygyny (which led to the abandonment of wives), support patriliny and encourage the joint owner-

Fig. 24. Labour recruitment in the north, 1953. This photograph was taken on behalf of the State Information Service in Pretoria, and probably shows would-be migrant labourers lined up for a medical examination. Such examinations were a persistent source of tension. (Reproduced courtesy of the National Archives of Namibia [no. 3270]).

ship of property also acted to undermine women's economic and political position; from 1947, when Harold Eedes replaced Hahn as Native Commissioner, the missionaries received active state support in these aims.[52]

Conditions in the north may have been deteriorating, but the economy of the territory, sustained as it was by the system of reserves and contract work, was booming. GDP increased phenomenally from £6.1 million in 1942 to £72.3 million in 1956. This was the beginning of a long period of growth lasting until the 1970s, involving a rapid expansion in the mining and fishing sectors and, from the 1960s, in manufacturing. By the mid-1950s, mining had overtaken agriculture in importance for the first time since the 1920s: the two sectors now respectively made up 53 and 23 per cent of Namibia's gross domestic product. This growth was made possible by South Africa's decision to encourage investment by international capital. The Tsumeb copper mine, for example, was bought by American, British and South African interests in 1945, although CDM (owned by De Beers and ultimately by the South African company Anglo-American) retained ownership of the territory's diamond interests. One consequence of this strategy was that a large proportion of GDP was remitted abroad, reaching a peak of 40 per cent in 1956. At the same time, Namibia's economy became increasingly dependent on that of South Africa, so that, for example, by the mid-1960s cattle and meat sales were controlled by the latter.[53]

Despite the rise in the value of mining, agriculture remained of critical importance, particularly in view of the post-war growth in white settlement. Moreover, since much of the best land had already been taken by earlier settlers, the new farms were economically marginal, and their need for cheap labour immense: at this period they still employed almost as many contract workers as the mining sector. These farms were particularly vulnerable to the vagaries of Namibia's climate, and many were severely affected by the drought of the late 1950s. They were also threatened by competition from black farmers, and until about 1960 the administration intervened directly to protect them by discouraging karakul farming in the reserves.[54]

In Namibia's unequal economy, levels of discontent among workers were high, and there were strikes nearly every year between 1946 and 1959. These occurred mainly on the mines at Luderitz, Tsumeb and Oranjemund, and in other places where workers were massed together, including fish processing at Walvis Bay, where conditions were particularly harsh. Although not focused on a formal organisation before the establishment of the OPO in 1959, labour unrest was informed by a sense of solidarity among migrant workers—an emphasis on the importance of 'brotherhood'—which ultimately strengthened the impulse for nationalism. In the 1950s, there was also a sharp rise in the number of migrant workers prepared to resist the system by 'breaking contract', moving from job to job, even though this was a criminal offence under Masters and Servants legislation. As Sam Nujoma among others found, labour shortages meant that employers were willing to turn a blind eye to this practice of 'desertion'.[55]

In the north, too, activist leaders had emerged well before the foundation of the OPO. The best-known were the Rev. Theophilus Hamutumbangela and Eliaser Tuhadeleni, nicknamed Kaxumba kaNdola (after the organ, *kaxumba*, he brought back to his village of Endola), who operated clandestinely, holding meetings after church services and using the Bible's rich idiom of the condemnation of injustice to educate and mobilise supporters; they may have been at the centre of a wider network represented as *Nghuwoyepongo*, as noted above. Both were arrested and maltreated by the authorities, although Tuhadaleni managed to continue his political activities in the north for over a decade. Another notable activist was Helao Shityuwete, who by about 1960 was secretly carrying messages between the north and Windhoek. This community activism, like the organised labour action, fed directly into the emerging nationalist movements. It was also provoked in part by the failure of the traditional leaders in the north, whose cooperation with the state in the running of the migrant labour system and increasing rapaciousness had, by about 1960, destroyed their credibility with most of the population.[56]

Nationalism in the 1960s

At the beginning of the 1960s, the differences between SWAPO and SWANU concerned their support bases within Namibia more than their political programmes. Although SWANU had rather more radical tendencies, both organisations were founded as, and remained, primarily nationalist movements. Both called for self-determination and independence for Namibia and supported Pan-Africanism, and both were strongly influenced by the experience of Ghana, which in 1957 became the first British colony in Africa to achieve independence. SWAPO's programme, which was first formulated in 1960, included the introduction of democracy and free speech, the abolition of the migrant labour system and racial discrimination, and the nationalisation of major industries.

Despite this convergence of aims, the two movements were dogged by competition, particularly outside Namibia. At the UN in New York there was considerable antagonism between Kozonguizi (for SWANU) and Kerina (for SWAPO, until he parted company with the movement in 1962). Further attempts to unify the two organisations, notably the creation in 1963 of the short-lived South West Africa National Liberation Front (SWANLIF), ended in failure. Their strategies also began to diverge. SWANU, whose policies included a strong emphasis on self-reliance and anti-imperialism, took an anti-Western stance and became closely aligned with China, while SWAPO placed much more emphasis on Namibia's special status at the UN as a means of unlocking political change. When the Soviet Union and China came into conflict in 1964,

SWANU naturally found itself on the Chinese side of the divide, while SWAPO, which already had some backing among the Western powers, was also able to capitalise on Soviet support. It was now in a more powerful and better-funded position internationally. SWAPO had also been strengthened by its relationship with the Organisation of African Unity (OAU), founded in 1963, which offered funds to both SWAPO and SWANU on condition that they planned military action in support of the liberation of Namibia. SWAPO produced such plans in 1964, but SWANU did not, and in 1965 the OAU recognised SWAPO as the only Namibian nationalist organisation it would support.

Although SWANU survived these various setbacks, it was never to achieve either a strong international position or a broad base within Namibia, where SWAPO was gaining increasing popular and cross-ethnic support. In Owambo, the movement grew as, from about 1961, SWAPO representatives began to speak out at the public meetings called by traditional leaders and to campaign on behalf of individuals.[57] In addition to its existing base among contract workers, SWAPO remained close to the Herero Chief's Council (which however formed its own political party, the National Unity Democratic Organisation (NUDO), in 1964). Adolf Gariseb, a member of the Damara Tribal Executive Committee (which opposed the pro-South African Chief Goraseb), became SWAPO chairman in 1962. Most significantly, in November 1964 the Caprivi African National Union (CANU) merged with SWAPO. In the Caprivi—which in many ways had developed a separate identity from the rest of Namibia—a small elite had been educated in Northern and Southern Rhodesia, and activists had been campaigning against South African rule and contesting local issues such as cattle prices since the early part of the decade; CANU was founded in 1964 and was immediately subjected to very severe repression.[58] As a result of the merger with SWAPO, CANU's leaders, Brendan Simbwaye and Mishake Muyongo, took up senior positions in SWAPO. The alliance finally dissolved in 1980, but in the meantime had strengthened SWAPO at a critical time.[59]

Campaigning at the UN began to bear fruit with the establishment of a Permanent Committee on South West Africa (1954–61). A 'Good Offices Committee' was also set up in 1957, under the leadership of the US, the UK and Brazil, to negotiate with South Africa. This body temporarily considered a plan to split Namibia, allowing the incorporation of the south, including all the white-owned farmland, into South

Africa, while the northern areas were to be administered by South Africa under UN trusteeship arrangements, but this was resisted by the Committee on South West Africa as being in contravention of the mandate. In 1960 the Committee planned a mission to Namibia with the aim of preparing the ground for the eventual achievement of 'complete independence', but was refused entry both to Namibia and (by the British government) to Botswana. In 1962 the South African government did permit a UN mission, led by Vittorio Carpio and Martinez de Alva, to visit the country, but this initiative lost its credibility when it issued a statement (not agreed by Carpio) jointly with the South African government.[60]

Meanwhile, in 1960, the governments of Ethiopia and Liberia-African countries that had been members of the League of Nations—initiated a case against South Africa at the International Court of Justice (ICJ), hoping to have the South African occupation of Namibia ruled illegal. The wheels of justice ground exceeding slow, and it was not until six years later, in July 1966, that the ICJ ruled, controversially and on the strength of the judge president's casting vote, that Ethiopia and Liberia did not have the right to bring the case. The UN General Assembly was dissatisfied with this result and resolved to end the mandate (Resolution 2145/1966), a decision eventually endorsed by the Security Council in 1969. It also voted to set up the United Nations Council for South West Africa (later the United Nations Council for Namibia). Legally, this body had responsibility for administering Namibia until independence, but in practice the South African occupation prevented it from fulfilling this role.[61]

Odendaal and Apartheid[62]

Towards the end of the 1962 the South African government established a Commission of Inquiry into South West African affairs, headed by Frans Hendrik Odendaal (the administrator of the Transvaal):

to enquire thoroughly into further promoting the material and moral welfare and the social progress of the inhabitants of South West Africa, and more particularly its non-White inhabitants, and to submit a report with recommendations on a comprehensive five-year plan for the accelerated development of the various non-White groups of South West Africa...[63]

The Odendaal Commission, which finished its report on 12 December 1963, signalled both the intensification of apartheid in Namibia, and the increased integration of Namibia's government and civil service with that of South Africa. These processes were to reach a peak over the next decade, before internal and external pressure started to undermine them. The Commission concluded that apartheid should remain 'the basic principle of political, economic and social organisation, as in South Africa';[64] the long-term intention was to create a system of (theoretically) independent black 'homelands', while those areas defined as 'white' should fall within South Africa itself.[65] The Commission also made a number of detailed recommendations for the development of the infrastructure of the territory, including the homelands, and increases in social and welfare provision to the African and Coloured population.

Two main considerations lay behind the Odendaal Commission. In recommending increased government expenditure and modernisation, it hoped to deflect some of the adverse criticism that South African rule in Namibia was receiving internationally, and to encourage foreign investment (which would in turn benefit the South African economy). More importantly, its conclusions flowed from the Bantustan policy that was being developed in South Africa, where independent 'homelands' for the different 'native races' were also envisaged. The Transkei received 'self-government' as early as 1963, and Bophuthatswana, Ciskei, Transkei and Venda were all subsequently granted nominal independence, as from 1976.[66] In Namibia, although the groundwork for Odendaal had begun to be laid by the reserves policy of the early 1950s, the Commission's recommendations nevertheless signalled the implementation of a policy that was radically new in its scope, the resources devoted to it, and its ambition that the reserves were to function, not simply as pools of cheap labour, but also as politically independent territories.

The intellectual basis for these policies was provided by a new effort to construct and reinforce ethnic boundaries, with the support of contemporary ethnographic scholarship, aided by the presence on the Commission of the ethnologist J.P. Bruwer. The final report identified twelve separate 'population groups',[67] and bluntly stated the rigid and crude position that lay at the heart of apartheid thought, ignoring the complexities of historical development, identity formation and settlement patterns in Namibia:

In the course of...the country's history various ethnic groups have settled as separate peoples in certain areas of the present Territory...the respective groups all retained their individual identity and are still distinguishable as such in the present population...These separate groups are distinguished from one another by their different languages, cultures and physical appearance, and to a large extent also according to the areas in which they...now live.[68]

In the Police Zone, the new homelands policy meant that the administration now embarked on the consolidation of the existing scattered, ethnically mixed reserves, which had hitherto acted as relatively local labour pools, into single, larger blocs—a process that encountered much resistance. In the north, where Africans still retained much of their land, the immediate consequences of Odendaal were less severe, although the enforcement of the reserve boundaries had long-term negative consequences. The homelands proposed by the Commission were: Ovamboland, for the Ovambos; Kaokoveld, for the 'Kaoko-velders' (defined mainly as Himba and Tjimba); Okavangoland, for five different groups; the Eastern Caprivi homeland, mainly for the Subia, Fwe and a number of smaller groups; Bushmanland, to the east of Grootfontein, and a further area of land for the San in Western Caprivi, between the Okavango and Mashi Rivers; and south of the Red Line, Damaraland, Hereroland, Namaland, Tswanaland and the Rehoboth Gebiet. Had independence ever been achieved on this pattern, the result would have been one state (Ovamboland) of 239,000 people, and 'eight to eleven dwarf states',[69] each with populations of less than 100,000.[70] For the white population there was to be no homeland; the entire Police Zone, apart from the reserves, was considered to be the 'white area'. The Commission also recommended that the Coloured population be accommodated in separately laid-out urban townships. Enforcing segregation in the towns, where the locations were coming under further control, remained an important component of the state's overall strategy, although the Natives (Urban Areas) Ordinance of 1951 remained the key tool for implementing this.

Overall, the Odendaal Plan recommended an increase of 26 per cent in the land area of the reserves. It also marked an end to the expansion of white territorial settlement.[71] Most of the new reserve land, however, was arid. Damaraland was to be composed of the existing reserve, further marginal land in the Outjo and Karibib districts, the (mainly Herero) Otjohorongo reserve and 223 white farms; as established, it was 40 per cent desert. Under the Odendaal Plan, the new integrated Hereroland would be based on four of the existing areas (Epukiro, Otjituo, Waterberg East and the Eastern Reserve), while Otjiherero-speakers would lose the best land at their disposal, at Aminuis, to white farming. The additional territory assigned to Hereroland was observed by one critic to be the 'same *omaheke* that the Hereros scorned as "wild beast country" when they were first allotted reserves in the early years of the mandate, only now it include[d] a greater area of waterless land near the eastern border'.[72] These changes, nevertheless, were also to put an end to 'the last vestiges of Jul'hoan autonomy in the Omaheke'[73]—already largely undermined by the establishment of white farms—as the existing Hereroland East reserve expanded eastwards. Namaland was to be created from the Berseba, Tses, Krantzplatz and Soromas reserves and the Gibeon town and townlands, consolidated into one bloc by the addition of white farms and crown land; at the same time, the Bondels, Warmbad and Neuhof reserves were to be closed. Plans for the removal of groups not mentioned under Odendaal, for example of the Kuiseb Topnaar and the Red Nation at Hoachanas, were made in the early 1970s.[74]

Much of the Odendaal Plan was implemented, but there is no overall study of the process: how much extra land was acquired, how many white farms compulsorily purchased, how many people forcibly removed within rural or urban areas and from the towns to the reserves, how much resistance offered—nor indeed what gains were made by whom. There was certainly a large number of forced removals, particularly in the Police Zone: the full implementation of the plan demanded the uprooting of as many as 130,000 Africans (29 per cent of the black population).[75] There was also a significant increase in the size of the reserves. By 1971/2, their land area totalled 32,629,364 ha., as opposed to 20,644,392 ha. at the time of the Odendaal Report, and at least 426 white farms had been bought by the state and added to the reserves; many of these, on marginal land, had been willingly offered for sale.[76] Black urban growth slowed in the period 1960–70, probably as a result of the homelands policy.[77]

Despite this expansion, the apartheid blueprint could only partially be put into practice. It was hampered by widespread resistance, covert and overt, to forced removals, the making of political compromises, and its own internal contradictions. In the south, there were protests when the plan began to be implemented in 1968, and by 1971 there were still over three hundred people living on the Bondels reserve and at Warmbad. In 1975 approximately eight hundred people were permitted to stay at Hoachanas after resistance to a removal order of

1969. The Bondelswarts also eventually succeeded in keeping their land by having it recognised as part of Namaland. These successes point not only to the inability of the state to force all the planned changes through, but also to the continued political importance of groups like the Bondelswarts and Witboois, with relatively deep historical roots, which the administration was now officially subsuming under a broad 'Nama' identity.[78]

In the case of the Herero reserves, too, there were varied outcomes. In the south, Otjiherero-speakers in the Tses reserve were removed to Epukiro in the early 1970s, but the people at Vaalgras (the 'Nama-speaking Herero') succeeded in holding onto their land. In the east, Herero were granted the right to remain at Aminuis in 1974 after sustained opposition by Clemens Kapuuo and his followers to the planned removal; this development also meant that plans for a Tswana reserve had to be dropped. The following year Kapuuo joined the Turnhalle Constitutional Conference (for which see the next chapter), probably in return for the land at Aminuis. His willingness to co-operate with the authorities was limited, however, since in 1977 he opposed the creation of a Herero Legislative Assembly and Bantustan.[79]

There were a number of forced removals to Damaraland, in the west (including one from Riemvasmaak in South Africa), but the reserve was never home to a majority of Damara: by 1981, only 24,000 out of a total 76,000 lived there. Damara ethnic politics came to express both rural-urban tensions and the difficulties of life in one of the most barren areas of Namibia. The Damara Tribal Executive, which drew its support from the urban areas, rejected the homelands policy and supported Namibian independence. In the reserve, power rested with the Damara Advisory Council, which was also prepared to contest South African policies in a general context of radicalisation. In mid-1972 some thousand Damara-speakers went on strike to protest at conditions in the homeland and in employment, and there was also some support for SWAPO in the reserve.[80]

The strategy delineated by the Odendaal Commission was put into effect through three major pieces of legislation. The Development of Self-Government for Native Nations in South West Africa Act (1968) set up the major homelands, allowing (in preparation for 'self-government') for legislative councils in each one, with powers over aspects of local government including education, water and revenue-raising, subject to the South African president's approval. In 1968 a legislative council was indeed appointed for Ovamboland, structured in such a way as to empower the 'traditional' leadership, with six representatives from each of the seven traditional authorities. Similar bodies were created in the following years in a number of other homelands, both north and south of the Red Line.[81]

The government of the 'white areas' of Namibia (as defined under Odendaal) was laid down by the South West Africa Constitution Act (1968), which provided for an Administrator as chief executive, a Legislative Assembly of eighteen white members and an Executive Committee of four. The powers of the Assembly were curtailed the following year by the South West Africa Affairs Act, bringing its status close to 'that of a South African provincial council';[82] this Act also began to integrate the South West African administration more closely with the South African government, apportioning many of its previous activities to South African government departments. New apartheid legislation was also introduced in the form of the Mines, Works and Minerals Regulations of 1968. This was the first law in Namibia to limit jobs by race, reserving a number of skilled and semi-skilled mining occupations to whites. In the following year the administration of the Coloured, Nama and Baster populations, who were not defined as 'Bantu' under Odendaal, was transferred to the South African Department of Coloured, Nama and Rehoboth Relations.

Apart from its well-known consequences in developing and entrenching 'second-stage apartheid' in Namibia, the Odendaal Commission also triggered increased government spending in a number of areas. It presented three five-year development plans, which resulted among other things in investment in infrastructure, both generally and in the reserves. In particular, efforts were made to ensure supplies of water and electricity, notably through the Kunene hydroelectric scheme at Ruacana, the drilling of boreholes in the reserves and, in Owambo, the construction of dams and canals. There was also development of other facilities including roads, air transport, postal and telephone communications and radio—a process that, through integration with existing South African services, increased Namibia's dependence on South Africa. The state also promoted agricultural improvement ('betterment') in the reserves, building on previous policies introduced by the NAD; such programmes, however, were frequently double-edged and aimed also at increasing state control over farming in the homelands, thus sparking some resistance. Industrial development in the reserves, particularly the establishment of factories in the north, was promoted through the (state-funded) Bantu Investment Corporation. In the Caprivi, a 'Planning Committee' effectively ran local government between 1964 and 1972, introducing some agricultural development, although not on the scale envisaged by Odendaal.[83]

Spending on education, health and welfare for Africans also increased as a result of the Commission, although it was always to lag far behind the amounts spent on whites. From the mid-1960s, old age pensions were made available. After Odendaal there was increased expenditure on health provision, with the result that by 1966, there were 4,631 hospital beds for blacks (as against 1,035 for whites, who constituted about 12 per cent of the population). As far as education was concerned, Odendaal essentially confirmed and extended the decision to implement Bantu education under the Education Ordinance of 1962 (as mentioned above), and education financing rose considerably in the decades before independence. With the establishment of the 'homelands', education in theory became a local responsibility—for example, with the passing of the Ovamboland Education Act in 1973—but in practice control remained with South Africa.[84]

One result of these developments was the creation, for the first time, of significant numbers of jobs within the reserves. By the early 1970s, in Owambo, some 3,000 people were employed directly by the local authority (as labourers and civil servants) and 1,500 by the Bantu Investment Corporation; there were also about 1,000 teachers. Trade also began to open up once more as an income-generating activity: in Owambo, restrictions were relaxed, with the result that by 1973, 1,388 residents of the reserve held trading licences.[85]

While an African bourgeoisie was thus beginning to emerge—although it remained small and fragile until after independence—the reserves nevertheless also became places of extreme poverty. In South Africa, estimates put the number of children dying before their fifth birthday in the 1960s and 1970s in some rural homelands as high as 30 per cent. In the absence of either contemporary debate or social histories, we know little of conditions in the homelands in Namibia, but similar levels of poverty would be unsurprising given the barrenness of the reserves, particularly in the west and south. Certainly, in 1976, 14 per cent of the population of Namaland was without small stock altogether; the level of social differentiation is illustrated by the fact that 27 per cent owned over 400 goats and sheep each.[86]

The Move to War[87]

The implementation of Odendaal embodied South Africa's intransigence over Namibia and its determination to entrench apartheid in the territory. This had much to do with SWAPO's decision to adopt a military strategy, given the apparent failure of peaceful protest against apartheid, although the organisation, like other African liberation movements, had in fact begun preparing for armed action in the early 1960s. Volunteers were trained initially in Ghana, Egypt and Algeria, and later Russia and even China and North Korea. Hifekepunye Pohamba (later President of Namibia) was among the first recruits to the armed struggle; in mid-1962 he slipped into Namibia, where he spent over a year clandestinely mobilising support.

The final decision to fight may not have been taken until the ICJ's failure in July 1966 to declare the South African occupation illegal. SWAPO stated that this relieved '...[our people] once and for all from any illusions which they may have harboured about the United Nations as some kind of saviour in their plight...We have no alternative but to rise in arms and bring about our own liberation'.[88]

In March, Nujoma and Pohamba had flown to Windhoek, only to be immediately expelled, thus underlining South Africa's intransigence. In fact, however, SWAPO fighters had already made contact with Tuhadaleni in the north of Namibia the previous year, and had set up a base at Omugulu gwombashe,[89] near Tsandi in north-western Owambo. It was here that the war between SWAPO and South Africa began when, on 26 August, the latter's forces discovered and overwhelmed the base.

This first engagement was, in itself, a minor battle, and easily won by South Africa, but its effects were far-reaching. The battle became a symbolic focus for SWAPO's mobilisation in support of its military campaign, but it also made war, and the strength of South African firepower, a reality for the first time in the north since the attack on Iipumbu three decades earlier. Johannes Silas, an eye-witness, remembered later that 'the whole Omugulu gwombashe attack brought bitterness to our community. The litany of horrors, the deafening sounds from the bombing and shooting, the shaking of the earth, the crying voices of children, the attack itself defied all reason...'[90]

Over the next few years SWAPO continued its armed campaign with guerrilla-style attacks, at a low level and mainly in the Caprivi, which was relatively accessible from the movement's bases further north, but difficult for the South Africans to defend because road communications to the south were very poor. The 1964 agreement between CANU and SWAPO also gave the latter political support within the region. In May 1967 Thomas Hainyeko, in charge of SWAPO's military operations, was killed in a boat on the Zambezi River; the following year South Africa seems to have killed sixty-three civilians as a reprisal after SWAPO attacked an army camp.[91]

The battle of Omugulu gwombashe was followed by widespread arrests and harassment in the north; tension throughout the country increased when the South African Prime Minister, Hendrik Verwoerd, was assassinated two weeks later. Nevertheless, some political mobilisation also took place in Owambo. Staff at the Ongwediva Teacher Training College secretly produced and distributed leaflets in the name of SWAPO; their leaders were eventually arrested and tortured. This was, it seems, the first use of electric shock torture in Owambo (although it had been used on SWAPO fighters in Rundu as early as March 1966), and local people commented in song:

| mOshakati mu n'emwangha | There is a bear in Oshakati |
| Tali li ovanhu | Eating up people[92] |

John Ya Otto, who faced electric shock torture at about the same time, described it thus: 'Each time it felt as if a bomb of a thousand sharp needles was exploding inside me, tearing my guts apart, pushing my eyes out from their sockets, bursting my skin open in a dozen places'.[93] These events, together with the Odendaal Report, first inspired church leaders to make (low-key) protests to the authorities.

By mid-1967, somewhere between 150 and 200 people had been arrested in Namibia and detained and tortured in South Africa. They included PLAN fighters and most of SWAPO's internal leadership, including Toivo Ya Toivo, Eliaser Tuhadeleni, John Ya Otto, Nathaniel Maxuilili and Jason Mutumbulua. The detainees' relatives in the north also faced severe hardships: Tuhadeleni's family, who remained active in the nationalist struggle after he had been imprisoned, suffered poverty, isolation and police harassment. In 1967, thirty-seven Namibians— twenty-seven combatants and ten members of SWAPO's internal leadership—were brought to trial in Pretoria under the Terrorism Act, passed while they were in detention but made retroactive to 1962. The case caused an international outcry, and this—together with the efforts of the defence lawyer Joel Carlson—perhaps saved the defendants from the death penalty. Over half the accused received life sentences, while nine, including Ya Toivo, were sentenced to twenty years' imprisonment.[94]

A string of other trials was to follow—in 1969, for example, guerrilla fighters were put on trial in Windhoek for the first time—but it was the Terrorism Trial that became particularly symbolic in SWAPO's struggle for Namibia, galvanising the movement and its international supporters. In this it holds a position analogous to the 1963–64 Rivonia Trial, at which Nelson Mandela and other African National Congress leaders were imprisoned for their part in the South African armed struggle. The Namibian court case, like the Rivonia Trial, both highlighted the ruthlessness of the South African state and allowed the nationalist leaders a stage on which to demonstrate their defiance, publicise the injustices of apartheid and put their case. Ya Toivo's speech from the dock in February 1968 was an emphatic statement of nationalist principles. The defendants, he declared, were 'Namibians and not South Africans':

We do not now, and will not in the future recognise your right to govern us, to make laws for us under which we had [sic] no say; to treat our country as if it were your property, and us as if you were our masters. We have always regarded South Africa as an intruder in our country.

Ya Toivo emphasised Namibia's status as a mandate—'South Africa has abused that trust because of its belief in racial supremacy'—and the importance of actively resisting South African rule, giving qualified support to the armed struggle. He finished by declaring presciently: 'If you [South Africa] choose to crush us and impose your will on us... you will live in security for only so long as your power is greater than ours'.[95]

Most of the defendants in the Treason Trial were imprisoned on Robben Island, off Cape Town—as were Nelson Mandela and many activists of the African National Congress and Pan Africanist Congress. Despite the harsh conditions they experienced, the island became a political and educational hothouse, and the prisoners were to play a key political role in the campaign for independence after their release in 1985. They were also joined over the years by other Namibian political prisoners, including the acting president of SWANU, Hitjevi Veii, who in 1967 was charged with sabotage and sentenced to five years' imprisonment.

By the end of the decade, SWAPO in exile had gained considerable international support. Nevertheless, the external wing of the movement remained small, its organisation rudimentary, and the resources devoted to the armed struggle minimal. This caused some discontent in SWAPO's armed wing, and in 1968 a group of seven military train-ees returned from China to the Kongwa camp in Tanzania, where they protested at what they perceived as poor organisation, corruption and military inactivity within the movement. The protest was treated as mutiny and quashed by the arrest of the group and their imprisonment in Tanzania. Nevertheless, and probably in response to concerns widely held within the movement, SWAPO went on to hold its first Consulta-tive Congress from 26 December 1969 to 2 January 1970, in Tanga in Tanzania. Although not all the causes of protest were addressed, the Congress ratified the decision to adopt the armed struggle and set up a number of new structures including a Women's Council, a Youth League, a Department of Labour and an Elders' Council.[96]

The crisis foreshadowed later conflict within SWAPO. A heavy-handed and authoritarian response to crisis allowed Sam Nujoma and those around him to stamp their authority on the movement, and resulted in the imprisonment of members expressing dissent. These actions were, however, followed by a limited willingness to make con-cessions. The Tanga Conference also presaged the sometimes uneasy relationship between SWAPO inside and outside Namibia; while the external wing acted nominally in the name of the internal movement, in practice, with widespread diplomatic influence and, increasingly, strong financial resources, it was already becoming the more powerful of the two.

By 1970, then, the groundwork had been laid for the struggles of the next two decades. Nationalist movements had built support both inside and outside the country; the South African authorities had laid down, and begun to implement, a comprehensive apartheid plan; mili-tary struggle had commenced; detention, torture and harassment of Namibians, particularly in the north, had begun; and conflict had emerged within SWAPO in exile. In the 1970s, these processes intensi-fied to the point of forcing the South African administration into sig-nificant retreat over its apartheid policies. Nevertheless, it was not until 1990 that independence was finally achieved.

10

LIBERATION STRUGGLES AND THE
RETREAT FROM APARTHEID, 1971–90

As the imposition of racial domination became harsher and more systematic, so protest grew. In 1971, the tensions in the migrant labour system exploded into a general strike that led to the mass deportation of workers to the north, and the shutdown of most mines and large industrial enterprises. At this period, too, Namibian nationalism—now dominated by SWAPO—became a far stronger force, offering a serious diplomatic, political and to some extent military challenge to the South African regime. In the 1970s and 1980s, South Africa was forced into a number of constitutional experiments in an attempt to retain as much control over Namibia as it could. In the end, however, renewed internal protest, international pressure and, above all, the costs of long and bitter warfare in Angola and Namibia led to a UN-sponsored transition process, culminating in independence on 21 March 1990.

It would be wrong, however, to cast this period as only one of polarisation between liberation and oppression, or between SWAPO and the South African administration. Much of the literature of the time, written in the heat of struggle, does just this. While the present book tries in some respects to move beyond this dialectic, fuller social histories of the period are still to be written, and our understanding of the development of the politics of identity, patronage, ethnicity, gender and power during the final decades of South African rule in Namibia remains rudimentary. A start can be made here, but the task of unpacking these themes remains an important one for future historical writing.[1]

Protest in the Early 1970s

In June 1971 the International Court of Justice, following an application by an Ad Hoc Sub-Committee of the UN Security Council, reversed its stance on Namibia. It now declared that the occupation was 'illegal' and that South Africa was 'under obligation to withdraw its administration from Namibia immediately...'[2] The General Assembly followed this with a resolution condemning the occupation.

In Namibia, the Lutheran churches (ELOK and ELC), supported by widespread opposition to South African rule,[3] now took the momentous decision to write to the South African Prime Minister, John Vorster, to protest at the occupation. At the same time they had a pastoral epistle, later dubbed the 'Open Letter', read out in every Lutheran church in the country. To Vorster they protested that the racial policies in the territory, and the lack of freedom of speech and voting rights, were violations of the United Nations Declaration of Human Rights of 1948: 'Our people are not free and by the way they are treated they do not feel safe'. In the pastoral letter they argued that apartheid was contrary to the work of the church: '...true development on a Christian basis ought to lead to unity and fraternity between the races'.[4]

The churches' action was inspired by Zephania Kameeta, a future radical theologian but then a student, and supported by their leaders, Bishop Leonard Auala (who was close to Ya Toivo) and Moderator Paul Gowaseb. The impetus behind the letters also stemmed from processes of transformation within the Namibian churches, which were changing from mission institutions 'into a fundamentally Black peasant church... It was the interpenetration of Church and people which bestowed on Church leaders their awareness and their strength and drove them into the open to recreate the "prophetic role" of the church'.[5]

From about this time, the churches began to expound and practise a radical new liberation theology (although their teachings on other matters, including sexual morality, remained largely conservative). They encouraged political mobilisation and communicated information from outside the country; increasingly they also aligned themselves explicitly with SWAPO, although the question of armed struggle remained a dilemma. The administration responded, among other measures, with the deportation of the Anglican bishop, Robert Mize, in 1968, followed in 1972 by that of his successor Colin Winter, a vocal campaigner against apartheid in the mould of predecessors such as Michael Scott.

The churches also became an important conduit for political and material support from abroad, particularly after the Lutheran World Federation declared itself against apartheid in 1970.[6]

The ICJ decision and the Open Letter helped to catalyse mobilisation against the South African presence in Namibia, particularly among the youth. In 1971, hundreds of students were expelled from their schools after taking part in protest marches at Ongwediva in the north. This movement, led by Kandy Nehova, Ndali Kamati, Helao Nafidi, Ndaxu Namolo and David Shikomba among others, was to become the SWAPO Youth League (SYL). Many of the expelled activists travelled south to obtain work and, in Walvis Bay in particular, they began to organise among workers, who, as we have seen, already had a long tradition of protest against the migrant labour system.[7]

This chain of events sparked a general strike of contract workers, which broke out on 13 December 1971 and quickly spread across the country. The central demand of the workers was '*Odalate Naiteke*', 'Let's break the wire [contract]'.[8] They aimed both to end the migrant labour system as an institution, and to achieve higher wages for their work in the south. By this time, the system was making deeper inroads than ever before into the lives of families in the increasingly impoverished Oshiwambo-speaking areas. In 1971–2 the number of recruits reached a new high of 43,890, and, by 1973, three-quarters or more of men in the north had been on contract at least once in their lives.[9] The potential for strike action was heightened by the concentration of workers on the mines and in the large factories, usually housed together in compounds, which greatly facilitated communication and organisation; on the other hand, agricultural workers, who were more isolated, generally shared a deep resentment at the system that made them quick to take action when they found out about the stoppage—which many did from radio broadcasts.[10] The strike also had immediate triggers. One was a recent tightening of control through identity cards, which now had to contain photographs, making it much harder for migrant labourers to switch identities.[11] In addition, when the Bantu Commissioner,[12] General Jannie de Wet, claimed in November 1971 that the contract labour system—felt by many migrants to be a form of slavery—was 'voluntary', he threw a spark onto dry timber.

Once lit, the fire spread rapidly. By 4 January 12,000 migrants had stopped work. Although the strike was not quite universal (it was undermined at Walvis Bay and at the CDM mine, by intimidation and conciliation respectively), it was on a scale never before seen in Namibia. At its peak, the strikers numbered at least 13,500, and eleven mines and twenty-three other workplaces had closed. Although the action was initially peaceful, some of the organisers were put on trial. In addition, the workers were immediately sent back to the north, where there were attacks 'on the symbols, fixtures and black personnel of colonial rule';[13] the border fence was also cut. De Wet testified in a later interview to the disarray of the authorities:

[The striking workers] destroyed the fence between Ovambo and Angola... they broke down that whole thing...we had no control whatsoever and this lasted for December and January and then they started to shoot and kill some of the headmen, those headmen who were working with us. And they drew up lists, protest lists, and complained about slavery and all that...I didn't know what to do...there was no law and order. Everything just went bang...[14]

At the beginning of January 1972, a Contract Committee was formed, under the leadership of Johannes Nangutuuala, to represent the workers in the north, who now drew up resolutions condemning many aspects of the contract system. On 20 January the Minister of Bantu Administration came to an agreement with the Ovambo and Kavango Legislative Councils which, although not discussed with the Contract Committee, effectively ended the strike. The workers' action had indeed won them some victories. Breaking contract was no longer to be a criminal offence, and the medical examination of workers in order to categorise them according to fitness was to be discontinued. However, most parts of the system were left unaltered. Migrant labourers were still to be housed in compounds without their families, and their movement controlled by passes. This led to some continued unrest: in early February workers broke up over four thousand beds in the Katutura compound. Although wages did rise a little as a result of the strike, and SWANLA was abolished and replaced by other agencies, employers combined to try to reduce competition for labour.

The government was obviously shaken by the strike, and in February 1972 introduced Proclamations R17 and R26, which imposed a virtual state of martial law in Owambo, banning public meetings and allowing indefinite detention without trial. The war also intensified now, as SWAPO's military capacity grew. The South Africans responded by transferring responsibility for the Angolan border area from the police to the army, sending increasing numbers of troops to Namibia, and giving traditional leaders arms.[15]

The strike also influenced the United Nations Security Council, which passed a resolution calling for negotiations leading to self-determination in Namibia. This resulted in visits to Namibia by Kurt Waldheim, the Secretary General, in March 1972, and his representative Alfred Escher in the following October. To the latter the authorities proposed a new constitutional arrangement: an Advisory Council, established on an ethnic basis, at national level. Namibia would thus remain a single unit—a limited concession to the UN, in that the Odendaal Plan had envisaged slicing Namibia into ten homelands, with the 'white areas' incorporated into South Africa. Nevertheless, the South African proposals fell far short of self-government and independence and the UN rejected them. When the Advisory Council was created in March 1973 it became clear that it was to be part of a federal structure incorporating a number of Bantustans.[16]

The Council's members came from most of Namibia's eleven supposed 'population groups'. It was, however, rejected by SWAPO, SWANU, Clemens Kapuuo (who had become Herero paramount after the death of Hosea Kutako in 1970) and, shortly after it first met, by the Mbanderu *omuhona* Munjuku II; it only survived until 1974. Early in the previous year, the government also amended the Development of Self-government for Native Nations in South West Africa Act to allow 'homelands' to become 'self-governing'. In Owambo and Kavango, elected legislative assemblies replaced the previous appointed bodies. In addition, in 1974 a SWA Coloured Council was set up, quickly becoming a focus for protest against racial discrimination; in 1976, Rehoboth became self-governing; in the same year, a Nama Council was established for the first time, based on five previously existing 'tribal' administrative bodies; and in 1977 the Damara Council gained more powers.

The move to 'self-government' was met by a new wave of protest, particularly in Katutura and Owambo, in which the SYL was a prime mover. In Owambo, where, in the elections of August 1973, the Ovambo Independence Party of Chief Filemon Elifas was the only party on the ballot paper, a boycott campaign was phenomenally successful and the turnout reached only 2.5 per cent. In Kavango, however, there was a 66 per cent vote. After the elections, the new Ovamboland Bantustan government instituted floggings of political opponents, women and men, using a palm tree branch[17] (these were eventually declared illegal when challenged in court by the SYL and the Lutheran and Anglican churches). Protest and unrest reached a crescendo in 1973–75. In August 1973 a crowd of three thousand marched on the magistrates' court in Ondangwa, where three activists were on trial, and a riot ensued. On the same day a large and peaceful SYL rally was held in Katutura, but the event ended in mass arrests, and public meetings were then banned. In this period hundreds of SWAPO and SYL supporters were arrested, detained and tortured, in the north and beyond, and some of the leaders were tried in court. Jerry Ekandjo, Jacob Ngidinua and Eshriel Taapopi (all of the SYL) were sent to Robben Island; David Meroro, SWAPO's Vice-president, was tortured and held in solitary confinement; and John Ya Otto, also of SWAPO, went into exile.

The SYL used a newly radical rhetoric, calling on Namibians to campaign directly for their liberation rather than waiting for the UN to act—'every Namibian must join in the struggle for freedom'[18]—and even declaring that 1974 would be the year of independence. This boldness caused some nervousness among the SWAPO leadership inside the country, who for their part were now campaigning for independence through the National Convention, a coalition formed in 1971. Headed by Clemens Kapuuo, the Convention incorporated SWAPO, SWANU, NUDO, the Herero Chief's Council, and smaller parties representing Nama and Damara groups and some Rehobothers. However, tensions soon surfaced between Kapuuo and the external leadership of SWAPO, particularly when, in 1973, the UN General Assembly recognised SWAPO as the 'authentic representative of the Namibian people'.[19] In the following year, anxious to safeguard Herero possession of the land they then occupied, Kapuuo entered into negotiations with the South African authorities over the future of the reserve at Aminuis (as noted in the previous chapter); he also became the only black political figure of any standing to enter the new round of constitutional negotiations (the Turnhalle talks, to be described below). In February 1975 the National Convention broke apart, and SWAPO, with SWANU and other parties, established the Namibia National Convention (NNC). The split between SWAPO and the Herero leadership proved of long duration. Kapuuo's outlook was at odds with nationalist ideology in that it remained essentially tied to Herero claims to identity and land; his major historical reference point was the land loss of the German period whose memory, he argued, SWAPO as an Ovambo organisation did not share.[20]

The Border Opens

In 1974 a major shift in the international situation led to the intensification of conflict both inside and outside Namibia. In April, the government of Portugal was overthrown in a coup, and its successor quickly moved to grant the Portuguese colonies independence. In Angola there were three competing groups: the National Front for the Liberation of Angola (FNLA); the National Union for the Total Independence of Angola (UNITA); and the Popular Front for the Liberation of Angola (MPLA). Although a plan for the transition to independence was agreed in January 1975, it broke down and civil war ensued, in which South Africa and the US supported the FNLA and UNITA, while the Soviet Union backed the MPLA. South Africa, encouraged by the US, intervened directly in this maelstrom and invaded Angola in August 1975, but was repelled by the MPLA, with the help of Cuban troops and Soviet armaments. In March 1976 South Africa pulled out, and the MPLA established itself as the first government of independent Angola. In December, after US involvement became known to the American public, Congress banned further secret aid.[21]

The new situation posed a number of challenges for the SWAPO leadership in exile. The end of Portuguese colonial rule meant that Namibia's northern border with Angola effectively opened in mid-1974, making it possible to send fighters of the People's Liberation Army of Namibia (PLAN)[22] directly into SWAPO's heartland of Owambo, where military action escalated from mid-1975.[23] It also raised the diplomatic problem of choosing an allegiance in the initially confused situation in Angola: SWAPO briefly sided with UNITA, before throwing in its lot with the MPLA. At the same time, the movement's position in Zambia, to which it had transferred its headquarters (from Tanzania) after the 1969–70 Tanga Congress, had become precarious. The move south had been made possible by Zambia's independence in 1964 and President Kaunda's support for the Namibian liberation movement (he also backed those of other countries, including South Africa). In 1974, however, relations between Kaunda and South African Prime Minister Vorster briefly improved, and SWAPO's continued ability to conduct military action from Zambia was thus thrown into doubt.

A further, and most far-reaching, consequence of the opening of the border was to precipitate the journey into exile of 'a very large part of the country's literate Oshiwambo-speaking youth', male and female, together with a minority of older people. Perhaps 6,000 left the country between June 1974 and early 1975; there were also later 'waves' of flight into exile, particularly in 1976 and 1978. Those who left did so for a variety of reasons, the strongest being opposition to apartheid and the South African occupation: the younger generation in particular had been politicised through the war, the activities of the SYL and their experience of Bantu education. Many were also keen to pursue their education.[24]

SWAPO, which in 1974 had only small-scale facilities in Zambia,[25] had considerable problems finding accommodation and supplies for the new arrivals. As large numbers of new, enthusiastic recruits joined PLAN, they became increasingly disillusioned by their experience of shortages of food and other essential supplies; there were also high levels of discontent among the small core of long-standing members of PLAN (which probably numbered only between two and three hundred at any one time before 1974). Rumours of badly planned and executed missions flourished, as well as allegations of corruption, and there was much unhappiness with SWAPO's initial closeness to UNITA. The SYL leaders, who had gone into exile together and established offices in Lusaka, also played an important role in these events. By early 1975 they were voicing concerns about inefficiency and finance, the lack of a clear political programme and the unwillingness of SWAPO leaders to allow debate or, apparently, to move in the direction of socialism. This widespread discontent crystallised into vociferous demands for a new congress, as promised at Tanga.

Negotiations failed to resolve the situation, and in April 1976 tensions finally exploded. At the SWAPO leadership's request, the Zambian army arrested an estimated 1,600–1,800 SWAPO members and detained them at a camp at Mboroma, near Kabwe, north of Lusaka. Eleven prominent leaders, including the SYL group and five of the SWAPO executive who had been sympathetic to them (among them Andreas Shipanga and Solomon Mifima), were imprisoned in Tanzania, with President Nyerere's cooperation. This group was freed in 1978 as a result of international pressure. Those in the Mboroma camp experienced harsh conditions, particularly a very severe food shortage. Two of the detainees eventually escaped and made the camp's existence known internationally, whereupon those imprisoned were offered the choice of leaving SWAPO under United Nations protection or rehabilitation within

SWAPO, at Mboroma; the latter option was accepted by all but two to three hundred. Conditions in the camp improved, but during this period there may have been killings of perhaps forty-five to fifty individuals.[26]

The events of the mid-1970s—and indeed those of the 1980s, when the 'spy crisis' within SWAPO led to a new wave of detentions, as we shall see below—are still highly contested in Namibia, where the issues they raise have not been resolved. That these events occurred, however, has been shown by substantial research and cannot now be in any serious doubt.[27]

The actions of the SWAPO leadership in exile can be understood partly as a reaction to increasingly difficult circumstances in a genuinely perilous war situation, as the volume of new arrivals put its logistics under considerable stress. The leadership thus treated the dissension essentially as a military mutiny, rather than a legitimate demand for democratic accountability. These considerations, however, hardly justify SWAPO's extreme reaction to the crisis, which resulted in large-scale human rights violations. The heavy-handedness of its response was partly due to the threat felt by those in power from the young, relatively well-educated people now joining the ranks and questioning the actions of the leadership. In these circumstances SWAPO's office-holders opted for authoritarianism, a course that was possible because they were, essentially, running a 'state within a state', supported by the presidents of the neighbouring countries (and, indeed, much of the international community) but without the checks and balances to which an elected government would have been subject.

In the aftermath of the crisis, SWAPO appointed a commission under John Ya Otto, which, in Dobell's words, defended the organisation on the grounds that it had been 'responding to a counter-revolutionary uprising led by reactionary elements in the movement'.[28] The Commission blamed a supposed international plot involving among others South Africa, West Germany, Shipanga and Mifima. At the same time, however, it admitted that SWAPO had been partly at fault, and that structural problems existed within the movement.

The Commission's recommendations for dealing with these problems were discussed at an Enlarged Central Committee Meeting (although not a full Congress) in July–August 1976 in Zambia. As well as restructuring and formalising the practical functioning of the movement, including its finances, the meeting agreed a new Political Programme. This document once again committed SWAPO to fight for national independence through organising the 'broad masses', to encourage national consciousness and do away with tribalism, and to build 'a classless, non-exploitative society based on the ideals and principles of scientific socialism'.[29] It went on to promise economic justice as well as education and medical care for all. The language of the movement had become infused with the vocabulary of socialism: members were 'comrades'; Namibians suffered from capitalist as well as apartheid exploitation. There was no detailed economic argument, however, and critics are probably right to argue that the programme reflected the need to please SWAPO's Eastern bloc sponsors rather more than a deep engagement with socialism. Nor, despite the call for mass mobilisation, did a meaningful commitment to the empowerment of people at grassroots level emerge.[30]

The Ya Otto Commission smoothed over the crisis both internally and with SWAPO's international supporters. Indeed, the movement's ability to make limited reforms after a crisis became part of a characteristic pattern: SWAPO's activities and policies continued to be contested, and authoritarianism did not always win out. The organisation's limited, but nevertheless significant, flexibility over gender roles in particular demonstrates this. Political office within the movement had hitherto been almost exclusively dominated by men; one resident of the north observed later, 'We [women] were not really counted, you see, women were equated with children'.[31] Nevertheless, women had long been involved in protest and political activism, and supported the liberation movements in numerous ways. The SWAPO Women's Council (SWC) was founded in exile in 1969/70, with Libertine Amathila as its first secretary. With the arrival in exile of thousands of young women in the mid-1970s, demands for women's rights grew stronger. At the 1976 Enlarged Central Committee meeting, five women were voted onto SWAPO's governing body, and the movement added 'combating sexism' to its aims; women were also allowed to join PLAN, in which some attained leadership positions. In 1980 the SWC held its first congress and appointed Gertrud Kandanga, then in prison in Namibia, as its deputy secretary. SWAPO did not become a bastion of gender equality, but there was significant change in this area.[32]

From the mid to late 1970s, the movement became increasingly well organised in both Zambia and Angola in order to provide for its members, who eventually numbered between forty and fifty thousand.[33] A large settlement was opened at Nyango in Zambia, and another at

Kwanza Sul in Angola; there were also facilities at Lubango and Cassinga (the latter set up in 1977) in Angola, as well as a network of smaller camps. SWAPO assumed the functions of education, health and defence provision for the exile community. The first school in the camps was opened in 1973, and by 1984 there were between eight and ten thousand pupils in education in Kwanza Sul, and between two and two and a half thousand in Zambia; there was a secondary school at Loudima in Congo; and about a thousand were also being educated in Cuba, with smaller numbers in East Germany and other Eastern bloc countries, where many children were sent for safety after the attack on Cassinga in 1978 (when over six hundred exiles were killed in a bombing raid by the South African Defence Force—see below). In the 1980s literacy and other forms of basic education, run partly by the SWAPO Women's

Fig. 25. Dr Libertine Amathila working at a clinic in Nyango refugee camp, Zambia (undated). SWAPO ran extensive programmes in health care and education and training for its exiled population, and was very successful in obtaining aid funding for this purpose. Amathila, one of SWAPO's most prominent female members, was the first Secretary of the SWAPO Women's Council; in 2005, she became Deputy Prime Minister. (Reproduced courtesy of the National Archives of Namibia [no. 13203]. From the collections of the International Defence and Aid Fund [IDAF]).

283

Council, were provided in particular for women who lacked formal schooling; the SWC also played a leading role in delivering health care for the camps. Vocational education was provided at Sumbe in Angola. For post-school education SWAPO had its own college, the United Nations Institute for Namibia (UNIN), founded in 1976 in Lusaka, and large numbers of scholarships to universities around the world were also made available. It is estimated that up to 15 per cent of the exile community received 'comprehensive post-secondary training'.[34]

This educational and health provision was made possible by donor aid which, because of Namibia's special international status, was generous. In 1979, for example, aid arriving through the UN alone amounted to US $15 million.[35] Assistance came not only from aid agencies and governments, but also from a large number of solidarity organisations around the world, whose main activity was political campaigning against apartheid.[36] The level of political and practical support that SWAPO was able to elicit was a measure of its success, not only in continuing to make its case at the UN, but also in creating an international infrastructure which, among other things, co-operated with solidarity organisations and was highly effective in distributing information and campaign literature.[37]

Morale and conditions in the camps varied with time and place. A UNICEF delegation to Cassinga in April 1978—a month before it was attacked—reported high levels of motivation among the refugees, as they directed their thoughts towards independence: 'They [the Namibians at Cassinga] are a community which, despite the adversity of the conditions in which they live, displays very high social organisation... Both men and women, as well as the young people, participate in dynamic fashion...'[38]

In general, it seems that the administration and control of the camps was achieved through military-style discipline, and it is certainly true that some individual officers abused their powers. This did not, however, preclude active engagement by the exiles, among whom there developed a strong sense of community cohesion, and considerable belief in maintaining unity in the face of South Africa's military might. During the long grind of the 1980s, however, when initial hopes for independence had been disappointed, deep tensions emerged within SWAPO and, in Angola in particular, logistical difficulties meant that food was sometimes in short supply, while the war made the camps vulnerable to attack.[39]

The War in the Late 1970s

Inside Namibia, both armed conflict and other forms of protest escalated after the decolonisation of Angola. Even after the main flight
across the border began, demonstrations and unrest continued. However, in 1975 a new poll was held in Owambo in order to double the
number of elected members of the Legislative Assembly to forty-two.
On this occasion the turnout in the north, at 70 per cent, was much
higher than in the 1973 vote (although among Oshiwambo-speakers
in the south, who also took part, it was only 4.2 per cent), and Peter
Kalangula and his Christian Democratic Action party won the election.
The high voting figures were probably a result both of the flight into
exile of many SWAPO organisers and of South African coercion of the
voters through a strong military presence and threats to pensions, land
and jobs.

The remainder of the decade saw the north of Namibia increasingly
transformed into a war zone, as the South African military presence
grew, attacks by SWAPO fighters intensified and more repressive legislation was applied. In 1976, residents of Owambo were removed from
a kilometre-wide strip of land running along the Angolan border, and
South African troops were first brought into the north of Namibia by
air. By now, international observers were putting the numbers of South
African troops in the north of the country at anywhere between fifteen
and forty-five thousand.[40]

In Caprivi, several thousand FNLA troops who had retreated from
Angola with the South Africans in 1976 became part of the South
African Defence Force (SADF) as 32 Battalion, and launched raids
into Angola against civilians and SWAPO fighters. The Kavango also
became an important base for the provision of South African aid to
UNITA, whose strength in southern Angola increased dramatically in
1976–77. By the end of the decade, however, the Angolan government
had largely regained control, although UNITA retained a headquarters
at Jamba.[41]

Despite the South African government's new security measures,
PLAN's activity in Owambo continued to grow, peaking in 1978–80,
a time of high morale. In Oshiwambo-speaking areas (where the guerrillas carried out some political mobilisation) local people provided
food and shelter. Operating mainly in the north (and on foot), PLAN
fighters made attacks on the South African forces and planted mines in

order to blow up convoys. Some were also able to operate as far south as the Otavi triangle, the prosperous white farming area bounded by the three towns of Otavi, Grootfontein and Tsumeb.[42] However, although PLAN was intermittently able to cause a great deal of damage to its opponents, it remained overall much the weaker party, and its campaign was ultimately most effective as 'armed propaganda'. It was in Angola, not in Namibia, that the military conflict was finally to play a crucial role in forcing South Africa to the negotiating table.

The Turnhalle Constitutional Settlement and Resolution 435

By 1974 internal protest, continued pressure from the UN and the threat of international sanctions had forced the South African government into limited concessions. It now initiated a new constitutional process aimed at a settlement for Namibia that it could promote as 'independence' but that would, as far as possible, ensure that the South Africans retained some control over the territory: the latter could thus continue to act as a very broad defensive buffer between South Africa and the rest of Africa. The Turnhalle[43] Constitutional Conference, which replaced the 1973 Advisory Council, was based on an essentially federal and ethnic model. There were over one hundred and fifty delegates, selected on the basis of 'tribe' and drawn from all eleven 'population groups'.[44] The participant with the largest popular following was Clemens Kapuuo; other delegates included ministers and officials from the Bantustan administrations, among them Cornelius Ndjoba and Alfons Majavero, the Chief Ministers of Ovamboland and Kavango respectively, and Dirk Mudge and Eben van Zyl, members of the white Legislative Assembly's Executive Committee. Others who had resisted South African rule—Kozonguizi, Kerina and Emil Apollus—now returned from exile and became involved in the Turnhalle process. Neither SWAPO nor SWANU, however, agreed to participate.

In August 1976, the Turnhalle delegates proposed an independence date of 31 December 1978, with an interim government holding the reins in the meantime; in March 1977 they agreed a draft constitution and bill of rights. Constitutional change followed. On 1 September 1977 the Administrator was replaced by an Administrator-General (AG) with wide governmental powers,[45] whose task was to make preparations for what was billed as independence; Judge T.M. Steyn was the first to take the post. As a prelude to planned elections, the Turnhalle conference was disbanded on 7 November 1977, and most of its members (with the exception of the National Party) combined to form the multi-racial, but still white-dominated, Democratic Turnhalle Alliance (DTA). Its first office-holders included Clemens Kapuuo as president and Dirk Mudge as chairman. As part of the same process, white Namibians ceased to sit in the South African Parliament, and most of the powers for the direct rule of Namibia that had been taken by the South African government since the Second World War were returned to Windhoek.

In October 1977 the Administrator-General ended many aspects of the influx control system, abolishing passes, permits to stay in residential areas and the forced removal of unemployed Africans from the towns (although black Namibians still needed permission to seek work in urban areas and the registration of contracts remained compulsory). This was a further stage in the gradual weakening of the pass and labour laws that had occurred after the strike of 1971–72; in 1975 the Masters and Servants legislation and the Extra-territorial and Northern Natives Proclamation had both been repealed.[46] The AG also abolished legislation outlawing inter-racial sexual relations and marriage;[47] the end of Bantu education was announced in December 1977; and, in June 1978, equal pay for equal work was introduced—although this had limited practical effect.

Although these changes went much further than any previous reforms, the Turnhalle settlement essentially preserved many of the crucial constitutional features of the apartheid years. The path to genuine independence was barred by the fact that South Africa retained control over vital areas of government including military matters, foreign relations, finance, internal security, broadcasting and customs and excise. The possibility of full and viable independence was further undermined when South Africa directly annexed Walvis Bay, Namibia's only deep-water port, on 1 September 1977. Turnhalle meant, moreover, a reinvention of the Bantustan policy—under an increasingly complex federal structure—rather than its abandonment. The draft constitution set out a three-tier system, with eleven ethnic administrations forming a 'second tier' below the central government; the third and lowest level consisted of local and municipal authorities. The second-tier authorities were to have jurisdiction over people of the same ethnic group, whether resident in homelands or not.[48]

The new constitutional arrangements were actively promoted to white Namibians, who approved them by a 95 per cent vote in May

1977. Opposition to the Turnhalle process was led by SWAPO. In 1975 the internal leadership produced a 'Discussion Paper on the Constitution of Independent Namibia', advocating Western-style democracy, and the following year a conference in Walvis Bay helped to refocus the direction of the movement, rejecting the Turnhalle process in favour of full independence, and re-electing the external and internal leadership.[49] SWAPO now developed into a more truly national movement as other community leaders came to the belief that a decisive moment had been reached. In 1976 Hendrik Witbooi (the grandson of the famous Namibian leader) and other Nama-speaking leaders brought the communities at Gibeon, Vaalgras, Keetmanshoop and Hoachanas—about four-fifths of the Nama-speaking population of 37,000—into SWAPO. The south was now, they declared, 'politically lost to the South African government and its allies, the Turnhalle',[50] and students and teachers there went on strike in protest at apartheid legislation and Bantu education. Other groups to join SWAPO included, in 1977, the Association for the Preservation of the Tjamuaha/Maharero Royal House (which had opposed Kapuuo's succession).

As SWAPO's ranks swelled, the Namibia National Convention dissolved. A third, much smaller, political force, composed of groups willing neither to participate in Turnhalle nor to ally with SWAPO, also came together under the rubric of the Namibia National Front (NNF). One of its members was SWANU, which now saw sufficient potential in the changing political scene for its external leadership to return home. The NNF also included the Damara Council under Justus Garoeb,[51] the Mbanderu under Munjuku Nguvauva, some former SWAPO members, including Andreas Shipanga, and the white Federal Party under Bryan O'Linn. The less liberal—and majority—sections of the white political community split in 1977 between the Republican Party under Dirk Mudge, which co-operated in the Turnhalle process, and AKTUR (Action Committee for the Maintenance of Turnhalle Principles), which came to oppose Turnhalle and was also joined by Hans Diergaardt, leader of the Rehoboth Council.

In recognition of the growth of SWAPO's support, and in frustration at South Africa's continued intransigence, the UN had, in late 1976, now declared SWAPO the 'sole authentic' representative of the Namibian people. This significant and controversial decision recognised the fact that SWAPO represented the hopes and aspirations of the majority of the population of Namibia (as the results of the independence election thirteen years later were to prove). The new designation of SWAPO also placed emphasis on unity of purpose and action in a struggle in which South Africa was still very much the stronger party, and carried a clear message about the illegitimacy of Turnhalle and South African rule. Nevertheless, the decision also effectively ignored the political representation of a significant minority of Namibians, particularly the large part of the Otjiherero-speaking population that acknowledged Kapuuo's authority, and supporters of Namibia's oldest liberation movement, SWANU.

Politics were thus becoming increasingly polarised, a trend accentuated when Kapuuo was assassinated in Katutura in March 1978 (SWAPO, although accused by the DTA of his murder, denied responsibility). But while the split that opened up between SWAPO and Kapuuo was one in which traditionalism was pitted against nationalism and modernity, the division between the two ideologies was not always as clear-cut as it was painted at the time. The Witboois, for example, successfully meshed together the politics of tradition and resistance, while other hereditary leaders perhaps saw participation in Turnhalle as an engagement with modernity.[52] Nor was the struggle over national constitutional issues the only fault-line to cut across the complex terrain of Namibian politics. There were also political currents and contests for hegemony that apparently spoke primarily to older conflicts, identities and ways of belonging, as well as to local dynamics. For example the graves of Mureti and Vita Tom, both important figures in the history of Kaoko, were memorialised in the mid-1980s.[53]

At the same time as it was pursuing an internal constitutional settlement, South Africa continued to negotiate with the United Nations. In 1976 the UN Security Council passed Resolution 385, which laid down arrangements for the transition to independence in Namibia and stipulated that the South African administration was to give way to a temporary UN authority that would hold free and fair elections. In the same year, the UN formally adopted the name 'Namibia' for South West Africa.

South Africa would not agree to Resolution 385. In this it was supported by some Western countries, principally the USA, the UK and France, which wanted to see an independent Namibia sympathetic to their interests (unlike the new governments of Angola and Mozambique) and were also anxious to prevent the imposition of economic sanctions against South Africa—a goal of the increasingly influential anti-apartheid campaigns around the world. These political objectives were carried forward by the Western Contact Group, consisting of the USA, the UK, France, West Germany and Canada, which was now set up to hammer out a new deal with South Africa. The result of these negotiations was then accepted by the Security Council as Resolution 435/1978. The principal difference between the two resolutions was that, under 435, the South African government would remain in place and conduct elections 'under UN supervision'; the later agreement also excluded Walvis Bay, which under 385 would have been returned to Namibia.[54]

South Africa accepted Resolution 435 in 1978, but without retreating from Turnhalle, which was at odds with UN requirements. On 4 May 1978 South Africa moved to destabilise the situation further by launching Operation Reindeer, an air and ground attack on SWAPO bases in Angola. The main target was the refugee camp at Cassinga, 250 km north of the Namibian border, where over six hundred were killed and a similar number wounded; in all, over 1,200 people died as a result of Operation Reindeer. More than two hundred survivors from the Chetequera and Vietnam camps near to Cassinga were subsequently imprisoned at Hardap, south of Windhoek (they were released in 1984).

The Cassinga massacre became a focal point of the memorialisation of SWAPO's struggle. There has been much controversy as to whether Cassinga was a civilian or military base; the report of South Africa's Truth and Reconciliation Commission found that it was 'both a military base and a refugee camp. It housed a considerable number of combatants, including senior officers. It also housed considerable numbers of civilians'.[55] Certainly, women and children were killed in some numbers, and the first-hand accounts of camp residents recall an unprovoked attack on a refugee camp. Linda Nambadi, who was aged eleven at the time of the massacre, later remembered:

The battle lasted from seven in the morning to seven in the evening and all the time everybody was running, running hither and thither, running up and down...It was like this: I was running, then I found somebody and immediately we ran together; we ran until she was lying in a pool of blood, dead...But you continued running, running till you burst into smashed people. Some were wounded, crying for help...Oh, it was bad, very bad. The South Africans were bombing from above and soldiers were shooting at us.[56]

The apparent contradictions in South African policy at this time—which resulted in a recurring pattern of delaying and destabilising tactics—stemmed from the fact that the regime was attempting to keep its options open. Having failed to achieve the direct incorporation of Namibia, it veered, or appeared to veer, between two alternatives: either an internal settlement—Turnhalle—based on the establishment of Bantustans and given some of the trappings of independence in the hope of gaining acceptance by the international community; or engagement with the UN, allowing elections leading to Namibia's independence as a nation-state, but with the hope of manipulating the process in order to achieve an independent Namibia compliant with South Africa's interests.

Developments within South Africa added further layers of complication to this picture, particularly after P.W. Botha, the powerful Defence Minister, became President in September 1978. Botha claimed to be in favour of a reformist strategy, declaring to the white population that they must 'adapt or die', but nevertheless clearly intending to hold on to white power. At the same time, he unleashed his 'total strategy', which involved countering military opposition to South African rule in both that country and Namibia, as well as weakening and destabilising the other southern African states politically and economically. These objectives were pursued through a mixture of threats, the infiltration of opposing forces and military aggression, including large-scale invasions of neighbouring countries and armed raids, assassinations and the planting of car bombs on their territory. Indeed, the military wing of the South African state became so powerful that it was able to influence policy significantly, and at crucial moments the government was barely able to control it. Diplomacy was also an element of the 'total strategy', but a much less important one.[57]

Relations worsened rapidly after Cassinga, and both South Africa and SWAPO launched new attacks. Even then, however, SWAPO agreed to restart negotiations with South Africa and accepted Resolution 435. Such flexibility stemmed both from the movement's focus on the goal of national independence and its dependence on its allies, who encouraged it to make compromises at significant moments: for example, the Front-Line states (the independent countries bordering South Africa), while providing resources and bases for the struggle, were literally in the South African firing line and therefore had a strong interest in securing peace. SWAPO also accepted the 'Constitutional

Principles' drafted in 1981, which determined that the constitution of independent Namibia would be a liberal democracy—an indication that it was less committed to socialism than many of its statements suggested.[58] South Africa, however, moved in the opposite direction when it held internal elections (boycotted by SWAPO) for a Constituent Assembly at the end of 1978. The turnout in these elections officially stood at 80 per cent and was thus relatively high,[59] not least because registration and voting were both characterised by intimidation and coercion. The DTA also received significant South African funding. It did, however, also have genuine popular support.[60]

The DTA received 82 per cent of the vote[61] and was thus installed as the new government, but it could not achieve legitimacy nationally or internationally. In May 1979 the Constituent Assembly was converted into a National Assembly, with sweeping powers subject to veto by the Administrator-General. At the same time, however, because of white protest at the pace of change, Steyn was replaced as AG by Gerrit Viljoen, a former Broederbond chairman; in 1980 he reintroduced prohibitions on interracial sexual relations. The independence of Zimbabwe in the same year, however, increased pressure on South Africa to make progress with its 'internal solution', and elections were held for a number of 'second-tier' 'Representative Authorities' (under AG 8 of 1980). In most cases the DTA received a majority of the votes, although turnout was low, and the National Party gained the white administration, while the Damara vote was won by the Damara Council. The authorities avoided the political risk of holding an election in Owambo (the home of 47 per cent of the population) by installing Peter Kalangula and his party on the basis of the 1975 poll.[62]

The new DTA government continued the process of liberalisation begun by the AG. In 1979 it introduced the Abolition of Racial Discrimination (Urban Residential Areas and Public Amenities) Act, which abolished 'petty apartheid' (that is, racial separation in public places). This measure was partly aimed at creating a new, potentially compliant, black middle class. However, many forms of effective racial discrimination remained. Perhaps the most fundamental was the fact that because of unequal funding for the different authorities, in practice the best facilities and resources continued to be reserved for whites. In 1980, for example, only R135m went to the black 'Representative Authorities' out of a total national budget of R520m. In 1981, the health expenditure of the various ethnic authorities ranged from R4.70

to R56.84 per person, while the equivalent figure for whites was R233.70.[63] By 1983, weakened by such internal contradictions, lack of external support and the loss of Kapuuo, the DTA administration had collapsed.

The short period of the Turnhalle regime had seen further internal repression, militarisation and engagement in regional conflict. Rather than moving towards independence, Namibia was increasingly becoming both a target of, and a base for, South African military operations. New security and emergency regulations, targeted at internal dissent as well as insurgency, were imposed in 1977 and, after Kapuuo's assassination, in 1978. Ovamboland, the Kavango, the Caprivi, Windhoek and five other towns were proclaimed 'security districts', where detention without trial was permitted for up to thirty days and was automatically renewable. In 1979 a curfew was introduced in the north, under which anyone found outside at night was liable to be shot. In the 'homelands', the authorities implemented a series of reprisals against those who had refused to participate in Turnhalle. Hendrik Witbooi himself was placed in solitary confinement in 1978. SWAPO leaders and members were harassed, imprisoned and maltreated; eventually the repression reached such a pitch that, although the organisation was never actually banned, in June 1979 its deputy national chairman, Dan Tjongarero, closed down its headquarters in Windhoek.

SWAPO continued to operate informally, but Tjongarero's controversial decision left a vacuum. The churches now became increasingly outspoken. Having publicly opposed Turnhalle, they also critiqued Western proposals for Namibian independence in the Maseru Declaration (1978). Through the newly founded Council of Churches in Namibia (CCN), they engaged in practical activities including help for political prisoners. In the north, church newspapers acted as a means of communication about politics as well as religion. In response, the churches became targets: South African forces destroyed printing presses and buildings and intimidated congregations, sometimes violently. Some foreign church workers—Heinz Hunke, Ed Morrow and Justin Ellis—were deported for opposing torture.[64]

It was also during the Turnhalle period that the war became 'Namibianised' to an unprecedented degree. Although the recruiting of auxiliary forces, particularly among San, had started in 1974, it was in 1980 that the South African government began in earnest to give a local identity to some of the army units in Namibia. By this date there were about 70–80,000 troops in the territory as a whole, and South Africa had become the most heavily armed country in the southern African region.[65] In 1980 the South West Africa Territorial Force (SWATF)—the local arm of the SADF—was founded, to be followed in 1981 by the South West Africa Police (SWAP). The state also introduced compulsory military service for Namibian males over sixteen living outside the northern war zone, regardless of race. In 1980 local battalions were also founded in the different regions of Namibia. The best-known was 1 Ovambo Battalion, more commonly known as 101 Battalion, which consisted of Oshiwambo-speakers who acted as guides to the South African troops using their tracking skills and local knowledge. There were similar units in the other northern regions including 201 Battalion, consisting of San centred on the Omega Base in the Caprivi.[66] Local people were attracted into these units through the generous pay offered, and economic dependence on the army grew. By 1988 the forces employed 9,277 people across the north (34 per cent of those in formal employment).[67] Engagement with the army also became a survival and regeneration strategy in the severe drought of 1980–81: pastoralists in Kaoko, for instance, experienced a massive drop in stock numbers, and used cash raised through military service to rebuild their herds.[68] Whole communities of San, already marginalised and impoverished, became dependent on the army for subsistence.[69]

At the same time, the state redoubled its attempts, begun in the mid-1970s, to 'win hearts and minds' through a number of propaganda strategies, not least the sustained deployment of visuals such as posters.[70] As part of this effort, soldiers worked as teachers in schools in the north; in Kavango they also carried out building and water-supply work. Such activities had some success in eastern Kavango, but were generally viewed with suspicion in Owambo and western Kavango, where SWAPO was popular; soldiers were banned from schools by the Ovambo Chief Minister, Peter Kalangula, in 1985. In Owambo, support for SWAPO extended from migrant workers and peasant farmers to prosperous business people and educated professionals. Nevertheless, even here backing for the movement was not quite universal, partly because of the presence of locally recruited troops, and partly because SWAPO's policy of assassinating representatives of the occupying power—traditional leaders, those thought to be informers, and members of the South African security and police forces—created tensions. The best-known assassination was that of Chief Elifas, the head of the Bantustan government from 1973, who was shot dead in August 1975. In this instance, however, SWAPO denied responsibility, and indeed there were cases in which killings were actually carried out by members of the South African forces disguised as PLAN.

South African propaganda efforts were also undermined, especially in Owambo, by the aggression with which military and quasi-military units extended the war into the remotest communities of the north, hunting down PLAN fighters and using random violence as a weapon to try to detach them from the essential support of their rural base. This counter-insurgency strategy was put in place in 1977–78,[71] and the war of terror that it produced continued throughout the 1980s. By 1988, war-weariness, demoralisation and anger had become palpable. Women at Engela, questioned about their experiences of war, responded: 'We are not going to tell you of our problems, because we have told our story so many times, and still no help comes. To ask us again is like pouring petrol on fire...We are tired of telling. Our burden is too heavy to pick up. We are angry'.[72]

The most notorious of the special units was Koevoet, named after the Afrikaans for 'crowbar' and founded as a counter-insurgency section of the South West African Police in 1979 under Hans Dreyer, former head of the security police in Natal. It consisted of up to 3,000 personnel—mainly black Namibians, many of them recruited in Owambo—under the command of white officers, and it was responsible for inflicting much of the worst damage on the civilian population of northern Namibia in the last decade before independence. Its activities included hunting down and fighting SWAPO guerrillas with patrols of *casspir*s (tanks). If prisoners were taken, it seems that they were usually interrogated and 'turned' to become agents for the South African forces, or killed. The South African Truth and Reconciliation Commission found later that 'While combatants were initially put on trial and imprisoned...there is considerable evidence that, as the war progressed, South African security forces, especially Koevoet, resorted increasingly to summary executions of captured combatants'.[73]

There is also evidence that PLAN fighters were thrown from aeroplanes into the sea off Namibia. During the independence process South Africa seems to have released only twenty political prisoners; although it had already released some, this is probably also an indication that it held very few.[74]

It was, however, Koevoet's indiscriminate use of violence against civilians—often at night and sometimes posing as members of PLAN—that caused the most fear: shooting, killing, beatings, rape and the destruction of homesteads became weapons against the population of the north:

> They drive across the crops...They run to all the people in the *kraal* [homestead], slapping them, shouting 'where's the terri [terrorist]?'...If you don't produce your ID card immediately, you are beaten—children, the elderly, pregnant women...you know anything can happen. People can be shot, beaten to death, things will be destroyed or just taken...[75]

The bounty paid to individual Koevoet members for each 'kill' encouraged the murder of civilians and PLAN fighters alike. The population of the north also continued to be subject to arbitrary detention and frequent torture. Rauna Nambinga, for example, detained and interrogated about her brother, said that she 'was beaten almost after every question until the whole of my body was in extreme pain and... swollen'.[76]

There was also severe repression in Kavango, where forced removals away from the river in the mid-1970s, and back to it in 1982, led to a loss in agricultural production as well as resistance that was met with harsh tactics by Koevoet. At the same time, 15–40,000 refugees arrived from Angola. In Kaoko, some 2,000 rifles were distributed among the local population, to use against SWAPO; this influx of weapons is likely also to have resulted in an increase in day-to-day violence. The *omuhona* Vetamuna Tjambiru, a descendant of Kakurukouje, banned people from bringing firearms into his homestead.[77]

The 1980s: The Lost Decade?

By 1980, hopes for a swift transition to independence had been disappointed. The refusal of South Africa to engage with the UN process meant that war would intensify, with the loss of many more lives, in the following years; in 1981, talks on the implementation of Resolution 435 effectively came to an end for the best part of a decade. Nevertheless, it was also during the 1980s that a new flowering of activism inside Namibia helped to make the country increasingly ungovernable, and led to a significant strengthening of civil society.

South Africa justified its hard-line strategy, and promoted it to the US government, by constructing itself as a bastion against the spread of communism in Africa; the Soviet Union had been involved in Africa since the 1960s, and in Angola the Cubans had provided military support to the MPLA since the mid-1970s. The contest between SWAPO and South Africa thus remained embroiled in the power politics of the Cold War, just at the time that a hardening of positions took place internationally, as right-wing governments took power in the UK (1979) and the US (1981). The new American government under President Reagan now embarked on a policy of 'constructive engagement' with South Africa, which effectively removed the threat of sanctions. In 1979 both the Iranian revolution and Soviet intervention in Afghanistan also contributed to international tension. Cuba, the Soviet Union, South Africa and the US all became increasingly involved in Angola; South Africa also stepped up operations against PLAN guerrillas. In May 1980 it launched a ground invasion of 2,000 troops against SWAPO bases more than a hundred miles into Angolan territory, and in the following year Operation Protea saw a South African force of 10,000 attack the bases of SWAPO and FAPLA—which were fighting together—in southern Angola. As this suggests, SWAPO was being drawn into the broader conflict, fighting in Angola as well as sending soldiers across the border into Namibia; although PLAN operations declined from their peak in 1978–80, hundreds of guerrillas were still able to operate during the rainy season in Owambo, and to a lesser extent in Kavango, during the first half of the 1980s. Through 32 Battalion, South Africa also assisted UNITA to take large parts of Cuando Cubango province in southern Angola. Thus, in 1980–82, 'military pressure against Angola and Mozambique grew from low-level harassment to massive sustained assault'.[78]

In 1984 there was a brief lull in the fighting when, under American pressure, Angola and Mozambique both made peace agreements with South Africa (respectively the Lusaka and Nkomati Accords). South Africa largely failed to comply with the terms, however, and did not even withdraw its troops from Angola. US involvement in the situation increased when, in 1985, the Clark Amendment (which had banned secret aid to anti-government forces in Angola a decade before) was repealed, and US funds began to flow directly to UNITA. On the diplomatic front, the Western Contact Group had effectively disintegrated in 1982 following new US demands, not shared by the other participants, that South African withdrawal from Namibia take place in tandem with Cuban withdrawal from Angola. 'Linkage', as this came to be called, was opposed not only by SWAPO, Angola, the Soviet Union and Cuba, but also by Security Council resolutions (for example, UNSCR 539/1983), and resulted in political stalemate for most of the 1980s.[79]

Some commentators have implied that, after the initial agreement of Resolution 435 in 1978, independence was a foregone conclusion. More accurately, however, '...what remained in some doubt throughout this period, was whether and when Namibia's decolonisation from South Africa would take place'.[80] The stresses of this final decade of war contributed, at least in part, to an extreme escalation of human rights violations within SWAPO, which detained and tortured hundreds, and possibly thousands,[81] of its own members, accusing them of spying for South Africa. The detentions were carried out by SWAPO's new Security Organisation, established in 1981 under 'Jesus' Solomon Hawala. Hundreds were imprisoned in 'dungeons' in Lubango in Angola, where some died as a result of the harsh conditions. One detainee described being made to strip naked, '...and [then] beatings started, continuing for several days. They once put me in a bag, tied it and carried me to a big hole where they threw me in and out, telling me they would bury me alive. One evening they tied me to a car and pulled me'.[82] Torture resulted in the video 'confessions' of many of the detainees.

South Africa pursued ruthless counter-insurgency operations as part of its 'total strategy' against the Front-Line states and the liberation movements they accommodated. SWAPO was subjected to the infiltration of spies, propaganda and disinformation, and direct military attacks on its members.[83] These pressures helped to create the 'spy' crisis. But both SWAPO's long-standing authoritarian culture and the increasing power of its Security Organisation were crucial factors in the tragedy. The latter body became increasingly out of control in the 1980s and could not be brought into line by those who opposed its actions within the leadership. Even the President's authority in the situation was brought into question when Kovambo Nujoma, his wife, was detained for a few weeks in 1988. The tactics the Security Organisation adopted were hardly designed to be effective against genuine spies, but rather reflected divisions within SWAPO, as educated people and non-Oshiwambo speakers found themselves particularly targeted. During the independence election campaign of 1989, the extent of SWAPO's detention and torture of its own members was to become widely known for the first time, leading to a weakening of its support within Namibia, especially in the south; a Parents' Committee set up by Erica Beukes (whose brother had been detained) and others demanded justice for the detainees, as did some political parties. Towards the end of that year, one of SWAPO's leaders condemned the use of torture, and acknowledged that not all the detainees had been spies.[84]

In the end, changes in the military situation in southern Angola began to shift the diplomatic deadlock. In the second half of 1985, and again in August 1987, the Angolan army (FAPLA), with Soviet and Cuban (direct and indirect) support, moved south-east from the town of Cuito Cuanavale, with the aim of attacking Mavinga, UNITA's main logistical base. UNITA's headquarters were at Jamba, further to the south-east, and the rebel movement by now effectively controlled the Cuando Cubango province. On both occasions the Angolan forces were pushed back by UNITA, with strong South African and US support. However, the South Africans in their turn failed to take Cuito Cuanavale, despite six months of siege and bombardment in 1987–88. The stalemate thus reached, and the actual and potential losses suffered, encouraged both sides to talk, and the Angolans and their allies to entertain 'linkage' for the first time. Negotiations on the implementation of UN Resolution 435 began in London in May 1988. At the same time, Cuban forces began to mass 15,000 troops further west, north of the border with Owambo. This build-up posed a strong military threat to South African control of the north of Namibia and, although there was no fighting beyond a minor clash at Calueque, it was instrumental in persuading the South Africans to go through with the negotiations. UN Resolution 435/1978 was eventually implemented in 1989, leading to independence for Namibia in 1990.[85]

Factors other than the military stalemate had combined to bring about an end to the war. International politics had swung away from South Africa: there was increasing pressure for sanctions, and in 1986 the US had passed a Comprehensive Anti-Apartheid Act despite Reagan's attempts to veto it. South Africa was in internal turmoil, with a new rise in protest in the 1980s, and the ruling National Party had begun talks with the African National Congress in 1986. Perhaps most important, all sides were counting the cost and finding it too high. The South African economy was not performing well, and the financial cost of war—put by one estimate at $2bn per year (for the whole of its 'distant defensive perimeter')—was a substantial drain. The political cost, particularly as reckoned in the lives of young white conscripts, was also becoming significant. On the other side, the Soviet Union and Angola were increasingly unwilling to fund a force of as many as 55,000 Cuban soldiers. The Angolan government's solid support for the war had been fuelled not only by its immediate need to counter UNITA's attacks, but also by its hope that Namibian independence would put an end to South African destabilisation and support for UNITA. Nevertheless, it was Angola—and in particular its civilian population—that suffered most, as the war devastated the southern regions of the country. According to UN estimates, between 1980 and 1988 it caused the deaths of some 331,000 children in Angola, and in the same period the fighting in that country cost $30 billion. In the north of Namibia, although mortality was much lower, the population was, as we have seen, confronted with daily violence. The social consequences of war included large-scale internal displacement as areas of agricultural land became war zones, the growth of informal settlements in safer areas and a marked worsening of the population's public health conditions.[86]

South Africa's decision to agree to independence had also been influenced by the difficulties increasingly created for it by Namibia's internal politics. For one thing, its clients in Namibia had proved disappointingly unable to deliver a working form of government. After the collapse of the DTA administration, another similar experiment was tried, but with even less success. A Multi-Party Conference, composed of groups and individuals drawn from Namibia's various population groups, was set up. This led to the establishment in June 1985, under Proclamation 101, of an Interim Government of National Unity (also called the Transitional Government of National Unity, TGNU). This consisted of both a National Assembly and a Ministers' Council, but failed in its assigned task of agreeing a new constitution for Namibia in order to bring about an internal form of 'independence'. Proclamation 101 also introduced a Bill of Rights which, however, was more honoured in the breach than the observance.[87]

The second-tier administrations continued to operate, but the problems created by this clumsy and extravagant political solution soon became obvious. The regional authorities had been instituted with little financial control, to the point where the Thirion Commission, which reported in 1983, found numerous examples of corruption, favouritism and mismanagement. In some of the reserves these bodies were acting as a means to channel resources to the cattle-owning elite, promoting the growth of a rural bourgeoisie and chipping away at traditional communal land use arrangements. On the other hand, the Damara Council enjoyed some popularity because it was seen to be using its power in Damaraland even-handedly.[88]

The Thirion Commission called this proliferation of government—which had also created a large number of new government jobs—an 'unbearable burden'[89] on an economy now thrown into crisis by severe drought in the late 1970s and early 1980s. Up to this point, Namibia had experienced sustained growth since the Second World War. This had not resulted in self-sufficiency, however. The economy was still dominated by the export of raw materials: by the late 1970s Namibia, Zambia and Zaire ranked equally as the second largest producers of non-petroleum minerals in Africa,[90] and the multinational corporation Rio Tinto Zinc had also begun to mine uranium at Arandis, near Swakopmund, in 1976. There was still very little manufacturing, and the territory increasingly became a captive market for South African goods. Economic inequality, based on Namibia's racial hierarchy, was extreme: in the mid-1970s, the top 10 per cent of the population received 52.8 per cent of total income, while the bottom 40 per cent had to make do with 5.9 per cent. Black people living in rural areas were generally worse off than those in the towns.[91]

In the late 1970s the drought, combined with international recession, brought the post-war growth to an end, and caused crop failure and the virtual collapse of the karakul industry. This resulted in increasing poverty and unemployment, and a significant migration of Africans, particularly those living south of the Red Line, to the towns—a development also precipitated by the abolition of most aspects of the pass laws in 1977. For much of the colonial period, officials and employers had been confronted with labour shortages; by the late 1970s, however, the position had been decisively reversed and there were no longer enough jobs to go round. Indeed, concerns about 'overpopulation' began to characterise colonial discourse at this period, and in the early 1970s contraceptives, including Depo-Provera, were routinely given to black women without their knowledge or consent.[92]

By 1978, unemployment seems to have been around 25 per cent (but was probably closer to 50 per cent if those under-employed in the subsistence agriculture sector are included),[93] and further redundancies will have been caused by the recession. This generated a wave of community activism, as new groups emerged to fight against poverty and for independence, partially filling the political vacuum created by SWAPO's formal dissolution inside the country. Action was also catalysed by the introduction of conscription, which brought the war into homes south of the Red Line for the first time; the rise in the number of educated young people probably also played a role.[94]

The resistance began in 1983 with protests against rising electricity prices, and street committees were formed in Luderitz, Mariental, Okahandja and other towns. The following year, two national organisations, the Namibian National Students' Organisation (NANSO) and Namibia Women's Voice (NWV), were set up. A list published in 1987 named twenty-nine active community-based organisations, ranging from residents' associations to women's, church, educational and health groups. A number of independent community schools had also been established by the churches, and the SWAPO Women's Council had become active inside the country. Labour organisation also revived (the last period of activity, heavily repressed, had been in the second half of the 1970s, at the Rössing mine in particular). Now, in 1985, the community workers Rosalinde Namises, Lindy Kazombaue and Bob Kandetu established a Workers' Action Committee to address the many complaints they were receiving from employees. The new resistance received a substantial boost from the involvement of the Robben Island prisoners, who were released in the middle of the decade. There was also an increase in pro-independence communications, including the independent but broadly pro-SWAPO newspaper the *Namibian*. These varied initiatives received substantial international support and funding. In 1986, the case for independence and Resolution 435 was made in the |Ae-||Gams[95] declaration, signed by a broad alliance of the CCN, most of the churches, several political parties including SWAPO, and other organisations including the NWV.[96]

This new flowering of civil society was built partly on women's pre-existing support networks, including church groups, and women now took up leadership roles in greater numbers than ever before. Because of these dynamics, a new kind of gender politics began to take shape as organisations such as Namibia Women's Voice worked with the problems of those living in poverty, and made connections between these experiences and liberation politics. Emma Mujoro, churchwoman and activist, argued, 'We cannot sit back and then start working [after independence]. We have to prepare people now...women are so oppressed, they come to adopt it [oppression] as their way of thinking'.[97]

The later 1980s were characterised by large-scale expansion in the trade union movement, and by increased student activism. In September 1986 the first new union, the Namibian Food and Allied Union, was launched, followed in November by the Mineworkers Union of Namibia; these were headed by the former Robben Island prisoners John Pandeni and Ben Ulenga respectively. Between 1987 and 1990 five more new unions followed; an umbrella organisation, the National Union of Namibian Workers, led by Barnabas Tjizu, also emerged.[98] At the same time, labour militancy increased sharply, with 24 strikes taking place across the country in 1987, in contrast to the three reported strikes of the period 1980–85.

Like other civil society organisations, the trade unions were assisted by a certain liberalisation of the political climate begun under Turnhalle and continued under the Interim Government; and, again like the other groups, they tested the limits of the new freedoms and came up against the increasingly repressive tactics that the authorities continued to employ. Thus, although the TGNU gave symbolic (if not substantial) ground—the much-hated workers' compound in Katutura was closed down, and May Day was made a public holiday—it also raided union offices and detained leaders under the Terrorism Act. The government also undermined the trade unions and other community organisation deliberately, by encouraging and funding rival organisations (which were also able to draw on pre-existing opposition to SWAPO within the country). On the other hand, however, an attempt to deal non-violently with worker unrest was made when the Wiehahn Commission was appointed in late 1987. The Commission advocated the recognition of trade unions and the liberalisation and 'modernisation' of union and employment law. Its final report was made in December 1989 and many of its recommendations were implemented after independence.[99]

Popular protest inspired by the student movement came to a head in 1988. This time the impetus came from inside the war zone, where there was a policy of situating army bases next to schools. In 1987, explosions occurred at least fourteen primary schools near the border with Angola, and two students at Ponhofi Secondary School at Ohangwena, Albertina Nghikongelwa and Victoria Nghikofa, were killed in fighting centred on the neighbouring Koevoet base. In March 1988 this sparked a schools strike that spread across the north and to some towns in the south. It drew in perhaps 75,000 students, and was supported by a two-day general strike in June. The interim government responded with new legislative controls and by the detention and violent intimidation of the strikers. By July, approximately 5,600 students had left to join SWAPO in exile.[100]

The boycott did not achieve its immediate objective—the removal of the bases—but it did swell the great wave of protest sweeping Namibia in the 1980s, which in turn helped to undermine South Africa's ability to hold on to the territory. Nevertheless, the community-based movement was ultimately both fragile and the focus for significant tensions. Most of the civil society organisations gave explicit support to SWAPO, seeing national liberation as a necessary precursor of meaningful change, and adopted a policy of non-cooperation with the government.[101] For many in the SWAPO leadership in exile, who felt threatened by the success of the grass-roots movement, this was not enough:

Fig. 26. This photograph, taken by John Liebenberg, shows a demonstration by students at the Windhoek Academy (the forerunner of the University of Namibia) on 9 August 1988. The protest was held in support of the schools boycott, then in full swing, which was demanding the removal of military bases from schools. (© John Liebenberg, published in *Bush of Ghosts*, Umuzi, 2010.)

the emphasis on 'development now', they argued, might weaken the fight for political independence. In the case of NWV, this conflict was, argues Becker, typical of relations between male-dominated liberation movements and women's organisations; eventually, in March 1989, NWV agreed to dissolve itself.[102] This, together with the fact that the community movement emerged only in the 1980s, prevented many of these organisations from putting down strong roots, with the result that, at independence, Namibia's civil society was not very robust.

The Transition to Independence[103]

The negotiations begun in May 1988 led to the agreement of South Africa, Angola and Cuba to the 'Geneva protocols', which set out a timetable for the implementation of Resolution 435 in Namibia, and the withdrawal of both South African and Cuban troops from Angola. In Namibia, the transition to independence was to begin on 1 February 1989, with the arrival of UN personnel in the country, under the aegis of the United Nations Transition Assistance Group (UNTAG); this body, drawn from 109 countries, eventually reached a strength of 4,650 military and 1,498 civilian personnel. There was to be a cease-fire on 1 April, followed by the confinement to base and demobilisa-tion of both the SWATF and PLAN. Voter registration on a single voters' roll would lead to elections for a constituent assembly at the end of the year.

The transition was almost derailed at the outset. SWAPO wanted its troops to be confined to base inside Namibia (where it insisted, not very convincingly, that it had fighters permanently stationed), but the movement had not been a direct participant in the negotiating process, and no such provision had been made. SWAPO then took the rash decision—which also dismayed most of the Front-Line states—to send hundreds of PLAN fighters across the border into Namibia, where they broke cover on the first day of the ceasefire with the intention of hand-ing themselves in to the UN.[104] The SADF designated this an 'invasion', and the South African foreign minister, Pik Botha, pressurised the UN Secretary-General's Special Representative Maarti Ahtisaari (in consul-tation with the UK Prime Minister, Margaret Thatcher, on a brief visit to Namibia at the time) into agreeing to let South African forces out of base to contain the situation. Both Botha and Thatcher seem to have considered it necessary to make this concession in order to calm the

South African security establishment and to safeguard the peace process; the late deployment of the UN in Namibia also meant that it could not send its own troops to the north. In the days immediately following, SWATF troops attacked unprepared PLAN guerrillas, about 140 of whom were killed in the first three days. There were perhaps 250 deaths on all sides before the fighting wound down.[105]

Despite this rocky start, diplomatic efforts brought the transition process back on track by mid-May. It was still dogged by major problems, especially widespread intimidation of the electorate, particularly by Koevoet (officially a police rather than military unit and therefore not at first confined to base) but also by the DTA, which received substantial South African funding. A significant number of SWAPO members were killed during the transition, including the lawyer Anton Lubowski, who was shot dead outside his house.[106] Nevertheless, with UN perseverance and monitoring by Namibian and international observers, a concerted programme of voter education was put in place. The political climate began to change, SWAPO leaders and most of the exiled population returned—42,736 people from forty-two countries by the end of the year[107]—and the elections in December were declared free and fair by the international community. The success of the peace process was testimony to the decades of campaigning waged by Namibians for independence, as well as a considerable achievement on the part of the UN and Namibia's many international supporters. The sense of hope, indeed euphoria, brought by the dawning of independence was expressed in many ways, not least by the name 'Untag' being given to a number of babies born during 1989, and Windhoek's main thoroughfare, Kaiser Street, being spontaneously rechristened 'Independence Avenue' almost overnight.

The election was won by SWAPO, with 384,567 votes—57.3 per cent of the vote—and forty-one seats in the Constituent Assembly. The party gained 92 per cent of the vote in the Ovamboland electoral district, and 50 per cent or over in Tsumeb and Kavango. The DTA was second, with 191,532 votes (28.6 per cent; 21 seats), performing best in the south, Hereroland, Kaoko and other rural areas. Its vote was bolstered by the 'patronage of local affiliated parties that had access to the resources of second-tier administrations, plus the backing of whites, farm-workers, and residents from Angola and South Africa'.[108] Five other parties gained a total of ten seats amongst them. They included the Namibia National Front and the NPF, which each gained one seat; both organisations represented parts of the old SWANU, which had now split.

In the months following the election, the new Namibian constitution was negotiated in the Constituent Assembly with a speed and willingness to compromise that surprised many observers. SWAPO had not achieved a two-thirds majority of the vote, and therefore needed the cooperation of other parties in the talks. The party accepted proportional representation and a second chamber, while the DTA agreed to the creation of a presidency with effective rather than ceremonial power. A Bill of Fundamental Human Rights was incorporated into the constitution, although 'preventive detention' (that is, detention without trial) was only ruled out after the intervention of international organisations, and trade union rights were only partly guaranteed.

Independence was declared on 21 March 1990, and Sam Nujoma was sworn in as President. The success of the constitutional process, together with the changed international situation and SWAPO's flexibility, helped to ensure in the end—and apparently against the odds—that the transition was smooth, and that there was little flight of either capital or people from the country. SWAPO was also careful not to antagonise existing economic interests, doing little at this stage to challenge the ownership of land (the constitution allows compulsory purchase, but at market prices) or of the mines. There was, however, a swift move to increase spending on health, education and housing, end racially exclusive schools and provide free primary education.[109] Namibian territory was finally unified when Walvis Bay was transferred from South African to Namibian rule in 1994.

The history of South African rule in Namibia thus came to an end, seventy-five years after it had begun. That the actual transition to independence was ultimately achieved peacefully is all the more remarkable, considering the level of repression that South Africa had imposed on the territory, and the bitterness (on all sides) caused by war and violence. The experience of committed activists is perhaps best epitomised by the career of Axel Johannes, whose periods in detention reflected the rhythms of Namibia's politics. Having joined the OPO in 1959 Johannes became a prominent activist in the SWAPO Youth League. He was imprisoned for the first time in 1964; arrested again after Omugulu gwombashe and sent to Pretoria, but eventually released because he was a minor; and detained several more times, including in 1975, after the assassination of Chief Elifas, and in 1978 when Clemens Kapuuo was killed. At various points, he also experienced torture, and eventually went into exile in 1980.[110]

More generally, scholars have begun to start to try to quantify the violence of the war, particularly in the north. Research based on newspaper reports between 1979 and 1989 produced a preliminary figure of 1,268 civilian deaths, 929 of whom were identified by name.[111] Other figures on killings by Koevoet are available in the Report of the South African Truth and Reconciliation Commission, which saw documents showing that, over a ten-year period in the north of Namibia, approximately 250 white officers had 1,666 'contacts' with PLAN. Of these, fourteen officers (excluding the most prolific killer, Eugene de Kock) were engaged in battles that resulted in 3,323 deaths and 104 prisoners.[112] On the other side, off-duty Koevoet members were also a frequent target for assassination by SWAPO: the state public prosecutor put the figure for 1978–82 at a total of 198 deaths.[113] As we have seen, the number of those who lost their lives in SWAPO detention probably amounts to several hundred or more.[114] Thus, although Namibia was spared the intensity and terrible mortality of the conflict on the Angolan side of the border, the war for the territory nevertheless had very high human costs.

CONCLUSION

In the two decades since independence, Namibia has established itself as a stable, peaceful and relatively prosperous country, with regular elections to both national and (restructured) regional government.[1] Nevertheless, observers are seriously concerned about some aspects of the country's development. While this brief concluding chapter cannot analyse the postcolonial period in detail, I will nevertheless attempt here to summarise the main dynamics of Namibia's most recent history.

Namibia's relative stability has resulted in part from the political climate established immediately after independence. Through a policy of 'national reconciliation', the new government attempted to set aside the conflicts of the past, taking no action against individuals who had committed human rights violations under the old regime (nor, by the same token, did it investigate or pursue the question of those detained by SWAPO in exile).[2] At the same time, the government, armed with a constitution that bans discrimination 'on the grounds of sex, race, colour, ethnic origin, religion, creed or social or economic status',[3] was able to bring most forms of overt racism to an end (although racial discrimination continued—and still lingers—in some arenas). Together, the new constitution and the politics of national reconciliation provided the state with a mandate to abolish apartheid legislation, to enshrine new rights in law, and to embark on a process of nation-building.

The potential for violence was also very much reduced by the successful integration of troops from both sides into the new Namibian Defence Force (NDF); a number of other programmes, including 'Development Brigades' (work projects), though dogged by problems, provided subsistence for PLAN veterans.[4] The new government took over the existing civil service, adding posts for its own people rather than dismissing those already employed (a decision which also helped to create Namibia's current disproportionately large bureaucracy).

Such policy decisions on the part of SWAPO, as well as its adoption of a capitalist, neoliberal economic model, had much to do with the contemporary shift away from the antagonisms of the Cold War (which, as we have seen, had helped to make independence possible). This, together with the transition to democracy in South Africa in 1994, meant that Namibia did not follow the earlier unhappy example of Angola and Mozambique, which had been treated as pawns in conflicts between the superpowers and were torn apart by civil war.

It is true that there have been significant threats to internal and external peace since 1990. In December 1999, as war again intensified in Angola, Namibia allowed the Angolan government to use Namibian territory as a base for attacks on UNITA. The violence escalated, civilians were killed in northern Namibia and there were reports of human rights abuses by members of the NDF and of the (police) Special Field Force; however, peace returned after the Angolan ceasefire in April 2002. In addition, between 1998 and 2002 Namibia showed its willingness to engage in a wider (and geographically remote) African conflict by sending troops—initially through a unilateral decision of the President—to the Democratic Republic of Congo in support of President Laurent Kabila, acting together with Zimbabwean and Angolan forces.[5] There was also tension during the 1990s between Namibia and Botswana over the ownership of Kasikili Island, in the Chobe River, but in 1995 the presidents of the two countries agreed to refer the matter to the International Court of Justice, which subsequently ruled in favour of Botswana.[6]

The most serious incident, however, was an attempted coup by Caprivi separatists. On 2 August 1999, a movement calling itself the Caprivi Liberation Army and led by a former head of the DTA, Mishake Muyongo, attacked the police station, army base and Namibia Broadcasting Corporation headquarters in Katima Mulilo. The government responded by declaring a state of emergency and detaining hundreds of people; around 2,500 fled to Botswana, while more than a hundred others were charged with high treason. The case did not come to trial until 2004, and at the time of writing is still in process.[7]

Despite these problems, Namibia has, on the whole and with some important exceptions, been governed constitutionally and under the rule of law for the last two decades. The country has an executive president and a bicameral Parliament, consisting of a National Assembly, seventy-two of whose seventy-eight members are elected, and a National Council (which can review, but not veto, legislation), consisting of twenty-six members elected from the thirteen regional councils. Elections have been held regularly at the appropriate times (for national elections, at five-year intervals). SWAPO (now officially renamed the SWAPO party) has won every national election, increasing its share of the vote to two-thirds in 1994 and three-quarters in 1999 and 2004. In 1998, the constitution was amended to allow President Nujoma a third term; although this move was legal, it has been criticised as anti-democratic.

Nujoma was succeeded, in March 2005, by President Hifikepunye Pohamba. The former—now with the title 'Founding Father'—nevertheless remains influential. Indeed, despite the outward constitutionalism of the last two decades, SWAPO's drive to retain control, well evidenced in exile, is clearly still at play. The first major split within the party occurred in 1999, when Ben Ulenga (a former Robben Island prisoner, trade union leader and Namibian High Commissioner in London) headed the formation of the Congress of Democrats (CoD) in frustration, according to Ulenga, at 'the failure of SWAPO to transform itself from a secretive and exiled armed nationalist movement to a mass-based governing party'.[8] The CoD won seven seats in the 1999 elections, at which 'serious concerns' were recorded about the conduct of the poll.[9]

CoD support has since dwindled, but a new major opposition force has emerged in the form of the Rally for Democracy and Progress (RDP), led by Hidipo Hamutenya, one of SWAPO's former major figures and independent Namibia's first Minister for Trade and Industry. The November 2009 elections resulted in fifty-four seats for SWAPO (a loss of one) and eight for the RDP, which came in second. There had, however, been pre-election violence between supporters of SWAPO and the RDP, as well as evidence of questionable practices at the polling stations and campaigns by SWAPO against 'hibernators'—people claimed to be secret RDP supporters—in government employ. At the time of writing, most of the opposition parties have requested the High Court to set aside the election results or, failing that, to rule in favour of a recount.[10]

In the face of these pressures, civil society organisations play an important role in attempting to hold the government to account, although there are significant weaknesses in this sector. Such activity is an important legacy of the 1980s. The press remains largely free, despite some *de facto* censorship and smear campaigns by the government and SWAPO. The autonomy of the trade unions has been heavily undermined since 1990, but the churches and youth organisations have been better able to maintain an independent voice.[11] The Namibian NGO sector is substantial[12] and flourishing and some organisations have played effective advocacy roles, for example voicing the concerns of women, minorities and the poor, educating people about their rights, carrying out social and economic research and critiquing many aspects of legislation and policy.

Arguably, the most important development of the last twenty years has been the devastating AIDS epidemic. The first case was recorded in 1986, and, by 2002, 22 per cent of Namibian adults were thought to be HIV-positive—a figure among the highest in the world. In 2007 prevalence rates are thought to have dropped for the first time, to 19.9 per cent, but the epidemic remains extremely serious, with some 200,000 people, including 14,000 children, estimated to be living with AIDS;[13] among adults, slightly more than half of those with the infection are women.[14] Children have been disproportionately affected, many losing one or both parents. The disease has been catastrophic not only for individuals and families,[15] but for all areas of Namibian society, as mortality rates have increased, development gains lost and labour, production and education severely affected.[16]

In 2003 the Namibian government—which commendably adopted a very different policy from the dominant denialism in South Africa—launched a programme to make anti-retroviral drugs available to HIV/AIDS sufferers, assisted by generous donor funding. There have, however, been problems with implementation, and access to the drugs remains patchy.[17] Arguably, failure to match practice to rhetoric has been a feature of many areas of Namibian government policy, particularly with regard to poverty reduction.

It is true that, according to some measures of poverty, significant advances have been made: for example, the death rate among children under five years old dropped from 84 per 1,000 live births in 1990 to 63 in 2004.[18] The adult literacy rate stood at the impressively high figure of 88.2 per cent in 2008.[19] While there is no comprehensive welfare state, the government nevertheless pays allowances to AIDS orphans, people with disabilities and the elderly; in the community of Otjivero-Omitara, east of Windhoek, the provision of a small guaranteed income (basic income grant) to all adults has been piloted. Nevertheless, as Henning Melber has pointed out, Namibia is one of the most unequal countries in the world, and in 2006 it still remained at 125th place in the Human Development Index, showing no improvement since 1996.[20] The majority of Namibians are still living in grinding poverty and, while a black middle class consolidated itself soon after independence, little has been done to bring about the redistribution of wealth or, indeed, land (despite some sabre-rattling over the latter issue). Urban populations have increased rapidly since independence as the rural poor have migrated to the towns, where most live in peripheral informal settlements.[21] There are, however, limits to the accumulation of the elite. Although corruption has increased, and Namibia has dropped from thirtieth on the Transparency Index in 2001 to fifty-sixth in 2009, according to this measure it nevertheless still remains less corrupt than most African and a considerable number of other countries, including Italy, China, Russia and India.[22]

Poverty and HIV/AIDS have placed a disproportionately heavy burden on women. In some respects, independent Namibia has made considerable advances in gender equality and women's rights. Sexual equality is enshrined in the constitution, and legislation subsequently enacted has, among other things, introduced anti-discrimination measures in employment, improved women's rights within the family and marriage, made their tenure of land more secure, and provided protection against violence. In the middle of the first decade of the twenty-first century, women constituted nearly 30 per cent of MPs (although the proportion has since declined), and over 40 per cent of local councillors. Nevertheless, women's income remains 50 per cent lower than men's, fathers frequently fail to take financial responsibility for their children, and levels of violence against women are very high—as is child rape. There has been a backlash against the progress that women have achieved, and gender issues remain heavily contested.[23]

Namibian political discourse has also operated, to a greater or lesser extent, to exclude and marginalise some groups. The most obvious example is that of gay people, whom Nujoma first isolated for criticism in 1996 and who have since been subject to periodic verbal and physical attacks (although Namibian society also has more tolerant strands).[24] The government—through, for example, the construction of the grandiose 'Heroes' Acre' outside Windhoek—has increasingly promoted a national historical narrative that validates the pre-independence history of SWAPO and its allies and tends to marginalise those formerly on the opposing side. Similarly, SWAPO has attempted to close down discussion of the experience of the people whom the movement itself detained before independence.[25] The politics of memory are, nevertheless, both contested and complex; many communities have (re)-instituted forms of memorialisation since independence with, in some cases, traditional forms of authority being revived.[26]

Perhaps most strikingly, San people have largely failed to benefit from development initiatives in independent Namibia and in many cases are now poorer than before.[27] In this and other cases, some ethnic tension and resentments underlie Namibia's political dynamics. Nevertheless, both the inclusiveness of pre-independence nationalism and the emergence of a strong discourse of 'Namibianness' since 1990 have had a restraining effect on ethnic divisiveness. In terms of formal politics, SWAPO has always been careful to incorporate and field politicians of all ethnic groups, including Hage Geingob and Hendrik Witbooi, who were Namibia's first prime minister and deputy prime minister respectively. To date, the only serious ethnically (or regionally) determined violence has been the attempted coup in the Caprivi.

The ability of Namibia's inhabitants to overcome poverty and marginalisation depends, of course, not only on government policy and the efforts of aid agencies, but also on the state of the economy more generally. As we have seen, at independence the country adopted a neoliberal, capitalist model; the main sectors of the economy remained mining, farming and to some extent fishing. A major concession to the new political circumstances was the transformation of CDM into the Namdeb Diamond Corporation Ltd in 1994, with the government taking a 50 per cent stake.

Some attempts to encourage economic activity have been less than successful. The Namibian government has tried to encourage investment by the granting of very favourable terms to potential foreign investors; one example is the Malaysian company Ramatex Textiles, which never lived up to its potential and eventually pulled out altogether. Other economic changes and policies have, however, been much more effective at generating local employment and economic activity (even if some of this oversteps the borders of the legal). In 2004 a new bridge across the Zambezi brought to fruition long-held plans for a Trans Caprivi Corridor, which links Walvis Bay (where the port infrastructure has been expanded) to central Africa, particularly Zambia and the Democratic Republic of Congo. Peace in Angola has also led to the opening of numerous trading opportunities—legal and illicit—with northern Namibia. A third major transformation was the coming of Chinese investment to Namibia in the first decade of the twenty-first century. This has brought mixed and as yet uncertain consequences for the Namibian economy, but has certainly had the short-term effect of bringing consumer goods further within reach of the poor, as well as creating some employment.[28]

While it is relatively easy to summarise the dynamics of Namibia's post-independence development, it is more difficult to predict Namibia's future path. One key question, however, is whether serious and successful efforts will be made to tackle poverty and inequality. Although life has improved for some, for the majority of Namibians it remains a daily struggle. Another crucial issue is whether the rule of law will hold, or whether the government's actions will become increasingly undemocratic and unaccountable. In addition, as in the past, external factors—changes in the world economy, in the climate, in geopolitical power relations—will play an important rule in determining Namibia's internal dynamics.

What is beyond question is that the successful transition to democracy, after decades of nationalist struggle, in no way represented an end to history in Namibia. In many respects—although it is far more inclusive than before 1990—the state still represents the interests of only a part of the population; the history of the period remains, as it has always been, a story of power, inclusion and exclusion.

The presence of the colonial past is a very marked feature of the post-colonial period: Namibia's physical, political and economic landscapes have been profoundly shaped by its multiple experiences of colonisation, dispossession and war, and much of the contemporary contestation over memory and resources references and reflects this past. The present has been shaped, too, not only by the period of formal colonisation, but also by the way in which the advent of merchant capital, mission and migrants of various kinds had already transformed Namibia in earlier decades. Indeed, change—as historians ought to expect—has been a feature of Namibia's past for as long as humans have lived there and have seized opportunities to adopt new innovations. Yet, at the same time, the resilience of many 'traditional' forms of authority, custom, culture and practice—however changed and reinvented—is also a defining feature of the post-colonial Namibia.

This history has attempted to illuminate some of these dynamics. In particular, it has sought to investigate the history of the years for which documentary sources exist, while not neglecting the fact that by far the longest period of human settlement in Namibia must be researched principally through archaeological means. Even for the historical period, many uncertainties remain, much has not been analysed at all, and many things are a matter of lively debate. The opportunities for research are thus rich and promising, and it is to be hoped that historians will continue to take up the challenge.

NOTES

INTRODUCTION

1. The population according to the 2001 census was 1.83 million; the World Bank figure for 2008 was 2.13 million. John Mendelsohn, Alice Jarvis, Carole Roberts and Tony Robertson, *Atlas of Namibia: A Portrait of the Land and its People* (Cape Town: David Philip, 2002), pp. 159, 38; John Middleton and Joseph Miller (eds), *New Encyclopedia of Africa* (Detroit: Charles Scribner's Sons, 2008), vol. 4, p. 489; http://databank.world.org (seen 10.5.2010).

2. According to one interpretation of international law, the border also comes to a point with Zimbabwe.

3. Mendelsohn *et al.*, *Atlas of Namibia*, pp. 38–9, 85, 162–3.

4. Peter Katjavivi, *A History of Resistance in Namibia* (London: James Currey, 1988); Klaus Dierks, *Chronology of Namibian History: From Pre-historical Times to Independent Namibia* (Windhoek: Namibia Scientific Society, 2002).

5. Heinrich Vedder, *Das alte Südwestafrika: Südwestafrikas Geschichte bis zum Tode Mahareros, 1890* (Martin Warneck: Berlin, 1934), published in English as *South West Africa in Early Times: Being the Story of South West Africa up to the Date of Maharero's Death in 1890*, ed. Cyril Hall (Oxford University Press, 1938).

6. Brigitte Lau, 'Thank God the Germans Came: Vedder and Namibian Historiography' in *idem*, *History and Historiography: Four Essays in Reprint* (Windhoek: Discourse/Michael Scott Oral Records Project, 1995), pp. 1–16; Jill Kinahan, 'Heinrich Vedder's Sources for his Account of the Exploration of the Namib Coast', *Cimbebasia*, 11 (1989), pp. 33–9.

7. Nevertheless, the sources Vedder collected are held by the National Archives of Namibia and are still of value to historians.

8. Ruth First, *South West Africa* (Harmondsworth: Penguin, 1963).

9. Israel Goldblatt, *History of South West Africa From the Beginning of the Nineteenth Century* (Cape Town: Juta, 1971).

10. John Wellington, *South West Africa and its Human Issues* (Oxford: Clarendon Press, 1967).

11. Helmut Bley, *Namibia under German Rule* (Hamburg: Lit, 1996); Horst Drechsler, *'Let Us Die Fighting': The Struggle of the Herero and Nama against German Imperialism, 1884–1915* (Berlin: Akademie, 1966).

12. SWAPO Department of Information and Publicity, *To Be Born a Nation: The Liberation Struggle for Namibia* (London: Zed, 1981).

13. Zedekia Ngavirue, *Political Parties and Interest Groups in South West Africa (Namibia)* (Basel: P. Schlettwein, 1997), completed as a PhD thesis in 1972.

14. For example, Richard Moorsom, 'Underdevelopment, Contract Labour and Worker Consciousness in Namibia, 1915–72', *JSAS*, 4,10 (1977), pp. 52–87; Elia Kaakunga, *Problems of Capitalist Development in Namibia: The Dialectics of Progress and Destruction* (Turku: Abo Akademi, 1990).

15. Brigitte Lau, *Southern and Central Namibia in Jonker Afrikaner's Time* (Windhoek: Windhoek Archives, 1987). A useful bibliography is Tore Linné Eriksen with Richard Moorsom, *The Political Economy of Namibia: An Annotated Critical Bibliography* (Oslo: Norwegian Institute of International Affairs, 1985).

16. Ronald Segal and Ruth First (eds), *South West Africa: Travesty of Trust* (London: Andre Deutsch, 1967; papers from the International Conference on South West Africa, Oxford, 1996; Brian Wood (ed.), *Namibia 1884–1984: Readings on Namibia's History and Society* (London and Lusaka: Namibia Support Committee and United Nations Institute for Namibia, 1988; papers to International Conference on Namibia, 1884–1984, London, 1984).

17. Klaas van Walraven and Jon Abbink, 'Rethinking Resistance in African History: An Introduction' in Jon Abbink, Mirjam de Bruijn and Klaas van Walraven (eds), *Rethinking Resistance: Revolt and Violence in African History* (Leiden: Brill, 2003), pp. 1–40, p. 1.

18. SWAPO, *To Be Born a Nation*, p. 151.

19. James Scott, *Weapons of the Weak: Everyday Forms of Peasant Resistance* (New Haven: Yale University Press, 1985).

20. Van Walraven and Abbink, 'Rethinking Resistance', p. 15; E.S. Atieno Odhiambo, 'The Usages of the Past: African Historiographies since Independence', *African Research and Documentation*, 96 (2004), pp. 3–62.

21. Exceptions include First, *South West Africa*; there is, however, very little recent work.

22. Dag Henrichsen, 'Herrschaft und Identifikation im vorkolonialen Zentralnamibia: Das Herero- und Damaraland im 19 Jahrhundert' (PhD, University of Hamburg, 1997); Jan-Bart Gewald, *Herero Heroes: A Socio-Political History of the Herero of Namibia, 1890–1923* (London: James Currey, 1999); Felix Schürmann, 'Land zu Territorium? Zur Terri-

torialisierung von Herrschaftsstrategien im südwestlichen Afrika, ca. 1790–1890' (MA, University of Hanover, 2008).

23. Drechsler, 'Let Us Die Fighting', ch. 5.

24. 'Trees Never Meet', 1994; 'Public Histories, Forgotten Histories?', 2000; 'Decontaminating Namibian History', 2004.

25. For example, Bennett Kangumu Kangumu, 'Contestations over Caprivi Identities: From Pre-colonial Times to the Present' (PhD, University of Cape Town, 2008); Martha Akawa, 'The Sexual Politics of the Namibian Liberation Struggle' (PhD, University of Basel, forthcoming 2010); Napandulwe Shiweda, 'Omhedi: Displacement and Legitimacy in Kwanyama Politics, Namibia, 1915–2007' (PhD, University of the Western Cape, forthcoming 2010); Memory Biwa, 'Narratives, Commemorations and Historic Sites: The 1903–1908 War in Southern Namibia and the Politics of Memory' (PhD, University of the Western Cape, forthcoming 2011); Vilho Shigwedha, 'The Cassinga Massacre and Indescribable Memories' (PhD, University of the Western Cape, forthcoming 2010); see also Lovisa Nampala and Vilho Shigwedha, Aawambo Kingdoms, History and Cultural Change: Perspectives from Northern Namibia (Basel: P. Schlettwein, 2006).

26. Ellen Ndeshi Namhila 'Filling the Gaps in the Archival Record of the Namibian Struggle for Independence', IFLA Journal, 30, 3 (2004), pp. 224–30.

27. For example, see Udo Kaulich, Die Geschichte der ehemaligen Kolonie Deutsch-Südwestafrika (1884–1914): Eine Gesamtdarstellung (Frankfurt: Peter Lang, 2000), ch. 4, for a rather Eurocentric approach to the protection treaties; there has also arguably been an over-concentration on settler experiences, particularly during the German period.

28. Gesine Krüger, 'Koloniale Gewalt, Alltagserfahrungen und Überlebenstrategien' in Larissa Förster, Dag Henrichsen and Michael Bollig (eds), Namibia–Deutschland: Eine geteilte Geschichte (Cologne: Rautenstrauch-Jöst Museum für Völkerkunde, 2004), pp. 92–105.

29. For example, Giorgio Miescher, Lorena Rizzo and Jeremy Silvester (eds), Posters in Action: Visuality in the Making of an African Nation (Basel: BAB, 2009); Wolfram Hartmann, Jeremy Silvester and Patricia Hayes (eds), The Colonising Camera: Photographs in the Making of Namibian History (Cape Town: University of Cape Town Press, 1998).

30. For a discussion, see Odhiambo, 'Usages'.

31. Jeremy Silvester, 'Introduction: Changing Clothes, Changing Traditions' in Nampala and Shigwedha, Aawambo Kingdoms, pp. xi–xviii, p. xii.

32. Nampala and Shigwedha, Aawambo Kingdoms, passim.

33. Nancy Rose Hunt, 'Introduction', p. 8 in Nancy Rose Hunt, Tessie Liu and Jean Quataert (eds), Gendered Colonialisms in African History (Oxford: Blackwell, 1997). See Patricia Hayes, 'A Land of Goshen: Landscape and Kingdom in Nineteenth Century Eastern Owambo (Namibia)' in M. Bollig and O. Bubenzer (eds), African Landscapes (New York:

Springer, 2009), for an astute demonstration of *African* politics of representation.

34. Norman Etherington, *The Great Treks: The Transformation of Southern Africa, 1815–1854* (Harlow: Longman, 2001), p. xiii.

35. Giorgio Miescher, 'Die Rote Linie: Die Geschichte der Veterinär und Siedlungsgrenze in Namibia (1890er bis 1960er Jahre)' (PhD, University of Basel, 2009), pp. 9, 43–9, 84–91, 139–42, 173–84 and *passim*.

36. Mamadou Diouf, *Historians and Histories, What For? African Historiography between the State and the Communities* (Amsterdam: SEPHIS-CSSSC, 2002), pp. 14–15; Jean Allman, Susan Geiger and Nakanyike Musisi (eds), *Women in African Colonial Histories* (Bloomington: Indiana University Press, 2002), p. 5.

37. Verne Harris, *Archives and Justice: A South African Perspective* (Chicago: Society of American Archivists, 2007), p. 32.

38. Generally speaking, a strong historiography on gender in Africa has opened up space for disentangling gendered histories (and, among other things, revealing ways in which African and colonial male elites made alliances to extend control of women). See, for example, Allman *et al.* (eds), *Women*, and the review by Lynn Thomas in *Journal of Colonialism and Colonial History*, 4 (2003); Wendy Woodward, Patricia Hayes and Gary Minkley (eds), *Deep Histories: Gender and Colonialism in South Africa* (Amsterdam: Rodopi, 2002); Iris Berger, 'African Women's History: Themes and Perspectives', *Journal of Colonialism and Colonial History*, 4, 1 (2003); Hunt *et al.*, *Gendered Colonialisms*; Marc Epprecht, '*This Matter of the Women is Getting Very Bad': Gender, Development and Politics in Colonial Lesotho* (Pietermaritzburg: University of Natal Press, 2000); Helen Bradford, 'Women, Gender and Colonialism: Rethinking the History of the British Cape Colony and its Frontier Zones, c. 1806–70', *JAH*, 37 (1996), pp. 351–70.

39. Bley, *Namibia*, p. 173; Drechsler, *'Let Us Die Fighting'*, p. 231; Kaulich, *Deutsch-Südwestafrika*, pp. 270–1; Jürgen Zimmerer, *Deutsche Herrschaft über Afrikaner: Staatlicher Machtanspruch und Wirklichkeit im kolonialen Namibia* (Münster: Lit, 2004), p. 77.

40. Lita Webley, 'Wives and Sisters: Changing Gender Relations among Khoe Pastoralists in Namaqualand' in Lyn Wadley (ed.), *Our Gendered Past: Archaeological Studies of Gender in South Africa* (Johannesburg: Witwatersrand University Press, 1997), pp. 167–208, p. 170.

41. But see Akawa, 'Sexual Politics'.

42. Etherington, *Great Treks*, p. 6. See also (among many possible references) Donald Wright, '"What Do You Mean, There Were No Tribes in Africa?" Thoughts on Boundaries—and Related Matters—in Precolonial Africa', *History in Africa*, 26 (1999), pp. 409–26.

43. Cape Coloureds who migrated into Namibia before this date are an exception. I use the word 'Coloured' because, although originally imposed on

mixed-race populations, it is used today with a considerable degree of self-ascription.

44. Vansina, *How Societies are Born: Governance in West Central Africa before 1600* (Charlottesville: University of Virginia Press, 2004), p. 58; Adi Inskeep, *Heinrich Vedder's The Bergdama: An Annotated Translation of the German Original with Additional EthnographicMaterial by Adi Inskeep* (Cologne: Rüdiger Köppe, 2003), pp. 63–7; Wilfred Haacke, Eliphas Eiseb and Levi Namaseb, 'Internal and External Relations of Khoe-Khoe Dialects: A Preliminary Survey' in Wilfred Haacke and Edward Elderkin (eds), *Namibian Languages: Reports and Papers* (Cologne: Rüdiger Koppe, 1997), pp. 125–209. The latter research disproves Vedder's argument that Damara lost their language, at a much more recent date, through enslavement to the Nama.

45. Etherington, *Great Treks*, pp. 345–6.

46. Miescher, 'Rote Linie', p. 148.

47. On these issues see, for example, *ibid.*, pp. 15–16; Marion Wallace, '"Making Tradition": Healing, History and Ethnic Identity among Otjiherero-speakers in Namibia, c. 1850–1950', *JSAS*, 29, 2 (2003), pp. 355–72; Jan-Bart Gewald, 'Near Death in the Streets of Karibib: Famine, Migrant Labour and the Coming of Ovambo to Central Namibia', *JAH*, 44 (2003), pp. 211–39, p. 213.

48. Suzman, *'Things from the Bush': A Contemporary History of the Omaheke Bushmen* (Basel: P. Schlettwein, 2000), p. 7.

49. *Ibid.*, pp. 160–1; Robert Gordon and Stuart Sholto-Douglas, *The Bushman Myth: The Making of a Namibian Underclass* 2nd ed. (Boulder: Westview, 2000).

1. FROM THE BEGINNING: THE ARCHAEOLOGICAL EVIDENCE

1. Peter Robertshaw (ed.), *A History of African Archaeology* (London: James Currey, 1990).

2. *Ibid.*; Martin Hall, *Archaeology Africa* (London: James Currey, 1996); Bruce Trigger, *A History of Archaeological Thought* (Cambridge University Press, 1989).

3. Eric L.P. Stals (ed.), *The Commissions of W.C. Palgrave, Special Emissary to South West Africa 1876–1885* (Cape Town: Van Riebeeck Society, 1990).

4. The term 'Bushman' is considered by some writers as pejorative and sexist, although the people themselves use it, sometimes in preference to the more formal 'San'. The latter is used by some academic writers, but it too has negative connotations, being derived from the Khoekhoen Nama term for 'vagabond'.

5. Henri Breuil, 'The White Lady of the Brandberg, SWA, Her Companions and Her Guards', *South African Archaeological Bulletin*, 3 (1948), pp. 2–11;

and see also Reinhard Maack, 'Erstbesteigung des Brandberges und Entdeckung der "Weissen Dame"', *JSWASS*, 14 (1960), pp. 5–38.

6. John Schofield, 'The Age of the Rock Paintings of South Africa', *South African Archaeological Bulletin*, 3 (1948), pp. 79–88.

7. John Kinahan, 'Theory, Practice and Criticism in the History of Namibian Archaeology' in Peter Ucko (ed.), *Theory in Archaeology: A World Perspective* (London: Routledge, 1995), pp. 76–92.

8. Gordon and Sholto-Douglas, *Bushman Myth*; John Molin, 'Twyfelfontein—A Rock Art Site of Local Significance', *Studies in the African Past*, 5 (2006), pp. 34–46.

9. Kinahan, 'Theory, Practice'; *idem*, 'Traumland Südwest: Two Moments in the History of German Archaeological Enquiry in Namibia' in Heinrich Härke (ed.), *Archaeology, Ideology and Society: The German Experience* (Frankfurt: Peter Lang, 2000), pp. 353–74; *idem*, 'Weisser Riese–Schwarze Zwerge? Empirismus und ethnische Deutung in der Archäologie Namibia', *Archäologische Informationen*, 18, 1 (1995), pp. 7–18.

10. J. David Lewis-Williams, *Believing and Seeing: Symbolic Meanings in Southern African Rock Art* (London: Academic Press, 1981); *idem*, 'The Social and Economic Context of Southern San Rock Art', *Current Anthropology*, 23 (1982), pp. 429–49.

11. E.g. John Kinahan, *Pastoral Nomads of the Namib Desert: The People History Forgot* 2nd ed. (Windhoek: Namibia Archaeological Trust, 2001), Myra Shackley, *Palaeolithic Archaeology of the Central Namib Desert: A Preliminary Survey of Chronology, Typology and Site Location* (Windhoek: Cimbebasia Memoir 6, National Museum of Namibia, 1985); Beatrice Sandelowsky, 'Mirabib—An Archaeological Study in the Namib', *Madoqua*, 10, 4 (1977), pp. 221–83.

12. E.g. Revil Mason, 'Notes on the Recent Archaeology of the Scherz Basin, Brandberg', *South African Archaeological Bulletin*, 10 (1955), pp. 30–1; Harald Pager, 'Felsbildforschungen am Brandberg in Namibia', *Beiträge zur Allgemeinen und Vergleichenden Archäologie*, 2 (1980), pp. 351–7; Wolfgang Wendt, 'Preliminary Report on an Archaeological Research Programme in South West Africa', *Cimbebasia* (B), 2, 1 (1972), pp. 1–61.

13. John Kinahan and Jill Kinahan, 'Preliminary Report on the Late Holocene Archaeology of the Awasib–Gorrasis Basin Complex in the Southern Namib Desert', *Studies in the African Past*, 5 (2006), pp. 1–14.

14. E.g. Lyn Wadley, 'Big Elephant Shelter and its Role in the Holocene Prehistory of Central South West Africa', *Cimbebasia* (B), 3, 1 (1979), pp. 1–76; *idem*, 'On the Move: A Look at Prehistoric Food Scheduling in Central Namibia', *Cimbebasia* (B), 4, 4 (1984), pp. 41–50.

15. Leon Jacobson, 'On Artefact Analysis and the Reconstruction of Past Ethnic Groups', *Current Anthropology*, 21 (1980), p. 409; *idem*, 'The White Lady of the Brandberg, a Re-interpretation', *Namibiana*, 2 (1980), pp. 21–9.

16. Katjavivi, *History of Resistance*; Johan Malan, *Peoples of Namibia* (Wingate Park: Rhino, 1995); Kaire Mbuende, *Namibia: The Broken Shield. Anatomy of Imperialism and Revolution* (Lund: Liber, 1986).

17. Kinahan, 'Theory, Practice'.

18. Beatrice Sandelowsky, 'Kapako and Vungu Vungu: Iron Age Sites on the Kavango River' in Nikolaas van der Merwe and Thomas Huffman (eds), *Iron Age Studies in Southern Africa* (Claremont: South African Archaeological Society), pp. 52–61; M. Albrecht *et al.*, 'Oruwanje 95/1: A Late Holocene Stratigraphy in Northwestern Namibia', *Cimbebasia*, 17 (2001), pp. 1–22.

19. David Phillipson, *The Later Prehistory of Eastern and Southern Africa* (London: Heinemann, 1977); *idem*, *African Archaeology* (Cambridge University Press, 2005).

20. Frieda-Nela Williams, *Pre-colonial Communities of Southwestern Africa: A History of Owambo Kingdoms 1600–1920* (Windhoek: National Archives of Namibia, 1991).

21. Bennet Fuller, 'Institutional Appropriation and Social Change among Agropastoralists in Central Namibia, 1916–1988' (PhD, Boston University, 1993).

22. Lau, *Jonker Afrikaner's Time*.

23. Gewald, *Herero Heroes*.

24. John Kinahan, 'The Rise and Fall of Nomadic Pastoralism in the Central Namib Desert' in Thurstan Shaw, Paul Sinclair, Bassey Andah and Alex Okpoko (eds), *The Archaeology of Africa: Food, Metals and Towns* (London: Routledge, 1993), pp. 372–85.

25. Jill Kinahan, *Cattle for Beads: the Archaeology of Historical Contact and Trade on the Namib Coast* (Uppsala and Windhoek: University of Uppsala and Namibia Archaeological Trust, 2000).

26. See Peter Mitchell, *The Archaeology of Southern Africa* (Cambridge University Press, 2002).

27. That is, the period often referred to as the last Ice Age—although there was in fact no ice in southern Africa.

28. Chris Stringer and Clive Gamble, *In Search of the Neanderthals* (London: Thames & Hudson, 1993).

29. See Mitchell, *Archaeology*, pp. 107–36.

30. Jeanette Deacon and Nicholas Lancaster, *Late Quaternary Palaeoenvironments of Southern Africa* (Oxford: Clarendon, 1988).

31. Shackley, *Palaeolithic Archaeology*.

32. Gudrun Corvinus, *The Raised Beaches of the West Coast of South West Africa/Namibia: An Interpretation of their Archaeological and Palaeontological Data* (Munich: C.H. Beck, 1983).

33. Thomas Volman, 'Early Prehistory of Southern Africa' in R.G. Klein (ed.), *Southern African Prehistory and Palaeoenvironments* (Rotterdam: Balkema, 1984), pp. 169–220.

34. John Vogel and Ebbie Visser, 'Pretoria Radiocarbon Dates II', *Radiocarbon*, 23, 1 (1981), pp. 43–80; J.C. Freundlich, H. Schwabedissen and W. Wendt, 'Köln radiocarbon measurements II', *Radiocarbon*, 22, 1 (1980), pp. 68–81.

35. Sheridan Bowman, *Radiocarbon Dating* (London: British Museum, 1990).

36. Kinahan, *Cattle for Beads*.

37. Mitchell, *Archaeology*; Volman, 'Early Prehistory'.

38. Zenobia Jacobs *et al.*, 'Ages for the Middle Stone Age of Southern Africa: Implications for Human Behaviour and Dispersal', *Science*, 322 (2008), pp. 733–5.

39. Ralf Vogelsang, *Middle Stone Age Fundstellen in Südwest-Namibia* (Cologne: Heinrich Barth Institut, 1998); Katharine Cruz-Uribe and Richard Klein, 'Faunal Remains from Some Middle and Late Stone Age Sites in South West Africa', *JSWASS*, 36/37 (1983), pp. 91–114.

40. Deacon and Lancaster, *Palaeoenvironments*; Mitchell, *Archaeology*.

41. Ralf Vogelsang, 'The Middle Stone Age in South-western Namibia' in Gilbert Pwiti and Robert Soper (eds), *Aspects of African Archaeology: Papers from the 10th Congress of the PanAfrican Association for Prehistory and Related Studies, Harare* (Harare: University of Zimbabwe Publications, 1996), pp. 207–12.

42. Wolfgang Wendt, '"Art mobilier" aus der Apollo-11 Grotte in Südwest-Afrika', *Acta Praehistorica et Archaeologica*, 5 (1974), pp. 1–42; *idem*, 'Die ältesten datierten Kunstwerke Afrikas', *Bild der Wissenschaft*, 10 (1975), pp. 44–50; Ralf Vogelsang, 'The Rock Shelter Apollo 11–Evidence of Early Modern Humans in South-western Namibia' in Cornelia Limpricht and Megan Biesele (eds), *Heritage and Cultures in Modern Namibia—In-depth Views of the Country* (Windhoek: TUCSIN, 2008), pp. 183–92.

43. Christopher Henshilwood, 'Emergence of Modern Human Behaviour: Middle Stone Age Engravings from South Africa', *Science*, 295 (2002), pp. 1278–80.

44. Ralf Vogelsang, Barbara Eichorn and Jürgen Richter, 'Holocene Human Occupation and Vegetation History in Northern Namibia', *Die Erde*, 133 (2002), pp. 113–32.

45. E.g. N.J. Shackleton and N.D. Opdyke, 'Oxygen Isotope Palaeomagnetic Stratigraphy of Pacific Core V28–239 Late Pliocene to Latest Pleistocene', *Geological Society of America Memoirs*, 145 (1976), pp. 449–64.

46. Deacon and Lancaster, *Palaeoenvironments*.

47. Anthony J. Tankard and J. Rogers, 'Late Cenozoic Palaeoenvironments on the West Coast of Southern Africa', *Journal of Biogeography*, 5 (1978), pp. 319–37.

48. Gavin Birch, 'Surficial Sediments of Saldanha Bay and Langebaan Lagoon', *Transactions of the Geological Society of South Africa*, 79 (1976), pp. 293–300; B.W. Flemming, 'Distribution of Recent Sediments in

Saldanha Bay and Langebaan Lagoon', *Transactions of the Royal Society of South Africa*, 42, 3 & 4 (1977), pp. 317–40; John Compton, 'Holocene Evolution of the Anichab Pan on the South-west Coast of Namibia', *Sedimentology*, 54 (2007), pp. 55–70.

49. The term 'north-west' in this chapter indicates the geographic north-west quadrant of Namibia; in the rest of the book it generally applies to what later became known as the Kaoko region.

50. Ralf Vogelsang and Karl Peter Wendt, 'Changing Patterns of Settlement in Namibia during the Holocene' in O. Bubenzer, A. Bolten and F. Darius (eds), *Atlas of Cultural and Environmental Change in Arid Africa* (Cologne: Heinrich Barth Institut, 2007), pp. 68–72.

51. Sandelowsky, 'Mirabib'; Wendt, 'Preliminary Report'; Christine Sievers, 'Test Excavations at Rosh Pinah Shelter, Southern Namibia', *Cimbebasia* (B), 4, 3 (1984), pp. 29–40; John Kinahan and Jill Kinahan, 'Excavation of a Late Holocene Cave Deposit in the Southern Namib Desert', *Cimbebasia*, 18 (2003), pp. 1–10.

52. H. Walter and O.H. Volk, *Grundlagen der Weidewirtschaft in Südwestafrika*, Teil 1 (Stuttgart: Ulmer 1954); M.G. Little *et al.*, 'Trade Wind Forcing of Upwelling, Seasonality and Heinrich Events as a Response to Sub-Milankovitch Climate Variability', *Paleoceanography*, 12 (1997), pp. 568–76.

53. Bernt Eitel, 'Environmental History of the Namib Desert' in Mike Smith and Paul Hesse (eds), *23 Degrees South: Archaeology and Environmental History of the Southern Deserts* (Canberra: National Museum of Australia, 2005), pp. 45–55.

54. P. Tyson, *Climatic Change and Variability in Southern Africa* (Cape Town: Oxford University Press, 1986); Mary Seely and Gideon Louw, 'First Approximation of the Effects of Rainfall on the Ecology and Energetics of a Namib Desert Dune Ecosystem', *Journal of Arid Environments*, 3 (1980), pp. 25–54; Mendelsohn *et al.*, *Atlas of Namibia*.

55. E.g. the site Bushman's Paradise, described in John Kinahan, 'Four Thousand Years at the Spitzkoppe: Changes in Settlement and Land Use on the Edge of the Namib Desert', *Cimbebasia*, 12 (1990), pp. 1–14; also the site Big Elephant Shelter described in Wadley, 'Big Elephant Shelter'; Wendt, 'Preliminary Report'.

56. Kinahan, *Pastoral Nomads*.

57. Barbara Eichorn and Ralf Vogelsang, 'A Pristine Landscape? Archaeological and Archaeobotanical Research in the Skeleton Coast Park, Northwestern Namibia' in Michael Bollig *et al.* (eds), *Aridity, Change and Conflict in Africa* (Cologne: Heinrich Barth Institut, 2007), pp. 145–65.

58. John Kinahan, 'The Late Holocene Human Ecology of the Namib Desert' in Mike Smith and Paul Hesse (eds), *23 Degrees South: Archaeology and Environmental History of the Southern Deserts* (Canberra: National Museum of Australia, 2005), pp. 120–31; see also Wadley, 'Big Elephant Shelter'; Sandelowsky, 'Mirabib'.

59. Sievers, 'Test Excavations'.
60. Jurgen Richter, 'Messum I: A Later Stone Age Pattern of Mobility in the Namib Desert', *Cimbebasia* (B), 4, 1 (1984), pp. 1–12.
61. Jurgen Richter, '"Zu wenig Chalzedon"–kritischer Rohstoffmangel bei prähistorischen Wildbeutern in Namibia' in M. Bollig and F. Klees (eds), *Überlebens-strategien in Afrika* (Cologne: Heinrich Barth Institut, 1994), pp. 179–86.
62. Jurgen Richter, *Studien zur Urgeschichte Namibias–Holozäne Stratigraphien im Umkreis des Brandberges* (Cologne: Heinrich-Barth Institut, 1991).
63. Kinahan, *Pastoral Nomads*.
64. David Coulson and Alec C. Campbell, *African Rock Art: Paintings and Engravings on Stone* (New York: Abrams, 2001).
65. Kinahan 'Theory, Practice'.
66. Jürgen Richter and Ralf Vogelsang, 'Rock Art in Northwestern Central Namibia—Its Age and Cultural Background' in Cornelia Limpricht, and Megan Biesele (eds), *Heritage and Cultures in Modern Namibia—In-depth Views of the Country* (Windhoek: TUCSIN, 2008), pp. 37–46.
67. Lewis-Williams, *Believing and Seeing*.
68. J. David Lewis-Williams (ed.), *New Approaches to Southern African Rock Art* (South African Archaeological Society, 1983); Geoffrey Blundell (ed.), *Further Approaches to Southern African Rock Art* (Vlaeberg: South African Archaeological Society, 2005).
69. J. David Lewis-Williams, 'Ideological Continuities in Prehistoric Southern African Rock: The Evidence of Rock Art' in Carmel Schrire (ed.), *Past and Present in Hunter-gatherer Studies* (Orlando: Academic Press, 1984), pp. 225–52.
70. Kinahan, 'Theory, Practice'. Recent confirmation of this view is provided by William Challis, '"The Men with Rhebok's Heads: They Tame Elands and Snakes": Incorporating the Rhebok Antelope in the Understanding of Southern African Rock Art' in Blundell (ed.), *Further Approaches*, pp. 11–20, and J. Swart, 'Rock Art Sequences in uKhahlamba-Drakensberg Park, South Africa', *Southern African Humanities*, 16 (2004), pp. 13–35.
71. Alan Barnard, *Hunters and Herders of Southern Africa: A Comparative Ethnography of the Khoisan Peoples* (Cambridge University Press, 1992).
72. E.g. Harald Pager, *The Rock Paintings of the Upper Brandberg. Part 1: Amis Gorge* (Cologne: Heinrich Barth Institut, 1989).
73. J. David Lewis-Williams and Thomas Dowson, *Images of Power: Understanding Bushman Rock Art* (Johannesburg: Southern, 1989).
74. Ernst-Rudolf Scherz, *Felsbilder in Südwest-Afrika. Teil 2: Die Gravierungen im Nordwest Südwest-Afrika* (Cologne: Böhlau Verlag, 1975).
75. Similar depictions have been noted in South Africa by Jeremy Holleman, '"Big Pictures": Insights into Southern African San Rock Paintings of Ostriches', *South African Archaeological Bulletin*, 56 (2001), pp. 62–75.

76. Edwin Wilmsen, *Land Filled with Flies: A Political Economy of the Kalahari* (University of Chicago Press, 1989).

77. Principally in the work of Lorna Marshall, *The !Kung of Nyae Nyae* (Cambridge, Mass.: Harvard University Press 1976); Richard Lee, *The !Kung San: Men, Women and Work in a Foraging Society* (Cambridge University Press, 1979).

78. For example, Lyn Wadley, *Later Stone Age Hunters and Gatherers of the Southern Transvaal: Social Land Ecological Interpretations* (Oxford: British Archaeological Reports, 1987).

79. Summarised in Mitchell, *Archaeology*, pp. 222–6.

80. Sandelowsky, 'Kapako'.

81. Thomas Huffman, *Handbook to the Iron Age: The Archaeology of Precolonial Farming Societies in Southern Africa* (Pietermaritzburg: University of KwaZulu-Natal Press, 2007); Phillipson, *African Archaeology*.

82. Mendelsohn *et al.*, *Atlas of Namibia*.

83. John Kinahan, 'Settlement Patterns and Regional Exchange: Evidence from Recent Iron Age Sites on the Kavango River, North-eastern Namibia', *Cimbebasia* (B), 3 (1986), pp. 109–16.

84. K.J. Thomsen, A. Murray, L. Bøtter-Jensen and J. Kinahan, 'Determination of Burial Dose in Incompletely Bleached Fluvial Samples using Single Grains of Quartz', *Radiation Measurements*, 24, 2 (2007), pp. 270–9.

85. Frank Seidel, Eileen Kose and Wilhelm Möhlig, 'Northern Namibia—Overview of its Historiography Based on Linguistic and Extralinguistic Evidence' in O. Bubenzer, A. Bolton and F. Darius (eds), *Atlas of Cultural and Environmental Change in Arid Africa* (Cologne: Heinrich Barth Institut, 2007), pp. 152–5; Eileen Kose and Jürgen Richter, 'The Prehistory of the Kavango People', *Sprache und Geschichte in Afrika*, 18 (2007), pp. 103–29.

86. See Mitchell, *Archaeology*, pp. 227–37; E. Oswin Westphal, 'The Linguistic Prehistory of Southern Africa: Bush, Kwadi, Hottentot and Bantu Linguistic Relationships', *Africa*, 33 (1963), pp. 237–65; Barnard, *Hunters and Herders*; G. Nurse, John Weiner and Trefor Jenkins, *The Peoples of Southern Africa and their Affinities* (Oxford University Press, 1985); Anne Solomon, 'Division of the Earth: Gender, Symbolism and the Archaeology of the Southern San' (MA, University of Cape Town, 1989); Katherine Horsburgh, 'The Origins of Southwestern African Pastoralism: Addressing Classic Debates using Ancient DNA' (PhD, Stanford University, 2008).

87. Christopher Ehret, 'The First Spread of Food Production in Southern Africa' in Christopher Ehret and Merrick Posnansky (eds), *The Archaeological and Linguistic Reconstruction of African History* (Berkeley: University of California Press, 1982).

88. Richard Elphick, *Khoikhoi and the Founding of White South Africa* (Johannesburg: Ravan Press, 1985); Jeanette Deacon, *The Later Stone Age of Southernmost Africa* (Oxford: British Archaeological Reports, 1984).

89. Andrew Smith, *Pastoralism in Africa: Origins and Developmental Ecology* (London: Hurst, 1992).

90. Judith Sealy and Royden Yates, 'The Chronology of the Introduction of Pastoralism to the Cape, South Africa', *Antiquity*, 68 (1994), pp. 58–67.

91. Karim Sadr and Francois-Xavier Fauvelle-Aymar (eds), 'Khoekhoe and the Origins of Herding in Southern Africa', special issue, *Southern African Humanities*, 20, 1 (2008), pp. 1–248.

92. Deacon, *Later Stone Age*.

93. Kinahan, *Pastoral Nomads*, pp. 87–122.

94. Kinahan and Kinahan, 'Late Holocene Cave Deposit'.

95. Kinahan, *Pastoral Nomads*, p. 76; Sian Sullivan, 'Folk and Formal, Local and National—Damara Knowledge and Community Conservation in Southern Kunene, Namibia', *Cimbebasia*, 15 (1999), pp. 1–28.

96. Kinahan and Kinahan, 'Preliminary Report'.

97. E.g. Andrew Smith, 'On Becoming Herders: Khoikhoi and San Ethnicity in Southern Africa', *African Studies*, 49 (1990), pp. 50–73.

98. Beatrice Sandelowsky, Johan van Rooyen and John Vogel, 'Early Evidence for Herders in the Namib', *South African Archaeological Bulletin*, 34 (1979), pp. 50–1; Andrew Smith and Leon Jacobson, 'Excavations at Geduld and the Appearance of Early Domestic Stock in Namibia', *South African Archaeological Bulletin*, 50 (1995), pp. 3–14.

99. Mitchell, *Archaeology*, p. 231; Larry Robbins *et al.*, 'Excavations at the Tsodilo Hills Rhino Cave', *Botswana Notes and Records*, 28 (1996), pp. 23–45.

100. Kinahan, *Pastoral Nomads*.

101. Andrew Smith, 'Exploitation of Marine Mammals by Prehistoric Cape Herders', *South African Journal of Science*, 89 (1993), pp. 162–5.

102. John Kinahan, 'Towards an Archaeology of Mimesis and Rainmaking in Namibian Rock Art' in Peter Ucko and Robert Layton (eds), *The Archaeology and Anthropology of Landscape: Shaping Your Landscape* (London: Routledge, 1999), pp. 336–57; John Kinahan and John Vogel, 'Recent Copper-working Sites in the !Khuiseb Drainage, Namibia', *South African Archaeological Bulletin*, 37 (1982), pp. 44–5.

103. Kinahan, *Pastoral Nomads*, pp. 14–48.

104. Thomas Dowson, 'Reading Art, Writing History: Rock Art and Social Change in Southern Africa, *World Archaeology*, 25 (1994), pp. 332–44.

105. Mathias Guenther, 'The Trance Dancer as an Agent of Social Change among the Farm Bushmen of the Ghanzi District', *Botswana Notes and Records*, 7 (1975), pp. 161–6.

106. John Kinahan, 'Alternative Views on the Acquisition of Livestock by Hunter-gatherers in Southern Africa: A Rejoinder to Smith, Yates and Jacobson', *South African Archaeological Bulletin*, 51 (1996), pp. 106–8.

107. But see Tilman Lenssen-Erz, and Ralf Vogelsang, 'Populating No-man's-land—Rock Art in Northern Namibia' in Blundell (ed.), *Further Approaches*, pp. 54–62.

108. Mitchell, *Archaeology*, p. 231.

109. See Francois-Xavier Fauvell-Aymar and Karim Sadr, 'Trends and Traps in the Reconstruction of Early Herding Societies in Southern Africa', *Southern African Humanities*, 20 (2008), pp. 1–6; Benjamin Smith, and Sven Ouzman, 'Taking Stock: Identifying Khoekhoen Herder Rock Art in Southern Africa', *Current Anthropology*, 45 (2004), pp. 499–526.

110. John Kinahan, 'The Archaeological Structure of Pastoral Production in the Central Namib Desert', *South African Archaeological Society Goodwin Series*, 5 (1986), pp. 69–82.

111. Sullivan, 'Folk and Formal'.

112. Kuno Budack, 'The Aonin, or Topnaar, of the Lower !Khuiseb Valley and the Sea', *Khoisan Linguistic Studies*, 3 (1977), pp. 1–42.

113. Jill Kinahan, 'The Impenetrable Shield: HMS *Nautilus* and the Namib Coast in the Late Eighteenth Century', *Cimbebasia*, 12 (1990), pp. 23–61.

114. John Kinahan, 'Human and Domestic Animal Tracks in an Archaeological Lagoon Deposit on the Coast of Namibia', *South African Archaeological Bulletin*, 51 (1996), pp. 94–8.

115. Kinahan, *Cattle for Beads*.

116. John Parkington, 'Soaqua and Bushmen: Hunters and Robbers' in Carmel Schrire, *Past and Present in Hunter-gatherer Studies* (Orlando: Academic Press, 1984), pp. 151–74.

117. Budack, 'Aonin'.

118. John Alexander, *An Expedition of Discovery into the Interior of Africa* (2 vols) (London: Henry Colburn, 1838).

119. Kinahan, *Cattle for Beads*.

120. Goldblatt, *History*.

121. J. Du Bruyn, 'Oorlam Afrikaners: from Dependence to Domination, ca.1760–1832 (unpublished research paper, University of South Africa, 1981).

122. Lau, *Jonker Afrikaner's Time*.

123. Tilman Dedering, 'Review Article: Problems of Precolonial Namibian Historiography', *SAHJ*, 20 (1988), pp. 95–104; *idem, Hate the Old and Follow the New: Khoekhoe and Missionaries in Early Nineteenth Century Namibia* (Stuttgart: Franz Steiner, 1997).

124. But see Nigel Penn, *Forgotten Frontier: Colonist and Khoisan on the Cape's Northern Frontier in the Eighteenth Century* (Athens: Ohio University Press, 2005).

125. Benjamin Ridsdale, *Scenes and Adventures in Great Namaqualand* (London: Woolmer, 1883).

126. For a detailed description of the site, see John Kinahan, 'The Archaeology of Social Rank Among Eighteenth Century Nomadic Pastoralists in Southern Namibia', *African Archaeological Review*, 13, 4 (1996), pp. 225–45.

127. B. Berkovitch, *The Cape Gunsmith* (Stellenbosch: Museum Stellenbosch, 1976); Barbara Bradlow, 'The Significance of Arms and Ammunition on

the Cape's Northern Frontier at the Turn of the Eighteenth Century', *Historia*, 1 (1981), pp. 59–68; G. Swenson, *Pictorial History of the Rifle* (New York: Bonanza Books, 1972); Brigitte Lau, 'Conflict and Power in Nineteenth Century Namibia', *JAH*, 27 (1986), pp. 29–39.

128. Lau, *Jonker Afrikaner's Time*.

129. Jill Kinahan and John Kinahan, '"A Thousand Fine Vessels are Ploughing the Main": Archaeological Traces of the Nineteenth Century "Guano Rage" on the South-western Coast of Africa', *Australasian Historical Archaeology*, 27 (2009), pp. 43–54.

130. Herbert Schneider, *Animal Health and Veterinary Medicine in Namibia* (Windhoek: Agrivet, 1994).

131. John Kinahan, 'The Archaeological and Social Dimension of Wild Grass Seed Exploitation in the Namib Desert' (Paper to Third Southern Deserts Conference, Molopo, South Africa, 2008).

132. E.g. World Bank, 'Cultural Heritage in Environmental Assessment', *Environmental Assessment Sourcebook Update*, 8 (1994), pp. 1–8; see also Pwiti and Soper (eds), *Aspects*, pp. 783–854.

133. Superseding the National Monuments Act (28 of 1969) and subsequent amendments up to Act 35 of 1979.

134. Gilbert Pwiti and George Mvenge, 'Archaeologists, Tourists and Rain-makers in the Management of Rock Art Sites in Zimbabwe: A Case Study of Domboshava National Monument' in Pwiti and Soper (eds), *Aspects*, pp. 817–24; Webber Ndoro, 'The Evolution of a Management Policy at Great Zimbabwe' in Gilbert Pwiti (ed.), *Caves, Monuments and Texts: Zimbabwean Archaeology Today* (Uppsala University, 1997), pp. 109–24.

135. Carlos Ervedosa, *Arqueologia Angolana* (Lisbon: Ministério da Educação, República Popular de Angola, 1980).

136. Martin Hall, 'Frontiers in Southern African Archaeology' in Martin Hall *et al.* (eds), *Frontiers: Southern African Archaeology Today* (Oxford: British Archaeological Reports, 1984), pp. 1–11.

137. Michael Bollig, 'Risk and Risk Minimization among Himba Pastoralists in Northwestern Namibia', *Nomadic Peoples*, 1 (1997), pp. 66–87; John Kinahan, 'The Presence of the Past: Archaeology, Environment and Land Rights on the Lower Cunene River', *Cimbebasia*, 17 (2001), pp. 23–39.

138. Kinahan, 'Presence of the Past'.

2. POLITICS, TRADE AND TRANSFORMATION: SOUTHERN AND CENTRAL NAMIBIA, 1730–1870

1. Little Namaqualand was the area of the northern Cape.

2. Martina Gockel, 'Diversifizierung und politische Ökonomie der Damara im 19. Jahrhundert', in Wilhelm Möhlig (ed.), *Frühe Kolonialgeschichte Namibias, 1880–1930* (Cologne: Koppe, 2000), pp. 97–135, argues that

Damara cultivation (principally of tobacco and dagga) dated at least from the early nineteenth century.

3. There is, however, evidence of 'fever' outbreaks in the nineteenth century in central Namibia. See, for example, John Wallis, *Fortune my Foe* (London: Jonathan Cape, 1936), p. 123.

4. Winifred Hoernlé, ed. Peter Carstens, *The Social Organization of the Nama and Other Essays* (Johannesburg: Witwatersrand University Press, 1985), p. 41.

5. Henrichsen, 'Herrschaft', p. 59 (my translation).

6. Hoernlé, *Nama*, pp. 50, 42. A tradition of common origin may reflect historical reality, or it may be invented in order to justify and encourage networks of cooperation and rights.

7. Gockel, 'Diversifizierung'; Inskeep, *Heinrich Vedder's The Bergdama*, p. 92. One traveller's account of 1888/89, however, notes the existence of 'an extremely old Bergdama captain' who claimed authority over the population of the Brandberg. See *idem*, p. 132.

8. Thomas Widlok, 'On the Other Side of the Frontier: Relations between Herero and "Bushmen" in Michael Bollig and Jan-Bart Gewald, *People, Cattle and Land: Transformations of a Pastoral Society in Southwestern Africa* (Cologne: Rüdiger Köppe, 2000), pp. 497–522, p. 507. See also Ute Dieckmann, *Hai||Om in the Etosha Region: A History of Colonial Settlement, Ethnicity and Nature Conservation* (Basel: BAB, 2007), p. 46. Hai||Om were usually classed as 'San' or 'Bushmen', but spoke Khoekhoegowab rather than a San language. On the identity of 'Bushmen' in Namibia, see Barnard, *Hunters and Herders*, pp. 39, 45–6, 62–5, 213–14; Gordon and Sholto-Douglas, *Bushman Myth*, p. 7; Sian Sullivan, 'Difference, Identity and Access to Official Discourses: Hai||om, "Bushmen" and a Recent Namibian Ethnography', *Anthropos*, 96, pp. 179–192 (2001).

9. K.F.R. Budack, 'Weibliche Häuptlinge bei den Khoe-khoen (Nama und Oorlam)', *Namibiana*, 1, 2 (1979), pp. 7–14; Webley, 'Wives and Sisters'; Lau, *Jonker Afrikaner's Time*, pp. 68–74; Vedder, *The Bergdama*, p. 104.

10. Henrichsen, 'Herrschaft', pp. 311 ff., pp. 12–13. A major tenet of Henrichsen's thesis, as we shall see below, is that Otjiherero-speakers can only be understood as a people with cattle from the second half of the nineteenth century.

11. Dedering, *Hate the Old*, p. 174.

12. See, for example, Randolph Vigne, 'The Hard Road to Colonization: The Topnaar Aonin of Namibia, 1670–1878', *Journal of Colonialism and Colonial History*, 1, 2 (2000) and Wilmsen, *Land Filled with Flies*, p. 108 for Galton's expeditions.

13. Wayne Dooling, *Slavery, Emancipation and Colonial Rule in South Africa* (Scotsville: University of KwaZulu-Natal Press, 2007), p. 23.

14. The British took the Colony in 1795, the Dutch retook it in 1803, and the British finally retook it in 1806. On the expansion of the Cape frontier see, for instance, Dooling, *Slavery*; Nigel Penn, *Forgotten Frontier*.

15. Penn, *Forgotten Frontier*, pp. 60–78.
16. This uprising coincided with the last Khoekhoe war of resistance in the east, 1799–1803.
17. Penn, *Forgotten Frontier*, pp. 78–86, 202–10.
18. The section below draws heavily on Dedering, *Hate the Old*. See also Alvin Kienetz, 'The Key Role of the Orlam Migrations in the Early Europeanization of South-West Africa (Namibia)', *International Journal of African Historical Studies* 10, 4 (1977), pp. 553–72; Nigel Penn, *Rogues, Rebels and Runaways: Eighteenth Century Cape Characters* (Cape Town: David Philip, 1999); Penn, *Forgotten Frontier*, pp. 108–12 and *passim*.
19. There is a large literature on the concept and reality of the frontier in southern Africa; an early and major contribution was Martin Legassick, 'The Frontier Tradition in South African Historiography' in Shula Marks and Anthony Atmore (eds), *Economy and Society in Pre-Industrial South Africa* (London: Longman, 1980).
20. Penn, *Rogues, Rebels*, p. 96.
21. Dedering, *Hate the Old*, pp. 37–43; see also Lau, *Jonker Afrikaner's Time*, p. 6. The Dutch version of these groups' names probably developed from contact with the incoming Oorlams.
22. Penn, *Forgotten Frontier*, pp. 168, 187–94, 210–17.
23. Lau, in contrast to Dedering (whom I have followed here) identifies the Bethany people as the combined settlement of Vlermuis' and Boois' people at Bethany in the early decades of the century. This perhaps underlines the fluidity of these groups. Lau, *Jonker Afrikaner's Time*, pp. 22–3; Dedering, *Hate the Old*, pp. 37–9.
24. For background on the LMS see John de Gruchy (ed.), *The London Missionary Society in Southern Africa* (David Philip: Cape Town, 1999). This work includes very little mention of Namibia.
25. Ursula Trüper, *The Invisible Woman: Zara Schmelen, African Mission Assistant at the Cape and in Namaland* (Basel: BAB, 2006); Kathrin Roller, 'Mission und "Mischehen": Errinerung und Körper-geteiltes Gedächtnis an eine afrikanische Vorfahrin. Über die Familie Schmelen–Kleinschmidt—Hegner' in Förster *et al.* (eds), *Namibia–Deutschland*, pp. 194–211.
26. For this interpretation see Dedering, *Hate the Old*, pp. 119–30.
27. *Ibid.*, p. 27.
28. *Ibid.*, p. 117.
29. On these issues see Dedering, *Hate the Old*, especially pp. 115, 120–1; Lau, *Jonker Afrikaner's Time*, pp. 25–8.
30. For the following account see especially Kinahan, *Cattle for Beads*; Kinahan, *Pastoral Nomads*, ch. 4.
31. Kinahan, 'Impenetrable Shield', p. 40.
32. Allan Cooper, *US Economic Power and Political Influence in Namibia, 1750–1982* (Boulder: Westview, 1982), ch. 1; Jill Kinahan, *By Command of Their Lordships: The Exploration of the Namibian Coast by the Royal Navy, 1795–1895* (Windhoek: Namibia Archaeological Trust, 1992).

Between 1720 and 1730 there was also a short-lived attempt by the Dutch West India Company to engage in whaling at Walvis Bay. See Peter Dekker and Cornelis de Jong, 'Whaling Expeditions of the West India Company to Walvis Bay', *JNSS*, 46 (1998), pp. 47–63.

33. Wilmsen, *Land Filled with Flies*, pp. 86, 88.
34. Quoted in Jill Kinahan, 'Impenetrable Shield', p. 25. See also Randolph Vigne, 'Imperialism at One Remove: Britain and Namibia, 1785–1915' in Wood (ed.), *Namibia 1884–1984*, pp. 145–51.
35. See especially Lynn Berat, *Walvis Bay: Decolonization and International Law* (Yale University Press, 1990), pp. 17–18.
36. For the section below see especially Wilmsen, *Land Filled with Flies*, pp. 90–2; A. Kaputu, 'Mbaha', in Annemarie Heywood, Brigitte Lau and Raimund Ohly (eds), *Warriors Leaders Sages and Outcasts in the Namibian Past: Narratives Collected from Herero Sources for the MSORP Project 1985–6* (Windhoek: Michael Scott Oral Records Project, 1992), pp. 84–96; Theo Sundermeier (ed.), *The Mbanderu: Their History until 1914 as told to Theo Sundermeier in 1966 by Heinrich Tjituka, Heinrich Hengari, Albert Kajovi, Heinrich Kavari, Paul Katjivikua, Ernst Ketjipotu* (trans. Annemarie Heywood) (Windhoek: Michael Scott Oral Records Project, n.d.), pp. 6–8; Thomas Tlou, *A History of Ngamiland 1750 to 1906: The Formation of an African State* (Gaborone: Macmillan Botswana, 1985), pp. 42–3.
37. Kaputu, 'Mbaha', p. 91.
38. Wilmsen, *Land Filled with Flies*, p. 78.
39. This is the era generally referred to as the *mfecane*, when wars originating in Natal are supposed to have spread throughout the southern African region in a domino-like series of enforced migrations. Scholars have cast doubt on this narrative, however, and a more recent history of the period calls for the term *mfecane* to be abandoned. Etherington, *Great Treks*, pp. xx–xxii.
40. Note, however, that another Herero/Himba tradition places the War of the Shields in Kaoko. Michael Bollig (ed.), '*When War Came the Cattle Slept*': *Himba Oral Traditions* (Cologne: Rüdiger Köppe, 1997).
41. Henrichsen, 'Herrschaft', p. 134.
42. This section draws especially on Henrichsen, 'Herrschaft' and Lau, *Jonker Afrikaner's Time*. In this chapter, the term 'Afrikaner' refers to the Oorlam Afrikaners.
43. Quoted in Wallis, *Fortune my Foe*, pp. 66–7.
44. On the early years of Jonker Afrikaner's polity see in particular Lau, *Jonker Afrikaner's Time*, pp. 28–9; Dedering, *Hate the Old*, pp. 152–3; Henrichsen, 'Herrschaft', pp. 146–52.
45. Although the Afrikaners had horses, oxen were frequently also ridden.
46. Heinrich Loth, *Die christliche Mission in Südwestafrika: Zur destruktiven Rolle der Rheinischen Missionsgesellschaft beim Prozess der Staatsbildung in Südwestafrika (1842–1893)* (Berlin: Akademie, 1963), pp. 22, 46.

47. For the archaeology of this trade see Chapter 1. See also Wilmsen, *Land Filled with Flies*, pp. 105–6.

48. Sundermeier, *The Mbanderu*, p. 10. Kandjake was the father of Munjuku, whose son, Kahimemua, led armed resistance to German rule in 1896.

49. Henrichsen, 'Herrschaft', pp. 152–3, 174–80, 307–11; Gewald, *Herero Heroes*, pp. 14–18; Lau, *Jonker Afrikaner's Time*, pp. 122, 62; Dag Henrichsen, '*Ozongombe, Omavita* and *Ozondjembo*–The Process of (Re-) Pastoralization amongst Herero in Pre-colonial 19th Century Namibia' in Michael Bollig and Jan-Bart Gewald (eds), *People, Cattle and Land*, pp. 149–186, p. 158; Gockel, 'Diversifizierung', pp. 121, 124–5. Henrichsen notes that foraging does not necessarily imply hunger.

50. See in particular, Dedering, *Hate the Old*, pp. 160–7.

51. In Otjiherero it was called Otjomuise, in Khoekhoegowab, ǁAeǀGams. Both names allude to Windhoek's natural hot springs.

52. For oral traditions relating to Tseib's people see Hein Willemse, 'Textual Production and Contested Histories in a Performance of the Namibian Storyteller Dawid Plaatjies', *Research in African Literatures* 34, 3 (2003), pp. 27–45.

53. Lau, *Jonker Afrikaner's Time*, p. 36.

54. On these points see Nils Oermann, *Mission, Church and State Relations in South West Africa under German Rule, 1884–1915* (Stuttgart: Franz Steiner, 1999), p. 49; Schürmann, 'Land', pp. 37–8.

55. On the RMS at this period see Loth, *Christliche Mission*, pp. 46–51; Lau, *Jonker Afrikaner's Time*, pp. 33–40; Wolfram Hartmann, 'Sexual Encounters and their Implications on an Open and Closing Frontier: Central Namibia from the 1840s to 1905' (PhD, Columbia University, 2002), pp. 56–8, 76; Kurt Panzergrau, *Die Bildung und Erziehung der Eingeborenen Südwestafrikas (Hereroland und Gross-Namaqualand) durch die Rheinische Missionsgesellschaft von 1842–1914* (Akademischer Verlag, 1998), pp. 20–2; Oermann, *Mission, Church*, p. 48; Lau, *History and Historiography*, pp. 53–64; Roller, 'Mission', pp. 198–9; Inskeep, *The Bergdama*, p. 23.

56. This is a summary of the complex argument presented in Jean Comaroff and John Comaroff, *Of Revelation and Revolution*, vols 1 and 2 (University of Chicago Press, 1991 and 1997). See especially vol. 2, chs 3–7; quotation from vol. 2, p. 119.

57. Lau, *Jonker Afrikaner's Time*, pp. 73, 47.

58. Oermann, *Mission, Church*, p. 50; Hildi Hendrickson, 'The "London Dress" and the Construction of Herero Identities in Southern Africa', *African Studies*, 53, 2 (1994), pp. 25–54.

59. Lau, *Jonker Afrikaner's Time*, p. 108, quoting the trader and explorer Charles John Andersson.

60. *Ibid.*, pp. 90, 61–2; Henrichsen, 'Herrschaft', pp. 155–6; Carl Hugo Hahn, *Tagebücher 1837–1860. Diaries: A Missionary in Damaraland*, ed.

Brigitte Lau (Windhoek: Archives Service Division, 1984–85), vol. 1, p. 144.

61. Kinahan, *By Command*, pp. 63–73.

62. Lau, *Jonker Afrikaner's Time*, p. 89. Charles John Andersson was born in Sweden in 1827. In 1850 he arrived with Francis Galton (an explorer and eugenicist) at the Cape, and for the following decade he explored, hunted and traded in south-western Africa, penetrating from Walvis Bay to Lake Ngami in 1851. By 1860 he had become the most important trader in South West Africa, supplying capital to many others, but he went bankrupt in 1864 and died three years later.

63. On the effects and scale of hunting see, for example, Wilmsen, *Land Filled with Flies*, pp. 93, 106–7, 118–21; Harri Siiskonen, *Trade and Socioeconomic Change in Ovamboland, 1850–1906* (Helsinki: SHS, 1990), p. 107; Schürmann, 'Land'.

64. For a summary see J.H. Esterhuyse, *South West Africa 1880–1894: The Establishment of German Authority in South West Africa* (Cape Town: C. Struik, 1968), p. 10.

65. Kinahan, *Cattle for Beads*, p. 70.

66. Henrichsen, 'Herrschaft', pp. 167–8 (my translation).

67. See especially *ibid.*, pp. 156–7; Hartmann, 'Sexual Encounters', pp. 66–8, 71–6; Kinahan, *Cattle for Beads*, p. 70; Esterhuyse, *South West Africa*, p. 9–10.

68. Lau, *Jonker Afrikaner's Time*, ch. 5; Henrichsen, 'Herrschaft', pp. 159–64, 169–74, 180–7; Gewald, *Herero Heroes*, p. 21; Esterhuyse, *South West Africa*, p. 10.

69. The section below draws largely on Henrichsen, 'Herrschaft', and Lau, *Jonker Afrikaner's Time*, ch. 7.

70. For an oral account of Tjamuaha's death and the wars that followed see A. Kaputu, 'The War Between the Nama and Herero' in Heywood *et al.* (eds), *Warriors*, pp. 1–49.

71. Henrichsen, 'Ozongombe', p. 164.

72. For this interpretation of Herero involvement see Henrichsen, 'Herrschaft', pp. 187–92, also Gewald, *Herero Heroes*, pp. 21–2. Henrichsen (p. 192, n. 258) argues that Maharero entered Otjimbingwe shortly before the battle and that Lau was wrong to state that he was not involved. For other aspects see Lau, *Jonker Afrikaner's Time*, ch. 7.

73. Vedder, *South West Africa*, p. 325; Kaputu, 'War', p. 23; Loth, *Christliche Mission*; Lau, *Jonker Afrikaner's Time*.

74. Henrichsen, 'Herrschaft', ch. 3. See also Kaputu, 'War', pp. 28–9.

75. Green to Andersson, 12 May 1864, in Brigitte Lau (ed.), *Charles John Andersson: Trade and Politics in Central Namibia, 1860–1864* (Windhoek Archives, 1989), p. 196.

76. For this argument see Henrichsen, 'Herrschaft', pp. 330–4.

77. On politics in the south see Esterhuyse, *South West Africa*, pp. 15–16.

78. Henrichsen, 'Herrschaft', pp. 159–64; *idem*, 'Ozongombe'; Lau, *Jonker Afrikaner's Time*, p. 133.
79. See especially Henrichsen, 'Herrschaft', pp. 82–3, 120; Hartmann, 'Sexual Encounters', pp. 54–5, 59–62, 66–7; Panzergrau, *Rheinische Missionsgesellschaft*, pp. 52–9.
80. Lau, *Jonker Afrikaner's Time*, pp. 140–1; Henrichsen, 'Herrschaft', pp. 335–40.

3. MONARCHY, POWER AND CHANGE: THE NORTH, 1750–1907

1. These definitions formed the basis of the Bantustans in the second half of the twentieth century, but were also in more general usage. They roughly correspond to the modern Kunene; Omusati, Oshana, Oshikoto, Ohangwena; Kavango; and Caprivi regions. For current mapping, see Mendelsohn *et al.*, *Atlas of Namibia*, pp. 20–7.
2. It should be borne in mind that colonial population estimates are notoriously unreliable, and that the population varied significantly (usually increasing) over time. There are several estimates for Owambo: see, for example, Martti Eirola, *The Ovambogefahr: The Ovamboland Reservation in the Making. Political Responses of the Kingdom of Ondonga to the German Colonial Power, 1884–1910* (Rovaniemi: Ponjois-Suomen Historialinen Yhdistys, 1992), p. 31; Siiskonen, *Trade*, pp. 42–3; Patricia Hayes, 'A History of the Ovambo of Namibia, c. 1880–1935' (PhD, University of Cambridge, 1992), p. 25. For Kavango there is an estimate of 1903 (Andreas Eckl, *Herrschaft, Macht und Einfluss: Koloniale Interaktionen am Kavango (Nord-Namibia) von 1891 bis 1921* (Cologne: Köppe, 2004), p. 13); for Caprivi, of 1908 (Maria Fisch, *The Caprivi Strip during the German Colonial Period, 1890 to 1914* (Windhoek: Out of Africa, 1999) p. 97); and for Kaoko, a census from the much later date of 1927 (Michael Bollig, 'The Colonial Encapsulation of the North-western Namibian Pastoral Economy', *Africa*, 68 4 (1988), pp. 506–35, p. 511; John Friedman, 'Making Politics, Making History: Chiefship and the Post-Apartheid State in Namibia', *JSAS*, 31 1 (2005), pp. 23–51, p. 32).
3. For analysis of these sources see, in particular, Hayes, 'Land of Goshen'; Meredith McKittrick, 'Landscapes of Power: Ownership and Identity on the Middle Kavango River, Namibia', *JSAS*, 34, 4 (2008), pp. 785–802; Patricia Hayes, 'When You Shake a Tree: The Precolonial and the Postcolonial in Northern Namibian History' in Derek Petersen and Giacomo Macola (eds), *Recasting the Past* (Athens, Ohio: Ohio University Press, 2009).
4. Unlike in areas inhabited by semi-nomadic peoples, fixed territorial boundaries existed in precolonial times in areas with more settled populations. See Wilhelm Möhlig, 'From Oral Tradition to Local History Textbook: Two Examples from the Kavango Region, Namibia' in Axel Harneit-Sievers (ed.), *A Place in the World: New Local Historiographies from Africa and*

South Asia (Leiden: Brill, 2002), pp. 181–99, p. 196; Gregor Dobler, 'Boundary Drawing and the Notion of Territoriality in Pre-Colonial and Early Colonial Ovamboland', *JNS*, 3 (2008), pp. 7–30; Andreas Eckl, 'Reports from "Beyond the Line": the Accumulation of Knowledge of Kavango and its Peoples by the German Colonial Administration, 1891–1911', *JNS*, 1 (2007), pp. 7–37, pp. 25–6.

5. Williams, *Precolonial Communities*; Axel Fleisch and Wilhelm Möhlig, *The Kavango Peoples in the Past: Local Historiographies from Northern Namibia* (Cologne: Rüdiger Köppe, 2002), p. 32; B. Hartmann, 'Die Tjaube, eine Vorbevölkerung im Kavangogebiet', *JSWASS*, 40/41 (1985/6–1985/7), pp. 75–95; Thomas Widlok, *Living on Mangetti: 'Bushman' Autonomy and Namibian Independence* (Oxford University Press, 1999), pp. 30–2, 64 and *passim*; Dieckmann, *Hai∥Om*, pp. 35–6.

6. Vansina, *Societies*, pp. 53–60, 134; see also Hayes, 'History of the Ovambo', p. 58.

7. Williams, *Precolonial Communities*, pp. 189–93, which gives the royal genealogies of five Ovambo kingdoms; Bollig (ed.), '*When War Came*', p. 13. Hans Namuhuja, *The Ondonga Royal Kings* (Windhoek: Out of Africa, 2002), gives the earliest dateable reign as 1650–90.

8. Patricia Hayes and Dan Haipinge (eds), *"Healing the land": Kaulinge's History of Kwanyama. Oral Tradition and History by the late Reverend Vilho Kaulinge of Ondobe as told to Patricia Hayes and Natangwe Shapange* (Cologne: Rüdiger Köppe, 1997), p. 23. For discussion of these processes, see especially Williams, *Precolonial Communities*, chs 1, 3.

9. Bollig, '*When War Came*', p. 13.

10. Williams, *Precolonial Communities*, especially pp. 63–5; Edwin Loeb, *In Feudal Africa* (Bloomington: Indiana University Research Center in Anthropology, Folklore and Linguistics, 1962), pp. 4–5, 365–73. Vilho Kaulinge, as recorded in Hayes and Haipinge, *Healing the Land*, p. 23, places the migration to Oshimholo after the settlement at Oshamba. All three sources also refer to the importance during the migrations of Ombwenge, which Loeb and Kaulinge place in Ondonga, and Williams on the Kwando River.

11. McKittrick, 'Landscapes', pp. 791–2; Vansina, *Societies*, pp. 182–6; Fleisch and Möhlig, *Kavango Peoples*, pp. 18, 21–3 and *passim*; Gordon Gibson, Thomas Larson and Cecilia McGurk, *The Kavango Peoples* (Wiesbaden: Steiner, 1981), p. 22.

12. D.M. Shamukuni, 'The baSubiya', *Botswana Notes and Records*, 4 (1972), pp. 161–84; Lawrence Flint, 'State-building in Central Southern Africa: Citizenship and Subjectivity in Barotseland and Caprivi', *International Journal of African Historical Studies*, 36, 2 (2003), pp. 393–428, p. 398; Louis L. van Tonder, 'The Hambukushu of Okavangoland: an Anthropological Study of A South-Western Bantu People in Africa' (PhD, University of Port Elizabeth, 1966), pp. 37, 48.

13. Fleisch and Möhlig, *Kavango Peoples*, Mangondo's Account: The Origin of the Kwangali, pp. 183–4.

14. Fleisch and Möhlig, *Kavango Peoples*, Frans Josef Haushiku's Chronicle of the Shambyu, p. 136.

15. For this paragraph see Williams, *Precolonial Communities*, pp. 92–3; Vilho Shigwedha, 'Mwaala gwa Nashilongo: a Twin with a Unique Personality' in Wolfram Hartmann (ed.), *More New Historical Writing from Namibia* (Windhoek: Namibian History Trust, 1999), pp. 37–52, pp. 40–3; Fleisch and Möhlig, *Kavango Peoples*, p. 129; Hayes, 'Landscapes'; Bollig, 'When War Came', p. 13.

16. Williams, *Precolonial Communities*, pp. 125–6, 142, 116–17; Widlok, *Living on Mangetti*, pp. 64–5, 234–6; Namuhuja, *Ondonga Royal Kings*, pp. 7–10. For examples of the conquest of Khoesan communities in the Kavango see Van Tonder, 'Hambukushu', pp. 47–9; Hartmann, 'Tjaube'.

17. For brief summaries of these decentralised communities, see Williams, *Precolonial Communities*, p. 11; Vilho Shigwedha, 'The Pre-Colonial Costumes of the Aawambo: Significant Changes under Colonialism and the Construction of Post-Colonial Identity' in Nampala and Shigwedha, *Aawambo Kingdoms*, pp. 111–274, pp. 115–16. Shigwedha calls the decentralised communities 'independent' or 'autonomous' territories.

18. Meredith McKittrick, *To Dwell Secure: Generation, Christianity and Colonialism in Ovamboland* (Portsmouth, NH: Heinemann, 2002), p. 30.

19. Williams, *Precolonial Communities*, pp. 98–101.

20. Hayes and Haipinge, *Healing the Land*, pp. 10–11; Emmanuel Kreike, 'Hidden Fruits: A Social Ecology of Fruit Trees in Namibia and Angola, 1820s–1980s' in William Beinart and JoAnn McGregor, *Social History and African Environments*, pp. 27–42; idem, *Re-creating Eden: Land Use, Environment, and Society in Southern Angola and Northern Namibia* (Portsmouth, NH: Heinemann, 2004), pp. 18–19; Hayes, 'History of the Ovambo', p. 47; Siiskonen, *Trade*, pp. 60–5, 70–9; McKittrick, 'Landscapes', p. 797.

21. On *efundula* and *ohango* see Lovisa Nampala, 'Christianisation and Social Change in Northern Namibia: A Comparative Study of the Impact of Christianity on Oukwanyama, Ondonga and Ombalantu, 1870–1971', in Nampala and Shigwedha, *Aawambo Kingdoms*, pp. 1–109, pp. 27–48; Patricia Hayes, 'Efundula and History: Female Initiation in Precolonial and Colonial Northern Namibia' in Tominaga Chizuko and Nagahara Yoko (eds), *Towards New Perspectives of African History: Women, Gender and Feminisms* (Osaka: Museum of Ethnology Japan, 2006); Heike Becker, 'Efundula: Women's Initiation, Gender and Sexual Identities in Colonial and Post-colonial Northern Namibia' in Arnfred (ed.), *Rethinking Sexualities in Africa*, pp. 35–56; Hayes, 'History of the Ovambo', pp. 68–9; McKittrick, *To Dwell Secure*, pp. 40–3, 65. Female initiation did not involve genital cutting.

22. Williams, *Precolonial Communities*, pp. 105–9, 126; Hayes, 'History of the Ovambo', pp. 48 ff.; Shigwedha, *Pre-Colonial Costumes*, ch. 1; Kreike, *Recreating Eden*, ch. 2.

23. Williams, *Precolonial Communities*, p. 94.

24. *Ibid.*, p. 97; Tlou, *Ngamiland*, pp. 19–21. Many of the polities, as a last resort, also sent to Evale for rain. See Nampala, 'Christianisation', pp. 54–8.

25. *Ibid.*, p. 30.

26. As McKittrick points out, stories of royal cruelty are too common in the oral traditions for this to have been a European invention. Shigwedha also notes the tendency of the royal clan to act without regard for the law. McKittrick, *To Dwell Secure*, pp. 66–9; Shigwedha, *Pre-colonial Costumes*, pp. 199–200.

27. Williams, *Precolonial Communities*, p. 121. Kaulinge, in Hayes and Haipinge, *Healing the Land*, pp. 24–5, attributes similar cruelties to King Shimbilinga rather than Haita.

28. Fleisch and Möhlig, *Kavango Peoples*, Haushiku's Chronicle of the Shambyu, pp. 137–8 (quote). For the two paragraphs above see Williams, *Precolonial Communities*, pp. 101–5, 122, 126, 135–7; Fleisch and Möhlig, *Kavango Peoples*, Michael Kativa Sirongo's Account of the History of Ukwangali, pp. 244–7, and *passim*; Hayes and Haipinge, *Healing the Land*, p. 28; McKittrick, *To Dwell Secure*, pp. 33–6, 26–7; Nampala, 'Christianisation', pp. 30–1.

29. Romanus Shiremo, 'Women Rule: Kavango Female Chiefs', *Namibian*, 17 May 2002.

30. In Owambo, newborn children were praised by referring to the roles they would take in production—boys were to 'look after the livestock and be a good shepherd', while girls were to 'make sure that people have *oshithima* [millet] to eat'. Nampala, 'Christianisation', pp. 66–7.

31. Pauline Peters, 'Revisiting the Puzzle of Matriliny in South-Central Africa', *Critique of Anthropology*, 17, 2 (1997), pp. 125–46, p. 134 (quote); Kari Miettinen, *On the Way to Whiteness: Christianization, Conflict and Change in Colonial Ovamboland, 1910–1965* (Helsinki: Suomalaisen Kirjallisuuden Seura, 2005), pp. 38, 52–3; Kreike, *Recreating Eden*; Robert Gordon, *Mines, Masters and Migrants: Life in a Namibian Mine Compound* (Johannesburg: Ravan, 1977), p. 245.

32. Williams, *Precolonial Communities*, pp. 132–4; Heike Becker, *Namibian Women's Movement 1980 to 1992: From Anti-colonial Resistance to Reconstruction* (Bonn: Informationsstelle Südliches Afrika, 1995), pp. 66–8.

33. Gordon Gibson and Cecilia McGurk, 'The Kwangari' in Gibson *et al.*, *Kavango Peoples*, pp. 35–79, 41–3; this total includes Queen Kanuni, who acceded in 1958. On this subject generally, see also Cecilia McGurk, 'The Mbundza' in *ibid.*, pp. 81–95, pp. 83–4; *idem*, 'The Sambyu' in *ibid.*, pp. 97–157, pp. 99–101; Thomas Larson, 'The Mbukushu' in *ibid.*,

pp. 211–67, 215–6; Fleisch and Möhlig, *Kavango Peoples*, pp. 130–1; Tlou, *Ngamiland*, pp. 19–21.

34. Fleisch and Möhlig, *Kavango Peoples*, Mangondo's Account, pp. 192–8.
35. Hayes, 'History of the Ovambo', pp. 41–5, 52–4; Siiskonen, *Trade*, pp. 203–6; Williams, *Precolonial Communities*, p. 122.
36. *Ibid.*, pp. 92–3, 117–18, 126, 133–4; Hayes, 'History of the Ovambo', p. 52.
37. These dates are given in Chris Maritz, 'The Subia and Fwe of Caprivi: Any Historical Grounds for *Primus inter Pares?*', *Africa Insight*, 26, 2 (1996), pp. 177–85, p. 178.
38. A.D. Roberts, *A History of Zambia* (London: Heinemann Educational, 1976), p. 98; Flint, 'State-building', pp. 393–6, 399–401; Shamukuni, 'The baSubiya'; Maritz, 'Subia and Fwe'; Bennett Kangumu, 'A Forgotten Corner of Namibia: Aspects of the History of the Caprivi Strip, 1939–1980' (MA, University of Cape Town, 2000), pp. 9–10.
39. Flint, 'State-building', p. 402.
40. Modern Linyanti is a newer foundation.
41. Tlou, *Ngamiland*, pp. 42–3; Mutumba Mainga, *Bulozi under the Luyana Kings: Political Evolution and State Formation in Pre-colonial Zambia* (Harlow: Longman, 1973), p. 70; Shamukuni, 'The baSubiya', pp. 173–4; Roberts, *History of Zambia*, p. 127; Flint, 'State-building', p. 403.
42. Siiskonen, *Trade*, pp. 60–79; Michael Bollig, 'Unmaking the Market: The Encapsulation of a Regional Trade Network. North-western Namibia between the 1880s and the 1950s' in Möhlig (ed.), *Frühe Kolonialgeschichte*, pp. 11–29, p. 12; Widlok, *Living on Mangetti*, pp. 30–2.
43. Joseph Miller, *Way of Death: Merchant Capitalism and the Angolan Slave Trade 1730–1830* (London: James Currey, 1988), ch. 5; Siiskonen, *Trade*, pp. 82–4; W.G. Clarence-Smith, *Slaves, Peasants and Capitalists in Angola 1840–1926* (Cambridge University Press, 1979), pp. 7–8; Eric Flint, 'Trade and Politics in Barotseland during the Kololo Period', *JAH*, 11, 1 (1970), pp. 71–86, pp. 71–2; Flint, 'State-building', p. 401.
44. Siiskonen, *Trade*, pp. 82–4, 89–92, 96–8; 102–4, 111; Clarence-Smith, *Slaves, Peasants*, pp. 14–15, 30–3.
45. Siiskonen, *Trade*, pp. 89–92; Hayes, 'History of the Ovambo', p. 73. Hayes notes that documentary evidence shows this contact, although oral traditions state that white traders did not enter Oukwanyama until the reign of Mweshipandeka (1850s–1881).
46. Williams, *Precolonial Communities*, pp. 142–4; Siiskonen, *Trade*, pp. 98–101; Bollig, 'When War Came', pp. 15–16; Hayes, 'History of the Ovambo', pp. 75–6.
47. Bollig, 'When War Came', pp. 15–19; *idem*, 'Power and Trade in Precolonial and Early Colonial Northern Kaokoland 1860s–1940s' in Patricia Hayes, Jeremy Silvester, Marion Wallace and Wolfram Hartmann (eds), *Namibia under South African Rule: Mobility and Containment, 1915–46* (London: James Currey, 1998), pp. 176–81.

48. One trader did, however, report in 1857 that the northern Ovambo societies had firearms. McKittrick, *To Dwell Secure*, p. 53.

49. Hahn, *Tagebücher*, pp. 1060–1; Siiskonen, *Trade*, pp. 98–101; Williams, *Precolonial Communities*, pp. 119–20. Williams suggests that the Ndonga warriors were attempting to confiscate the travellers' wagons in payment of tribute they believed due to the king; Hahn and his party had presented a number of items including clothing that the king did not value—another indication of the relative isolation of Owambo at this date.

50. Kalle Gustafsson, 'The Trade in Slaves in Ovamboland, *ca.* 1850–1910', *African Economic History*, 33 (2005), pp. 31–68, pp. 34–5, 39; Siiskonen, *Trade*, pp. 102–4; 109–10, 107–52; Kreike, *Recreating Eden*, p. 27; Clarence-Smith, *Slaves, Peasants*, p. 44; Hayes, 'History of the Ovambo', pp. 81–4; Peter Johannson, *The Trader King of Damaraland: Axel Eriksson. A Swedish Pioneer in South Africa* (Windhoek: Gamsberg Macmillan, 2007), chs 16, 17.

51. Flint, 'State-building', p. 406.

52. Flint, 'Trade'; Mainga, *Bulozi*, pp. 82–5; Roberts, *History of Zambia*, pp. 127–31; Andrew Ross, *David Livingstone, Mission and Empire* (London: Hambledon, 2002); Flint, 'State-building', pp. 402–5.

53. Tlou, *Ngamiland*, pp. 65–7, 75; Gibson, *Kavango Peoples*, pp. 24–5; Eckl, 'Reports', pp. 19–21.

54. Hayes and Haipinge, *Healing the Land*, p. 32.

55. A number of dates are given in the secondary sources: for a discussion, see Miettinen, *On the Way*, p. 71, n. 208. See also Williams, *Precolonial Communities*, pp. 151–3; Dobler, 'Boundary Drawing'.

56. Siiskonen, *Trade*, pp. 206–13, 224–9; Williams, *Precolonial Communities*, pp. 142–6, 151–3, 157–9; Gustafsson, 'Trade in Slaves', pp. 40–2; Hayes, 'History of the Ovambo', pp. 53–4, 88; McKittrick, *To Dwell Secure*, p. 58.

57. Magdalena Malonde, quoted in Kreike, *Recreating Eden*, p. 28.

58. Siiskonen, *Trade*, pp. 112–14, 213–24; Widlok, *Living on Mangetti*, pp. 30–2; Hayes, 'History of the Ovambo', pp. 85–6, 88–92, 94–7; Eirola, *Ovambogefahr*, pp. 57–9; McKittrick, *To Dwell Secure*, pp. 64–5, 70–9; Gustafsson, 'Trade in Slaves', pp. 41, 46–7, 50–1.

59. Although Siiskonen denies that traders operated on credit in the north, Hayes and Clarence-Smith both refer to this phenomenon. The creation of indebtedness by traders was so common in Africa that it seems highly probable that it occurred in the north of Namibia. Siiskonen, *Trade*, pp. 194–200; Hayes, 'History of the Ovambo', pp. 84–7; Clarence-Smith, *Slaves, Peasants*, pp. 66–7.

60. Siiskonen, *Trade*, pp. 136–57; Hayes, 'History of the Ovambo', pp. 100–12, 136–7; Kreike, *Recreating Eden*, pp. 37–42; McKittrick, *To Dwell Secure*, pp. 119–22; Clarence-Smith, *Slaves, Peasants*, pp. 87–8.

61. Bollig, 'Power and Trade', pp. 181–2; Fleisch and Möhlig, *Kavango Peoples*, Sirongo's Account of the History of Kwangali, p. 256.

62. Pers. comm., Lorena Rizzo, April 2010.

63. McKittrick, *To Dwell Secure*, pp. 55–62; Gustafsson, 'Trade in Slaves', p. 35.

64. Namuhuja, *Ondonga Royal Kings*, p. 26 (quote); Miettinen, *On the Way*, pp. 89–90; McKittrick, *To Dwell Secure*, pp. 94–8.

65. Hayes, 'History of the Ovambo', p. 80, 89–90; Williams, *Precolonial Communities*, pp. 151–3; Miettinen, *On the Way*, pp. 90–6.

66. Andreas Eckl, 'Serving the Kavango Sovereigns' Political Interests: The Beginnings of the Catholic Mission in Northern Namibia', *Le Fait Missionaire*, 14, 2004, 9–46; Fisch, *Caprivi Strip*, p. 58; Flint, 'State-building', pp. 409–10; Kangumu, 'Forgotten Corner', p. 19; Michael Bollig, 'Contested Places: Graves and Graveyards in Himba Culture', *Anthropos*, 92 (1977), 35–50, p. 45.

67. Hayes, 'History of the Ovambo', p. 80.

68. Miettinen, *On the Way*, pp. 90–1; Nampala and Shigwedha, *Aawambo Kingdoms*.

69. McKittrick, *To Dwell Secure*, pp. 79–83, 106–18; Shigwedha, *Pre-Colonial Costumes*, p. 185. The latter argues that children were forcibly kept away from their parents by the missionaries. This question is obscured by the fact that much of the evidence concerns the early twentieth rather than the nineteenth century.

70. Miettinen, *On the Way*, pp. 90–6.

71. Moorsom, 'Underdevelopment', pp. 182–5; Hayes, 'History of the Ovambo', pp. 148–57; McKittrick, *To Dwell Secure*, pp. 123–9; Becker, *Namibian Women's Movement*, p. 95.

72. Roberts, *History of Zambia*, pp. 131, 135; Eugenia Herbert, *Twilight on the Zambezi: Late Colonialism in Central Africa* (Basingstoke: Palgrave, 2002), pp. 4–5.

73. Kabunda Kayongo, *Reciprocity and Interdependence: The Rise and Fall of the Kololo Empire in Southern Africa in the Nineteenth Century* (n.p.: Almqvist & Wiksell International, 1987), pp. 140–4; Mainga, *Bulozi*, pp. 111–13; Roberts, *History of Zambia*, pp. 132–3; Flint, 'State-building', pp. 402–8; Maritz, 'Subia and Fwe', pp. 180–3; Shamukuni, 'The baSubiya', p. 174.

74. Mainga, *Bulozi*, pp. 118–29, 172; Roberts, *History of Zambia*, pp. 133–5; Maria Fisch, 'The Tawana's Military Campaign in the Kavango', *JNSS*, 55 (2007), pp. 109–31, pp. 115–16; Fleisch and Möhlig, *Kavango Peoples*, Haushiku's Chronicle of the Shambyu, pp. 160–1; Flint, 'State-building', pp. 401, 410; Fisch, *Caprivi Strip*, pp. 54–65.

75. Hayes, 'History of the Ovambo', pp. 114–15; Eckl, *Herrschaft*, p. 14; Herbert, *Twilight*, pp. 6–7; Flint, 'State-building', p. 411. The Caprivi Strip was named after the German Chancellor 1890–4, Count Leo von Caprivi. The name 'Caprivi Zipfel' (Caprivi Strip) originated in mockery of Count von Caprivi. See Wolfgang Zeller and Bennett Kangumu Kangumu, 'Caprivi Under Old and New Indirect Rule: Falling off the Map or

a 19th Century Dream Come True?' in Henning Melber (ed.), *Transitions in Namibia: Which Changes for Whom?* (Uppsala: Nordiska Afrikainstitutet, 2007), pp. 190–209, pp. 193–4.

76. Kreike, *Recreating Eden*, pp. 42–4; Hayes, 'History of the Ovambo', pp. 124–40; Siiskonen, *Trade*, pp. 114–16, 156–7; Clarence-Smith, *Slaves, Peasants*, pp. 15–16, 81.

77. Flint, 'State-building', p. 413; Fisch, *Caprivi Strip*, pp. 43–51, 61–3.

78. Bollig, 'Power and Trade', pp. 183–5; Eckl, 'Reports'. Kaoko, however, never supplied much labour to the Police Zone.

79. The Kavango area had fallen under the Grootfontein District in 1901.

80. Eckl, *Herrschaft*, pp. 34–53; *idem*, 'Serving', pp. 16–17; *idem*, 'Mit Kreuz, Gewehr und Handelskarre: der Kavango 1903 im deutschen Fokus' in Möhlig (ed.), *Frühe Kolonialgeschichte*, pp. 31–75, pp. 49–50; Fleisch and Möhlig, *Kavango Peoples*, p. 62 n. 14. The settlers Eduard Paasch and family had trekked to the Gciriku polity with their cattle, but he had been killed in a fight apparently provoked by his aggression towards the local people. His family escaped to the Shambyu polity but were all killed except his youngest daughter.

81. Fleisch and Möhlig, *Kavango Peoples*, Anna Mavandje's Chronicle of the Gciriku People, pp. 96–7.

82. Fisch, 'Tawana's Military Campaign'; Hartmann, 'Tjaube', pp. 78–84; Fleisch and Möhlig, *Kavango Peoples*, pp. 58–62; Gibson, *Kavango Peoples*, pp. 31–3. Fisch places the massacres in 1893, Fleisch and Möhlig in 1894.

83. Fleisch and Möhlig, *Kavango Peoples*, Alex Muranda Hamunyera's Account of the History of Ukwangali and Umbunza, p. 286. The passage refers to the time of the reign of Himarwa (1886–1910).

84. Kambonde and Nehale both had interests in the land at Upingtonia. See ch. 4.

85. For the dynamics of early colonialism in Owambo see Hayes, 'History of the Ovambo', pp. 113–19; Eirola, *Ovambogefahr*, pp. 64–5, 77–8, 84–7, 89, 98–9, 100–6, 118–36, 169–85, 187–99 and *passim*.

86. *Ibid.*, p. 87.

87. *Ibid.*, pp. 118–22 and *passim*.

88. *Ibid.*, pp. 60–1, 87; Hayes, 'History of the Ovambo', pp. 114–15; Kreike, *Recreating Eden*, pp. 41–2; Siiskonen, *Trade*, pp. 143–5, 178–83; Bollig, 'Power and Trade', pp. 183–5. The total arms trade ban of 1892 had been enforced at that time, and had stopped the supply of arms to Hendrik Witbooi from Owambo.

4. THE SHADOW OF PROTECTION, 1870–93

1. Henrichsen, 'Herrschaft', p. 186 (my translation).

2. *Ibid.*, p. 203.

3. Cape of Good Hope, *Report of W. Coates Palgrave, Special Commissioner… of His Mission to Damaraland and Great Namaqualand in 1876*

(Cape Town, 1877), pp. 83, 94. (It is not clear whether the total of Nama-Oorlam in Great Namaquland (16,850) given on p. 94 includes the total of Nama-Oorlam given for Damaraland (1,500) on p. 83).

4. Henrichsen, 'Herrschaft', pp. 198–202; see also Gewald, *Herero Heroes*, pp. 24–6.

5. Brigitte Lau (ed.), *The Hendrik Witbooi Papers* (Windhoek: National Archives of Namibia, trans. Annemarie Heyward and Eben Maasdorp, 2nd ed., 1995), pp. viii–ix.

6. On the Rehoboth Basters see Maximilian Bayer, *The Rehoboth Baster Nation of Namibia* (Basel: BAB, 1984, ed. Peter Carstens); Peter Carstens, 'Opting out of Colonial Rule: the Brown Voortrekkers of South Africa and their Constitutions', part one, *African Studies*, 42, 2 (1983), pp. 135–52 and part two, *African Studies*, 43, 1 (1984), pp. 19–30.

7. Henrichsen, 'Herrschaft', pp. 365–8; Joris de Vries, *Manasse Tjiseseta: Chief of Omaruru 1884–1898, Namibia* (Cologne: Rüdiger Köppe, 1999).

8. The letter is published in Cape of Good Hope, *Report of W. Coates Palgrave*, Annexures, pp. iv–vi. Although the 'Thirstland Trekkers' did not begin to leave the Transvaal until the following year, in 1874 there were enough rumours of their departure to alarm the Herero leaders.

9. On Palgrave's mission see Stals (ed.), *Commissions of Palgrave*, especially 'Introduction', pp. ix–xxxiv, and *passim*; Cape of Good Hope Legislative Council, *Report of W. Coates Palgrave*; Henrichsen, 'Herrschaft', pp. 372–83; idem, 'Pastoral Modernity, Territoriality and Colonial Transformations in Central Namibia, 1860s to 1904' in Peter Limb, Peter Midgley and Norman Etherington (eds), *Grappling with the Beast: Indigenous Southern African Responses to Colonialism, 1840–1930* (Leiden: Brill, 2010); Berat, *Walvis Bay*, pp. 31–7; Schürmann, 'Land', pp. 147–54; Jeremy Silvester, 'Portraits of Power and Panoramas of Persuasion: The Palgrave Album at the National Archives of Namibia' in Hartmann (ed.), *Hues*, pp. 131–60; Esterhuyse, *South West Africa*, pp. 16–24.

10. Dag Henrichsen, 'Claiming Space and Power in Pre-Colonial Central Namibia: The Relevance of Herero Praise Songs' (Basel: BAB Working Paper 1, BAB, 1999); idem, 'Herrschaft', pp. 62–8.

11. Isaak to Palgrave, 18 Jan. 1877, published in Cape of Good Hope, *Report of W. Coates Palgrave*, p. 108.

12. Willem Christian to Palgrave, 22 Dec. 1876, published in *ibid.*, p. 101.

13. Oermann, *Mission, Church*, p. 53. According to Palgrave, in 1876/77 in central Namibia there were 'Namaqua' missions at Bokberg (Erongo) and Windhoek, a 'Houquain' (Damara) station at Okombahe, and 'Damara' (Herero) missions at Otjimbingwe, Barmen (Otjikango), Okahandja, Otjozondjupa, Otjithwathu (Otjosazu), Omburu, Otjizeva and Okozondje (Omaruru). For the south Oermann gives Grootfontein, Hoachanas and Gobabis, but this list is likely to be incomplete. There was certainly also a

station at Gibeon at this date. Cape of Good Hope, *Report of W. Coates Palgrave*, pp. 85–6.

14. Henrichsen, 'Herrschaft', pp. 394–6, 112; Oermann, *Mission, Church*, p. 70; Hartmann, 'Sexual Encounters', pp. 87–8; Brigitte Lau, 'A Critique of the Historical Sources and Historiography Relating to the "Damaras" in Pre-colonial Namibia' (BA, University of Cape Town, 1979), p. 67; Ivan Gaseb, 'A Historical Hangover: The Absence of Damara from Accounts of the 1904–08 War' in Hartmann (ed.), *More New Historical Writing*, pp. 5–20, pp. 14–15; Gockel, 'Diversifizierung', pp. 113–14.

15. Henrichsen, 'Herrschaft', pp. 215–16, 220–39, 90–1; Hartmann, 'Sexual Encounters', pp. 88–9. On Eriksson see Peter Johansson, *The Trader King of Damaraland: Axel Eriksson. A Swedish Pioneer in Southern Africa* (Windhoek: Gamsberg Macmillan, 2007).

16. Henrichsen, 'Herrschaft', pp. 244–66; Wilmsen, *Land Filled with Flies*, pp. 120–5.

17. Lau (ed.), *Hendrik Witbooi Papers*, p. x.

18. See Lau (ed.), *Hendrik Witbooi Papers*, p. 39, n. 42. She estimates that 15–20 people were killed as a result in the Okahandja area, and a further 24 at Witvlei. This figure is considerably lower, and probably more accurate, than earlier estimates: Esterhuyse, for example, asserts that 200 were killed (*South West Africa*, p. 29).

19. Henrichsen, 'Herrschaft', pp. 292–9, 73; *idem*, '"Damara" Labour Recruitment to the Cape Colony and Marginalisation and Hegemony in Late Nineteenth Century Namibia', *JNS*, 3 (2008), pp. 63–82; Gewald, *Herero Heroes*, pp. 64–7.

20. Henrichsen, 'Herrschaft', pp. 212–16, 227–8, 266–79, 292–9, 413; Oermann, *Mission, Church*, p. 53; Brian Mokopakgosi, 'German Colonialism in Microcosm: A Study of the Role of the Concessionaire Companies in the Development of the German Colonial State' (PhD, University of London, 1998), pp. 144–7; Ronald Dreyer, *The Mind of Official Imperialism: British and Cape Government Perceptions of German Rule in Namibia from the Heligoland–Zanzibar Treaty to the Kruger Telegram (1890–1896)* (Essen: Hobbing, 1987), p. 105, n. 17.

21. Günter Reeh's biography, *Hendrik Witbooi: Ein Leben für die Freiheit. Zwischen Glaube und Zweifel* (Cologne: Rüdiger Köppe, 2000), elegantly recounts his life and explores his religious convictions, but has little to say about the social and economic foundations of his success. For an important analysis see also Tilman Dedering, 'Hendrik Witbooi, the Prophet', *Kleio*, 25 (1993), pp. 54–78. See also Ludwig Helbig and Werner Hillebrecht, *The Witbooi* (Windhoek: CASS, 1992), a useful but brief overview; Lau (ed.), *Hendrik Witbooi Papers* (see especially 'Introduction'); Gustav Menzel, *'Widerstand und Gottesfurcht': Hendrik Witbooi–eine Biographie in zeitgenössischen Quellen* (Cologne: Rüdiger Köppe, 2000), which consists mainly of citations of primary sources; George Gugelberger, *Nama/ Namibia: Diary and Letters of Nama Chief Hendrik Witbooi, 1884–1894*

(Boston University African Studies Centre, 1984); Hendrik Witbooi, *Die Dagboek van Hendrik Witbooi* (Cape Town: Van Riebeeck Society, 1929); idem, *Afrika den Afrikanern! Aufzeichnungen eines Nama-Häuptlings aus der Zeit der deutschen Eroberung Südwestafrikas 1884 bis 1894* (Berlin: Dietz, 1982). The account below is based mainly on the first four of these texts.

22. Lau (ed.), *Hendrik Witbooi Papers*, pp. iii–xi; Henrichsen, 'Herrschaft', pp. 284–5.

23. Reeh, *Hendrik Witbooi*, p. 26, using Missionary Rust's evidence; Dedering, 'Hendrik Witbooi', pp. 57–63. See also Menzel, '*Widerstand und Gottesfurcht*', pp. 89, 97.

24. It is possible, however, as Reeh argues, that the attack arose mainly from the tensions of the moment. See *Hendrik Witbooi*, p. 28.

25. See especially Witbooi's 1890 description of his religious experience: Witbooi to Johannes Olpp, 3 January 1890, in Lau (ed.), *Hendrik Witbooi Papers*, pp. 38–43.

26. For the third expedition see Menzel, *Widerstand und Gottesfurcht*, ch. 9; Esterhuyse, *South West Africa*, p. 112.

27. For a summary of this much-debated subject see W.O. Henderson, *The German Colonial Empire, 1884–1919* (London: Frank Cass, 1993), chs 3, 4. See also Mokopakgosi, 'German Colonialism', pp. 64–71.

28. Namibia's copper deposits were well known, and speculation about the existence of precious minerals was encouraged by the discovery of diamonds at Kimberley in the Cape in 1867 (although gold was not discovered on the Rand until 1886–88).

29. Drechsler notes that the German Commissioner Gustav Nachtigal, who arrived later in the year, rectified the position by deleting the word 'geographical'. However, because he died on the return journey to Europe, this change was not implemented. Drechsler, '*Let Us Die Fighting*', p. 24. For these land transactions in general see Schürmann, 'Land', pp. 160–73.

30. Oermann, *Mission, Church*, p. 68 (quote), pp. 54–63; Ngavirue, *Political Parties*, pp. 94–7.

31. For a map see Mokopgakgosi, 'German Colonialism', p. 194.

32. For the land treaties and related politics see Goldblatt, *History*, ch. 17, pp. 100–3; de Vries, *Manasse Tjiseseta*, pp. 28–35, 99; Drechsler, '*Let Us Die Fighting*', pp. 17–26, 37; Henderson, *German Colonial Empire*, pp. 24–5; Walter Moritz, *Die Swartboois in Rehoboth, Salem, Ameib und Franzfontein* (Tsumeb: Nation Press, 1998), p. 33; Ngavirue, *Political Parties*, p. 74; Schürmann, 'Land', pp. 161, 170. Historians disagree on the precise extent of the land affected by some of these transactions.

33. Quoted in Drechsler, '*Let Us Die Fighting*', p. 28.

34. Schürmann, 'Land', pp. 140–1. For the protection treaties see Drechsler, '*Let Us Die Fighting*', pp. 26–9.

35. On these negotiations, and Maharero's politics in particular, see Henrichsen, 'Herrschaft', pp. 372–414; *idem*, 'Pastoral Modernity'; Goldblatt,

History, pp. 100–3; Schürmann, 'Land', pp. 164–7, pp. 172–3; De Vries, *Manasse Tjiseseta*, pp. 35–6.

36. On Upingtonia see Henrichsen, 'Herrschaft', pp. 422 ff.; Gordon and Sholto-Douglas, *Bushman Myth*, pp. 40–2. The Thirstland Trekkers had crossed the Kalahari to arrive at Rietfontein in eastern Namibia in 1877; they then moved on to the Okavango, eventually arriving in Angola. Some of them returned to the Grootfontein area in 1885. Henrichsen attributes the collapse of Upingtonia to Maharero and his allies, Gordon to San resistance. The issue of Upingtonia was very complex, encompassing the rival claims to the land of Maharero and Kambonde, as well as involving Kambonde's rival Nehale, who had the Boers' leader Jordan killed, on which see Eirola, *Ovambogefahr*. On Herero—San contestation of the land around Grootfontein see also Thomas Widlok, 'On the Other Side of the Frontier: Relations between Herero and "the Bushmen"' in Bollig and Gewald (eds), *People, Cattle and Land*, pp. 487–522.

37. One reason for British acquiescence was the promise of German support in Egypt, where British and French economic interests were in conflict. See Dreyer, *Official Imperialism*, p. 58.

38. *Ibid.*, pp. 65–70, 98; Henderson, *German Colonial Empire*, pp. 42–3; Drechsler, *'Let Us Die Fighting'*, pp. 31–2.

39. Not to be confused with the Deutsche Kolonialgesellschaft (German Colonial Union; DKG) formed in 1887 in Germany through the amalgamation of two similar organisations, with the aim of promoting German colonial expansion.

40. Drechsler, *'Let Us Die Fighting'*, pp. 29–31, 35–7; Henderson, *German Colonial Empire*, p. 43; Dreyer, *Official Imperialism*, p. 104; Richard Voeltz, *German Colonialism and the South West Africa Company* (Athens, Ohio: Ohio University Press, 1988), pp. 1–2; Mokopakgosi, 'German Colonialism', pp. 90–105, pp. 113–14.

41. Drechsler, *'Let Us Die Fighting'*, pp. 37–9; quote p. 39.

42. Oermann, *Mission, Church*, p. 66.

43. Lau, (ed.), *Hendrik Witbooi Papers*, p. xvii.

44. *Ibid.*, pp. vii–ix.

45. Helbig and Hillebrecht, *The Witbooi*, p. 23, quoting unnamed German visitors to Hoornkrans.

46. *Ibid.*, pp. 25 (quoting an unnamed German visitor), 23. On livestock-rearing practices see Witbooi's letter to the Hoornkrans community, 27 July 1890 (Lau (ed.), *Hendrik Witbooi Papers*, pp. 55–6), in which he encourages the people to husband rather than squander their animals. See also *idem*, pp. 63–4, for the appointment of officers in the community in 1891.

47. Witbooi to Hermanus van Wyk, 9 June 1889, quoted in Lau (ed.), *Hendrik Witbooi Papers*, p. 34; Reeh, *Hendrik Witbooi*, pp. 27–30, 35–8.

48. Henrichsen, 'Herrschaft', pp. 425–31. Whether these troops were the forerunners of the *oturupa* movements (see Chapter 8) is a moot point.

While the young men partially copied German practices, these were real troops rather than a mock-military movement.

49. Drechsler, *'Let Us Die Fighting*, pp. 43–4; Gewald, *Herero Heroes*, pp. 33–7; Lau (ed.), *Hendrik Witbooi Papers*, pp. xix–xx, 45–6.

50. Oermann, *Mission, Church*, p. 69; Dreyer, *Official Imperialism*, p. 165; Gewald, *Herero Heroes*, pp. 39–41; Lau (ed.), *Hendrik Witbooi Papers*, pp. 48; Annemarie Heywood and Brigitte Lau, *Three Views into the Past of Windhoek* (Windhoek: Historical Conference, 1993), pp. 9–11.

51. Witbooi to Maharero, 30 May 1890, in Lau (ed.), *Hendrik Witbooi Papers*, pp. 50–3.

52. Drechsler, *'Let Us Die Fighting'*; Henderson, *German Colonial Empire*, p. 74.

53. Quoted in Drechsler, *'Let Us Die Fighting'*, p. 52.

54. For the concession companies and policy towards them see especially Drechsler, *'Let Us Die Fighting'*, pp. 44–53; Mokopakgosi, 'German Colonialism', pp. 123–4, 187–9, 190, 201–3, 214–15; Dreyer, *Official Imperialism*, ch. 3; Voeltz, *South West Africa Company*, ch. 1.

55. Mokopakgosi, 'German Colonialism', pp. 96–8, 209–11; Gewald, *Herero Heroes*, p. 48.

56. For the succession conflict see *ibid.*, pp. 41–6; Gerhard Pool, *Samuel Maharero* (Windhoek: Gamsberg Macmillan, 1991), p. 97; Bley, *Namibia*, pp. 17–18. Gewald argues that Riarua was the choice of the Okahandja Herero, Pool that Riarua supported Nikodemus Kavikunua in the leadership contest. Bley, following Lehmann and Vedder, makes the less credible argument that the *ovahona* chose Samuel Maharero, probably without German intervention.

57. Lau (ed.), *Hendrik Witbooi Papers*, pp. xvi–xvii, 45–6; Pool, *Samuel Maharero*, pp. 71, 84–92.

58. See Gewald, *Herero Heroes*, pp. 46–52. Gewald does not discuss in detail the reasons for the alliance between Samuel Maherero and Witbooi. See also Lau (ed.), *Hendrik Witbooi Papers*, *passim*.

59. Lau (ed.), *Hendrik Witbooi Papers*, pp. 126–7; see also pp. 207–10.

60. Quoted in Martha Mamozai, *Herrenmenschen: Frauen im deutschen Kolonialismus* (Reinbek bei Hamburg: Rohwohlt, 1982), p. 173 (my translation).

61. Theodor Leutwein, *Elf Jahre Gouverneur in Deutsch-Südwestafrika* (Windhoek: Namibia Scientific Society, 1997, first pub. 1906), p. 106 (my translation).

62. Wolfram Hartmann, 'Urges in the Colony: Men and Women in Colonial Windhoek, 1890–1905', *JNS*, 1 (2007), pp. 39–71, pp. 40–2; Lau (ed.), *Hendrik Witbooi Papers*, pp. xxi–xxii, 199–214; Oermann, *Mission, Church*, pp. 71–2; Drechsler, *'Let Us Die Fighting'*, pp. 69–71; Helbig and Hillebrecht, *The Witbooi*, pp. 33–4; Reeh, *Hendrik Witbooi*, pp. 42–4.

5. UNDER GERMAN RULE, 1894–1903

1. Leutwein arrived in SWA, like von François before him, as Landeshauptmann (the title used to describe the head of the government of a province). After the first phase of armed resistance had been defeated, he became Gouverneur (governor), signalling increased German control over the territory. See Hansjörg Huber, *Koloniale Selbstverwaltung in Deutsch-Südwestafrika* (Frankfurt: Peter Lang, 1999), p. 68.

2. Helbig and Hillebrecht, *The Witbooi*, p. 37.

3. Witbooi to Leutwein, 21 May 1894 and reply, 24 May 1894. Lau (ed.), *Hendrik Witbooi Papers*, pp. 163–5.

4. Another contemporary estimate by Lieut. F.J. Bulow, however, put the Witboois' troops at 600 at this time. See Drechsler, *'Let Us Die Fighting'*, pp. 72–3.

5. There has been little work on the extent to which limits on cattle raiding and tribute extraction were imposed on the Witboois and other groups after they came under German authority, but it is likely that these sources of income declined radically and that this also increased economic dependence.

6. This took place during the 1896 campaign against Kahimemua. See Ludwig von Estorff, *Kriegserlebnisse in Südwestafrika* (Berlin: Ernst Siegfried Mittler, 1911), p. 7.

7. Witbooi to Leutwein, 14 Nov. 1904, in Lau (ed.), *Hendrik Witbooi Papers*, p. 193. On the Khauas, Fransmanns and Witboois during this decade, see *idem*, pp. xxv–xxvi; *Bley, Namibia*, pp. 8–15, 27–38; Drechsler, *'Let Us Die Fighting'*, pp. 75–82.

8. Bley, *Namibia*, pp. 15–22; Gewald, *Herero Heroes*, pp. 56–60.

9. *Ibid.*, pp. 62–80; De Vries, *Manasse Tjiseseta*, ch. 3; Moritz, *Die Swartboois*, p. 33.

10. Bennet Fuller, 'Institutional Appropriation and Social Change among Agropastoralists in Central Namibia, 1916–1988' (PhD, Boston University, 1993), p. 178; Gewald, *Herero Heroes*, pp. 62–80; Bley, *Namibia*, pp. 23–7; Gordon and Sholto-Douglas, *Bushman Myth*, pp. 49–50, 64.

11. Pool, *Samuel Maharero*, chs 9, 10, p. 115; Gewald, *Herero Heroes*, pp. 81–102.

12. Mokopakgosi, 'German Colonialism', pp. 212–14.

13. Bley, *Namibia*, p. 56.

14. Gewald, *Herero Heroes*, pp. 83, 85; Pool, *Samuel Maharero*, pp. 119–23.

15. See Bley, *Namibia*, pp. 59–60 for Gobabis. Eventually Leutwein allowed Nicodemus Kavikunua the temporary use of the place, subject to some restrictions.

16. Kahimemua to Leutwein, 3 March 1896, quoted in Gewald, *Herero Heroes*, p. 102.

17. Nikodemus Kavikunua's involvement is agreed by most sources, but for an opposite view, see Pool, *Samuel Maharero*, ch. 11.

18. The German officer Richard Carow, who was present at the trial, records how Kahimemua 'recounted the plans that he had hatched together with Nicodemus, to destroy the *Schutztruppe*' (my translation). Richard Carow, *Die kaiserliche Schutztruppe in Deutsch Sudwest-Afrika unter Major Leutwein* (Leipzig: Freund und Wittig, 1898). Oral tradition, however, claims the opposite.

19. P.H. Van Rooyen and Peter Reiner, *Gobabis: Brief History of the Town and Region* (Gobabis: Municipality of Gobabis, 1995), p. 21.

20. Quoted in Sundermeier (ed.), *The Mbanderu*, p. 45.

21. Quoted in *ibid.*, p. 38.

22. Richard Carow, *Die kaiserliche Schutztruppe in Deutsch-Südwest-Afrika unter Major Leutwein* (Leipzig: Freund and Wittig, 1898), p. 86 (my translation).

23. For the 1896 war and its causes, see Sundermeier (ed.), *The Mbanderu*, pp. 39–48, including extracts from Kurt Schwabe's works, pp. 62–5, 67–8; Carow, *Die kaiserliche Schutztruppe*, pp. 58–96; Leutwein, *Elf Jahre Gouverneur*, ch. 3; Bley, *Namibia*, pp. 59–62; Drechsler, *'Let Us Die Fighting'*, pp. 92–6; Gewald, *Herero Heroes*, pp. 85–90, 107–8; Pool, *Samuel Maharero*, ch. 11, pp. 128–9.

24. Carow, *Die kaiserliche Schutztruppe*, pp. 86, 65. Carow also notes (p. 81) that many women and children were present in encampments around Otjunda.

25. Gewald, *Herero Heroes*, p. 108; see also Kaulich, *Deutsch-Südwestafrika*, p. 236.

26. Drechsler, *'Let Us Die Fighting'*, pp. 96–7; Huber, *Koloniale Selbstverwaltung*, p. 77; Jan-Bart Gewald, '"I was afraid of Samuel, therefore I came to Sekgoma": Herero Refugees and Patronage Politics in Ngamiland, Bechuanaland Protectorate, 1890–1914', *Journal of African History*, 43 (2002), pp. 211–34; *idem, Herero Heroes*, pp. 124–8.

27. This photograph, originally dated to 1904, was subsequently traced in a book published in 1899 where it was associated with the defeat of the Khauas. See Hartmann, *Hues*, p. 62.

28. *Ibid.*, pp. 81–106; Pool, *Samuel Maharero*, pp. 133–8; Bley, *Namibia*, pp. 50–7; Drechsler, *'Let Us Die Fighting'*, p. 87.

29. Comparable figures are not available for the south.

30. Gewald, *Herero Heroes*, p. 112; Oermann, *Mission, Church*, p. 84. Irle and German official sources concur in this estimate of mortality among Herero cattle; the missionary Viehe, however, reported the higher estimate of 90 per cent mortality.

31. Koch had identified the causative agent of tuberculosis in 1882 and that of cholera in 1883.

32. Drechsler, *'Let Us Die Fighting'*, p. 98.

33. For a detailed study of the effect of the rinderpest on Herero, see Gewald, *Herero Heroes*, ch. 4. For the account given here see also Drechsler, *'Let Us Die Fighting'*, p. 98; Bley, *Namibia*, pp. 124–6; Miescher, 'Rote Linie', pp. 43–9; Heywood *et al.* (eds), *Warriors*, p. 161.

34. Gordon and Sholto-Douglas, *Bushman Myth*, pp. 51–2.
35. Drechsler, '*Let Us Die Fighting*', pp. 99–100; Kaulich, *Deutsch-Südwestafrika*, p. 238.
36. Drechsler, '*Let Us Die Fighting*', pp. 100–3; Moritz, *Die Swartboois*, pp. 33–6; Kaulich, *Deutsch-Südwestafrika*, pp. 238–9.
37. Kaulich, *Deutsch-Südwestafrika*, pp. 239–41; Mokopakgosi, 'German Colonialism', p. 328; Leutwein, *Elf Jahre*, pp. 249–52; Heywood *et al.* (eds), *Warriors*, pp. 161 ff.; Sundermeier, *The Mbanderu*, p. 49.
38. I am grateful to Dag Henrichsen for his comments on this point.
39. Oermann, *Mission, Church*, p. 80.
40. Von Bülow is famous for his desire to give Germany a 'place in the sun'—that is, to gain an empire—but had no special interest in southern African expansion.
41. Matthew Seligmann, *Rivalry in Southern Africa, 1893–99: The Transformation of German Colonial Policy* (New York: St Martin's, 1998), pp. 3, 14–16, 21, 57, 76.
42. Bley, *Namibia*, p. 73. See also Robbie Aitken, *Exclusion and Inclusion: Gradations of Whiteness and Socio-economic Engineering in German Southwest Africa, 1884–1914* (Berne: Peter Lang, 2007), pp. 58–69; Daniel Walther, *Creating Germans Abroad: Cultural Policies and National Identity in Namibia* (Athens, Ohio: Ohio University Press, 2002), pp. 15–16, 28–9.
43. Wolfgang Werner, '*No One Will Become Rich*': *Economy and Society in the Herero Reserves in Namibia, 1915–1946* (Basel: P. Schlettwein, 1998), p. 44.
44. This was also true of the Settlement Syndicate, which became a commercial company in 1896 as the Siedlungsgesellschaft für Südwestafrika, and was granted 20,000 square kilometres of territory by the government in Berlin.
45. Mokopakgosi, 'German Colonialism', pp. 291–9; Gert Sudholt, *Die deutsche Eingeborenenpolitik in Südwestafrika von den Anfängen bis 1904* (Hildesheim: Georg Olms, 1975), pp. 61–8; Christo Botha, 'The Politics of Land Settlement in Namibia, 1890–1960', *SAHJ*, 42 (2000), pp. 232–75, p. 235.
46. Huber, *Koloniale Selbstverwaltung*, p. 73; Miescher, 'Rote Linie'; see also Eirola, '*Ovambogefahr*', p. 78.
47. For the complexities of this policy see Huber, *Koloniale Selbstverwaltung*, pp. 73, 79.
48. Bley, *Namibia*, pp. 46–50, 99–103; Gewald, *Herero Heroes*, p. 136; Leutwein, *Elf Jahre Gouverneur*, pp. 209–227; Zimmerer, *Deutsche Herrschaft*, p. 116; Kaulich, *Deutsch-Südwestafrika*, p. 90.
49. Mokopakgosi, 'German Colonialism', pp. 201–5. Mokopakgosi shows that SWACO share capital owned by Germans had exceeded that owned by British and South Africans by 1908/9.
50. On the concession companies and related issues see *ibid.*, pp. 209–11, 274–95, 221–5, 201–3, 217–20; Voeltz, *South West Africa Company*, p. 66; Kaulich, *Deutsch-Südwestafrika*, p. 460.

51. Sudholt, *Eingeborenenpolitik*, pp. 82–90; Kaulich, *Deutsch-Südwestafrika*, p. 460; Ursula Massman, *Swakopmund: A Chronicle of the Town's People, Places and Progress* (Swakopmund: Society for Scientific Development, 1983), pp. 9, 12–13.

52. Richard Moorsom, 'The Formation of the Contract Labour System in Namibia, 1900–1926' in Abebe Zegeye and Shuni Ishemo (eds), *Forced Labour and Migration: Patterns of Movement within Africa* (London: Hans Zell, 1989), pp. 55–108, p. 79. A similar number of Nkhumbi and Ovambo workers were also employed annually on works in southern Angola.

53. Gewald, *Herero Heroes*, pp. 132–3; Gordon and Sholto-Douglas, *Bushman Myth*, ch. 6; Zimmerer, *Deutsche Herrschaft*, pp. 179–81; Jan-Bart Gewald, 'The Road of the Man called Love and the Sack of Sero: the Herero-German War and the export of Herero Labour to the South African Rand', *JAH*, 40 (1999), pp. 21–40.

54. By the end of the century, efforts were being made to send German women to the colonies. The first shipment of white women, sixteen in number, sent by the Deutsche Kolonialgesellschaft to SWA, arrived in 1898. Lora Wildenthal, *German Women for Empire, 1884–1945* (Durham, NC: Duke University Press, 2002), p. 16.

55. Bley, *Namibia*, pp. 86–91; Zimmerer, *Deutsche Herrschaft*, pp. 84–97; Aitken, *Exclusion*, pp. 95–101; Dag Henrichsen, 'Heirat im Krieg: Erfahrungen von Kaera Ida Getzen-Leinhos' in Zimmerer and Zeller, *Völkermord*, pp. 160–8; Hartmann, 'Sexual Encounters', pp. 133–6, ch. 4, pp. 211–14. The authorities in SWA imposed a *de facto* ban on mixed marriages in the 1890s, which they were forced to rescind in 1899.

56. Gesine Krüger, *Kriegsbewältigung und Geschichtsbewusstsein: Realität, Deutung und Verarbeitung des deutschen Kolonialkrieges 1904 bis 1907* (Goettingen: Vandenhoek & Ruprecht), pp. 157–8 (my translation).

57. Hartmann, 'Urges', pp. 41–2.

58. Zimmerer, *Deutsche Herrschaft*, pp. 69–74.

59. *Ibid.*, pp. 28–9; Gordon and Sholto-Douglas, *Bushman Myth*, pp. 51–2 shows the punishments in the Grootfontein District in 1898–99 of labourers, especially San, who were widely employed on the farms. See also Bley, *Namibia*, pp. 95–8.

60. Gunther Wagner, 'Ethnographic Survey of the Windhoek District' (ms, 1950), gives a figure of 457 whites and 2,000 Africans in Windhoek in 1903; Bley, *Namibia*, gives a figure of 610 whites excluding the army, also for 1903.

61. *Ibid.*, p. 89; Marion Wallace, 'Looking at the Locations: The Ambiguities of Urban Photography' in Hartmann *et al.* (eds), *Colonising Camera*, 132–7, p. 132; Oswin Köhler, *A Study of the Karibib District (SWA)* (Pretoria: Union of South Africa, 1958), p. 58; *idem*, *A Study of the Omaruru District (SWA)* (Pretoria: Department of Bantu Administration and Development, 1959), p. 98. Karibib had two locations in 1902, and 204 Chris-

tians registered by the Rhenish Mission in 1903. For precolonial settlement patterns on mission stations, see Henrichsen, 'Herrschaft', pp. 110–13.

6. THE NAMIBIAN WAR, 1904–8

1. 'Reconcentration camps' were invented in Cuba in the late nineteenth century during a war over Spanish control; concentration camps were also used by the British in their war against the Boers in South Africa (1899–1902).
2. In common with some other recent histories, I have used the term 'Namibian War' advisedly. The word 'war' both denotes the scale of these events, and avoids implying the legitimacy of German rule, as 'uprising' or 'rebellion' perhaps do. The anachronism 'Namibian' is a usage adopted throughout this book, and enables us to move away from a description of the war in ethnic terms (particularly as 'Herero'). The term 'Namibian War' also emphasises the importance of this war, which led to greater loss of life in Namibia than any other in the nineteenth or twentieth centuries.
3. In 1900 the concession company SATCO selected 128 farms for settlers in the south of the country, 98 of which were on land sold by Willem Christian, then Bondelswarts *kaptein*, to the Kharaskhoma Syndicate in 1890. The community (and the mission) had been given shares in return. However, SATCO took over the Syndicate in 1895 and failed to honour these commitments, so the shareholdings were lost. By the time of the uprising in 1903, twenty-five of the designated farms had been sold or leased.
4. Earlier estimates put Ovambo losses at over 100, while Eirola has more recently put the number at about sixty. Eirola, *Ovambogefahr*, p. 168.
5. For the debate about the timing of these letters see below. As Krüger points out, Samuel Maharero may also have written previously to Hendrik Witbooi.
6. Jon Bridgman, *The Revolt of the Hereros* (Berkeley: University of California Press, 1981), p. 84. For the Bondelswarts uprising, and the outbreak of the Namibian War, see Mokopakgosi, 'German Colonialism', pp. 195, 274–80, 325–7; Drechsler, *'Let Us Die Fighting'*, pp. 106–11; Casper Erichsen, *'What the Elders Used to Say': Namibian Perspectives on the Last Decade of German Colonial Rule* (Windhoek: Namibia Institute for Democracy, 2008), pp. 21–4; Zimmerer, *Deutsche Herrschaft*, p. 34; Eirola, *Ovambogefahr*, pp. 163–9; Williams, *Precolonial Communities*, p. 149; Jeremy Silvester, 'Black Pastoralists, White Farmers: The Dynamics of Land Dispossession and Labour Recruitment in Southern Namibia' (PhD, University of London, 1993).
7. The evidence implying that the rising was pre-planned has been discussed in many accounts of this war; see, for example, Krüger, *Kriegsbewältigung*, pp. 56–9. On the other hand, Gewald (*Herero Heroes*, ch. 5) has argued that the uprising was in fact spontaneous and was caused by a series of overreactions on the part of Lieutenant Zürn, so that the Herero were effectively pushed into war by the Germans. Pool, *Samuel Maharero*, pp. 208–9 also gives evidence as to the patchy spread of the revolt.

Although there clearly was heightened tension in Okahandja at the time, and Gewald may be right, in my view the balance of evidence still tends to tip against him. To agree with him one would have to discount the evidence of Samuel Maharero's letters to van Wyk and Witbooi, dated before 12 January (for an argument against Gewald on this point see Oermann, *Mission, Church*, pp. 94–6, and for further insights Krüger, *Kriegsbewältigung*, p. 59), ignore all the circumstantial evidence that the rising was pre-planned, and dismiss the fact that it spread so quickly, and that military action was so effective, in the days after 12 January.

8. Heywood *et al.* (eds), *Warriors*, pp. 161 ff.
9. Pool, *Samuel Maharero*, chs 12, 13. For the opposing view—that land alienation was more a fear than a reality by 1904–see Bley, *Namibia*, pp. 133–4, 138; Gewald, *Herero Heroes*, pp. 142–4.
10. Oermann, *Mission, Church*, pp. 91–2; Drechsler, *'Let Us Die Fighting'*, pp. 133–6.
11. *Ibid.*, pp. 113–4,132–3; Mokgapakgosi, 'German Colonialism', pp. 364–7; Oermann, *Mission, Church*, pp. 87-91; Gewald, *Herero Heroes*, pp. 146–7.
12. For a summary of the debate see Krüger, *Kriegsbewältigung*, pp. 56–9.
13. Sundermeier (ed.), *The Mbanderu*, p. 49; Heywood *et al.* (eds), *Warriors*, pp. 161 ff.
14. Pool, *Samuel Maharero*, p. 181.
15. Bley, *Namibia*, pp. 142–3; Krüger, *Kreigsbewältigung*, pp. 116–19; Pool, *Samuel Maharero*, pp. 186–7; *Deutsches Kolonialblatt*, 1 June 1904, pp. 357–8; Bridgman, *Revolt of the Herero*, p. 108; Gewald, *Herero Heroes*, pp. 167–8.
16. Sundermeier (ed.), *The Mbanderu*, pp. 49 ff.; Gewald, '"I Was Afraid of Samuel"'.
17. Krüger, *Kriegsbewältigung*, pp. 71–3, 98–103; Dag Henrichsen, 'Ozombambuse and Ovasolondate: Everyday Military Life and African Service Personnel in German South West Africa' in Hartmann (ed.), *Hues*, pp. 161–84.
18. Gaseb, 'Historical Hangover', p. 6; Erichsen, *Elders*, pp. 18, 33–7.
19. For an account of this encampment see the report of the missionary Kuhlmann, *Deutsches Kolonialblatt*, 1 June 1904, pp. 357–8. See also Bridgman, *Revolt of the Herero*, ch. 4.
20. *Ibid.*, ch. 4, pp. 99, 106. On 12 March, at Owikokorero, near Onjatu, twenty-six Germans were killed and an unknown number, probably very small, of Herero. On 1 April, at Okaharui, the German advance party was attacked and 33 killed (out of 230); the Germans put Herero losses at more than 84, but Bridgman thinks this estimate very unreliable.
21. *Ibid.*, ch. 4. For a detailed description of the military campaign see also Pool, *Samuel Maharero*, chs 15–20.
22. Bridgmon, *Revolt of the Herero*, ch. 4. The figures quoted are on p. 113, but on p. 124 Bridgman gives a figure of 50,000 men, women and children in the 'rear area'. Oermann, *Mission, Church*, p. 97, draws on a variety of sources to give estimates of 50–60,000 Herero in total, including 6,000 armed men.

23. Bridgmon, *Revolt of the Herero*, p. 112; Jürgen Zimmerer, 'Krieg, KZ and Völkermord in Südwestafrika: Der erste deutsche Genozid' in Jürgen Zimmerer and Joachim Zeller (eds), *Völkermord in Deutsch-Südwestafrika: der Kolonialkrieg (1904–1908) in Namibia und seine Folgen* (Berlin: Links, 2003) (now published as *idem* (eds), *Genocide in German South-West Africa: The Colonial War of 1904–1908 and its Aftermath* (Monmouth: Merlin, 2008)), pp. 45–63, p. 49; Isabel Hull, *Absolute Destruction: Military Culture and the Practices of War in Imperial Germany* (Ithaca: Cornell University Press, 2006), pp. 21–7.

24. Zimmerer ('Krieg', p. 50) is among historians who have made this argument; the oral history narrated by Moses Maharero, Samuel's great-grandson, is recorded in Erichsen, *Elders*, pp. 52–3. Bridgman (*Revolt of the Herero*, ch. 5) argues that Samuel Maharero thought that he could win the battle.

25. Drechsler, *'Let Us Die Fighting'*; Neville Alexander, 'The Namibian War of Anti-colonial Resistance, 1904–7' in Wood (ed.), *Namibia 1884–1984*, pp. 193–204, pp. 194–5.

26. Krüger, *Kreigsbewältigung*, pp. 60–2.

27. From the orders issued by von Trotha for the battle at the Waterberg, quoted in Henrik Lundtofte, '"I Believe that the Nation as Such Must be annihilated"—The Radicalisation of the German Suppression of the Herero Rising in 1904' in Steven Jensen (ed.), *Genocide: Cases, Comparisons and Contemporary Debates* (Copenhagen: Danish Center for Holocaust and Genocide Studies, 2003), pp. 15–53, p. 30; see also pp. 30–31. The question of genocide in this context is discussed below.

28. These figures are given in Bridgman, *Revolt of the Herero*, p. 121, although he does not specify the relative numbers of combat and support troops. On p. 117 he mentions that on the eve of battle there were only 1,500 bayonets and 30 field pieces.

29. This summary is taken from contrasting accounts: Bridgman, *Revolt of the Herero*, ch. 5; Hull, *Absolute Destruction*, pp. 33–43. Hull argues convincingly against Drechsler's (and Bridgman's) argument (*'Let Us Die Fighting'*, pp. 154–5) that von Trotha deliberately planned to drive the Herero into the *omaheke* and posits instead that their escape was a setback for the general, who wanted a complete victory. Nevertheless, it is certainly true that von Trotha was quick to use the situation as a means of instituting mass killing. Tilman Dedering also cites evidence that von Trotha's staff thought a total victory was not possible ('A Certain Rigorous Treatment of All Parts of the Nation': The Annihilation of the Herero in German South West Africa, 1904' in Mark Levene and Penny Roberts (eds), *The Massacre in History* (Oxford: Berghahn Books, 1999), pp. 205–22). Hull also omits any consideration of Herero experience during the battle beyond stating that, although it was a defeat for the Herero, their 'warriors' suffered 'relatively light' casualties (pp. 41, 44). See also Lundtofte, '"Nation"', pp. 29–30.

30. See, for example, Karl-Johann Lindholm, *Wells of Experience: A Pastoral Land-use History of Omaheke, Namibia* (University of Uppsala, 2006), especially pp. 42 ff., 109 ff.

31. Adolf Fischer, *Menschen und Tiere in Deutsch-Südwest* (Stuttgart: Deutsche Verlagsanstalt, 1914), pp. 94–5, quoted in George Steinmetz, *The Devil's Handwriting: Precoloniality and the German State in Qingdao, Samoa and Southwest Africa* (University of Chicago Press, 2007), p. 190.

32. Larissa Förster, 'Land and Landscape in Herero Oral Culture: Cultural and Social Aspects of the Land Question in Namibia', *Analyses and Views*, 1 (2005), p. 16.

33. Orature presented by Adelheid Mbwaondjou and others, quoted and discussed in Anette Hoffmann, '"Since the Germans Came it Rains Less": Landscape and Identity in Herero Communities of Namibia' (PhD, University of Amsterdam, 2005), pp. 65–6.

34. Erichsen, *Elders*, pp. 53–4.

35. Kirsten Alnaes, 'Living with the Past: The Songs of the Herero in Botswana', *Africa*, 59 (1989), pp. 267–99, pp. 276–7.

36. From Festus Kandjo's evidence to Michael Scott in the late 1940s, quoted in Freda Troup, *In Face of Fear: Michael Scott's Challenge to South Africa* (Faber & Faber, 1950), p. 52. Gewald, '"Samuel"', discusses Samuel Maharero's arrival in Botswana, his conflicts with earlier Mbanderu arrivals and his attempt to rebuild his wealth as a recruiter for the South African mines.

37. Larissa Förster, 'Zwischen Waterberg und Okakarara: namibische Errinerungslandschaften' in Larissa Förster, Dag Henrichsen and Michael Bollig (eds), *Namibia–Deutschland: Eine geteilte Geschichte* (Cologne: Rautenstrauch-Jöst Museum für Völkerkunde, 2004), pp. 164–79, pp. 170–4; Hull, *Absolute Destruction*, p. 45.

38. The events after Waterberg are covered in a variety of sources. For a careful consideration of the evidence see Hull, *Absolute Destruction*, ch. 2, who finds that 'the indiscriminate shooting of civilians had become common practice' (p. 49).

39. In the literature this document has been dubbed the '*Vernichtungsbefehl*' (extermination order) or '*Schiessbefehl*' (order to shoot). Quotation as translated in Drechsler, '*Let Us Die Fighting*', pp. 156–7.

40. *Ibid.*, p. 157.

41. The main sources for this section are Andreas Bühler, *Der Namaaufstand gegen die deutsche Kolonialherrschaft in Namibia von 1904–1913* (Frankfurt: IKO, 2003), especially pp. 161–81, 215, 217, 231 ff., 244, 255–9, 261–94; Bridgman, *Revolt of the Herero*, ch. 6; John Masson, *Jakob Marengo: An Early Resistance Hero of Namibia* (Windhoek: Out of Africa, 2001). For the military history see also Walter Nuhn, *Feind überall: der grosse Nama-Aufstand (Hottentottenaufstand) 1904–1908 in Deutsch-Südwestafrika (Namibia). Der erste Partisanenkrieg in der Geschichte der deutschen Armee* (Bonn: Bernard & Graefe, 2000).

42. Werner Hillebrecht, 'Die Nama und der Krieg im Süden' in Zimmerer and Zeller (eds), *Völkermord*, pp. 121–33.

43. Witbooi's letters make it clear that he had reservations about this course of action.

44. Hendrik Witbooi to Karl Schmidt, July 1905, *Hendrik Witbooi Papers*, pp. 195 (quote), p. 190. For these events see also Tilman Dedering, 'The Prophet's "War against Whites": Shepherd Stuurman in Namibia and South Africa, 1904–7', *JAH*, 40 (1999), pp. 1–19; *idem*, 'Hendrik Witbooi the Prophet', p. 66; Drechsler, '*Let Us Die Fighting*', pp. 181–3.

45. This is Bühler's estimate, using official figures (*Der Namaaufstand*, pp. 181–8); Bridgman's figure for Nama fighters is 1,260–1,400 (*Revolt of the Herero*, p. 140).

46. On politics in Germany see, for example, Henderson, *German Colonial Empire*, pp. 83–92.

47. Witbooi losses numbered about seventy.

48. Tilman Dedering, 'War and Mobility in the Borderlands of Southwestern Africa in the Early Twentieth Century', *International Journal of African Historical Studies*, 39, 2 (2006), pp. 275–94.

49. For example, four surrenders in the south are listed by Bridgman (*Revolt of the Herero*, pp. 153–4) between November 1905 and March 1906; they consisted of a total of 315 men and 342 women and children.

50. Jeremia Rooi jr, quoted in Erichsen, *Elders*, p. 31.

51. *Auflösung* has a number of alternative translations including 'elimination', 'dissolution', 'disappearance' and 'disintegration'.

52. Kurd Schwabe, *Im deutschen Diamantenlande: Deutsch-Südwestafrika von der Errichtung der deutschen Herrschaft bis zur Gegenwart (1884–1910)* (Berlin: n.p., 1909), pp. 319–20 (my translation). Although Schwabe does not say whether the women and children were given water, we know that they were refused at Aninhoos near Aminuis (where Hendrik Witbooi has sent them with a white flag) and at Gamib (Bühler, *Der Namaaufstand*, pp. 257–8, 262–3). On the sealing off of waterholes see also Jürgen Zimmerer, 'Das deutsche Reich und der Genozid–Überlegungen zum historischen Ort des Völkermordes an den Herero und Nama', in Förster *et al.*, *Namibia–Deutschland*, pp. 106–21, p. 111.

53. The proclamation defines these people as '...those who at the beginning of the uprising murdered whites or ordered others to do so...'.

54. Quoted for example in Bridgman, *Revolt of the Herero*, p. 145; Bühler, *Der Namaaufstand*, p. 244.

55. In fact, it was misunderstood by the Germans in charge of Warmbad, who released their Bondelswarts prisoners, thus allowing Johannes Christian and his people to join the African forces.

56. These numbers are derived from official figures and are scattered through published sources. See especially Bühler, *Der Namaaufstand*, pp. 265–70; Nuhn, *Feind überall*, p. 178.

57. Dedering, 'Shepherd Stuurman', pp. 9–11.

58. These groups must be assumed, however, to have encompassed other Nama-speakers and perhaps members of other ethnic groups. The Nama-speaking groups remained fluid, a fact illustrated when, in late 1905, a group of Witbooi women and children crossed the border to Bechuanaland ostensibly as Simon Kopper's people becaue, as Witboois, they would have been barred from entering. Bühler, *Der Namaaufstand*, pp. 261–70.

59. Quoted in Drechsler, '*Let Us Die Fighting*', pp. 192–3.

60. Lukas Afrikaner, quoted in Erichsen, *Elders*, p. 29.

61. Bridgman, *Revolt of the Herero*, p. 160.

62. On border relations in general see Dedering, 'War and Mobility'; on the Boer factor, see *idem*, 'The Ferreira Raid of 1906: Boers, Britons and Germans in Southern Africa in the Aftermath of the South African War', *JSAS*, 26 (1), 2000, pp. 43–60. In 1902, there were 1,455 Boers out of 4,635 whites in the territory, and 400 more emigrated there during the Namibian War. *Ibid.*, p. 51.

63. Drechsler, '*Let Us Die Fighting*', p. 186. (As noted earlier, the total of Nama fighters was, according to official figures, around 2,350.)

64. For the concentration camps see in particular Casper Erichsen, '*The Angel of Death has Descended Violently Among Them*': *Concentration Camps and Prisoners-of-war in Namibia, 1904–1908* (Leiden: African Studies Centre, 2005), especially p. 45, ch. 2 (for Shark Island), pp. 76–7, 102–10; Joachim Zeller, '"Ombepera i koza–Die Kälte tötet mich": Zur Geschichte des Konzentrationslagers in Swakopmund (1904–1908)' in Zimmerer and Zeller (eds), *Völkermord*, pp. 64–79; Krüger, *Kriegsbewältigung*, pp. 126–37; Drechsler, '*Let Us Die Fighting*', pp. 204–14; Hull, *Absolute Destruction*, ch. 3.

65. After the closure of the mission camps in late 1906 and early 1907, raids were resumed, continuing to the end of the German period.

66. Chief Kaveriua Hoveka, a descendant of Nikanor Hoveka, quoted in Erichsen, *Elders*, p. 49.

67. Rainer-Maria Kiel, 'Der Hereroaufstand in Deutsch-Südwestafrika: Zeitgenössische Originalfotografien als Leihgabe des Historischen Vereins für Oberfranken in der Universitätsbibliothek Bayreuth', *Archiv für Geschichte von Oberfranken*, 85 (2005), pp. 267–78.

68. Quoted in Krüger, *Kriegsbewältigung*, p. 176 (my translation).

69. On these deportations see Drechsler, '*Let Us Die Fighting*', pp. 185–6; Krüger, *Kriegsbewältigung*, pp. 138–40.

70. Wolfgang Eckart, 'Medizin und kolonialer Krieg: Die Niederschlagung der Herero-Nama-Erhebung im Schutzgebiet Deutsch-Südwestafrika, 1904–1907' in Peter Heine and Ulrich van der Heyden (eds), *Studien zur Geschichte des deutschen Kolonialismus in Afrika* (Pfaffenweiler: Centaurus, 1995), pp. 220–35, pp. 227–8.

71. Quoted in Zeller, '"Ombepera"', p. 64 (my translation).

72. Less positive missionary roles are, however, attested (for example) in oral records. See Erichsen, *Elders*, pp. 29–31.

73. Erichsen, 'The Angel of Death', p. 119.
74. Krüger, Kriegsbewältigung, pp. 131–2. OMEG did, however, improve conditions and pay a small wage, since it placed a higher priority on obtaining a workforce able to work than on punishing a defeated enemy.
75. From an affidavit by Jack Seti, John Culayo and James Tolibandi to the Governor of the Cape, Aug. 1906, quoted in Erichsen, 'The Angel of Death', pp. 60–1.
76. Zimmerer, '"Ombepera"', pp. 73–4; Erichsen, 'The Angel of Death', pp. 76–7.
77. Krüger, 'Koloniale Gewalt', p. 103.
78. Henrichsen, 'Heirat im Krieg', p. 167. Kaera was the daughter of a Herero woman, Betji Kahitjene, and the Anglo-Canadian trader Frederick Green.
79. Chief Zeraua, Ngatitwe's great-grandson, quoted in Erichsen, Elders, pp. 58–9. Erichsen does not discuss the reliability of this account, which perhaps tells us more about Ngatitwe's courage than about any change in German policy.
80. Krüger, Kriegsbewältigung, p. 130.
81. Quoted in Erichsen, 'The Angel of Death', p. 78.
82. Ibid., ch. 2. Photographs of the concentration camps have additionally been published in, for example, Hartmann, Hues, passim.
83. This is Erichsen's estimate, based on a detailed review of the figures ('The Angel of Death', pp. 132–3).
84. Ibid., pp. 131–2.
85. Ibid., pp. 125–31, 154; Drechsler, 'Let Us Die Fighting', pp. 211–13.
86. Zimmerer, Deutsche Herrschaft, p.48
87. Quoted, for example, in Werner Hillebrecht, '"Certain Uncertainties": Or Venturing Progressively into Colonial Apologetics?', JNS, 1 (2007), pp. 73–96, p. 93.
88. Bühler, Der Namaaufstand, p. 337, gives the totals of 'Eingeborenenzählungen' (native population counts) from 1908 and 1913 held in the Bundesarchiv in Koblenz in Germany (file reference N 1037, Nachlaß Hintrager, Band 9, Statistische Materialen). The figure for Herero in 1913 was 21,611. Hillebrecht, '"Certain Uncertainties"', pp. 82–3, gives the 1911 census figure from the records in the National Archives of Namibia. He notes that Drechsler ('Let Us Die Fighting', p. 214 and n. 189), relied on the figures from the 1911 census given in the Blue Book, which gives the rather lower (and necessarily inaccurate) figure of 15,130.
89. Küger, Kriegsbewältigung, pp. 123–6. The range of figures mainly reflects two different estimates of the numbers arriving in Botswana.
90. Leutwein, Elf Jahre Gouverneur, p. 11. Drechsler gives the pre-war total as 20,000, without, however, quoting his source. 'Let Us Die Fighting', p. 181.
91. Bühler, Der Namaaufstand, p. 337; NAN, ZBU 172 A.VI.d.4, population census 1911. Again, Drechsler, using the Blue Book, gives a lower figure of 9,781.

92. Erichsen, 'The Angel of Death', pp. 125–31, 154, 158, 131n, 253. The discrepancy in the figures for Shark Island is that between the official figures of the District Commissioner, according to which there were about 450 survivors of the original total of over 2,000 Nama prisoners in April 1907, and von Estorff's estimate that 1,900 Nama had died on the island.

93. Zimmerer, 'Deutsche Reich', p. 109; Hull, *Absolute Destruction*, pp. 47–51.

94. *Ibid.*, ch. 1, essentially argues that von Trotha adopted his genocidal strategy as a result of his failure to achieve total victory at Ohamakari; see also Lundtofte, '"Nation"', pp. 33–8. Jürgen Zimmerer, however, argues that von Trotha's June order essentially set the genocide in motion. Zimmerer, 'Deutsche Reich', p. 109; *idem*, 'Rassenkrieg und Völkermord: Der Kolonialkrieg in Deutsch-Südwestafrika und die Globalgeschichte des Genozids' in Henning Melber (ed.), *Genozid und Gedenken: Namibisch–deutsche Geschichte und Gegenwart* (Frankfurt: Brandes und Apsel, 2005), pp. 23–48, p. 30.

95. Hull, *Absolute Destruction*, p. 52.

96. Tilman Dedering, 'The German-Herero War of 1904: Revisionism of Genocide or Imaginary Historiography?', *Journal of Southern African Studies*, 19 1 (1993), pp. 80–88. The quotation (p. 85) is from von Estorff's *Wanderungen und Kämpfe in Südwestafrika, Ostafrika und Südafrika 1904–1910* (Wiesbaden: privately pub., 1968). For a discussion of the meaning of the word '*Vernichtung*' (destruction/annihilation/ extermination) see Steinmetz, *Devil's Handwriting*, pp. 188–9.

97. Hull, *Absolute Destruction*, pp. 54–9.

98. Von Trotha to Leutwein, 5 Nov. 1904, quoted in Drechsler, '*Let Us Die Fighting*', p. 154.

99. Leutwein to Colonial Dept, 23 Feb. 1904, quoted in *ibid.*, p. 148.

100. Hull, *Absolute Destruction*, pp. 63–5.

101. Erichsen, 'The Angel of Death', pp. 151–6; see also Steinmetz, *Devil's Handwriting*, pp. 173–5.

102. Zimmerer, 'Deutsche Reich', p. 117.

103. Bühler, *Der Namaaufstand*, pp. 234–5.

104. For this argument see Casper Erichsen, '"The Angel of Death has Descended Violently among them": A Study of Namibia's Concentration Camps and Prisoners-of-war, 1904–1908' (MA, University of Namibia, 2004), pp. 264–6.

105. In fact, very few German women were killed; usually they, and their children, were spared, and on a number of occasions they were escorted to safety by the Herero fighters.

106. Krüger, *Kreigsbewältigung*, pp. 104–15; Joachim Zeller, 'Images of the South West African War: Reflections on the 1904–1907 Colonial War in Contemporary Photo Reportage and Book Illustration' in Hartmann (ed.), *Hues*, pp. 309–23. For a detailed analysis of German stereotypes of Herero and Nama see also Steinmetz, *Devil's Handwriting*, part 1.

107. Krüger, *Kreigsbewältigung*, pp. 95–103; Patricia Hayes, Jeremy Silvester and Wolfram Hartmann, '"Picturing the Past" in Namibia: The Visual Archive and its Energies' in Carolyn Hamilton *et al.* (eds), *Refiguring the Archive* (Dordrecht: Kluwer Academic, 2002), pp. 102–33, p. 103; Erichsen, '*The Angel of Death*', pp. 140–4. Africans were believed to be at a lower stage of evolutionary development than Europeans.

108. Hillebrecht, 'Certain Uncertainties', p. 73. Whether what happened in Namibia prefigured the Holocaust is a related and complex debate, which falls outside the scope of this book.

109. The argument for genocide was forcefully put by Drechsler in the 1960s; among its opponents were Gert Sudholt, Brigitte Lau, Karla Poewe and, somewhat later, Claus Nordbruch. See, for example, Sudholt, *Eingeborenenpolitik*; Lau, 'Uncertain Certainties: The Herero-German War of 1904' in *idem*, *History and Historiography*, pp. 39–52; Claus Nordbruch, *Völkermord an den Herero in Deutsch-Südwestafrika? Widerlegung einer Lüge* (Tübingen: Grabert, 2004). For incisive rebuttals of their arguments see Dedering, 'German–Herero War' and Hillebrecht, 'Certain Uncertainties'. For an article by an academic historian that seeks (with, in this author's view, very limited success) to cast doubt on the genocide narrative, see Andreas Eckl, 'The Herero Genocide of 1904: Source-critical and Methodological Considerations', *JNS*, 3 (2008), pp. 31–61.

110. It should be noted that Riruako probably represents a majority of Otjiherero-speakers, but not all.

111. The *Namibian*, 16 Aug. 2004. The apology was a new departure, but the German government has continued to resist the payment of reparations. For a lucid and wide-ranging explanation and discussion of these issues of memory and commemoration, see the contributions to Melber (ed.), *Genozid und Gedenken*.

112. For example, Hull, *Absolute Destruction*; Steinmetz, *Devil's Handwriting*.

113. Sources giving Africans' point of view are sparse. Samuel Maharero left a number of letters, but these have not been collected and published (but see Gewald, *Herero Heroes, passim*); Hendrik Witbooi's letters have, however, survived. The testimonies of survivors were collected by Major O'Reilly in 1917 for the controversial 'Blue Book', *Report on the Natives of South-West Africa and their Treatment by Germany* (London: HMSO, 1918), republished as Jeremy Silvester and Jan-Bart Gewald (eds), *Words Cannot be Found: German Colonial Rule in Namibia. An Annotated Reprint of the 1918 Blue Book* (Leiden: Brill, 2003). See the present author's review in *African Research and Documentation*, 99 (2005), pp. 57–60, and Hull, *Absolute Destruction*, pp. 47–9 for arguments in favour of relying on the witness statements published here. There is now also a small body of work on, of, or using oral history and orature, including Alnaes, 'Living with the Past'; Heywood *et al.*, *Warriors*,

pp. 114–17, 143; Sundermeier, *The Mbanderu*, pp. 51–6; Ernst Damman (ed.), *Herero-Texte erzählt von Pastor Andreas Kukuri* (Berlin: Dietrich Reimer, 1983); Förster, 'Land and Landscape'; *idem*, 'Zwischen Waterberg'; Hoffmann, '"Since the Germans Came"'; Erichsen, *Elders*; Gewald, 'Road of the Man Called Love'; *idem*, '"I was Afraid of Samuel"'; Henrichsen, 'Heirat im Krieg'.

114. Exceptions have been quoted throughout this chapter; see especially (for Herero internal dynamics) Gewald, *Herero Heroes*.

7. BUILDING A GERMAN COLONY, 1908–15

1. Gewald, *Herero Heroes*, p. 220; Silvester *et al.*, 'Trees Never Meet', pp. 4–5.
2. Zimmerer, *Deutsche Herrschaft*, pp. 183–7. In 1912, 7,618 people out of a workforce of 69,003 moved between districts (that is, both *Bezirke* and *Distrikte*); many more would have moved illegally.
3. Krüger, *Kriegsbewältigung*, pp. 190–3, quote p. 193 (my translation).
4. Werner, 'No One Will Become Rich', p. 52. See also Zimmerer, *Deutsche Herrschaft*, pp. 258–67 for 1909 statistics of African stock ownership (which show only a small number of large herds).
5. Zimmerer, *Deutsche Herrschaft*, pp. 84, 93 (quotes, my translation), 68–9, 77–93, also 250–81; see also Drechsler, 'Let Us Die Fighting', pp. 231–2; Bley, *Namibia*, pp. 172–3.
6. These arrangements seem to have led to the *de facto* creation of reserves, even though no formal reserves policy was instituted during the German period. A full list of such reserves remains elusive, but it seems likely that it also included Okombahe, Gunichas in the Gobabis district, Otjimbingwe Nord and Soromas, and possibly Sesfontein and Fransfontein. See, for example, Wellington, *South West Africa*, pp. 280–1; Rheinhart Kößler, *In Search of Survival and Dignity: Two Traditional Communities in Southern Namibia under South African Rule* (Windhoek: Gamsberg Macmillan, 2005), pp. 43–5.
7. Zimmerer, *Deutsche Herrschaft*, pp. 56–66, 167–75; Drechsler, 'Let Us Die Fighting', pp. 241–3; Steinmetz, *Devil's Handwriting*, pp. 216–39; Rheinhart Kößler, '"A Luta Continua": Strategische Orientierung und Erinnerungspolitik am Beispiel des "Heroes Day" der Witbooi in Gibeon' in Zimmerer and Zeller (eds), *Völkermord*, pp. 180–91, pp. 181–2.
8. Friedrich von Lindequist was Governor 1905–7, followed by Bruno von Schuckmann (1907–10) and Theodor Seitz (1910–15).
9. Birthe Kundrus, *Moderne Imperialisten: das Kaiserreich im Spiegel seiner Kolonien* (Cologne: Böhlau, 2003), pp. 61–2; Aitken, *Exclusion*, pp. 91–3; Zimmerer, *Deutsche Herrschaft*, pp. 161–7.
10. Zimmerer, *Deutsche Herrschaft*, p. 204. Oermann, *Mission, Church*, p. 176, gives a figure of 697 Africans subjected to physical punishment in

the Windhoek District in 1913–14 (the district with the highest number of such sentences).

11. The farmers on trial were Oehlsen, Schneidewind, Cramer, Baas and Berner; sentences were generally very light. See especially Bley, *Namibia*, pp. 260–7. Drechsler (*'Let Us Die Fighting'*, pp. 234–7), draws on the controversial 'Blue Book' (Great Britain, *Report on the Natives*), but Bley does not. See also Philipp Prein, 'Guns and Top Hats: African Resistance in German South West Africa, 1907–1915', *JSAS*, 20, 1, pp. 99–121; Krista O'Donnell, 'Poisonous Women: Sexual Danger, Illicit Violence, and Domestic Work in German Southern Africa, 1904–1915', *Journal of Women's History*, 11, 3 (1999), pp. 31–54; Oermann, *Mission, Church*, pp. 172–7.

12. Gordon and Sholto-Douglas, *Bushman Myth*, p. 65. The figures are from the 1912 census.

13. *Ibid.*, chs 7–9.

14. Gewald, *Herero Heroes*, pp. 208–11. Kanjemi was hanged, while Kandiapu died in prison while awaiting deportation to Cameroon. Very little has been written about Damara communities in this context, but Drechsler (*'Let Us Die Fighting'*, p. 234) quotes a 1911 passage from the *Deutsche Kolonial-Zeitung* arguing for the draconian punishment of vagrancy: '*The Kaffirs in their hide-out in the mountains*, the Herero lurking in the bushveld and the Bushmen wandering over the savannah—all of them must not feel secure for a single moment [my emphasis]'. Damara were commonly called 'Klip Kaffirs'. Zimmerer, *Deutsche Herrschaft*, p. 87, notes that Streitwolf brought in Damara from the *veld* in 1907 and put them to work.

15. Zimmerer, *Deutsche Herrschaft*, pp. 110, 177.

16. William Beinart, '"Jamani": Cape Workers in German South West Africa, 1904–12' in William Beinart and Colin Bundy (eds), *Hidden Struggles in Rural South Africa: Politics and Popular Movements in the Transkei and Eastern Cape, 1890–1930* (London: James Currey, 1987), pp. 166–90; Zimmerer, *Deutsche Herrschaft*, pp. 228–36, who notes (pp. 228–9) that 2,540 workers were recruited from South Africa in 1910, 6,439 in 1911 and 2,089 in 1913.

17. Quoted in Bley, *Namibia*, p. 264.

18. Zimmerer, *Deutsche Herrschaft*, pp. 115–18, 126–41; Krüger, *Kriegsbewältigung*, pp. 186–7; Gewald, *Herero Heroes*, p. 224. The projected strength of the police was 720 white officers, but at its peak it reached only 569, plus 370 African auxiliaries.

19. For the argument in favour of African political reconstitution see among others Bley, *Namibia*, and for the counter-argument Prein, 'Guns', pp. 104–7.

20. Bley, *Namibia*, pp. 252–5.

21. Alnaes, 'Living with the Past', p. 279.

22. Bley, *Namibia*, pp. 228–32, 237, 274–9; Zimmerer, *Deutsche Herrschaft*, pp. 203–28; L.H. Gann and Peter Duignan, *The Rulers of German Africa, 1884–1914* (Stanford, Calif.: Stanford University Press, 1977), pp. 53–4, 181–3; Prein, 'Guns', pp. 113–14. The German Colonial Office replaced the Colonial Department of the Foreign Office as a fully fledged ministry in 1907.

23. Lothar Engel, *Kolonialismus und Nationalismus im deutschen Protestantismus in Namibia 1907 bis 1945* (Herbert Lang, 1976), p. 38 n. 3; Oermann, *Mission, Church*, p. 134.

24. Gewald, *Herero Heroes*, pp. 193–204, 220–5; *idem*, 'Chief Hosea Kutako: A Herero Royal and Namibian Nationalist's Life against Confinement 1870–1970' in De Bruijn *et al.* (eds), *Strength Beyond Structure*, pp. 83–113, p. 88; Ernst Damman (ed.), *Herero-Texte erzählt von Pastor Andreas Kukuri* (Berlin: Dietrich Reimer, 1983), pp. 6, 61; Engel, *Kolonialismus*, pp. 103–21. Where Christian names only are given, this reflects the usage in the published source. The absence of work on the role of African women in the churches at this period does not mean that they were inactive in this field.

25. Oermann, *Mission, Church, passim*.

26. Dag Henrichsen, '*Ozombambuse* and *Ovasolondate*: Everyday Military Life and African Service Personnel in German South West Africa' in Hartmann (ed.), *Hues*, pp. 161–84; Gewald, *Herero Heroes*, pp. 204–6, 227–9; Damman (ed.), *Herero-Texte*, pp. 42–3. According to Kukuri, von Estorff asked his father for permission to employ him and others as *Bambusen*.

27. Marion Wallace, *Health, Power and Politics in Windhoek, Namibia, 1915–1945* (Basel: P. Schlettwein, 2002), p. 40; *idem*, 'The Process of Urbanisation', paper to Trees Never Meet conference, Windhoek, 1994; *idem*, 'Looking at the Locations', p. 135; Zimmerer, *Deutsche Herrschaft*, p. 79; Prein, 'Guns', pp. 113–14; Bley, *Namibia*, p. 263.

28. Prein, 'Guns'; Engel, *Kolonialismus*, pp. 88–101; Oermann, *Mission, Church*, pp. 162–5; Gewald, *Herero Heroes*, pp. 226–7.

29. For example, in both the Schneidewind and Cramer cases, women were responsible for cattle. Bley, *Namibia*, pp. 264–5.

30. Wallace, *Health*, pp. 46, 259.

31. O'Donnell, 'Poisonous Women'; Zimmerer, *Deutsche Herrschaft*, pp. 262–3, 278–9; Prein, 'Guns', pp. 113–14.

32. Bley, *Namibia*, p. 264.

33. This argument is made by O'Donnell ('Poisonous Women'), who mainly uses the Cramer case but also looks at manifestations of the wider discourse. German attitudes to African women were also revealed, for example, in the novels of Hans Grimm (Aitken, *Exclusion*, ch. 4), and in caricatures published in German newspapers (Edward Norris with Arnold Beukes, 'Kolonialkrieg und Karikatur in Deutschland: Die Aufstände der Herero und der Nama und die Zeichnungen der deutschen satirischen

Zeitschriften' in Heine and Heyden, *Studien*, pp. 377–98). See also the discussion of mixed marriages below.

34. For a brief discussion see Eckhart, 'Medizin', pp. 220–35 (but for a contrary view see Hartmann, 'Urges', p. 43). Eckhart warns of the complexities of the history of VD and war; on this see also Wallace, *Health*, p. 101.

35. Oermann, *Mission, Church*, pp. 210–12; Gewald, *Herero Heroes*, pp. 201–2; Bley, *Namibia*, p. 214; Wildenthal, *German Women*, p. 47. Bley states that, because of the protests, compulsory examinations were restricted to prostitutes in 1910, but Oermann and Gewald suggest merely that the process became less brutal at this point.

36. For German imperialism and *Deutschtum* in the colonies see especially Kundrus, *Moderne Imperialisten*, pp. 1–38, 56–9; also, for example, Bley, *Namibia, passim*; Aitken, *Exclusion*, pp. 49–55; Wildenthal, *German Women*, pp. 55–6, 99–104. Von Bülow and Peters were mainly associated with East Africa, but their ideas had a wider reach.

37. Zimmerer, *Deutsche Herrschaft*, p. 97. Church marriages were not recognised by the state without a civil ceremony.

38. The question of mixed marriages and sexual relationships in German South West Africa has been covered in many accounts. See, for example, Dag Henrichsen, '"…Unerwuenscht im Schutzgebiet…nicht schlechtin unsittlich": "Mischehen" und deren Nachkommen im Visier der Kolonialverwaltung in Deutsch-Südwestafrika' in Marianne Bechhaus-Gerst and Mechthild Leutner (eds), *Frauen in den deutschen Kolonien* (Berlin: Links, 2009), pp. 80–90; Aitken, *Exclusion*, ch. 3; Zimmerer, *Deutsche Herrschaft*, pp. 94–109; Bley, *Namibia*, pp. 212–19; Kundrus, *Moderne Imperialisten*, ch. 4; Wildenthal, *German Women*, ch. 3; Hartmann, 'Urges'; Karen Smidt, '"Germania führt die deutsche Frau nach Südwest": Auswanderung, Leben und soziale Konflikte deutscher Frauen in der ehemaligen Kolonie Deutsch-Südwestafrika 1884–1920' (PhD, Otto-von-Guericke Universität Magdeburg, 1995), ch. 2. For a discussion of colonial constructions of race among the Rehobothers see Steinmetz, *Devil's Handwriting*, pp. 218–39.

39. The reverse would not have been true because, under German law, a woman took her husband's citizenship. Such marriages, although much discussed, were, in any case, very rare: Smidt cites one definite case in SWA, although there were more in Germany itself. Smidt, '"Germania"', pp. 167–70; Aitken, *Exclusion*, p. 98.

40. *Ibid.*, p. 129.

41. See, in particular, Henrichsen, '"Mischehen"', p. 89, n. 47.

42. Originally called the Deutschkolonialer Frauenbund, it soon changed its name to the Frauenbund der Deutsche Kolonialgesellschaft; it had had a predecessor in the Verein Frauenwohl. Wildenthal, *German Women*, pp. 131–2.

43. Aitken, *Exclusion*, p. 183; Brigitta Schmidt-Laubner, *Die Abhängigen Herren: deutsche Identität in Namibia* (Münster: Lit, 1993), pp. 57–9.

44. On this point see Wildenthal, *German Women*, p. 102: 'Colonial freedom also meant acting without compunction against those who would never be part of the national polity. Külz [the commissioner for self-administration appointed in 1906] felt so free in the colonial space' that he fired into a peaceable San encampment in order to obtain a souvenir.

45. Bley, *Namibia*, p. 233.

46. Aitken, *Exclusion*, p. 86, chs 2, 5. German attitudes to Afrikaners became more favourable over time, particularly because of German sympathy with the Boer side in the South African War.

47. Kundrus, *Moderne Imperialisten*, pp. 176 ff.; Jeremy Silvester, '"Sleep with a Southwester": Monuments and Settler Identity in Namibia' in Elkins and Pedersen (eds), *Settler Colonialism in the Twentieth Century*, pp. 271–86, pp. 275–6. On town planning see Walter Peters, 'Grundlagen des Städtebaus in Namibia' in Heine and Heyden, *Studien*, pp. 429–52.

48. Bley, *Namibia*, pp. 181–96; Kaulich, *Deutsch Südwestafrika*, pp. 112–18, 157–8, 341–2; Zimmerer, *Deutsche Herrschaft*, pp. 183–7; Botha, 'Land Settlement', p. 235. After the Namibian War farmers were supposed to possess 10,000 Marks before being granted land, but this rule was not always observed—for example in the settlement of members of the *Schutztruppe*.

49. On the economy, infrastructure and administration of the colony see Zimmerer, *Deutsche Herrschaft*, pp. 110–11, 115–18, 243–50; Kaulich, *Deutsch Südwestafrika*, pp. 308–14; 92–100, 157–8, 378–9; Helmuth Stoecker (ed.), *German Imperialism in Africa: From the Beginnings until the Second World War* (London: C. Hurst & Co., 1986), p. 200; Gann and Duignan, *German Africa*, pp. 53–5, 87–9; Henderson, *German Colonial Empire*, pp. 100–5; Christo Botha, 'Internal Colonisation and an Oppressed Minority? The Dynamics of Relations between Germans and Afrikaners against the Background of Constructing a Colonial State in Namibia, 1884–1990', *JNS*, 2, 2007, pp. 7–50, pp. 14–15.

50. Kambonde kAngula succeeded Kambonde kaMpingana, who died of alcohol poisoning, in 1909. For the succession see Namuhuja, *Ondonga Royal Kings*.

51. Eirola, *Ovambogefahr*, pp. 230–62, 269–75. Görgens did in fact very briefly establish a small base without authorisation in 1910.

52. Hayes and Haipinge, *'Healing the Land'*, p. 63 (quote), pp. 42–63; Hayes, 'When You Shake a Tree'.

53. Eirola, *Ovambogefahr*, pp. 225–6, 269–75; McKittrick, *To Dwell Secure*, pp. 137–44; Hayes, 'History of the Ovambo', pp. 157–77; Hayes and Haipinge, *'Healing the Land'*; Namuhuja, *Ondonga Royal Kings*, pp. 38–43.

54. Moorsom, 'Formation', pp. 79, 81–7; Hayes, 'History of the Ovambo', pp. 153–6; Zimmerer, *Deutsche Herrschaft*, pp. 211–28.

55. Flint, 'State-building', pp. 413–17; Fisch, *Caprivi Strip*, pp. 24, 71–127; Zeller and Kangumu, 'Caprivi', p. 194. Flint (p. 414) places Streitwolf's arrival in the Caprivi in November 1908, but according to both Fisch (p. 77) and Dierks (*Chronology*, p. 80) he arrived in January 1909; Dierks gives his departure date from the Police Zone as November 1908, which is the most likely explanation of this confusion.

56. Eckl, *Herrschaft*, p. 227.

57. *Ibid.*, pp. 62–106, 183–235; *idem*, 'Serving', *passim*.

8. SOUTH AFRICAN RULE, 1915–46

1. Fisch, *Caprivi Strip*, pp. 137–40; Kangumu, 'Forgotten Corner', p. 13; Hayes, 'History of the Ovambo', pp. 178–85; Eckl, *Herrschaft*, pp. 252–62, quote (in English) p. 261.

2. On the campaign see especially Hew Strachan, *The First World War*, vol. 1, *To Arms* (Oxford University Press, 2001), pp. 543–69; Gerald L'Ange, *Urgent Imperial Service: South African Forces in German South West Africa, 1914–1915* (Rivonia: Ashanti, 1991).

3. The secondary sources differ wildly on the number of South African troops. Strachan, *First World War*, p. 560, gives 43,000; other estimates range from 8,000 to 60,000. See Wallace, *Health*, p. 71, n. 2. The Germans had about 2,000 regular troops and 7,000 reservists.

4. *Ibid.*, ch 3.

5. For this section see especially Hayes, 'History of the Ovambo', pp. 178–250; McKittrick, *To Dwell Secure*, ch. 5.

6. Hayes, 'History of the Ovambo', p. 205; Patricia Hayes, pers. comm., 2002.

7. McKittrick, *To Dwell Secure*, p. 151.

8. Such mobility was possible at the time because the South Africans had not yet imposed restrictions on migration from Owambo into the Police Zone (although in 1916 they did clamp down on the migration of whites into the northern areas). See Miescher, 'Rote Linie', pp. 139–42.

9. Jan-Bart Gewald, 'Karibib'. For the medical offcer Andrew Neethling's account of the famine victims see NAN, A.173, Neethling correspondence, 1915–16.

10. Eckl, *Herrschaft*, pp. 321–7. These figures cover the period Jan.–Sept. and are the first available for this period.

11. Hayes, 'History of the Ovambo', p. 273.

12. On these developments see especially Cooper, *Ovambo Politics*, pp. 75–8 (quote on p. 75); McKittrick, *To Dwell Secure*, pp. 152–3.

13. This is Hayes's best guess; she argues that Portuguese estimates of 50,000 are exaggerated. 5,000 Kwanyama may have had modern rifles. Hayes, 'History of the Ovambo', pp. 192–3.

14. Patricia Hayes, pers. comm., April 2010.

15. Quoted in *ibid.*, p. 224.

16. On these traditions, and for the photographs, see Margo Timm, 'Transpositions: The Reinterpretation of Colonial Photographs of the Kwanyama King Mandume ya Ndemufayo in the Art of John Ndevasia Muafangejo' in Hartmann *et al.* (eds), *Colonising Camera*, pp. 145–50.

17. Hayes, 'History of the Ovambo', p. 226.

18. *Ibid.*, pp. 237–40.

19. Meredith McKittrick, 'Conflict and Social Change in Northern Namibia, 1850–1954' (PhD, Stanford University, 1995), pp. 86–7.

20. Michael Bollig, 'The Colonial Encapsulation of the North: Western Namibian Pastoral Economy', *Africa*, 68, 4 (1998), pp. 506–535, p. 508; Friedman, 'Making Politics', pp. 26–8; Eckl, *Herrschaft*, ch. 4.

21. Zimmerer, *Deutsche Herrschaft*, p. 175; Jeremy Silvester, 'Beasts, Boundaries and Buildings: The Survival and Creation of Pastoral Economies in Southern Namibia, 1915–35' in Hayes *et al.* (eds), *Namibia under South African Rule*, pp. 95–116, p. 99; Steinmetz, *Devil's Handwriting*, pp. 237–9; Werner, *'No One Will Become Rich'*, pp. 56–7.

22. *Ibid.*, pp. 59, 62, 68–9; J.J. Bruwer, *Aus 1915–1919: Errichtung, Bestehen und Schließung des Kriegsgefangenenlagers bei Aus* (Windhoek: Historic Monuments Commission, 1985).

23. Gewald, *Herero Heroes*, p. 253; Ben Fuller, '"We Live in a *Manga*": Constraint, Resistance and Transformation on a Native Reserve' in Hayes *et al.*, *Namibia*, pp. 194–216, p. 197; Silvester, 'Beasts, Boundaries and Buildings', p. 102; Werner, *'No One Will Become Rich'*, pp. 58–61.

24. Jeremy Silvester, Marion Wallace and Patricia Hayes, '"Trees Never Meet": Mobility and Containment: An Overview, 1915–1946' in Hayes *et al.*, *Namibia*, pp. 3–48, pp. 4–6; Gesine Krüger and Dag Henrichsen, '"We Have Been Captives Long Enough. We Want to Be Free": Land, Uniforms and Politics in the History of Herero in the Interwar Period' in *ibid.*, pp. 149–174, pp. 150–1; Kößler, '"A Luta Continua"', p. 181; Gewald, 'Hosea Kutako', pp. 89–92; Engel, *Kolonialismus*, p. 100.

25. Ngavirue, *Political Parties*, p. 193 (quote); Wolfgang Werner, '"Playing Soldiers": The Truppenspieler Movement Among the Herero of Namibia, 1915 to ca. 1945', *JSAS*, 16, 3 (1990), pp. 476–502, p. 484. The term *otjiserandu* is often used to describe the movement as a whole, but it is properly applied to Maharero's people, and was named for the red flag and red armband used by the latter as identifying symbols. Other Otjiherero-speaking groups had their own *oturupa* movements. Its members were mainly Herero, and mainly men, although women could be members in the Omaruru district in 1927.

26. Werner, *'No One Will Become Rich'*, p. 55. See also Gewald, *Herero Heroes*, p. 232.

27. Tony Emmett was the first to propose this break between the German and South African periods; his work remains the standard source on this legislation. See Tony Emmett, *Popular Resistance and the Roots of National-*

ism in Namibia, 1915–1966 (Basel: P. Schlettwein, 1999), ch. 2; also Werner, 'No One Will Become Rich', ch. 2.

28. Emmett, *Popular Resistance*, pp. 76–7; United Kingdom, *Report on the Natives*; see also above, p. 182 and footnote 112.

29. Werner, 'No One Will Become Rich', p. 67.

30. For a discussion of state weakness in this period see in particular Silvester *et al.*, 'Trees Never Meet', p. 25.

31. André du Pisani, *SWA/Namibia: The Politics of Continuity and Change* (Johannesburg: Jonathan Ball, 1986), p. 47. Strachan, however (*First World War*, p. 568) gives the number of German dead as 103.

32. Werner, 'No One Will Become Rich', pp. 61–4; Du Pisani, *Continuity and Change*, p. 52.

33. Wallace, *Health*, pp. 82–95; M. Chambikabalenshi Musambachime, '"*Kapitohanga*: The Disease that Killed Faster than Bullets". The Impact of the Influenza Pandemic in the South West Africa Protectorate (Namibia) from October 1918 to December 1919' (BAB Working Paper No. 4 1999, Basel: BAB) (with thanks to the author for permission to use this paper). One could speculate that Owambo may have been protected from the first wave by the sheer virulence of the virus: anyone infected in the Police Zone would not have had the strength to complete the journey to the north. It did, however, reach the Kavango (Eckl, *Herrschaft*, p. 329).

34. Allan Cooper, *The Occupation of Namibia: Afrikanerdom's Attack on the British Empire* (Lanham: University Press of America, 1991), pp. 31–2; Silvester *et al.*, 'Trees Never Meet', pp. 7–8.

35. Martin Chanock, *Unconsummated Union: Britain, Rhodesia and South Africa, 1900–45* (Manchester University Press, 1977), p. 2.

36. Silvester *et al.*, 'Trees Never Meet', p. 8. On South African strategy at this period see Chanock, *Unconsummated Union*, pp. 108–17; Maynard Swanson, 'South West Africa in Trust, 1915–1939' in Prosser Gifford and Wm Roger Louis, *Britain and Germany in Africa: Imperial Rivalry and Colonial Rule* (New Haven: Yale University Press, 1967), pp. 632–6; Wm Roger Louis, 'The Origins of the "Sacred Trust"' in Segal and First (eds), *Travesty of Trust*, pp. 54–86; du Pisani, *Continuity and Change*, p. 46.

37. Cooper, *Occupation of Namibia*, p. 37. Cooper argues that it was only with the National Party victory in South Africa in 1924 that a specifically Afrikaner identity began to be imposed on the state in Namibia.

38. Quoted in Silvester, 'Black Pastoralists', p. 31.

39. Emmett, *Popular Resistance*, p. 69; Werner, 'No One Will Become Rich', p. 65; Duncan Innes, *Anglo American and the Rise of Modern South Africa* (New York: Monthly Review Press, 1984), p. 98; SWAPO, *To Be Born a Nation*, p. 21.

40. Cooper, *Occupation of Namibia*, pp. 33–8; Swanson, 'South West Africa in Trust'.

41. Quoted, for example, in Wellington, *South West Africa*, p. 275.

42. NASA, GG 1418, 45/96. Petitions from representatives of Cape Coloured of SWA, Herero & Ovambanderu, Damara, and Nama of Windhoek and district, and Herero of Okahandja and district, 1922.
43. Wellington, *South West Africa*, pp. 277.
44. For a summary and these quotations see *ibid.*, pp. 275–8. On the Commission see also especially Silvester, 'Black Pastoralists'; Kößler, *Survival*, pp. 35 ff.
45. NAN SWAA A50/1, quoted in Silvester, 'Black Pastoralists', p. 37. For segregation in South Africa see, in particular, William Beinart and Saul Dubow, *Segregation and Apartheid in Twentieth-Century South Africa* (London: Routledge, 1995).
46. Silvester, 'Black Pastoralists'; Werner, 'No One Will Become Rich', p. 107.
47. Silvester, 'Beasts, Boundaries and Buildings', p. 105.
48. Wellington, *South West Africa*, p. 273; Katjavivi, *History of Resistance*, p. 14; Emmett, *Popular Resistance*, pp. 97–8; Werner, 'No One Will Become Rich', p. 146.
48. Silvester, 'Beasts, Boundaries and Buildings', pp. 96, 105–7.
50. Fencing of the reserves in the south, for example, only became the norm in the 1940s. Silvester, 'Black Pastoralists'.
51. South Africa, *Report of the Government of the Union of South Africa on South West Africa* (Pretoria: Government Printer, 1926), p. 59, quoted in Silvester *et al.*, 'Trees Never Meet', p. 20.
52. On urbanization see Wallace, *Health*, chs 1, 2 and *passim*; *idem*, 'Looking at the Locations'.
53. Such employment was normally on the farms since, as a result of competition between the mining and agricultural sectors, the Police Zone workforce was generally reserved to the farms rather than mines. Emmett, *Popular Resistance*, p. 176.
54. *Ibid.*, p. 118; Gordon and Sholto-Douglas, *Bushman Myth*, chs 10–12, 14.
55. See Robert Gordon, 'Vagrancy, Law and "Shadow Knowledge": Internal Pacification, 1915–1939' in Hayes *et al.*, *Namibia*, pp. 51–76, p. 56. The decision not to bring women under the pass laws may have had to do with the resistance of women in South Africa to similar restrictions.
56. Wellington, *South West Africa*, pp. 282–3, 308–9; Silvester, 'Black Pastoralists'; Mbuende, *Namibia*, p. 79; Kößler, *Survival*, pp. 50–2, 63, 71 ff.; Emmett, *Popular Resistance*, p. 91.
57. Silvester *et al.*, 'Trees Never Meet', p. 35–6; Emmett, *Popular Resistance*, pp. 101–2; Wallace, *Health*, p. 153. The Natives Land Act of 1913 was not introduced into Namibia.
58. Gordon, 'Vagrancy', p. 61 and *passim*; Silvester, 'Black Pastoralists'; Wellington, *South West Africa*, p. 309; Emmett, *Popular Resistance*, pp. 92–7; Werner, 'No One Will Become Rich', pp. 86–91.
59. Wellington, *South West Africa*, pp. 280–2; Silvester, 'Black Pastoralists'; Kößler, *Survival*, pp. 44–5; Fuller, '"Manga"', pp. 197–202 (quote on

p. 201). A part of the Otjimbingwe reserve had already been declared a reserve in 1907; the new reserve was gazetted in 1926.

60. Silvester, 'Black Pastoralists', p. 203 (referring here specifically to the Bondelswarts after 1922).

61. *Ibid.*, pp. 195–203; Emmett, *Popular Resistance*, pp. 111–24; First, *South West Africa*, pp. 101–4.

62. Kößler, *In Search*, p. 207.

63. Quoted in Troup, *In Face of Fear*, p. 76.

64. Jan-Bart Gewald, *'We Thought We Would Be Free': Socio-cultural Aspects of Herero History in Namibia, 1915–1940* (Cologne: Rüdiger Köppe, 2000), pp. 50–65; Troup, *In Face of Fear*, pp. 72–9; see also Gewald, 'Kutako', pp. 98–100.

65. I am indebted to Regula Iselin of the Basler Afrika Bibliographien for this information.

66. Silvester *et al.*, 'Trees Never Meet', pp. 23–4; Wallace, *Health*, ch. 2; Gordon and Sholto-Douglas, *Bushman Myth*, pp. 127–8.

67. Patrick Pearson, 'The Rehoboth Rebellion' in Philip Bonner (ed.), *Working Papers in Southern African Studies*, vol. 2 (Johannesburg: Ravan, 1981), pp. 31–51; Emmett, *Popular Resistance*, pp. 155–63.

68. Aaron Mungunda, speaking at Usakos in 1922, quoted in Emmett, *Popular Resistance*, p. 146.

69. On these movements see especially Emmett, *Popular Resistance*, pp. 125–54; Gregory Pirio, 'The Role of Garveyism in the Making of Namibian Nationalism' in Wood (ed.), *Namibia 1884–1984*, pp. 259–67.

70. Withdrawal from the church was not necessarily absolute, nor can it be equated with withdrawal from Christianity; various forms of dualism and syncretism began to develop at this period. See, for instance, Wallace, *Health*, p. 136.

71. Krüger and Henrichsen, '"Captives"'; Emmett, *Popular Resistance*, pp. 227–49; Werner, *'No One Will Become Rich'*, pp. 109–23, 133–7; *idem*, '"Playing Soldiers"'; Wallace, *Health*, pp. 135–7; Gewald, *Herero Heroes*, pp. 274–84.

72. Emmett, *Popular Resistance*, p. 166.

73. For these and more detailed figures see Wellington, *South West Africa*, pp. 299–300; Emmett, *Popular Resistance*, pp. 180–5; Werner, *'No One Will Become Rich'*, pp. 139–42. Retrenchment from the mines began in 1930 and by 1933, the year in which the CDM diamond mines closed, nearly all the mines in Namibia had shut down.

74. Wallace, *Health*, chs 1, 2.

75. For the north at this period see especially Hayes, 'History of the Ovambo', chs 6 and 7; *idem*, 'The Famine of the Dams: Gender, Labour and Politics in Colonial Ovamboland' in Hayes *et al.*, *Namibia*, pp. 117–46; McKittrick, *To Dwell Secure*, ch. 6; *idem*, 'Northern Namibia', chs 3–5; idem, 'Generational Struggles and Social Mobility in Western Ovambo Communities, 1915–54' in Hayes *et al.*, *Namibia*, pp. 241–62.

76. Petrus Ndongo, 'The Borderline: "Onhaululi"' in Hayes *et al.*, *Namibia*, pp. 289–91, p. 291.

77. Kreike, *Recreating Eden*, pp. 57–80, ch. 7.

78. Hayes, 'History of the Ovambo', p. 297. On Hahn see, in particular, Patricia Hayes, '"Cocky" Hahn and the "Black Venus": The Making of a Native Commissioner in South West Africa, 1915–46' in Hunt *et al.* (eds), *Gendered Colonialisms*, pp. 42–70.

79. Calculated from figures given in Emmett, *Popular Resistance*, p. 181 (and including workers from Owambo, Kavango and southern Angola).

80. Cooper, *Ovambo Politics*, pp. 82–3, 151–65; Miescher, 'Rote Linie', pp. 173–108, 248–50. On migrant labour see also Moorsom, 'Underdevelopment'; *idem*, 'Formation'; Allan Cooper, 'The Institutionalization of Contract Labour in Namibia', *JSAS*, 25 1 (1999), pp. 121–38; and the works of McKittrick and Hayes cited above.

81. Bollig, 'Colonial Encapsulation'; Lorena Rizzo, 'N.J. van Warmelo: Anthropology and the Making of a Reserve', in Miescher and Henrichsen, *New Notes on Kaoko: The Northern Kunene Region (Namibia) in Texts and Photographs* (Basel: BAB, 2000), pp. 189–206; McGurk, 'Sambyu', pp. 141–2; McKittrick, 'Landscapes', pp. 798–9; Kangumu, 'Forgotten Corner', p. 13; *idem*, 'Contestations', pp. 108–11.

82. Hayes, '"Famine of the Dams"', p. 134.

83. Petrus Amutenya, quoted in *ibid.*, p. 131.

84. McKittrick, *To Dwell Secure*, pp. 182, 198; Cooper, *Ovambo Politics*, pp. 85–6; Kreike, *Recreating Eden*, p. 68; Loeb, *In Feudal Africa*, pp. 77–8.

85. Gibson, *Kavango Peoples*, p. 170.

86. Bollig, 'Colonial Encapsulation', quote on p. 511; *idem*, 'Power and Trade'; Rizzo, 'Van Warmelo'.

87. For a detailed account see Wolfram Hartmann, '"Ondillimani!" Iipumbu ya Tshilongo and the Ambiguities of Resistance in Ovambo' in Hayes *et al.*, *Namibia*, pp. 263–88 (quote on p. 264).

88. McKittrick, *To Dwell Secure*, pp. 194–9; Miettinen, *'On the Way'*, p. 112.

89. Shigwedha, 'Mwaala gwa Nashilongo', p. 51 and *passim*.

90. Lorena Rizzo, 'The Elephant Shooting: Colonial Law and Indirect Rule in Kaoko, Northwestern Namibia, in the 1920s and 1930s', *JAH*, 48 (2007), pp. 245–66; Friedman, 'Making Politics', pp. 28–30. As Rizzo points out (pp. 259–60), violence was not only a feature of life in Kaoko in this period, it was also an integral part of the experience of Hahn as well as Tom and Mutate.

91. Fleisch and Möhlig, *Kavango Peoples*, p. 27; Kangumu, 'Contestations', pp. 115–21, quote p. 113; *idem*, 'Forgotten Corner', pp. 13–16; Rainer Bruchmann, *Caprivi: An African Flashpoint. An Illustrated History of Namibia's Tropical Region Where Four Countries Meet* (Northcliff: Rainer Bruchmann, 2000), pp. 58–62.

92. Miettinen, *On the Way*, pp. 183–5, 196–204.

93. McKittrick, *To Dwell Secure*, p. 172.

94. *Idem*, pp. 188–93; Kreike, *Recreating Eden*, pp. 110–22; Patricia Hayes, 'Northern Exposures: The Photography of C.H.L. Hahn, Native Commissioner of Ovamboland 1915–1946', in Hartmann *et al.* (eds), *Colonising Camera*, pp. 171–87; *idem*, '"Cocky Hahn"'; Shigwedha, 'Pre-colonial Costumes', *passim*; Becker, *Namibian Women's Movement*, pp. 78 ff.

95. Emmett, *Popular Resistance*, pp. 181, 200; Ngavirue, *Political Parties*, p. 234 n. 61; Cooper, *Ovambo Politics*, pp. 94–5.

96. Silvester *et al.*, 'Trees Never Meet', pp. 28–9; Silvester, 'Black Pastoralists'; Emmett, *Popular Resistance*, pp. 184–5; Cooper, *Ovambo Politics*, pp. 107–8.

97. Fuller, '"We Live in a *Manga*"', p. 208.

98. Werner, '*No One Will Become Rich*', pp. 160–8; Emmett, *Popular Resistance*, pp. 229–30 (quotes p. 229); Silvester, 'Black Pastoralists'; Kößler, *In Search*, p. 122 ff.

99. This has not been researched for towns outside Windhoek, where there were small removals in the period; Köhler, however, refers to a location removal at Usakos in 1928, and several (undated) in Karibib. Oswin Köhler, *A Study of the Karibib District (SWA)* (Pretoria: Union of South Africa, Dept of Native Affairs, 1958), pp. 84, 58.

100. Wallace, *Health*, especially ch. 11; *idem*, '"A Person is Never Angry for Nothing": Women, VD and Windhoek' in Hayes *et al.*, *Namibia under South African Rule*, pp. 77–94.

101. For ethnic stereotyping in the German period, see especially Steinmetz, *Devil's Handwriting*, part 1; Peter Scheulen, *Die 'Eingeborenen' Süd-westafrikas: Ihr Bild in deutschen Kolonialzeitschriften von 1884 bis 1918* (Cologne: Rüdiger Köppe, 1998).

102. Vedder had arrived in Namibia as a missionary in 1903 and played a major role in the RMS, becoming the defining voice in both the mission and the ethnography of SWA in the first half of the twentieth century. See Silvester *et al.*, 'Trees Never Meet', p. 44, n. 175.

103. C.H.L. Hahn, Louis Fourie and Heinrich Vedder, *The Native Tribes of South West Africa* (Cape Town: Cape Times, 1928).

104. Hayes *et al.*, 'Trees Never Meet', pp. 43–6; Lau, 'Thank God the Germans Came'; Robert Gordon, *Picturing Bushmen: The Denver Expedition of 1925* (Athens, Ohio: Ohio University Press, 1997). For the construction of ethnicity at this period see also, in particular, Hartmann *et al.* (eds), *Colonising Camera*, especially Robert Gordon, 'Backdrops and Bushmen: An Expeditious Comment', pp. 111–17; Hayes, 'Northern Exposures'.

105. Lau, 'Thank God the Germans Came'; Gordon and Sholto-Douglas, *Bushman Myth*, pp. 153–4; Gordon, 'Backdrops'; *idem*, *Denver Expedition*.

106. Fuller, "'We Live in a Manga'", pp. 211–13; Kößler, *In Search*, pp. 89–91; Werner, *'No One Will Become Rich'*, pp. 210–11.

107. Silvester, 'Beasts, Boundaries and Buildings', p. 107; Silvester *et al.*, 'Trees Never Meet', p. 38. For most of the inter-war years there seems not to have been an identified (or self-identified) 'Coloured' group, with the exception of those Cape Coloureds living in SWA, although such a process of ethnic construction may have been under way by 1946.

108. South Africa, *Report on the Natives*.

109. 261 Germans refused South African citizenship, while 3,489 accepted. Mbuende, *Namibia*, p. 74.

110. On these constitutional arrangements see especially Wellington, *South West Africa*, pp. 274, 291; J. Kozonguizi and A. O'Dowd, 'The Legal Apparatus of Apartheid' in Segal and First (eds), *Travesty of Trust*, pp. 118–27. On white politics at this period, see also Botha, 'Internal Colonisation'.

111. South Africa's constitutional status is complex and cannot be discussed in detail here. Briefly, the dominions were effectively given independence by the Statute of Westminster (1931); this was enacted in South Africa itself through the Status of the Union Act (1934). In 1961 South Africa increased its distance from Britain by declaring itself a republic.

112. Cooper, *Occupation of Namibia*, pp. 47–67; Randolph Vigne, 'The Moveable Frontier: The Namibia–Angola Boundary Demarcation, 1926–1928' in Hayes *et al.*, *Namibia*, pp. 289–304, p. 300.

113. For these divisions see, for example, Klaus Rüdiger, *Die Namibia-Deutschen: Geschichte einer Nationalität im Werden* (Stuttgart: Steiner, 1993), p. 74; Schmidt-Laubner, *Abhängige Herren*, pp. 69–70.

114. Ngavirue, *Political Parties*, ch. 5; Cooper, *Occupation of Namibia*, ch. 3; Du Pisani, *Continuity and Change*, pp. 71–8.

115. Hartmann *et al.* (eds), *Colonising Camera*, p. 62 (quote); Ngavirue, *Political Parties*, pp. 147–64.

116. Ngavirue, *Political Parties*, p. 139. See also Martin Eberhardt, *Zwischen Nationalismus und Apartheid: Die deutsche Bevölkerungsgruppe Südwestafrikas 1915–1965* (Münster: Lit, 2007).

117. On the Commission see Wellington, *South West Africa*, pp. 305–10.

118. Negley Farson, *Behind God's Back* (London: Victor Gollancz, 1940), quoted in Robert Gordon, 'The Impact of the Second World War on Namibia', *JSAS*, 19, 1 (1993), pp. 147–65, p. 149. The account below draws on this article.

119. Gordon, 'Second World War', p. 151.

120. McKittrick, 'Northern Namibia', pp. 186–8, discusses forced recruitment in western Owambo, in contrast to Gordon, 'Second World War', who argues that recruitment in the region was largely voluntary and mainly from the eastern kingdom of Oukwanyama. Hileni Elago, 'Ovambo Men's Experiences of Participation in the Second World War (1939–1945)' in Wolfram Hartmann (ed.), *New Historical Writing in Namibia:*

Three Research Papers (Windhoek: Namibia History Trust), pp. 20–3, also argues that recruitment was voluntary.

121. Kangumu, 'Forgotten Corner', p. 16.
122. Gordon, 'Second World War', p. 164.

9. NATIONALISM AND APARTHEID, 1946–70

1. For this and the following chapter I have drawn heavily on Katjavivi, *History of Resistance*. This work remains very useful for many aspects of this period, although it deals mainly with political history and its intellectual framework relates closely to the politics of the independence struggle. Other sources used throughout are Gretchen Bauer, *Labor and Democracy in Namibia, 1971–1996* (Athens, Ohio: Ohio University Press), which includes a useful summary of the constitutional history of this period (pp. 21–33) and Denis Herbstein and John Evenson, *The Devils are Among Us: The War for Namibia* (London: Zed, 1989), which (despite its obvious political agenda) brings together much evidence on the history of this period, particularly the war.

2. For this section see especially Wellington, *South West Africa*, pp. 320–9; Katjavivi, *History of Resistance*, ch. 6; Werner, 'No One Will Become Rich', p. 185; Silvester, 'Black Pastoralists'; Emmett, *Popular Resistance*, pp. 250–5, 268–99; Du Pisani, *Continuity and Change*, ch. 5; Hellberg, *Mission, Colonialism*, pp. 238–44; Ngavirue, *Political Parties*, pp. 21, 212–9.

3. For South African strategy see Peter Henshaw, 'South African Territorial Expansion and International Reaction to South African Racial Policies, 1939 to 1948', *SAHJ*, 50 (2004), pp. 65–76.

4. Emmett, *Popular Resistance*, p. 252.

5. Quoted in Katjavivi, *History of Resistance*, p. 34.

6. Silvester, 'Black Pastoralists', p. 190.

7. See also Katesa Schlosser, *Eingeborenenkirchen in Süd und Südwestafrika, ihre Geschichte und Sozialstruktur* (Kiel: W.G. Mühlau, 1958), ch. 3.

8. Zedekia Ngavirue, 'The Land Theft' in Segal and First (eds), *Travesty of Trust*, pp. 178–88, pp. 186–7.

9. The last such report had been made in 1946.

10. Anne Yates and Lewis Chester, *The Troublemaker: Michael Scott and his Lonely Struggle against Injustice* (London: Aurum, 2006), chs 10, 12, 13, 15; Troup, *In Face of Fear*; Gewald, 'Kutako', pp. 104–7. For extracts from UN petitions from Namibians see Mburumba Kerina, *Namibia: The Making of a Nation* (New York: Books in Focus, 1981), pp. 134–41.

11. Quoted in Katjavivi, *History of Resistance*, p. 38.

12. Vedder had retired from the RMS in 1947; he was replaced by Hans Karl Diehl.

13. Miettinen, *On the Way*, pp. 99, 183, 233–48, 362–3, Appx 1; McKittrick, *To Dwell Secure*, ch. 8, which see in particular for the social meanings of the *Epaphuduko* movement.

14. Solomon Mifima, a founder of the OPO, quoted in Emmett, *Popular Resistance*, p. 268. Nevertheless, the degree to which the African population was in touch with wider events can be overstated. The family of Eliaser Tuhadeleni (for whom see below) seems not to have known for years that he was imprisoned on Robben Island, even though this had been reported by the international press. Ellen Ndeshi Namhila, *Kaxumba kaNdola: Man and Myth. The Biography of a Barefoot Soldier* (Basel: BAB, 2005), pp. 75 ff.

15. Emmett, *Popular Resistance*, pp. 266–8; Kangumu, 'Forgotten Corner', p. 72 ff.

16. Namhila, *Kaxumba*, pp. 35–7. The OPC may, in fact, never have left the planning stage—see Emmett, *Popular Resistance*, p. 276.

17. In 1960 the FMS ran 243 schools for a total of 26,846 pupils; the vast majority of these learners (26,046) were in elementary schools whose maximum highest level was Standard II. Miettinen, *On the Way*, p. 92.

18. Emmett, *Popular Resistance*, pp. 287–8. By 1962 there were twelve government schools for black pupils in the territory, nine of them in mainly Herero reserves.

19. Cynthia Cohen, *Administering Education in Namibia: The Colonial Period to the Present* (Windhoek: Namibia Scientific Society, 1994).

20. Katjavivi, *History of Resistance*, p. 30.

21. Dag Henrichsen (ed.), *A Glance at Our Africa: Facsimile Reprint of: South West News, the Only Non-racial Newspaper in the Territory, 1960* (Basel: BAB, 1997).

22. In addition to the works quoted at the beginning of this section, on the early history of OPO and SWANU see Lauren Dobell, *Swapo's Struggle for Namibia, 1960–1991: War by other Means* (Basel: P. Schlettwein, 1998), ch. 1.

23. Jeremy Silvester, 'Assembling and Resembling: Herero History in Vaalgras, southern Namibia' in Bollig and Gewald (eds), *People, Cattle and Land*, pp. 473–92.

24. Although the succession to Kutako was a live issue at this date, Kapuuo did not in fact succeed until Kutako died at the age of 100 in 1970. Katjavivi, *History of Resistance*, p. 92.

25. Katjavivi (*ibid.*, p. 45) dates this event to June 1960, arguing that the 19 April date frequently given is actually the anniversary of the foundation of the OPO. Examples of dates and places given in other sources for the foundation of SWAPO are: 19 April 1960, New York (Bauer, *Labor and Democracy*, p. 32); the official version, 19 April 1960, Ovamboland (Herbstein and Evenson, *Devils*, pp. 7–9); 1960, Dar-es-Salaam (Colin Leys and Susan Brown (eds), *Histories of Namibia: Living through the Liberation Struggle* (London: Merlin, 2001), p. 2).

26. Four representatives were elected to the Senate, and six to the Assembly. The members of the Legislative Assembly in SWA were also all now elected by the white population (some had previously been appointed by the Administrator).

27. Miescher, 'Rote Linie', pp. 268–90; Emmett, *Popular Resistance*, pp. 262–3.
28. See, for example, Ngavirue, *Political Parties*, pp. 170–9; Wellington, *South West Africa*, p. 379.
29. In 1958 the NAD was split into two: the Department of Bantu Administration and Development (DBAD) and the Department of Bantu Education.
30. On apartheid in South Africa in the 1950s, see, for example, William Beinart, *Twentieth-century South Africa* (Oxford University Press, 1994), ch. 6; Paul Maylam, *South Africa's Racial Past: The History and Historiography of Racism, Segregation and Apartheid* (Aldershot: Ashgate, 2001), pp. 183–7, ch. 6.
31. Ngavirue, *Political Parties*, p. 237.
32. Emmett, *Popular Resistance*, pp. 283. These figures include contract workers.
33. Part of the Act was applied to Namibia as the Identity Documents in South West Africa Act (1970), in order to implement a measure of control over white and Coloured rather than black people. Elizabeth Landis, *Laws and Practices established in Namibia by the Government of South Africa which are Contrary to the Purposes and Principles of the Charter of the United Nations and to the Universal Declaration of Human Rights* (New York: Office of the UN Commissioner for Namibia, 1975), pp. 89–91.
34. The Proclamation was similar to previous legislation of the same name, particularly the Natives (Urban Areas) Proclamation (1945); it consolidated and repealed the urban areas legislation of 1924. Landis, *Laws and Practices*, p. 324.
35. This is made clear in Muriel Horrell, *South West Africa* (Johannesburg: South African Institute of Race Relations, 1967) (despite some confusion in the literature).
36. On apartheid in Namibia see Ngavirue, *Political Parties*, pp. 235–6; Landis, *Law and Practices*, pp. 248, 324–32; Horrell, *South West Africa*; First, *South West Africa*, pt 4 and *passim*; Jacques-Roger Booh Booh, *La décolonisation de la Namibie: un mandat usurpé* (Paris: Les Publications Universitaires, 1982), pp. 99–100; David Simon, 'Aspects of Urban Change in Windhoek, Namibia, during the Transition to Independence' (PhD, University of Oxford, 1983), p. 204 (who states explicitly that the Group Areas Act was not applied to Namibia); Astrid Seckelmann, *Siedlungsentwicklung im unabhängigen Namibia: Transformationsprozesse in Klein- und Mittelzentren der Farmzone* (Hamburg: Institut für Afrika-Kunde, 2000), p. 43; Volker Winterfeldt, 'Labour Migration in Namibia—Gender Aspects' in *idem et al.*, *Namibia Society Sociology*, pp. 39–74; Bruce Frayne, *Urbanisation in Post-independence Windhoek* (Windhoek: Namibian Institute for Social and Economic Research, 1992), p. 40; Justin Ellis, *Education, Repression and Liberation: Namibia* (London: World University Service, 1984), pp. 21–6. There is no overall study of the impo-

sition of apartheid legislation on Namibia, but Horrell's outline is the most coherent.

37. Rizzo, 'Van Warmelo'; Fuller, '"Manga"', pp. 213–15; Kößler, *In Search*, pp. 89–91. Kößler argues that by the mid-twentieth century, many of those classified as 'Nama' also saw themselves as such.

38. On the Etosha eviction see Dieckmann, *Hai//Om*, pp. 186–208.

39. See Amenda Zingelwa, 'The Campaign for Khomasdal: The Building of a Coloured Community in Windhoek' in Hartmann (ed.), *More New Historical Writing*, pp. 22–36 for the complexities of the Coloured population in Windhoek at this date. Zingelwa argues that it was mainly members of the Cape Coloured community who were interested in developing their rights and identity as Coloureds, and who fought for the new township at Khomasdal.

40. The representative body for the Old Location, which was subject to the authority of the (white) location superintendent.

41. For a detailed account of the removal and resistance to it, see Milly Jafta *et al.*, *An Investigation of the Shooting at the Old Location on 10 December 1959* (Windhoek: Namibian History Trust, 1999).

42. Eleven is the generally accepted figure. A list of thirteen names is published in *ibid.*, p. 39.

43. The exact sequence and nature of events on the night of 10 December are contested. For a critical view of *ibid.*, see Bryan O'Linn, *Namibia: The Sacred Trust of Civilization. Ideal and Reality* (Windhoek: Gamsberg Macmillan, 2003), pp. 40–59. O'Linn's exploration of apparent inconsistencies in existing accounts of the events is suggestive, if flawed, but in my view his focus on the issue of culpability for the shootings prevents his seeing the episode in its wider historical context, and causes him to underestimate the importance of the interviews with community members published in Jafta *et al.*, *Old Location*. He also takes at face value the evidence of the police to the subsequent commission of inquiry.

44. Gerson Veii, quoted in *ibid.*, p. 44.

45. See Wade Pendleton, *Katutura: A Place Where We Do Not Stay. The Social Structure and Social Relationships of People in an African Township in South West Africa* (San Diego: San Diego State University Press, 1974), for a detailed picture of the township in the late 1960s and early 1970s.

46. For migrancy, and the state's policy on migrant labour, see especially Emmett, *Popular Resistance*, chs 8, 9, 11, 12; Ngavirue, *Political Parties*, ch. 8; John ya Otto, *Battlefront Namibia: An Autobiography* (London: Heinemann, 1982); Vinnia Ndadi, *Breaking Contract: The Story of Vinnia Ndadi* (London: IDAF Publications, 1989), pt 1; Helao Shityuwete, *Never Follow the Wolf: The Autobiography of a Namibian Freedom Fighter* (London: Kliptown, 1990).

47. Emmett, *Popular Resistance*, p. 181.

48. The population doubled in some areas of the north in the 1940s, and growth continued until the 1970s and 1980s, when it was halted because

of the war. Veijo Notkola and Harri Siiskonen, *Fertility, Mortality and Migration in sub-Saharan Africa: The Case of Ovamboland in North Namibia, 1925–90* (Basingstoke: Macmillan, 1999), pp. 17–19.

49. On Owambo see especially Moorsom, 'Underdevelopment', pp. 60–5; also Kreike, *Recreating Eden*, pp. 92–6, 148 ff. On Kavango see Gordon, *Mines, Masters*, pp. 22 ff. Of the total of 30,129 workers recruited in 1960, only 2,623 were recruited in the Kavango, of whom only 612 actually came from the area.

50. Cooper, *Ovambo Politics*, p. 131.

51. Namhila, *Kaxumba*, p. 16, quoting Ndeshihafela Hangula-Haimbangu.

52. Becker, *Namibian Women's* Movement, pp. 94–100; Miettinen, *On the Way to Whiteness*, pp. 292–6; McKittrick, *To Dwell Secure*, pp. 220–44.

53. See, in particular, *Namibia: Perspectives for National Reconstruction and Development* (Lusaka: United Nations Institute for Namibia, 1986), pp. 65, 300–1, 305–6, 337–8.

54. Kößler, *In Search*, pp. 74–5. In the mid-1950s karakul sales made an income of £3,500 p.a. for the Berseba reserve.

55. Gordon, *Mines, Masters*; Sam Nujoma, *Where Others Wavered: The Autobiography of Sam Nujoma* (London: Panaf Books, 2001); Ndadi, *Breaking Contract*; Cooper, *Ovambo Politics*, pp. 131–2.

56. Emmett, *Popular Resistance*, pp. 279–81; Namhila, *Kaxumba*, chs 1–2; Shityuwete, *Never Follow the Wolf*; Cooper, *Ovambo Politics*, pp. 237–59.

57. Cooper, *Ovambo Politics*, pp. 252–62. By this time K.R. Crossman had replaced Eedes, who retired in 1954, as Native Commissioner.

58. Kangumu, 'Forgotten Corner', ch. 3.

59. On SWAPO and SWANU see among other sources Dobell, *Swapo's Struggle for Namibia*, pp. 31–5. The agreement between SWAPO and CANU became a point of contestation when a secessionist movement emerged in the Caprivi after independence. The secessionist leaders claimed that the agreement had promised independence for the Caprivi. The *Namibian*, however, reported later (24 Jan. 2007) that it had seen the merger document of 1964 and that it contained no such promise.

60. The South African government tried to prevent the delegation from speaking to the opposition, but SWAPO leaders quickly mobilised and managed to meet them. Shityuwete, *Never Follow the Wolf*, ch. 6.

61. Katjavivi, *History of Resistance*, pp. 55–8; O'Linn, *Sacred Trust*, ch. 2; Du Pisani, *Continuity and Change*, pp. 135 ff.

62. For this section see, in particular, Wellington, *South West Africa*, pp. 379–91; Du Pisani, *Continuity and Change*, pp. 162–6, 243–4, 286.

63. Quoted in Wellington, *South West Africa*, p. 376. Published as South Africa, *Report of the Commission of Enquiry into South West Africa Affairs 1962–63* (Pretoria: 1964); generally known as the Odendaal Report.

64. Quoted in Katjavivi, *History of Resistance*, p. 72.

65. Lionel Cliffe *et al.*, *The Transition to Independence in Namibia* (Boulder: Lynne Rienner, 1994), p. 34.

66. Beinart, *South Africa*, p. 207.

67. The way in which these were constructed was in many cases arbitrary. For example, the five main ethnic groups in the Kavango area were simply classified as 'Kavango', and whites of all three language groups—Afrikaans, German and English—were given the label 'white'.

68. South Africa, *Commission 1962–3*, p. 29 (quotation); Robert Gordon, 'The Making of Modern Namibia: A Tale of Anthropological Ineptitude?', *Kleio*, 37 (2005), pp. 26–49, pp. 37–9, 44–5.

69. Hans Jenny, *South West Africa: Land of Extremes* (Windhoek: South West Africa Scientific Society, 1976), p. 198.

70. According to the official figures quoted in the Odendaal Report, the population of each ethnic group in 1960 was: Ovambo, 239,363; whites, 73,464; Damara, 44,353; Herero, 35,354; Nama, 34,806; Okavango, 27,871; Coloureds, 12,708; Bushmen, 11,762; Rehoboth Basters, 11,257; Kaokovelders, 9,234, East Caprivians, 15,840; Tswana and others, 9,992 totalling 526,004. South Africa, *Commission 1962–3*, p. 29.

71. Du Pisani, *Continuity and Change*, p. 162; Miescher, 'Rote Linie', p. 281.

72. Wellington, *South West Africa*, p. 386 (quotation); Richard Rohde, *Afternoons in Damaraland: Common Land and Common Sense in One of Namibia's Former Homelands* (University of Edinburgh Centre of African Studies, 1993), p. 18.

73. Suzman, '*Things from the Bush*', p. 83.

74. Kößler, *In Search*, p. 94; Adelheid Iken, *Woman-headed Households in Southern Namibia: Causes, Patterns and Consequences* (Frankfurt: IKO, 1999), p. 41.

75. Du Pisani, *Continuity and Change*, p. 163.

76. *Ibid.*, p. 162 (figure from the *SWA Handbook* for 1971/2); South Africa, *Commission 1962–3*, p. 29; the figure is given as 79,708 square miles.

77. David Simon, 'Recent Trends in Namibian Urbanization', *Tijdschrift voor economische en sociale Geographie*, 73, 4 (1982), pp. 237–49.

78. Kößler, *In Search*, p. 94; Iken, *Woman-headed Households*, p. 41; *Namibia: The Facts* (London: IDAF, 1990), p. 22.

79. Silvester, 'Assembling and Resembling', p. 491; Du Pisani, *Continuity and Change*, p. 286; Jan-Bart Gewald, 'Who Killed Clemens Kapuuo?', *JSAS*, 30, 3 (2004), pp. 559–76, pp. 563–5.

80. Du Pisani, *Continuity and Change*, pp. 243–4; Rohde, *Afternoons*, p. 31.

81. Gerhard Tötemeyer, *Namibia Old and New: Traditional and Modern Leaders in Ovamboland* (London: C. Hurst & Co., 1978), ch. 3; Katjavivi, *History of Resistance*, pp. 72–3; Bauer, *Labor and Democracy*, p. 21; p. 21, n. 8; p. 46; Herbstein and Evenson, *Devils*, p. 22.

82. Bauer, *Labor and Democracy*, p. 21, n. 7.

83. Gordon, *Mines, Masters*, pp. 32–6; Jenny, *South West Africa*, ch. 12; Michael Bollig, 'Success and Failure of CPR Management in an Arid Environment: Access to Pasture, Environment and Political Economy in Northwestern Namibia' in Hartmut Leser (ed.), *The Changing Culture and Nature of Namibia: Case Studies* (Basel: BAB, 2006), pp. 37–68, p. 43; Andre du Pisani, 'Beyond the Transgariep: South Africa in Namibia, 1915–89', *Politikon*, 16, 1 (1989), pp. 26–43, p. 33; Kangumu, 'Forgotten Corner', pp. 22–4, 69–71; Walter Louw, *Owambo* (Sandton: Southern African Freedom Foundation, n.d.), ch. 7. The last of these is a work of propaganda that praises South African development in the largest of the homelands.

84. Horrell, *South West Africa*, p. 80l; Cohen, *Administering Education*, chs 5, 6.

85. Gordon, *Mines, Masters*, pp. 27–8; Moorsom, 'Underdevelopment', p. 69.

86. Beinart, *South Africa*, p. 204; Iken, *Female-Headed Households*, p. 43. See Kößler, *In Search, passim*, for a discussion of deteriorating conditions in the reserves.

87. For this section, in addition to the works quoted at the beginning of this chapter, see Namhila, *Kaxumba* pp. 59 ff., 79–83, 102–113; Nujoma, *Where Others Wavered*, pp. 126–8; Dobell, *SWAPO's Struggle*, pp. 35–6; Oswin Namakalu, *Armed Liberation Struggle: Some Accounts of PLAN's Combat Operations* (Windhoek: Gamsberg Macmillan, 2004), pp. 10–23.

88. Quoted in Katjavivi, *History of Resistance*, p. 59.

89. Referred to in many accounts as Omgulumbashe or Ongulumbashe.

90. Quoted in Namhila, *Kaxumba*, p. 67.

91. There is, however, some conflicting evidence. See Kangumu, 'Forgotten Corner', pp. 31, 53–5.

92. Quoted in Namhila, *Kaxumba*, p. 82. See also Shityuwete, *Never Follow the Wolf*.

93. Quoted in Katjavivi, *History of Resistance*, p. 61.

94. Katjavivi, *History of Resistance*, pp. 61–3; Namhila, *Kaxumba*, pp. 79–83, 102–113; David Soggot, *Namibia: The Violent Heritage* (London: Collings, 1986), pp. 30–2.

95. The full text of the speech is given in SWAPO, *To Be Born a Nation*, pp. 311–16.

96. John Saul and Colin Leys, 'SWAPO: The Politics of Exile' in Leys and Saul (eds), *Namibia's Liberation Struggle*, pp. 40–65, pp. 43–6; Dobell, *SWAPO's Struggle*, pp. 37–40.

10. LIBERATION STRUGGLES AND THE RETREAT FROM APARTHEID, 1971–90

1. For this chapter, I have drawn heavily, as for Chapter 9 (see n. 1), on Katjavivi, *History of Resistance*; Bauer, *Labor and Democracy*, especially

pp. 21–33; and Herbstein and Evenson, *Devils*. For the present chapter, Soggot, *Violent Heritage* is also used throughout.

2. Katjavivi, *History of Resistance*, p. 65.

3. In an unsuccessful attempt to delay the ICJ decision, the South African authorities asked the Lutheran church in the north (ELOK) to put a questionnaire to its members, but the plan backfired when the vast majority rejected South African rule.

4. Quoted in Peter Katjavivi, Per Frostin and Kaire Mbuende (eds), *Church and Liberation in Namibia* (London: Pluto, 1989), pp. 134–8.

5. Soggot, *Violent Heritage*, pp. 37, 43. On p. 33 Soggot gives the membership of the two Lutheran churches as 300,000, and that of the Anglicans as 50,000. Comparable figures for 1989 are: ELCIN (northern Lutherans) 360,000; ELK (southern Lutherans) 193,000; Anglicans 120,000; Catholics 195,000. The *Oruuano* and AMEC were smaller but remained important.

6. See especially Katjavivi *et al.* (eds), *Church and Liberation*, pp. 5–7, 12 and *passim*.

7. This point is carefully argued in Bauer, *Labor and Democracy*, pp. 34–5; n. 82.

8. *Ibid.*, p. 34. For the strike in general see especially *idem*, pp. 34–41; also Soggot, *Violent Heritage*, ch. 7; Moorsom, 'Underdevelopment'; Katjavivi, *History of Resistance*, pp. 67–71; Cooper, *Ovambo Politics*, pp. 138–40.

9. Emmett, *Popular Resistance*, p. 181; Moorsom, 'Underdevelopment', p. 70. Emmett gives the total number of recruits for 1966 as 39,033 and for 1960 as 30,129.

10. In 1968, 32% of SWANLA employees were on the mines, 27% in non-fishing industries, 6% in fishing, 28% on farms and 7% in the domestic sector. Cooper, *Ovambo Politics*, p. 137.

11. Bauer, *Labor*, p. 34, n. 78, referencing Robert Gordon, 'A Note on the History of Labour Action in Namibia', *South African Labour Bulletin*, 1 (1975), pp. 7–17.

12. Officially, the Commissioner-General of the Indigenous Peoples of South West Africa.

13. Moorsom, 'Underdevelopment', p. 85.

14. Quoted in Bauer, *Labor and Democracy*, p. 37, n. 100.

15. Herbstein and Evenson, *Devils*, p. 27.

16. On the retreat from the Odendaal Plan see Cliffe *et al.*, *Transition*, p. 34.

17. This genre of punishment was not new. For example, the first Native Commissioner for Owambo, Hahn, had been known as 'Shongola', the whip. Johanna Mweshida, 'Nicknames in Ovambo: Some Preliminary Deliberations' in Hartmann (ed.), *New Historical Writing*, pp. 4–12; Hayes, '"Cocky Hahn"'.

18. Quoted in Katjavivi, *History of Resistance*, p. 78.

19. The title of 'sole and authentic representative' was to be granted by the General Assembly in December 1976.

20. For Kapuuo's politics see Gewald, 'Who Killed Clemens Kapuuo?', pp. 563–5.

21. William Minter, *Apartheid's Contras: An Inquiry into the Roots of War in Angola and Mozambique* (Johannesburg: Witwatersrand University Press, 1994), pp. 3, 20–1.

22. SWAPO's armed force was initially called the South West Africa Liberation Army, then the Namibian People's Liberation Army. It was renamed the People's Liberation Army of Namibia after the Tanga Congress of 1969–70.

23. Susan Brown, 'Diplomacy By Other Means: SWAPO's Liberation War' in Leys and Saul, *Namibia's Liberation Struggle*, pp. 19–39, pp. 23–5.

24. For a summary, and these figures, see Leys and Brown (eds), *Histories of Namibia*, pp. 6–8; see also Herbstein and Evenson, *Devils*, pp. 40–1.

25. In 1973 there were approximately 600 Namibians under SWAPO's control in Zambia, and a further 1,000 under the United Nations High Commission for Refugees. There were also about a thousand Namibian refugees in Botswana. Tor Sellström, *Sweden and National Liberation in Southern Africa* (Uppsala: Nordiska Afrikainstitutet, 1999–2002), vol. 2, p. 262, n. 3.

26. For a detailed account of these events see Colin Leys and John Saul, 'Liberation without Democracy? The Swapo Crisis of 1976', *JSAS*, 20, 1 (1994), pp. 123–48; also Saul and Leys, 'SWAPO: The Politics of Exile'.

27. As well as the work of Colin Leys and John Saul quoted above, see, for example, Gustine [*sic*] Hunter, *Die Politik der Erinnerung und des Vergessens in Namibia: Umgang mit schweren Menschenrechtsverletzungen der Ära des bewaffneten Befreiungskampfes 1966 bis 1989* (Frankfurt: Peter Lang, 2008); Cliffe *et al.*, *Transition*, pp. 167–75; Justine Hunter, 'No Man's Land of Time: Reflections on the Politics of Memory and Forgetting in Namibia' in Gary Baines and Peter Vale (eds), *Beyond the Border War*, pp. 302–21; Siegfried Groth, *Namibia: The Wall of Silence. The Dark Days of Liberation* (Wuppertal: Peter Hammer, 1995); Richard Pakleppa (director), 'Nda Mona: I Have Seen' (film, Johannesburg, 1999).

28. Dobell, *SWAPO's Struggle*, p. 50.

29. *Ibid.*, p. 57.

30. For the Political Programme, and these general conclusions on SWAPO policy, see *ibid.*, pp. 55–9, 92; Axel Harneit-Sievers, *SWAPO of Namibia: Entwicklung, Programmatik und Politik seit 1959* (Hamburg: Institut fur Afrika-Kunde, 1985), pp. 91–7.

31. Namhila, *Kaxumba*, p. 98, quoting Meme Loini Shivute.

32. Becker, *Namibian Women's Movement*, pp. 149–66. See also, for example, Tessa Cleaver and Marion Wallace, *Namibia: Women in War* (London: Zed, 1990), ch. 6; interviews with Netumbo Nandi and Mathilda Amoomo in Liberation Support Movement (ed.), *Namibia: SWAPO Fights for Freedom* (Oakland, CA: LSM Information Center, 1978), pp. 60–7;

Iina Soiri, *The Radical Motherhood: Namibian Women's Independence Struggle* (Uppsala: Nordic Africa Institute, 1996), pp. 74–84.

33. This figure is given in Chris Tapscott, 'National Reconciliation, Social Equity and Class Formation in Independent Namibia', *JSAS*, 19, 1 (1993), pp. 29–39, p. 32.

34. For this figure see Chris Tapscott, 'National Reconciliation', p. 32. For the camps in general see Ellis, *Education, Repression*, pp. 55–8; *Namibia: Perspectives for National Reconstruction*, pp. 895–9; Sellström, *Sweden and National Liberation*, pp. 262–72; Stig Nielsen, 'A Refugee School 1 400 km, 850 Miles from Home' in Flemming Gjedde-Nielsen, *Namibia: Landet uden overgivelse* (Copenhagen: WUS, 1988); Constance Kenna (ed.), *Homecoming: The GDR Kids of Namibia* (Windhoek: New Namibia Books, 1999). For an account of the camps in Angola in the 1970s and 1980s see Ellen Ndeshi Namhila, *The Price of Freedom* (Windhoek: New Namibia Books, 1997). See also Giorgio Miescher's very useful bibliographical essay on SWAPO in *idem* (ed.), *Registratur AA.3 (Enlarged and Revised Edition): Guide to the SWAPO Collection in the Basler Afrika Bibliographien* (Basel: BAB, 2006).

35. Dobell, *SWAPO's Struggle*, p. 64, n. 163.

36. On the solidarity movements see, for example, Sellström, *Sweden and National Liberation*; Tore Linné Eriksen (ed.), *Norway and National Liberation in Southern Africa* (Uppsala: Nordic Institute of African Studies, 1999); Christopher Morgenstierne, *Denmark and National Liberation in Southern Africa: A Flexible Response* (Uppsala: Nordic Africa Institute, 2003); Chris Saunders, 'Namibian Solidarity: British Support for Namibian Independence', *JSAS*, 35, 2 (2009), pp.437–54.

37. For visual aspects of this propaganda effort see Giorgio Miescher *et al.* (eds), *Posters in Action: Visuality in the Making of an African Nation* (Basel: BAB, 2009), *passim*.

38. Quoted in Mvula Ya Nangolo and Tor Sellström, *Kassinga: A Story Untold* (Windhoek: Namibia Book Development Council, 2005), pp. 28–9.

39. For the insecurity of the refugees in Angola see Namhila, *The Price of Freedom*.

40. Soggot, *Violent Heritage*, pp. 178–9.

41. Minter, *Apartheid's Contras*, pp. 30–2. Several 'insider' accounts of 32 Battalion also exist, including Jan Breytenbach, *The Buffalo Soldiers: The Story of South Africa's 32-Battalion, 1975–1993* (Alberton: Galago, 2002).

42. Susan Brown, 'Diplomacy by Other Means: SWAPO's Liberation War' in Leys and Saul (eds), *Namibia's Liberation Struggle*, pp. 19–39, pp. 29–34; see also Soiri, *Radical Motherhood*, pp. 67–74.

43. The Turnhalle was the German-era gymnasium building in Windhoek, in which the conference met.

44. The total population of Namibia, in fact, remained very small—761,562 according to the 1970 census—and out of proportion to these elaborate

arrangements. The census showed 75% defined as 'black', 10% as Nama, Coloured and Baster, 12% as white and 3% as 'Bushmen'. About 25% lived in urban areas, of which Windhoek was the largest, with a population of 75,026. Bauer, *Labor and Democracy*, p. 26.

45. Soggot, *Violent Heritage*, p. 208.
46. Winterfeldt, 'Labour Migration', p. 61.
47. The Immorality Proclamation (1934), the Prohibition of Mixed Marriages Act (1953) and the Immorality Amendment Ordinances (1953, 1954).
48. Du Pisani, *Continuity and Change*, p. 331.
49. Dobell, *SWAPO's Struggle*, pp. 45 ff. The conference did not directly address the crisis of SWAPO in exile, then at its height, and the relationship between the two events remains unclear. There was clearly some tension between 'internal' and 'external' SWAPO at the time; it was also very difficult for those inside the country to obtain accurate information about events outside. For these issues see Leys and Saul, 'SWAPO inside Namibia' in *idem* (eds), *Namibia's Liberation Struggle*, pp. 66–93, pp. 73–4.
50. Quoted in Katjavivi, *History of Resistance*, p. 100. See also SWAPO, *To Be Born a Nation*, p. 231.
51. The Damara Tribal Executive also remained outside the Turnhalle process. Du Pisani, *Continuity and Change*, pp. 290–2.
52. Kößler, *In Search*, ch. 3. Fleisch and Möhlig, *Kavango Peoples*, pp. 114–16, note the involvement of Kamwanga, the Gciriku king, in the Advisory Council (1973), Turnhalle (1975) and the Kavango Council (1980).
53. Itaru Ohta, 'Drought and Mureti's Grave: the "we/us" boundaries between Kaokolanders and the People of the Okakarara Area in the Early 1980s' in Bollig and Gewald, *People, Cattle and Land*, pp. 299–317.
54. Cliffe *et al.*, *Transition*, pp. 65–9.
55. South Africa, *Truth and Reconciliation Commission of South Africa Report* (London: Macmillan, 1999), vol. 2, pp. 46–55, quote on p. 50. On the same page the *Report* states that Cassinga had a self-defence unit of three hundred male and female PLAN fighters with two anti-aircraft guns: it is not clear whether the *Report*'s authors think that these three hundred equalled the 'considerable' number of PLAN fighters to whom they refer earlier. See also Ya Nangolo and Sellström, *Kassinga*; Annemarie Heywood, *The Cassinga Event: An Investigation of the Records* (Windhoek: National Archives of Namibia, 1994); Christopher Saunders, 'South Africa in Namibia/Angola: The Truth and Reconciliation Commission's Account' in Baines and Vale (eds), *Beyond the Border War*, pp. 267–80, pp. 273–4; Cliffe *et al.*, *Transition*, pp. 43–56; Minter, *Apartheid's Contras*, pp. 37–9.
56. Quoted in Barbara Becker (ed.), *Speaking Out: Namibians Share their Perspectives on Independence* (Windhoek: Out of Africa, 2005), p. 64. See also Namhila, *Price of Freedom*, pp. 40–1.

57. Newell Stultz, 'South Africa in Angola and Namibia' in Thomas Weiss and James Blight (eds), *The Suffering Grass: Superpowers and Regional Conflict in Southern Africa and the Caribbean* (Boulder, Colo.: Lynne Riener, 1992), pp. 79–99, p. 87; J.E. Davies, *Constructive Engagement? Chester Crocker and American Policy in South Africa, Namibia and Angola, 1981–8* (Oxford: James Currey, 2007), chs 4, 5 and *passim*; Cedric Thornberry, *A Nation is Born: The Inside Story of Namibia's Independence* (Windhoek: Gamsberg Macmillan, 2004), *passim*; Lindsay Eades, *The End of Apartheid in South Africa* (Westport, Conn.: Greenwood, 1999), pp. 22–3.

58. Cliffe *et al.*, *Transition*, p. 53.

59. Soggot, *Violent Heritage*, p. 256.

60. On this point, see, for example, Kletus Muhena Likuwa and Bertha Nyambe, 'Posters, T-shirts and Placards: Images and Popular Mobilisation in Rundu during the Liberation Struggle' in Miescher *et al.* (eds), *Posters*, pp. 87–99.

61. Soggot, *Violent Heritage*, p. 256.

62. Du Pisani, *Continuity and Change*, p. 451; Cliffe *et al.*, *Transition*, p. 38.

63. Tim Lobstein, *Namibia: Reclaiming the People's Health* (London: AON Publications, 1984), p. 13.

64. Peter Katjavivi, 'The Role of the Church in the Struggle for Independence' in *idem et al.* (eds), *Church and Liberation*, pp. 3–26.

65. *Idem, History of Resistance*, p. 88; Minter, *Apartheid's Contras*, pp. 37–9.

66. For the role of Namibians as guides to the South African troops see *i.a.* Anthony Feinstein, *In Conflict* (Windhoek: New Namibia Books, 1999).

67. I.J. van der Merwe, 'The Role of War and Urbanization in the Regional Development of Namibia', *Africa Urban Quarterly*, 4, 3/4 (1989), pp. 263–74, p. 267.

68. Ohta, 'Drought and Mureti's Grave'.

69. Kangumu, 'Forgotten Corner', pp. 34–7, argues that the members of the San battalions were used as 'human shields' by the South African forces.

70. Jeremy Silvester, '"The Struggle is Futile": A Short Overview of Anti-SWAPO Visual Propaganda' in Miescher *et al.* (eds), *Posters*, pp. 187–201.

71. Emmanuel Kreike, 'War and the Environmental Effects of Displacement in Southern Africa (1970s–1990s)' in William Moseley and B. Ikubolajeh Logan (eds), *African Environment and Development: Rhetoric, Program and Realities* (Aldershot: Ashgate, 2004), pp. 90–110, pp. 91–2.

72. Quoted in Cleaver and Wallace, *Namibia: Women in War*, p. 1.

73. South Africa, *Truth and Reconciliation Commission Report*, vol. 2, p. 70. For further evidence supporting the conclusions of the TRC see Cleaver and Wallace, *Namibia: Women in War*, p. 2; Thornberry, *A Nation is Born*, p. 93; David Lush, *Last Steps to Uhuru: An Eyewitness Account of Namibia's Transition to Independence* (Windhoek: New Namibia Books, 1993), p. 147; Robert Gordon, 'Marginalia on "Grensliteratur": Or how/

why is Terror Culturally Constructed in Namibia?', *Critical Arts*, 5, 3 (1991), pp. 79–99.

74. Saunders, 'South Africa', p. 271; Thornberry, *A Nation is Born*, pp. 169–73.

75. Interview (1987), quoted in Herbstein and Evenson, *Devils*, p. 84

76. Quoted in *ibid.*, p. 82.

77. Tony Weaver, 'The War in Namibia: Social Consequences' in Gerhard Tötemeyer, Vezera Kandetu and Wolfgang Werner (eds), *Namibia in Perspective* (Windhoek: Council of Churches in Namibia, 1987), pp. 239–55; Inge Brinkman and Axel Fleisch (eds), *Grandmother's Footsteps: Oral Tradition and South-east Angolan Narratives on the Colonial Encounter* (Köln: Koppe, 1999), p. 19; Christofer Wärnlöf, 'The Politics of Death: Demarcating Land through Ritual Performance' in Bollig and Gewald, *People, Cattle and Land*, pp. 449–69.

78. Minter, *Apartheid's Contras*, pp. 39–42, quote on p. 42; Brown, 'Diplomacy', p. 32; Davies, *Constructive Engagement, passim* and p. 149 for a list of South African attacks in Angola in 1978–88.

79. *Ibid.*, pp. 42–9; Cliffe *et al.*, *Transition*, ch. 3.

80. *Ibid.*, p. 68.

81. In November 1989 the UN reported on the cases of around a thousand people thought to have been detained. A UN mission to Angola in September of that year found that, of this number, 517 had been set free and/or returned to Namibia, 57 were reported not to have been imprisoned, 123 were dead, 52 could not be identified and 263 could not then be found. These figures were finalised on 31 Oct. 1989, revised downwards from an earlier estimate of 11 Oct. See Cliffe *et al.*, *Transition*, p. 172. Cliffe, and also Hunter ('No-man's Land', pp. 310–11), note that the UN investigation was widely seen to lack credibility. Hunter describes a further ICRC investigation in 1993, in which SWAPO gave answers to queries concerning 556 out of 2,161 people thought missing, and Lauren Dobell notes the probable existence in 1994 of an 'official list', apparently containing the names of approximately 2,100 people unaccounted for. The ICRC's estimate was 1,600. Dobell, 'Review Article: Silence in Context. Truth and/or Reconciliation in Namibia', *JSAS*, 23, 2 (1997), pp. 371–82.

82. Emma Kambangula, quoted in Groth, *Wall of Silence*, p. 116.

83. See, for example, South Africa, *Truth and Reconciliation Report*, pp. 46–55.

84. See, in particular, Saul and Leys, 'SWAPO: The Politics of Exile'; Cliffe *et al.*, *Transition*, pp. 151–3, 167–75, 193–4.

85. Cliffe *et al.*, *Transition*, pp. 27–8, 55–60, ch. 3. For the Cuban, and especially Castro's, point of view, see David Deutschmann (ed.), *Changing the History of Africa: Angola and Namibia* (Melbourne, Vic.: Occan, 1989).

86. Robert Rotberg, *Ending Autocracy, Enabling Democracy: The Tribulations of Southern Africa, 1960–2000* (Cambridge, Mass.: World Peace Foundation, 2002) (quote), p. 129; Minter, *Apartheid's Contras*, p. 4; Weaver, 'War in Namibia'.

87. Cooper, *Occupation of Namibia*, p. 110; David Smuts, 'The Interim Government and Human Rights' in Tötemeyer *et al.* (eds), *Namibia in Perspective*, pp. 219–26.

88. Wolfgang Werner, 'Ethnicity and Reformism in Namibia' in *ibid.*, pp. 69–81; Rohde, *Afternoons in Damaraland*, pp. 32–3.

89. *Namibia: Perspectives*, p. 83.

90. Reginald Green and Kimmo Kiljunen, 'The Colonial Economy: Structures of Growth and Exploitation' in Reginald Green, Kimmo Kiljunen and Marja-Liisa Kiljunen (eds), *Namibia: The Last Colony* (Harlow: Longman, 1981), pp. 30–58, p. 35.

91. *Namibia: Perspectives*, p. 856.

92. Jenny Lindsay, *Population Control Policies in Namibia* (Leeds: University of Leeds, 1989), pp. 11–12.

93. *Namibia: Perspectives*, p. 856.

94. By 1988 there were over 311,000 black and Coloured school students, in contrast to the total of a little over 53,000 in 1962. Cohen, *Education*, pp. 130, 158.

95. The Khoekhoegowab name for Windhoek; the Otjiherero name is 'Otjomuise'.

96. Becker, *Namibian Women's Movement*, pp. 171 ff.; André Strauss, 'Community Organisations in Namibia', in Tötemeyer *et al.*, *Namibia in Perspective*, pp. 184–95; Bauer, *Labor and Democracy*, pp. 52–61; William Heuva, 'Voices in the Liberation Struggle: Discourse and Ideology in the SWAPO Exile Media' in Henning Melber (ed.), *Re-examining Liberation in Namibia: Political Culture since Independence* (Uppsala: Nordic Africa Institute, 2003), pp. 25–33; Cleaver and Wallace, *Namibia: Women and War*, p. 109.

97. Quoted in *ibid.*, p. 95. See also *idem*, ch. 7; Becker, *Namibian Women's Movement*, p. 189.

98. There had been efforts to set up the NUNW inside the country at Rössing in the late 1970s, but in the event it did not take shape until the mid-1980s, and it was in fact only formally constituted in 1989.

99. Bauer, *Labor and Democracy*, pp. 62–7, 72–9, 88–90.

100. Cleaver and Wallace, *Namibia: Women in War*, ch. 5. Herbstein and Evenson, *Devils*, pp. 116–18, give a lower figure of 40,000 participants in the schools strike.

101. For the trade unions in this respect see Bauer, *Labor and Democracy*, pp. 68–9, ch. 4.

102. Becker, *Namibian Women's Movement*, p. 189.

103. For this section see especially Cliffe *et al.*, *Transition*, chs 4, 6, 8 and specifically pp. 63, 84–91, 97–110, 134–6, 170, 172, 194; also Brian Harlech-Jones, *A New Thing? The Namibian Independence Process, 1989–1990* (Windhoek: EIN Publications, 1997).

104. UN personnel in Namibia were aware of the PLAN fighters' intentions by early on 2 April. Thornberry, *A Nation is Born*, pt 2.

105. Cliffe *et al.*, *Transition*, pp. 84–91 (figures on p. 85, from Legal Assistance Centre, Windhoek); Thornberry, *A Nation is Born*, pt 2, ch 6; Lush, *Last Steps*, ch. 6.
106. Cliffe *et al.*, *Transition*, p. 99–100; they note that one person was killed by SWAPO supporters.
107. Thornberry, *A Nation is Born*, p. 161.
108. Cliffe *et al.*, *Transition*, p. 194.
109. Health spending was doubled, and education spending trebled.
110. Herbstein and Evenson, *Devils*, pp. 35–6.
111. Martha Akawa and Jeremy Silvester, 'Their Blood Waters our Freedom. Naming the Dead: Civilian Casualties in the Liberation Struggle', *Namibian*, 24 August 2007.
112. South Africa, *Truth and Reconcilation Commission Report*, vol. 2, p. 77. The *Report* does not state which side the deaths were on, although the implication is clearly that they were all, or mainly, SWAPO. Presumably civilian deaths are included within these figures.
113. For Koevoet see Herbstein and Evenson, *Devils*, ch. 3; Soggot, *Violent Heritage*, ch. 36.
114. For a discussion of the figures, see n. 81 above.

CONCLUSION

1. For the constitutional and political history of the period, I have relied heavily on Gretchen Bauer and Scott Taylor, *Politics in Southern Africa: State and Society in Transition* (Boulder, CO: Lynne Riener, 2005), ch. 8. Melber, *Transitions*, and Graham Hopwood, *Guide to Namibian Politics* (Windhoek: Namibia Institute for Democracy, 2007) are also useful guides to many of the themes discussed here.
2. See, for example, John Saul and Colin Leys, 'Truth, Reconciliation, Amnesia: The "Ex-detainees'" Fight for Justice' in Melber (ed.), *Re-examining Liberation*, pp. 69–86, pp. 70–2.
3. *Constitution of the Republic of Namibia, Adopted by the Constituent Assembly in Windhoek, Namibia on 9th February 1990* (n. p.), Article 10.
4. Rosemary Preston, 'Integrating Fighters after War: Reflections on the Namibian Experience, 1989–1993', *JSAS*, 23, 2 (1997), pp. 453–72.
5. Bauer and Taylor, *Politics*, pp. 218–19.
6. For the documentation see the ICJ's website at http://www.icj-cij.org/docket/index.php?p1=3&p2=3&code=bona&case=98&k=b7.
7. Bauer and Taylor, *Politics*, pp. 219–20; Henning Melber, 'One Namibia, One Nation? The Caprivi as Contested Territory', *Journal of Contemporary African Studies*, 27, 4 (2009), pp. 463–81.
8. Quoted in Bauer and Taylor, *Politics*, p. 224.
9. *Ibid.*, p. 223.

10. 'Election Case Heats Up', *Namibian*, 15.1.2010. On Namibia's election history since independence see especially Henning Melber, 'Analysis: Namibia's Elections 2009. Democracy without Democrats?', Heinrich Böll Stiftung, Dec. 2009, http://www.boell.org.za/web/144–487.html; Bauer and Taylor, *Politics*, ch. 8.

11. Bauer and Taylor, *Politics*, pp. 225–8; Herbert Jauch, 'Between Politics and Shop Floor: Which Way for Namibia's Labour Movement?' in Melber, *Transitions*, pp. 50–64.

12. Bauer and Taylor, *Politics*, p. 225, cites a 'recent survey' giving a total of 220 NGOs.

13. These prevalence rates are based on surveys of women attending antenatal clinics and are therefore approximate. For the figures quoted here see Republic of Namibia, Ministry of Health and Social Services, *United Nations General Assembly Special Session (UNGASS) Country Report*, April 2006–Mar. 2007, http://data.unaids.org/pub/Report/2008/namibia_2008_country_progress_report_en.pdf (download 25.1.10), pp. 7–8; also Ida Susser, *Aids, Sex and Culture: Global Politics and Survival in Southern Africa* (Chichester: Wiley-Blackwell, 2009), p. 155.

14. Kaiser Family Foundation, 'The HIV/AIDS Epidemic in Namibia', Oct. 2005, http://www.kff.org/hivaids/upload/7362.pdf (download 25.1.10).

15. For personal accounts by young people of the impact of the epidemic, see Reimer Gronemeyer and Matthias Rompel (eds), *Today It's Your Family, Tomorrow It's You: Essays by Young Namibians on the Social Impact of HIV and AIDS* (Windhoek: Gamsberg Macmillan, 2003).

16. For a discussion of the broad social implications of the epidemic see Bauer and Taylor, *Politics*, ch. 10.

17. UNAIDS Country Situation Fact Sheet, 'Namibia', July 2008, http://data.unaids.org/pub/FactSheet/2008/sa08_nam_en.pdf (download 25.1.10).

18. WHO 'Country Health System Fact Sheet 2006 Namibia', p. 6, http://www.afro.who.int/home/countries/fact_sheets/namibia.pdf.

19. World Bank, World Development Indicators, http://data.worldbank.org/indicator/SE.ADT.LITR.ZS (accessed 10.5.10).

20. Henning Melber, 'Poverty, Politics and Privilege: Namibia's Black Economic Elite Formation' in *idem* (ed.), *Transitions in Namibia*, pp. 110-29, p. 115.

21. Winterfeldt, 'Labour Migration', p. 64.

22. Corruption Perceptions Index published by Transparency International, 2009 and 2001, http://www.transparency.org/policy_research/surveys_indices/cpi/2009/cpi_2009_table, http://www.transparency.org/policy_research/surveys_indices/cpi/2001 (25.1.10).

23. Dianne Hubbard, 'Gender and Sexuality: The Law Reform Landscape' in Suzanne LaFont and Dianne Hubbard (eds), *Unravelling Taboos: Gender and Sexuality in Namibia* (Windhoek: Legal Assistance Centre, 2007), pp. 99–128; *idem*, 'Ideas about Equality in Namibian Law' in Melber (ed.), *Transitions*, pp. 209–29; Bauer and Taylor, *Politics*, p. 207; Suzanne

LaFont, 'An Overview of Gender and Sexuality in Namibia' in *idem* and Hubbard (eds), *Unravelling Taboos*, pp. 1–38; Rachel Jewkes, Hetty Rose-Junius and Loveday Penn-Kekana, 'The Social Context of Child Rape in Namibia' in *ibid.*, pp. 167–80.

24. LaFont, 'Overview', pp. 11–14.

25. Ironically, a similar debate about prisoners taken by the South African forces has not emerged because, as we have seen, the latter took few prisoners and killed or 'turned' a high proportion of those they did take.

26. Christopher Saunders, 'History and the Armed Struggle: From Anti-colonial Propaganda to "Patriotic History"?' in Melber (ed.), *Transitions*, pp. 13–29; Lalli Metsola, 'Out of Order? The Margins of Namibian Ex-combatant "Reintegration"' in *ibid.*, pp. 130–52; Lauren Dobell, 'Review Article: Silence in Context', *JSAS*, 23, 2 (1997), pp. 371–82; Reinhart Kößler, 'Public Memory, Reconciliation and the Aftermath of War' in Melber (ed.), *Re-examining Liberation*, pp. 99–110; Henning Melber, '"Namibia, Land of the Brave": Selective Memories on War and Violence within Nation Building' in Abbink *et al.* (eds), *Rethinking Resistance*, pp. 305–27.

27. James Suzman, 'Difference, Domination and "Underdevelopment": Notes on the Marginalisation of Namibia's San Population' in Winterfeldt *et al.* (eds), *Namibia Society Sociology*, pp. 125–35.

28. Martin Boer and Robin Sherbourne, 'Getting the Most our of our Diamonds: Namibia, De Beers and the Arrival of Lev Leviev' (Windhoek, IPPR, Briefing Paper 20, 2003), p. 2; Volker Winterfeldt, 'Liberated Economy: The Case of Ramatex Textiles Namibia' in Melber (ed.), *Transitions*, pp. 65–93; *Namibian*, 7 March 2008, 'Ramatex ups and offs'; Gregor Dobler, 'Old Ties or New Shackles? China in Namibia' in *ibid.*, pp. 94–109; Wolfgang Zeller, 'Danger and Opportunity in Katima Mulilo: A Namibian Border Boomtown at Transnational Crossroads', *JSAS*, 35, 1 (2009), pp. 133–54.

BIBLIOGRAPHY

Unpublished works

Akawa, Martha (2010), 'The Sexual Politics of the Namibian Liberation Struggle' (PhD, University of Basel).

Biwa, Memory (forthcoming 2011), 'Narratives, Commemorations and Historic Sites: The 1903–1908 War in Southern Namibia and the Politics of Memory' (PhD, University of the Western Cape).

Du Bruyn, J. (1981), 'Oorlam Afrikaners: From Dependence to Domination, ca.1760–1832' (unpublished research paper, University of South Africa).

Erichsen, Casper (2004), '"The Angel of Death has Descended Violently among them": A Study of Namibia's Concentration Camps and Prisoners-of-war, 1904–1908' (MA, University of Namibia).

Fuller, Bennet (1993), 'Institutional Appropriation and Social Change among Agropastoralists in Central Namibia, 1916–1988' (PhD, Boston University).

Hartmann, Wolfram (2002), 'Sexual Encounters and their Implications on an Open and Closing Frontier: Central Namibia from the 1840s to 1905' (PhD, Columbia University).

Hayes, Patricia (1992), 'A History of the Ovambo of Namibia, c. 1880–1935' (PhD, University of Cambridge).

Henrichsen, Dag (1997), 'Herrschaft und Identifikation im vorkolonialen Zentralnamibia: Das Herero- und Damaraland im 19. Jahrhundert' (PhD, University of Hamburg).

Henrichsen, Dag (1999), 'Claiming Space and Power in Pre-Colonial Central Namibia: The Relevance of Herero Praise Songs' (Basel: BAB Working Paper 1, BAB).

Hoffmann, Anette (2005), '"Since the Germans Came it Rains Less": Landscape and Identity in Herero Communities of Namibia' (PhD, University of Amsterdam, 2005).

Horsburgh, Katherine (2008), 'The Origins of Southwestern African Pastoralism: Addressing Classic Debates using Ancient DNA' (PhD, Stanford University).

Kangumu, Bennett (2000), 'A Forgotten Corner of Namibia: Aspects of the History of the Caprivi Strip, 1939–1980' (MA, University of Cape Town).

——— (2008), 'Contestations over Caprivi Identities: From Pre-colonial Times to the Present' (PhD, University of Cape Town), now published as *idem* (2010), *Contesting Caprivi: A History of Colonial Isolation and Regional Nationalism in Namibia* (Basel: BAB).

Kinahan, John (2008), 'The Archaeological and Social Dimension of Wild Grass Seed Exploitation in the Namib Desert' (Paper to Third Southern Deserts Conference, Molopo, South Africa).

Lau, Brigitte (1979), 'A Critique of the Historical Sources and Historiography Relating to the "Damaras" in Pre-colonial Namibia' (BA (Honours), University of Cape Town).

McKittrick, Meredith (1995), 'Conflict and Social Change in Northern Namibia, 1850–1954' (PhD, Stanford University).

Miescher, Giorgio (2009), 'Die Rote Linie: Die Geschichte der Veterinär und Siedlungsgrenze in Namibia (1890er bis 1960er Jahre)' (PhD, University of Basel).

Mokopakgosi, Brian (1998), 'German Colonialism in Microcosm: A Study of the Role of the Concessionaire Companies in the Development of the German Colonial State' (PhD, University of London).

Musambachime, M. Chambikabalenshi (1999), '"*Kapitohanga*: The Disease that Killed Faster than Bullets". The Impact of the Influenza Pandemic in the South West Africa Protectorate (Namibia) from October 1918 to December 1919' (BAB Working Paper No. 4, Basel: BAB).

Schürmann, Felix (2008), 'Land zu Territorium? Zur Territorialisierung von Herrschaftsstrategien im südwestlichen Afrika, ca. 1790–1890' (MA, University of Hanover).

Shigwedha, Vilho (forthcoming 2010), 'The Cassinga Massacre and Indescribable Memories' (PhD, University of the Western Cape).

Shiweda, Napandulwe (forthcoming 2010), 'Omhedi: Displacement and Legitimacy in Kwanyama Politics, Namibia, 1915–2007' (PhD, University of the Western Cape).

Simon, David (1983), 'Aspects of Urban Change in Windhoek, Namibia, during the Transition to Independence' (PhD, University of Oxford).

Silvester, Jeremy (1993), 'Black Pastoralists, White Farmers: The Dynamics of Land Dispossession and Labour Recruitment in Southern Namibia' (PhD, University of London).

Smidt, Karen (1995), '"Germania führt die deutsche Frau nach Südwest": Auswanderung, Leben und soziale Konflikte deutscher Frauen in der ehemaligen Kolonie Deutsch-Südwestafrika 1884–1920' (PhD, Otto-von-Guericke Universität Magdeburg).

Solomon, Anne (1989), 'Division of the Earth: Gender, Symbolism and the Archaeology of the Southern San' (MA, University of Cape Town).

van Tonder, Louis (1966), 'The Hambukushu of Okavangoland: An Anthropological Study of A South-Western Bantu People in Africa' (PhD, University of Port Elizabeth).

Wagner, Gunther (1950), 'Ethnographic Survey of the Windhoek District' (unpublished ms, held by NAN).

Wallace, Marion (1994), 'The Process of Urbanisation', paper to Trees Never Meet conference, Windhoek.

Published works

Abbink, Jon Mirjam de Bruijn and Klaas van Walraven (eds) (2003), *Rethinking Resistance: Revolt and Violence in African History* (Leiden: Brill).

Aitken, Robbie (2007), *Exclusion and Inclusion: Gradations of Whiteness and Socio-economic Engineering in German Southwest Africa, 1884–1914* (Berne: Peter Lang).

Akawa, Martha and Jeremy Silvester, 'Their Blood Waters our Freedom. Naming the Dead: Civilian Casualties in the Liberation Struggle', *Namibian*, 24 August 2007.

Albrecht, M. *et al.* (2001), 'Oruwanje 95/1: A Late Holocene Stratigraphy in Northwestern Namibia', *Cimbebasia*, 17, pp. 1–22.

Alexander, John (1838), *An Expedition of Discovery into the Interior of Africa* (2 vols) (London: Henry Colburn).

Alexander, Neville (1988), 'The Namibian War of Anti-colonial Resistance, 1904–7' in Wood (ed.), *Namibia 1884–1984*, pp. 193–204.

Allman, Jean, Susan Geiger and Nakanyike Musisi (eds) (2002), *Women in African Colonial Histories* (Bloomington: Indiana University Press).

Alnaes, Kirsten (1989), 'Living with the Past: The Songs of the Herero in Botswana', *Africa*, 59, pp. 267–99.

L'Ange, Gerald (1991), *Urgent Imperial Service: South African Forces in German South West Africa, 1914–1915* (Rivonia: Ashanti).

Baines, Gary and Peter Vale (eds) (2008), *Beyond the Border War: New Perspectives on Southern Africa's Late-Cold War Conflicts* (n.p.; UNISA Press).

Barnard, Alan (1992), *Hunters and Herders of Southern Africa: A Comparative Ethnography of the Khoisan Peoples* (Cambridge University Press).

Bauer, Gretchen (1998), *Labor and Democracy in Namibia, 1971–1996* (Athens, Ohio: Ohio University Press).

―――― and Scott Taylor (2005), *Politics in Southern Africa: State and Society in Transition* (Boulder, CO: Lynne Riener).

Bayer, Maximilian (1984), *The Rehoboth Baster Nation of Namibia* (Basel: BAB, ed. and trans. Peter Carstens).

Becker, Barbara (ed.) (2005), *Speaking Out: Namibians Share their Perspectives on Independence* (Windhoek: Out of Africa).

Becker, Heike (1995), *Namibian Women's Movement 1980 to 1992: From Anti-colonial Resistance to Reconstruction* (Bonn: Informationsstelle Südliches Afrika).

―――― (2004), '*Efundula*: Women's Initiation, Gender and Sexual Identities in Colonial and Post-colonial Northern Namibia' in Signe Arnfred (ed.), *Rethinking Sexualities in Africa* (Uppsala: Nordic Africa Institute), pp. 35–56.

Beinart, William (1987), '"Jamani": Cape Workers in German South West Africa, 1904–12' in William Beinart and Colin Bundy (eds), *Hidden Struggles in Rural South Africa: Politics and Popular Movements in the Transkei and Eastern Cape, 1890–1930* (London: James Currey), pp. 166–90.

—— (1994), *Twentieth-century South Africa* (Oxford University Press).

—— and Saul Dubow (1995), *Segregation and Apartheid in Twentieth-Century South Africa* (London: Routledge).

Berat, Lynn (1990), *Walvis Bay: Decolonization and International Law* (New Haven: Yale University Press).

Berger, Iris (2003), 'African Women's History: Themes and Perspectives', *Journal of Colonialism and Colonial History*, 4, 1.

Berkovitch, B. (1976), *The Cape Gunsmith* (Stellenbosch: Museum Stellenbosch).

Birch, Gavin (1976), 'Surficial Sediments of Saldanha Bay and Langebaan Lagoon', *Transactions of the Geological Society of South Africa*, 79, pp. 293–300.

Bley, Helmut (1996), *Namibia under German Rule* (Hamburg: Lit; first published as *Kolonialherrschaft und Sozialstruktur in Deutsch-Südwestafrika 1894–1914* (Hamburg: Leibniz, 1968).

Blundell, Geoffrey (ed.) (2005), *Further Approaches to Southern African Rock Art* (Vlaeberg: South African Archaeological Society).

Boer, Martin and Robin Sherbourne (2003), 'Getting the Most out of our Diamonds: Namibia, De Beers and the Arrival of Lev Leviev' (Windhoek: IPPR, Briefing Paper 20).

Bollig, Michael (1977), 'Contested Places: Graves and Graveyards in Himba Culture', *Anthropos*, 92, pp. 35–50.

—— (1997), 'Risk and Risk Minimization among Himba Pastoralists in Northwestern Namibia', *Nomadic Peoples*, 1, pp. 66–87.

Bollig, Michael (ed.) (1997), *'When War Came the Cattle Slept': Himba Oral Traditions* (Cologne: Rüdiger Köppe).

—— (1998), 'Power & Trade in Precolonial and Early Colonial Northern Kaokoveld, 1860s–1940s', in Hayes *et al.*, *Namibia under South African Rule*, pp. 175–93.

—— (1998), 'The Colonial Encapsulation of the North-western Namibian Pastoral Economy', *Africa*, 68, 4, pp. 506–35.

—— (2000), 'Unmaking the Market: The Encapsulation of a Regional Trade Network. North-western Namibia between the 1880s and the 1950s' in Möhlig (ed.), *Frühe Kolonialgeschichte*, pp. 11–29.

—— (2006), 'Success and Failure of CPR Management in an Arid Environment: Access to Pasture, Environment and Political Economy in Northwestern Namibia' in Hartmut Leser (ed.), *The Changing Culture and Nature of Namibia: Case Studies* (Basel: BAB), pp. 37–68.

—— and Jan-Bart Gewald (eds) (2000), *People, Cattle and Land: Transformations of a Pastoral Society in Southwestern Africa* (Cologne: Rüdiger Köppe).

Bollig, Michael and Jan-Bart Gewald (eds) (2000), 'People, Cattle and Land—Transformations of a Pastoral Society' in idem, *People, Cattle and Land*, pp. 3–52.

Booh Booh, Jacques-Roger (1982), *La décolonisation de la Namibie: un mandat usurpé* (Paris: Les Publications Universitaires).

Botha, Christo (2000), 'The Politics of Land Settlement in Namibia, 1890–1960', *SAHJ*, 42, pp. 232–75.

——— (2007), 'Internal Colonisation and an Oppressed Minority? The Dynamics of Relations between Germans and Afrikaners against the Background of Constructing a Colonial State in Namibia, 1884–1990', *JNS*, 2, pp. 7–50.

Bowman, Sheridan (1990), *Radiocarbon Dating* (London: British Museum).

Bradford, Helen (1996), 'Women, Gender and Colonialism: Rethinking the History of the British Cape Colony and its Frontier Zones, c. 1806–70', *JAH*, 37, pp. 351–70.

Bradlow, Barbara (1981), 'The Significance of Arms and Ammunition on the Cape's Northern Frontier at the Turn of the Eighteenth Century', *Historia*, 1, pp. 59–68.

Breytenbach, Jan (2002), *The Buffalo Soldiers: The Story of South Africa's 32-Battalion, 1975–1993* (Alberton: Galago).

Breuil, Henri (1948), 'The White Lady of the Brandberg, SWA, her Companions and her Guards', *South African Archaeological Bulletin*, 3, pp. 2–11.

Bridgman, Jon (1981), *The Revolt of the Hereros* (Berkeley: University of California Press).

Brinkman, Inge and Axel Fleisch (eds) (1999), *Grandmother's Footsteps: Oral Tradition and South-east Angolan Narratives on the Colonial Encounter* (Cologne: Rüdiger Koppe).

Brown, Susan (1995), 'Diplomacy By Other Means: SWAPO's Liberation War' in Leys and Saul (eds), *Namibia's Liberation Struggle*, pp. 19–39.

Bruchmann, Rainer (2000), *Caprivi: An African Flashpoint. An Illustrated History of Namibia's Tropical Region Where Four Countries Meet* (Northcliff: Rainer Bruchmann).

Bruwer, J.J. (1985), *Aus 1915–1919: Errichtung, Bestehen und Schließung des Kriegsgefangenenlagers bei Aus* (Windhoek: Historic Monuments Commission).

Budack, Kuno (1977), 'The Aonin, or Topnaar, of the Lower !Khuiseb Valley and the Sea', *Khoisan Linguistic Studies*, 3, pp. 1–42.

Budack, K.F.R. (1979), 'Weibliche Häuptlinge bei den Khoe-khoen (Nama und Oorlam)', *Namibiana*, 1, 2, pp. 7–14.

Bühler, Andreas (2003), *Der Namaaufstand gegen die deutsche Kolonialherrschaft in Namibia von 1904–1913* (Frankfurt: IKO).

Cape of Good Hope (1877), *Report of W. Coates Palgrave, Special Commissioner to the Tribes North of the Orange River, of His Mission to Damaraland and Great Namaqualand in 1876* (Cape Town).

Carow, Richard (1898), *Die kaiserliche Schutztruppe in Deutsch-Südwest-Afrika unter Major Leutwein* (Leipzig: Freund and Wittig).

Carstens, Peter (1983), 'Opting out of Colonial Rule: The Brown Voortrekkers of South Africa and their Constitutions', part one, *African Studies*, 42, 2, pp. 135–52.

―――― (1984), 'Opting out of Colonial Rule: The Brown Voortrekkers of South Africa and their Constitutions', part two, *African Studies*, 43, 1 (1984), pp. 19–30.

Challis, William (2005), '"The Men with Rhebok's Heads: They Tame Elands and Snakes": Incorporating the Rhebok Antelope in the Understanding of Southern African Rock Art' in Blundell (ed.), *Further Approaches*, pp. 11–20.

Chanock, Martin (1977), *Unconsummated Union: Britain, Rhodesia and South Africa, 1900–45* (Manchester University Press).

Clarence-Smith, W.G. (1979), *Slaves, Peasants and Capitalists in Angola 1840–1926* (Cambridge University Press).

Cleaver, Tessa and Marion Wallace (1990), *Namibia: Women in War* (London: Zed).

Cliffe, Lionel *et al.* (1994), *The Transition to Independence in Namibia* (Boulder: Lynne Rienner).

Cohen, Cynthia (1994), *Administering Education in Namibia: The Colonial Period to the Present* (Windhoek: Namibia Scientific Society).

Comaroff, Jean and John Comaroff (1991), *Of Revelation and Revolution: Christianity*, vol. 1, *Colonialism and Consciousness in South Africa* (University of Chicago Press).

―――― (1997), *Of Revelation and Revolution: Christianity*, vol. 2, *The Dialectics of Modernity on a South African Frontier* (University of Chicago Press).

Compton, John (2007), 'Holocene Evolution of the Anichab Pan on the South-west Coast of Namibia', *Sedimentology*, 54, pp. 55–70.

Constitution of the Republic of Namibia Adopted by the Constituent Assembly in Windhoek, Namibia on 9ᵗʰ February 1990.

Cooper, Allan (1982), *US Economic Power and Political Influence in Namibia, 1750–1982* (Boulder: Westview).

―――― (1991), *The Occupation of Namibia: Afrikanerdom's Attack on the British Empire* (Lanham: University Press of America).

―――― (1999), 'The Institutionalization of Contract Labour in Namibia', *JSAS*, 25, 1, pp. 121–38.

Corvinus, Gudrun (1983), *The Raised Beaches of the West Coast of South West Africa/Namibia: An Interpretation of their Archaeological and Palaeontological Data* (Munich: C.H. Beck).

Coulson, David and Alec C. Campbell (2001), *African Rock Art: Paintings and Engravings on Stone* (New York: Abrams).

Cruz-Uribe, Katharine and Richard Klein (1983), 'Faunal Remains from Some Middle and Late Stone Age Sites in South West Africa', *JSWASS*, 36/37, pp. 91–114.

Damman, Ernst (ed.) (1983), *Herero-Texte erzählt von Pastor Andreas Kukuri* (Berlin: Dietrich Reimer).

Davies, J.E. (2007), *Constructive Engagement? Chester Crocker and American Policy in South Africa, Namibia and Angola, 1981–8* (Oxford: James Currey).

Deacon, Jeanette (1984), *The Later Stone Age of Southernmost Africa* (Oxford: British Archaeological Reports).

—— and Nicholas Lancaster (1988), *Late Quaternary Palaeoenvironments of Southern Africa* (Oxford: Clarendon).

Dedering, Tilman (1988), 'Review Article: Problems of Precolonial Namibian Historiography', *SAHJ*, 20, pp. 95–104.

—— (1993), 'The German-Herero War of 1904: Revisionism of Genocide or Imaginary Historiography?' *JSAS*, 19, 1, pp. 80–8.

—— (1993), 'Hendrik Witbooi, the Prophet', *Kleio*, 25, 54–78.

—— (1997), *Hate the Old and Follow the New: Khoekhoe and Missionaries in Early Nineteenth Century Namibia* (Stuttgart: Franz Steiner).

—— (1999), '"A Certain Rigorous Treatment of All Parts of the Nation": The Annihilation of the Herero in German South West Africa, 1904' in Mark Levene and Penny Roberts (eds), *The Massacre in History* (Oxford: Berghahn Books), pp. 205–22.

—— (1999), 'The Prophet's "War against Whites": Shepherd Stuurman in Namibia and South Africa, 1904–7', *JAH*, 40, pp. 1–19.

—— (2000), 'The Ferreira Raid of 1906: Boers, Britons and Germans in Southern Africa in the Aftermath of the South African War', *JSAS*, 26 (1), pp. 43–60.

—— (2006), 'War and Mobility in the Borderlands of Southwestern Africa in the Early Twentieth Century', *International Journal of African Historical Studies*, 39, 2, pp. 275–94.

De Gruchy, John (ed.) (1999), *The London Missionary Society in Southern Africa* (Cape Town: David Philip).

Dekker, Peter and Cornelis de Jong (1998), 'Whaling Expeditions of the West India Company to Walvis Bay', *Namibia Scientific Society Journal*, 46, pp. 47–63.

Deutsches Kolonialblatt.

David Deutschmann (ed.), *Changing the History of Africa: Angola and Namibia* (Melbourne, Vic.: Occan, 1989).

Dieckmann, Ute (2007), *Hai∥Om in the Etosha Region: A History of Colonial Settlement, Ethnicity and Nature Conservation* (Basel: BAB).

Dierks, Klaus (2002), *Chronology of Namibian History: From Pre-historical Times to Independent Namibia* (Windhoek: Namibia Scientific Society).

Diouf, Mamadou (2002), *Historians and Histories, What For? African Historiography between the State and the Communities* (Amsterdam: SEPHIS-CSSSC).

Dobell, Lauren (1997), 'Review Article: Silence in Context. Truth and/or Reconciliation in Namibia', *JSAS*, 23, 2, pp. 371–82.

——— (1998), *Swapo's Struggle for Namibia, 1960–1991: War by other Means* (Basel: P. Schlettwein).

Dobler, Gregor (2007), 'Old Ties or New Shackles? China in Namibia' in Melber, *Transitions*, pp. 94–109.

——— (2008), 'Boundary Drawing and the Notion of Territoriality in Pre-Colonial and Early Colonial Ovamboland', *JNS*, 3, pp. 7–30.

Dooling, Wayne (2007), *Slavery, Emancipation and Colonial Rule in South Africa* (Scotsville: University of KwaZulu-Natal Press).

Dowson, Thomas (1994), 'Reading Art, Writing History: Rock Art and Social Change in Southern Africa', *World Archaeology*, 25, pp. 332–44.

Drechsler, Horst (1966), *'Let Us Die Fighting': The Struggle of the Herero and Nama against German Imperialism, 1884–1915* (Berlin: Akademie).

Dreyer, Ronald (1987), *The Mind of Official Imperialism: British and Cape Government Perceptions of German Rule in Namibia from the Heligoland–Zanzibar Treaty to the Kruger Telegram (1890–1896)* (Essen: Hobbing).

Du Pisani, Andre (1986), *South West Africa/Namibia: The Politics of Continuity and Change* (Johannesburg: Jonathan Ball).

——— (1989), 'Beyond the Transgariep: South Africa in Namibia, 1915–89', *Politikon*, 16, 1, pp. 26–43.

Eades, Lindsay (1999), *The End of Apartheid in South Africa* (Westport, Conn.: Greenwood).

Eberhardt, Martin (2007), *Zwischen Nationalismus und Apartheid: Die deutsche Bevölkerungsgruppe Südwestafrikas 1915–1965* (Münster: Lit).

Eckart, Wolfgang (1995), 'Medizin und kolonialer Krieg: Die Niederschlagung der Herero-Nama-Erhebung im Schutzgebiet Deutsch-Südwestafrika, 1904–1907' in Heine and Heyden (eds), *Studien*, pp. 220–35.

Eckl, Andreas (2000), 'Mit Kreuz, Gewehr und Handelskarre: der Kavango 1903 im deutschen Fokus' in Möhlig (ed.), *Frühe Kolonialgeschichte*, pp. 31–75.

——— (2004), *Herrschaft, Macht und Einfluss: Koloniale Interaktionen am Kavango (Nord-Namibia) von 1891 bis 1921* (Cologne: Rüdiger Köppe).

——— (2004), 'Serving the Kavango Sovereigns' Political Interests: The Beginnings of the Catholic Mission in Northern Namibia', *Le Fait Missionaire*, 14, pp. 9–46.

——— (2007), 'Reports from "Beyond the Line": The Accumulation of Knowledge of Kavango and its Peoples by the German Colonial Administration, 1891–1911', *JNS*, 1, pp. 7–37.

——— (2008), 'The Herero Genocide of 1904: Source-critical and Methodological Considerations', *JNS*, 3, pp. 31–61.

Ehret, Christopher (1982), 'The First Spread of Food Production in Southern Africa' in Christopher Ehret and Merrick Posnansky (eds), *The Archaeological and Linguistic Reconstruction of African History* (Berkeley: University of California Press).

Eichorn, Barbara and Ralf Vogelsang (2007), 'A Pristine Landscape? Archaeological and Archaeobotanical Research in the Skeleton Coast Park, Northwestern Namibia' in Michael Bollig *et al.* (eds), *Aridity, Change and Conflict in Africa* (Cologne: Heinrich Barth Institut), pp. 145–65.

Eirola, Martii (1992), *The* Ovambogefahr: *The Ovamboland Reservation in the Making. Political Responses of the Kingdom of Ondonga to the German Colonial Power 1884–1910* (Rovaniemi: Historical Association of Northern Finland).

Eitel, Bernt (2005), 'Environmental History of the Namib Desert' in Mike Smith and Paul Hesse (eds), *23 Degrees South: Archaeology and Environmental History of the Southern Deserts* (Canberra: National Museum of Australia), pp. 45–55.

Elago, Hileni (1997), 'Ovambo Men's Experiences of Participation in the Second World War (1939–1945)' in Hartmann (ed.), *New Historical Writing*, pp. 20–3.

Ellis, Justin (1984), *Education, Repression and Liberation: Namibia* (London: World University Service).

Elphick, Richard (1985), *Khoikhoi and the Founding of White South Africa* (Johannesburg: Ravan).

Emmett, Tony (1999), *Popular Resistance and the Roots of Nationalism in Namibia, 1915–1966* (Basel: P. Schlettwein).

Engel, Lothar (1976), *Kolonialismus und Nationalismus im deutschen Protestantismus in Namibia 1907 bis 1945* (Berne: Herbert Lang).

Epprecht, Marc (2000), *'This Matter of the Women is Getting Very Bad': Gender, Development and Politics in Colonial Lesotho* (Pietermaritzburg: University of Natal Press).

Erichsen, Casper (2005), *'The Angel of Death has Descended Violently Among Them': Concentration Camps and Prisoners-of-war in Namibia, 1904–1908* (Leiden: African Studies Centre).

——— (2008), *'What the Elders Used to Say': Namibian Perspectives on the Last Decade of German Colonial Rule* (Windhoek: Namibia Institute for Democracy).

Eriksen, Tore Linné (ed.) (1999), *Norway and National Liberation in Southern Africa* (Uppsala: Nordic Institute of African Studies).

Eriksen, Tore Linné with Richard Moorsom (1985), *The Political Economy of Namibia: An Annotated Critical Bibliography* (Oslo: Norwegian Institute of International Affairs).

Ervedosa, Carlos (1980), *Arqueologia Angolana* (Lisbon: Ministério da Educação, República Popular de Angola).

Esterhuyse, J.H. (1968), *South West Africa 1880–1894: The Establishment of German Authority in South West Africa* (Cape Town: C. Struik).

Etherington, Norman (2001), *The Great Treks: The Transformation of Southern Africa, 1815–1854* (Harlow: Longman).

Estorff, Ludwig von (1911), *Kriegserlebnisse in Südwestafrika* (Berlin: Ernst Siegfried Mittler).

——— (1968), *Wanderungen und Kämpfe in Südwestafrika, Ostafrika und Südafrika 1904–1910* (Wiesbaden: privately pub.).

Farson, Negley (1940), *Behind God's Back* (London: Victor Gollancz).

Fauvell-Aymar, Francois-Xavier and Karim Sadr (2008), 'Trends and Traps in the Reconstruction of Early Herding Societies in Southern Africa', *Southern African Humanities*, 20, pp. 1–6.

First, Ruth (1963), *South West Africa* (Harmondsworth: Penguin).

Fisch, Maria (1999), *The Caprivi Strip during the German Colonial Period, 1890 to 1914* (Windhoek: Out of Africa).

—— (2007), 'The Tawana's Military Campaign in the Kavango', *JNSS*, 55, pp. 109–31.

Fischer, Adolf (1914), *Menschen und Tiere in Deutsch-Südwest* (Stuttgart: Deutsche Verlagsanstalt).

Fleisch, Axel and Wilhelm Möhlig (2002), *The Kavango Peoples in the Past: Local Historiographies from Northern Namibia* (Cologne: Rüdiger Köppe).

Flemming, B.W. (1977), 'Distribution of Recent Sediments in Saldanha Bay and Langebaan Lagoon', *Transactions of the Royal Society of South Africa*, 42, 3 & 4, pp. 317–40.

Flint, Eric (1970), 'Trade and Politics in Barotseland during the Kololo Period', *JAH*, 11, 1, pp. 71–86.

Flint, Lawrence (2003), 'State-building in Central Southern Africa: Citizenship and Subjectivity in Barotseland and Caprivi', *International Journal of African Historical Studies*, 36, 2, pp. 393–428.

Förster, Larissa (2004), 'Zwischen Waterberg und Okakarara: namibische Errinerungslandschaften' in Förster *et al.* (eds), *Namibia–Deutschland*, pp. 164–79.

—— (2005), 'Land and Landscape in Herero Oral Culture: Cultural and Social Aspects of the Land Question in Namibia', *Analyses and Views*, 1.

Förster, Larissa, Dag Henrichsen and Michael Bollig (eds) (2004), *Namibia–Deutschland: Eine geteilte Geschichte* (Cologne: Rautenstrauch-Jöst Museum für Völkerkunde).

Frayne, Bruce (1992), *Urbanisation in Post-independence Windhoek* (Windhoek: Namibian Institute for Social and Economic Research).

Freundlich, J.C., H. Schwabedissen and W. Wendt (1980), 'Köln Radiocarbon Measurements II', *Radiocarbon*, 22, 1, pp. 68–81.

Friedman, John (2005), 'Making Politics, Making History: Chiefship and the Post-apartheid State in Namibia', *JSAS*, 31, 1, pp. 23–51.

Fuller, Ben (1998), '"We Live in a *Manga*": Constraint, Resistance and Transformation on a Native Reserve' in Hayes *et al.*, *Namibia under South African Rule*, pp. 194–216.

Gann, L.H. and Peter Duignan (1977), *The Rulers of German Africa, 1884–1914* (Stanford, Calif.: Stanford University Press).

Gaseb, Ivan (1999), 'A Historical Hangover: The Absence of Damara from Accounts of the 1904–08 War' in Hartmann (ed.), *More New Historical Writing in Namibia* (Windhoek: Namibia History Trust), pp. 5–20.

BIBLIOGRAPHY

Gewald, Jan-Bart (1999), *Herero Heroes: A Socio-Political History of the Herero of Namibia, 1890–1923* (London: James Currey).

—— (1999), 'The Road of the Man called Love and the Sack of Sero: the Herero–German War and the export of Herero Labour to the South African Rand', *JAH*, 40, pp. 21–40.

—— (2000), *'We Thought We Would Be Free': Socio-cultural Aspects of Herero History in Namibia, 1915–1940* (Cologne: Rüdiger Köppe).

—— (2002), '"I was afraid of Samuel, therefore I came to Sekgoma": Herero Refugees and Patronage Politics in Ngamiland, Bechuanaland Protectorate, 1890–1914', *JAH*, 43, pp. 211–34.

—— (2003), 'Near Death in the Streets of Karibib: Famine, Migrant Labour and the Coming of Ovambo to Central Namibia', *JAH*, 44, pp. 211–39.

—— (2004), 'Who Killed Clemens Kapuuo?', *JSAS*, 30, 3, pp. 559–76.

—— (2007), 'Chief Hosea Kutako: A Herero Royal and Namibian Nationalist's Life against Confinement 1870–1970' in Miriam de Bruijn, Rijk van Dijk and Jan-Bart Gewald (eds), *Strength Beyond Structure: Social and Historical Trajectories of Agency in Africa* (Leiden: Brill), pp. 83–113.

Gibson, Gordon, Thomas Larson and Cecilia McGurk (1981), *The Kavango Peoples* (Wiesbaden: Steiner).

—— and Cecilia McGurk (1981), 'The Kwangari' in Gibson *et al.*, *Kavango Peoples*, pp. 35–79.

Gifford, Prosser and Wm Roger Louis (1967), *Britain and Germany in Africa: Imperial Rivalry and Colonial Rule* (New Haven: Yale University Press).

Gockel, Martina (2000), 'Diversifizierung und politische Ökonomie der Damara im 19. Jahrhundert', in Möhlig (ed.), *Frühe Kolonialgeschichte*, pp. 97–135.

Goldblatt, Israel (1971), *History of South West Africa from the Beginning of the Nineteenth Century* (Cape Town: Juta).

Gordon, Robert (1975), 'A Note on the History of Labour Action in Namibia', *South African Labour Bulletin*, 1, pp. 7–17.

—— (1977), *Mines, Masters and Migrants: Life in a Namibian Mine Compound* (Johannesburg: Ravan).

—— (1991), 'Marginalia on "Grensliteratur": Or how/why is Terror Culturally Constructed in Namibia?', *Critical Arts*, 5, 3, pp. 79–99.

—— (1993), 'The Impact of the Second World War on Namibia', *JSAS*, 19, 1, pp. 147–65.

—— (1997), *Picturing Bushmen: The Denver Expedition of 1925* (Athens, Ohio: Ohio University Press).

—— (1998), 'Backdrops and Bushmen: An Expeditious Comment' in Hartmann *et al.* (eds), *Colonising Camera*, pp. 111–17.

—— (1998), 'Vagrancy, Law and "Shadow Knowledge": Internal Pacification, 1915–1939' in Hayes *et al.*, *Namibia under South African Rule*, pp. 51–76.

—— (2005), 'The Making of Modern Namibia: A Tale of Anthropological Ineptitude?', *Kleio*, 37, pp. 26–49.

—— and Stuart Sholto-Douglas (2000), *The Bushman Myth: The Making of a Namibian Underclass* 2nd ed., (Boulder: Westview).

Green, Reginald and Kimmo Kiljunen (1981), 'The Colonial Economy: Structures of Growth and Exploitation' in Reginald Green, Kimmo Kiljunen and Marja-Liisa Kiljunen (eds), *Namibia: The Last Colony* (Harlow: Longman), pp. 30–58.

Gronemeyer, Reimer and Matthias Rompel (eds) (2003), *Today It's Your Family, Tomorrow It's You: Essays by Young Namibians on the Social Impact of HIV and AIDS* (Windhoek: Gamsberg Macmillan).

Groth, Siegfried (1995), *Namibia: The Wall of Silence. The Dark Days of Liberation* (Wuppertal: Peter Hammer).

Guenther, Mathias (1975), 'The Trance Dancer as an Agent of Social Change among the Farm Bushmen of the Ghanzi District', *Botswana Notes and Records*, 7, pp. 161–6.

Gugelberger, George (1984), *Nama/Namibia: Diary and Letters of Nama Chief Hendrik Witbooi, 1884–1894* (Boston University African Studies Centre).

Gustafsson, Kalle (2005), 'The Trade in Slaves in Ovamboland, *ca.* 1850–1910', *African Economic History*, 33, pp. 31–68.

Haacke, Wilfred, Eliphas Eiseb and Levi Namaseb (1997), 'Internal and External Relations of Khoe-Khoe Dialects: A Preliminary Survey' in Wilfred Haacke and Edward Elderkin (eds), *Namibian Languages: Reports and Papers* (Cologne: Rüdiger Koppe), pp. 125–209.

Hahn, Carl Hugo (1984–85), *Tagebücher 1837–1860. Diaries: A Missionary in Damaraland*, ed. Brigitte Lau (Windhoek: Archives Service Division).

Hahn, C.H.L., Louis Fourie and Heinrich Vedder (1928), *The Native Tribes of South West Africa* (Cape Town: Cape Times).

Hall, Martin (1984), 'Frontiers in Southern African Archaeology' in Martin Hall *et al.* (eds), *Frontiers: Southern African Archaeology Today* (Oxford: British Archaeological Reports), pp. 1–11.

—— (1996), *Archaeology Africa* (London: James Currey).

Harlech-Jones, Brian (1997), *A New Thing? The Namibian Independence Process, 1989–1990* (Windhoek: EIN Publications).

Harneit-Sievers, Axel (1985), *SWAPO of Namibia: Entwicklung, Programmatik und Politik seit 1959* (Hamburg: Institut fur Afrika-Kunde).

Harris, Verne (2007), *Archives and Justice: A South African Perspective* (Chicago: Society of American Archivists).

Hartmann, B. (1985/86–1985/87), 'Die Tjaube, eine Vorbevölkerung im Kavangogebiet', *JSWASS*, 40/41, pp. 75–95.

Hartmann, Wolfram (1998), '"Ondillimani!" Iipumbu ya Tshilongo and the Ambiguities of Resistance in Ovambo' in Hayes *et al.*, *Namibia under South African Rule*, pp. 263–88.

—— (ed.) (1997), *New Historical Writing in Namibia: Three Research Papers* (Windhoek: Namibia History Trust).

—— (ed.) (1999), *More New Historical Writing from Namibia* (Windhoek: Namibia History Trust).

—— (ed.) (2004), *Hues Between Black and White: Historical Photography from Colonial Namibia 1860s to 1915* (Windhoek: Out of Africa).

—— (2007), 'Urges in the Colony: Men and Women in Colonial Windhoek, 1890–1905', *JNS*, 1, pp. 39–71.

—— Jeremy Silvester and Patricia Hayes (eds) (1998), *The Colonising Camera: Photographs in the Making of Namibian History* (Basel: BAB).

Hayes, Patricia (1997), '"Cocky" Hahn and the "Black Venus": The Making of a Native Commissioner in South West Africa, 1915–46' in Hunt *et al.* (eds), *Gendered Colonialisms*, pp. 42–70.

—— (1998), 'The Famine of the Dams: Gender, Labour and Politics in Colonial Ovamboland' in Hayes *et al.*, *Namibia under South African Rule*, pp. 117–46.

—— (1998), 'Northern Exposures: The Photography of C.H.L. Hahn, Native Commissioner of Ovamboland 1915–1946', in Hartmann *et al.* (eds), *Colonising Camera*, pp. 171–87.

—— (2006), '*Efundula* and History: Female Initiation in Precolonial and Colonial Northern Namibia' in Tominaga Chizuko and Nagahara Yoko (eds), *Towards New Perspectives of African History: Women, Gender and Feminisms* (Osaka: Museum of Ethnology Japan).

—— (2009), 'A Land of Goshen: Landscape and Kingdom in Nineteenth Century Eastern Owambo (Namibia)' in M. Bollig and O. Bubenzer (eds), *African Landscapes* (New York: Springer).

—— (2009), 'When You Shake a Tree: The Precolonial and the Postcolonial in Northern Namibian History' in Derek Petersen and Giacomo Macola (eds), *Recasting the Past* (Athens, Ohio: Ohio University Press).

—— and Dan Haipinge (eds) (1997), *'Healing the land': Kaulinge's History of Kwanyama. Oral Tradition and History by the late Reverend Vilho Kaulinge of Ondobe as told to Patricia Hayes and Natangwe Shapange* (Cologne: Rüdiger Köppe).

Hayes, Patricia, Jeremy Silvester, Marion Wallace and Wolfram Hartmann (eds) (1998), *Namibia under South African Rule: Mobility and Containment, 1915–46* (London: James Currey).

Hayes, Patricia, Jeremy Silvester and Wolfram Hartmann (2002), '"Picturing the Past" in Namibia: The Visual Archive and its Energies' in Carolyn Hamilton *et al.* (eds), *Refiguring the Archive* (Dordrecht: Kluwer Academic), pp. 102–33.

Heine, Peter and Ulrich van der Heyden (eds) (1995), *Studien zur Geschichte des deutschen Kolonialismus in Afrika* (Pfaffenweiler: Centaurus, 1995).

Helbig, Ludwig and Werner Hillebrecht (1992), *The Witbooi* (Windhoek: CASS and Longman Namibia).

Henderson, W.O. (1993), *The German Colonial Empire, 1884–1919* (London: Frank Cass).

Hendrickson, Hildi (1994), 'The "London Dress" and the Construction of Herero Identities in Southern Africa', *African Studies*, 53, 2, pp. 25–54.

Henrichsen, Dag (2000), '*Ozongombe, Omavita* and *Ozondjembo*—The Process of (Re-)Pastoralization amongst Herero in Pre-colonial 19th Century Namibia' in Michael Bollig and Jan-Bart Gewald (eds), *People, Cattle and Land*, pp. 149–86.

———— (2003), 'Heirat im Krieg: Erfahrungen von Kaera Ida Getzen-Leinhos' in Zimmerer and Zeller (eds), *Völkermord*, pp. 160–8.

———— (2004), '*Ozombambuse* and *Ovasolondate*: Everyday Military Life and African Service Personnel in German South West Africa' in Hartmann (ed.), *Hues*, pp. 161–84.

———— (2008), '"Damara" Labour Recruitment to the Cape Colony and Marginalisation and Hegemony in Late Nineteenth Century Namibia', *JNS*, 3, pp. 63–82.

———— (2009), '"…Unerwuenscht im Schutzgebiet…nicht schlechtin unsittlich": "Mischehen" und deren Nachkommen im Visier der Kolonialverwaltung in Deutsch-Südwestafrika' in Marianne Bechhaus-Gerst and Mechthild Leutner (eds), *Frauen in den deutschen Kolonien* (Berlin: Links), pp. 80–90.

———— (2010), 'Pastoral Modernity, Territoriality and Colonial Transformations in Central Namibia, 1860s to 1904' in Peter Limb, Peter Midgley and Norman Etherington (eds), *Grappling with the Beast: Indigenous Southern African Responses to Colonialism, 1840–1930* (Leiden: Brill).

Henrichsen, Dag (ed.) (1997), *A Glance at Our Africa: Facsimile Reprint of: South West News, the Only Non-racial Newspaper in the Territory, 1960* (Basel: BAB).

Henshaw, Peter (2004), 'South African Territorial Expansion and International Reaction to South African Racial Policies, 1939 to 1948', *SAHJ*, 50, pp. 65–76.

Henshilwood, Christopher (2002), 'Emergence of Modern Human Behaviour: Middle Stone Age Engravings from South Africa', *Science*, 295, pp. 1278–80.

Herbert, Eugenia (2002), *Twilight on the Zambezi: Late Colonialism in Central Africa* (Basingstoke: Palgrave).

Herbstein, Denis and John Evenson (1989), *The Devils are Among Us: The War for Namibia* (London: Zed).

Heuva, William (2003), 'Voices in the Liberation Struggle: Discourse and Ideology in the SWAPO Exile Media' in Melber (ed.), *Re-examining Liberation*, pp. 25–33.

Heywood, Annemarie (1994), *The Cassinga Event: An Investigation of the Records* (Windhoek: National Archives of Namibia).

———— Brigitte Lau and Raimund Ohly (eds) (1992), *Warriors Leaders Sages and Outcasts in the Namibian Past: Narratives Collected from Herero Sources for the MSORP Project 1985–6* (Windhoek: Michael Scott Oral Records Project).

Heywood, Annemarie and Brigitte Lau (1993), *Three Views into the Past of Windhoek* (Windhoek: n. p.).

Hillebrecht, Werner (2003), 'Die Nama und der Krieg im Süden' in Zimmerer and Zeller (eds), *Völkermord*, pp. 121–33.

—— (2007), '"Certain Uncertainties": Or Venturing Progressively into Colonial Apologetics?', *JNS*, 1, pp. 73–96.

Hoernlé, Winifred, ed. Peter Carstens (1985), *The Social Organization of the Nama and Other Essays* (Johannesburg: Witwatersrand University Press).

Holleman, Jeremy (2001), '"Big Pictures": Insights into Southern African San Rock Paintings of Ostriches', *South African Archaeological Bulletin*, 56, pp. 62–75.

Hopwood, Graham (2007), *Guide to Namibian Politics* (Windhoek: Namibia Institute for Democracy).

Horrell, Muriel (1967), *South West Africa* (Johannesburg: South African Institute of Race Relations).

Hubbard, Dianne (2007), 'Gender and Sexuality: The Law Reform Landscape' in LaFont and Hubbard (eds), *Unravelling Taboos*, pp. 99–128.

—— (2007), 'Ideas about Equality in Namibian Law' in Melber (ed.), *Transitions*, pp. 209–29.

Huber, Hansjörg (1999), *Koloniale Selbstverwaltung in Deutsch-Südwestafrika* (Frankfurt: Peter Lang).

Huffman, Thomas (2007), *Handbook to the Iron Age: The Archaeology of Pre-colonial Farming Societies in Southern Africa* (Pietermaritzburg: University of KwaZulu-Natal Press).

Hull, Isabel (2006), *Absolute Destruction: Military Culture and the Practices of War in Imperial Germany* (Ithaca: Cornell University Press).

Hunt, Nancy Rose (1997), 'Introduction', in Nancy Rose Hunt, Tessie Liu and Jean Quataert (eds), *Gendered Colonialisms*.

—— Tessie Liu and Jean Quataert (eds) (1997), *Gendered Colonialisms in African History* (Oxford: Blackwell).

Hunter, Gustine [*sic*—i.e. Justine] (2008), *Die Politik der Erinnerung und des Vergessens in Namibia: Umgang mit schweren Menschenrechtsverletzungen der Ära des bewaffneten Befreiungskampfes 1966 bis 1989* (Frankfurt: Peter Lang).

—— (2008), 'No Man's Land of Time: Reflections on the Politics of Memory and Forgetting in Namibia' in Gary Baines and Peter Vale (eds), *Beyond the Border War*, pp. 302–21.

Iken, Adelheid (1999), *Woman-headed Households in Southern Namibia: Causes, Patterns and Consequences* (Frankfurt: IKO).

Innes, Duncan (1984), *Anglo American and the Rise of Modern South Africa* (New York: Monthly Review Press).

Inskeep, Adi (2003), *Heinrich Vedder's The Bergdama: An Annotated Translation of the German Original with Additional Ethnographic Material by Adi Inskeep* (Cologne: Rüdiger Köppe).

Irle, Jakob (1906), *Die Herero: Ein Beitrag zur Landes-, Volks und Mission-skunde* (Gütersloh: C. Bertelsmann).

Jacobs, Zenobia *et al.* (2008), 'Ages for the Middle Stone Age of Southern Africa: Implications for Human Behaviour and Dispersal', *Science*, 322, pp. 733–5.

Jacobson, Leon (1980), 'On Artefact Analysis and the Reconstruction of Past Ethnic Groups', *Current Anthropology*, 21, p. 409.

——— (1980), 'The White Lady of the Brandberg, a Re-interpretation', *Namibiana*, 2, pp. 21–9.

Jafta, Milly, Nicky Kautja, Magda Oliphant, Dawn Ridgway, Kapofi Shipin-gana, Ussiel Tjijenda and Gerson Veii (1999), *An Investigation of the Shooting at the Old Location on 10 December 1959*, (ed.) Brigitte Lau, 2nd ed. (Windhoek: Namibian History Trust).

Jauch, Herbert (2007), 'Between Politics and Shop Floor: Which Way for Namibia's Labour Movement?' in Melber, *Transitions*, pp. 50–64.

Jenny, Hans (1976), *South West Africa: Land of Extremes* (Windhoek: South West Africa Scientific Society).

Jewkes, Rachel, Hetty Rose-Junius and Loveday Penn-Kekana (2007), 'The Social Context of Child Rape in Namibia' in Lafont and Hubbard (eds), *Unravelling Taboos*, pp. 167–80.

Johannson, Peter (2007), *The Trader King of Damaraland: Axel Eriksson. A Swedish Pioneer in South Africa* (Windhoek: Gamsberg Macmillan).

Kaakunga, Elia (1990), *Problems of Capitalist Development in Namibia: The Dialectics of Progress and Destruction* (Turku: Abo Akademi).

Kaputu, A. (1992), 'Mbaha' in Heywood *et al.* (eds), *Warriors Leaders Sages and Outcasts*, pp. 84–96.

——— (1992), 'The War Between the Nama and Herero' in *ibid.*, pp. 1–49.

Katjavivi, Peter (1988), *A History of Resistance in Namibia* (London: James Currey).

——— (1989), 'The Role of the Church in the Struggle for Independence' in *idem et al.* (eds), *Church and Liberation*, pp. 3–26.

——— Per Frostin and Kaire Mbuende (eds) (1989), *Church and Liberation in Namibia* (London: Pluto).

Kaulich, Udo (2000), *Die Geschichte der ehemaligen Kolonie Deutsch-Süd-westafrika (1884–1914): Eine Gesamtdarstellung* (Frankfurt: Peter Lang).

Kayongo, Kabunda (1987), *Reciprocity and Interdependence: The Rise and Fall of the Kololo Empire in Southern Africa in the Nineteenth Century* (n.p.: Almqvist & Wiksell International).

Kenna, Constance (ed.) (1999), *Homecoming: The GDR Kids of Namibia* (Windhoek: New Namibia Books).

Kerina, Mburumba (1981), *Namibia: The Making of a Nation* (New York: Books in Focus).

Kiel, Rainer-Maria (2005), 'Der Hereroaufstand in Deutsch-Südwestafrika: Zeitgenössische Originalfotografien als Leihgabe des Historischen Vereins für Oberfranken in der Universitätsbibliothek Bayreuth', *Archiv für Geschichte von Oberfranken*, 85, pp. 267–78.

Kienetz, Alvin (1977), 'The Key Role of the Orlam Migrations in the Early Europeanization of South-West Africa (Namibia)', *International Journal of African Historical Studies*, 10, 4, pp. 553–72.

Kinahan, Jill (1989), 'Heinrich Vedder's Sources for his Account of the Exploration of the Namib Coast', *Cimbebasia*, 11, pp. 33–9.

———— (1990), 'The Impenetrable Shield: HMS *Nautilus* and the Namib Coast in the Late Eighteenth Century', *Cimbebasia*, 12, pp. 23–61.

———— (1992), *By Command of Their Lordships: The Exploration of the Namibian Coast by the Royal Navy, 1795–1895* (Windhoek: Namibia Archaeological Trust).

———— (2000), *Cattle for Beads: The Archaeology of Historical Contact and Trade on the Namib Coast* (Uppsala and Windhoek: University of Uppsala and Namibia Archaeological Trust).

———— and John Kinahan (2009), '"A Thousand Fine Vessels are Ploughing the Main": Archaeological Traces of the Nineteenth Century "Guano Rage" on the South-western Coast of Africa', *Australasian Historical Archaeology*, 27, pp. 43–54.

Kinahan, John (1986), 'The Archaeological Structure of Pastoral Production in the Central Namib Desert', *South African Archaeological Society Goodwin Series*, 5, pp. 69–82.

———— (1986), 'Settlement Patterns and Regional Exchange: Evidence from Recent Iron Age Sites on the Kavango River, North-eastern Namibia', *Cimbebasia* (B), 3, pp. 109–16.

———— (1990), 'Four Thousand Years at the Spitzkoppe: Changes in Settlement and Land Use on the Edge of the Namib Desert', *Cimbebasia*, 12, pp. 1–14.

———— (1993), 'The Rise and Fall of Nomadic Pastoralism in the Central Namib Desert' in Thurstan Shaw, Paul Sinclair, Bassey Andah and Alex Okpoko (eds), *The Archaeology of Africa: Food, Metals and Towns* (London and New York: Routledge), pp. 372–85.

———— (1995), 'Theory, Practice and Criticism in the History of Namibian Archaeology', in Peter Ucko (ed.), *Theory in Archaeology: A World Perspective* (London: Routledge), pp. 76–92.

———— (1995), 'Weisser Riese–Schwarze Zwerge? Empirismus und ethnische Deutung in der Archäologie Namibia', *Archäologische Informationen*, 18, 1, pp. 7–18.

———— (1996), 'Alternative Views on the Acquisition of Livestock by Hunter-gatherers in Southern Africa: A Rejoinder to Smith, Yates and Jacobson', *South African Archaeological Bulletin*, 51, pp. 106–8.

———— (1996), 'Human and Domestic Animal Tracks in an Archaeological Lagoon Deposit on the Coast of Namibia', *South African Archaeological Bulletin*, 51, pp. 94–8.

—— (1996), 'The Archaeology of Social Rank among Eighteenth-Century Nomadic Pastoralists in Southern Namibia', *African Archaeological Review*, 13, 4, pp. 225–45.

—— (1999), 'Towards an Archaeology of Mimesis and Rain-making in Namibian Rock Art' in Peter Ucko and Robert Layton (eds), *The Archaeology and Anthropology of Landscape: Shaping your Landscape* (London: Routledge), pp. 336–57.

—— (2000), 'Traumland Südwest: Two Moments in the History of German Archaeological Enquiry in Namibia', in Heinrich Härke (ed.), *Archaeology, Ideology and Society: The German Experience* (Frankfurt: Peter Lang), pp. 353–74.

—— (2001), *Pastoral Nomads of the Namib Desert: The People History Forgot* (Windhoek: Namibia Archaeological Trust and New Namibia Books, 2nd ed.).

—— (2001), 'The Presence of the Past: Archaeology, Environment and Land Rights on the Lower Cunene River', *Cimbebasia*, 17, pp. 23–39.

—— (2005), 'The Late Holocene Human Ecology of the Namib Desert' in Mike Smith and Paul Hesse (eds), *23 Degrees South: Archaeology and Environmental History of the Southern Deserts* (Canberra: National Museum of Australia), pp. 120–31.

—— and Jill Kinahan (2003), 'Excavation of a Late Holocene Cave Deposit in the Southern Namib Desert', *Cimbebasia*, 18, pp. 1–10.

Kinahan, John and Jill Kinahan (2006), 'Preliminary Report on the Late Holocene Archaeology of the Awasib–Gorrasis Basin Complex in the Southern Namib Desert', *Studies in the African Past*, 5, pp. 1–14.

—— and John Vogel (1982), 'Recent Copper-working Sites in the !Khuiseb Drainage, Namibia', *South African Archaeological Bulletin*, 37, pp. 44–5.

Köhler, Oswin (1958), *A Study of the Karibib District (SWA)* (Pretoria: Union of South Africa, Department of Native Affairs).

—— (1959), *A Study of the Omaruru District (SWA)* (Pretoria: Department of Bantu Administration and Development).

Kose, Eileen and Jürgen Richter (2007), 'The Prehistory of the Kavango People', *Sprache und Geschichte in Afrika*, 18, pp. 103–29.

Kößler, Reinhart (2003), 'Public Memory, Reconciliation and the Aftermath of War' in Melber (ed.), *Re-examining Liberation*, pp. 99–110.

—— (2004), '"A Luta Continua": Strategische Orientierung und Erinnerungspolitik am Beispiel des "Heroes Day" der Witbooi in Gibeon' in Zimmerer and Zeller (eds), *Völkermord*, pp. 180–91.

—— (2005), *In Search of Survival and Dignity: Two Traditional Communities in Southern Namibia under South African Rule* (Windhoek: Gamsberg Macmillan).

Kozonguizi, J. and A. O'Dowd (1967), 'The Legal Apparatus of Apartheid' in Segal and First (eds), *Travesty of Trust*, pp. 118–27.

Kreike, Emmanuel (2003), 'Hidden Fruits: A Social Ecology of Fruit Trees in Namibia and Angola, 1820s–1980s' in William Beinart and JoAnn McGregor, *Social History and African Environments* (Oxford: James Currey), pp. 27–42.

—— (2004), *Re-creating Eden: Land Use, Environment, and Society in Southern Angola and Northern Namibia* (Portsmouth, NH: Heinemann).

—— (2004), 'War and the Environmental Effects of Displacement in Southern Africa (1970s–1990s)' in William Moseley and B. Ikubolajeh Logan (eds), *African Environment and Development: Rhetoric, Program and Realities* (Aldershot: Ashgate), pp. 90–110.

Kriegskarte von Deutsch-Südwestafrika (Berlin: Dietrich Reimer, 1904, reprinted Windhoek: National Archives of Namibia, 1987).

Krüger, Gesine (1999), *Kriegsbewältigung und Geschichtsbewusstsein: Realität, Deutung und Verarbeitung des deutschen Kolonialkrieges 1904 bis 1907* (Goettingen: Vandenhoek and Ruprecht).

—— (2004), 'Koloniale Gewalt, Alltagserfahrungen und Überlebenstrategien' in Förster *et al.* (eds), *Namibia–Deutschland*, pp. 92–105.

Krüger, Gesine and Dag Henrichsen (1998), '"We Have Been Captives Long Enough. We Want to Be Free": Land, Uniforms and Politics in the History of Herero in the Interwar Period' in Hayes *et al.*, *Namibia under South African Rule*, pp. 149–74.

Kundrus, Birthe (2003), *Moderne Imperialisten: das Kaiserreich im Spiegel seiner Kolonien* (Cologne: Böhlau).

LaFont, Suzanne (2007), 'An Overview of Gender and Sexuality in Namibia' in *idem* and Hubbard (eds), *Unravelling Taboos*, pp. 1–38.

—— and Dianne Hubbard (eds) (2007), *Unravelling Taboos: Gender and Sexuality in Namibia* (Windhoek: Legal Assistance Centre).

Landis, Elizabeth (1975), *Laws and Practices established in Namibia by the Government of South Africa which are Contrary to the Purposes and Principles of the Charter of the United Nations and to the Universal Declaration of Human Rights* (New York: Office of the UN Commissioner for Namibia).

Larson, Thomas (1981), 'The Mbukushu' in Gibson *et al.*, *Kavango Peoples*, pp. 211–67.

Lau, Brigitte (1986), 'Conflict and Power in Nineteenth Century Namibia', *JAH*, 27, pp. 29–39.

—— (1987), *Southern and Central Namibia in Jonker Afrikaner's Time* (Windhoek Archives).

Lau, Brigitte (ed.) (1989), *Charles John Andersson: Trade and Politics in Central Namibia, 1860–1864* (Windhoek Archives).

—— (ed.) (1995), *The Hendrik Witbooi Papers* (Windhoek: National Archives of Namibia, 2nd ed., trans. Annemarie Heywood and Eben Maasdorp).

—— (1995), *History and Historiography: Four Essays in Reprint* (Windhoek: Discourse/Michael Scott Oral Records Project).

—— (1995), 'Uncertain Certainties: The Herero–German War of 1904' in *idem*, *History and Historiography*, pp. 39–52.

——— (1995), 'Thank God the Germans Came: Vedder and Namibian Historiography' in *idem*, *History and Historiography*, pp. 1–16.

Lee, Richard (1979), *The !Kung San: Men, Women and Work in a Foraging Society* (Cambridge University Press).

Legassick, Martin (1980), 'The Frontier Tradition in South African Historiography' in Shula Marks and Anthony Atmore (eds), *Economy and Society in Pre-industrial South Africa* (London: Longman).

Lenssen-Erz, Tilman and Ralf Vogelsang (2005), 'Populating No-man's-land—Rock Art in Northern Namibia' in Blundell (ed.), *Further Approaches*, pp. 54–62.

Leutwein, Theodor (1997), *Elf Jahre Gouverneur in Deutsch-Südwestafrika* (Windhoek: Namibia Scientific Society 1997, first pub. 1906).

Lewis-Williams, J. David (1981), *Believing and Seeing: Symbolic Meanings in Southern African Rock Art* (London: Academic Press).

——— (1982), 'The Social and Economic Context of Southern San Rock Art', *Current Anthropology*, 23, pp. 429–49.

——— (ed.) (1983), *New Approaches to Southern African Rock Art* (Cape Town: South African Archaeological Society).

——— (1984), 'Ideological Continuities in Prehistoric Southern African Rock: The Evidence of Rock Art' in Carmel Schrire (ed.), *Past and Present in Hunter-gatherer Studies* (Orlando: Academic Press), pp. 225–52.

——— and Thomas Dowson (1989), *Images of Power: Understanding Bushman Rock Art* (Johannesburg: Southern).

Leys, Colin and Susan Brown (eds) (2005), *Histories of Namibia: Living through the Liberation Struggle* (London: Merlin Press).

Leys, Colin and John Saul (eds) (1994), 'Liberation without Democracy? The Swapo Crisis of 1976', *JSAS*, 20, 1, pp. 123–48.

——— (eds) (1995), *Namibia's Liberation Struggle: The Two-Edged Sword* (London: James Currey).

——— (1995), 'SWAPO inside Namibia' in *ibid.*, pp. 66–93.

Liberation Support Movement (ed.) (1978), *Namibia: SWAPO Fights for Freedom* (Oakland, CA: LSM Information Center).

Likuwa, Kletus Muhena and Bertha Nyambe (2009), 'Posters, T-shirts and Placards: Images and Popular Mobilisation in Rundu during the Liberation Struggle' in Miescher *et al.* (eds), *Posters in Action*, pp. 87–99.

Lindholm, Karl-Johann (2006), *Wells of Experience: A Pastoral Land-use History of Omaheke, Namibia* (University of Uppsala).

Lindsay, Jenny (1989), *Population Control Policies in Namibia* (University of Leeds).

Little, M.G. *et al.* (1997), 'Trade Wind Forcing of Upwelling, Seasonality and Heinrich Events as a Response to Sub-Milankovitch Climate Variability', *Paleoceanography*, 12, pp. 568–76.

Lobstein, Tim (1984), *Namibia: Reclaiming the People's Health* (London: AON Publications).

Loeb, Edwin (1962), *In Feudal Africa* (Bloomington: Indiana University Research Center in Anthropology, Folklore and Linguistics).

Loth, Heinrich (1963), *Die christliche Mission in Südwestafrika: Zur destruktiven Rolle der Rheinischen Missionsgesellschaft beim Prozess der Staatsbilduing in Südwestafrika (1842–1893)* (Berlin: Akademie).

Louis, Wm Roger (1967), 'The Origins of the "Sacred Trust"' in Ronald Segal and Ruth First, *South West Africa: Travesty of Trust* (Andre Deutsch, 1967), pp. 54–86.

Louw, Walter (n.d.), *Owambo* (Sandton: Southern African Freedom Foundation).

Lundtofte, Henrik (2003), '"I Believe that the Nation as Such Must be Annihilated"—The Radicalisation of the German Suppression of the Herero Rising in 1904' in Steven Jensen (ed.), *Genocide: Cases, Comparisons and Contemporary Debates* (Copenhagen: Danish Center for Holocaust and Genocide Studies), pp. 15–53.

Lush, David (1993), *Last Steps to Uhuru: An Eyewitness Account of Namibia's Transition to Independence* (Windhoek: New Namibia Books).

Maack, Reinhard (1960), 'Erstbesteigung des Brandberges und Entdeckung der "Weissen Dame"', *JSWASS*, 14, pp. 5–38.

Mainga, Mutumba (1973), *Bulozi under the Luyana Kings: Political Evolution and State Formation in Pre-colonial Zambia* (Harlow: Longman).

Malan, Johan (1995), *Peoples of Namibia* (Wingate Park: Rhino).

Mamozai, Martha (1982), *Herrenmenschen: Frauen im deutschen Kolonialismus* (Reinbek bei Hamburg: Rohwohlt).

Maritz, Chris (1996), 'The Subia and Fwe of Caprivi: Any Historical Grounds for *Primus inter Pares?*', *Africa Insight*, 26, 2, pp. 177–85.

Marshall, Lorna (1976), *The !Kung of Nyae Nyae* (Cambridge, Mass.: Harvard University Press).

Mason, Revil (1955), 'Notes on the Recent Archaeology of the Scherz Basin, Brandberg', *South African Archaeological Bulletin*, 10, pp. 30–1.

Massman, Ursula (1983), *Swakopmund: A Chronicle of the Town's People, Places and Progress* (Swakopmund: Society for Scientific Development).

Masson, John (2001), *Jakob Marengo: An Early Resistance Hero of Namibia* (Windhoek: Out of Africa).

Maylam, Paul (2001), *South Africa's Racial Past: The History and Historiography of Racism, Segregation and Apartheid* (Aldershot: Ashgate).

Mbuende, Kaire (1986), *Namibia: The Broken Shield. Anatomy of Imperialism and Revolution* (Lund: Liber).

McGurk, Cecilia (1981), 'The Mbundza' in Gibson *et al.*, *Kavango Peoples*, pp. 81–95.

——— (1981), 'The Sambyu' in *ibid.*, pp. 97–157.

McKittrick, Meredith (1998), 'Generational Struggles and Social Mobility in Western Ovambo Communities, 1915–54' in Hayes *et al.*, *Namibia under South African Rule*, pp. 241–62.

——— (2002), *To Dwell Secure: Generation, Christianity and Colonialism in Ovamboland* (Portsmouth, NH: Heinemann).

——— (2008), 'Landscapes of Power: Ownership and Identity on the Middle Kavango River, Namibia', *JSAS*, 34, 4, pp. 785–802.

Melber, Henning (2003), '"Namibia, Land of the Brave": Selective Memories on War and Violence within Nation Building' in Abbink *et al.* (eds), *Rethinking Resistance*, pp. 305–27.

———— (ed.) (2003), *Re-examining Liberation in Namibia: Political Culture since Independence* (Uppsala: Nordic Africa Institute).

———— (ed.) (2005), *Genozid und Gedenken: Namibisch–deutsche Geschichte und Gegenwart* (Frankfurt: Brandes und Apsel), pp. 23–48.

———— (ed.) (2007), *Transitions in Namibia: Which Changes for Whom?* (Uppsala: Nordic Africa Institute).

———— (2007), 'Poverty, Politics and Privilege: Namibia's Black Economic Elite Formation' in *idem* (ed.), *Transitions*, pp.110–29.

———— (2009), 'One Namibia, One Nation? The Caprivi as Contested Territory', *Journal of Contemporary African Studies*, 27, 4 (2009), pp. 463–81.

———— (2009), 'Analysis: Namibia's Elections 2009. Democracy without Democrats?', Heinrich Böll Stiftung, Dec. 2009, http://www.boell.org.za/web/144-487.html.

Mendelsohn, John, Alice Jarvis, Carole Roberts and Tony Robertson (2002), *Atlas of Namibia: A Portrait of the Land and its People* (Cape Town: David Philip).

Menzel, Gustav (2000), *'Widerstand und Gottesfurcht': Hendrik Witbooi–eine Biographie in zeitgenössischen Quellen* (Cologne: Rüdiger Köppe).

van der Merwe, I.J. (1989), 'The Role of War and Urbanization in the Regional Development of Namibia', *Africa Urban Quarterly*, 4, 3/4, pp. 263–74.

Metsola, Lalli (2007), 'Out of Order? The Margins of Namibian Ex-combatant "Reintegration"' in Melber (ed.), *Transitions*, pp. 130–52.

Middleton, John and Joseph Miller (eds) (2008), *New Encyclopedia of Africa* (Detroit: Charles Scribner's Sons).

Miescher, Giorgio (ed.) (2006), *Registratur AA.3 (Enlarged and Revised Edition): Guide to the SWAPO Collection in the Basler Afrika Bibliographien* (Basel: BAB).

———— and Dag Henrichsen (eds) (2000), *New Notes on Kaoko: The Northern Kunene Region (Namibia) in Texts and Photographs* (Basel: BAB).

————, Lorena Rizzo and Jeremy Silvester (eds) (2009), *Posters in Action: Visuality in the Making of an African Nation* (Basel: BAB).

Miettinen, Kari (2005), *On the Way to Whiteness: Christianization, Conflict and Change in Colonial Ovamboland, 1910–1965* (Helsinki: Suomalaisen Kirjallisuuden Seura).

Miller, Joseph (1988), *Way of Death: Merchant Capitalism and the Angolan Slave Trade 1730–1830* (London: James Currey).

Minter, William (1994), *Apartheid's Contras: An Inquiry into the Roots of War in Angola and Mozambique* (Johannesburg: Witwatersrand University Press).

Mitchell, Peter (2002), *The Archaeology of Southern Africa* (Cambridge University Press).

Möhlig, Wilhelm (ed.) (2000), *Frühe Kolonialgeschichte Namibias, 1880–1930* (Cologne: Rüdiger Koppe).

—— (2002), 'From Oral Tradition to Local History Textbook: Two Examples from the Kavango Region, Namibia' in Axel Harneit-Sievers (ed.), *A Place in the World: New Local Historiographies from Africa and South Asia* (Leiden: Brill), pp. 181–99.

Molin, John (2006), 'Twyfelfontein—A Rock Art Site of Local Significance', *Studies in the African Past*, 5, pp. 34–46.

Moorsom, Richard (1977), 'Underdevelopment, Contract Labour and Worker Consciousness in Namibia, 1915–72', *JSAS*, 4, 1, pp. 52–87.

—— (1989), 'The Formation of the Contract Labour System in Namibia, 1900–1926' in Abebe Zegeye and Shuni Ishemo (eds), *Forced Labour and Migration: Patterns of Movement within Africa* (London: Hans Zell), pp. 55–108.

Morgenstierne, Christopher (2003), *Denmark and National Liberation in Southern Africa: A Flexible Response* (Uppsala: Nordic Africa Institute).

Moritz, Walter (1998), *Die Swartboois in Rehoboth, Salem, Ameib und Franzfontein* (Tsumeb: Nation Press).

Mweshida, Johanna, 'Nicknames in Ovamboland: Some Preliminary Deliberations' in Hartmann (ed.), *New Historical Writing*, pp. 4–12.

Namakalu, Oswin (2004), *Armed Liberation Struggle: Some Accounts of PLAN's Combat Operations* (Windhoek: Gamsberg Macmillan).

Namhila, Ellen Ndeshi (1997), *The Price of Freedom* (Windhoek: New Namibia Books).

—— (2004), 'Filling the Gaps in the Archival Record of the Namibian Struggle for Independence', *IFLA Journal*, 30, 3, pp. 224–30.

—— (2005), *Kaxumba kaNdola: Man and Myth. The Biography of a Barefoot Soldier* (Basel: BAB).

Namibia: Perspectives for National Reconstruction and Development (Lusaka: United Nations Institute for Namibia, 1986).

Namibia: The Facts, (London: IDAF, 1990).

Nampala, Lovisa (2006), 'Christianisation and Social Change in Northern Namibia: A Comparative Study of the Impact of Christianity on Oukwanyama, Ondonga and Ombalantu, 1870–1971', in Nampala and Shigwedha, *Aawambo Kingdoms*, pp. 1–109.

—— and Vilho Shigwedha (2006), *Aawambo Kingdoms, History and Cultural Change: Perspectives from Northern Namibia* (Basel: P. Schlettwein).

Namuhuja, Hans (2002), *The Ondonga Royal Kings* (Windhoek: Out of Africa).

Ndadi, Vinnia (1989), *Breaking Contract: The Story of Vinnia Ndadi* (London: IDAF Publications).

Ndongo, Petrus (1998), 'The Borderline: "Onhaululi"' in Hayes *et al.*, *Namibia under South African Rule*, pp. 289–91.

Ndoro, Webber (1997), 'The Evolution of a Management Policy at Great Zimbabwe' in Gilbert Pwiti (ed.), *Caves, Monuments and Texts: Zimbabwean Archaeology Today* (Uppsala University), pp. 109–24.

Nielsen, Stig (1988), 'A Refugee School 1 400 km, 850 Miles from Home' in Flemming Gjedde-Nielsen, *Namibia: Landet uden overgivelse* (Copenhagen: WUS).

Ngavirue, Zedekia (1967), 'The Land Theft' in Segal and First (eds), *Travesty of Trust*, pp. 178–88.

——— (1997), *Political Parties and Interest Groups in South West Africa (Namibia): A Study of a Plural Society (1972)* (Basel: P. Schlettwein).

Nordbruch, Claus (2002), *Der Hereroaufstand, 1904* (Stegen am Ammersee: K. Vowinckel).

Norris, Edward with Arnold Beukes (1995), 'Kolonialkrieg und Karikatur in Deutschland: Die Aufstände der Herero und der Nama und die Zeichnungen der deutschen satirischen Zeitschriften' in Heine and Heyden, *Studien*, pp. 377–98.

Notkola, Veijo and Harri Siiskonen (1999), *Fertility, Mortality and Migration in sub-Saharan Africa: The Case of Ovamboland in North Namibia, 1925–90* (Basingstoke: Macmillan).

Nuhn, Walter (2000), *Feind überall: der grosse Nama-Aufstand (Hottentottenaufstand) 1904–1908 in Deutsch-Südwestafrika (Namibia). Der erste Partisanenkrieg in der Geschichte der deutschen Armee* (Bonn: Bernard & Graefe).

Nujoma, Sam (2001), *Where Others Wavered: The Autobiography of Sam Nujoma* (London: Panaf Books).

Nurse, G., John Weiner and Trefor Jenkins (1985), *The Peoples of Southern Africa and their Affinities* (Oxford University Press).

Odhiambo, E.S. Atieno (2004), 'The Usages of the Past: African Historiographies since Independence', *African Research and Documentation*, 96, pp. 3–62.

O'Donnell, Krista (1999), 'Poisonous Women: Sexual Danger, Illicit Violence, and Domestic Work in German Southern Africa, 1904–1915', *Journal of Women's History*, 11, 3, pp. 31–54.

Oermann, Nils (1999), *Mission, Church and State Relations in South West Africa under German Rule, 1884–1915* (Stuttgart: Franz Steiner).

Ohta, Itaru (2000), 'Drought and Mureti's Grave: the "we/us" boundaries between Kaokolanders and the People of the Okakarara Area in the Early 1980s' in Bollig and Gewald (eds), *People, Cattle and Land*, pp. 299–317.

O'Linn, Bryan (2003), *Namibia: The Sacred Trust of Civilization. Ideal and Reality* (Windhoek: Gamsberg Macmillan).

Pager, Harald (1980), 'Felsbildforschungen am Brandberg in Namibia', *Beiträge zur Allgemeinen und Vergleichenden Archäeologie*, 2, pp. 351–7.

——— (compiled Tilman Lenssen-Erz, ed. Rudolph Kuper) (1989), *The Rock Paintings of the Upper Brandberg. Part 1: Amis Gorge* (Cologne: Heinrich Barth Institut).

Pakleppa, Richard (director) (1999), 'Nda Mona: I Have Seen' (film, Johannesburg).

Panzergrau, Kurt (1998), *Die Bildung und Erziehung der Eingeborenen Süd-westafrikas (Hereroland und Gross-Namaqualand) durch die Rheinische Missionsgesellschaft von 1842–1914* (Munich: Akademischer Verlag).

Parkington, John (1984), 'Soaqua and Bushmen: Hunters and Robbers' in Carmel Schrire, *Past and Present in Hunter-gatherer Studies* (Orlando: Academic Press), pp. 151–74.

Pearson, Patrick (1981), 'The Rehoboth Rebellion' in Philip Bonner (ed.), *Working Papers in Southern African Studies*, vol. 2 (Johannesburg: Ravan), pp. 31–51.

Pendleton, Wade (1974), *Katutura: A Place Where We Do Not Stay. The Social Structure and Social Relationships of People in an African Township in South West Africa* (San Diego: San Diego State University Press).

Penn, Nigel (1999), *Rogues, Rebels and Runaways: Eighteenth Century Cape Characters* (Claremont: David Philip).

——— (2005), *Forgotten Frontier: Colonist and Khoisan on the Cape's Northern Frontier in the Eighteenth Century* (Athens: Ohio University Press).

Peters, Pauline (1997), 'Revisiting the Puzzle of Matriliny in South-Central Africa', *Critique of Anthropology*, 17, 2, pp. 125–46.

Peters, Walter (1995), 'Grundlagen des Städtebaus in Namibia' in Heine and Heyden, *Studien*, pp. 429–52.

Phillipson, David (1977), *The Later Prehistory of Eastern and Southern Africa* (London: Heinemann).

——— (2005), *African Archaeology* (Cambridge University Press).

Pirio, Gregory (1988), 'The Role of Garveyism in the Making of Namibian Nationalism' in Wood (ed.), *Namibia 1884–1984*, pp. 259–67.

Pool, Gerhard (1991), *Samuel Maharero* (Windhoek: Gamsberg Macmillan).

Prein, Philipp (1994), 'Guns and Top Hats: African Resistance in German South West Africa, 1907–1915', *JSAS*, 20, 1, pp. 99–121.

Preston, Rosemary (1997), 'Integrating Fighters after War: Reflections on the Namibian Experience, 1989–1993', *JSAS*, 23, 2, pp. 453–72.

Pwiti, Gilbert and George Mvenge (1996), 'Archaeologists, Tourists and Rainmakers in the Management of Rock Art Sites in Zimbabwe: A Case Study of Domboshava National Monument' in Pwiti and Soper (eds), *Aspects*, pp. 817–24.

——— and Robert Soper (eds) (1996), *Aspects of African Archaeology: Papers from the 10th Congress of the PanAfrican Association for Prehistory and Related Studies, Harare* (Harare: University of Zimbabwe Publications).

Reeh, Günter (2000), *Hendrik Witbooi: Ein Leben für die Freiheit. Zwischen Glaube und Zweifel* (Cologne: Rüdiger Köppe).

Republic of Namibia, Ministry of Health and Social Services (April 2006–Mar. 2007), *United Nations General Assembly Special Session (UNGASS) Country Report*.

Richter, Jurgen (1984), 'Messum I: A Later Stone Age Pattern of Mobility in the Namib Desert', *Cimbebasia* (B), 4, 1, pp. 1–12.

———— (1991), *Studien zur Urgeschichte Namibias–Holozäne Stratigraphien im Umkreis des Brandberges* (Cologne: Heinrich-Barth Institut).

———— (1994), '"Zu wenig Chalzedon"—kritischer Rohstoffmangel bei prähistorischen Wildbeutern in Namibia', in M. Bollig and F. Klees (eds), *Überlebens-strategien in Afrika* (Cologne: Heinrich Barth Institut), pp. 179–86.

———— and Ralf Vogelsang (2008), 'Rock Art in Northwestern Central Namibia—Its Age and Cultural Background' in Cornelia Limpricht and Megan Biesele (eds), *Heritage and Cultures in Modern Namibia—In-depth Views of the Country* (Windhoek: TUCSIN), pp. 37–46.

Ridsdale, Benjamin (1883), *Scenes and Adventures in Great Namaqualand* (London: Woolmer).

Rizzo, Lorena (2000), 'N.J. van Warmelo: Anthropology and the Making of a Reserve' in Miescher and Henrichsen, *New Notes on Kaoko*, pp. 189–206.

———— (2007), 'The Elephant Shooting: Colonial Law and Indirect Rule in Kaoko, Northwestern Namibia, in the 1920s and 1930s', *JAH*, 48, pp. 245–66.

Robbins, Larry *et al.* (1996), 'Excavations at the Tsodilo Hills Rhino Cave', *Botswana Notes and Records*, 28, pp. 23–45.

Roberts, A.D. (1976), *A History of Zambia* (London: Heinemann Educational).

Robertshaw, Peter (ed.) (1990), *A History of African Archaeology* (London: James Currey).

Rohde, Richard (1993), *Afternoons in Damaraland: Common Land and Common Sense in One of Namibia's Former Homelands* (University of Edinburgh Centre of African Studies).

Roller, Kathrin (2004), 'Mission und "Mischehen": Errinerung und Körpergeteiltes Gedächtnis an eine afrikanische Vorfahrin. Über die Familie Schmelen–Kleinschmidt–Hegner' in Förster *et al.* (eds), *Namibia–Deutschland*, pp. 194–211.

van Rooyen, P.H. and Peter Reiner (1995), *Gobabis: Brief History of theTown and Region* (Gobabis: Municipality of Gobabis).

Ross, Andrew (2002), *David Livingstone, Mission and Empire* (London: Hambledon).

Rotberg, Robert (2002), *Ending Autocracy, Enabling Democracy: The Tribulations of Southern Africa, 1960–2000* (Cambridge, Mass.: World Peace Foundation).

Rüdiger, Klaus (1993), *Die Namibia-Deutschen: Geschichte einer Nationalität im Werden* (Stuttgart: Steiner).

Sadr, Karim and Francois-Xavier Fauvelle-Aymar (eds) (2008), 'Khoekhoe and the Origins of Herding in Southern Africa', special issue, *Southern African Humanities*, 20, 1, pp. 1–248.

Sandelowsky, Beatrice (1977), 'Mirabib—An Archaeological Study in the Namib', *Madoqua*, 10, 4, pp. 221–83.

———— (1979), 'Kapako and Vungu Vungu: Iron Age Sites on the Kavango River', in Nikolaas van der Merwe and Thomas Huffman (eds), *Iron Age*

Studies in Southern Africa (Claremont: South African Archaeological Society), pp. 52–61.

Sandelowsky, B.H., J.H. van Rooyen and J.C.Vogel (1979), 'Early Evidence for Herders in the Namib', *South African Archaeological Bulletin*, 34, pp. 50–1.

Saul, John and Colin Leys (1995), 'SWAPO: The Politics of Exile' in Leys and Saul (eds), *Namibia's Liberation Struggle*, pp. 40–65.

——— (2003), 'Truth, Reconciliation, Amnesia: The "Ex-detainees'" Fight for Justice' in Melber (ed.), *Re-examining Liberation*, pp. 69–86.

Saunders, Christopher (2007), 'History and the Armed Struggle: From Anti-colonial Propaganda to "Patriotic History"?' in Melber (ed.), *Transitions*, pp. 13–29.

——— (2008), 'South Africa in Namibia/Angola: The Truth and Reconciliation Commission's Account' in Baines and Vale (eds), *Beyond the Border War*, pp. 267–80.

——— (2009), 'Namibian Solidarity: British Support for Namibian Independence', *JSAS*, 35, 2, pp. 437-54.

Scherz, Ernst-Rudolf (1975), *Felsbilder in Südwest-Afrika. Teil 2: Die Gravierungen im Nordwest Südwest-Afrika* (Cologne: Böhlau Verlag).

Scheulen, Peter (1998), *Die 'Eingeborenen' Südwestafrikas: Ihr Bild in deutschen Kolonialzeitschriften von 1884 bis 1918* (Cologne: Rüdiger Köppe).

Schlosser, Katesa (1958), *Eingeborenenkirchen in Süd und Südwestafrika, ihre Geschichte und Sozialstruktur* (Kiel: W.G. Mühlau).

Schmidt-Laubner, Brigitta (1993), *Die abhängigen Herren: deutsche Identität in Namibia* (Münster: Lit).

Schneider, Herbert (1994), *Animal Health and Veterinary Medicine in Namibia* (Windhoek: Agrivet).

Schofield, John (1948), 'The Age of the Rock Paintings of South Africa', *South African Archaeological Bulletin*, 3, pp. 79–88.

Schwabe, Kurd (1909), *Im deutschen Diamantenlande: Deutsch-Südwestafrika von der Errichtung der deutschen Herrschaft bis zur Gegenwart (1884–1910)* (Berlin: n.p.).

Scott, James (1985), *Weapons of the Weak: Everyday Forms of Peasant Resistance* (New Haven: Yale University Press, 1985).

Sealy, Judith and Royden Yates (1994), 'The Chronology of the Introduction of Pastoralism to the Cape, South Africa', *Antiquity*, 68, pp. 58–67.

Seckelmann, Astrid (2000), *Siedlungsentwicklung im unabhängigen Namibia: Transformationsprozesse in Klein- und Mittelzentren der Farmzone* (Hamburg: Institut für Afrika-Kunde).

Seely, Mary and Gideon Louw (1980), 'First Approximation of the Effects of Rainfall on the Ecology and Energetics of a Namib Desert Dune Ecosystem', *Journal of Arid Environments*, 3, pp. 25–54.

Segal, Ronald and Ruth First (eds) (1967), *South West Africa: Travesty of Trust* (London: André Deutsch).

419

Seidel, Frank, Eileen Kose and Wilhelm Möhlig (2007), 'Northern Namibia—Overview of its Historiography Based on Linguistic and Extralinguistic Evidence' in O. Bubenzer, A. Bolton and F. Darius (eds), *Atlas of Cultural and Environmental Change in Arid Africa* (Cologne: Heinrich Bart Institut), pp. 152–5.

Seligmann, Matthew (1998), *Rivalry in Southern Africa, 1893–99: The Transformation of German Colonial Policy* (New York: St Martin's).

Sellström, Tor (1999–2002), *Sweden and National Liberation in Southern Africa* (Uppsala: Nordic Africa Institute).

Shackleton, N.J. and N.D. Opdyke (1976), 'Oxygen Isotope Palaeomagnetic Stratigraphy of Pacific Core V28–239 Late Pliocene to Latest Pleistocene', *Geological Society of America Memoirs*, 145, pp. 449–64.

Shackley, Myra (1985), *Palaeolithic Archaeology of the Central Namib Desert: A Preliminary Survey of Chronology, Typology and Site Location* (Windhoek: Cimbebasia Memoir 6, National Museum of Namibia).

Shamukuni, D.M. (1972), 'The baSubiya', *Botswana Notes and Records*, 4, pp. 161–84.

Shigwedha, Vilho (1999), 'Mwaala gwa Nashilongo: A Twin with a Unique Personality' in Hartmann (ed.), *More New Historical Writing*, pp. 37–52.

———— (2006), 'The Pre-colonial Costumes of the Aawambo: Significant Changes under Colonialism and the Construction of Post-Colonial Identity' in Nampala and Shigwedha, *Aawambo Kingdoms*, pp. 111–274.

Shityuwete, Helao (1990), *Never Follow the Wolf: The Autobiography of a Namibian Freedom Fighter* (London: Kliptown).

Sievers, Christine (1984), 'Test Excavations at Rosh Pinah Shelter, Southern Namibia', *Cimbebasia* (B), 4, 3, pp. 29–40.

Siiskonen, Harri (1990), *Trade and Socioeconomic Change in Ovamboland, 1850–1906* (Helsinki: SHS).

Silvester, Jeremy (1998), 'Beasts, Boundaries and Buildings: The Survival and Creation of Pastoral Economies in Southern Namibia, 1915–35' in Hayes *et al.*, *Namibia under South African Rule*, pp. 95–116.

———— (2000), 'Assembling and Resembling: Herero History in Vaalgras, southern Namibia' in Bollig and Gewald (eds), *People, Cattle and Land*, pp. 473–92.

———— (2004), 'Portraits of Power and Panoramas of Persuasion: The Palgrave Album at the National Archives of Namibia' in Hartmann (ed.), *Hues*, pp. 131–60.

———— (2005), '"Sleep with a Southwester": Monuments and Settler Identity in Namibia' in Caroline Elkins and Susan Pedersen (eds), *Settler Colonialism in the Twentieth Century: Projects, Practices, Legacies* (New York: Routledge), pp. 271–86.

———— (2006), 'Introduction: Changing Clothes, Changing Traditions' in Nampala and Shigwedha, *Aawambo Kingdoms*, pp. xi–xviii.

———— (2009), '"The Struggle is Futile": A Short Overview of Anti-SWAPO Visual Propaganda' in Miescher *et al.* (eds), *Posters*, pp. 187–201.

—— and Jan-Bart Gewald (eds) (2003), *Words Cannot be Found: German Colonial Rule in Namibia. An Annotated Reprint of the 1918 Blue Book* (Leiden: Brill).

Silvester, Jeremy, Marion Wallace and Patricia Hayes (1998), '"Trees Never Meet": Mobility and Containment: An Overview, 1915–1946' in Hayes *et al.*, *Namibia under South African Rule*, pp. 3–48.

Simon, David (1982), 'Recent Trends in Namibian Urbanization', *Tijdschrift voor economische en sociale Geographie*, 73, 4, pp. 237–49.

Smith, Andrew (1990), 'On Becoming Herders: Khoikhoi and San Ethnicity in Southern Africa', *African Studies*, 49, pp. 50–73.

—— (1992), *Pastoralism in Africa: Origins and Developmental Ecology* (London: Hurst).

—— (1993), 'Exploitation of Marine Mammals by Prehistoric Cape Herders', *South African Journal of Science*, 89, pp. 162–5.

—— and Leon Jacobson (1995), 'Excavations at Geduld and the Appearance of Early Domestic Stock in Namibia', *South African Archaeological Bulletin*, 50, pp. 3–14.

Smith, Benjamin and Sven Ouzman (2004), 'Taking Stock: Identifying Khoekhoen Herder Rock Art in Southern Africa', *Current Anthropology*, 45, pp. 499–526.

Smuts, David (1987), 'The Interim Government and Human Rights' in Tötemeyer *et al.*, *Namibia in Perspective*, pp. 219–26.

Soggot, David (1986), *Namibia: The Violent Heritage* (London: Collings).

Soiri, Iina (1996), *The Radical Motherhood: Namibian Women's Independence Struggle* (Uppsala: Nordic Africa Institute).

South Africa (1926), *Report of the Government of the Union of South Africa on South West Africa* (Pretoria: Government Printer).

—— (1964), *Report of the Commission of Enquiry into South West Africa Affairs 1962–63* (Pretoria).

—— (1999), *Truth and Reconciliation Commission of South Africa Report* (London: Macmillan).

Stals, Eric L.P. (ed.) (1991), *The Commissions of W. C. Palgrave, Special Emissary to South West Africa, 1876–1885* (Cape Town: Van Riebeeck Society).

Steinmetz, George (2007), *The Devil's Handwriting: Precoloniality and the German State in Qingdao, Samoa and Southwest Africa* (University of Chicago Press).

Stoecker, Helmuth (ed.) (1986), *German Imperialism in Africa: From the Beginnings until the Second World War* (London: Hurst).

Strachan, Hew (2001), *The First World War*, vol. 1, *To Arms* (Oxford University Press, 2001).

Strauss, André (1987), 'Community Organisations in Namibia', in Tötemeyer *et al.*, *Namibia in Perspective*, pp. 184–95.

Stringer, Chris and Clive Gamble (1993), *In Search of the Neanderthals* (London: Thames & Hudson).

Stultz, Newell (1992), 'South Africa in Angola and Namibia' in Thomas Weiss and James Blight (eds), *The Suffering Grass: Superpowers and Regional Conflict in Southern Africa and the Caribbean* (Boulder, Colo: Lynne Rienner), pp. 79–99.

Sudholt, Gert (1975), *Die deutsche Eingeborenenpolitik in Südwestafrika von den Anfängen bis 1904* (Hildesheim: Georg Olms).

Sullivan, Sian (1999), 'Folk and Formal, Local and National—Damara Knowledge and Community Conservation in Southern Kunene, Namibia', *Cimbebasia*, 15, pp. 1–28.

—— (2001), 'Difference, Identity and Access to Official Discourses: Haillom, "Bushmen" and a Recent Namibian Ethnography', *Anthropos*, 96, pp. 179–192.

Sundermeier, Theo (1977), *Die Mbanderu: Studien zu ihrer Geschichte und Kultur* (St Augustin: Anthropos Institut).

—— (ed) (n.d.), *The Mbanderu: Their History until 1914 as told to Theo Sundermeier in 1966 by Heinrich Tjituka, Heinrich Hengari, Albert Kajovi, Heinrich Kavari, Paul Katjivikua, Ernst Ketjipotu* (trans. Annemarie Heywood) (Windhoek: Michael Scott Oral Records Project).

Susser, Ida (2009), *Aids, Sex and Culture: Global Politics and Survival in Southern Africa* (Chichester: Wiley-Blackwell).

Suzman, James (2000), *'Things from the Bush': A Contemporary History of the Omaheke Bushmen* (Basel: P. Schlettwein Publishing).

—— (2002), 'Difference, Domination and "Underdevelopment": Notes on the Marginalisation of Namibia's San Population' in Winterfeldt *et al.* (eds), *Namibia Society Sociology*, pp. 125–35.

Swanson, Maynard (1967), 'South West Africa in Trust, 1915–1939' in Gifford and Louis, *Britain and Germany in Africa*, pp. 632–6.

SWAPO Department of Information and Publicity (1981), *To Be Born a Nation: The Liberation Struggle for Namibia* (London: Zed).

Swart, J. (2004), 'Rock Art Sequences in uKhahlamba-Drakensberg Park, South Africa', *Southern African Humanities*, 16, pp. 13–35.

Swenson, G. (1972), *Pictorial History of the Rifle* (New York: Bonanza Books).

Tankard, Anthony J. and J. Rogers (1978), 'Late Cenozoic Palaeoenvironments on the West Coast of Southern Africa', *Journal of Biogeography*, 5, pp. 319–37.

Tapscott, Chris (1993), 'National Reconciliation, Social Equity and Class Formation in Independent Namibia', *JSAS*, 19, 1, pp. 29–39.

Thomsen, K.J., A. Murray, L. Bøtter-Jensen and J. Kinahan (2007), 'Determination of Burial Dose in Incompletely Bleached Fluvial Samples using Single Grains of Quartz', *Radiation Measurements*, 24, 2, pp. 270–9.

Thornberry, Cedric (2004), *A Nation is Born: The Inside Story of Namibia's Independence* (Windhoek: Gamsberg Macmillan).

Timm, Margo (1998), 'Transpositions: The Reinterpretation of Colonial Photographs of the Kwanyama King Mandume ya Ndemufayo in the Art of

John Ndevasia Muafangejo' in Hartmann *et al.*, *Colonising Camera*, pp. 145–50.

Tlou, Thomas (1985), *A History of Ngamiland 1750 to 1906: The Formation of an African State* (Gaborone: Macmillan Botswana).

Tötemeyer, Gerhard (1978), *Namibia Old and New: Traditional and Modern Leaders in Ovamboland* (London: Hurst).

——— Vezera Kandetu and Wolfgang Werner (eds) (1978), *Namibia in Perspective* (Windhoek: Council of Churches in Namibia).

Trigger, Bruce (1989), *A History of Archaeological Thought* (Cambridge University Press).

Troup, Freda (1950), *In Face of Fear: Michael Scott's Challenge to South Africa* (London: Faber & Faber).

Trüper, Ursula (2006), *The Invisible Woman: Zara Schmelen, African Mission Assistant at the Cape and in Namaland* (Basel: BAB).

Tyson, P. (1986), *Climatic Change and Variability in Southern Africa* (Cape Town: Oxford University Press).

United Kingdom (1916), *Papers Relating to Certain Trials in German South West Africa* (Parliamentary paper: vol. 20, cd 8371).

——— (1916), *German Atrocities and Breaches of the Rules of War, in Africa* (Parliamentary paper: vol. 20, cd 8306).

——— (1918), *Report on the Natives of South West Africa and their Treatment by Germany* (Parliamentary paper: vol. 17, cd. 9146).

——— (1921), *Correspondence Relating to the Wishes of the Natives of the German Colonies as to their Future Government* (Parliamentary paper: vol. 43, 1921).

Vansina, Jan (2004), *How Societies are Born: Governance in West Central Africa before 1600* (Charlottesville: University of Virginia Press).

Vedder, Heinrich (1934), *Das alte Südwestafrika: Südwestafrikas Geschichte bis zum Tode Mahareros, 1890* (Martin Warneck: Berlin), published in English as *South West Africa in Early Times: Being the Story of South West Africa up to the Date of Maharero's Death in 1890*, (ed.) Cyril Hall (Oxford University Press, 1938).

Vigne, Randolph (1988), 'Imperialism at One Remove: Britain and Namibia, 1785–1915' in Wood (ed.), *Namibia 1884–1984*, pp. 145–51.

——— (1998), 'The Moveable Frontier: The Namibia–Angola Boundary Demarcation, 1926–1928' in Hayes *et al.*, *Namibia under South African Rule*, pp. 289–304.

——— (2000), 'The Hard Road to Colonization: The Topnaar Aonin of Namibia, 1670–1878', *Journal of Colonialism and Colonial History*, 1, 2.

Voeltz, Richard (1988), *German Colonialism and the South West Africa Company* (Athens, Ohio: Ohio University Press).

Vogel, John and Ebbie Visser (1981), 'Pretoria Radiocarbon Dates II', *Radiocarbon*, 23, 1, pp. 43–80.

Vogelsang, Ralf (1996), 'The Middle Stone Age in South-western Namibia' in Pwiti and Soper (eds), *Aspects of African Archaeology*, pp. 207–12.

—— (1998), *Middle Stone Age Fundstellen in Südwest-Namibia* (Cologne: Heinrich Barth Institut).

—— (2008), 'The Rock Shelter Apollo 11—Evidence of Early Modern Humans in South-western Namibia' in Cornelia Limpricht and Megan Biesele (eds), *Heritage and Cultures in Modern Namibia—In-depth Views of the Country* (Windhoek: TUCSIN), pp. 183–92.

—— Barbara Eichorn and Jürgen Richter (2002), 'Holocene Human Occupation and Vegetation History in Northern Namibia', *Die Erde*, 133, pp. 113–32.

Vogelsang, Ralf and Karl Peter Wendt (2007), 'Changing Patterns of Settlement in Namibia during the Holocene' in O. Bubenzer, A. Bolten and F. Darius (eds), *Atlas of Cultural and Environmental Change in Arid Africa* (Cologne: Heinrich Barth Institut), pp. 68–72.

Volman, Thomas (1984), 'Early Prehistory of Southern Africa' in R.G. Klein (ed.), *Southern African Prehistory and Palaeoenvironments* (Rotterdam: Balkema), pp. 169–395.

de Vries, Joris (1999), *Manasse Tjiseseta: Chief of Omaruru 1884–1898, Namibia* (Cologne: Rüdiger Köppe).

Wadley, Lyn (1979), 'Big Elephant Shelter and its Role in the Holocene Prehistory of Central South West Africa', *Cimbebasia* (B), 3, 1, pp. 1–76.

—— (1984), 'On the Move: A Look at Prehistoric Food Scheduling in Central Namibia', *Cimbebasia* (B), 4, 4, pp. 41–50.

—— (1987), *Later Stone Age Hunters and Gatherers of the Southern Transvaal: Social and Ecological Interpretations* (Oxford: British Archaeological Reports).

Wallace, Marion (1998), '"A Person is Never Angry for Nothing": Women, VD and Windhoek' in Hayes *et al.*, *Namibia under South African Rule*, pp. 77–94.

—— (1998), 'Looking at the Locations: The Ambiguities of Urban Photography' in Hartmann *et al.* (eds), *Colonising Camera*, pp. 132–7.

—— (2002), *Health, Power and Politics in Windhoek, Namibia, 1915–1945* (Basel: P. Schlettwein).

—— (2003), '"Making Tradition": Healing, History and Ethnic Identity among Otjiherero-speakers in Namibia, c. 1850–1950', *JSAS*, 29, 2, pp. 355–72.

Wallis, John (1936), *Fortune my Foe* (London: Jonathan Cape).

van Walraven, Klaas and Jon Abbink (2003), 'Rethinking Resistance in African History: An Introduction' in Abbink et al. (eds), *Rethinking Resistance*, pp. 1–40.

Walter, H. and O.H. Volk (1954), *Grundlagen der Weidewirtschaft in Südwestafrika*, Teil 1 (Stuttgart: Ulmer).

Walther, Daniel (2002), *Creating Germans Abroad: Cultural Policies and National Identity in Namibia* (Athens, Ohio: Ohio University Press).

Wärnlöf, Christofer (2000), 'The Politics of Death: Demarcating Land through Ritual Performance' in Bollig and Gewald, *People, Cattle and Land*, pp. 449–69.

Weaver, Tony (1987), 'The War in Namibia: Social Consequences' in Töte-meyer *et al.* (eds), *Namibia in Perspective* (Windhoek: Council of Churches in Namibia).

Webley, Lita (1997), 'Wives and Sisters: Changing Gender Relations among Khoe Pastoralists in Namaqualand' in Lyn Wadley (ed.), *Our Gendered Past: Archaeological Studies of Gender in South Africa* (Johannesburg: Witwatersrand University Press, 1997), pp. 167–208.

Wellington, John (1967), *South West Africa and its Human Issues* (Oxford: Clarendon Press).

Wendt, Wolfgang (1972), 'Preliminary Report on an Archaeological Research Programme in South West Africa', *Cimbebasia* (B), 2, 1, pp. 1–61.

——— (1974), '"Art mobilier" aus der Apollo-11 Grotte in Südwest-Afrika', *Acta Praehistorica et Archaeologica*, 5, pp. 1–42.

——— (1975), 'Die ältesten datierten Kunstwerke Afrikas', *Bild der Wissenschaft*, 10, pp. 44–50.

Werner, Wolfgang (1987), 'Ethnicity and Reformism in Namibia' in Tötemeyer *et al.* (eds), *Namibia in Perspective*, pp. 69–81.

——— (1990), '"Playing Soldiers": The Truppenspieler Movement Among the Herero of Namibia, 1915 to ca. 1945', *JSAS*, 16, 3, pp. 476–502.

——— (1998), *'No One Will Become Rich': Economy and Society in the Herero Reserves in Namibia, 1915–1946* (Basel: P. Schlettwein).

Westphal, E. Oswin (1963), 'The Linguistic Prehistory of Southern Africa: Bush, Kwadi, Hottentot and Bantu Linguistic Relationships', *Africa 33*, pp. 237–65.

Widlok, Thomas (1999), *Living on Mangetti: 'Bushman' Autonomy and Namibian Independence* (Oxford University Press).

——— (2000), 'On the Other Side of the Frontier: Relations between Herero and "the Bushmen"' in Bollig and Gewald (eds), *People, Cattle and Land*, pp. 497–522.

Wildenthal, Lora (2002), *German Women for Empire, 1884–1945* (Durham, NC: Duke University Press).

Willemse, Hein (2003), 'Textual Production and Contested Histories in a Performance of the Namibian Storyteller Dawid Plaatjies', *Research in African Literatures*, 34, 3, pp. 27–45.

Williams, Frieda-Nela (1991), *Pre-colonial Communities of Southwestern Africa: A History of Owambo Kingdoms 1600–1920* (Windhoek: National Archives of Namibia).

Wilmsen, Edwin (1989), *Land Filled with Flies: A Political Economy of the Kalahari* (University of Chicago Press).

Winterfeldt, Volker (2002), 'Labour Migration in Namibia—Gender Aspects' in *idem et al.*, *Namibia Society Sociology*, pp. 39–74.

——— (2007), 'Liberated Economy: The Case of Ramatex Textiles Namibia' in Melber (ed.), *Transitions*, pp. 65–93.

———, Tom Fox and Pempelani Mufume (eds) (2002), *Namibia, Society, Sociology* (Windhoek: University of Namibia Press).

Witbooi, Hendrik (1929), *Die Dagboek van Hendrik Witbooi* (Cape Town: Van Riebeeck Society).

───── (1982), *Afrika den Afrikanern! Aufzeichnungen eines Nama-Häuptlings aus der Zeit der deutschen Eroberung Südwestafrikas 1884 bis 1894* (Berlin: Dietz).

Wood, Brian (ed.) (1988), *Namibia 1884–1984: Readings on Namibia's History and Society* (London and Lusaka: Namibia Support Committee and United Nations Institute for Namibia).

Woodward, Wendy, Patricia Hayes and Gary Minkley (eds) (2002), *Deep Histories: Gender and Colonialism in South Africa* (Amsterdam: Rodopi).

World Bank (1994), 'Cultural Heritage in Environmental Assessment', *Environmental Assessment Sourcebook Update*, 8, pp. 1–8.

Wright, Donald (1999), '"What Do You Mean, There Were No Tribes in Africa?" Thoughts on Boundaries—and Related Matters—in Precolonial Africa', *History in Africa*, 26, pp. 409–26.

Ya Nangolo, Mvula and Tor Sellström (2005), *Kassinga: A Story Untold* (Windhoek: Namibia Book Development Council).

Ya Otto, John (1982), *Battlefront Namibia: An Autobiography* (London: Heinemann).

Yates, Anne and Lewis Chester (2006), *The Troublemaker: Michael Scott and his Lonely Struggle against Injustice* (London: Aurum).

Zeller, Joachim (2003), '"Ombepera i koza—Die Kälte tötet mich": Zur Geschichte des Konzentrationslagers in Swakopmund (1904–1908)' in Zimmerer and Zeller (eds), *Völkermord*, pp. 64–79.

───── (2004), 'Images of the South West African War: Reflections on the 1904–1907 Colonial War in Contemporary Photo Reportage and Book Illustration' in Hartmann (ed.), *Hues*, pp. 309–23.

Zeller, Wolfgang (2009), 'Danger and Opportunity in Katima Mulilo: A Namibian Border Boomtown at Transnational Crossroads', *JSAS*, 35, 1, pp. 133–54.

───── and Bennett Kangumu Kangumu (2007), 'Caprivi Under Old and New Indirect Rule: Falling off the Map or a 19th Century Dream Come True?' in Melber (ed.), *Transitions*, pp. 190–209.

Zimmerer, Jürgen (2004), 'Krieg, KZ and Völkermord in Südwestafrika: Der erste deutsche Genozid' in Zimmerer and Zeller (eds), *Völkermord*, pp. 45–63.

───── (2004), 'Das deutsche Reich und der Genozid—Überlegungen zum historischen Ort des Völkermordes an den Herero und Nama', in Förster *et al.*, *Namibia–Deutschland*, pp. 106–21.

───── (2004), *Deutsche Herrschaft über Afrikaner: Staatlicher Machtanspruch und Wirklichkeit im kolonialen Namibia* (Münster: Lit).

───── (2005), 'Rassenkrieg und Völkermord: Der Kolonialkrieg in Deutsch-Südwestafrika und die Globalgeschichte des Genozids' in Henning Melber (ed.), *Genozid und Gedenken*, pp. 23–48.

―――― and Joachim Zeller (eds) (2003), *Völkermord in Deutsch-Südwestafrika: Der Kolonialkrieg (1904–1908) in Namibia und seine Folgen* (Berlin: Links), published in English as *idem* (eds), *Genocide in German South-West Africa: The Colonial War of 1904–1908 and its Aftermath* (Monmouth: Merlin, 2008).

Zingelwa, Amenda (1999), 'The Campaign for Khomasdal: The Building of a Coloured Community in Windhoek' in Hartmann (ed.), *More New Historical Writing*, pp. 22–36.

INDEX

Abrahams, Kenneth, 248
Abrahams, Ottilie Schimming, 248
Action Committee for the Main-
tenance of Turnhalle Principles
(AKTUR): eventual opposition to
Turnhalle, 288
African Improvement Society, 248
African Methodist Episcopal Church
(AMEC): secession to, 244
African National Congress (ANC),
247, 270, 299; led by Dr. A.B.
Xuma, 244
Afrikaner, Christian: death of
(1863), 68–9; response to *ovita
vyongombongange* (1863), 69
Afrikaner, Jager: attacks on Warmbad, 53–4; baptism of (1815), 52;
family of, 52, 59
Afrikaner, Jan Jonker, 68, 118,
122; attempt to sell Windhoek to
Adolf Lüderitz, 118; conflict with
Rehoboth Basters, 111; peace
treaty with Maharero (1870), 72;
protection treaty (1885), 119
Afrikaner, Jonker, 112, 115; alliances with other Nama-Oorlam
kapteins, 61, 68; and ‖Oaseb, 59,
61; and Amraal Lambert, 61; cattle loans to Tjimba, 60; conflict
with RMS, 63; death of (1861),
59, 68; control of Cape trade,

73; established trading route to
Walvis Bay, 38, 59–60; family of,
52, 59; military campaigns of, 60;
polities of, 61; raids on Ovambo
territory, 87
Afrikaner, Klaas: family of, 40, 59;
responsible for murder of Pieter
Pienaar (1796), 38, 52; use of
‖Khauxa!nas, 40
Afrikaners (Nama-Oorlam group):
competition with ‖Oaseb over
control of Otjiherero-speakers,
61; concession granted to
WBMC (1854), 67; conflict with
Bondelswarts, 59; conflict with
Germany (1897), 145; earliest
records of, 57
Afrikaners (white ethnic group):
policy towards, 251; settlers
('Angola Boers'), 240; soldiers
granted farms, 241; rebellion
(1914), 216. *See also* Boers
Ahtisaari, Maarti: UN Secretary-
General Special Representative,
305
Aipanda: appointed as spokesman
for Ombalantu (1917), 210
Albrecht, Johann: appeal to Cape
for commando to be raised
against Afrikaners, 54